Lecture Notes in Computer Science   2562

Edited by G. Goos, J. Hartmanis, and J. van Leeuwen

Springer
Berlin
Heidelberg
New York
Barcelona
Hong Kong
London
Milan
Paris
Tokyo

Veronica Dahl   Philip Wadler (Eds.)

Practical Aspects of Declarative Languages

5th International Symposium, PADL 2003
New Orleans, LA, USA, January 13-14, 2003
Proceedings

 Springer

Series Editors

Gerhard Goos, Karlsruhe University, Germany
Juris Hartmanis, Cornell University, NY, USA
Jan van Leeuwen, Utrecht University, The Netherlands

Volume Editors

Veronica Dahl
Simon Fraser University, Computer Science Department
Logic and Functional Programming Group
8888 University Drive, Burnaby B.C. V5A 1S6, Canada
E-mail: veronica@cs.sfu.ca

Philip Wadler
Avaya Labs
233 Mount Airy Road, Basking Ridge, NJ 07920, USA
E-mail: wadler@avaya.com

Cataloging-in-Publication Data applied for

A catalog record for this book is available from the Library of Congress.

Bibliographic information published by Die Deutsche Bibliothek.
Die Deutsche Bibliothek lists this publication in the Deutsche Nationalbibliografie;
detailed bibliographic data is available in the Internet at <http://dnb.ddb.de>.

CR Subject Classification (1998): D.3, D.1, F.3, D.2

ISSN 0302-9743
ISBN 3-540-00389-4 Springer-Verlag Berlin Heidelberg New York

Springer-Verlag Berlin Heidelberg New York
a member of BertelsmannSpringer Science+Business Media GmbH

http://www.springer.de

© Springer-Verlag Berlin Heidelberg 2002
Printed in Germany

Typesetting: Camera-ready by author, data conversion by PTP-Berlin, Stefan Sossna e.K.
Printed on acid-free paper   SPIN: 10871827   06/3142   5 4 3 2 1 0

Preface

The Fifth International Symposium on Practical Aspects of Declarative Languages (PADL 2003) was held in New Orleans on 13–14 January 2003. It was colocated with the 30th Annual ACM Symposium on Principles of Programming Languages (POPL 2003).

We received 57 submissions, a record for PADL. One of the strengths of PADL is that it draws papers from both sides of the declarative divide, from both the functional and logic programming communities. Of the 57 submissions, 25 were functional and 32 were logical, with some notable overlaps.

The program committee was divided on the approach to take to the conference. Those from the logic programming community preferred to have parallel sessions in order to accept more papers, those from the functional programming community preferred to avoid parallel sessions though it meant accepting fewer papers. We decided to find strength in diversity, and experiment with taking both paths. We accepted 8 papers on functional programming, each presented in its own slot, and 15 papers on logic programming, 10 of which are presented in parallel sessions. We felt that papers from both communities were comparable in quality. The ratio of 4 hours of functional talks to 5 hours of logic talks matches the ratio of submissions.

While most papers submitted to PADL are traditional research papers, some were submitted as Application Letters or Declarative Pearls. Traditional papers may be judged on whether they present a crisp new research result; Application Letters may be judged according to the interest in the application and the novel use of declarative languages; and Declarative Pearls may be judged according to the elegance of the development and the clarity of the expression.

This year PADL instituted a "Most Practical" paper award, for the paper that best exemplified the goals of PADL. The award went to "Data mining the yeast genome in a lazy functional language", Amanda Clare and Ross D. King, University of Wales, Aberystwyth, which describes a real-word application running on multiprocessors, drawing on techniques from both the functional and logic programming communities.

Special thanks are due: to Shriram Krishnamurthi, Dave Tucker, and Paul Graunke of Brown University, for running the website of the PADL submission and review process (see Krishnamurthi's invited talk in this volume); to Martina Sharp of Avaya Labs and Kimberly Voll of Simon Fraser University, for help with preparing this volume; and to Gopal Gupta of the University of Texas at Dallas, for serving as general chair. We thank Avaya Labs, Brown University, Simon Fraser University, Université de Provence, and the University of Texas at Dallas for their support.

Our thanks to the program committee members and referees for their reviewing and for their advice. Finally, our thanks to all those who submitted papers to or participated in PADL 2003.

November 2003
                                                                    Veronica Dahl
                                                                    Philip Wadler

Preface

Program Committee

Table of Contents

Invited Papers

Papers

The Role of Declarative Languages in Mining Biological Databases

David Page

Dept. of Biostatistics and Medical Informatics
and Dept. of Computer Sciences
University of Wisconsin
1300 University Ave.
Madison, WI 53706
U.S.A.
page@biostat.wisc.edu

Abstract. Biological and biomedical databases have become a primary application area for data mining. Such databases commonly involve multiple relational tables and a variety of data types, as in the biological databases that formed the basis for the KDD Cup 2001 and 2002 competitions. The diversity of such "multi-relational" data is likely to increase dramatically in the near future. For example, patient records at major medical institutions are being augmented to include a variety of genetic data, including data on single-nucleotide polymorphisms (SNPs) and mRNA levels from gene expression microarrays, in addition to clinical data. Data mining tools based on declarative languages are able to naturally integrate data of diverse types, from multiple tables, to arrive at novel discoveries.

V. Dahl and P. Wadler (Eds.): PADL 2003, LNCS 2562, p. 1, 2003.
© Springer-Verlag Berlin Heidelberg 2003

The CONTINUE Server
(or, How I Administered PADL 2002 and 2003)

Shriram Krishnamurthi*

Computer Science Department
Brown University
Providence, RI, USA
sk@cs.brown.edu

Abstract. Conference paper submission and reviewing is an increasingly electronic activity. Paper authors and program committee members expect to be able to use software, especially with Web interfaces, to simplify and even automate many activities. Building interactive Web sites is a prime target of opportunity for sophisticated declarative programming languages. This paper describes the PLT Scheme application CONTINUE, which automates many conference paper management tasks.

1   Introduction

The submission and review phases of computer science conferences have become increasingly electronic. Indeed, many conferences operate without using any paper until the copyright forms come due. The many phases of this process—paper submission, download by reviewers, review submission, paper discussion, review dissemination and final paper submission—all employ electronic media and formats.

The increasing use of automation benefits authors and reviewers alike. Authors no longer need to mail bulky cartons containing several copies of their submissions. Program chairs no longer need to receive and store these cartons. And having the papers in electronic form helps reviewers search and bookmark fragments of a paper.

All this automation places immense pressure on one group of individuals: the program committee (PC) chairs. They are forced to install servers, which is often an onerous task, and worse, to maintain them. They must fret about privacy and security, which they may ill-understand. They need to support a variety of platforms and formats, all while providing a reasonable user interface. Finally, they must support the electronic management of the review process.

In the early days of (partial) conference automation, interfaces tended to demand that authors FTP to a particular site, save their paper in a hopefully unique filename, and then notify the maintainer by email of their upload. Server installation and maintenance was therefore easy, because host departments usually provided FTP facilities. Security was usually accomplished by making the

---

* This work is partially supported by NSF grants ESI-0010064 and ITR-0218973.

V. Dahl and P. Wadler (Eds.): PADL 2003, LNCS 2562, pp. 2–16, 2003.

directory unreadable, but this made it difficult for authors to ensure their file had been uploaded successfully. Invariably, authors would forget to, say, set the transmission type to binary, causing an entirely avoidable exchange to ensure. Those were not halcyon days.

The development of the Web as a medium for interaction has greatly helped conference submission. The Web provides many of the benefits of the FTP approach, while tying it to a better interface. As a result, several servers now perform conference paper management. Unfortunately, some of these servers are difficult to install, and some are even commercial enterprises (in return for which they ostensibly provide professional, around-the-clock service).

The computer science community could benefit from a simple yet powerful server that provides most of the features currently available from existing servers. By exploiting the powerful features of declarative languages, such a server can demonstrate the benefits of declarative programming to a wider audience. This paper presents CONTINUE, a Web package that meets both these requirements.

2   CONTINUE as an Application

CONTINUE has two heads. It presents one face to the submitter, and entirely another to PC members. We will describe each of these in turn, focusing on the most useful or interesting features.

In general, CONTINUE looks much like any other server program or conference manager: maybe a little less slick than others, but also less garish. This commonness of interface is important, because it means users are less likely to be confounded by the interface, and consequently less likely to blame a language for the program's author's faults.

2.1   Submitting Papers

One of the more vexing problems that PC chairs face is incorrect contact information for an author. The first line of defense against this is to ensure that authors provide valid email addresses. And the simplest way of ensuring an address is valid is to actually use the address to establish contact. This is a common pattern now used by many registration sites, and we view the act of submitting a paper as a form of registration. (Erecting a barrier is also a valuable safeguard against junk submissions, spam, etc.)

To wit, the primary submission page asks authors to enter an email address and other contact information (particularly their Web page URL). It sends a message containing a special URL to the address input. The author needs to use the transmitted URL to continue the submission process and, in particular, to obtain a form that permits file upload. CONTINUE implements the standard HTTP upload protocol, so users will find nothing unfamiliar about using this server. (The actual protocol implementation is part of the PLT Web server API.)

Fig. 1. Reviewer Interface

2.2   Reviewing Papers

Papers are assigned to PC members by the PC chairs. A chair's interface provides access to this feature, but it is not made available to individual PC members. Only a PC member assigned to a paper can submit a review for it (though I plan to add a feature whereby *any* PC member can submit a "note" to the authors: see section 4.1). To make assigning PC members more flexible, CONTINUE offers PC chairs the option of downloading a list of all the papers as an XML document. The chairs can use XSLT or other transformation tools to endow each paper with reviewers. CONTINUE accepts the resulting XML document and converts the embellishments into reviewer preferences in its internal format.

Each PC member logs in using a unique username and password to obtain their assigned papers. The default page a PC member sees lists the following:

- a progress bar showing how many papers they've reviewed, and how many remain;
- a link (anchored by the text "How are the others doing?") that lets them compare their progress against that of the other PC members;
- a link to all submitted papers;
- papers for which their review is pending;
- papers they have finished reviewing (see figure 1).

PC members have two incentives for completing reviews. One, of course, is the progress bar comparator. The other is that they cannot see reviews by other PC members until they have filed their own review. While this feature is obviously easy to circumvent (by submitting a blank review), we hope social forces will prevent most PC members from doing so. At any rate, it does ensure that a PC member cannot accidentally view another member's review before completing their own, thereby reducing bias in their own evaluation.

One vexing question that faces authors of conference managers is how to cleanly summarize reviews. This in turn depends on the reviewing system the conference adopts. Because of this dependency, in principle, the paper management software should be parameterized over the review regime, and should perhaps offer a domain-specific language for specifying how to summarize data.[1]

CONTINUE does not currently adopt this complex strategy. Instead, it implements Oscar Nierstrasz's "Identify the Champion" (henceforth, ItC) pattern for program committees [14]. Like most review regimes, ItC includes two summary data on each paper: the overall evaluation, and the reviewer's expertise. What distinguishes ItC is, rather than using passive terms such as "good" and "bad", it uses active phrases such as "I will champion [this paper] at the PC meeting" and "I will argue to reject this paper". Nierstrasz argues that this language, and the notion of making champions explicit, will help a PC more rapidly converge on papers that it is actually going to accept.

While ItC prescribes codes for reviews (A (will champion)–D (argue against) for overall quality, X (expert)–Z (non-expert) for expertise), it does not dictate a presentation mechanism. We therefore experimented with a number of different schemes that kept the two units of data separate. These were somehow unsatisfying, because they cluttered the screen without providing appreciably more information. The clutter was increased by the presence of another, unavoidable, field: the final decision.

The present scheme, implemented by CONTINUE, is due to Phil Wadler. Wadler's scheme is to ignore the expertise (since this is often reflected in the overall rating) and deal with *ranges* of overall ratings. The lexicographically ordered pairs of ratings form a triangular matrix. Wadler's scheme assigns a color to each corner, and lets them (roughly) fade toward one another. It puts the most visually striking colors at the corner where there is most need for discussion due to the greatest variance of opinion (A–D). To wit:

A	B	C	D	
yellow	yellow	orange	red	A
	yellow	green	purple	B
		green	blue	C
			blue	D

CONTINUE designates the final decision using the same color scheme. Thus, accepted papers get a yellow tick, and rejected papers a blue cross. (The blue cross on a white background looks remarkably like an inverted Saltaire.)

---

[1] An alternative is to use a swarm of colors and codes to cover almost every possible situation. One popular conference manager uses so many colors, it pops up a window of color codes every time a PC member logs in. Since pop-ups usually contain advertisements, many Web users have come to regard pop-ups as nuisances and close them immediately. The unfortunate PC member must then click on a link to see the color codes explained again. Convenience notwithstanding, I believe having a pop-up to explain color codes is a symptom, not a solution.

3   CONTINUE as a Program

The slogan for the implementation of CONTINUE is

CONTINUE = functional programming + interactivity + databases

The API design means the interactive portions also appear functional, resulting in a very elegant and maintainable program.

3.1   Caching and Performance

At the outset, CONTINUE had to decide how much to generate dynamically and how much should be cached statically. For instance, should Web pages of review summaries always be regenerated, or should they be stored and updated only when a review changes? The tradeoffs are fairly obvious, but worth recounting. Static caches increase performance, but also introduce cache effects: delayed propagation, concurrency, and so forth. So the decision hinges on the frequency of updates and the need for up-to-date information.

For a conference paper review system, performance is governed by the following parameters:

- The load distribution is not uniform. Most days few or no reviews are logged. There is a flurry of submissions as the deadline approaches, and a few may come in only after the deadline.[2]
- Reviewers are often spread around the globe, so there is no "safe" time for re-generating caches.
- The cost of stale data can be high. When discussing papers, for instance, it sometimes really matters whether a paper was assigned a slightly favorable or slightly unfavorable review. PC members need to be able to instantaneously see recent additions as well as changes.

An early version of CONTINUE (used for PADL 2002) performed extensive caching. Unfortunately, this led to greater manual overhead for the server maintainer to ensure that information propagated quickly enough. For the 2003 edition, I therefore decided to experiment with generating all information dynamically. Would the server cope?

With CONTINUE, there is an additional performance parameter that needs tuning. Every interaction point captures a new continuation; as we have explained elsewhere [9], these continuations are difficult to garbage collect, because a server cannot know when a client might still maintain a reference to them.[3] The PLT Scheme Web server provides a parameter that allows the user to specify a timeout period following which continuations are reaped. Because this timeout

---

[2] We won't name names.

[3] Though there are space-efficient implementations of continuations [10], PLT Scheme cannot exploit them because of the constraints of interoperability with languages hostile to garbage collection.

can be inconvenient to users, and also as an experiment, we ran CONTINUE with no timeouts.

I'm happy to report that, for the reviewing phase of PADL 2003 (which received 58 submissions), CONTINUE held fast. There were no appreciable lags, nor did space usage skyrocket. The decision phase consumed the following resources (these figures represent an instantaneous snapshot taken just after decisions were made):

total memory: 159 Mb
resident set size: 159 Mb
CPU time: 49 minutes

These are modest numbers for a modern server application!

3.2   Functional Programming

A good portion of CONTINUE code is straight-up functional programming: maps, filters and folds. This is hardly surprising, because these looping paradigms accurately capture many presentation tasks. Want to turn database records into HTML rows? Map the row constructor over them. Want to select a reviewer's papers out of all submitted ones? Filter by whether they have been assigned to the paper. And so on.

CONTINUE also benefits from the ability to conveniently construct HTML using Scheme s-expressions (a benefit noted by several others). In general, programmers are more likely to construct abstractions if the language makes this easy. The ease with which s-expressions support HTML construction makes it convenient to define style sheets, resulting in benefits both external (interface consistency) and internal (code reuse). For instance, this template generates all conference pages:

```
(define (generate-web-page title bodies)
  '(html
    (head
     (title ,conference-short-name ": " ,title))
    (body [(bgcolor "white")]
          (p (h3 (a [(href ,conference-home-page-url)]
                    ,conference-short-name)))
          (p (h4 ,title))
          (hr)
          ,@bodies
          (hr)
          (p ((align "RIGHT"))
             (small
              "Web site implemented using the "
              (a ((href "http://www.plt-scheme.org/"))
                 "PLT Scheme Web server")))))))
```

Here is one more example, which combines higher-order function use with s-expression based HTML generation. This function generates the progress bar of PC member reviews (see section 2.2):

```
(define (make-pc-progress-list)
  `((p [(align "center")]
     (table
      [(width "90%")]
      ,@(map (lambda (pc-member)
               `(tr
                 (td  [(width "30%")
                       (align "right")]
                  ,pc-member)
                 (td  [(width "70%")]
                  (table [(width "100%")]
                   (tr
                    ,@(pc-member-progress-bar pc-member))))))
             pc-keys)))))
```

3.3 Interactivity

CONTINUE's name pays tribute in two directions: to the START conference manager by Gerber, Hollingsworth and Porter at Maryland, an early utility of this kind, and to continuations, which are at the heart of CONTINUE's interactive capabilities. Graham [4], Hughes [11], Queinnec [15] and others have all noticed the profound utility of continuations to Web programming; CONTINUE puts this observation to work.

The PLT Scheme Web server provides a primitive called **send/suspend** [9]. This primitive captures the current continuation and stores it in a hash table, associated with a unique name. It then generates a URL which includes that name such that visiting the URL results in the Web server extracting the continuation from the table and invoking it. **send/suspend** takes as an argument a function of one argument, which it invokes on this generated URL. (As we will see below, this function usually—but not always!—generates a Web form with the provided URL as the form's handler.)

The **send/suspend** primitive makes writing interactive Web programs considerably easier. Instead of breaking down a single program into multiple subprograms, which must then carefully orchestrate their communication, storing data in hidden fields, cookies, databases and so on, **send/suspend** permits the programmer to code in direct style, so all the benefits of lexical scope are conveniently at hand.

For instance, here is a typical use of **send/suspend**. This is the top-level routine for PC members:[4]

---

[4] Some code fragments have been cleansed slightly for presentation purposes.

```
(define (go pc-member)
  (choose-action
    (request-bindings
      (send/suspend
        (lambda (k-url)
          (generate-web-page "All Your Papers" ···)))))
    pc-member))
```

Note how the use of **send/suspend** makes the structure of this program as simple as if it had been reading input from the keyboard. In particular, the program can refer to identifiers such as *pc-member*, which are lexically bound, without the contortions that the CGI protocol normally engenders [8].

Not all uses look quite so functional. Here is a sequence of interactions with the user, extracted from the code where CONTINUE requests and then saves a paper's review:

```
(begin
  (send/suspend
    (lambda (k-url)
      (show-submission-page-w-review-link key k-url)))
  (write-review pc-member
                key
                (request-bindings
                  (send/suspend
                    (lambda (k-url)
                      (show-submission-and-review-page
                       key k-url
                       (read-review pc-member key))))))
  ···)
```

In this fragment, the first **send/suspend** returns no useful value. It simply generates a page that the user must click through to generate the review form. The second page actually receives a value from the form, extracts the essential data, and saves the PC member's review. (Note that *pc-member* is a reference to a lexically scoped identifier.)

There is one other interesting use of **send/suspend**, for handling email confirmation (see section 2.1). It's worth stepping through most of this function (figure 2). First, the header is in $\boxed{0}$. The first thing the function body does is ask the user for their contact information ($\boxed{1}$). If the user enters invalid information, CONTINUE signals an error and asks again ($\boxed{2}$). Otherwise, it installs an exception handler (elided) and sends the URL in a mail message ($\boxed{3}$).

In particular, after sending the message, this code generates a page so the user can verify the address to which the server sent the message. If the user detect an error, he can click on a button, which resumes computation with *get-contact-info*—thereby generating the contact information form all over again. In contrast, if he does actually receive the URL in his mail and pastes it, computation

```
⎡0⎤ = (define (get-contact-info email name url) ⎡1⎤)
⎡1⎤ = (let* ([contact-bindings
              (request-bindings
                (send/suspend
                  (page/email-info email name url)))]
             [email (get-binding 'cont-auth-email contact-bindings)]
             [name (get-binding 'cont-auth-name contact-bindings)]
             [url (get-binding 'cont-auth-web-page contact-bindings)])
         ⎡2⎤)
⎡2⎤ = (if (or (string=? email "") (string=? name ""))
           (begin (send/suspend (page/empty-inputs email name))
                  (get-contact-info email name url))
           ⎡3⎤)
⎡3⎤ = (begin
        (send/suspend
          (lambda (k-url)
            (send-email email name url k-url)
            (send/suspend (page/verifying-email-address email))
            (get-contact-info email name url)))
        (get-submission email name url))
```

Fig. 2. Email Confirmation Code

resumes at the **send/suspend**, whose continuation is the invocation of *get-submission*—which enables the user to actually upload the paper.

These examples illustrate how continuations greatly simplify the construction of powerful interactive Web programs. The last use was an unexpected benefit of having the full power of continuations available to the programmer, because this was not an application we foresaw when first designing the server.

3.4   The Database

CONTINUE uses a database that

— is relatively fast,
— supports concurrent access,
— has been tested extensively,
— is easy to install, and
— on most systems, is supported by backup:

the *filesystem!*

There are natural reasons for using a traditional database manager for storing records. But there are several equally good reasons for CONTINUE's choice:

Installation Simplicity. No installation is necessary. The filesystem is already "running" when the user installs CONTINUE. Database managers are often not trivial to install, and CONTINUE's design goal is to make it easy for people to run conference sites. Even just the installation instructions become vastly more complex, and become highly dependent on the individual platform.

Maintenance Simplicity. Once installed, someone needs to keep an eye on the database manager, and introducing an additional component results in an extra point of failure. It's pretty easy to diagnose that the filesystem is down and, if it is, it doesn't matter whether the database is up.

Programming Simplicity. There is admittedly an allure to keeping the program simple also. Though most languages offer database primitives (PLT Scheme's database manager, SrPersist [18], supports the standard ODBC protocol), sometimes quite nicely (SchemeQL [19] provides an elegant Scheme interface to SQL), the installation and maintenance overhead do not appear to justify the effort.

Ease of Access. In an emergency, the filesystem is easy to access without knowing to use query languages or sophisticated clients.

It would appear that the main reasons for *not* using the filesystem are efficiency and concurrent semantics. CONTINUE uses files thoughtfully to minimize the possibility of concurrent writes, so that the only circumstances under which one document might overwrite another are the same that would occur with a database.[5] We have not found efficiency to be a problem in practice (especially given the latency introduced by the network). Most reviews and other data files tend to be small. CONTINUE stores them as Scheme s-expressions, and Scheme implementations tune the *read* primitive to operate as efficiently as possible.

3.5   Security and Privacy

Security is vital in an application such as CONTINUE. The need for security, however, creates a constant conflict against the desire for convenience. CONTINUE cannot protect against the malicious or careless PC member handing out their password, thereby compromising the entire process. But it can create mechanisms that make it less necessary for PC members to be tempted to disperse this information.

The tradeoff classically arises when a PC member P wants to request a subreviewer S to examine a paper. P does not want to have to download the paper and a form, save them to files, mail the files, then manually copy S's feedback back into a form. In turn, S is likely to perform their service better if they were given a pleasant interface. This may tempt P to send S a password. CONTINUE makes this unnecessary by creating one-shot passwords *implicitly*.

The URL that CONTINUE (really, the PLT server) generates has this form:

```
http://host/servlets/pc-member.ss;id281*k2-95799725
```

This URL is essentially unforgeable. Therefore, P can send the URL generated for the review form to S. The review form contains all the necessary data (the

---

[5] CONTINUE could easily keep backups of all overridden files, though this would require designing an interface for recovering data from the backups.

abstract, paper and review form), so P does not need to send other files as attachments. In turn, once S submits a review, the URL *ceases to be active*! CONTINUE enforces this by using the **send/finish** primitive in place of **send/suspend** after receiving the review. The **send/finish** primitive reaps the continuation after its use, so subsequent attempts to access it will not succeed. Though **send/finish** was defined primarily to control resource usage, it has proven extremely valuable for defining policies such as this. Once S has submitted his review, P can edit it, secure in the knowledge that her changes cannot even be seen, much less changed, by S. P must explicitly generate a fresh URL for S so if she wants S to make changes.

CONTINUE also uses the traditional HTTP password mechanism to protect against inadvertent access. Therefore, simply stripping off part of the generated URL is insufficient: the intruder must know the username and password of a PC member also. This appears to be about the same level of security that other Web conference managers employ.

CONTINUE does assume that the PC chair(s) can see all decisions. This appears to inevitable for an effective decision-making process. Since many conferences disallow submissions by PC chairs, this seems to be a reasonable decision.

Finally, CONTINUE does ensure a paper co-authored by a PC member is treated with care. It prevents the PC chair from (accidentally) adding the PC member as a reviewer of their own paper, and anyway ensures that the paper does not show up on the PC member's view of assigned or all papers. Thus, a PC member should not be able to determine who wrote their reviews.

4   Future Directions

First we'll examine some observations about users and uses, then discuss some interesting research questions that CONTINUE engenders, and conclude with intended features.

4.1   Usability Issues

Observing the use of a running program raised several usability concerns to contemplate and address.

First, PC members sometimes sent the same review URL to more than one sub-reviewer. The second sub-reviewer who attempted to submit a review found that their URL had expired (see section 3.5). This was clearly a failing on my part, because I hadn't adequately explained this to users. (It's easy to say this should be in the documentation, but as Joel Spolsky notes, "Users don't have the manual, and if they did, they wouldn't read it" [17].) It is anyway unclear what to do in this case, since one PC member can't count themselves twice!

CONTINUE currently does not allow a PC member to file *comments*—or even the equivalent of an amicus brief—as distinct from *reviews*. Yet PC members often have a brief note to make to the author, but haven't read the paper in enough detail (or lack the authority) to file a full review. This would be a valuable feature, along with room for comments from the PC meeting.

There may be a bug in CONTINUE. A PC member complained that the server had lost one prior review. Investigation suggests that the fault may partially have been the user's (a sub-reviewer): it appears that they may have made the browser stop part-way through the review submission process. Since we have seen this behavior only once, it's unclear where the problem lies.

Finally, some mail agents take undue liberties with email messages. In particular, they feel free to reformat mail text by inserting line breaks at apparently appropriate locations. Sometimes, however, the text they break may be a URL, such as that for continuing the submission process (this process is described in sections 2.1 and 3.3). For PADL 2002, we received some complaints of non-functional URLs that we traced to this problem. (One paper submitter, in particular, initiated the process five times!) We could have used MIME-formatted messages, but instead made some changes to the URL the PLT server generates. As a result, we received no complaints for PADL 2003 (or other conferences that have used CONTINUE), nor saw instances of repeated initiation.

4.2   Research Problems

Since I also do research in computer-aided verification, I have thought about modeling and verifying CONTINUE's behavior. CONTINUE has several behavioral properties worth verifying. For instance: No PC member should have access to reviews for their own paper (because this would compromise the identity of the reviewers). PC members should not be given access to their paper when they ask to see all submitted papers. A paper may have *multiple* PC member authors, and the software should be sensitive to this fact.[6] No sub-reviewer can override the review of a PC member without permission (in the form of a fresh URL). The reviewers of a paper should only be in the set of those assigned to review it by the PC chairs. A PC member should (presumably) not have both a note and a review for the same paper. The list continues.

It should be clear from surveying this list that most properties involve a strong interplay between data and control. While automated tools such as model checkers [2] are very good at verifying control properties, it is unclear that they are appropriate here for two reasons: (1) they are generally weak at modeling rich data, and (2) it is unclear how to effectively model continuations (beyond unfettered nondeterministic jumps, which would greatly increase the expense of verification). Theorem provers are generally effective for reasoning about data, but may not have sufficient automation for discharging some of these properties, especially the temporal ones. Paul Graunke and I attempted to construct a model using Alloy [12], but had difficulty effectively representing continuations. At any rate, I believe this remains an open problem for verification research.

---

[6] One manual mailing in 2002 failed to account for this, but the other PC member was kind enough to point out the mistake before any information was compromised.

4.3   Features

CONTINUE currently provides no useful sorting features. A PC member—and PC chair, in particular—might want to sort papers by status, quality and so on, to better order an upcoming discussion. It would be relatively easy to implement each feature, but I need to experiment with different interfaces for presenting the numerous options: Clicking on table headers? Buttons? Pull-down menus?

I believe the most significant missing feature is discussion tracking. Experience suggests that PC members are loath to discuss over almost any medium other than email. In particular, Web forms are often unwieldy, especially due to the poor editing interfaces in most Web browsers. Editing tools aside, the problem remains: how to associate messages with papers? Invariably, a discussion will span more than one paper (especially if the conference has related submissions), and it must then be associated with each of those papers.[7] It is especially frustrating when a message is stuck in the archive corresponding to a different paper—some messages really should be in multiple archives.

The easiest proposal is to ask authors to annotate each message with paper identifiers, perhaps by decorating the subject line. Needless to say, this is hopelessly error prone *and* unlikely to be effective in practice. Another possibility is to use a rule-based approach, but this requires generating a suitable set of rules for classifying messages. Anyone who has wrestled with rules for spam filtering is probably aware of the difficulty of doing this effectively. Worse, the design of rules usually comes about through experience, but there is relatively little time to gain experience with a set of messages in this domain.

The problem reduces to one of artificial intelligence. The machine learning community uses Bayesian [13] and other approaches in place or in addition to rule-based learning for classification. Some authors have, for instance, recently begun to use this corpus to classify messages as spam [16]; Androutsopoulos, et al. analyze this approach [1] and Graham reports success (with some interesting observations) with it [7]. In turn, we can ask of each message and each paper, "Relative to this paper, is this message spam?" The success of this approach depends on having a corpus for identification, and in this domain, the corpus should be effective from the very beginning. I think the title, author list, abstract, keywords and paper number would be a sufficient positive corpus for this purpose. There are some subtleties: for instance, if multiple papers have authors of the same name, we'd need a way to make that name insignificant for the purpose of classification. Nevertheless, this seems like a promising direction to explore: It will permit PC members to adhere to a comfortable interface, it requires relatively little manual setup or intervention, and it should make discussion and debate more effective by providing useful archives at no human cost.

---

[7] This raises an interesting privacy-related verification question about ensuring PC members do not inadvertently see discussion about their submission amidst messages about related ones. The odds of this increase since, given their expertise, they are likely to be judging related submissions. The Web, and passwords, offer a privacy mechanism; this section suggests a way of implementing the corresponding policy.

5   Conclusion

CONTINUE appears to be successful. It has twice supported a conference of nontrivial size with virtually no errors. It is in its "second system" phase, which has made its design more extensible. It appears to present a credible alternative to commercial and other conference paper management systems.

CONTINUE depends heavily on the PLT Scheme [3] implementation. The (live) experiments indicate that PLT Scheme can handle these workloads. The language and implementation offer very high cross-platform portability, so PC chairs are not bound to specific platforms (and can even more the sever across platforms amidst the process). In addition, the PLT Scheme Web server offers a convenient interface for writing interactive programs, and its primitives make it easier to construct interesting security and privacy protocols.

This experience contains a broader message for declarative programmers: Paul Graham is right [6]. If you can build your software as a Web application, you have the flexibility of choosing a better programming language. The Web largely frees programmers from the constraints of platform independence, ease of interface generation, ease of upgrading[8], absence of complex installation problems, absence of library dependencies .... It is possible to oversell the case, but there's no doubt that the Web does give programmers new powers. (Indeed, Graham and his partners illustrated this through Viaweb/Yahoo! Store [4], and ITA Software is doing so through Orbitz [5].)

Program declaratively, and seek the comforts that the Web affords. If you write a useful enough application, make it stable and evolve it rapidly, eventually others may want to know how you produced it.

Acknowledgments. I thank C.R. Ramakrishnan and Gopal Gupta for supporting my proposal to run PADL 2002 on a server that I hadn't yet written. Thanks to Gopal, Phil Wadler and Veronica Dahl for permitting the experiment to continue in PADL 2003. All of them, Phil in particular, suggested numerous improvements. The authors and reviewers of PADL 2002 and 2003 bore CONTINUE with remarkably good cheer. Thanks also to the other workshops that have permitted its use.

Paul Graunke was of immense help by maintaining the PLT Web server and assisting with PADL 2002. David Tucker similarly helped me with PADL 2003. Oscar Nierstrasz provided helpful encouragement as we devised a visual scheme for identifying champions. Finally, special thanks to the PLT Scheme team, especially Matthew Flatt, Robby Findler and Matthias Felleisen, whose credo of testing languages through applications pervades this work.

---

[8] Indeed, the server was constantly in development during the review period. I did some of the development while in Edinburgh for a conference. Thanks to the Web, changes were easy to prototype, test and install from a (considerable) distance.

References

1. Androutsopoulos, I., J. Koutsias, K. Chandrinos, G. Paliouras and C. Spyropoulos. An evaluation of naive Bayesian anti-spam filtering, 2000.
2. Clarke, E., E. Emerson and A. Sistla. Automatic verification of finite-state concurrent systems using temporal logic specifications. *ACM Transactions on Programming Languages and Systems*, 8(2):244–263, 1986.
3. Findler, R. B., J. Clements, C. Flanagan, M. Flatt, S. Krishnamurthi, P. Steckler and M. Felleisen. DrScheme: A programming environment for Scheme. *Journal of Functional Programming*, 12(2):159–182, 2002.
4. Graham, P. Beating the averages, April 2001.
   http://www.paulgraham.com/avg.html.
5. Graham, P. Carl de Marcken: Inside Orbitz, January 2001.
   http://www.paulgraham.com/carl.html.
6. Graham, P. The other road ahead, September 2001.
   http://www.paulgraham.com/carl.html.
7. Graham, P. A plan for spam, August 2002.
   http://www.paulgraham.com/spam.html.
8. Graunke, P. T., R. B. Findler, S. Krishnamurthi and M. Felleisen. Automatically restructuring programs for the Web. In *IEEE International Symposium on Automated Software Engineering*, pages 211–222, November 2001.
9. Graunke, P. T., S. Krishnamurthi, S. van der Hoeven and M. Felleisen. Programming the Web with high-level programming languages. In *European Symposium on Programming*, pages 122–136, April 2001.
10. Hieb, R., R. K. Dybvig and C. Bruggeman. Representing control in the presence of first-class continuations. In *ACM SIGPLAN Conference on Programming Language Design and Implementation*, 1990.
11. Hughes, J. Generalising monads to arrows. *Science of Computer Programming*, 37(1–3):67–111, May 2000.
12. Jackson, D. Alloy: a lightweight object modelling notation. Technical Report 797, MIT Laboratory for Computer Science, Feburary 2000.
13. Lewis, D. D. Naive (Bayes) at forty: The independence assumption in information retrieval. In Nédellec, C. and C. Rouveirol, editors, *Proceedings of the European Conference on Machine Learning*, pages 4–15. Springer-Verlag, 1998.
14. Nierstrasz, O. Identify the champion. In Harrison, N., B. Foote and H. Rohnert, editors, *Pattern Languages of Program Design*, volume 4, pages 539–556. Addison-Wesley, 2000.
15. Queinnec, C. The influence of browsers on evaluators or, continuations to program web servers. In *ACM SIGPLAN International Conference on Functional Programming*, 2000.
16. Sahami, M., S. Dumais, D. Heckerman and E. Horvitz. A Bayesian approach to filtering junk email. In *AAAI Workshop on Learning for Text Categorization*, July 1998.
17. Spolsky, J. User interface design for programmers.
    http://www.joelonsoftware.com/uibook/fog0000000249.html.
18. Steckler, P. SrPersist. http://www.plt-scheme.org/software/srpersist/.
19. Welsh, N., F. Solsona and I. Glover. SchemeUnit and SchemeQL: Two little languages. In *Scheme and Functional Programming*, 2002.

Zen and the Art of Symbolic Computing: Light and Fast Applicative Algorithms for Computational Linguistics

Gérard Huet

INRIA Rocquencourt,
BP 105, 78153 Le Chesnay Cedex, France,
Gerard.Huet@inria.fr,
http://pauillac.inria.fr/~huet

Abstract. Computational linguistics is an application of computer science which presents interesting challenges from the programming methodology point of view. Developing a realistic platform for the treatment of a natural language in its phonological, morphological, syntactic, and ultimately semantic aspects demands a principled modular architecture with complex cooperation between the various layers. Representing large lexical data bases, treating sophisticated phonological and morphological transformations, and processing in real time large corpuses demands fast finite-state methods toolkits. Analysing the syntactic structure, computing anaphoric relations, and dealing with the representation of information flow in dialogue understanding, demands the processing of complex constraints on graph structures, with sophisticated sharing of large non-deterministic search spaces.

The talk reports on experiments in using declarative programming for the processing of the sanskrit language, in its phonological and morphological aspects. A lexicon-based morphological tagger has been designed, using an original algorithm for the analysis of euphony (the so-called *sandhi* process, which glues together the words of a sentence in a continuous stream of phonemes). This work, described in [2], has been implemented in a purely applicative core subset of Objective Caml [5]. The basic structures underlying this methodology have been abstracted in the Zen toolkit, distributed as free software [3]. Two complementary techniques have been put to use. Firstly, we advocate the systematic use of *zippers* [1] for the programming of mutable data structures in an applicative way. Zippers, or *linear contexts*, are related to the interaction combinators of linear logic. Secondly, a *sharing functor* allows the uniform minimisation of inductive data structures by representing them as shared dags. This is similar to the traditional technique of bottom-up hashing, but the computation of the keys is left to the client invoking the functor, which has two advantages: keys are computed along with the bottom-up traversal of the structure, and more importantly their computation may profit of specific statistical properties of the data at hand, optimising the buckets balancing in ways which would be unattainable by generic functions. These two complementary technologies are discussed in [4].

The talk discusses the use of these tools in the uniform representation of finite state automata and transducers as *decorated* lexical trees (also

V. Dahl and P. Wadler (Eds.): PADL 2003, LNCS 2562, pp. 17–18, 2003.

called *tries*). The trie acts as a spanning tree of the automaton search space, along a preferred deterministic skeleton. Non deterministic transitions are constructed as choice points with virtual addresses, which may be either absolute words (locating the target state by a path from the starting state) or relative *differential words* (bytecode of the trie zipper processor, representing the shortest path in the spanning tree of the state graph). Sharing such automata structures gives uniformly an associated equivalent minimal automaton. For instance, the lexicon is itself represented by its characteristic minimal recognizer. But this applies as well to possibly non-deterministic transducers. Thus our segmenting sandhi analyser compiles a lexicon of 120000 flexed forms with a data base of 2800 string rewrite rules into a very compact transducer of 7300 states fitting in 700KB of memory, the whole computation taking 9s on a plain PC.

We believe that our experiment with functional programming applied to lexical and morphological processing of natural language is a convincing case that direct declarative programming techniques are often superior to more traditional imperative programming techniques using complex object-oriented methodologies. Our programs are very short, easy to maintain and debug, though efficient enough for real-scale use. It is our belief that this extends to other areas of Computational Linguistics, and indeed to most areas of Symbolic Computation.

References

1. Gérard Huet. "The Zipper". J. Functional Programming 7,5 (Sept. 1997), pp. 549–554.
2. Gérard Huet. "Transducers as Lexicon Morphisms, Segmentation by Euphony Analysis, And Application to a Sanskrit Tagger". Draft available as
   http://pauillac.inria.fr/~huet/FREE/tagger.pdf.
3. Gérard Huet. "The Zen Computational Linguistics Toolkit". ESSLLI 2002 Lectures, Trento, Italy, Aug. 2002. Available as:
   http://pauillac.inria.fr/~huet/PUBLIC/esslli.pdf.
4. Gérard Huet. "Linear Contexts and the Sharing Functor: Techniques for Symbolic Computation". Submitted for publication, 2002.
5. Xavier Leroy et al. "Objective Caml." See:
   http://caml.inria.fr/ocaml/index.html.

Data Mining the Yeast Genome in a Lazy Functional Language

Amanda Clare and Ross D. King

Computational Biology Group, Department of Computer Science,
University of Wales Aberystwyth, Penglais, Aberystwyth, SY23 3DB, UK
Tel: +44-1970-622424 Fax: +44-1970-628536
rdk@aber.ac.uk

Abstract. Critics of lazy functional languages contend that the languages are only suitable for toy problems and are not used for real systems. We present an application (PolyFARM) for distributed data mining in relational bioinformatics data, written in the lazy functional language Haskell. We describe the problem we wished to solve, the reasons we chose Haskell and relate our experiences. Laziness did cause many problems in controlling heap space usage, but these were solved by a variety of methods. The many advantages of writing software in Haskell outweighed these problems. These included clear expression of algorithms, good support for data structures, abstraction, modularity and generalisation leading to fast prototyping and code reuse, parsing tools, profiling tools, language features such as strong typing and referential transparency, and the support of an enthusiastic Haskell community. PolyFARM is currently in use mining data from the *Saccharomyces cerevisiae* genome and is freely available for non-commercial use at http://www.aber.ac.uk/compsci/Research/bio/dss/polyfarm/.

1 Declarative Languages in Data Mining

Data mining may at first seem an unusual area for applications for declarative languages. The requirements for data mining software used to be simply speed and ability to cope with large volumes of data. This meant that most data mining applications have been written in languages such as C and C++[1]. Java has also become very popular recently with the success of the Weka toolkit [1]. However, as the volumes of data grow larger, we wish to be more selective and mine only the interesting information, and so emphasis begins to fall on complex data structures and algorithms in order to achieve good results [2].

The declarative community have in fact been involved in data mining right from the start with Inductive Logic Programming (ILP) [3,4]. ILP uses the language of logic (and usually Prolog or Datalog) to express relationships in the data. Machine learning is used to induce generalisations of these relationships,

---

[1] A selection of current data mining software can be found at
http://www.kdnuggets.com/software/

V. Dahl and P. Wadler (Eds.): PADL 2003, LNCS 2562, pp. 19–36, 2003.

which can be later applied to future data to make classifications. The advantage of ILP is that complex results can be extracted, but as the results are expressed symbolically (in logic) the results are still more intelligible and informative than traditional numerical learners such as neural networks.

Some of the earliest successful applications of ILP were to computational biology. Perhaps the best known example was the mutagenesis problem [5]: the task of learning whether a chemical is mutagenic or not, given the atoms, bonds and structures within its molecules. Computational biology is a new and exciting field. Recent advances in DNA sequencing, microarray technology and other large-scale biological analysis techniques are now producing vast databases of information. These databases await detailed analysis by biologists. Due to the amount of data, automatic techniques such as data mining will be required for this task. The explosion in computational biology data will revolutionise biology, and new algorithms and solutions are needed to process this data.

For our work in computational biology, we needed to develop a data mining algorithm that would find frequent patterns in large amounts of relational data. Our data concerns the 6000 genes in the yeast genome (*Saccharomyces cerevisiae*) and our aim is to use these patterns as the first stage in learning about the biological functions of the genes. The data is both structured and relational. We also wanted a solution that was capable of running in a distributed fashion on a Beowulf cluster to make best use of the hardware resources we have available.

In the following sections of this paper we describe the problem we wish to solve, the solution we produced, the reasons we chose to use Haskell for the implementation and the problems and advantages we had using Haskell.

2   The Requirements

2.1   The Data

There are more than 6000 potential genes of the yeast *S. cerevisiae*. The yeast genome was sequenced in 1996 [6] and has been well studied as a model organism both before and after it was sequenced. However, despite its relatively small size and intensive study, the biological function of 30% of its genes is still unknown. We would like to apply machine learning to learn the relationship between properties of yeast genes and their biological functions, and hence make predictions for the functions of the genes that currently have no known function.

For each gene we collect as much information as possible from public data sources on the Internet. This includes data that is relational in nature, such as predicted secondary structure and homologous proteins.

Predicted secondary structure is useful because the shape and structure of a gene's product can give clues to its function. Protein structure can be described at various levels. The primary structure is the amino acid sequence itself. The secondary structure and tertiary structure describe how the backbone of the protein is arranged in 3-dimensional space. The backbone of the protein makes hydrogen bonds with itself, causing it to fold up into arrangements known as alpha helices, beta sheets and random coils. Alpha helices are formed when the backbone twists into right-handed helices. Beta sheets are formed when the backbone folds back on itself to make pleats. Random coils are neither random, nor coils, but are connecting loops that join together the alpha and beta regions. The alpha, beta and coil components are what is known as secondary structure. The secondary structures then fold up to give a tertiary structure to the protein. This makes the protein compact and globular. Our data is composed of predicted secondary structure information, which has a sequential aspect - for example, a gene might begin with a short alpha helix, followed by a long beta sheet and then another alpha helix. This spatial relationship between the components is important.

Data about homologous proteins is also informative. Homologous proteins are proteins that have evolved from the same ancestor at some point in time, and usually still share large percentages of their DNA composition. We can search publicly available databases of known proteins to find such proteins that have sequences similar to our yeast genes. These proteins are likely to be homologous, and to share common functions, and so information about these is valuable. For example, if we knew that the yeast genes that have homologs very rich in the amino acid lysine tend to be involved in ribosomal work, then we could predict that any of the genes of unknown function that have homologs rich in lysine could also be producing ribosomal proteins.

Figures 1 and 2 demonstrate the contents of our databases.

The overall method we use is the same as the method used in our work on predicting the functions of genes in the *M. tuberculosis* and *E. coli* genomes [7]. For this we use association mining to discover frequent patterns in the data. Then we use these patterns as attributes into a machine learning algorithm in order to predict gene function. The association mining stage is the concern of this paper.

2.2   Association Rule Mining

Association rule mining is a common data mining technique that can be used to produce interesting patterns or rules. Association rule mining programs count frequent patterns (or "associations") in large databases, reporting all that fall above a minimum frequency threshold known as the "support". The standard example used to describe this problem is that of analysing supermarket basket data, to see which products are frequently bought together. Such an association might be "minced beef and pasta are bought by 30% of customers". An association rule might be "**if** a customer buys minced beef and pasta **then** they are 75% likely to also buy spaghetti sauce".

The amount of time taken to count associations in large databases has led to many clever algorithms for counting, and investigations into aspects such as minimising candidate associations to count, minimising IO operations to read the database, minimising memory requirements and parallelising the algorithms. Certain properties of associations are useful when minimising the search space. Frequency of associations is **monotonic**: if an association is not frequent, then orf(yor034c).

hom(yor034c,p31947,b1.0e-8_4.0e-4).
sq_len(p31947,b16_344).
mol_wt(p31947,b1485_38502).
classification(p31947,homo).
db_ref(p31947,prints).
db_ref(p31947,embl).
db_ref(p31947,interpro).

hom(yor034c,p29431,b4.5e-2_1.1).
sq_len(p29431,b483_662).
mol_wt(p29431,b53922_74079).
classification(p29431,buchnera).
keyword(p29431,transmembrane).
keyword(p29431,inner_membrane).
db_ref(p29431,pir).
db_ref(p29431,pfam).

hom(yor034c,q28309,b4.5e-2_1.1).
sq_len(q28309,b16_344).
mol_wt(q28309,b1485_38502).
classification(q28309,canis).
keyword(q28309,transmembrane).
db_ref(q28309,prints).
db_ref(q28309,gcrdb).
db_ref(q28309,interpro).

hom(yor034c,p14196,b0.0_1.0e-8).
sq_len(p14196,b344_483).
mol_wt(p14196,b38502_53922).
classification(p14196,dictyostelium).
keyword(p14196,repeat).
db_ref(p14196,embl).

orf(yil137c).

ss(yil137c,1,c).
coil_len(1,gte10).
ss(yil137c,2,b).
beta_len(2,gte7).
ss(yil137c,3,c).
coil_len(3,b6_10).
ss(yil137c,4,b).
beta_len(4,gte7).
ss(yil137c,5,c).
coil_len(5,b3_4).
ss(yil137c,6,b).
beta_len(6,b6_7).
ss(yil137c,7,c).
coil_len(7,b3_4).
ss(yil137c,8,b).
beta_len(8,gte7).
ss(yil137c,9,c).
coil_len(9,b6_10).
ss(ytyil137c,10,b).
beta_len(10,b3_4).
alpha_dist(yil137c,b36.2_47.6).
beta_dist(yil137c,b19.1_29.1).
coil_dist(yil137c,b6.2_39.5).
neighbour(1,2,b).
neighbour(2,3,c).
neighbour(3,4,b).
neighbour(4,5,c).
neighbour(5,6,b).
neighbour(6,7,c).
neighbour(7,8,b).
neighbour(8,9,c).
neighbour(9,10,b).

Fig. 1. A simplified portion of the homology data for the yeast gene YOR034C. Details are shown of four SWISSPROT proteins (p31947, p29431, q28309, p14196) that are homologous to this gene. Each has facts such as sequence length, molecular weight, keywords and database references. The classification is part of a hierarchical taxonomy.

Fig. 2. A portion of the structure data for the yeast gene YIL137C. The secondary structure elements (a - alpha, b - beta, c - coil) are numbered sequentially, their lengths are given, and neighbours are made explicit. Overall distributions are also given.

no specialisations of this association are frequent (if *pasta* is not frequent, then *pasta* ∧ *mince* cannot be frequent). And if an association is frequent, then all of its parts or subsets are also frequent.

Perhaps the best known association rule algorithm is APRIORI [8]. It works on a levelwise basis, guaranteeing to take at most $d + 1$ passes through the database, where d is the maximum size of a frequent association. First a pass is made through the database where all singleton associations are discovered and counted. All those falling below the minimum support threshold are discarded. The remaining sets are "frontier sets". Next, another pass through the database is made, this time discovering and counting frequencies of possible 1-extensions that can be made to these frontier sets by adding an item. For example, {*pasta*} could be extended to give {*pasta, mince*}, {*pasta, sauce*}, {*pasta, wine*}. Whilst the basic idea is a brute force search through the space of associations of ever increasing length, APRIORI reduces the amount of associations that have to be counted by an intelligent algorithm (APRIORI_GEN) for generation of candidate associations. APRIORI was one of the early association mining algorithms, but its method of generating candidate associations to count is so efficient that it has been popular ever since.

APRIORI, along with most other association rule mining algorithms, applies to data represented in a single table, i.e non-relational data. For relational data we need a different representation.

2.3   First Order Association Mining

When mining relational data we need to extend ordinary association mining to relational associations, expressed in the richer language of first order predicate logic. The associations are existentially quantified conjunctions of literals.

Definition 1. *A term is either a constant or a variable, or an expression of the form $f(t_1, ..., t_n)$ where f is an n-place function symbol and $t_1, ..., t_n$ are terms.*

Definition 2. *An atom is an expression of the form $p(t_1, ..., t_n)$ where p is an n-place predicate symbol and $t_1, ..., t_n$ are terms.*

Definition 3. *A literal is an atom or the negation of an atom.*

Some examples of associations are:

$\exists X, Y : buys(X, pizza) \land friend(X, Y) \land buys(Y, coke)$

$\exists X, Y : gene(X) \land similar(X, Y) \land classification(Y, virus) \land mol\_weight(Y, heavy)$

Dehaspe and DeRaedt [9] developed the WARMR algorithm for data mining of first order associations. It works in a similar manner to APRIORI, extending associations in a levelwise fashion, but with other appropriate methods for candidate generation, to eliminate counting unnecessary, infrequent or duplicate associations. WARMR also introduces a language bias that allows the user to specify modes, types and constraints for the predicates that will be used to construct associations and hence restrict the search space. The language bias of a learning algorithm is simply the set of factors which influence hypothesis selection [10]. Language bias is used to restrict and direct the search.

2.4   Distributed Association Mining

As the size of data to be mined has increased, algorithms have been devised for parallel rule mining, both for machines with distributed memory [11,12,13, 14] ("shared-nothing" machines), and, more recently, for machines with shared memory [15]. These algorithms have introduced more complex data representations to try to speed up the algorithms, reduce I/O and use less memory. Due to the size and nature of this type of data mining, it is often the case that even just keeping the candidate associations in memory is too much and they need to be swapped out to disk, or recalculated every time on the fly. The number of I/O passes through the database that the algorithm has to make can take a substantial proportion of the running time of the algorithm if the database is large. Parallel rule mining also raises issues about the best ways to partition the work.

This type of rule mining is of interest to us because we have a Beowulf cluster of machines, which can be used to speed up our processing time. This cluster is a network of around 60 shared-nothing machines each with its own processor and between 256M and 1G memory per machine, with one machine acting as scheduler to farm out portions of work to the others.

2.5   Distributed First Order Association Mining

The version of WARMR that was available at the time was unable to handle the quantity of data that we had, so we needed to develop a WARMR-like algorithm that would deal with an arbitrarily large database.

The program should count associations in relational data, progressing in a levelwise fashion, and making use of the parallel capabilities of our Beowulf cluster. We use Datalog[2] as the language to represent the database. When the database is represented as a flat file of Datalog facts in plain uncompressed text, each gene has on average 150K of data associated with it (not including background knowledge). This is in total approximately 1G for the whole yeast genome when represented in this way. Scaling is a desirable feature of any such algorithm - it should scale up to genomes that are larger than yeast, it should

---

[2] Datalog [16] is the language of function free and negation free Horn clauses (Prolog without functions) and as a database query language it has been extensively studied. Datalog and SQL are incomparable in terms of expressiveness. Recursive queries are not possible in SQL, and Datalog needs the addition of negation to be more powerful than SQL

be able to make use of additional processors if they are added to the Beowulf cluster in the future, and indeed should not rely on any particular number of processors being available.

The two main options for parallelisation considered by most association mining algorithms are partitioning the associations or partitioning the database.

Partitioning the candidate associations. In this case, it is difficult to find a partition of the candidate associations that optimally uses all available nodes of the Beowulf cluster without duplication of work. Many candidates share substantial numbers of literals, and it makes sense to count these common literals only once, rather than repeatedly. Keeping together candidates that share literals makes it difficult to produce a fair split for the Beowulf nodes.

Partitioning the database. The database is more amenable to partitioning, since we have more than 6000 genes, each with their own separate data. Division of the database can take advantage of many Beowulf nodes. Data can be partitioned into pieces that are small enough to entirely fit in memory of a node, and these partitions can be farmed out amongst the nodes, with nodes receiving extra partitions of work when they finish. Partitioning the database means that we can use the levelwise algorithm, which requires just d passes through the database to produce associations of length d. In this application we expect the size of the database to be more of an issue than the size of the candidates.

Although a distributed algorithm necessarily will do extra work to communicate the counts, candidates or data between the machines, the investment in this distributed architecture pays off as the number of machines is increased.

3   The Solution

The system would serve two purposes:

1. To provide a immediate solution to mine the homology and structure data.
2. To become a platform for future research into incorporating more knowledge of biology and chemistry into this type of data mining (for example, specific biological constraints and hierarchies).

3.1   Associations

The patterns to be discovered are first order associations. An association is a conjunction of literals (actually existentially quantified, but written without the quantifier where it is clear from the context). Examples of associations are:

$$pizza(X) \land buys(bill, X) \land likes(sam, X)$$
$$gene(X) \land similar(X, Y) \land keyword(Y, transmembrane)$$

Associations are constructed in a levelwise manner. At each level, new, candidate associations are generated by specialisation of associations from the previous level under θ-subsumption.

Definition 4. *An association a_1 θ-subsumes an association a_2 if and only if there exists a substitution θ such that $a_1\theta \subseteq a_2$.*

This specialisation is achieved by extension of each of the previous associations by each of the literals in the language that are allowed by the language bias. Candidate associations are counted against the database, and pruned away if their support does not meet the minimum support threshold (θ-subsumption is monotonic with respect to frequency). The surviving candidates become the frequent association set for that level and are used to generate the next level. The algorithm can be used to generate all possible frequent associations, or to generate associations up to a certain length (level).

3.2   Farmer, Worker, and Merger

The system we developed is called PolyFARM (Poly-machine First-order Association Rule Miner). To the best of our knowledge PolyFARM is the first system to do distributed first order association mining. There are three main parts to the PolyFARM system:

Farmer. Reporting of results so far, and candidate association generation for the next level
Worker. Candidate frequency counting on a subset of the database
Merger. Collation and compaction of Worker results to save filespace

The candidate associations are generated once, centrally, by the Farmer process, using the language bias and the frequent associations from the previous level. The generation process also checks candidates against a list of infrequent associations from the previous level, to ensure that no part of an association is already known to be infrequent.

The database is partitioned and each Worker process reads in all the candidates, its own database partition and the common background knowledge. Candidates are evaluated (counted) against the database partition, and the results are saved to file (the Beowulf has no shared memory, and we do not rely on any PVM-like architectures). When all Workers have completed, the Farmer collects in the files of counts produced by the Workers. It prunes away the infrequent associations (saving them for future reference), and displays the results so far. Then the Farmer generates the next level of candidates, and the cycle begins again.

A single Worker represents counting of a single partition of a database. On the Beowulf cluster, each node will be given a Worker program to run. When the node has completed, and the results have been saved to a file, the node can run another Worker program. In this way, even if there are more partitions of the database than nodes in the Beowulf cluster, all partitions can be counted within the memory available.

In generating a file of counts from each Worker (each database partition), so many files can be generated that filespace could become an issue. So we introduce the third step - Merger. Merger collates together many Worker files into one single file, saving space. Merger can be run at any time, when filespace needs compacting. Finally, Farmer will simply read in the results from Merger, rather than collating Workers' results itself. A diagram of how the three steps interact is given in Figure 3.

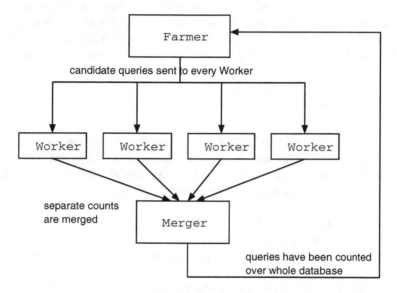

Fig. 3. Farmer, Worker and Merger

This solution addresses 2 aspects of scaling:

- Memory: Partitioning data for the Workers means that no Worker need handle more data than can fit in its main memory, no matter how large the database becomes.
- Filespace: Merger means that the buildup of intermediate results is not a filespace issue.

3.3   Association Trees

New candidates are generated by extending associations from the previous level. Any literals from the language can be added, as long as they agree with the modes, types and constraints of the language bias, and the whole association does not contain any part that is known to be infrequent. As each previous association can usually be extended by several literals, this leads naturally to a tree-like structure of associations, where literals are nodes in the tree and children of a node are the possible extensions of the association up to that point. Each level in the tree corresponds to a level in the levelwise algorithm (or the length of an association). At the root of the tree is a single literal, which all associations must contain.

Allowing common parts of associations to be collected up into a tree structure in this way provides several advantages, and was suggested in Luc Dehapse's PhD thesis [17] (p104) as an improvement that could be made to WARMR. Not only is it a compact way of representing associations, but it means that counting can be done efficiently, since common subparts are counted just once. As the associations are first order, some thought is required to make sure that the various possibilities for variable bindings are consistent within an association.

4 Why Haskell?

Why choose a language such as Haskell for an application such as data mining? Haskell was considered because in previous smaller applications it had proved to be an excellent tool for quickly prototying ideas. Initial concerns about choosing Haskell as a language for this project were

- Would it be fast enough?
- Would the resource usage be reasonable?
- Would there be enough help and support if problems occurred?

Our application does not need to run in real time, and is not time critical, though a reasonable running speed is required. We have complex data and wish to extract complex information. We are searching through large amounts of genomic information, and algorithm correctness is important, because the results can have biological significance and debugging rare or special cases that show up in large amounts of data is extremely time consuming.

Like many other software projects this required many of the techniques at which Haskell excels:

- Complex algorithms and clarity of code
- Data structures and abstraction
- Parsers and pretty printing
- Modularity and fast prototyping
- Good programming support through language features and on-line help

Whilst all of these are arguably available in any programming language if code is written well, high level declarative languages such as Haskell provide more support for the programmer. Since the application uses data expressed in Datalog and methods such as θ-subsumption, we considered using Prolog as an implementation language. However we were reluctant to give up features such as higher order functions, strong typing and profiling tools, and given the knowledge that our input data would consist of ground terms only, we would not be needing full Prolog to deal with it.

5   Disadvantages of Using Haskell

Execution time did not turn out to be a major problem. The run time is adequate for our purposes. Time profiling was used to tune the system, and it became apparent that testing for θ-subsumption accounted for most of the time taken. This is due to both the number of subsumption tests required, and the relatively expensive nature of this test. This time was then substantially alleviated and reduced by restricting the database literals to be tested - firstly to those with the correct predicate symbol, and secondly to those whose constant arguments match exactly with the constants in the literal of the association.

The main disadvantage that was faced was dealing with unwanted laziness. In a data mining environment, where all data needs to be read and counted, and all calculations will be used, laziness provides few advantages, and usually takes up huge amounts of heap space while delaying all computation until the last minute. At every step of the coding process it was found that code was easy to get right, but then difficult to get working in practice without running out of memory.

5.1   Reading Data

Much of the memory was being used by lazy reading of data. When data was lazily held in string form, it would consist of repetitions of literals and constants, and occupy far more memory than the compiled form that the program actually used.

If Haskell is to be used in earnest for real-world programs it needs to have to have good methods of reading and writing persistent data. Using the built-in **read** function for large amounts of user data or complex data structures (for example large trees of associations) is not appropriate. Apart from being slow, it is also difficult to force code using **read** to be strict. Using a parser generator tool such as Happy (http://haskell.cs.yale.edu/happy/) to generate specialist parsers helps by giving an enormous speed increase, and some memory reduction too. The disadvantages were the difficulty in tracking down the source of type errors in generated code (Happy itself provides little in the way of error checking, and type errors come to light only when using the generated Haskell), and the fact that Happy currently doesn't return anything until the whole input is parsed, and then it returns a tree of thunks. However, in the latest version of Happy, there is now a **--strict** flag to make all the productions strict. We used Happy generated parsers for all user-generated data (knowledge base, settings, and background knowledge).

Malcolm   Wallace   and   Colin   Runciman's   **Binary**   library   ([18]) (http://www.cs.york.ac.uk/fp/nhc98/libs/Binary.html)   was   considered. Currently only available for the nhc98 compiler, this provides binary data reading and writing. Data can be read and written to file or to memory, and due to the compression used, the amount of data stored will generally be an order of magnitude smaller than if it were stored as text. This also means an order of magnitude saving in memory costs too, as there are no strings to remain on the heap, because the data is read in directly. The single disadvantage of Binary at the moment is that it is not Standard Haskell, so is not portable between the compilers, and the only compiler providing support for this is nhc98.

The final solution we chose for reading and writing the counted associations that were to be communicated between Beowulf nodes was a simple strict IO class[3] providing operations `fromSeq` and `toSeq` that read and wrote data from/to a file handle. Instances of this class were written so that `seq` was applied at every stage, and data was then read and written strictly. This provided a Standard Haskell solution.

5.2   Strictness Annotations

Laziness elsewhere in the code was also a problem. Several approaches were used to enforce stricter execution and reduce heap usage. The Haskell language provides support for strictness annotations to data and functions. The `seq` function is provided in Haskell to enforce evaluation. x `seq` y will evaluate x, enough to check that x is not bottom, then discard the result and return y. This means that x is guaranteed to be evaluated before y is considered. However, `seq` forces evaluation only of the top level construct, so its argument is reduced only to weak head normal form. This was often not enough to remove the laziness. Haskell also allows user-defined data types to contain strictness annotations, specifying that each annotated argument to a data constructor will evaluated when the constructor is applied. This evaluation will also be to weak head normal form only. Careful use of the combination of strictness annotations on data types and `seq` should be enough to force complete evaluation.

`DeepSeq` is a module that provides the `deepSeq` function, which forces complete evaluation rather than the partial evaluation of `seq`. `DeepSeq` is not part of the standard libraries, but has been requested many times by users, so is easy to access on the Internet.

However, all such ways of enforcing evaluation and strictness are the programmer's responsibility, and in practice, their use is not obvious to the average programmer. `DeepSeq` is not yet automatically derivable, and instances must be written for all our datatypes. Finding the correct places in the code to use `seq` or `deepSeq` after the code has been written is not always obvious, and code can still be lazy if any necessary places are overlooked. `deepSeq` can also be an additional time overhead: if a computation is repeatedly carried out on an ever-growing datastructure, then it may be necessary to re-deepSeq the whole structure each iteration, even though most of it will have already been evaluated the previous time. Sometimes it can be difficult to find a place to put the `seq` or `deepSeq` functions and extra code needs to be written.

5.3   CPS

Use of Continuation Passing Style (CPS) was another technique we used to enforce evaluation order. By converting parts of the program into CPS some

---

[3] We would like to thank Julian Seward for this solution

control could be gained over the order of evaluation. CPS gives the programmer a handle on the continuation computation, the computation that comes next, and so this computation can be moved over a part of the code that will force execution, such as a conditional, case expression or a pattern match. CPS is a purely functional style of coding, and fits elegantly into Haskell's character. However, encoding parts of the evaluation order in this manner tends to make the code less readable (and occasionally unintelligible!), which negates one of the main reasons for using Haskell. We look forward to the day when automatic code refactoring tools are available that can analyse laziness and automatically reorganise code in a readable manner.

6   Advantages of Using Haskell

6.1   Laziness as an Advantage?

The main place in the program where laziness was an advantage was in matching associations to the data (testing for subsumption).

A tree structure of associations makes counting efficient since subparts are not repeatedly counted. For example, the associations

$$gene(X) \land similar(X, Y) \land mol\_weight(Y, heavy)$$
$$gene(X) \land similar(X, Y) \land mol\_weight(Y, light)$$
$$gene(X) \land seq\_length(X, long)$$
$$gene(X) \land seq\_length(X, short)$$

would be stored in the natural tree structure shown in Figure 4.

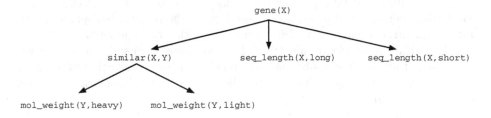

Fig. 4. Associations stored in a tree structure

As we test the associations to see whether or not they match the data for a particular gene in our database, we are aware that individual literals within the association may match the database with more than one possible binding of its variables. The variable bindings must be consistent along a path from root to leaf of the tree. The WARMR system, on which this work is based, was written in Prolog. In order to efficiently make use of both this tree structure and Prolog's built-in query subsumption test without repeatedly backtracking and redoing the variable bindings, the authors of WARMR devised the concept of "query packs" [19], requiring an extension to the standard Prolog system. In Haskell, calculating a lazy list of possible variable bindings at each node in the tree ensures that no unnecessary computation is needed. When a complete match is found the alternative possible bindings are no longer required but do not need pruning, since they will never be evaluated due to laziness.

6.2   Algorithm Expression

Haskell makes algorithm expression elegant, clear and simple. It simplifies the process of debugging by allowing each function to be tested independently and modified without side effects to other code. Higher order functions and polymorphic types can allow generalisations that make code shorter. We frequently used the predefined higher order functions, such as "map", "fold", "filter" and "any". However, we seldom defined our own, which indicates that we are still not using the full power of Haskell. Pattern matching on datatypes allows complex problems to be broken down into manageable parts. In this code there are algorithms for pruning infrequent associations, generating new extensions to associations given the modes and types supplied by the user for the predicates, testing for θ-subsumption, and various other non-trivial tasks. Haskell is a very clean and concise language, allowing the program to be easily expressed and almost self documenting. We illustrate some of the elegance of Haskell by demonstrating the `makeCombs` function in Figure 5.

`makeCombs` is the function that is responsible for constructing all the possible sets of correct arguments for a new literal that is to be added, given the type constraints and mode constraints for this literal. We work through a list of arguments, each of which has a mode (`Plus`, `Minus`, `PlusMinus` or `ConstList`). Prolog variables will be represented by Ints, and constants by PackedStrings. We wish to construct all possible combinations of the results, and remember the maximum variable number used in each combination of arguments.

Each case can be clearly identified. List comprehensions give a concise way to construct all possible combinations of results without generating many intermediate data structures, and they also allow us to test for constraints such as our type constraints.

6.3   Data Structures

The associations are stored in a tree structure to make best use of their common subparts and hence much of the program is based on handling tree-structured data (merging, searching, pruning and path-finding). We also allow hierarchically structured values for the arguments within a literal, and support counts must be propagated through these hierarchies. Haskell provides good support for trees with variable branching factors. In many other parts of the code variable length lists are ideal, since we rarely know in advance how many possible elements

```
makeCombs :: PredID -> [(ArgPosition,Mode)] -> MaxVarNum -> [Pred]
          -> Type -> [(VarCount, [Arg])]

-- When we reach the end of the argument list, just note the
-- maximum variable number used so far
makeCombs predID [] maxVar preds typenums = [(maxVar,[])]

-- if the mode is Plus then this argument must be a variable or constant of
-- the correct type which already exists in the association
makeCombs predID ((n,Plus):otherArgModes) maxVar preds types =
  let otherArgCombs = makeCombs predID otherArgModes maxVar preds types in
  [ (v, (Var i) : alist) | i <- [1..maxVar] ,
                           correctVarType i n predID types preds,
                           (v, alist) <- otherArgCombs]
  ++ [ (v, a : alist) | a <- correctAtomicTypes n predID types preds,
                        (v, alist) <- otherArgCombs]

-- if the mode is Minus then we need to create a new variable, which is
-- numbered 1 greater than the current maximum variable number for this
-- association
makeCombs predID ((n,Minus):otherArgModes) maxVar preds types =
  let otherArgCombs = makeCombs predID otherArgModes maxVar preds types in
  [ (newMaxVar+1, (Var (newMaxVar+1)) : alist) |
                           (newMaxVar,alist) <- otherArgCombs]

-- if the mode is PlusMinus, we want both options, Plus and Minus
makeCombs predID ((n,PlusMinus):otherArgModes) maxVar preds types =
  makeCombs predID ((n,Plus):otherArgModes) maxVar preds types
  ++ makeCombs predID ((n,Minus):otherArgModes) maxVar preds types

-- if the argument is to be a constant, we generate all possible constants
makeCombs predID ((n,ConstList cs):otherArgModes) maxVar preds types =
  let otherArgCombs =  makeCombs predID otherArgModes maxVar preds types in
  [ (v, (Atomic (packString c)) : alist) | c <- cs ,
                          (v,alist) <- otherArgCombs]
```

Fig. 5. The makeCombs function is responsible for constructing all the possible sets of correct arguments for a new literal that is to be added, given type and mode constraints.

will be needed. We had little use for random access arrays since in data mining we usually have to test or count all elements. Lists of lists and other nested structures have been invaluable. We make use of partially indexed lists when the search space can be reduced. Easily definable groupings of data into new data types greatly enhanced code readability and understanding. Haskell has many more useful features that we did not use, such as parameterised data structures. However, we used many of the pre-defined parameterised data structures such as lists and FiniteMap.

6.4 Parsers and Pretty Printing

Various parsers are needed to read in the knowledge base (a Datalog file), a user settings file describing the language bias and several other parameters, a background knowledge file including hierarchical data, and data which is to be exchanged by nodes of the Beowulf cluster during distributed processing. We also need pretty printing of results.

6.5 Modularity and Fast Prototyping

Modularity is very important for future experimentation, additions, redesign and modification. Abstraction allowed data types to be changed easily, to give faster execution via a different data structure. Lack of side effects in Haskell means that any changes to code are guaranteed not to interfere with any existing code. When developing this application there were many instances where an algorithm could be achieved via a number of different methods and there were several decisions to be made. The ability to prototype quickly allowed experimentation with research ideas, and this made the project less prone to retention of bad design due to the time invested in writing it, or the time to redesign it.

6.6 Good Programming Support

In spite of the lack of available books on the language, the wealth of friendly, free and expert advice available from the Haskell community, the various mailing lists and on-line Internet documentation is tremendous. Other good support comes from the tools available, such as time and heap profiling, make-tools, interpreters for easy testing, and features of the language itself such as strong static typing and referential transparency meaning that the compilers can catch most errors.

7   Conclusions

PolyFARM is a data mining application written entirely in Standard Haskell. It is currently in use for analysing computational biology data from the genome of the yeast *S. cerevisiae*. We hope to apply this to the 25,000 genes of the plant genome *A. thaliana* next, and to other genomes in future. This application is not limited to computational biology data, but can be used to mine frequent associations in any relational data expressed as Datalog. In future we also hope to extend the interface to connect directly to data in standard relational databases, as an additional alternative to using the Datalog format inherited from the field of ILP. We plan to further develop this application for future research in the field of data mining of biological data.

The use of Haskell was a success for this project. A prototype was correctly working within a remarkably short time frame (3 man-weeks), which encouraged us to continue using Haskell. However, we encountered problems with unexpected laziness frequently filling up the heap space. A further 2 months were needed to obtain reasonable resource usage. The heap problems were resolvable with the aid of the excellent profiling tools available, but profiling took time, and solutions required tricks and intuition that are not obvious. Finding all the correct places to use seq after the code has been written was difficult. Transforming code into CPS style can make code obscure, and tax the programmer. We would like to see more support for refactoring code to control heap usage.

Haskell was an excellent language for coding the application due to many features, including clear expression of complex algorithms, good support for data structures, abstraction, modularity and generalisation leading to fast prototyping and code reuse, parsing tools, profiling tools, language features such as strong typing and referential transparency which allowed for easy modification of code, and the helpful support of an enthusiastic Haskell community.

PolyFARM is freely available for non-commercial use at http://www.aber.ac.uk/compsci/Research/bio/dss/polyfarm/.

References

1. Witten, I.H., Frank, E.: Data Mining: Practical machine learning tools with Java implementations. Morgan Kaufmann, San Francisco (1999)
2. Mannila, H.: Methods and problems in data mining. In: International Conference on Database Theory. (1997)
3. Muggleton, S., ed.: Inductive Logic Programming. Academic Press (1992)
4. Wrobel, S., Džeroski, S.: The ILP description learning problem: Towards a general model-level definition of data mining in ILP. In: FGML-95 Annual Workshop of the GI Special Interest Group Machine Learning (GI FG 1.1.3). (1995)
5. King, R., Muggleton, S., Srinivasen, A., Sternberg, M.: Structure-activity relationships derived by machine learning: The use of atoms and their bond connectives to predict mutagenicity by inductive logic programming. Proc. Nat. Acad. Sci. USA **93** (1996) 438–442
6. Goffeau, A., Barrell., B., Bussey, H., Davis, R., Dujon, B., Feldmann, H., Galibert, F., Hoheisel, J., Jacq, C., Johnston, M., Louis, E., Mewes, H., Murakami, Y., Philippsen, P., Tettelin, H., Oliver, S.: Life with 6000 genes. Science **274** (1996) 563–7
7. King, R., Karwath, A., Clare, A., Dehaspe, L.: Genome scale prediction of protein functional class from sequence using data mining. In: KDD 2000. (2000)
8. Agrawal, R., Srikant, R.: Fast algorithms for mining association rules in large databases. In: 20th International Conference on Very Large Databases (VLDB 94). (1994) Expanded version: IBM Research Report RJ9839, June 1994.
9. Dehaspe, L., De Raedt, L.: Mining association rules in multiple relations. In: 7th International Workshop on Inductive Logic Programming. (1997)
10. Utgoff, P.: Shift of bias for inductive concept learning. In Michalski, R., Carbonell, J., Mitchell, T., eds.: Machine Learning: An Artificial Intelligence Approach, Volume II. Morgan Kaufmann (1986)
11. Park, J.S., Chen, M., Yu, P.: Efficient parallel data mining for assocation rules. In: CIKM '95. (1995)
12. Agrawal, R., Shafer, J.: Parallel mining of assocation rules. IEEE Trans. on Knowledge and Data Engineering **8(6)** (1996) 962–969

13. Cheung, D., Ng, V., Fu, A., Fu, Y.: Efficient mining of assocation rules in distributed databases. IEEE Trans. on Knowledge and Data Engineering **8(6)** (1996) 911–922
14. Han, E., Karypis, G., Kumar, V.: Scalable parallel data mining for assocation rules. In: SIGMOD '97. (1997)
15. Parthasrathy, S., Zaki, M., Ogihara, M., Li, W.: Parallel data mining for association rules on shared-memory systems. Knowledge and Information Systems **3(1)** (2001) 1–29
16. Ullman, J.D.: Principles of Database and Knowledge-Base Systems, Vol. 1 and 2. Computer Science Press, Rockville, Md. (1988)
17. Dehaspe, L.: Frequent Pattern Discovery in First Order Logic. PhD thesis, Department of Computer Science, Katholieke Universiteit Leuven (1998)
18. Wallace, M., Runciman, C.: The bits between the lambdas: Binary data in a lazy functional language. In: Proceedings of the International Symposium on Memory Management. (1998)
19. Blockeel, H., Dehaspe, L., Demoen, B., Janssens, G., Ramon, J., Vandecasteele, H.: Improving the efficiency of Inductive Logic Programming through the use of query packs. Journal of Artificial Intelligence Research **16** (2002) 135–166

Non-monotonic Reasoning on Beowulf Platforms

E. Pontelli[1], M. Balduccini[2], and F. Bermudez[1]

[1] Dept. Computer Science
New Mexico State University
epontell@cs.nmsu.edu
[2] Dept. Computer Science
Texas Tech University
marcello.balduccini@ttu.edu

Abstract. Non-monotonic logic programming systems, such as the various implementations of Answer Set Programming (ASP), are frequently used to solve problems with large search spaces. In spite of the impressive improvements in implementation technology, the sheer size of realistic computations required to solve problems of interest often makes such problems inaccessible to existing sequential technology. This paper presents some preliminary results obtained in the development of solutions for execution of Answer Set Programs on parallel architectures. We identify different forms of parallelism that can be automatically exploited in a typical ASP execution, and we describe the execution models we have experimented with to take advantage of some of these. Performance results obtained on a Beowulf system are presented.

1 Introduction

In recent years we have witnessed a rapid development of logical systems—*non-monotonic logics*—that provide the ability to retract existing theorems via introduction of new axioms. In the context of logic programming, non-monotonic behavior has been accomplished by allowing the use of negation as failure (NAF) in the body of clauses. The presence of NAF leads to a natural support for non-monotonic reasoning, allowing for intelligent reasoning in presence of incomplete knowledge. NAF is also important for various forms of database technology (e.g., deductive databases). Stable model semantics [8] is one of the most commonly accepted approaches to provide semantics to logic programs with NAF. Stable model semantics relies on the idea of accepting multiple minimal models as a description of the meaning of a program. In spite of its wide acceptance and its extensive mathematical foundations, stable models semantics have only recently found its way into mainstream "practical" logic programming. The recent successes have been sparked by the availability of very efficient inference engines (such as *smodels* [15], DeRes [3], and DLV [6]) and a substantial effort towards *understanding* how to write programs under stable models semantics [14,12]. This has led to the development of a novel *programming paradigm*, commonly referred to as *Answer Set Programming (ASP)*. ASP is a computation paradigm

V. Dahl and P. Wadler (Eds.): PADL 2003, LNCS 2562, pp. 37–57, 2003.

in which logical theories (Horn clauses with NAF) serve as problem specifications and solutions are represented by *collection of models*. ASP has been concretized in a number of related formalism—e.g., disjunctive logic programming and Datalog with constraints [6,5]. In comparison to other non-monotonic logics, ASP is syntactically simpler and, at the same time, very expressive. The mathematical foundations of ASP have been extensively studied; in addition, there exist a large number of *building block* results about specifying and programming using ASP—e.g., results about dealing with incomplete information and abductive assimilation of new knowledge. ASP has been successfully adopted in various domains (e.g., [1,2,11,16]).

In spite of the continuous effort in developing fast execution models for ASP [6,5,15], computation of significant programs remains a challenging task, limiting the scope of applicability of ASP in a number of domains (e.g., planning). In this work we propose the use of *parallelism* to improve performance of ASP engines and improve the scope of applicability of this paradigm. The core of our work is the identification of potential sources for *implicit* exploitation of parallelism from a basic execution model for ASP programs—specifically the execution model proposed in the *smodels* system [15]. We show that ASP has the potential to provide considerable amounts of independent tasks, which can be concurrently explored by different ASP engines. Exploitation of parallelism can be accomplished in a fashion similar to the models proposed to parallelize Prolog [10] and constraint propagation [13].

Building on recent theoretical results regarding efficiency of parallel search in computation trees [19], we provide the design of an engine which exploits the two forms of parallelism identified (*Vertical Parallelism* and *Horizontal Parallelism*). The engine design is optimized to take advantage of the specific features of the *smodels* execution, including features such as *lookahead*. The effectiveness of our engine design in extracting parallelism is demonstrated via implementations on a *distributed memory system* (a Pentium-based Beowulf architecture) and the execution of a number of ASP benchmarks. We also investigate the use of parallelism to improve the performance of the local grounding preprocessor [22] used in *smodels*-type systems. The work proposed—which continues the work on shared memory platforms presented in [18]—along with the work concurrently conducted by Finkel et al. [7], represents the first exploration in the use of scalable architectures for ASP computations ever proposed.

The paper is organized as follows. In the next section we present an introduction to answer set programming. In Section 3 we describe the parallelization of local grounding. In Sections 4, 5, and 6 we discuss the design of the engine for the computation of the answer sets of logic programs. Performance results are presented in Section 7, while optimization, related work and conclusions are discussed in Sections 8 and 9.

2   Answer Set Programming

From Answer Set Semantics to Answer Set Programming: *Answer Sets Semantics (AS)* [8] (a.k.a. *Stable Models Semantics*) was designed in the mid eighties as a tool to provide semantics for logic programming with *negation as failure*. The introduction of NAF in logic programming leads to various complications. In particular, it leads to the loss of a key property of logic programming: the existence of a *unique* intended model for each program. In standard logic programming there is no ambiguity in what is true and what is false w.r.t. a given program. This property does not hold true anymore when NAF is allowed in the programs—i.e., programs may admit distinct independent models. Various classes of proposals have been developed to tackle the problem of providing semantics to logic programs with NAF. In particular, one class of proposals allows the existence of a *collection* of intended models (*answer sets*) for a program [8]. *Answer Sets Semantics (AS)* (also known as *Stable Models Semantics*) is the most representative approach in this class, and there is intuitive as well as formal evidence showing that AS "properly" deals with negation as failure. AS relies on a simple definition: Given a ground program P and given a "tentative" model M, we can define a new program P^M (the *reduct* of P w.r.t. M) by: *(i)* removing all rules containing atoms under NAF which are contradicted by M, and *(ii)* removing all the atoms under NAF from the remaining rules. P^M contains only those rules of P that are applicable given M. P^M is a standard logic program, without negation as failure, which admits a unique intended model M'. M is an *answer set* (or *stable model*) if M and M' coincide. In general, a program with NAF may admit multiple answer sets.

Example 1. Given a database containing information regarding people working in different departments, e.g.,

```
dept(hartley,cs). dept(pfeiffer,cs). dept(gerke,math). dept(prasad,ee).
```

we would like to select the existing departments and one (arbitrary) representative employee from each of them:

```
depts_employee(Name,Dep) :- dept(Name,Dep), not other_emps(Name,Dep).
other_emps(Name,Dep) :- dept(Name1,Dep), depts_employee(Name1,Dep), Name ≠ Name1.
```

The rules assert that Name/Dep should be in the solution only if no other member of the same department has already been selected. AS produces 2 possible answer sets (for the depts_employee predicate):

$$\{\langle \text{hartley}, \text{cs}\rangle, \langle \text{gerke}, \text{math}\rangle, \langle \text{prasad}, \text{ee}\rangle\}$$
$$\{\langle \text{pfeiffer}, \text{cs}\rangle, \langle \text{gerke}, \text{math}\rangle, \langle \text{prasad}, \text{ee}\rangle\}$$

As recognized by a number of authors [12,14], the adoption of AS requires a *paradigm shift* to reconcile the peculiar features of AS with the traditional program view of logic programming. First of all, we need to provide programmers with a way of handling multiple answer sets. One could attempt to restore a more "traditional" view, where a single "model" exists. This has been attempted, for example, using *skeptical semantics* [12], where a formula is considered entailed from the program only if it is entailed in *each* answer set. Nevertheless, skeptical semantics is often inadequate—e.g., in many situations it does not provide the desired result, and in its general form provides excessive expressive power [12]. The additional level of non-determinism, is indeed a real need for a number of applications. Maintaining multiple answer sets bears also close resemblance to similar proposals put forward in other communities—such as the *choice* and *witness* constructs used in the database community. This creates an additional level of *non-determinism* on top of the non-determinism in traditional logic programming. Both are forms of *don't know* non-determinism: the difference is in the granularity of the choices made at each level.

Additionally, the presence of multiple answer sets leads to a new set of requirements on the *computational mechanisms* used. Given a program, the goal of the computation is not to provide a goal-directed tuple-at-a-time answer (i.e., a true/false answer or a substitution), as in traditional logic programming, but the objective is to return *whole answer sets*—i.e., set-at-a-time answers. The traditional resolution-based control used in logic programming is largely inadequate, and should give place to different control and execution mechanisms.

To accommodate for all these novel aspects, we embrace a different view of logic programming under AS, interpreted as a *novel programming paradigm*—that we will refer to as *Answer Sets Programming (ASP)* [14,12]. In simple terms, the goal of an ASP program is to identify a *collection of answer sets*—i.e., each program is interpreted as a specification of a *collection of sets of atoms*. Each rule in the program plays the role of a *constraint* [14] on the collection of sets specified by the program: a generic rule $Head : - B_1, \dots, B_n, not\, G_1, \dots, not\, G_m$ indicates that, whenever $B_1, \dots, B_n$ are part of an answer set and $G_1, \dots, G_m$ are not, then $Head$ has to be in the answer set as well. The shift of perspective from traditional logic programming to ASP is very important. The programmer is led to think about writing programs as manipulating *sets* of elements, and the outcome of the computation is a collection of sets. This perspective comes natural in a large number of application domains—e.g., graph problems deal with set of nodes/edges, planning problems deal with sets of actions. ASP has received consideration in knowledge representation and deductive database communities, as it enables to represent default assumptions, constraints, uncertainty and non-determinism *in a direct way* [2].

Sequential Implementation Technology: Various execution models have been proposed in the literature to support computation of answer sets and some of them have been applied as inference engines to support ASP systems [3,14,6]. In this work we adopt an execution model which is built on the ideas presented in [14] and effectively implemented in the popular *smodels* system [15]. The choice is dictated by the relatively simplicity of this execution model and its apparent suitability to exploitation of parallelism. The system consists of two parts: a preprocessor (called *lparse* in the *smodels* system [22]) that is in charge of creating atom tables and performing program grounding, and an engine, which is in charge of computing the answer sets of the ground program. The work performed by the preprocessor is based on a local grounding for programs with a restricted syntax (strongly range restricted programs [22]). Intuitively, rules are required to contain *domain predicates*—i.e., predicates not relying on any recursive definition—and each variable in a rule is required to appear in a domain predicate. Domain predicates and their extensions are identified and computed through dependency graphs. These are used to perform local grounding of each rule—taking a natural join of the positive domain predicates in the body and then checking them against the negative ones.

Our main interest is focused on the engine component. A detailed presentation of the structure of the *smodels* engine [15] is outside the scope of this paper. In this section we propose an *intuitive* overview of the basic execution algorithm. Fig. 1 presents the overall execution cycle for the computation of stable models: the computation of answer sets can be described as a non-deterministic process—since each program Π may admit multiple distinct answer sets. The computation is an alternation of two operations, expand and choose_literal. The expand operation is in charge of computing the truth value of all those atoms that have a determined value in the current answer set (i.e., there is no ambiguity on whether they are true or false). The choose_literal is in charge of arbitrarily choosing one of the atoms not present in the current answer set (i.e., atoms which do not have a determined value) and "guessing" a truth value for it. We will refer to B as *partial answer set*. The general objective is to try to expand a partial answer set into a stable model.

The meaning of the partial answer set is that, if atom a belongs to B, then a will belong to the final model. If *not* a belongs to B, a will *not* belong to the final model.

Non-determinism originates from the execution of choose_literal(Π, B), which selects an atom l such that neither l nor its negation are present in B. The *chosen* atom is added to the partial answer set and the expansion process is restarted. The choice of literals makes use of *lookahead* [15] to quickly exclude literals not leading to answer sets (see Sect. 6).

```
function compute (Π : Program)
    B := expand(Π, ∅);
    while ( (B is consistent) and
            (B is not complete) )
        l := choose_literal(Π, B);
        B := expand(Π , B ∪ { l });
    endwhile
    if (B stable model of Π) then
        return B;
```

```
function expand (Π : Program, A : LiteralsSet)
    B := A ;
    do
        B' := B;
        B := apply_rule(Π, B);
    while ( B ≠ B' );
    return B;
```

Fig. 1. Basic Execution Model for ASP   **Fig. 2.** Expand procedure

Each non-deterministic computation can terminate either successfully—i.e., B assigns a truth value to all the atoms and it represents an answer set of Π—or unsuccessfully—if either the process tries to assigns two distinct truth values to the same atom or if B does not represent an answer set of the program (e.g., truth of certain selected atoms is not "supported" by the rules in the program). As in traditional logic programming, non-determinism is handled via backtracking to the choice points generated by choose_literal. Observe that each choice point produced by choose_literal has only two alternatives: one assigns the value true to the chosen literal, and one assigns the value false to it. The expand procedure mentioned in the algorithm in Figure 1 is intuitively described in Figure 2. This procedure repeatedly applies expansion rules to the given set of literals until no more changes are possible. The expansion rules are derived from the program Π and allow to determine which literals have a definite truth value w.r.t. the existing partial answer set. This is accomplished by applying the rules of the program Π in different ways [15]. Efficient implementation of this procedure requires care to avoid unnecessary steps, e.g., by dynamically removing invalid rules and by using smart heuristics in choose_literal [15].

3   Parallel Local Grounding

The first phase of the execution is characterized by the grounding of the input program. Although most interesting programs invest the majority of their execution time in the actual computation of models, the execution of the local grounding can still require a non-negligible amount of time. We decided to

> **function ParallelGround(Π)**
> $\Pi_G = \{a \mid a$ *is instance of domain predicate*$\}$
> $\Pi = \Pi \setminus \Pi_G$
>   **forall** $R^i \in \Pi$
> $R_G^i = \texttt{GroundRule}(R^i)$
>   **endall**
> $\Pi_G = \bigcup R_G^i$
> **end**

Fig. 3. Parallel Preprocessing

investigate simple ways to exploit parallelism also from the preprocessing phase. The structure of the local grounding process, as illustrated in [22], is based on taking advantage of the strong range restriction to individually ground each rule in the program. The process can be parallelized by simply distributing the task of grounding the different rules to different agents, as in Fig. 3. The **forall** indicated in the algorithm represents a parallel computation: the different iterations are independent of each other. The actual solution adopted in our system is based on the use of a *distribution function* which statically computes a partition of the program Π (after removing all rules defining the domain predicates) and assigns the elements of the partition to the available computing agents. The choice of performing a static assignment is dictated by *(i)* the large amount of work typically generated, and *(ii)* the desire to avoid costly dynamic scheduling in a distributed memory context. The various computing agents provide as result the ground instantiations of all the rules in their assigned component of the partition of Π. The partitioning of Π is performed in a way to attempt to balance the load between processors. The heuristic used in this context assigns a weight to each rule (an estimation of the number of instances based on the size of the relations of the domain predicates in the body of the rule) and attempts to distribute balanced weight to each agent. Although simplistic in its design, the heuristics have proved effective in the experiments performed.

The preprocessor has been implemented as part of our ASP system, and it is designed to be compatible in input/output formats with the *lparse* preprocessor used in *smodels*. The preprocessor makes use of an internal representation of the program based on structure sharing—the input rule acts as skeleton and the different instantiations are described as environments for such skeleton. The remaining data structures are essentially identical to those described for the *lparse* system [22]. The implementation of the preprocessor, developed on a Beowulf system, has been organized as a master-slave structure, where the master agent is in charge of computing the program partition while the slaves are in charge of grounding the rules in each partition.

4   Parallelizing the ASP Engine

The structure of the computation of answer sets previously illustrated can be easily interpreted as an instance of a constraint-based computation [21], where the application of the expansion rules (**expand** procedure) represents the *propagation* step of the constraint computation, and the selection of a literal in **choose_literal** represents a *labeling* step. From this perspective, it is possible to identify two sources of non-determinism: **horizontal non-determinism:** which arises from the choice of the next expansion rule to apply (in **expand**), and **vertical non-determinism:** which arises from the choice of the literal to add to the partial answer set (in **choose_literal**). These two forms of non-determinism bear strong similarities respectively to the *don't care* and *don't know* non-determinism traditionally recognized in constraint and logic programming [10]. The goal of this project is to explore avenues for the exploitation of parallelism from these two sources of non-determinism—by exploring the different alternatives available in each point of non-determinism in parallel. In particular, we will use the terms *(i) Vertical Parallelism* to indicate a situation where separate threads of computation are employed to explore alternatives arising from vertical non-determinism; and, *(ii) Horizontal Parallelism* to indicate the use of separate threads of computation to concurrently apply different expansion rules to a given set of literals. Horizontal parallelism is aimed at the use of different computation agents to construct *one* of the models of the program—thus, the different agents cooperate in the construction of one solution to the program. Vertical Parallelism on the other hand makes use of separate computing agents for the computation of *different* models of the program—each execution thread is working on a differen answer set of the program. In the rest of this paper we focus on the exploitation of Vertical Parallelism, and on a particular form of Horizontal Parallelism, that we call *Parallel Lookahead*.

5   Vertical Parallelism

The essential idea behind Vertical Parallelism is the concurrent exploration of different alternatives associated to the guessing of the truth value of chosen literals (**choose_literal** operation). Each time a literal is guessed, two independent computations can be spawned, one which assumes the literal to be true and one that assumes the literal to be false. Exploitation of Vertical Parallelism shares the same roots as or-parallelism for Prolog [10] and search parallelism in constraint programming [20,17]. Recent studies have underlined the inherent complexity of maintaining the correct view of execution during parallel search [19].

The overall design of the engine used for our experiments has been directly derived from the design of the engine used in the *smodels* system [15]. In this paper we are drawing our experience from two prototypical implementations (both having a very similar structure), one developed at New Mexico State University (NMSU) and one concurrently developed at Texas Tech University (TTU). The design used builds on the design previously proposed by the authors for executing ASP on shared memory architectures [18].

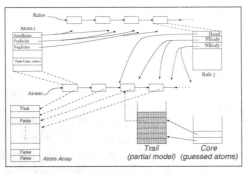

Fig. 4. Structure of an Engine

Answer set programs are internally represented using a collection of structures (both for rules and atoms) which are interlinked to allow direct access from each rule to the associated atoms and from each atom to the rules in which such atom appears (following the scheme for linear-time computations originally described in [4]). Since we are relying on a share-nothing model, each processor maintains a copy of the representation of the program. Each agent makes use of two stacks for supporting its computation. One stack (called *trail*) is used to represent the current partial answer set—each element in the current answer set is represented by an entry in the stack. Each entry is a pointer to the data structure representing the atom–and the truth value in the data structure identifies whether the atom appears positively or negatively in the answer set. For efficiency reasons the truth values are maintained in a separate array structure (the *Atom Array* in Fig. 4). The second stack, called *core*, keeps track of the answer set elements which have been "guessed" during the computation. The elements in the core allow to identify the computation points where unexplored alternatives may be available—to support backtracking and/or work sharing between agents. This structure is depicted in Fig. 4.

The architecture for vertical parallel ASP that we envision is based on the use of a number of ASP engines (*or-agents*) which are concurrently exploring the search tree generated by the search for answer sets—specifically the search tree whose nodes are generated by the execution of the `choose_literal` procedure. Each or-agent explores a distinct branch of the tree; idle agents are allowed to acquire unexplored alternatives generated by other agents.

As ensued from research on parallelization of search tree applications and non-deterministic languages [19,10], the issue of designing the appropriate data structures to maintain the correct state in the different concurrent branches is essential to achieve efficient parallel behavior. Straightforward solutions have been formally proved to be inefficient, leading to unacceptable overheads [19]. The major issue in the design of such architecture is to provide efficient mechanisms to support sharing of unexplored alternatives between agents. Each node P of the tree is associated to a partial answer set $B(P)$—the partial answer set computed in the part of the branch preceding P. An agent acquiring an unexplored alternative from P needs to continue the execution by expanding $B(P)$ together with the literal selected by choose_literal in node P. Efficiently computing $B(P)$ for the different nodes P in the tree is a known difficult problem [19]. Due to the irregular structure of the computation (branches in the computation tree may have different and unpredictable size) effective parallel implementation of ASP requires the use of dynamic distribution of work. Mechanisms have to be designed to allow dynamic exchange of tasks during the computation.

Exploitation of Vertical Parallclism requires tackling two major issues: *(i)* work sharing: i.e., allowing idle agents to acquire unexplored tasks from active agents, efficiently reproducing the necessary computation state to restart execution; *(ii)* scheduling: i.e., guiding idle agents in the search for unexplored tasks. In [18] we have sketched solutions to these issues in the context of shared memory architectures. In the successive sections we explore how these problems have been tackled and solved in the context of share-nothing architectures.

5.1   Work Sharing

The results presented in [19] lead to the following conclusions in the context of parallel ASP: at least one of the following operations will incur a cost which is $\Omega(\lg n)$ (where n is the size of the computation tree): *(i)* access to the atoms in the partial answer set; *(ii)* execution of a choose_literal operation; *(iii)* acquisition of unexplored alternatives from another agent. Practical experience [10] suggests that parallel engine designs where operations *(i)* and *(ii)* are performed in constant time are preferable—i.e., the non-constant time cost should be concentrated in operation *(iii)*. The intuition behind this is that, since the non-constant time cost is unavoidable, it is favorable to locate it in operations whose frequency can be controlled by the engine—and only operation *(iii)* has this property. On top of this, the majority of the methods proposed in the literature for handling work sharing in parallel search (see [10] for a survey on the topic) heavily rely on the use of shared data structures, and are thus unsuitable for a share-nothing architecture—as the Beowulf platforms we intend to use in this project. We have identified two methods suitable to support ASP on a distributed memory architectures: *model copying* and *model recomputation*.

Model Recomputation: The idea of recomputation-based sharing of work is derived by similar schemas adopted in the context of *or-parallel* execution of logic programs [10]. In the recomputation-based scheme, an idle agent obtains a partial answer set from another agent in an *implicit* fashion. Let us assume that agent $\mathcal{A}$ wants to send its partial answer set B to agent $\mathcal{B}$. To avoid copying the whole partial answer set B, the agents exchange only a list containing the literals which have been chosen by $\mathcal{A}$ during the construction of B. These literals represent the "core" of the partial answer set. In particular, we are guaranteed that an **expand** operation applied to this list of literals will correctly produce the whole partial answer set B. This communication process is illustrated in Fig. 5. The core of the current answer set is represented by the set of literals which are pointed to by the choice points in the core stack (see Fig. 4). In particular, to make the process of sharing work more efficient, we have modified the core stack so that each choice point not only points to the trail, but also contains the corresponding chosen literal (the literal it is pointing to in the trail stack). As a result, when sharing of work takes place between agent A and agent B, the only required activity is to transfer the content of the core stack from A to B. Once B receives the chosen literals, it will proceed to install their truth values (by recording the literals' truth values in the Atom Array) and perform an **expand** operation to reconstruct (on the trail stack) the partial answer set. The last chosen literal will be automatically complemented to obtain the effect of backtracking and constructing the "next" answer set. This copying process can be also made more efficient by making it *incremental*: agents exchange only the *difference* between the content of their core stacks. This reduces the amount of data exchanged and allows to reuse part of the partial answer set already existing in the idle agent.

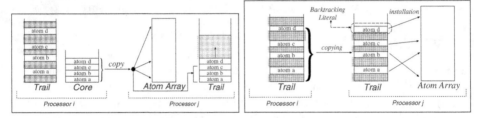

Fig. 5. Recomputation Sharing of Work   **Fig. 6.** Copy-based Sharing of Work

Model Copying: The copying-based approach to work sharing adopts a simpler approach then recomputation. Upon work sharing from agent A to B, the entire partial answer set existing in A is directly copied to agent B. The use of copying has been frequently adopted to support computation in constraint programming systems [20] as well as to support or-parallel execution of logic and constraint programs [10]. The partial answer set owned by A has an explicit representation within the agent A: it is completely described by the content of the trail stack. Thus, copying the partial answer set from A to B can be simply reduced to the copying of the trail stack of A to B. This is illustrated in Figure 6. Once this copying has been completed, B needs to install the truth value of the atoms in the partial answer set—i.e., store the correct truth values in the atom array. Computation of the "next" answer set is obtained by identifying the most recently literal whose value has been "guessed" and performing local backtracking to it. The identification of the backtracking literal is immediate as this literal lies always at the top of copied trail stack. As in the recomputation case, we can improve performance by performing incremental copying, i.e., by copying not the complete answer set but only the difference between the answer set in A and the one in B.

Hybrid Scheme: The experiments performed on shared memory architectures [18] have indicated that Model Copying behaves better than Model Recomputation in most of the cases. This is due to the high cost of recomputing parts of the answer set w.r.t. the cost of simply performing a memory copying operation. This property does not necessarily hold any longer when we move to distributed memory architectures (as the Beowulf platform used in this project), due to the considerably higher cost for copying data between agents.

To capture the best of both worlds, we have switched in our prototype to a hybrid work sharing scheme, where both Model Recomputation and Model Copying are employed. The choice of which method to use is performed dynamically (*each time* a sharing operation is required). Various heuristics have been considered for this selection, which take into account the size of the core and the size of the partial answer set. Some typical observations that have been made from our experiments include: *(i)* if the size of the core is sufficiently close to the size of the answer set, then recomputation would lead to a loss w.r.t. copying. *(ii)* if the size of the answer set is very large compared to the size of the core, then copying appears still to be more advantageous than recomputation. This last property is strongly related to the speed of the underlying interconnection network—the slower the interconnection network, the larger is the partial answer set that we can afford to recompute. We have concretized these observations by experimentally identifying two thresholds (*low* and *high*) and a function f which relates the size of the core and the size of the answer set; Recomputation is employed whenever $low \leq f(\ sizeof(Core), sizeof(Partial\ Answer\ Set)\ ) \leq high$.

5.2 Scheduling

In the context of our system, two scheduling decisions have to be taken by each idle processor in search of work: *(1)* select from which agent work will be taken; *(2)* select which unexplored alternative will be taken from the selected agent. In the current prototype, we have tackled the first issue by lazily maintaining in each agent ($\mathcal{P}$): **(a)** an approximated view of the load in each other agent. Each agent maintains an array with an entry for each agent in the system; the ith entry in the array indicates what is believed to be the load in the ith agent. The entries in the load array are managed by broadcasting the updated load whenever a sharing operation occurs; **(b)** an approximated view of what is the lowest choice point in common with each other agent in the system. This information is updated via multicast each time an agent backtracks over a copied choice point. The scheduling strategy gives preference to agents which are "near" the idle one (allowing for incremental copying) and which have a sufficiently high load.

Regarding the selection of the unexplored alternatives, in [18] we explored two approaches, respectively called *top* and *bottom* scheduling. Top scheduling selects alternatives from choice points which lie closer to the root of the tree (i.e., the oldest choices made during the computation), while in bottom scheduling the most recently guessed literals are considered. From the experiments reported in [18] we observed that in general top scheduling leads to faster sharing operations (as they typically allows the agents to deal with smaller answer sets), but to more frequent calls to the scheduler. Considering the higher cost of communication in presence of share-nothing architectures, we have reverted to a variation of bottom scheduling, similar to the *Stack Splitting* method presented in [9]. In a single sharing operation, two agents share not just one unexplored alternative (taken from the youngest choice point), but a set of them—half of the unexplored alternatives available in the active agent. This method has been implemented as follows: *(i)* the last choice point is easily detected as it lies on the top of the core stack; this allows to determine what is the part of the trail that has to be copied/recomputed; *(ii)* splitting is performed by allowing the idle agent to take control of each other choice point in the core stack.

6   Horizontal Parallelism: Parallel Lookahead

The (sequential) *smodels* algorithm presented earlier builds the stable models of an answer set program incrementally. The algorithm presented in Fig. 1 can be refined to introduce the use of lookahead during the "guess" of a literal. The algorithm is modified as follows: *(1)* Before guessing a literal to continue expansion, unexplored literals are tested to verify whether there is a literal l such that expand$(\Pi, B \cup \{l\})$ is consistent and expand$(\Pi, B \cup \{not\ l\})$ is inconsistent. Such literals can be immediately added to B. *(2)* After such literals have been found, choose_literal can proceed by guessing an arbitrary unexplored literal. Step 1 is called the `lookahead` step. It is important to observe that any introduction of literals performed in this step is *deterministic* and does not require the creation of a choice point. In addition, the work performed while testing for the various unexplored literals can be used to choose the "best" literal to be used in step 2, according to some heuristic function.

During the lookahead step, every test performed on a pair $\langle l, not\ l \rangle$ is substantially independent from the tests run on any other pair $\langle l', not\ l' \rangle$. Each test involves up to two calls to expand (one for l, the other one for $not\ l$), thus resulting in a comparatively expensive computation. These characteristics make the lookahead step a natural point where the algorithm could be parallelized. Notice that *Parallel Lookahead* is an instance of the general concept of Horizontal Parallelism, since the results of the parallel execution of lookahead are combined, rather than being considered alternative to each other, as in Vertical Parallelism. The appeal of exploiting Horizontal Parallelism at the level of `lookahead`, rather than at the level of `expand`, lies in the fact that the first involves a coarser-grained type of parallelism.

Basic Design: The parallelization of the lookahead step is obtained in a quite straightforward way by splitting the set of unexplored literals, and assigning each subset to a different agent. Each agent then performs the test described in step 1 on the unexplored literals that it has been assigned. Finally, a new partial answer set, B' is built by merging the results generated by the agents. Work sharing is based on the Model Copying technique.

Notice that, even in the parallel implementation, the lookahead step can be exploited in order to determine the best literal to be used in `choose_literal` (provided that the results returned by the agents are suitably combined). This significantly reduces the computation performed by `choose_literal`, and provides a simple way of combining Vertical and Horizontal Parallelism by applying a work-sharing method similar to the *Basic Andorra Model* [10], studied for parallelization of Prolog computation.

Scheduling: The key for the integration of Vertical and Horizontal Parallelism is in the way work is divided in work units and assigned to the agents. Our system is based on a central scheduler, and a set of agents that are dedicated to the actual computation of the answer sets. Every work unit corresponds to a lookahead step performed on a partial answer set, B, using a set of unexplored literals, U. Work units related to different partial answer sets can be processed at the same time by the system. Whenever all the work units associated with certain partial answer set have been completed, the scheduler gathers the results and executes `choose_literal` – which, as we stated before, requires a very small amount of computation, and can thus be executed directly on the scheduler. `choose_literal` returns two (possibly) partial answer sets[1], and the scheduler generates work units for both of them, thus completing a (parallel) iteration of the algorithm in Fig. 1, extended with `lookahead`. Under this perspective, Horizontal Parallelism corresponds to the parallel execution of work units related to the same partial answer set. Vertical Parallelism, instead, is the parallel execution of work units related to different partial answer sets. The way the search space is traversed, as well as the balance between Vertical and Horizontal Parallelism, are determined by: *(1)* the number agents among which the set of unexplored literals is split, and *(2)* the priority given to pending work units. In our implementation we assign priorities to pending work units according to a "simulated depth first" strategy, i.e., the priority of a work unit depends first on the depth, d, in the search space, of the corresponding node, n, and second on the number of nodes of depth d present to the left of n. This choice guarantees that, if a computation based only on Horizontal Parallelism is selected, the order in which nodes are considered is the same as in a sequential implementation of our algorithm. This is an important feature, because it allows us to exploit the same search heuristics present in the original smodels algorithm. These heuristics have been thoroughly tested in the past few years and proved to perform very well in most applications.

The number of agents among which the set of unexplored literals is split is selected at run-time. This allows the user to decide between a computation based on Horizontal Parallelism, useful if the answer set(s) are expected to be found with little backtracking, and a computation based on Vertical Parallelism, useful if more backtracking is expected.

---

[1] Our version of `choose_literal` runs `expand` on the two partial answer sets before returning them.

7   Performance Results

In this section we show some of the experimental results collected from the implementation of the ideas presented in the previous sections. The results have been obtained on the Pentium-based Beowulf (purely distributed memory architectures) at NMSU—Pentium II (333Mhz) connected via Myrinet. The results reported have been obtained from two similar implementations of ASP, one developed at NMSU and one at TTU. Both systems have been constructed in C using MPI for dealing with interprocessor communication. The experiments have been performed by executing a number of ASP programs (mostly obtained from other researchers) and the major objective was to validate the feasibility of parallel execution of ASP programs on Beowulf platforms.

Parallel Local Grounding: We have analyzed the performance of the parallel preprocessor by comparing its execution speed with varying number of processors. The parallel preprocessor is in its first prototype and it is very unoptimized (compared to *lparse* we have observed differences in speed ranging from 4% to 48%). Nevertheless, the current implementation was mostly meant to represent a proof of concept concerning the feasibility of extracting parallelism from the preprocessing phase. The first interesting result that we have observed is that the rather embarrassingly parallel structure of the computation allowed us to make the parallel overhead (i.e., the added computation cost due to the exploitation of parallelism) almost negligible. This can be seen in Fig. 7, which compares the execution times for a direct sequential implementation of the grounding algorithm with the execution times using a single agent in the parallel preprocessor. In no cases we have observed overhead higher than 4.1%. Very good speedups have been observed in each benchmark containing a sufficient number of rules to keep the agents busy. Fig. 8 shows the preprocessing time for two benchmarks using different numbers of processors. Note that for certain benchmarks the speedup is slightly lower than linear due to slightly unbalanced distribution of work between the agents—in the current scheme we are simply relying on a static partitioning without any additional load balancing activities.

Parallel Literal Selection: The experiments for exploitation of Vertical Parallelism through parallel literal selection have been conducted using the Beowulf ASP engine developed at NMSU—an evolution of the shared memory engine previously described in [18]. All timings presented have been obtained as average over 10 runs. As mentioned in Sect. 5.1, in our design we have decided to adopt a Hybrid Method to support exchange of unexplored tasks between agents. This is different from what we have observed in [18], where Model Copying was observed to be the winning strategy in the last majority of the benchmarks. In the context of distributed memory architectures, the higher cost of communication between processors leads to a higher number of situations where the model copying provides sub-optimal performances.

Table 1 reports the execution times observed on a set of benchmarks, while Fig. 9 illustrates the speedups observed using the hybrid scheme on a set of ASP benchmarks. Some of the benchmarks, e.g., T8 and P7, are synthetic benchmarks developed to study specific properties of the inference engine, while others are

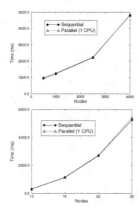

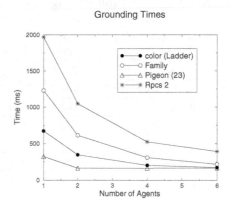

Fig. 7. Preproc. Overhead
(Pigeon, Coloring)

Fig. 8. Parallel Exec. of the Preprocessor

ASP programs obtained from other researchers. Color is a graph coloring problem, Logistics and Strategic are scheduling problems, while sjss is a planner. Note also that sjss is executed searching for a single model while all others are executed requiring all models to be produced. The tests marked [*] in Fig. 9 indicate those cases where Recomputation instead of Copying has been triggered the majority of the times. The results presented have been accomplished by using an experimentally determined threshold to discriminate between copying and recomputation. The rule adopted in the implementation can be summarized as: if $min \leq \frac{size(Partial\ Answer\ Set)}{size(Core)} \leq max$ then model recomputation is applied, otherwise model copying is used. The intuition is that *(i)* if the ratio is too low, then, there is no advantage in copying just the core, while *(ii)* if the ratio is too high, then the cost of recomputing the answer set is likely to be excessive. The *min* and *max* used for these experiments where set to 1.75 and 12.5. Fig. 10 shows the impact of using recomputation in the benchmarks marked with [*] in Fig. 9. Some benchmarks have shown rather low speedups—e.g., Color on a ladder graph and Logistics. The first generates very fine grained tasks and suffers the penalty of the cost of communication between processors—the same benchmarks on a shared-memory platform produces speedups close to 4. For what concerns Logistics, the results are, after all, quite positive, as the maximum speedup possible is actually 5 and there seem to be no degradation of performance when the number of agents is increased beyond 5.

It is interesting to compare the behavior of the distributed memory implementation with that of the shared memory engine presented in [18]. Fig. 11 presents a comparison between the speedups observed on selected benchmarks in the shared memory and the distributed memory engines. In the majority of the cases we observed relatively small degradation in the speedup. Only bench-

Table 1. Execution Times (in μs.) on Beowulf

Name	1 Agent	2 Agents	3 Agents	4 Agents	8 Agents
Color (Ladder)	345201	249911	235421	292932	295420
Color (Random2)	2067987	1162905	829685	604586	310622
Logistics 2	3937246	2172124	1842695	1652869	1041534
Strategic	76207	40169	28327	21664	12580
sjss	93347226	46761140	31012367	22963465	13297326
T8	1770106	865175	590035	444730	226930
P7	1728001	918172	690924	536646	216040

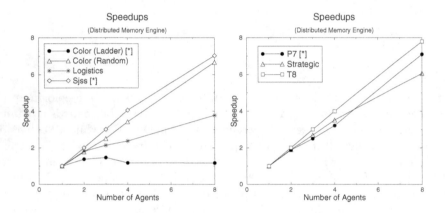

Fig. 9. Speedups from Vertical Parallelism

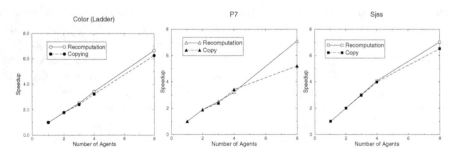

Fig. 10. Impact of using Recomputation

marks where frequent scheduling of small size tasks is required lead to a more relevant difference (e.g., `Color` for the ladder graph).

Parallel Lookahead: The experiments on Parallel Lookahead have been conducted using the distributed ASP engine developed at TTU.

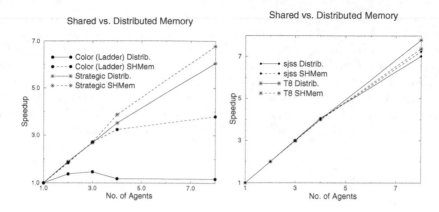

Fig. 11. Comparison of Shared and Distributed Memory Engines

For our tests, we have used a subset of the benchmarks available at `http://www.tcs.hut.fi/pub/smodels/tests/lp-csp-tests.tar.gz`: *(1)* `color`: c-colorability (4 colors, 300 nodes), *(2)* `pigeon`: put N pigeons in M holes with at most one pigeon in a hole ($N = 24, M = 24$), *(3)* `queens`: N-queens problem ($N = 14$), and *(4)* `schur`: put N items in B boxes such that, for any $X, Y \in \{1, \ldots, N\}$: items labeled X and $2X$ are in different boxes, and if X and Y are in the same box, then $X + Y$ is in a different box ($N = 35, B = 15$).

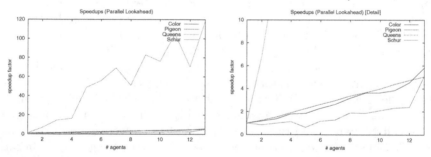

Fig. 12. Speedups for Parallel Looka-head

Fig. 13. Speedups for Parallel Looka-head

The tests consisted in finding one answer set for each of these programs. Since, for all of these programs, this can be accomplished with a comparatively small amount of backtracking, the engine was run so that Horizontal Parallelism was given a higher priority than Vertical Parallelism by acting on the number of agents among which the set of unexplored literals is split. The experiments show, in general, a good speedup for all programs. The speedup, for 13 processors, is 5 for `schur` and `pigeon`, almost 6 for `color`, and 120 for `queens`. The speedup measured for `queens` is indeed surprising. It is interesting to note that `queens` requires (with *smodels*) the highest amount of backtracking. We conjecture that the speedup observed is the result of the combined application of both types of parallelism. However this issue deserves further investigation before any precise statement can be made. The results are definitely encouraging if we consider that: to the best of our knowledge, our system is one of the first exploiting Horizontal Parallelism; the way parallelism is handled is still very primitive if compared with the other existing parallel systems; the level of refinement of the algorithms for the computation of answer sets is still far beyond *smodels* (we expect the optimizations exploited in *smodels* to significantly improve speedup).

8   Optimizations

Optimizing Vertical Parallelism: Various optimizations can be envisioned to improve the performance of the basic vertical parallel engine. Many of the general optimization principles discussed for parallel execution of Prolog [10] are likely to reduce the parallel overhead. We have applied two optimizations in the development of the parallel engine. Whenever a sharing operation is performed (either using copying or recomputation), the copying agent needs to perform an "installation" operation used to erase the truth value of those literals which have been removed from the partial answer set and add the truth value of those literals copied from the remove agent. This process is typically accomplished by forcing the copying agent to backtrack to the nearest common ancestor in the computation tree between the position of the two agents (for removing literals) and by an explicitly installing the truth value of the copied literals. While the installation is a fairly fast operation (especially when recomputation is used), the backtracking step can be fairly expensive. We have introduced an optimization which trades the cost of backtracking for the cost of copying additional data from the remote agent. The idea is that if the common ancestor is "too far away" and close to the root of the tree, it may be cheaper to avoid backtracking, removing *all* the literals from the partial answer set (using a brute force operation, e.g., the system call `memzero`), and then copy the complete answer set from the remote agent. Fig. 14 shows the improvements observed by triggering this optimization whenever the size of the answer set at the common ancestor is less than 512.

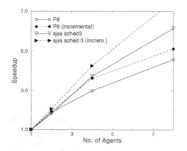 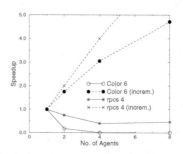

Fig. 14. Speedup Curves with and without Memory Zeroing Optimization

Optimizing Parallel Lookahead: Further research is needed in order to improve the efficiency of the system. Different types of improvements can be identified.

(1) Design improvements, aimed at decreasing the overhead due to communications. Improvements will probably need to be focused on the selection of the correct work sharing model, for which the hybrid method is a good candidate. The development of better scheduling techniques will also be important to achieve a higher efficiency.

(2) Optimization of the heuristic function used to find the "best" literal for `choose_literal`, in order to exploit the features of the parallel implementation: we are currently using a heuristic function close to the one used in *smodels*, designed for sequential implementations.

(3) Improvements aimed at making the system able to *self-adapt* according the type of logic program whose answer sets are to be found. Research has to be conducted on techniques for selecting the correct balance between Vertical Parallelism and Horizontal Parallelism depending on the task to be performed.

9   Related Work and Conclusions

The problem tackled in this work is the efficient execution of Answer Set Programs. Real-life ASP applications can easily become very time consuming, to the point that various programs (e.g., large planning applications) are beyond the computational capabilities of existing inference engines. The goal of this work is to explore the use of parallelism to improve execution performance of ASP engines. Starting from the basic design of an inference engine for ASP (the one proposed in the *smodels* system) we have identified two major sources of parallelism—*Horizontal* and *Vertical* Parallelism. We have focused on the design of technology to allow the exploitation of Vertical Parallelism in the context of a distributed memory architecture. Within Vertical Parallelism, we have distinguished between standard parallel branching and parallel lookahead to provide further scope of exploitation of parallelism. The various issues related to the exploitation of this form of parallelism have been analyzed and solutions proposed. We have also briefly explored the issue of parallelization of the pre-processing phase required for the execution of answer set programs.

The potential for exploitation of parallelism from ASP computations has been recently recognized by other authors as well: [7] proposes a PVM-based implementation of a *smodels*-type engine with Vertical Parallelism—parallelism is extracted from the actual operation of guessing the truth value of a chosen literal, and scheduling is centralized. The work we propose has also strong ties to the work on parallel execution of logic programs [10] and non-deterministic languages [19]. With respect to parallel execution of logic programs, the vertical parallelism used in our work can be related to or-parallelism in Prolog, and horizontal parallelism can be related to deterministic parallelism. With respect to non-deterministic languages, there are similar aspects in the construction of the search tree – each branch represents a solution, and the way nodes are handled involves the ability to reconstruct part of the computation (e.g., "environments").

Acknowledgments. The authors wish to thank G. Gupta, S. Tran, and M. Gelfond for their help. E. Pontelli and F. Bermudez were partially supported by NSF grants CCR9875279, CCR9900320, CDA9729848, EIA0130887, EIA9810732, and HRD9906130. M. Balduccini was partially supported by United Space Alliance under Research Grant 26-3502-21 and Contract COC6771311.

References

1. M. Balduccini and M. Gelfond. Diagnostic Reasoning with A-Prolog. *Theory and Practice of Logic Programming* (to appear), 2002.
2. C. Baral and M. Gelfond. Logic Programming and Knowledge Representation. *Journal of Logic Programming*, 19/20:73–148, 1994.
3. P. Cholewinski et al. Default Reasoning System DeReS. In *Int. Conf. on Principles of Knowledge Representation and Reasoning*, pages 518–528. Morgan Kauffman, 1996.
4. W.F. Dowling and J.H. Gallier. Linear-time Algorithms for Testing the Satisfiability of Propositional Horn Formulae. *Journal of Logic Programming*, 3, 1984.
5. D. East and M. Truszczyński. Datalog with Constraints. In *National Conference on Artificial Intelligence*, pages 163–168. AAAI/MIT Press, 2000.
6. T. Eiter et al. The KR System dlv: Progress Report, Comparisons, and Benchmarks. In *Int. Conf. on Principles of Knowledge Representation and Reasoning*, 1998.
7. R. Finkel et al. Computing Stable Models in Parallel. In *AAAI Spring Symposium on Answer Set Programming*, pages 72–75, 2001. AAAI/MIT Press.
8. M. Gelfond and V. Lifschitz. The Stable Model Semantics for Logic Programs. In *Int. Symposium on Logic Programming*, pages 1070–1080. MIT Press, 1988.
9. G. Gupta and E. Pontelli. Stack-splitting: A Simple Technique for Implementing Or-Parallelism on Distributed Machines. In *ICLP*, pages 290–304, 1999. MIT Press.
10. G. Gupta, E. Pontelli, M. Carlsson, M. Hermenegildo, and K.M. Ali. Parallel Execution of Prolog Programs: a Survey. *ACM TOPLAS*, 23(4):472–602, 2001.
11. K. Heljanko and I. Niemela. Answer Set Programming and Bounded Model Checking. In *AAAI Spring Symposium*, pages 90–96, 2001.
12. V.W. Marek and M. Truszczyński. Stable Models and an Alternative Logic Programming Paradigm. In *The Logic Programming Paradigm*. Springer Verlag, 1999.
13. T. Nguyen and Y. Deville. A Distributed Arc-Consistency Algorithm. *Science of Computer Programming*, 30(1–2):227–250, 1998.
14. I. Niemela. Logic Programs with Stable Model Semantics as a Constraint Programming Paradigm. *Annals of Mathematics and AI*, 2001.
15. I. Niemela and P. Simons. Smodels - An Implementation of the Stable Model and Well-Founded Semantics for Normal LP. In *LPNMR*, Springer Verlag, 1997.
16. M. Nogueira, M. Balduccini, M. Gelfond, R. Watson, and M. Barry. An A-Prolog Decision Support System for the Space Shuttle. In *PADL*, Springer Verlag, 2001.
17. L. Perron. Search Procedures and Parallelism in Constraint Programming. In *Int. Conf. on Principles and Practice of Constraint Programming*, 1999. Springer Verlag.

18. E. Pontelli and O. El-Kathib. Construction and Optimization of a Parallel Engine for Answer Set Programming. In *PADL*, 2001. Springer Verlag.

19. D. Ranjan, E. Pontelli, and G. Gupta. On the Complexity of Or-Parallelism. *New Generation Computing*, 17(3):285–308, 1999.

20. C. Schulte. Comparing Trailing and Copying for Constraint Programming. In *International Conference on Logic Programming*, pages 275–289. MIT Press, 1999.

21. V.S. Subrahmanian, D. Nau, and C. Vago. WFS + Branch and Bound = Stable Models. *Transactions on Knowledge and Data Engineering*, 7(3):362–377, 1995.

22. T. Syrjanen. Implementation of Local Grounding for Logic Programs with Stable Model Semantics. Technical Report B-18, Helsinki University of Technology, 1998.

DATALOG with Constraints: A Foundation for Trust Management Languages

Ninghui Li and John C. Mitchell

Department of Computer Science, Stanford University
Gates 4B, Stanford, CA 94305-9045
{ninghui.li, jcm}@cs.stanford.edu

Abstract. Trust management (TM) is a promising approach for authorization and access control in distributed systems, based on signed distributed policy statements expressed in a policy language. Although several TM languages are semantically equivalent to subsets of DATALOG, DATALOG is not sufficiently expressive for fine-grained control of structured resources. We define the class of linearly decomposable unary constraint domains, prove that DATALOG extended with constraints in any combination of such constraint domains is tractable, and show that permissions associated with structured resources fall into this class. We also present a concrete declarative TM language, RT_1^C, based on constraint DATALOG, and use constraint DATALOG to analyze another TM system, KeyNote, which turns out to be less expressive than RT_1^C in significant respects, yet less tractable in the worst case. Although constraint DATALOG has been studied in the context of constraint databases, TM applications involve different kinds of constraint domains and have different computational complexity requirements.

1 Introduction

One main goal of computer security is to ensure that access to resources is restricted to parties with legitimate access permissions. Traditional *access control* mechanisms process requests from authenticated users of an operating system or a database system and make authorization decisions based on the identity of the requester. However, in decentralized, open, distributed systems, the resource owner and the requester often are unknown to one another, and access control based on identity may be ineffective. In the "trust-management" approach to distributed authorization, articulated in [4], access control decisions are based on *policy statements* made by multiple principals. Some statements are digitally signed to ensure their authenticity and integrity; these are called *credentials*. Some statements may be stored in local trusted storage and do not need to signed, we call these *access rules*. In a TM scenario, a *requester* submits a request, possibly supported by a set of credentials issued (signed) by other parties, to an *authorizer*, who specifies access rules governing access to the requested resources. The authorizer then decides whether to authorize this request by answering the *proof-of-compliance* question: "Do the access rules and credentials authorize

V. Dahl and P. Wadler (Eds.): PADL 2003, LNCS 2562, pp. 58–73, 2003.

the request?" Digitally signed credentials document authenticated attributes of entities. These attributes may be group membership, membership in a role within an organization, or being delegated of a permission or role. Access rules can specify what attributes are required to access a resource and other conditions of access, such as time or auditing requirements. There are good reasons to prefer TM languages that are declarative and have a formal foundation.

Several TM languages are based on DATALOG, e.g., Delegation Logic [14,13], the RT (Role-based Trust-management) framework [15,16], SD3 (Secure Dynamically Distributed DATALOG) [10], and Binder [6]. However, DATALOG has limitations as a foundation of TM languages. One significant limitation is the inability to describe structured resources. For example, a project manager may want to grant permission to read the entire document tree under a given URI, assign responsibility for associating public keys with all DNS names in a given domain, restrict network connections to port numbers in a limited range, or approve routine transactions with value below an upper limit. The permission to access all files and subdirectories under a directory "/pub/rt" represents permissions to access a potentially infinite set of resources that seems most naturally expressed using a logic programming language with function symbols. However, the tractability of DATALOG is a direct consequence of the absence of function symbols. Previous TM languages that can express certain structured resources, e.g., SPKI [7], have not had a formal foundation; some studies suggest that SPKI may be ambiguously specified and intractable [8,1].

In this paper, we show that DATALOG extended with constraints (denoted by DATALOG$^\mathcal{C}$) can define access permissions over structured resources without compromising the properties of DATALOG that make it attractive for trust management, thus establishing a suitable logical foundation for a wider class of TM languages. DATALOG$^\mathcal{C}$ allows first-order formulas in one or more constraint domains, which may define file hierarchies, time intervals, and so on, to be used in the body of a rule, thus representing access permissions over structured resources in a declarative language. We study several constraint domains that are useful for representing structured resources, e.g., tree domains and range domains, and show that DATALOG$^\mathcal{C}$ with these domains can be evaluated efficiently. We also define a general class of tractable constraint domains, called linearly decomposable unary constraint domains and present a concrete declarative TM language, $RT_1^\mathcal{C}$, that is based on DATALOG$^\mathcal{C}$. We show how to translate credentials in $RT_1^\mathcal{C}$, which extends the DATALOG-based RT_1 language from the RT framework [15,16] with constraints, into DATALOG$^\mathcal{C}$ over tractable constraint domains. We also use DATALOG$^\mathcal{C}$ to analyze another prominent TM systems KeyNote [3], and show that KeyNote uses constraint domains that are too expressive.

Constraint DATALOG has been studied extensively in the Constraint Database (CDB) literature [11,12,18,19,20,21]. However, TM applications involve constraint domains that are outside the scope of previous CDB research. Moreover, TM applications have different computational complexity requirements. In the CDB literature, tractability is often measured using data complexity, which considers the processing time for a fixed query (set of rules) as the size of the database (set of facts) grows. Data complexity is appropriate for CDB applications where the size of the input databases dominates the size of the queries by several orders of magnitude. However, expressing the access control policy in trust management and distributed access control requires both rules and facts. In particular, delegation, a characteristic feature of trust management, is represented using rules rather than facts. To guarantee that queries can be answered in time related to the complexity of the access control policy, TM applications require efficient computation as a function of the size of the set of rules and facts.

The rest of this paper is organized as follows. Some background on constraint DATALOG appears in Section 2. Tractability of constraint domains is studied in Section 3, with RT_1^C in Section 4 and an analysis of KeyNote in Section 5. We conclude in Section 6.

2   Background on Constraint DATALOG

Constraint DATALOG is a restricted form of Constraint Logic Programming (CLP) [9], and is also a class of query languages for CDB.

2.1   DATALOG

DATALOG is a restricted form of logic programming with variables, predicates, and constants, but without function symbols. A DATALOG *rule* has the form

$$R_0(t_{0,1}, \ldots, t_{0,k_0}) :- R_1(t_{1,1}, \ldots, t_{1,k_1}), \ldots, R_n(t_{n,1}, \ldots, t_{n,k_n})$$

where $R_0, \ldots, R_n$ are predicate (relation) symbols and each term $t_{i,j}$ is either a constant or a variable ($0 \leq i \leq n$ and $1 \leq j \leq k_i$). The formula $R_0(t_{0,1}, \ldots, t_{0,k_0})$ is called the *head* of the rule and the sequence $R_1(t_{1,1}, \ldots, t_{1,k_1}), \ldots, R_n(t_{n,1}, \ldots, t_{n,k_n})$ the *body*. If $n = 0$, then the body is empty and the rule is called a *fact*. A rule is *safe* if all variables occurring in the head also appear in the body. A DATALOG *program* is a finite set of DATALOG rules. DATALOG is attractive for trust management because of the following reasons.

1. DATALOG is declarative and is a subset of first-order logic; therefore, the semantics of a DATALOG-based TM language is declarative, unambiguous, and widely understood.
2. DATALOG has been extensively studied both in logic programming, and in the context of relational databases as a query language that supports recursion. TM languages based on DATALOG can benefit from past results and future advancements in those fields.
3. The function-symbol-free property of DATALOG ensures its tractability. For a safe DATALOG program with fixed maximum number of variables per rule, construction of its minimal model takes time polynomial in the size of the program.
4. There are efficient goal-directed evaluation procedures for answering queries.

2.2   Constraint Domains and Constraint Databases

The notion of constraint databases was introduced in [11], and grew out of the research on DATALOG and CLP. It generalizes the relational model of data by allowing infinite relations that are finitely representable using constraints. Constraint databases find many applications in spatial and temporal databases. For recent surveys, see [12,18].

Intuitively, a constraint domain is a domain of objects, such as numbers, points in the plane, or files in a file hierarchy, together with a language for speaking about these objects. The language is typically defined by a set of first-order constants, function symbols, and relation symbols.

Definition 1. A *constraint domain* Φ is a 3-tuple $(\Sigma, \mathcal{D}, \mathcal{L})$. Here Σ is a signature; it consists of a set of constants and a collection of predicate and function symbols, each with an associated "arity", indicating the number of arguments to the symbol. $\mathcal{D}$ is a Σ-structure; it consists of the following: a set D called the universe of the structure, a mapping from each constant to an element in D, a mapping from each predicate symbol in Σ of degree k to a k-ary relation over D, and a mapping from each function symbol in Σ of degree k to a function from D^k into D. $\mathcal{L}$ is a class of quantifier-free first-order formulas over Σ, called the *primitive constraints* of this domain.

Following common conventions, we assume that the binary predicate symbol $=$ is contained in Σ and is interpreted as identity in $\mathcal{D}$. We also assume that $\top$ (true) and $\bot$ (false) are in $\mathcal{L}$, and that $\mathcal{L}$ is closed under variable renaming.

The following are examples of classes of constraint domains that have been studied in the CDB literature; they are listed in order of increasing expressive power.

Equality constraint domains. The signature Σ consists of a set of constants and one predicate $=$. A primitive constraint has the form $x = y$ or $x = c$, where x and y are variables, and c is a constant. DATALOG can be viewed as one specific instance of DATALOG$^{\mathcal{C}}$ with an equality constraint domain.

Order constraint domains. The signature Σ has two predicates: $=$ and $<$. The Σ-structure is linearly ordered. A primitive constraint has the form $x\theta y$, $x\theta c$, or $c\theta x$ where θ is one of $=, <$.

Order and inequality constraint domains. The signature Σ has predicates $\{=, \neq, <, >, \geq, \leq\}$. The Σ-structure is linearly ordered. A primitive constraint has the form $x\theta y$ or $x\theta c$, where θ is any predicate in Σ.

The structures in order constraint domains and order and inequality constraint domains can be integers, rational numbers, real numbers, or some subset of them.

Linear constraint domains. The signature Σ has function symbols $+$ and $*$ and predicates $\{=, \neq, <, >, \geq, \leq\}$. A primitive constraint has the form $c_1 x_1 + \cdots + c_k x_k \theta b$, where c_i is a constant and x_i is a variable for each $1 \leq i \leq k$, θ is any predicate in Σ, and b is a constant.

Polynomial constraint domains. The signature Σ has the same functions symbols and predicate symbols as linear constraint domains. A primitive constraint has the form $p(x_1, \ldots, x_k)\theta 0$, where p is a polynomial in variables $x_1, \ldots, x_k$, and θ is any predicate in Σ.

Linear constraints and polynomial constraints may be interpreted over integers, rational numbers, or real numbers.

Definition 2. Let Φ be a constraint domain.

1. A *constraint k-tuple*, or a *constraint*, (in variables $x_1, \ldots, x_k$) is a finite conjunction $\phi_1 \wedge \cdots \wedge \phi_N$, where each $\phi_i, 1 \leq i \leq N$, is a primitive constraint in Φ. Furthermore, the variables in each ϕ_i are all free and among $x_1, \ldots, x_k$.
2. A *constraint relation of arity k* is a finite set $r = \{\psi_1, \ldots, \psi_M\}$, where each $\psi_i, 1 \leq i \leq M$ is a constraint k-tuple over the same variables $x_1, \ldots, x_k$.
3. The *formula corresponding to* the constraint relation r is the disjunction $\psi_1 \vee \cdots \vee \psi_M$.
4. A *constraint database* is a finite collection of constraint relations.

Relational calculus, relation algebra, and DATALOG can all be enhanced with constraints as query languages for constraint databases. Our focus in this paper is DATALOG extended with constraints, DATALOG$^\mathcal{C}$.

2.3   Evaluation of Datalog$^\mathcal{C}$

A *constraint* (DATALOG) *rule* has the form:

$$R_0(x_{0,1}, \ldots, x_{0,k_0}) :- R_1(x_{1,1}, \ldots, x_{1,k_1}), \ldots, R_n(x_{n,1}, \ldots, x_{n,k_n}), \psi_0$$

where ψ_0 is a constraint in the set of all variables in the rule. When $n = 0$, the constraint rule is called a *constraint fact*. A constraint rule with n hypotheses may be applied to n constraint facts to produce m facts. The process of applying a rule to a set of facts requires a form of quantifier elimination, made precise in the following two definitions.

Definition 3. Given a rule of the form above and n facts of the form

$$R_i(x_{i,1}, \ldots, x_{i,k_i}) :- \psi_i(x_{i,1}, \ldots, x_{i,k_i})$$

where each ψ_i is a constraint, $1 \leq i \leq n$, a *constraint rule application* produces $m \geq 0$ facts

$$R_0(x_1, \ldots, x_k) :- \psi'_j(x_1, \ldots, x_k),$$

where each ψ'_j is a constraint, $1 \leq j \leq m$, and $\psi'_1(x_1, \ldots, x_k) \vee \cdots \vee \psi'_m(x_1, \ldots, x_k)$, or $\perp$ when $m = 0$, is equivalent to the formula

$$\exists * (\psi_1(x_{1,1}, \ldots, x_{1,k_1}) \wedge \cdots \wedge \psi_n(x_{n,1}, \ldots, x_{n,k_n}) \wedge \psi_0),$$

where "$*$" is the list of the variables that appear in the body but not the head of the rule.

Intuitively, a rule means that the head of the rule holds if the body holds, where variables that appear only in the body are implicitly existentially quantified. Therefore, the head of the rule holds if the displayed $\exists *$ formula is true. When the $\exists *$ formula is equivalent to a disjunction $\psi'_1(x_1, \ldots, x_k) \vee \cdots \vee \psi'_m(x_1, \ldots, x_k)$, then the rule reduces to a set of facts (rules with only constraints in the body).

The form of constraint rule application defined above is called *closed-form* because the outputs $\psi'_1, \ldots, \psi'_m$ are constraints in the same constraint domain as the input facts. Closed-form application requires quantifier elimination.

Definition 4. Let $x_1, \ldots, x_k$ be a set of variables, $* \subseteq \{x_1, \ldots, x_k\}$ some subset, and $\overline{*} = \{x_1, \ldots, x_k\} - *$ its complement. A constraint domain $(\Sigma, \mathcal{D}, \mathcal{L})$ *admits quantifier elimination* if, for every formula $\exists * \psi(x_1, \ldots, x_k)$ with ψ any constraint (a conjunction of several constraints is still a constraint), it is possible to compute an equivalent quantifier-free disjunction of constraints $\psi'_1(\overline{*}) \vee \cdots \vee \psi'_m(\overline{*})$ with the same free variables.

Linear constraint domains (and other less expressive domains) admit quantifier elimination. On the other hand, the domain of polynomial constraints over integers does not admit quantifier elimination. This follows from the fact that it is undecidable to determine whether constraints of the form $p(x_1, \ldots, x_k) = 0$, known as Diophantine equations, have integer solutions or not [17]. The domain of polynomial constraints over real numbers admits quantifier elimination, but the complexity is very high.

The least fixpoint of a DATALOG$^\mathcal{C}$ program over any constraint domain that admits quantifier elimination may be computed by iterated rule application. The following algorithm terminates when all derivable new facts are already implied by previous results of the algorithm.

Definition 5 (The Datalog$^\mathcal{C}$ least fixpoint algorithm).

```
constraintFixpoint(Facts, Rules) {
  Results = Facts;  Changed = true;
  while (Changed) {
    Changed = false;
    foreach Rule = "R₀(...) :- R₁(...),...,Rₖ(...), ψ₀" in Rules
      foreach Tuple <(R₁ :- ψ₁),...,(Rₖ :- ψₖ)>
                        constructed from Results {
        NewResults = constraintRuleApplication(Rule, Tuple)
        foreach Fact in NewResults {
          if (Fact is not implied by any fact in Results) {
            Results = Results ∪ {Fact};  Changed=true; } } }
  }
  return Results;
}
```

The set of facts produced by this algorithm is called the *constraint least fixpoint* of the program. Even when a constraint domain admits quantifier elimination, the least fixpoint algorithm may not terminate. An example arises in

DATALOG$^\mathcal{C}$ with linear constraints over the integers, which can express any computable function. More efficient least fixpoint algorithms exist. Also, resolution-style goal-directed evaluation procedures for DATALOG can be adapted to work with DATALOG$^\mathcal{C}$ [20].

In the CDB literature, most complexity results are about data complexity, which is a measure of running time for a fixed query as the size of the input database grows. Some constraint domains that can be evaluated in closed-form with DATALOG with PTIME data complexity are: equality constraints, order and inequality constraints over dense linear order domains [11], and integer periodicity constraints ($x \equiv_k y$, $x \equiv_k c$) for fixed set of k's [21].

As mentioned in the introduction, a more restrictive DATALOG$^\mathcal{C}$ complexity measure is appropriate for TM applications.

Definition 6. A constraint domain Φ is *tractable*, if evaluating any DATALOG$^\mathcal{C}$ program with constraints in Φ has time complexity polynomial in the size of the program, when the size of each rule is bounded by a fixed value. One good measure of rule size is the sum of all the arities of the predicates in a rule.

3   Tractable Constraint Domains in Trust Management

In TM languages, it is useful to appeal to constraints from several domains. It is straightforward to define multi-sorted DATALOG$^\mathcal{C}$, following the standard definition of multi-sorted first-order logic. In order to keep each constraint domain separate from the others, we assume that when constraint domains are combined, each domain is given a separate sort, all predicate symbols are only applicable to arguments from the appropriate constraint domain, and each variable belongs to only one sort. It is straightforward to verify, by inspection of the algorithm in Definition 5, that any multi-sorted combination of tractable domains remains tractable.

Theorem 1. *A multi-sorted DATALOG$^\mathcal{C}$ program with constraints in several domains can be evaluated in time polynomial in the size of the program if all involved constraint domains are tractable.*

We now give several classes of constraint domains that are useful in TM.

Tree domains. Each constant of a tree domain takes the form $\langle a_1, \ldots, a_k \rangle$. Imagine a tree in which every edge is labelled with a string value. The constant $\langle a_1, \ldots, a_k \rangle$ represents the node for which $a_1, \ldots, a_k$ are the strings on the path from root to this node. A primitive constraint is of the form $x = y$ or $x\theta\langle a_1, \ldots, a_k \rangle$, in which $\theta \in \{=, <, \leq, \prec, \preceq\}$, $x < \langle a_1, \ldots, a_k \rangle$ means that x is a child of the node $\langle a_1, \ldots, a_k \rangle$, and $x \prec \langle a_1, \ldots, a_k \rangle$ means that x is a descendant of $\langle a_1, \ldots, a_k \rangle$.

Range domains. Range domains are syntactically sugared order domains. A primitive constraint has the form $x = y$, $x = c$ or $x \in (c_1, c_2)$, in which c is a constant, each of c_1 and c_2 is either a constant or a special symbol "$*$", meaning unbounded. And when c_1 is not $*$, "(" can also be "["; similarly, ")" can be "]" when c_2 is not $*$.

Discrete domains with sets. This is syntactically sugared version of equality domains. A primitive constraint has the form $x = y$, or $x \in \{c_1, \ldots, c_\ell\}$, in which $c_1, \ldots, c_\ell$ are constants.

The following is an example that uses three sorts: one tree domain and two range domains.

Example 1. An entity A grants to an entity B the permission to connect to machines in the domain "stanford.edu" at port number 80, and allows B to further delegate any part of the permission, the validity period of this grant is from time t_1 to time t_3. To represent this, we need to use a tree domain for DNS names, a range domain for port number, and another range domain for time. The above grant and delegation can be represented using the following constraint fact and rule.

$$\text{grantConnect}(A, B, h, p, v) :- h \prec \langle\text{edu,stanford}\rangle, p = 80, v \in [t_1, t_3].$$
$$\text{grantConnect}(A, x, h, p, v) :- \text{grantConnect}(B, x, h, p, v),$$
$$h \prec \langle\text{edu,stanford}\rangle, p = 80, v \in [t_1, t_3].$$

If B grants to another entity D the permission to connect to the host "cs.stanford.edu" and any machine in the domain "cs.stanford.edu" at any port number, with validity period from t_2 to t_4. Then we have:

$$\text{grantConnect}(B, D, h, p, v) :- h \preceq \langle\text{edu,stanford,cs}\rangle, v \in [t_2, t_4].$$

From the above, we can conclude the following, assuming that $t_1 \leq t_2 \leq t_3 \leq t_4$:

$$\text{grantConnect}(A, D, h, p, v) :- h \preceq \langle\text{edu,stanford,cs}\rangle, p = 80, v \in [t_2, t_3].$$

3.1 Hierarchical Domains Are Tractable

We first show that tree domains are tractable, using a specialized property of unary statements about tree orderings.

Definition 7. A constraint domain is *unary* if each primitive constraint either has the form $x = y$, where x and y are variables, or contains only one variable. We call a unary primitive constraint a *basic constraint*.

Definition 8. A unary constraint domain is *hierarchical* if, for any two basic constraints $\phi_1(x)$ and $\phi_2(x)$, either $\phi_1(x) \wedge \phi_2(x)$ is unsatisfiable or one of the constraints implies the other.

It is not difficult to verify that tree domains are hierarchical.

Theorem 2. *Hierarchical domains are tractable.*

Proof. Consider the algorithm in Definition 5 and the process of constraint rule application. The key step is quantifier elimination, i.e., finding a formula equivalent to $\exists * \psi(x_1, \ldots, x_k)$, in which $\psi(x_1, \ldots, x_k)$ is a conjunction of primitive constraints and $* \subseteq \{x_1, \ldots, x_k\}$. In hierarchical constraint domains, this can be done as follows. First, we transform ψ to an equivalent constraint that is free of equality constraints. For every constraint $x_i = x_j$ in ψ, we remove $x_i = x_j$ and replace every occurrence of x_j in ψ with x_i. Next, if any variable x_i has two basic constraints, by the property of hierarchical domains, either their conjunction is unsatisfiable, in which case $\exists * \psi(x_1, \ldots, x_k)$ is equivalent to $\bot$, or one of them implies the other, in which case we can remove the less restrictive one. Repeating the above step until either we know that $\exists * \psi(x_1, \ldots, x_k)$ is not satisfiable, or we have a constraint that has at most one basic constraint per variable. In the latter case, we simply remove the constraints about variables occurring in $*$ (since any one basic constraint is satisfiable) and get an constraint equivalent to $\exists * \psi(x_1, \ldots, x_k)$.

Following this process for quantifier elimination, the fixpoint computation for any hierarchical domains does not introduce any new basic constraints. If the algorithm begins with a set of constraint rules that have total size N (and fixed rule size), there are at most polynomial number of different constraint facts as possible results, giving us a computational complexity of PTIME. ∎

3.2 Linearly Decomposable Domains Are Tractable

Range domains are not hierarchical. The conjunction of two basic constraints $x \in (c_1, *)$ and $x \in (*, c_2)$ results in a new constraint $x \in (c_1, c_2)$, which is not equivalent to either.

Definition 9. A unary constraint domain is said to be *linearly decomposable* if there exists a constant d such that, given any set C of basic constraints about one variable x, there exists a set C' of basic constraints about x such that $|C'| \leq d|C|$, where $|C|$ is the sum of the sizes of constraints in C for some appropriate notion of size (e.g., number of symbols in a constraint), and the conjunction of any subset of $C \cup C'$ can be represented by the disjunction of constraints in C'. We say that C' is a decomposition of C.

Clearly, all hierarchical domains are linearly decomposable. Range domains are also linearly decomposable. For example, a set of constraints $C = \{x \in (*, 10], x \in [5, *), x \in [1, 5]\}$ can be decomposed into $C' = \{x \in (*, 1), x \in [1, 4], x \in [5, 5], x \in (5, 10], x \in (10, *)\}$. Discrete domains with sets are also linearly decomposable, as each constraint $x \in \{c_1, \ldots, c_\ell\}$ is equivalent to the disjunction of ℓ constraints $x = c_1, \cdots, x = c_\ell$. This is linear because the size of the original constraint is $\Theta(\ell)$.

Theorem 3. *Linearly decomposable domains are tractable.*

Proof. Given a DATALOG^C program, one can collect all the basic constraints in it, rename them so that all the constraints are about the same variable, and compute a linear decomposition of them. During quantifier elimination, a conjunction of multiple constraints on one variable can be replaced with a disjunction of constraints in C'. The fixpoint computation does not need to introduce any new basic constraints beyond those in C', and the size of C' is bounded by dN. The rest follows from the proof of Theorem 2.

3.3   Not All Unary Domains Are Tractable

The key reason that linearly decomposable domains are tractable is that although new basic constraints are introduced by the conjunction of existing constraints, the number of these new constraints are still linear in the total size of the original constraints. The tractability result in Theorem 3 can be generalized to the case of polynomially decomposable domains. We now show that some unary constraint domains are not polynomially decomposable and are intractable.

Example 2. The universe of the constraint domain is all the subsets of

$$A = \{a_{11}, \cdots, a_{1n}, a_{21}, \cdots, a_{2n}, \cdots, a_{n1}, \cdots, a_{nn}\}$$

and the only predicates are $=$ and $\subseteq$. We show a program that has n^2 constraint rules and total size n^4:

$$\{p_1(x) :- x \subseteq A - \{a_{1i}\}. \qquad \mid 1 \le i \le n\}$$
$$\{p_2(x) :- p_1(x), \, x \subseteq A - \{a_{2i}\}. \quad \mid 1 \le i \le n\}$$
$$\cdots$$
$$\{p_n(x) :- p_{n-1}(x), \, x \subseteq A - \{a_{ni}\}. \mid 1 \le i \le n\}$$

The constrain least fixpoint is

$$\{p_n(x) :- x \subseteq A - \{a_{1i_1}, a_{2i_2}, \cdots, a_{ni_n}\} \mid 1 \le i_1 \le n, \ldots, 1 \le i_n \le n\},$$

which has size n^n. In this example, answering a single query is still tractable, computing the fixpoint is not.

3.4   Discussion

There are tractable constraint domains that are not unary; for example, order and inequality constraints over densely ordered structures. In this paper, we limit our attention to unary constraint domains. Unary domains are not very interesting from the point of view of constraint satisfaction. However, we find them attractive for the following reasons. First, DATALOG$^\mathcal{C}$ with unary domains strictly generalizes DATALOG, yet preserves the features of DATALOG that makes it attractive for trust management. Second, DATALOG$^\mathcal{C}$ with unary domains can express most useful assertions in trust management, because describing permissions or attributes of entities typically does not involve constraints relating two variables in ways other than equality. Third, DATALOG$^\mathcal{C}$ with unary domains is easier to understand and to implement than more complicated domains. Ease of understanding is an important advantage, since authors of TM policy statements need to understand their meanings.

4 RT_1^C: A Declarative TM Language Based on Datalog^C

In this section, we introduce RT_1^C, a constraint-based extension to the RT_1 language in the RT framework [15,16], as a concrete example of declarative TM languages based on DATALOG^C. Each statement in RT_1^C can be translated into an equivalent rule in DATALOG^C with linearly decomposable domains.

4.1   Overview of the RT Framework

The RT framework is a family of Role-based Trust-management languages. The basic concepts of RT include entities and roles. *Entities* can issue statements and make requests. RT assumes that one can determine which entity issued a particular statement or request. Public/private key pairs clearly make this possible. We use A, B, and D, sometimes with subscripts, to denote entities.

A *role* in RT takes the form of an entity followed by a role name, separated by a dot. The simplest kinds of role names, used in RT_0, are identifiers. We use R, often with subscripts, to denote role names. A *role* is similar to a group; it defines a set of entities who are members of this role. Each entity A has the authority to define who are the members of each role of the form $A.R$, and A does so by issuing statements. Each statement defines one role to contain either an entity, another role, or certain other expressions that evaluate to a set of entities. A role may be defined by multiple statements. Their effect is union.

We now describe four kinds of statements for defining roles in RT_1; for simplicity, we assume that role names are simple identifiers.

- *Type-1*: $A.R \longleftarrow B$
  A and B are (possibly the same) entities, and R is a role name. This means that A defines B to be a member of A's R role.
- *Type-2*: $A.R \longleftarrow B.R_1$
  This statement means that A defines its R role to include (all members of) B's R_1 role.
- *Type-3*: $A.R \longleftarrow A.R_1.R_2$
  We call $A.R_1.R_2$ a *linked role*. This means that A defines its R role to include (members of) every role $B.R_2$ in which B is a member of $A.R_1$ role.
- *Type-4*: $A.R \longleftarrow A_1.R_1 \cap A_2.R_2 \cap \cdots \cap A_\ell.R_\ell$
  This means that A defines its R role to include the intersection of the ℓ roles.

Following is an example from [16], illustrating the use of these statements.

Example 3. A fictitious Web publishing service, EPub, offers a discount to anyone who is both an ACM member and a preferred customer of EOrg, the parent organization of EPub. EOrg considers students of all universities to be preferred customers, and delegate the authority over the identification of students to entities that EOrg believes are legitimate universities. EOrg additionally delegates the authority over identifying universities to a fictitious Accrediting Board for

Universities, ABU. Alice is an ACM member and a student of StateU, which is accredited by ABU.

EPub.discount ⟵ EOrg.preferred ∩ ACM.member
EOrg.preferred ⟵ EOrg.university.student
EOrg.university ⟵ ABU.accredited
ABU.accredited ⟵ StateU
StateU.student ⟵ Alice
ACM.member ⟵ Alice

In the above example, role names are simple identifiers. In RT_1, more generally, role names can have parameters. Parameterized roles can represent access permissions that take parameters identifying resources and access modes, role templates (e.g., leader of a project), relationships between entities (e.g., manager of an employee), and attributes that have fields (e.g., digital driver licenses, digital diplomas).

4.2 RT_1^C

RT has *application domain specification documents (ADSDs)* and statements. Each ADSD defines a vocabulary, which is a suite of related data types and role identifiers (role ids for short).

RT_1^C has several categories of types: integer types, float types, enumeration types, string types, tree types. Integer types, float types, and ordered enumeration types correspond to range domains. Unordered enumeration types and string types correspond to discrete domains with sets. And tree types correspond to tree domains. Each type category has a syntax for defining *value sets*, for each value set S, $x \in S$ corresponds to a basic constraint in the corresponding constraint domain. In an ADSD, to declare a role id, one needs to declare the parameters. Each parameter has a name and a data type.

An RT_1^C *statement* has the same structure as an RT_0 statement. The difference is that each role name takes the form of $r(h_1, \ldots, h_n)$, in which r is a role identifier, and for each i in $1..n$, h_i takes one of the following three forms: $f = c$, $f \in S$, and $f = ref$, in which f is the name of one of r's parameters that has type τ, c is a constant of type τ, S is a value set of type τ, and ref is a reference to another parameter in the same statement, also of type τ.

We now describe how to translate RT_1^C statements into DATALOG^C rules. Each type is mapped to a constraint domain, and each role id r is mapped to a corresponding predicate symbol $\bar{r}$. Role names in RT_1^C have named parameters; these can be easily translated into unnamed (position-based) parameters by choosing an order among parameters.

1. From $A.r(h_1, \ldots, h_n) \longleftarrow D$ to

   $\bar{r}(A, D, x_1, \ldots, x_k) :- \psi$

   In which k is the arity of r and ψ is a conjunction of primitive constraints corresponding to parameters $h_1, \ldots, h_n$. A parameter like $f_j = c$ is translated into a basic constraint $x = c$. A parameter like $f_i \in S$ is translated into a corresponding basic constraint. And a parameter like $f_j = ref$ is translated into an equality constraint involving two variables.

2. From $A.r(h_1, \ldots, h_n) \longleftarrow B.r_1(s_1, \ldots, s_m)$ to

$$\overline{r}(A, y, x_1, \ldots, x_k) :- \overline{r_1}(B, y, x_{1,1}, \ldots, x_{1,k_1}), \psi$$

In which k and k_1 are the arities of r and r_1, ψ is a constraint corresponding to the parameters $h_1, \ldots, h_n, s_1, \ldots, s_m$.

3. From $A.r(h_1, \ldots, h_n) \longleftarrow A.r_1(s_{1,1}, \ldots, s_{1,m_1}).r_2(s_{2,1}, \ldots, s_{2,m_2})$ to

$$\overline{r}(A, y, x_1, \ldots, x_k) :- \overline{r_1}(A, z, x_{1,1}, \ldots, x_{1,k_1}), \overline{r_2}(z, y, x_{2,1}, \ldots, x_{2,k_2}), \psi$$

In which ψ is a constraint corresponding to the parameters in the statement.

4. From $A.r(h_1, \ldots, h_n) \longleftarrow A_1.r_1(s_{1,1}, \ldots, s_{1,m_1}) \cap \cdots \cap A_\ell.r_\ell(s_{\ell,1}, \ldots, s_{\ell,m_\ell})$ to

$$\overline{r}(A, y, x_1, \ldots, x_k) :- \overline{r_1}(A_1, y, x_{1,1}, \ldots, x_{1,k_1}), \cdots, \overline{r_\ell}(A_\ell, y, x_{\ell,1}, \ldots, x_{\ell,k_\ell}), \psi$$

In which ψ is a constraint corresponding to the parameters in the statement.

As shown in [15,16], the RT framework supports for flexible delegation relationships and distributed credential chain discovery. RT_1 requires that every variable in a statement must appear in the body, to guarantee that the resulting DATALOG rule is safe. As a result, one cannot represent granting the permissions of connecting to any port number in a range to an entity. In RT_1^C, this restriction is not needed anymore. The addition of constraints enables one to represent permissions involving ranges and structured resources. Using DATALOG^C as the foundation of RT_1^C provides a sound semantics foundation and tractability guarantee.

5   Using Datalog^C to Analyze KeyNote

KeyNote [3] is a TM system that is based on PolicyMaker [4]. A KeyNote *assertion* is essentially a delegation from its issuer to its licensees, which in the simplest case is a single entity. A KeyNote *request* is characterized by a list of fields, which are name/value pairs. An assertion also has *conditions* written in an expression language, which refers to fields in requests. The intuitive meaning of an assertion is that, if the licensees support a request, and the request satisfies the conditions, then the issuer supports the request as well. KeyNote can be roughly captured by DATALOG^C with several very expressive constraint domains. One domain is integers with function symbols $\{+, -, *, /, \%, \hat{}\}$, predicates $\{=, \neq, <, >, \leq, \geq\}$, and any quantifier-free first-order formula as a primitive constraint. The fragment of that domain without function symbols $\{/, \%, \hat{}\}$ is polynomial constraints over integers, which, as we discussed in Section 2.3, does not admit quantifier elimination.

Theorem 4. *It is undecidable to compute the set of all requests that a set of KeyNote assertions authorizes.*

Note that the above theorem does not rule out that possibility to determine whether any specific request is authorized by a set of assertions. In fact, this only involves arithmetic computation and comparison. The above result means that there does not exist an algorithm to perform analysis of all the requests being authorized by a set of assertions. In fact, this is so even when there is only one assertion with a single entity as the licensees, and the question is just whether the assertion authorizes any request at all. We view this as a significant disadvantage, because it would be desirable to evaluate and analyze the effect of security assertions.

We want to point out that examples given in [3] do not use the expressive power that leads to undecidability. In fact, we have not encountered any TM example both in our research and in literature that requires such expressive power; therefore, we argue that the expression language in KeyNote is too expressive. On the other hand, it has been shown that the delegation structure in KeyNote is too limited in TM applications [14,15].

Related Work

Several TM languages were designed based on DATALOG without constraints. DATALOG with periodicity constraints is used in [2] in an access control language that supports periodic temporal constraints; however, this work does not deal with representation of structured resources and the general tractability of different constraint domains.

In comparison with work on constraint databases, Chomicki et al. [5] state "Recent developments in constraint databases, in particular the research on aggregation and spatiotemporal applications, suggest a need for *middle-ground* formalisms that preserve some of the expressive power of constraint databases and constraint query languages, while at the same time generalizing in a natural way the basic assumptions underlying the classical relational model of data." In [5], Chomicki et al. study constraint databases with variable independence conditions, which is a property of constraint relations. Our work to find tractable domains is also a search for useful middle-grounds, but our motivations are different, namely, usefulness in trust management, simplicity, and tractability. These motivations led us to take a different approach; we study properties of constraint domains, rather than properties of constraint relations. Moreover, properties like hierarchical and linearly decomposable are not limited to one class of constraint domains; our approach is thus similar to yet different from that in [19], in which Revesz studies the complexity of DATALOG^C with various limited form of linear constraints. We believe that DATALOG^C with unary constraint domains provides a useful middle-ground that generalizes DATALOG in a natural and useful way while preserving many nice properties of DATALOG.

6   Conclusion and Future Directions

Trust management (TM) languages need a declarative and formal foundation. Although DATALOG has been the best logical foundation for distributed access control decisions to date, DATALOG does not meet the practical need for policies about common structured resources. Our work with the RT family of TM languages [15,16], and demonstration applications such as a distributed scheduling system and web-based file-sharing system, underscore the need for a more expressive logical foundation. DATALOG with constraints is a promising and expressive alternative that eliminates some deficiencies of DATALOG without sacrificing any of the attractive features that make DATALOG appealing for trust management.

In this paper, we identify a class of constraint domains called linearly decomposable unary domains, prove that DATALOG with any combination of such constraint domains is tractable, and show that permissions associated with structured resources, including tree domains and range domains, fall into this class. To illustrate the value of constraint DATALOG for designing TM languages, we present a declarative TM language, RT_1^C, based on constraint DATALOG. We also use DATALOG to analyze KeyNote, which turns out to be less expressive than RT_1^C in significant respects, yet less tractable in the worst case.

Further study is needed on the tractability of unary constraint domains and non-unary constraint domains useful for trust management. We showed that linearly decomposability is a sufficient condition for tractability; however, we have not identified necessary and sufficient conditions for a unary constraint domain to be tractable. Other constraint domains worthy of investigation include strings with constraints involving regular expressions.

References

1. Olav Bandmann and Mads Dam. A note on SPKI's authorization syntax. In *Pre-Proceedings of 1st Annual PKI Research Workshop*, April 2002. Available from http://www.cs.dartmouth.edu/~pki02/.
2. Elisa Bertino, Claudio Bettini, Elena Ferrari, and Pierangela Samarati. An access control model supporting periodicity constraints and temporal reasoning. *ACM Transactions on Database Systems*, 23(3):231–285, 1998.
3. Matt Blaze, Joan Feigenbaum, John Ioannidis, and Angelos D. Keromytis. The KeyNote trust-management system, version 2. IETF RFC 2704, September 1999.
4. Matt Blaze, Joan Feigenbaum, and Jack Lacy. Decentralized trust management. In *Proceedings of the 1996 IEEE Symposium on Security and Privacy*, pages 164–173. IEEE Computer Society Press, May 1996.
5. Jan Chomicki, Dina Goldin, Gabriel Kuper, and David Toman. Variable independence in constraint databases, November 2001. In final review for IEEE Transactions on Knowledge and Data Engineering.
6. John DeTreville. Binder, a logic-based security language. In *Proceedings of the 2002 IEEE Symposium on Security and Privacy*, pages 105–113. IEEE Computer Society Press, May 2002.
7. Carl Ellison, Bill Frantz, Butler Lampson, Ron Rivest, Brian Thomas, and Tatu Ylonen. SPKI certificate theory. IETF RFC 2693, September 1999.
8. Jonathan R. Howell. *Naming and sharing resources acroos administrative boundaries*. PhD thesis, Dartmouth College, May 2000.
9. Joxan Jaffar and Michael J. Maher. Constraint logic programming: A survey. *Journal of Logic Programming*, 19/20:503–580, 1994.

10. Trevor Jim. SD3: A trust management system with certified evaluation. In *Proceedings of the 2001 IEEE Symposium on Security and Privacy*, pages 106–115. IEEE Computer Society Press, May 2001.

11. Paris C. Kanellakis, Gabriel M. Kuper, and Peter Z. Revesz. Constraint query languages. *Journal of Computer and System Sciences*, 51(1):26–52, August 1995. Preliminary version appeared in *Proceedings of the 9th ACM Symposium on Principles of Database Systems (PODS)*, 1990.

12. Gabriel Kuper, Leonid Libkin, and Jan Paredaens, editors. *Constraint Databases*. Springer, 2000.

13. Ninghui Li, Benjamin N. Grosof, and Joan Feigenbaum. A practically implementable and tractable Delegation Logic. In *Proceedings of the 2000 IEEE Symposium on Security and Privacy*, pages 27–42. IEEE Computer Society Press, May 2000.

14. Ninghui Li, Benjamin N. Grosof, and Joan Feigenbaum. Delegation Logic: A logic-based approach to distributed authorization. *ACM Transaction on Information and System Security (TISSEC)*, February 2003. To appear.

15. Ninghui Li, John C. Mitchell, and William H. Winsborough. Design of a role-based trust management framework. In *Proceedings of the 2002 IEEE Symposium on Security and Privacy*, pages 114–130. IEEE Computer Society Press, May 2002.

16. Ninghui Li, William H. Winsborough, and John C. Mitchell. Distributed credential chain discovery in trust management. To appear in *Journal of Computer Security*. Extended abstract appeared in *Proceedings of the Eighth ACM Conference on Computer and Communications Security (CCS-8)*, November 2001.

17. Yuri V. Matiyasevich. *Hilbert's Tenth Problem*. The MIT Press, 1993.

18. Peter Z. Revesz. Constraint databases: A survey. In L. Libkin and B. Thalheim, editors, *Semantics in Databases*, number 1358 in LNCS, pages 209–246. Springer, 1998.

19. Peter Z. Revesz. Safe Datalog queries with linear constraints. In *Proceedings of the 4th International Conference on Principles and Practice of Constraint Programming (CP98)*, number 1520 in LNCS. Springer, 1998.

20. David Toman. Memoing evaluation for constraint extensions of Datalog. *Constraints: An International Journal*, 2:337–359, 1997.

21. David Toman and Jan Chomicki. Datalog with integer periodicity constraints. *Journal of Logic programming*, 35:263–290, 1994.

Web Programming with SMLserver

Martin Elsman* and Niels Hallenberg

IT University of Copenhagen.
Glentevej 67, DK-2400 Copenhagen NV, Denmark
{mael,nh}@it.edu

Abstract. SMLserver is an efficient multi-threaded Web server platform for Standard ML programs. It provides access to a variety of different Relational Database Management Systems (RDBMSs), including Oracle, MySQL, and PostgreSQL. We describe the execution model and the region-based memory model of SMLserver and explain our solutions to the design issues we were confronted with in the development. We also describe our experience with programming and maintaining Web applications using Standard ML, which provides higher-order functions, static typing, and a rich module system. Through experiments based on user scenarios for some common Web tasks, the paper demonstrates the efficiency of SMLserver, both with respect to script execution and database connectivity.

1   Introduction

Higher-order functions and a modules language for exposing the functionality of composable components are promising features for Web application development, where code reuse and separation of programming tasks (layout from implementation) are of primary concern.

The rapid change and development of Web applications combined with the way that Web applications are exposed to users also suggests that Web applications should be particularly robust to changes and easy to maintain. This observation is in contrast to how most Web applications are built—namely with scripting languages that have only limited support for finding errors in the program before it is exposed to users. A powerful static type system, on the other hand, enforces many programming errors to be found and fixed at compile time, although with the cost of an imposed compilation step in the development cycle.

SMLserver [7] is a Web server platform for Standard ML [14], a programming language which provides the features requested above, namely higher-order functions, a rich module system, and a powerful static type system. SMLserver builds on a bytecode backend and interpreter for the ML Kit [22], a compiler for the full Standard ML programming language. The interpreter, called the *Kit Abstract Machine* (KAM) [6], is embedded in a module for AOLserver, an open source Web server provided by America Online.[1] The KAM supports caching of

---

* Part time at Royal Veterinary and Agricultural University of Denmark.
[1] A port of SMLserver to the open source Web server Apache is ongoing.

V. Dahl and P. Wadler (Eds.): PADL 2003, LNCS 2562, pp. 74–91, 2003.
© Springer-Verlag Berlin Heidelberg 2003

loaded code, multi-threaded execution, and other features, including database interoperability.

The focus of this work is two-fold. We first demonstrate that programming Web applications with Standard ML provides many useful programming idioms, based on higher-order functions, static typing, and the rich Standard ML module system. Second, we present evidence that Web server support for high-level functional programming languages, such as Standard ML, can be as efficient as the use of highly tuned scripting languages, such as TCL and PHP.

1.1 Background

The ideas behind SMLserver came to mind in 1999 when the first author was attending a talk by Philip Greenspun, the author of the book "Philip and Alex's Guide to Web Publishing" [11]. Philip and his coworkers had been writing an astonishing 250,000 lines of dynamically typed TCL code to implement a community system that they planned to maintain, extend, and even customize for different Web sites. Although Philip and his coworkers were very successful with their community system, the dynamic typing of TCL makes such a large system difficult to maintain and extend, not to mention customize.

The SMLserver project was initiated at the end of 2000 by the construction of an embeddable runtime system and a bytecode backend for the ML Kit. Once the bytecode backend and the embeddable runtime system was in place, the KAM was embedded in an AOLserver module in such a way that requests for files with extension .sml and .msp (also called *scripts*) cause the corresponding compiled bytecode files to be loaded and executed. In April 2001, the basic system was running, but more work was necessary to support caching of loaded code, multi-threaded execution, and other features, such as database interoperability and a type safe caching interface. SMLserver is open source and distributed under the GNU General Public License (GPL).

1.2 Outline of the Paper

The paper proceeds as follows. In Sect. 2, we describe how SMLserver serves requests by loading and executing compiled scripts. In Sect. 3, we demonstrate the use of higher-order functions and type polymorphism for providing a type safe caching (i.e., memoization) interface for SMLserver Web scripts. In Sect. 4, we describe how SMLserver scripts may interface to an RDBMS through a generic interface, which makes extensive use of higher-order functions and type polymorphism for convenient access and manipulation of data in an RDBMS.

In Sect. 5, we describe how the region based memory model scales to a multi-threaded environment where programs run shortly, but are executed often. In Sect. 6, we demonstrate the efficiency of SMLserver, both with respect to script execution and database connectivity, by comparing the number of requests SMLserver may serve each second with numbers for other Web server platforms. We also measure the effect that some of the design decisions we were confronted with in the development have on script execution time. Finally, we describe related and future work and conclude.

2   Serving Pages to Users

We shall now see how to create a small Web service for presenting the time-of-day to a user. The example uses the `Time.now` function from the Standard ML Basis Library to obtain the present time of day. HTML code to send to the user's browser is constructed using Standard ML string primitives:

```
val time_of_day = Date.fmt "%H.%M.%S" (Date.fromTimeLocal(Time.now()))
val _ = Ns.Conn.return
   "<html><head><title>Time of day</title></head> \
   \   <body bgcolor=white><h2>Time of day</h2> \
   \      The time of day is " ^ time_of_day ^ ".<hr></i> \
   \      Served by <a href=http://www.smlserver.org>SMLserver</a></i> \
   \</body></html>"
```

The result of a user requesting the file `time_of_day.sml` from the Web server is shown in Fig. 1. The script uses the function `Ns.Conn.return` to send an HTTP response with HTTP status code 200 (Page found) and MIME type `text/html` to the browser along with HTML code passed in the argument string.

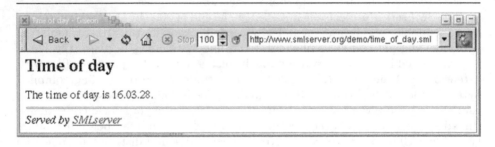

Fig. 1. The result of requesting the script `time_of_day.sml`.

In Sect. 2.2 we shall see how support for quotations may be used to embed HTML code in Web applications somewhat more elegantly than using Standard ML string literals. SMLserver also supports an alternative to quotations and strings in the form of an abstract combinator library for constructing HTML code. Although the use of the combinator library does not guarantee the validity of the generated HTML code, it may help eliminate certain types of errors at compile time. In addition, SMLserver has support for ML Server Pages, which provides a notation for embedding Standard ML code in HTML code, similar to PHP and Microsoft's Active Server Pages (ASP). ML Server Pages are stored in files with extension `.msp`.

2.1   Loading and Serving Pages

SMLserver is implemented as a module `nssml.so`, which is loaded into the AOLserver Web server when the Web server starts. At this time, future requests for *scripts* (i.e., `.sml`-files and `.msp`-files) are served by interpreting the bytecode file that is the result of compiling the requested script. Compilation of scripts into bytecode files is done by the user explicitly invoking the SMLserver compiler `smlserverc`. The SMLserver compiler takes as argument a *project file*, which lists the scripts that a client may request along with Standard ML library code to be used by the scripts.

The first time a script is requested, SMLserver executes initialization code for each library file and caches the resulting initial heap, which can then be used for execution of the requested script and future requests. To serve a script, SMLserver first loads the requested script and caches the result (if it is not already in the cache), after which the script is executed. After execution, the heap is restored and made available for future requests.

Thus, SMLserver initiates execution in identical initial heaps each time a request is served, which means that it is not possible to maintain state implicitly in Web applications using Standard ML references or arrays. Instead, state must be maintained explicitly using a Relational Database Management System (RDBMS) or the cache primitives supported by SMLserver. Another possibility is to emulate state behavior by capturing state in form variables or cookies.

At first, this limitation may seem like a major drawback. However, the limitation has several important advantages:

- Good memory reuse. When a request has been served, memory used for serving the request may be reused for serving other requests.
- Support for a threaded execution model. Requests may be served simultaneously by interpreters running in different threads without the need for maintaining complex locks.
- Good scalability properties. For high volume Web sites, the serving of requests may be distributed to several different machines that communicate with a single database server. Serving many simultaneous requests from multiple clients is exactly what an RDBMS is good at.
- Good durability properties. Upon Web server and hardware failures, data stored in Web server memory is lost, whereas data stored in an RDBMS may be restored using the durability features of the RDBMS.

The limitation does not suggest that session support is impossible; sessions with timeout semantics can be encoded using SMLserver's caching features.

2.2   Quotations for HTML Embedding

Although SMLserver supports generation of HTML code through HTML combinators, it is sometimes more convenient to write HTML code directly. In this section we introduce the notion of *quotations* [19], an elegant extension to Standard ML, which eases readability and maintainability of embedded object language fragments (e.g., HTML code) within Standard ML programs. Although quotations are not officially Standard ML [14], many compilers provide support for quotations, including Moscow ML, SML/NJ, and the ML Kit. Here is a small quotation example that demonstrates the basics of quotations:

```
val text = "fun"
val ulist : string frag list =
  '<ul><li>Web programming is ^text
    </ul>'
```

The program declares a variable `text` of type `string`, a variable `ulist` of type `string frag list`, and indirectly makes use of the constructors of this predeclared datatype:

```
datatype 'a frag = QUOTE of string | ANTIQUOTE of 'a
```

What happens is that the quotation bound to `ulist` evaluates to the list:

```
[QUOTE "<ul><li>Web programming is ", ANTIQUOTE "fun", QUOTE "\n</ul>"]
```

Using the `Quot.flatten` function, which has type `string frag list->string`, the value bound to `ulist` may be turned into a string (which can then be sent to a browser.)

To be precise, a quotation is a particular kind of expression that consists of a non-empty sequence of (possibly empty) fragments surrounded by back-quotes:

exp	::=	'*frags*'	quotation
frags	::=	*charseq*	character sequence
	|	*charseq* ^*id frags*	anti-quotation id
	|	*charseq* ^(*exp*) *frags*	anti-quotation exp

A *character sequence*, written *charseq*, is a possibly empty sequence of printable characters or spaces or tabs or newlines, with the exception that the characters ^ and ' must be escaped using the notation ^^ and ^', respectively.

A quotation evaluates to a value of type `ty frag list`, where `ty` is the type of all anti-quotation variables and anti-quotation expressions in the quotation. A character sequence fragment *charseq* evaluates to `QUOTE "`*charseq*`"`. An anti-quotation fragment ^*id* or ^(*exp*) evaluates to `ANTIQUOTE` *value*, where *value* is the value of the variable *id* or the expression *exp*, respectively.

To ease programming with quotations, the type constructor `quot` is declared at top-level as an abbreviation for the type `string frag list`. Moreover, the symbolic identifier ^^ is declared as an infix identifier with type `quot * quot -> quot` and associativity similar to `@`.

2.3   Obtaining Data from Users

The following example demonstrates the use of quotations for embedding HTML code and the use of the SMLserver Library structure `FormVar` for accessing and validating user input and so-called "hidden" form variables for emulating state in a Web application. The example that we present is a simple Web game, which, by use of the functionality in the structure `Random`, asks the user to guess a number between zero and 100:

```
fun returnPage title pic body = Ns.return
  '<html><head><title>^title</title></head>
    <body bgcolor=white> <center>
    <h2>^title</h2> <img src=^pic> <p>
     ^(Quot.toString body) <p> <i>Served by <a
        href=http://www.smlserver.org>SMLserver</a>
    </i> </center> </body>
    </html>'

fun mk_form (n:int) =
  '<form action=guess.sml method=post>
     <input type=hidden name=n value=^(Int.toString n)>
     <input type=text name=guess>
     <input type=submit value=Guess>
   </form>'

fun processGuess n =
  case FormVar.wrapOpt FormVar.getNat "guess"
    of NONE => returnPage "You must type a number - try again"
                          "bill_guess.jpg" (mk_form n)
     | SOME g => if g > n then
                     returnPage "Your guess is too big - try again"
                                "bill_large.jpg" (mk_form n)
                 else if g < n then
                     returnPage "Your guess is too small - try again"
                                "bill_small.jpg" (mk_form n)
                 else
                     returnPage "Congratulations!" "bill_yes.jpg"
                        'You guessed the number ^(Int.toString n) <p>
                         <a href=guess.sml>Play again?</a>'
val _ =
  case FormVar.wrapOpt FormVar.gotNat "n"
    of NONE => let (* generate new random number *)
                   val n = Random.range(0,100) (Random.newgen())
               in returnPage "Guess a number between 0 and 100"
                             "bill_guess.jpg" (mk_form n)
               end
     | SOME n => processGuess n
```

The functions returnPage and mk_form use quotations for embedding HTML code. The function Ns.return, which takes a value of type quot as argument, returns the argument to the client.

The expression FormVar.wrapOpt FormVar.getNat results in a function of type string -> int option. The function takes the name of a form variable as argument and returns SOME(i), where i is an integer obtained from the string value associated with the form variable. If the form variable does not occur in the query data, is not a well-formed natural number, or its value does not fit in 32 bits, the function returns NONE. The argument given to FormVar.wrapOpt, namely FormVar.getNat, is a function with type string -> int and the property that it raises an exception if its argument is not a proper natural number. The use of higher-order functions for form variable validation is necessary to obtain a shallow interface and gain a high degree of code reuse. In particular, the FormVar structure provides wrapper functions that make it possible to report multiple error messages to the user concerning invalid form content.

In the case that no form variable n exists, a new random number is generated and the game is started by presenting an introduction line to the player along with a form for entering the first guess. The game then proceeds by returning different pages to the user depending on whether the user's guess is greater than, smaller than, or equal to the random number n.

Notice that the game uses the HTTP request method POST, so that the random number that the user is to guess is not shown in the browser's location field. It is left as an exercise to the reader to find out how—with some help from the Web browser—it is possible to "guess" the number using only one guess. Figure 2 shows three different pages served by the "Guess a Number" game.

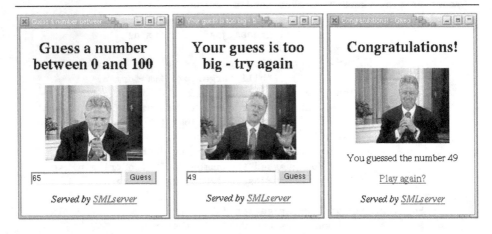

Fig. 2. Three different pages served by the "Guess a Number" game.

3   Caching Support

SMLserver has a simple type safe caching interface that can be used to cache data so that information computed by some script invocation can be used by subsequent script invocations. The cache functionality is implemented as a structure Cache, which matches the signature CACHE listed in Fig. 3.

A cache of type (α, β) cache maps keys of type α Type to values of type β Type. The cache interface defines a set of *base types* (e.g., Int, Real and String) and a set of type constructors to build new types (e.g., Pair, List, and Option). A cache has a *cache name*, which is represented by a Standard ML string. SMLserver supports three *kinds* of caches:

```
signature CACHE =
  sig
    datatype kind = WhileUsed of int | TimeOut of int | Size of int
    type ('a,'b) cache
    type 'a Type
    type name = string

    val get      : 'a Type * 'b Type * name * kind -> ('a,'b) cache
    val memoize  : ('a,'b) cache -> ('a -> 'b) -> 'a -> 'b

    val Int      : int Type
    val Real     : real Type
    val String   : string Type
    val Pair     : 'a Type -> 'b Type -> ('a*'b) Type
    val Option   : 'a Type -> 'a option Type
    val List     : 'a Type -> 'a list Type
    ...
  end
```

Fig. 3. The cache interface.

- Size caches. Entries in caches of kind Size(n) expire when there is not enough room for a new entry (maximum cache size is n bytes). Oldest entries expire first.
- Timeout caches. For caches of kind TimeOut(t), an entry expires t seconds after it is inserted. This kind of cache guarantees that the cache is updated with freshly computed information, even if the cache is accessed constantly.
- Keep-while-used caches. An entry in a cache of kind WhileUsed(t) expires when it has not been accessed in t seconds. This kind of cache is useful for caching authentication information, such as passwords, so as to lower the pressure on the RDBMS.

The function get obtains a cache given a domain type, a range type, a cache name, and a kind. The first time get is called with a particular domain type, a particular range type, and a particular cache name, a new cache is constructed. Conceptually one can think of the function get as having the constrained (or bounded) polymorphic type [8]

$$\forall \alpha \leq \mathsf{Type},\ \beta \leq \mathsf{Type} \ .\ \mathsf{name} * \mathsf{kind} \ \text{->}\ (\alpha, \beta)\ \mathsf{cache}$$

where Type denotes the set of types supported by the cache interface. As an example, the following expression constructs a cache named mycache, which maps pairs of integers to lists of reals:

```
get (Pair Int Int, List Real, "mycache", Size (9*1024))
```

The function memoize adds caching functionality (i.e., memoization) to a function. Assuming that the function f has type int -> string * real and

c is an appropriately typed cache, the expression `memoize` c f returns a new function f', which caches the results of evaluating the function f. Subsequent calls to f' with the same argument results in cached pairs of strings and reals, except when a result no longer lives in the cache, in which case f is evaluated again.

The cache interface also provides functions for flushing caches, adding entries, and deleting entries (not shown in the signature above).

We now present a currency exchange rate service that uses the function `memoize` to cache an exchange rate obtained from a foreign Web site. The Web service is implemented as a single file `exchange.sml`:

```
structure C = Cache
val c = C.get (C.String, C.Option C.Real, "currency", C.TimeOut 300)
val form = '<form method=post action=exchange.sml>
              <b>Dollar amount</b><br><input type=text name=a>
              <input type=submit value="Value in Danish Kroner">
            </form>'
fun fetchRate url =
  case Ns.fetchUrl url of
    NONE => NONE
  | SOME pg => let val pattern = RegExp.fromString
                    ".+USDDKK.+<td>([0-9]+).([0-9]+)</td>.+"
                in case RegExp.extract pattern pg
                    of SOME [r1,r2] => Real.fromString (r1^"."^r2)
                     | _ => NONE
               end
val fetch = C.memoize c fetchRate
val url = "http://se.finance.yahoo.com/m5?s=USD&t=DKK"
val body = case FormVar.wrapOpt FormVar.getReal "a"
             of NONE => form
              | SOME a =>
                case fetch url
                  of NONE  => 'The service is currently not available'
                   | SOME rate =>
                     '^(Real.toString a) USD gives
                      ^(Real.fmt (StringCvt.FIX(SOME 2)) (a*rate)) DKK.
                     <p>' ^^ form
val _ = Page.return "Currency Exchange Service" body
```

The program creates a cache c that maps strings (base type `String`) to optional reals (constructed type `Option Real`). The cache kind `TimeOut` is used to limit the pressure on the foreign site and to make sure that the currency rate is updated every five minutes.

The exchange rate (American dollars to Danish kroner) is obtained by fetching a Web page using the function `Ns.fetchUrl`, which takes an URL as argument and returns the contents of the page as a string. Once the page is received, support for regular expressions is used to extract the appropriate information (the currency exchange rate) from the Web page.

The function `Page.return` is used to return HTML code to the client; the function takes two arguments, a string denoting a title for the page and a body for the page in terms of a value of type `quot`.

4   Interfacing with an RDBMS

In this section we present an interface for connecting to an RDBMS from within Web scripts written with SMLserver. We shall not argue here that it is a good idea to use an RDBMS for keeping state on a Web server, but just mention that a true RDBMS provides data guarantees that are difficult to obtain using other means. RDBMS vendors have also solved the problem of serving simultaneous users, which make RDBMSs ideal for Web purposes.

The language used to communicate with the RDBMS is the standardized Structured Query Language (SQL). Although each RDBMS has its own extensions to the language, to some extent, it is possible with SMLserver to write Web services that are indifferent to the RDBMS of choice. SMLserver scripts may access and manipulate data in an RDBMS through the use of a structure that matches the `NS_DB` signature:

```
signature NS_DB =
  sig
    structure Handle : ...
    val dml          : quot -> unit
    val foldr        : ((string->string)*'a->'a)->'a->quot->'a
    val qq           : string -> string
    val qqq          : string -> string
    ...
  end
```

Because SMLserver supports the Oracle RDBMS, the PostgreSQL RDBMS, and MySQL, there are three structures in the `Ns` structure that matches the `NS_DB` signature, namely `Ns.DbOra`, `Ns.DbPg`, and `Ns.DbMySQL`. The example Web server project file includes a file `Db.sml`, which binds a top-level structure `Db` to the structure `Ns.DbPg`; thus, in what follows, we shall use the structure `Db` to access the PostgreSQL RDBMS.

A *database handle* identifies a connection to an RDBMS and a *pool* is a set of database handles. When the Web server is started, a configurable number of pools are created. At any time, a database handle is owned by at most one script. Moreover, the database handles owned by a script at any one time belong to different pools. The database functions request database handles from the initialized pools and release the database handles again in such a way that deadlocks are avoided; with the use of only one pool with two database handles, say, a simple form of deadlock would appear if two scripts executing simultaneously each had obtained a database handle from the pool and were both requesting a second database handle.

The `NS_DB` function `dml` with type `quot->unit` is used to execute SQL *data manipulation language* statements (i.e., `insert` and `update` statements) in the RDBMS. On error, the function raises the top-level exception `Fail`.

The function `foldr`, is used to access data in the database. A `select` statement is passed as an argument to the function. The function is similar to the Basis Library function `List.foldr`. An application `foldr f b sql` executes the SQL statement given by the quotation sql and folds over the result set, similarly to how `List.foldr` folds over a list. The function f is the function used in the folding with base b. The first argument to f is a function of type `string->string` that maps column names into values for the row. Because the number of database handles owned by a script at any one time is limited to the number of initialized pools, nesting of applications of database access functions (such as `foldr`) is limited by the number of initialized pools. On error, the function raises the top-level exception `Fail` and all involved database handles are released appropriately.

The function `qq`, which has type `string->string`, returns the argument string in which every occurrence of a quote (`'`) is replaced with a double occurrence (`''`), which is how quotes are escaped in SQL string literals. The function `qqq` is similar to the `qq` function with the extra functionality that the result is encapsulated in quotes (`'...'`).

We now show a tiny "Guest Book" example, which demonstrates the database interface. The example consists of the file `guest.sml`, which presents guest book entries and a form for entering new entries, and a file `guest_add.sml`, which processes a submitted guest book entry. The data model, which is the basis for the guest book service, consists of a simple SQL table:

```
create table guest (
   email    varchar(100),
   name     varchar(100),
   comment  varchar(2000)
);
```

The table `guest` contains the three columns `email`, `name`, and `comment`. A row in the table corresponds to a form entry submitted by a user; initially, the table contains no rows. The file `guest.sml` includes the following code:

```
val form = '<form method=post action=guest_add.sml><table>
            <tr><td valign=top colspan=3>New comment<br>
                <textarea name=c cols=65 rows=3
                  wrap=virtual>Fill in...</textarea></tr>
            <tr><td>Name<br><input type=text size=25 name=n>
                <td>Email<br><input type=text size=25 name=e>
                <td><br><input type=submit value="Add">
            </tr></table></form>'

fun layoutRow (f,acc) =
  '<li> <i>^(f "comment")</i>
   -- <a href="mailto:^(f "email")">^(f "name")</a><p>' ^^ acc

val rows = Db.foldr layoutRow ''
  'select email,name,comment from guest order by name'

val _ = Page.return "Guest Book" ('<ul>' ^^ rows ^^ '</ul>' ^^ form)
```

The function `Db.foldr` is used to query the database for rows in the table; the function `layoutRow`, which has type `(string->string)*quot->quot` is used to format each row appropriately. The first argument passed to this function is a function, which returns the contents of the given column in the row. Notice also that quotations are used to embed SQL statements in the code. Figure 4 shows the result of requesting the file `guest.sml`. The file `guest_add.sml`, which we

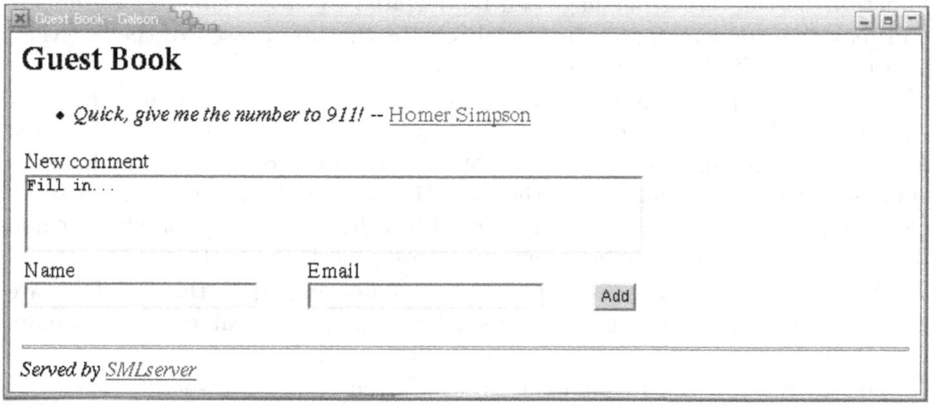

Fig. 4. The result of requesting the file `guest.sml`.

shall not list here, uses the `FormVar` functionality for extracting form variables and the function `Db.dml` to add an entry in the `guest` table.

For databases that support transactions, SMLserver supports transactions through the use of the `Handle` structure.

5   The Execution Model

Before we describe how SMLserver caches loaded bytecode to gain efficiency and how a multi-threaded execution model makes it possible for SMLserver to serve multiple requests simultaneously, we describe the region-based memory management scheme used by SMLserver.

5.1   Region-Based Memory Management

The memory management system used in SMLserver is based on region inference [23], but extended appropriately to deal correctly with multi-threaded program execution. Region inference inserts allocation and deallocation directives in the program at compile time; no pointer-tracing garbage collection is used at run-time.

In the region memory model, the store consists of a stack of regions. Region inference turns all value producing expressions e in the program into e at ρ, where ρ is a region variable, which denotes a region in the store at runtime. Moreover, when e is an expression in the source program, region inference may turn e into the target expression letregion ρ in e' end, where e' is the target of analyzing sub-expressions in e and ρ is a region variable. At runtime, first an empty region is pushed on the stack and bound to ρ. Then, the sub-expression e' is evaluated, perhaps using ρ for allocation. Finally, upon reaching end, the region is deallocated from the stack. Safety of region inference guarantees that a region is not freed until after the last use of a value located in that region [23]. Functions in the target language can be declared to take regions as arguments and may thus, depending on the actual regions that are passed to the function, produce values in different regions for each call.

After region inference, the region-annotated program is compiled into byte-code for the KAM through a series of compilation phases [5,1,6]. Dynamically, a region is represented as a linked list of constant-sized region pages, which are chunks of memory allocated from the operating system. When a region is deallocated, region pages in the region are stored in a *free list*, also from which region pages are obtained when more memory is requested for allocation.

A consequence of region-based memory management is that no tags are needed at runtime to distinguish between different types of values, as are usually necessary for pointer tracing garbage collection.

For all the programs that we have developed using SMLserver, region inference has proven to recycle memory sufficiently without using a combination of region inference and garbage collection [12] or enforcing the programmer to write region-friendly programs.

5.2 Multi-threaded Execution

SMLserver supports multi-threaded execution of scripts with a shared free list of region pages. The memory model allows two threads executing simultaneously to own the same region page at two different points in time. This property, which can potentially reduce the overall memory usage, is obtained by protecting the free list with mutual exclusion locks (i.e., mutex's).

SMLserver also maintains a mutex-protected *pool of initial heaps*, which makes it possible to eliminate the overhead of library initialization in the presence of multi-threaded execution. Before a script is executed, an initial heap is obtained from the pool. After execution, the heap is recovered before it is given back to the pool. For type safety, the process of recovering the pool involves restoring the initial heap to ensure that mutable data (e.g., references) in the initial heap are reinitialized.

For the Standard ML Library, approximately 18kb of region pages, containing mostly closures, are copied each time a heap is recovered. By storing mutable data (i.e., references and arrays) in distinct regions, most of the copying can be avoided, which may further improve the efficiency of SMLserver.

6 Measurements

In this section, we measure the performance of SMLserver with respect to script execution time and compare it to a CGI-based ML Server Pages implementation, TCL on AOLserver, and PHP on Apache (Apache 1.3.22). We also measure the effect that caching of compiled scripts has on performance. Finally, we measure the overhead of interpreting initialization code for libraries for each request.

All measurements are performed on an 850Mhz Pentium 3 Linux box, equipped with 384Mb RAM. The program we use for benchmarking is ApacheBench, Version 1.3d.

The benchmark scripts include eight different scripts. The `hello` script returns a small constant HTML document. The `date` script uses a library function to show the current date. The script `db` connects to a database and executes a simple query. The script `guest` returns three guest list entries from the database. The script `calendar` returns 13 formatted calendar months. The script `mul` returns a simple multiplication table. The script `table` returns a 500 lines HTML table. The script `log` returns a 500 lines HTML table with database content.

The use of higher-order functions, such as `List.foldl` and `List.map`, in the MSP version of the `calendar` script are translated into explicit `while` loops in the TCL and PHP versions of the script.

Performance figures for SMLserver on the eight benchmark scripts are shown in the fourth column of Table 1. The column shows, for each benchmark, the number of requests that SMLserver serves each second when ApacheBench is instructed to have eight threads issue requests simultaneously for 60 seconds. Measurements for the Web server platforms MosML/MSP, AOLserver/TCL, and Apache/PHP are shown in the first three columns. There are two observations to point out:

1. For all scripts, SMLserver performs better than any of the other Web server platforms.
2. The MosML/MSP platform performs worse than any of the other three platforms on any of the benchmark scripts, most probably due to the CGI approach used by MosML/MSP.

The fifth column of Table 1 shows the efficiency of SMLserver with caching of script bytecode disabled (caching of library bytecode is still enabled). The measurements demonstrate that caching of script bytecode improves performance between 3 and 53 percent with an average of 37 percent.

The sixth column of Table 1 shows the efficiency of SMLserver with library execution enabled on all requests (library and script code is cached). Execution of library code on each request degrades performance between 10 and 74 percent with an average of 44 percent. The performance degrade is highest for less involved scripts. The four scripts `hello`, `date`, `db`, and `guest` use more time on library execution than executing the script itself.

7 Related Work

Related work fall into several categories. First, there is much related work on improving the efficiency of CGI programs [15], in particular by embedding in-

Table 1. The first four columns compares script execution times for SMLserver with three other Web server platforms. Caching of loaded script bytecode improves performance between 3 and 53 percent (column five). Column six shows that execution of library code on each request degrades performance between 10 and 74 percent.

	Requests / second					
Program	MosML MSP	AOLserver TCL	Apache PHP	SMLserver MSP	No script caching	With library execution
hello	55	724	489	**1326**	916	349
date	54	855	495	**1113**	744	337
db	27	558	331	**689**	516	275
guest	25	382	274	**543**	356	249
calendar	36	27	37	**101**	69	80
mul	50	185	214	**455**	300	241
table	21	59	0.7	**93**	84	75
log	8	12	0.4	**31**	30	28

terpreters within Web servers [20], which may drastically decrease script initialization time. In particular, expensive script forking and script loading may be avoided and a *pool of database connections* can be maintained by the Web server, so that scripts need not establish individual connections to a database.

Second, there is a large body of related work on using functional languages for Web programming. Meijer's library for writing CGI scripts in Haskell [13] provides low-level functionality for accessing CGI parameters and sending responses to clients. Thiemann extends Meijer's work by providing a library WASH/CGI [21], which supports sessions and typing of forms and HTML using combinators. The mod_haskell project [4] takes the approach of embedding the Hugs Haskell interpreter as a module for the Apache Web server. Also, Peter Sestoft's ML Server Pages implementation for Moscow ML [17] provides good support for Web programming, although it is based on CGI and thus does not provide high efficiency (see Table 1).

Graunke et al. [10] demonstrate that programming a Web server infrastructure in a high-level functional language can be as efficient as utilizing an existing Web server infrastructure. Their work does not suggest, however, how multi-threaded execution of scripts can be supported in the context of server state. Using an existing Web server infrastructure, such as Apache or AOLserver, also has the advantage of pluggable modules for providing SSL (Secure Socket Layer) support and efficient pool-based database drivers for a variety of database systems.

Queinnec [16] suggests using continuations to implement the interaction between clients and Web servers. In a separate paper, Graunke et al. [9] demonstrate how Web programs can be written in a traditional direct style and transformed into CGI scripts using CPS conversion and lambda lifting. In contrast to Queinnec, their approach uses the client for storing state information (i.e, continuation environments) between requests. It would be interesting to investigate if this approach works for statically typed languages, such as Standard ML.

Finally, <bigwig> [18,2] provides a type system, which guarantees that Web applications return proper HTML to clients. To support typing of forms and sessions (to ensure type safety), <bigwig> programs are written in a special domain-specific language. Also, the session support provided by <bigwig> raises the question of when session state stored on the Web server should be garbage collected.

8   Future Directions

There are many directions for future work. One ongoing direction is the development of an SMLserver Community Suite (SCS), which already contains composable modules for user authentication, multi-lingual Web sites, and much more. SMLserver and SCS is used at the IT University of Copenhagen for running a course evaluation system and other administrative systems, which amounts to approximately 30,000 lines of Standard ML (excluding the Basis Library).

Not surprisingly, we have experienced that the static type system of Standard ML eases development and maintenance of Web applications. However, there are three aspects of Web application development with SMLserver where further work may give us better static guarantees:

1. Embedded HTML code is untyped. Data sent to a browser is not guaranteed to be valid HTML. Use of HTML combinators for constructing HTML code could increase faith in our code, but to completely ensure validity of HTML code requires dynamic tests for text embedded in HTML code.
2. Form variables are untyped. The correspondence between form variables expected by a script and the form variables provided by a request is not modeled by the Standard ML type system. A solution to this problem and the problem that HTML code is untyped has been proposed in the <bigwig> project [18,2], but the solution builds on a new language tailored specifically to Web applications.
3. Embedded SQL queries are untyped. An extension to the Standard ML type system to support embedding of SQL queries has been proposed [3], but it requires a drastic departure from the Standard ML language with the addition of extensible records and variant types. Another possibility is to separate database queries from the program logic and have a tool generate type safe query functions from query specifications. In this way, queries that are invalid with respect to the underlying data model can be rejected at compile time.

9   Conclusion

In this paper, we have presented SMLserver, a multi-threaded Web server platform for executing Web applications written in Standard ML. Making use of the advanced language features of Standard ML provides many advantages for Web programming:

- Higher-order functions combined with the rich module language of Standard ML, provide mechanisms to gain a high degree of code reuse and means for constructing shallow interfaces; examples include modules for form variable validation, database interaction, and data caching.
- The static type system of Standard ML provides very good maintenance properties, which is particularly important for Web programming where, often, program modifications are exposed to users early. Experience with writing large Web applications (+30,000 lines of code) with SMLserver demonstrates the importance of the maintenance properties and that SMLserver scales to the construction of large systems.

Measurements demonstrate that Web applications written with SMLserver perform better than Web applications written with often used scripting languages, both with respect to script execution time and database connectivity.

Finally, we have shown that the region-based memory model scales to a multi-threaded environment where programs run shortly but are executed often. More information about SMLserver is available from http://www.smlserver.org.

Acknowledgments. We would like to thank Lars Birkedal, Ken Friis Larsen, Peter Sestoft, and Mads Tofte for many fruitful discussions about this work.

References

1. Lars Birkedal, Mads Tofte, and Magnus Vejlstrup. From region inference to von Neumann machines via region representation inference. In *Proceedings of the 23rd ACM SIGPLAN-SIGACT Symposium on Principles of Programming Languages*, pages 171–183. ACM Press, January 1996.
2. Claus Brabrand, Anders Møller, and Michael I. Schwartzbach. The <Bigwig> project. *ACM Transactions on Internet Technology*, 2(2), May 2002.
3. Peter Buneman and Atsushi Ohori. Polymorphism and type inference in database programming. *ACM Transactions on Database Systems*, 21(1):30–76, 1996.
4. Eelco Dolstra and Armijn Hemel. *mod_haskell*, January 2000. http://losser.st-lab.cs.uu.nl/mod_haskell.
5. Martin Elsman. Static interpretation of modules. In *Procedings of Fourth International Conference on Functional Programming (ICFP'99)*, pages 208–219. ACM Press, September 1999.
6. Martin Elsman and Niels Hallenberg. A region-based abstract machine for the ML Kit. Technical Report TR-2002-18, IT University of Copenhagen, August 2002.
7. Martin Elsman and Niels Hallenberg. *SMLserver—A Functional Approach to Web Publishing*. The IT University of Copenhagen, February 2002. (154 pages). Available via http://www.smlserver.org.
8. Matthew Fluet and Riccardo Pucella. Phantom types and subtyping. In *Second IFIP International Conference on Theoretical Computer Science (TCS'02)*, pages 448–460, August 2002.
9. Paul Graunke, Shriram Krishnamurthi, Robert Bruce Findler, and Matthias Felleisen. Automatically restructuring programs for the web. In *17th IEEE International Conference on Automated Software Engineering (ASE'01)*, September 2001.

10. Paul Graunke, Shriram Krishnamurti, Steve Van Der Hoeven, and Matthias Felleisen. Programming the web with high-level programming languages. In *European Symposium On Programming (ESOP'01)*, April 2001.
11. Philip Greenspun. *Philip and Alex's Guide to Web Publishing*. Morgan Kaufmann, May 1999. 596 pages. ISBN: 1558605347.
12. Niels Hallenberg, Martin Elsman, and Mads Tofte. Combining region inference and garbage collection. In *ACM SIGPLAN Conference on Programming Language Design and Implementation (PLDI'02)*. ACM Press, June 2002. Berlin, Germany.
13. Erik Meijer. Server side Web scripting in Haskell. *Journal of Functional Programming*, 10(1):1–18, January 2000.
14. Robin Milner, Mads Tofte, Robert Harper, and David MacQueen. *The Definition of Standard ML (Revised)*. MIT Press, 1997.
15. Open Market, Inc. *FastCGI: A High-Performance Web Server Interface*, April 1996. Technical white paper. Available from http://www.fastcgi.com.
16. Christian Queinnec. The influence of browsers on evaluators or, continuations to program web servers. In *Fifth International Conference on Functional Programming (ICFP'00)*, September 2000.
17. Sergei Romanenko, Claudio Russo, and Peter Sestoft. *Moscow ML Owner's Manual*, June 2000. For version 2.00. 35 pages.
18. Anders Sandholm and Michael I. Schwartzbach. A type system for dynamic web documents. In *Proceedings of the ACM SIGPLAN-SIGACT Symposium on Principles of Programming Languages (POPL)*. ACM Press, January 2000.
19. Konrad Slind. Object language embedding in Standard ML of New Jersey. In *Proceedings of the Second ML Workshop, CMU SCS Technical Report*. Carnegie Mellon University, Pittsburgh, Pennsylvania, November 1991.
20. Lincoln Stein and Doug MacEachern. *Writing Apache Modules with Perl and C*. O'Reilly & Associates, April 1999. ISBN 1-56592-567-X.
21. Peter Thiemann. Wash/CGI: Server-side Web scripting with sessions and typed, compositional forms. In *Procedings of Practical Aspects of Declarative Languages (PADL'02)*. Springer-Verlag, January 2002. Portland, Oregon.
22. Mads Tofte, Lars Birkedal, Martin Elsman, Niels Hallenberg, Tommy Højfeld Olesen, and Peter Sestoft. Programming with regions in the ML Kit (for version 4). Technical Report TR-2001-07, IT University of Copenhagen, October 2001.
23. Mads Tofte and Jean-Pierre Talpin. Region-based memory management. *Information and Computation*, 132(2):109–176, 1997.

An Integrated Information System Powered by Prolog

António Porto

Departamento de Informática
Faculdade de Ciências e Tecnologia
Universidade Nova de Lisboa
ap@di.fct.unl.pt

Abstract. Our Faculty embarked a few years ago on an ambitious
project to redesign itself around an integrated information system, aimed
at supporting all information handling activities and deployed through
dynamic Web interfaces automatically customized for individual users.
The project includes both the design of the services and the development
of appropriate software technology to implement them. It led already to a
running system, supporting many official academic procedures, which is
under constant evolution. The system architecture is fully based on Prolog, connected to an external database engine. This paper summarizes
and discusses the characteristics that make Prolog a vehicle of choice for
the implementation, along with a sketch of main aspects of the system
architecture and the specific declarative techniques that were developed
for them. The recurring methodological gain is the ease of building abstraction layers supported by specific term sub-languages, due to the
combination of flexible operator syntax with the power of the underlying machinery to define new constructs. The basic programming layer
evolved from standard Prolog to a novel structured version of it, with
compositional semantics (no cuts) and direct support for structural abstraction and application, combining in practice the logic programming
style with the higher-order power and some of the programming flavour
of functional languages. The system's main architectural glue is the conceptual scheme, for which a definition language was developed whose
expressions are compiled (by Prolog) to induce the database tables and
(the instantiation of) a query/update language with a syntax based on
compositionality principles of natural language, whose expressions are
both more natural and much more compact than the equivalent in SQL.

1 Introduction

A few years ago our Faculty decided to redesign itself around a fully integrated
information system. The aim is that all information handling (creation, transmission, storage, retrieval) relative to all aspects of school life (students' records,
schedules, discussion groups, library use, accounting, etc.) is carried out through
a single system, with a comprehensive and coherent data model, and Web interfaces automatically customized for each individual user. The project is doubly

V. Dahl and P. Wadler (Eds.): PADL 2003, LNCS 2562, pp. 92–109, 2003.
© Springer-Verlag Berlin Heidelberg 2003

ambitious, as it comprises not only the redesign of the way people act and interact within the institution, but also the development of appropriate software technology to implement such functionalities. A first report on the objectives and results can be found in [6]. The system is up and running, albeit with a coverage still limited mostly to academic services (course enrollment, grading, student records, schedules, statistics, etc.).

The system architecture is based on Prolog, the only outside components being a database engine and an http server with a small servlet. The choice of Prolog represents neither an arbitrary option among many possibilities, nor an experiment in forced adequacy, but a genuine belief, based on many years of experience, that it contains essential ingredients for bootstrapping an architecture exhibiting required features of structural richness, modularity and multi-layered abstractions, translatable as declarativeness, which ultimately have a decisive impact on development and maintenance costs. This belief can now be substantiated, that being the purpose of this paper.

The word "declarative", in the context of logic programming, is traditionally equated with logic-based model-theoretic semantics of "pure" programs, and extra-logical features of real programs are hopelessly dismissed as not declarative. This is unfortunate and rather myopic. We found that the essential operational aspects of Prolog can be given a perfectly declarative status, by choosing the right semantic domain and a syntactic variant with operators that are compositional in that domain. On the other hand we often code in syntactic terms certain information structures that are declaratively understood only by implicit reference to application-specific semantic domains. A crucial point of view of ours is that syntax, by itself, has no semantics, and it is only in a given *context* that syntax acquires meaning through a given semantics. A system is declarative if all contexts are clearly identifiable and are given proper semantics. We claim to do it in our system, which has a large variety of such contexts.

This paper cannot aim at presenting in sufficient breadth or depth the various mechanisms that were devised to push the declarative agenda into the architecture of our system. We must perforce only hint at their variety and properties through chosen examples, and adopt an informal if rigorous style of presentation.

2   The System

2.1   Vision

This project was born out of a vision that it should be possible and desirable to bring together under a single coherent system all aspects of information handling that can be carried out through a standard computer interface. This is in sharp contrast to the current practice (virtually everywhere) of having different systems for different tasks, with their own databases and interfaces. The perceived benefits are to get rid of data inconsistencies, to explore the relationships among everything, and to provide uniform user access, in terms of interfaces, control and deployment. The drawbacks are the necessity to (re)code all services, rather than using ready-made solutions, and the needed development of a suitable software architecture to support the system. We were convinced that we could provide the latter, using Prolog technology, in such a way as to minimize the costs of the coding effort. This confidence was key to launching the project.

The requirement of universal accessibility (independence from place and platform) let to the obvious choice of relying on the Web to channel every service provided by the system, i.e. the sole user interface to the system is a Web browser. The other essential requirements of our vision are *integration, individuality* and *instantaneity*.

By integration we mean that all information processed by the system must be captured by a unique coherent data model, and correspondingly stored in a single database and accessed through a query/update language with integral relationship power.

Individuality refers to the level of automatic customization of available services. A typical user (student or staff), authenticated through a single personal signature (identifier and password), gains access to exactly those services that are allowed to him or her at the moment. The bonus of integration is maximum flexibility in access control, since the database can be queried with arbitrary expressions about user properties. Thus a student may access her record of course enrollments and results, and also the news/messages of an interest group she belongs to, a professor may manage the courses he is teaching, and also access his department's budget, etc.

Instantaneity is required of the effects of information update, i.e. there must be no intermediate delayed processes between information sources and all the possible uses of the conveyed information. Thus students are able to see their grades on a course right after they are entered by the grader, and the course instructors may also immediately see the overall statistics. Notice that a single update action affecting the status of someone immediately and implicitly impacts on the range of services accessible to that person, e.g. the moment a teacher is assigned the responsibility of a course (through the system, by someone else having the power to do it) he gains access to certain management facilities for that course edition (through links previously unavailable to him).

2.2   Realization

The vision is being realized by jointly developing a generic software architecture for building integrated information systems, called PETISCO, and the particular information system for our Faculty, called MIAU (pronounced "meow").

MIAU went into operation in 2000, with the progressive replacement of the existing student record management system, which was strictly a back-office operation, with no public interfaces. In 2000/01 we achieved exclusive use of MIAU for introducing final course grades by instructors, as well as access by students to their records, and global access to grade statistics by department and course. The registration and enrollment process is now completely done on the Web by the students themselves. Another novelty is a systematic enquiry of all students about their academic experience in the previous semester, with automatic availability of results. System integration allows in this case the authorization of course-related answers only for courses in which a student was enrolled and not excluded in the final grading. Students now use the system to get the codes needed for paying tuition fees in ATM machines, while staff from the Academic Division manage tuition exemptions, and may check statistics and individual situations. Detailed plans of studies for each degree program are available for consultation, and so are schedules, be they for a given student, teacher, course, room, or curricular semester of a degree program. This flexibility attests the power of an integrated system. There are management services such as the automatic compilation of departmental indexes of teaching load. The system has already spread to non-academic areas, namely the Technical Support and Personnel divisions.

2.3   Basic Runtime Architecture

A Web browser being the sole interface, any user request is conveyed to the system through a URL, possibly adjoined with submitted form data. It always specifies the user (the code of a person in the database) and a channel for accessing a service. Different channels may exist for the same service, corresponding to different navigation paths, authorization policies or parameterizations.

Instantaneity demands that any request must be evaluated dynamically, i.e. there must be a corresponding program which is run to compute, using up-to-date information in the database, the content that is delivered to the user's browser. We use a standard http server, but, rather than using the CGI method of dynamic content generation, each request is passed to a small servlet (a permanent autonomous process) that triggers the execution of a Prolog program, by initializing it with the specific request data. This Prolog process acts as the real request server, and produces the content (typically an HTML page) through computations that generally involve querying (and possibly updating) the database. The servlet actually manages a pool of ready Prolog server processes, one of which is consumed for each request. A small protocol between servlet and Prolog is used to pass the relevant request data, and to exchange information on authenticated user sessions, whose persistent data is kept by the servlet.

A request server is a Prolog runtime environment process, pre-loaded with generic definitions for handling requests, and performing a read/execute loop for commands input from the servlet. The initialization commands convey information from the URL—user code, channel path, and possibly parameters (name/value pairs)—, any available post data (parameters from forms) and active user sessions. After these the starting command is issued, triggering a series of validation steps whose success leads to the processing of a required service. First the channel is validated. It must correspond to a path in a channel directory, along which are files containing declarative local definitions that are compositionally assembled. The result usually specifies a required service, in the form of a path in a service directory, along which can be found files containing definitions of allowed parameters and their types. These are used to validate the parameters that were sent. Furthermore, the channel definition may require certain parameters to be present, in which case their presence is also checked. Next comes the authorization. Each channel specifies one, defined with the full power of conceptual expressions over the database scheme and denoting an arbitrary group of persons. Its validation is carried out by checking if the user belongs to the group. The channel also specifies the needed authentications, that correspond to sessions. If a required session is inactive the relevant authentication page is issued, whose form submission is a request similar to the original one but with added authentication data, whose successful check is reported to the servlet to set up an active session. The service is finally processed, by first consulting files along the service path containing specific procedure definitions and then executing goals read from the service execution file that is found at the end of the service path.

2.4 Software Challenges

If there is one word summarizing the methodological challenges for this kind of system it is *flexibility*. An integrated information system is under constant change, because the full coverage must be gradually implemented (there are no ready-made solutions), organizations frequently reorganize themselves (their structure, activities and rules) and there are always new ideas for information services (facilitated by integration) even within an otherwise stable organization.

The key interrelated notions that are crucial for achieving flexibility are *structure* and *abstraction*. System development is a permanent exercise in generalization, as there inevitably come up analogies, commonalities and variants over what is being developed. The challenge is to have the linguistic and computational means to turn those generalizations into suitable abstractions, and their application and composition options into suitable structures. These often correspond to sub-languages, used in particular contexts, and an essential requirement is the ability to manipulate their expressions both syntactically (structure inspection and construction) and semantically (achieving intended effects).

While developing PETISCO/MIAU, as with any other large system, it was obviously hard to come up with the right solutions from the start. A fair degree of flexibility was achieved in the first running version, but accumulated experience with its major limitations led to a complete overhaul, not only of the PETISCO architecture but even of the basic Prolog platform, in order to increase the structural cleanliness of the code at all levels, including the ability to adequately write truly generic code.

3   Semantics and Declarativeness

Over the years, the major influence in preaching the virtues of the logic programming paradigm has been the quite impressive body of work on so-called declarative semantics, i.e. logic-based model-theoretic semantics. Impressive as such semantics are, their application is limited to truly logic-based concerns, such as arise in knowledge representation, but fail to address other crucial concerns of many practical applications such as our integrated information system. Why? First, model-theoretic semantics are mostly ground, being defined over variants of the Herbrand base consisting of ground literals, whereas we often need to reason about actual variable bindings, i.e. to think of calls with free variables as queries whose answers are the constructed bindings for those variables. Furthermore, the Herbrand semantics are based on *sets*, whereas in practice it may be imperative to consider the *order* of those answers to queries. Finally, logic-based semantics are usually first-order, but a vitally important feature of Prolog, that we use extensively to write generic code, is the higher-order meta-call facility, that allows the execution of dynamically constructed calls.

We should, therefore, give more importance to such operational aspects of the Prolog machinery. But can it ever be considered "declarative"? In some sense declarativeness is in the eyes of the beholder, but there are some important criteria for any reasonable notion of it: one must define denotational semantics that attribute meaning to syntax fragments, its semantic domain must be intuitively clear, and the semantics must be *compositional* for the operators available to construct programs—an essential feature for allowing modular local reasoning and its progressive lifting through the operator applications. We claim that a declarative semantics satisfying these criteria can indeed be defined for Prolog, addressing the non-logic-based concerns alluded to above. This paper is not the proper vehicle to formally present such semantics, so we just sketch below the main ideas.

A major difference between the paradigms of logic and functional programming is that a call in the former may produce any number of results (what is usually called "don't know" non-determinism) and in the latter exactly one. We need to have clear, compositional denotational semantics associated with Prolog's way of exploring the multiple result space. Intuitively, the denotational semantics of Prolog maps any term t to a *sequence* of results, each being a set of bindings (a substitution) for the free variables of t.[1] Let us call this the *polyresult* semantics. Failure corresponds to the empty sequence, and the "don't know" non-determinism allows for more than one result in the sequence (whose ordered nature actually makes "non-determinism" a misnomer). The meaning of extra-logical built-in Prolog predicates such as var is easily captured in this semantics. The basic control operators are ',' and ';', whose usual names, 'conjunction' and 'disjunction', reflect the logic-based reading; in the polyresult semantics they represent a sort of 'product' and 'sum' of results, where sum is just sequence concatenation and the product involves "multiplying" each result of the first term by the results of (its application to) the second term. They remain associative but not commutative as in the logic reading. To handle the power of Prolog's cut we need another control operator that has a filtering (cutting) effect on sequences but is compositional. This is 'until' (see later), with which we can define the other familiar control constructs such as 'not' and 'if-then-else'.

---

[1] This can of course be generalized to constraint logic programming, by considering that results contain more general constraints than just equalities.

Is this *the* semantics of Prolog programs? To us, the question is not well phrased. The polyresult semantics is what we associate with terms *when* invoked as goals. But terms can be arguments of other terms, their meaning depending *then* on what these are and how they, in turn, are interpreted. In short, syntax *by itself* has no meaning, semantics being for syntax *in context*. This is intuitively obvious to programmers. In a Prolog goal (X is A+B) the term A+B means the sum of A and B, but the same term as argument of another predicate may have a totally different meaning, and yet another when invoked as a goal. A constant activity in the development of systems such as PETISCO/MIAU is the design of term languages (i.e. defining subsets of "valid" terms) of various degrees of complexity, to specify information structures that are useful in particular contexts, and therefore each have their own semantics.

What about side-effects? Although if freely used they can generate a semantic nightmare, in practice they can and should be used in principled ways whose semantics are actually quite simple to grasp. Take for example output operations. In PETISCO the main purpose of the request server is to output the content to the user's browser, there being no escape from this reality. For flexibility, content is generated by executing a series of Prolog calls read from a file associated with the requested service, each call naturally having a single result. It being so, and there being no feedback loop between produced output and the calls producing it, these can in fact be viewed through the lens of a purely functional semantics, where the output is the resulting value. This is another instance of the phenomenon of attributing semantics to syntax in context. In this functional output semantics the 'conjunction' is a simple concatenation operator, the 'disjunction' is not used, and 'if-then-else' is used but reading the 'if' part (yet again, context) through its polyresult semantics (non-empty or empty result sequence). Often we need to glue, under 'conjunction' and using a common variable, a binding-producing call with a binding-consuming output-producing call, e.g. produce(X),display(X). We have to mix the polyresult reading of ',' for deriving the dataflow of X's binding from produce to display, and the functional output reading of the same ',' for checking that output comes only from display. The two relevant "functions" can be made more visible with the functional notation produce\display, that is read as applying display to the result of evaluating produce. This is one of several mechanisms designed to express in Prolog functional notions of structural abstraction and application [5] that are discussed further ahead.

How can we cleanly mix genuine multiple results with side effects? The answer is through *iterators*, mentioned in the next section.

4   The Prolog Platform

The Prolog system we use was totally developed in-house. The basis is Nano-Prolog, a compact portable implementation developed by Artur Miguel Dias that provides an interpreter environment but internally compiles into WAM code.

There are several non-standard low-level extensions, notably a few predicates for interfacing with an external database engine.

The first implementation of PETISCO/MIAU used basically standard Prolog (syntax and built-in predicates), but our experience and continuous search for declarative methodologies for writing code, so necessary to achieve the level of genericity demanded by this kind of application, actually led us to design a major overhaul of the language, involving both the control primitives and the syntax of predicate definitions. This was brought about by two essential realizations. One is that the practical operational semantics can be defined in a fully compositional way (the polyresult semantic framework), by keeping some operators, replacing others and introducing new ones. The other is that there are very flexible but principled ways to use the flavour of functional programming and its power of higher-order abstraction, within the polyresult framework.

Standard Prolog's most spectacular flaw is with respect to compositionality, by making available to the programmer the non-compositional 'cut'. But this problem can be elegantly solved. We intend to present the formal details elsewhere, and only informally summarize the solution here.

The simplest and intuitively well-understood use of the cut is to implement if-then-else, through a clause with the pattern $H:-C,!,B$. We write instead $H<-C<>B$. The limit cases where C or B are empty are written respectively as $H<>B$ and $H<-C!$. What if B is a conjunction containing other cuts, say $X,!,Y$? The global effect (for the whole predicate definition) is already achieved by $<>$, and the local effect amounts to allowing only the first result of X. We write $H<-C<>$ once X,Y. The more complex cases are those where cuts appear inside disjunctions. These can be coded by resorting to the new operators until and unless. The sequence of results of (X unless C) is the maximum prefix of the sequence of results of X for which C has no result. For until, the sequence is similar but extended with the first result, if it exists, for which C also has one.

Another helpful control concept is that of the *iterator* $G=>A$, resulting in the execution of (the corresponding instance of) an action A *for each* result of a generator G. The standard use is when A (but not G) produces side-effects such as output, for example when the results of G are answers to a database query and A outputs an answer tuple in a table row format.

We have by now fully reprogrammed PETISCO and parts of MIAU using the "reinvented" compositional Prolog. The result is much more compact, readable and understandable than the previous version.

5 Structural Abstraction and Application

We introduced into Prolog a powerful set of mechanisms meant to achieve, in principled but flexible ways, the higher-order power of functional languages, following and expanding on an old suggestion by David Warren [7]. The fundamentals have been presented in [5]. The main idea is to be able to interpret terms (in certain contexts) as implicit abstractions of their extensions with one more start- or end-argument, i.e. p(1) as $\lambda x.p(x,1)$ or $\lambda y.p(1,y)$, and to define a variety of application operators that provide contexts for applying such abstractions to arguments and then execute the resulting terms as goals. For example, the explicit end-application p(1) \: 2 is equivalent to p(1,2), the pipe p(1)\q(2) implicitly performs end- and start-applications on a new variable X to become (p(1,X),q(X,2)) and similarly the piped iterator g \=> a rewrites as g(X) => a(X). Notice that the two first constructs suggest functional application, respectively to literal and evaluated arguments, but the application is actually taking place in the polyresult framework. Of course the real interest is to use the application operators with variable arguments, e.g. Gen \=> Act, to obtain generic code relying on the dynamic interpretation of argument bindings, akin to the use of functions as arguments of other functions in functional programming.

We next motivate the introduction of some of these mechanisms with particular aspects of our system that are at the origin of their development.

5.1   HTML Generation

Most of the services correspond to HTML pages. In the future we will use XML, but for now HTML is still the common denominator among widespread browsers. So, a question of paramount importance is how best to write code to generate HTML. This is a case where it can be argued that Prolog allowed us to implement a wonderful solution, mixing a simple and very readable syntax with generic parametricity and ultimately a highly flexible abstraction power that transcends its use in HTML generation and is of much more general applicability.

We took a different approach from that of the well-known P*i*LL*o*W system [1], for reasons that will presently become clear. In order to output HTML content in P*i*LL*o*W one has to invoke output_html(t) where t is an HTML term, this being a very direct term encoding of an explicit HTML structure, for example [img$[src='phone.gif'],h2(a([href=Phone_ref],'Phone'))].

We opt for a much more lightweight and uniform syntax. All tag and attribute names become prefix operators (of the same right-associative precedence) and as such are used to bind their attributes. For grouping we use conjunctive notation (comma separation) instead of lists. Tag terms, consisting of just tag atoms or tag prefixes applied to attributes, are connected to their argument representations through the right-associative infix operator ':'. The example above is rewritten as img src -- 'phone.gif', h2 : a href Phone_ref : -- 'Phone', a lighter syntactic variant but with a crucial semantic difference: this term is actually meant to be directly executed, resulting in the outputting of the desired HTML string. So we totally avoid the wrapping with something like output_html. A purist reader may at first be disgusted by our implicit use of side-effects, but is this really any less declarative than P*i*LL*o*W's solution? We honestly think rather the contrary. Terms such as the one above can be readily understood as denoting *both* the (functional) process of producing an HTML fragment *and* the structure of the produced output.

Why did we write (-- 'Phone') rather than just 'Phone'? Because a goal t:x, when t represents an HTML tag, means "*execute* x in the tag environment t". The prefix (--) is just a synonym of write. So we can pass as the argument of a tag any kind of executable expression. This is a plus for the readability of our scheme, as it allows the local use of simple compact terms that are calls to possibly complex procedures whose definitions lie elsewhere. E.g. `table : ( tr : titles, data_tuple \=> tr : data_display )`, with `titles`, `data_tuple` and `data_display` referring to application-specific predicates, has a very direct declarative reading: "in a table, a row with the titles followed by, for each data tuple, a row displaying it". To achieve the same effect in PiLLoW, the application-specific predicates must generate a term rather than producing the corresponding output, we must call them before the final output is assembled, and the equivalent of the iterator must be a `bagof` or equivalent predicate that explicitly constructs a list:

```
titles( T ),
bagof( tr(DD), ( data_tuple(D), data_display(D,DD) ), TR_ ),
output_html( table( [ tr( T ), TR_ ] ) ).
```

Going back to the first example of our HTML notation, note that the argument of attribute `src` is also an executable term. In our definitions we have split the HTML attributes in two groups: the call attributes, such as `src`, that expect the argument to be an output-producing call, and the text attributes, such as `align`, whose argument term is directly written as output (these attributes are unlikely to require procedural abstractions to specify the required values).

The *generalized application* operator ':' is of much wider applicability than HTML generation, as we show next.

5.2   The Power of Generalized Application

A goal $e:x$ is generally interpreted as the application of an environment e to x, the exact meaning depending on e. Upon invocation e must be bound to a non-variable term, that always stands for some structural abstraction $\lambda a.t[a]$, which is applied to x, the resulting term $t[x]$ being invoked as a goal.

Our flexibility requirements led us to the following definition:

```
Env : X  <-  Env :=: E
         <>  E : X.

(A:B):X  <>  A : B : X.

Abs : X  <>  Abs \: X.
```

The first clause allows environment equations. An HTML tag such as `table` is in fact defined with the clauses

```
table    :=:  tag( table, [] )  !.
table A  :=:  tag( table, A )   !.
```

The base case of ':' treats environment application as end-application, whose default case is end-argument term extension, so (`table bgcolor red : X`) calls (`tag(table,bgcolor red) \: X`), which calls `tag(table,bgcolor red,X)`.[2]

---

[2] This actually produces the output `<table bgcolor="#ff0000">`...`</table>`, where the dots stand for the output resulting from the execution of X.

The middle clause allows environment chains by applying associativity, a declaratively important feature. Take this example of a padded, coloured background in HTML:

```
table(B,S,P,C)   :=:   table ( border S, cellspacing S,
                               cellpadding P, bgcolor C )   !.


background(P,C)   :=:   table(0,0,P,C) : tr : td   !.
```

A goal such as `background(2,red):X` invokes `(table(0,0,2,red):tr:td):X` which invokes `table(0,0,2,red):(tr:td):X`. When the time comes to execute `(tr:td):X` associativity is used again to call `tr:td:X`.

HTML tags (and compositions thereof) are just examples of environments whose application is invoked with ':'. We use many others, notably *generators*. A call `G:X` where `G` is bound to a generator is invoked with `X` a free variable, in order to *generate* bindings for it. For example, if `G` is bound to `member([1,2])` then `G:X` will call `member([1,2],X)` (through the base cases of both ':' and '\:') and `X` will get bound successively to 1 and 2. In MIAU we faced the problem of often wishing to write generic code that could use either a generator of values or a list of precomputed values. This was solved by making lists actually behave as generators of their own elements! Since, as remarked above, the base case of the execution of `G:X` calls for the application of `X` as an extra end-argument of the generator term bound to `G`, we need only to define a predicate for the ternary version of the list constructor '.', of which regular lists become implicit end-abstractions:

```
.( X, _, X ).
.( _, L, X )   <>   member( L, X ).
```

Thus the list `[1,2]` becomes a generator equivalent to `member([1,2])`.

A typical example of using these mechanisms is the following procedure for filling HTML tables (we omit some extra parameter details):

```
fill_table(  C )   <>   table : fill_rows( C ).
fill_rows(   C )   <>   C \=> fill_row.
fill_row(    C )   <>   tr : fill_colums( C ).
fill_colums( C )   <>   C \=> fill_column.
fill_colum(  C )   <>   td : C.
```

The first two clauses show that the argument of `fill_table` is expected to be a generator, i.e. a term interpreted (by the pipe semantics) as the abstraction of a goal with an extra end-argument, whose solutions are passed to `fill_row`. Each such solution must itself be a generator (see the next clauses) for a column's data items. A typical example of use is with structured answers to database queries that consist of lists of lists, say of courses and students enrolled in each of them. As we've shown, the lists behave as generators.

6   The Conceptual Scheme

An essential feature of a PETISCO system, addressing the requirement of integration, is the existence of one coherent conceptual scheme, expressing the terminology, structure and constraints among all the organizational concepts that the system may handle, and whose instances are stored in the system database.

The way the conceptual scheme is incorporated in PETISCO is a testimony to the ease and power of using Prolog to implement the syntax and operational semantics of particular sub-languages whose expressions are themselves amenable to manipulation inside the system. We have devised a scheme *definition* language, in which the scheme of a particular system such as MIAU is expressed. The files containing the compact definitions are processed by a PETISCO package, that compiles them into a lower-level expanded representation of the scheme, in the form of a Prolog program consisting only of facts for a few predicates that capture the structural relationships in any scheme. Interestingly, inference over the compiled scheme is used by the processor itself while compiling the definition of a concept that refers to others (as most do).

The compiled scheme is used by several other Prolog processors for various purposes. One automatically generates the scheme documentation as a set of linked HTML pages. Another generates the code for creating the database tables in the particular database system in use. A third one is a module inside the PETISCO runtime environment (request server) that implements the conceptual query/update language, yet another sub-language which is of paramount importance. It takes advantage of inference over the compiled scheme to provide a much more compact syntax and higher level of abstraction than SQL.

The use of our scheme definition language in PETISCO substitutes the use of development tools of the database system. The obvious advantage, as explained, is the tight integration with the runtime PETISCO architecture through the high-level query language. This paper cannot aim at an in-depth discussion of the model behind the scheme definition language and all its features, so we settle for a brief informal summary and some examples.

6.1   The Conceptual Model

Our conceptual model is simple but richer than is strictly needed for implementing a relational database, namely through the use of conceptual (high-level) attributes besides the lexical (low-level) ones. The reason is that this extra terminology is used in the real world being modeled and allows more compact (abstract) and natural expressions both in the definition language and in the query/update language.

There is no distinction between entities and relationships. A *concept* is syntactically an atomic name and semantically a set of abstract individuals (objects, relationships, situations, events, etc.), for example `student`, `course_edition`, `annual_registration`. A conceptual type is a conjunction of disjunctions of concepts, denoting the intersection of unions thereof. The basic concepts are the data types (`integer`, `real`, `string`), that have no inner structure. Each non-basic concept has a set of *attributes*, syntactically atomic names and semantically functions between individuals. The *lexical* attributes range over data types, whereas the *conceptual* ones range over conceptual types. Each concept has a subset of *referential* attributes, from which there is a functional dependency to the concept, i.e. a tuple of values for the referential attributes uniquely determines an individual belonging to the concept. A concept's type, if it exists, is the minimal conceptual type that includes it other than the concept itself. In many cases it is simply another concept, expressing a direct sub-concept relationship.

Each concept with its lexical attributes gives rise to a database table. The referential lexical attributes constitute its primary key. Each conceptual attribute gives rise to foreign keys from its lexical attributes to every minimal concept that includes its type (usually just one). A concept's type, similarly, induces foreign keys (one or more) from the referential lexical attributes.

6.2 The Scheme Definition Language

We illustrate just some of the features, through examples adapted from MIAU.

We can define abstractions on data types, using the logic variable for parametricity, as in this example with the string size:

```
d  name(X) : string(X).
```

A simple concept definition is that of a person:

```
c( person, [ sex : string(1),
             name(80)         ] ).
```

In this case, as in many others, there is by default an implicit referential attribute `code` of type `integer`. The outcome of the compilation is the following set of clauses (presented with their predicate meaning):

`d_c(person).`	database concept
`gsc(person,person).`	greatest super concept
`ref(person,[code]).`	referent
`r_a(person,code,i,l(integer)).`	referential attribute
`n_a(person,sex,p,l(string(1))).`	non-referential attribute
`n_a(person,name,p,l(string(80))).`	

Sub-concepts (concept types) may be expressed via name composition operators, such as in the following example defining `authenticated_person` as a sub-concept of `person`:

```
c( authenticated / person, [ identifier : string(20),
                             encrypted_password : string(34) ] ).
```

A concept's referent can be explicitly defined between braces, for example:[3]

---

[3] A student is a person enrolled in a degree program; the same person when enrolled in another degree program is a different student with another number.

```
c( student, { number : integer }, [ < person,
                                     degree \\ program ] ).
```

In this case the non-referential attributes are conceptual: person[4] of type person (implicit by being a defined concept) and program of type degree_program (as meant by the name composition degree\\program). The scheme compiler infers the corresponding lexical attributes' names and types, using the referred concepts' referent descriptions (the ref and r_a clauses) and the local attribute and concept names. In this case the inferred lexical attributes have the same name as their conceptual counterparts (person and program) because such is the policy for code referents, encoded in the value i (invisible) of the third argument of r_a (see above). The compiled information on the program attribute is this:

```
n_a(student,program,p,l(integer)).   lexical
n_a(student,program,p,c([program])). conceptual
ndr(student,program,degree_program). non-referential database reference
```

One can also define virtual concepts, i.e. concept templates used to define other concepts or attributes but not giving rise to database tables. Here is an example illustrating also the use of more than one referential attribute:

```
c_( period, { year     : int,
              semester : int  } ).
```

This can then be used to define other derived concepts, for example:

```
c( course_edition, { course,
                     period  }, [ master : professor ] ).
```

In this case three lexical attributes are generated, namely course (with foreign key to course.code), year and semester.

Now consider enrollments of students in course editions:

```
c( enrollment, { student,
                 course_edition }, [ date ] ).
```

The table enrollment has five lexical attributes (four being referential), with a foreign key from (course, year, semester) to the referential attributes of course_edition, which in this case have the same names although in general this might be otherwise.

6.3   The Query Language

Any interface code for accessing the database is written in our conceptual query language, which is based on compositional principles inspired by natural language, e.g. prepositional phrases, relative clauses, and determiners, with just a few connectors. The concrete language is the instantiation of a generic linguistic framework through the conceptual scheme, the atomic names in the expressions being the scheme's concept and attribute names.

---

[4] The '<' notation signals sub-attribute inheritance, commented in the next section.

The very basic idea for a query is to select (the values of) an attribute of a concept. We write `name/person` to express 'name of person'. Generally concepts need to be qualified by constraints. We write `name/person$(code<100)` to mean 'name of person with code less than 100'. Referential equalities can be simply expressed by values inside braces, eg. `student${1234}`.

The language makes full use of Prolog's inferential power over the compiled scheme to allow for compact and natural expressions, notably by avoiding in many cases the explicit mention of join conditions. The simplest such case is the cascading of attributes, e.g. we write `name/student/enrollment$(year=2002)` to get the names of students enrolled in 2002. Compare this with the generated SQL where the join appears explicitly:

```
select s.name from  student s, enrollment e
                where s.number=e.student and e.year=2002
```

A more sophisticated example is the use of inherited attributes. In the definition of `student` its attribute `person` was '<'-prefixed to mean that the defined concept inherits the attributes of that attribute's type. This corresponds to the particular semantics of the verb 'to be' used when we say that a student is a person,[5] which allows us to talk of a student's name. We can indeed use `name/student` to mean 'name of student', because although `name` is not a direct attribute of `student` it is inherited through its attribute `person`, and our translation into SQL infers the needed selection of `name` from `person` with the join condition `student.person=person.code`. Better still, `identifier/student` can also be used, demanding the selection from `authenticated_person` through the join `student.person=authenticated_person.code`, because although `identifier` is not an attribute of (every) `person`, it is of its sub-concept. The dual search in super-concepts is also available, so `name/authenticated_person` also works.

Another important feature, exemplary of the achieved tight integration, is the ability to use references to parameters whose values are passed in the URL or hidden as post data (from forms), and whose names are those of attributes of certain concepts. Imagine a service that displays the names of students enrolled in a particular course edition. The corresponding query can be naturally expressed by `name/student/enrollment$(@course,@period)`, where '@' reads as 'the', and the implicit values are assumed to have been passed as parameters, e.g. through a URL ending with `period(2002,1)course(56)`. Notice the usefulness of conceptual attributes such as `period`. The '@' construction can also be used inside a constraint, say `year >= @year`.

The language includes the ability to use inner references, typically in nested conceptual expressions. As an example, suppose that there is a need to count the number of students which are enrolled in just one course, in a given period. We can express this with

```
# / enrollment$( @period, student:S, course:C,
                 ~ enrollment$( @period, :S, course \= :C ) ).
```

---

[5] Remember that a person can become more than one student.

The '~' prefix reads as 'there is no'. The infix use of ':' corresponds to an indefinite article plus a local name, e.g. 'a student S', and later prefix occurrences are definite references such as '(the student) S'.

One may ask for more than one attribute, recursively apply them, and factorize such applications. For example, assume that a department has a name, and a course has a department and credits. Then this form of query is valid: (name/department,credits)/course/ enrollment$... It returns pairs of department names and credit values. Should one wish to retrieve also the code (referent) of the course it would be enough to prefix course with '?'.

The language having been designed with preoccupations of non-verbosity, all queried attributes are implicitly assumed to return ordered values, and group functions such as count or sum implicitly require grouping on the remaining attributes, e.g. the query (name/department/course,#)/enrollment$... returns pairs consisting of a department name and the number of its courses, for the given enrollment conditions.

Updates rely on the same syntax of constrained concepts that is used in queries. For example, - enrollment$(@student,@period) is used to erase all enrollments of a given student in a given period.

6.4   Groups

The definition of groups of people is of paramount importance in organizational information systems, be they authorization groups, discussion groups, news recipients, or whatever. We have set up a standard way to deal with groups, that takes advantage of the power of the conceptual query language.

A group has a name and an intensional definition, built out of other groups and/or conceptual expressions using union, intersection and difference operators. The allowed conceptual expressions are restricted only by the requirement that they represent groups of people, naturally. Further abstraction is achieved by parametric group names, using numbered parametric references in the conceptual expressions. As an example we can define a parametric group sector with the expression staff/working_position$(acronym/sector = @1) and then invoke a particular group such as sector:'DI'.

Associated to group membership is the notion of level, expressing the rights to grant ad-hoc membership to new members. A member of level 0 cannot bring in new members, while one of level 1 can designate new members of level 0, etc. This is very useful for implementing *delegation* of authorizations. A user is authorized to use a certain channel for services if he belongs to its authorization group. In case his membership is of level 1 he can introduce a new level 0 member, which in practice means delegating to that person the power to use that channel's services, in this case without granting the power to sub-delegate.

7   Conclusions and Further Work

PETISCO/MIAU is a Prolog-based system that has been in daily use for more than two years by a population of currently over 6,000 people, supporting official academic procedures such as enrollments, grades, certificates, etc. Its performance and the ease with which it is being continuously updated attest to the practicality of the declarative approach for building real-life large-scale integrated information systems.

Somewhat remarkable is the fact that the practical needs of such an application, namely the flexibility required for the continued refactoring of code dictated by manageable system growth, actually led to theoretically interesting basic language developments.

Regarding future work, among many other issues we single out three on which we briefly comment.

7.1   Performance

Contrary to many disbelievers' expectations, MIAU has a quite respectable performance, even running on low-end server hardware. Our peak loads so far have been in the first days of enrollments in September 2002, where hourly rates of about 10,000 hits were handled, originating about 5,000 database update transactions and many more queries. We have observed that the architectural bottleneck is typically not on the Prolog side but on the database server.

However, with the growth of services and the ensuing growth of abstraction layers it makes sense to worry about performance optimization. Fortunately the opportunities abound for doing so. Precisely due to the systematic use of generic code at many levels and compact sublanguages for many purposes, large parts of the code are deterministic and can be statically unfolded through the definitions by a partial evaluator. It is a crucially important property of our structured version of Prolog that, due to its compositional semantics, we can indeed build with relative ease a partial evaluator for the whole language. "Nothing is so practical as a good theory."

7.2   Programming Environment

The sort of envisaged compilation remains valid, of course, only up to changes in the used definitions. This puts a burden on constructing a better programming environment, distinguishing between development (no need to compile) and production (up-to-date compilation), and addressing the incrementality issue through inference of inter- and intra-module code dependencies.

Someone trying to understand real code needs to be aware of the semantic contexts of the pieces, but the fact remains that not everything can be locally explicit in the code itself. Our longer term aim, to help in solving this problem, is to develop our Prolog system into a *literate programming* [2] environment as advocated and used by Knuth, whereby proper documentation can be produced in tight integration with the code.

We also intend to explore more fully the potential of the contextual logic programming modularity model [3,4], already available in our implementation, and indeed use the practical needs of the growing system as a guide on best practice and possible modifications to the model.

7.3   Conceptual Scheme and Database Management

We plan to use the system's own architecture to implement Web interfaces for managing changes in the scheme, rather than explicitly editing files and invoking processors at the operating system shell level. The crucial issues to tackle are modularity and incrementality, on the one hand, and how to efficiently handle the kind of scheme changes that result in non-trivial reorganization of the database involving table drops and data migration.

Another important direction for improvement regards views and triggers in the database. Currently this is done in an ad-hoc way, but the interesting challenge is to come up with a richer syntax and semantics for the scheme definition language that will at least partly automate this process while generating appropriate documentation.

References

1. Daniel Cabeza and Manuel Hermenegildo. Distributed WWW programming using (Ciao-)Prolog and the PiLLoW library. *Theory and Practice of Logic Programming*, 1(3):251–282, May 2001.
2. Donald Knuth. *Literate Programming*, volume 27 of *CSLI Lecture Notes*. Center for the Study of Language and Information, 1992.
3. Luís Monteiro and António Porto. Contextual logic programming. In Giorgio Levi and Maurizio Martelli, editors, *Logic Programming, Proceedings of the Sixth International Conference*, pages 284–299. MIT Press, 1989.
4. Luís Monteiro and António Porto. A language for contextual logic programming. In K.R. Apt, J.W. de Bakker, and J.J.M.M. Rutten, editors, *Logic Programming Languages: Constraints, Functions and Objects*. MIT Press, 1993.
5. António Porto. Structural abstraction and application in logic programming. In Zhenjiang Hu and Mario Rodriguez-Artalejo, editors, *FLOPS 2002, Sixth International Symposium on Functional and Logic Programming, Proceedings*. Springer, 2002.
6. António Porto. Towards fully integrated information services. In Lígia Maria Ribeiro and José Marques dos Santos, editors, *The Changing Universities: The Challenge of New Technologies, Eunis 2002, The 8th International Conference of European University Information Systems, Proceedings*, pages 319–324. FEUP edições, University of Porto, Portugal, 2002.
7. D. H. Warren. Higher-order extensions to PROLOG: are they needed? In J.E. Hayes, Donald Michie, and Y-H. Pao, editors, *Machine Intelligence 10*, pages 441–454. Ellis Horwood, 1982.

JMatch: Iterable Abstract Pattern Matching for Java

Jed Liu and Andrew C. Myers

Computer Science Department
Cornell University, Ithaca, New York

Abstract. The JMatch language extends Java with *iterable abstract pattern matching*, pattern matching that is compatible with the data abstraction features of Java and makes iteration abstractions convenient. JMatch has ML-style deep pattern matching, but patterns can be abstract; they are not tied to algebraic data constructors. A single JMatch method may be used in several modes; modes may share a single implementation as a boolean formula. Modal abstraction simplifies specification and implementation of abstract data types. This paper describes the JMatch language and its implementation.

1 Introduction

Object-oriented languages have become a dominant programming paradigm, yet they still lack features considered useful in other languages. Functional languages offer expressive pattern matching. Logic programming languages provide powerful mechanisms for iteration and backtracking. However, these useful features interact poorly with the data abstraction mechanisms central to object-oriented languages. Thus, expressing some computations is awkward in object-oriented languages. In this paper we present the design and implementation of JMatch, a new object-oriented language that extends Java [GJS96] with support for *iterable abstract pattern matching*—a mechanism for pattern matching that is compatible with the data abstraction features of Java and that makes iteration abstractions more convenient. This mechanism subsumes several important language features:

- convenient use and implementation of iteration abstractions (as in CLU [L+81], ICON [GHK81], and Sather [MOSS96].)
- convenient run-time type discrimination without casts (for example, Modula-3's `typecase` [Nel91])
- deep pattern matching allows concise, readable deconstruction of complex data structures (as in ML [MTH90], Haskell [Jon99] and Cyclone [JMG+02].)
- multiple return values
- views [Wad87]
- patterns usable as first-class values [PGPN96,FB97]

Email: jed@cs.washington.edu, andru@cs.cornell.edu. Jed Liu is now at the University of Washington, Seattle, WA. This research was supported by DARPA Contract F30602-99-1-0533, monitored by USAF Rome Laboratory, by ONR Grant N00014-01-1-0968, and by an Alfred P. Sloan Research Fellowship. The U.S. Government is authorized to reproduce and distribute reprints for Government purposes, notwithstanding any copyright annotation thereon.

V. Dahl and P. Wadler (Eds.): PADL 2003, LNCS 2562, pp. 110–127, 2003.
© Springer-Verlag Berlin Heidelberg 2003

JMatch exploits two key ideas: *modal abstraction* and *invertible computation*. Modal abstraction simplifies the *specification* (and use) of abstractions; invertible computation simplifies the *implementation* of abstractions.

JMatch constructors and methods may be modal abstractions: operations that support multiple *modes* [SHC96]. Modes correspond to different directions of computation, where the ordinary direction of computation is the "forward" mode, but backward modes may exist that compute some or all of a method's arguments using an expected result. Pattern matching uses a backward mode. A mode may specify that there can be multiple values for the method outputs; these can be easily iterated over in a predictable order. Modal abstraction simplifies the specification and use of abstract data type (ADT) interfaces, because where an ADT would ordinarily have several distinct but related operations, in JMatch it is often natural to have a single operation with multiple modes.

The other key idea behind JMatch is invertible computation. Computations may be described by boolean formulas that express the relationship among method inputs and outputs. Thus, a single formula may implement multiple modes; the JMatch compiler automatically decides for each mode how to generate the outputs of that mode from the inputs. Each mode corresponds to a different direction of evaluation. Having a single implementation helps ensure that the modes implement the abstraction in a consistent manner, satisfying expected equational relationships.

These ideas appear in various logic programming languages, but it is a challenge to integrate these ideas into an object-oriented language in a natural way that enforces data abstraction, preserves backwards compatibility, and permits an efficient implementation. JMatch is not a general-purpose logic-programming language; it does not provide the full power of unification over logic variables. This choice facilitates an efficient implementation. However, JMatch does provide more expressive pattern matching than logic-programming, along with modal abstractions that are first-class values (objects).

Although JMatch extends Java, little in this paper is specific to Java. The ideas in JMatch could easily be applied to other garbage-collected object-oriented languages such as C# [Mic01] or Modula-3 [Nel91].

A prototype compiler for JMatch is available for download. It is built using the Polyglot extensible Java compiler framework [NCM02], which supports source-to-source translation into Java.

The rest of this paper is structured as follows. Section 2 provides an overview of the JMatch programming language. Section 3 gives examples of common programming idioms that JMatch supports clearly and concisely. Section 4 describes the implementation of the prototype compiler. Section 5 discusses related work. Section 6 summarizes and concludes with a discussion of useful extensions to JMatch.

2   Overview of JMatch

JMatch provides convenient specification and implementation of computations that may be evaluated in more than one direction, by extending expressions to *formulas* and *patterns*. Named abstractions can be defined for formulas and patterns; these abstractions are called *predicate methods*, *pattern methods*, and *pattern constructors*. JMatch extends the meaning of some existing Java statements and expressions, and adds some new forms. It is backwards compatible with Java.

2.1 Formulas

Syntactically, a JMatch formula is similar to a Java expression of boolean type, but where a Java expression would permit a subexpression of type T, a formula may include a variable declaration with type T. For example, the expression 2 + int x == 5 is a formula that is satisfied when x is bound to 3.

JMatch has a `let` statement that tries to satisfy a formula, binding new variables as necessary. For example, the statement `let 2 + int x == 5;` causes x to be bound to 3 in subsequent code (unless it is later reassigned). If there is no satisfying assignment, an exception is raised. To prevent an exception, an `if` statement may be used instead. The conditional may be any formula with at most one solution. If there is a satisfying assignment, it is in scope in the "then" clause; if there is no satisfying assignment, the "else" clause is executed but the declared variables are not in scope. For example, the following code assigns y to an array index such that a[y] is nonzero (the `single` restricts it to the first such array index), or to −1 if there is no such index:

```
int y;
if (single(a[int i] != 0)) y = i;
else y = -1;
```

A formula may contain free variables in addition to the variables it declares. The formula expresses a relation among its various variables; in general it can be evaluated in several modes. For a given mode of evaluation these variables are either *knowns* or *unknowns*. In the *forward mode*, all variables, including bound variables, are knowns, and the formula is evaluated as a boolean expression. In backward modes, some variables are unknowns and satisfying assignments are sought for them. If JMatch can construct an algorithm to find satisfying assignments given a particular set of knowns, the formula is *solvable* in that mode. A formula with no satisfying assignments is considered solvable as long as JMatch can construct an algorithm to determine this.

For example, the formula a[i] == 0 is solvable if the variable i is an unknown, but not if the variable a is an unknown. The modes of the array index operator [] do not include any that solve for the array, because those modes would be largely useless (and inefficient).

Some formulas have multiple satisfying assignments; the JMatch `foreach` statement can be used to iterate through these assignments. For example, the following code adds the indices of all the non-zero elements of an array:

```
foreach(a[int i] != 0) n += i;
```

In formulas, the single equals sign (=) is overloaded to mean equality rather than assignment, while preserving backwards compatibility with Java. The symbol = corresponds to semantic equality in Java (that is, the `equals` method of class `Object`). Formulas may use either pointer equality (==) or semantic equality (=); the difference between the two is observable only when an equation is evaluated in forward mode, where the Java `equals` method is used to evaluate =. Otherwise an equation is satisfied by making one side of the equation pointer-equal to the other—and therefore also semantically equal. Because semantic equality is usually the right choice for JMatch programs, concise syntax is important. The other Java meanings for the symbol = are initialization and assignment, which can be thought of as ways to satisfy an equation.

2.2 Patterns

A pattern is a Java expression of non-boolean type except that it may contain variable declarations, just like a formula. In its forward mode, in which all its variables are knowns, a pattern is evaluated directly as the corresponding Java expression. In its backward modes, the value of the pattern is a known, and this value is used to reconstruct some or all of the variables used in the pattern. In the example above, the subexpression 2 + int x is a pattern with type int, and given that its value is known to be 5, JMatch can determine x = 3. Inversion of addition is possible because the addition operator supports the necessary computational mode; not all binary operators support this mode. Another pattern is the expression a[int i]. Given a value v to match against, this pattern iterates over the array a finding all indices i such that v = a[i]. There may be many assignments that make a pattern equal to the matched value. When JMatch knows how to find such assignments, the pattern is *matchable* in that mode. A pattern p is matchable if the equation $p = v$ is solvable for any value v.

The Java switch statement is extended to support general pattern matching. Each of the case arms of a switch statement may provide a pattern; the first arm whose pattern matches the tested value is executed.

The simplest pattern is a variable name. If the type checker cannot statically determine that the value being matched against a variable has the same type, a dynamic type test is inserted and the pattern is matched only if the test succeeds. Thus, a typecase statement [Nel91] can be concisely expressed as a switch statement:

```
Vehicle v; ...
switch (v) {
    case Car c: ...
    case Truck t: ...
    case Airplane a: ...
}
```

For the purpose of pattern matching there is no difference between a variable declaration and a variable by itself; however, the first use of the variable must be a declaration.

2.3 Pattern Constructors

One way to define new patterns is *pattern constructors*, which support conventional pattern matching, with some increase in expressiveness. For example, a simple linked list (a "cons cell", really) naturally accommodates a pattern constructor:

```
public class List implements Collection {
    Object head;
    List tail;
    public List(Object h, List t) returns(h, t) (
        head = h && tail = t
    )
    ...
}
```

This constructor differs in two ways from the corresponding Java constructor whose body would read {head = h; tail = t; }. First, the mode clause returns(h,t) indicates that in addition to the implicit forward mode in which the constructor makes a new object, the constructor also supports a mode in which the result object is a known and the arguments h and t are unknowns. It is this backward mode that is used for pattern matching. Second, the body of the constructor is a simple formula (surrounded by parentheses rather than by braces) that implements both modes at once. Satisfying assignments to head and tail will build the object; satisfying assignments to h and t will deconstruct it.

For example, this pattern constructor can be applied in ways that will be familiar to ML programmers:

```
List l;
...
switch (l) {
    case List(Integer x, List(Integer y, List rest)): ...
    default: ...
}
```

The switch statement extracts the first two elements of the list into variables x and y and executes the subsequent statements. The variable rest is bound to the rest of the list. If the list contains zero or one elements, the default case executes with no additional variables in scope. Even for this simple example, the equivalent Java code is awkward and less clear. In the code shown, the constructor invocations do not use the new keyword; the use of new is optional.

The List pattern constructor also matches against subclasses of List; in that case it inverts the construction of only the List part of the object.

It is also possible to match several values simultaneously:

```
List l1, l2; ...
switch (l1, l2) {
    case List(Object x, List(Integer y,List r)), List(y, _): ...
    default: ...
}
```

The first case executes if the list l1 has at least two elements, and the head of list l2 exists and is an Integer equal to the second element of l1. The remainder of l2 is matched using the wildcard pattern "_".

In this example of a pattern constructor, the constructor arguments and the fields correspond directly, but this need not be the case. More complex formulas can be used to implement views as proposed by Wadler [Wad87] (see Section 3.4).

The example above implements the constructor using a formula, but backwards compatibility is maintained; a constructor can be written using the usual Java syntax.

2.4   Methods and Modal Abstraction

The language features described so far subsume ML pattern matching, with the added power of invertible boolean formulas. JMatch goes further; pattern matching coexists with abstract data types and subtyping, and it supports iteration.

Methods with `boolean` return type are *predicate methods* that define a named abstraction for a boolean formula. The forward mode of a predicate method expects that all arguments are known and executes the method normally. In backward modes, satisfying assignments to some or all of the method arguments are sought. Assuming that the various method modes are implemented consistently, the corresponding forward invocation using these satisfying assignments would have the result `true`.

Predicate methods with multiple modes can make ADT specifications more concise. For example, in the Java Collections framework the `Collection` interface declares separate methods for finding all elements and for checking if a given object is an element:

```
boolean contains(Object o);
Iterator iterator();
```

In any correct Java implementation, there is an equational relationship between the two operations: any object x produced by the iterator object satisfies `contains(x)`, and any object satisfying `contains(x)` is eventually generated by the iterator. When writing the specification for `Collection`, the specifier must describe this relationship so implementers can do their job correctly.

By contrast, a JMatch interface can describe both operations with one declaration:

```
boolean contains(Object o) iterates(o);
```

This declaration specifies two modes: an implicit forward mode in which membership is being tested for a particular object o, and a backward mode declared by `iterates(o)`, which iterates over all contained objects. The equational relationship is captured simply by the fact that these are modes of the same method.

An interface method signature may declare zero or more additional modes that the method implements, beyond the default, forward mode. A mode $returns(x_1, \ldots, x_n)$, where $x_1, \ldots, x_n$ are argument variable names, declares a mode that generates a satisfying assignment for the named variables. A mode $iterates(x_1, \ldots, x_n)$ means that the method iterates over a *set* of satisfying assignments to the named variables.

Invocations of predicate methods may appear in formulas. The following code iterates over the Collection c, finding all elements that are lists whose first element is a green truck; the loop body executes once for each element, with the variable t bound to the Truck object.

```
foreach (c.contains(List(Truck t, _)) && t.color() = GREEN)
    System.out.println(t.model());
```

2.5   Implementing Methods

A linked list is a simple way to implement the `Collection` interface. Consider the linked list example again, where the `contains` method is no longer elided:

```
public class List implements Collection {
    Object head; List tail;
    public List(Object h, List t) returns(h, t) ...
    public boolean contains(Object o) iterates(o) (
        o = head || tail.contains(o)
    )
}
```

As with constructors, multiple modes of a method may be implemented by a formula instead of a Java statement block. Here, the formula implements both modes of `contains`. In the forward mode there are no unknowns; in the backward mode the only unknown is o, as the clause `iterates(o)` indicates.

In the backward mode, the disjunction signals the presence of iteration. The two subformulas separated by | | define two different ways to satisfy the formula; both will be explored to find satisfying assignments for o.

The modes of a method may be implemented by separate formulas or by ordinary Java statements, which is useful when no single boolean formula is solvable for all modes, or it leads to inefficient code. For example, the following code separately implements the two modes of `contains`:

```
public boolean contains(Object o) {
    if (o.equals(head)) return true;
    return tail.contains(o);
} iterates(o) {
    o = head;
    yield;
    foreach (tail.contains(Object tmp)) {
    o = tmp;
    yield;
    }
}
```

For backward modes, results are returned from the method by the `yield` statement rather than by `return`. The `yield` statement transfers control back to the iterating context, passing the current values of the unknowns. While this code is longer and no faster than the formula above, it is simpler than the code of the corresponding Java iterator object. The reason is that iterator objects must capture the state of iteration so they can restart the iteration computation whenever a new value is requested. In this example, the state of the iteration is implicitly captured by the position of the `yield` statement and the local variables; restarting the iteration is automatic. In essence, iteration requires the expressive power of coroutines [Con63,L+81,GHK81]. Implementing iterator objects requires coding in continuation-passing style (CPS) to obtain this power [HFW86], which is awkward and error-prone [MOSS96]. The JMatch implementation performs a CPS conversion behind the scenes.

2.6   Pattern Methods

JMatch methods whose return type is not boolean are *pattern methods* whose result may be matched against other values if the appropriate mode is implemented. Pattern methods provide the ability to deconstruct values even more abstractly than pattern constructors do, because a pattern method declared in an interface can be implemented in different ways in the classes that implement the interface.

For example, many data structure libraries contain several implementations of trees (e.g., binary search trees, red-black trees, AVL trees). When writing a generic tree-walking algorithm it may be useful to pattern-match on tree nodes to extract left and

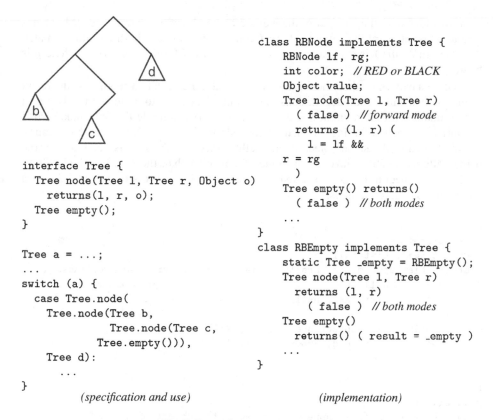

```
interface Tree {
  Tree node(Tree l, Tree r, Object o)
    returns(l, r, o);
  Tree empty();
}

Tree a = ...;
...
switch (a) {
  case Tree.node(
    Tree.node(Tree b,
            Tree.node(Tree c,
          Tree.empty())),
    Tree d):
      ...
}
```

(specification and use)

```
class RBNode implements Tree {
  RBNode lf, rg;
  int color;  // RED or BLACK
  Object value;
  Tree node(Tree l, Tree r)
    ( false )  //forward mode
    returns (l, r) (
      l = lf &&
      r = rg
    )
  Tree empty() returns()
    ( false )  // both modes
    ...
}
class RBEmpty implements Tree {
  static Tree _empty = RBEmpty();
  Tree node(Tree l, Tree r)
    returns (l, r)
    ( false )  // both modes
  Tree empty()
    returns() ( result = _empty )
    ...
}
```

(implementation)

Fig. 1. Deep abstract pattern matching

right children, perhaps deep in the tree. This would not be possible in most languages with pattern matching (such as ML or Haskell) because patterns are built from constructors, and thus cannot apply to different types. An abstract data type is implemented in these languages by hiding the actual type of the ADT values; however, this prevents any pattern matching from being performed on the ADT values. Thus, pattern matching is typically incompatible with data abstraction.

By contrast, in JMatch it is possible to declare pattern methods in an interface such as the Tree interface shown on the left side of Figure 1. As shown in the figure, these pattern methods can then be used to match the structure of the tree, without knowledge of the actual Tree implementation being matched.

An implementation of the pattern methods node and empty for a red-black tree is shown on the right side of Figure 1. Here there are two classes implementing red-black trees. For efficiency there is only one instance of the empty class, called _empty. The node and empty pattern methods are only intended to be invoked in the backwards mode for pattern-matching purposes. Thus, the ordinary forward mode is implemented by the unsatisfiable formula false.

As this example suggests, the rule for resolving method invocations is slightly different for JMatch. A non-static pattern method m of class T can be invoked using the syntax

$T.m$, in which case the receiver of the method is the object being matched. JMatch has a pattern operator as; the pattern (P_1 as P_2) matches a value if both P_1 and P_2 match it. A pattern $T.m()$ is syntactic sugar for the pattern (T y as $y.m()$) where y is fresh.

Within a pattern method there is a special variable result that represents the result of the method call. Mode declarations may mention result to indicate that the result of the method call is an unknown. In the default, forward mode the only unknown is the variable result. During the method calls shown in Figure 1, the variable result will be bound to the same object as the method receiver this. This need not be true if the pattern method is invoked on some object other than the result—which allows the receiver object to be used as a first-class pattern. (The expression this is always a known in non-static methods.)

```
class List {
  Object head; List tail;
  static List append(List prefix, Object last) returns(prefix, last) (
      prefix = null &&                      // single element
      result = List(last, null)
    else                                    // multiple elements
      prefix = List(Object head, List ptail) &&
      result = List(head, append(ptail, last))
  )
}
List l; ...
switch(l) {
  case List.append(List.append(_, Object o1), Object o2): ...
}
```

Fig. 2. Reversible list append

Figure 2 shows an example of a static pattern method; append appends an element to the list in the forward direction but inverts this operation in the backward direction, splitting a list into its last element and a prefix list. In this version of List, empty lists are represented by null. The append method is static so that it can be invoked on empty lists. The switch statement shows that pattern matching can extract the last two elements of a list.

This example uses a disjunctive logical connective, else, which behaves like || except that the right-hand disjunct generates solutions only if the left-hand disjunct has not. An else disjunction does not by itself generate multiple solutions in backward modes; both else and || are short-circuit operators in the forward mode where the proposed solution to the formula is already known.

This example also demonstrates reordering of conjuncts in different modes. The algorithm for ordering conjuncts is simple: JMatch solves one conjunct at a time, and always picks the leftmost solvable conjunct to work on. This rule makes the order of evaluation easy to predict, which is important if conjuncts have side effects. While JMatch tends to encourage a functional programming style, it does not attempt to guarantee that formulas are free of side-effects, because side-effects are often useful.

In this example, in the backward mode the first conjunct is not initially solvable, so the conjuncts are evaluated in reverse order—in the multiple-element case, `result` is first broken into its parts, then the prefix of its tail is extracted (recursively using the append method), and finally the new prefix is constructed.

Pattern methods and pattern constructors obey similar rules; the main difference is that when `result` is an unknown in a pattern constructor, the variable `result` is automatically bound to a new object of the appropriate type, and its fields are exposed as variables to be solved. The list-reversal example shows that pattern methods can construct and deconstruct objects too.

2.7 Built-in Patterns

Many of the built-in Java operators are extended in JMatch to support additional modes. As mentioned earlier, the array index operator [] supports new modes that are easy to specify if we consider the operator on the type T[] (array of T) as a method named `operator[]` after the C++ idiom:

```
static T operator[](T[] array, int index)
   iterates(index, result)
```

That is, an array has the ability to automatically iterate over its indices and provide the associated elements. Note that other than the convenient syntax of array indexing and the type parameterization that arrays provide, there is no special magic here; it is easy to write code using the `yield` statement to implement this signature, as well as for the other built-in extensions.

The arithmetic operations + and − are also able to solve for either of their arguments given the result. In Java, the operator + also concatenates strings. In JMatch the concatenation can be inverted to match prefixes or suffixes; all possible matching prefix/suffix pairs can also be iterated over.

Within formulas, relational expressions are extended to support a chain of relational comparisons. Certain integer inequalities are treated as built-in iterators: formulas of the form $(a_1 \, \rho_1 \, a_2 \, \rho_2 \, \ldots \, \rho_{n-1} \, a_n)$, where a_1 and a_n are solvable, and all of the ρ_i are either < or <= (or else all > or >=). These formulas are solved by iteration over the appropriate range of integers between a_1 and a_n. For example, the following two statements are equivalent except that the first evaluates a.length only once:

```
foreach (0 <= int i < a.length) { ... }
for (int i = 0; i < a.length; i++) { ... }
```

2.8 Iterator Objects

Java programmers are accustomed to performing iterations using objects that implement the `Iterator` interface. An `Iterator` is an object that acts like an input stream, delivering the next object in the iteration whenever its next() method is called. The hasNext() method can be used to test whether there is a next object.

Iterator objects are usually unnecessary in JMatch, but they are easy to create. Any formula F can be converted into a corresponding iterator object using the special expression syntax `iterate` $C(F)$. Given a formula with unknowns $x_1, \ldots, x_n$, the expression produces an iterator object that can be used to iterate over the possible solutions to the formula. Each time the `next()` method of the iterator is called, a container object of class C is returned that has public fields named $x_1, \ldots, x_n$ bound to the corresponding solution values.

Iterator objects in Java sometimes implement a `remove` method that removes the current element from the collection. Iterators with the ability to remove elements can be implemented by returning the (abstract) context in which the element occurs. This approach complicates the implementation of the iterator and changes its signature. Better support for such iterators remains future work.

2.9 Exceptions

The implementation of forward modes by boolean formulas raises the question of what value is returned when the formula is unsatisfiable. The `NoSuchElementException` exception is raised in that case.

Methods implemented as formulas do not have the ability to catch exceptions raised during their evaluation; a raised exception propagates out from the formula to the context using it. If there is a need to catch exceptions, the method must be implemented as a statement block instead.

In accordance with the expectations of Java programmers, exceptions raised in the body of a `foreach` iteration cannot be intercepted by the code of the predicate being tested.

3 Examples

A few more detailed examples will suggest the added expressive power of JMatch.

3.1 Functional Red-Black Trees

A good example of the power of pattern matching is the code for recursively balancing a red-black tree on insertion. Cormen et al. [CLR90] present pseudocode for red-black tree insertion that takes 31 lines of code yet gives only two of the four cases necessary. Okasaki [Oka98a] shows that for functional red-black trees, pattern matching can reduce the code size considerably. The same code can be written in JMatch about as concisely. Figure 3 shows the key code that balances the tree. The four cases of the red-black rotation are handled by four cases of the `switch` statement that share a single `return` statement, which is permitted because they solve for the same variables (a–d, x–z).

3.2 Binary Search Tree Membership

Earlier we saw that for lists, both modes of the `contains` method could be implemented as a single, concise formula. The same is true for red-black trees:

```
static Node balance(int color, int value, RBTree left, RBTree right) {
  if (color == BLACK) {
    switch (value, left, right) {
      case int z,
           Node(RED, int y, Node(RED,int x,RBTree a,RBTree b), RBTree c),
           RBTree d:
      case z, Node(RED,x,a,Node(RED,y,b,c)), d:
      case x, c, Node(RED,z,Node(RED,y,a,b),d):
      case x, a, Node(RED,y,b,Node(RED,z,c,d)):
          return Node(RED,y,Node(BLACK,x,a,b), Node(BLACK,z,c,d));
    }
  }
  return new Node(color, value, left, right);
}
```

Fig. 3. Balancing red-black trees

```
public boolean contains(int x) iterates(x) (
  left != null && x < value && left.contains(x) ||
  x = value ||
  right != null && x > value && right.contains(x)
)
```

In its forward mode, this code implements the usual $O(\log n)$ binary search for the element. In its backward mode, it iterates over the elements of the red-black tree in ascending order, and the tests x < value and x > value superfluously check the data-structure invariant. Automatic removal of such checks is future work.

3.3 Hash Table Membership

The hash table is another collection implementation that benefits in JMatch. Here is the contains method, with three modes implemented by a single formula:

```
class HashMap {
  HashBucket[] buckets;
  int size;
  ...
  public boolean contains(Object key, Object value)
    returns(value) iterates(key, value) (
    int n = key.hashCode() % size &&
    HashBucket b = buckets[n] &&
    b.contains(key, value)
  )
}
```

In the forward mode, the code checks whether the (key,value) binding is present in the hash table. In the second mode, a key is provided and a value efficiently located if available. The final mode iterates over all (key,value) pairs in the table. The hash table has chained buckets (HashBucket) that implement contains similarly to the earlier List implementation. In the final, iterative mode, the built-in array iterator generates the individual buckets b; the check n = hash(key) becomes a final consistency check on the data structure, because it cannot be evaluated until key is known.

The signature of the method HashBucket.contains is the same as the signature of HashMap.contains, which is not surprising because they both implement maps. The various modes of HashMap.contains use the corresponding modes of HashBucket.contains and different modes of the built-in array index operator. This coding style is typical in JMatch.

A comparison to the standard Java collection class HashMap [GJS96] suggests that modal abstraction can substantially simplify class signatures. The contains method provides the functionality of methods get, iterator, containsKey, containsValue, and to a lesser extent the methods keySet and values.

3.4   Simulating Views

Wadler has proposed views [Wad87] as a mechanism for reconciling data abstraction and pattern matching. For example, he shows that the abstract data type of Peano natural numbers can be implemented using integers, yet still provide the ability to pattern-match on its values. Figure 4 shows the equivalent JMatch code. Wadler also gives an example of a view of lists that corresponds to the modes of the method append shown in Section 2.6.

```
class Peano {
    private int n;
    private Peano(int m) returns(m) ( m = n )
    public Peano succ(Peano pred) returns(pred) (
    pred = Peano(int m) && result = Peano(m+1)
    )
    public Peano zero() returns() ( result = Peano(0) )
}
```

Fig. 4. Peano natural numbers ADT

In both cases, the JMatch version of the code offers the advantage that the forward and backwards directions of the view are implemented by a single formula, ensuring consistency. In the views version of this code, separate *in* and *out* functions must be defined and it is up to the programmer to ensure that they are inverses.

4   Semantics and Implementation

We now touch on some of the more interesting details of the semantics of JMatch and its implementation. The JMatch compiler is built using the Polyglot compiler framework for Java language extensions [NCM02]. Polyglot supports both the definition of languages that extend Java and their translation into Java. For more details see the technical report on JMatch and the implementation notes available with the current version of the compiler [LM02].

4.1 Static Semantics

Type-checking JMatch expressions, including formulas and patterns, is little different from type-checking Java expressions, since the types are the same in all modes, and the forward mode corresponds to ordinary Java evaluation.

The Java interface and abstract class conformance rules are extended in a natural way to handle method modes: a JMatch class must implement all the methods in all their modes, as declared in the interface or abstract class being implemented or extended. A method can add new modes to those defined by the super class.

The introduction of modes does create a new obligation for static checking. In JMatch it is a static error to use a formula or pattern with multiple solutions in a context (such as a let) where a single solution is expected, because solutions might be silently discarded. Thus, the JMatch type system is extended so that every expression has a multiplicity in addition to its ordinary Java type. The single operator may be used to explicitly discard the extra solutions of an expression and reduce its static multiplicity.

For each invocation of a built-in or user-defined predicate or pattern method, the compiler must select a mode to use to solve the expression in which the invocation appears. There may be more than one usable mode; the compiler selects the best mode according to a simple ordering. Modes are considered better if (in order of priority) they are not iterative, if they avoid constructing new objects, if they solve for fewer arguments, and if they are declared earlier.

One change to type checking is in the treatment of pattern method invocations. When a non-static method is invoked with the syntax $T.m$, it is a pattern method invocation of method m of type T. It would be appealing to avoid naming T explicitly but this would require type inference.

4.2 Translation to Java

In the current implementation, JMatch is translated into Java by way of an intermediate language called $\text{Java}_{\text{yield}}$, which is the Java 1.4 language extended with a limited yield statement that can only be used to implement Java iterator objects. Executing yield causes the iterator to return control to the calling context. The iterator object constructor and the methods next and hasNext are automatically implemented in $\text{Java}_{\text{yield}}$. Each subsequent invocation of next on the iterator returns control to the point just after the execution of the previous yield statement.

The benefit of the intermediate language is that the translation from JMatch to $\text{Java}_{\text{yield}}$ is straightforwardly defined using a few mutually inductively defined syntax-directed functions. The translation from $\text{Java}_{\text{yield}}$ to Java 1.4 is also straighforward; it is essentially a conversion to continuation-passing style. While the performance of the translated code is acceptable, several easy optimizations would improve code quality. See the technical report [LM02] for more details on the translation.

5 Related Work

Prolog is the best-known declarative logic programming language. It and many of its descendents have powerful unification in which a predicate can be applied to an expression containing unsolved variables. JMatch lacks this capability because it is not targeted specifically at logic programming tasks; rather, it is intended to smoothly incorporate some expressive features of logic programming into a language supporting data abstraction and imperative programming. ML [MTH90] and Haskell [HJW92,Jon99] are well-known functional programming languages that support pattern matching, though patterns are tightly bound to the concrete representation of the value being matched. Because pattern matching in these languages requires access to the concrete representation, it does not coexist well with the data abstraction mechanisms of these languages. However, an advantage of concrete pattern matching is the simplicity of analyzing *exhaustiveness*; that is, showing that some arm of a `switch` statement will match.

Pattern matching has been of continuing interest to the Haskell community. Wadler's views [Wad87] support pattern matching for abstract data types. Views correspond to JMatch constructors, but require the explicit definition of a bijection between the abstract view and the concrete representation. While bijections can be defined in JMatch, often they can be generated automatically from a boolean formula. Views do not provide iteration.

Burton and Cameron [BC93] have also extended the views approach with a focus on improving equational reasoning. Fähndrich and Boyland [FB97] introduced first-class pattern abstractions for Haskell, but do not address the data abstraction problem. Palao Gonstanza et al. [PGPN96] describe first-class patterns for Haskell that work with data abstraction, but are not statically checkable. Okasaki has proposed integrating views into Standard ML [Oka98b]. Tullsen [Tul00] shows how to use combinators to construct first-class patterns that can be used with data abstraction. Like views, these proposals do not provide iterative patterns, modal abstraction, or invertible computation.

A few languages have been proposed to integrate functional programming and logic programming [Han97,Llo99,CL00]. The focus in that work is on allowing partially instantiated values to be used as arguments, rather than on data abstraction.

In the language Alma-0, Apt et al. [ABPS98] have augmented Modula-2, an imperative language, with logic-programming features. Alma-0 is tailored for solving search problems and unlike JMatch, provides convenient backtracking through imperative code. However, Alma-0 does not support pattern matching or data abstraction.

Mercury [SHC96] is a modern declarative logic-programming language with modularity and separate compilation. As in JMatch, Mercury predicates can have several modes, a feature originating in some versions of Prolog (e.g., [Gre87]). Modal abstractions are not first-class in Mercury; a single mode of a predicate can be used as a first-class function value, but unlike in JMatch, there is no way to pass several such modes around as an object and use them to uniformly implement another modal abstraction. Mercury does not support objects.

CLU [L+81], ICON [GHK81], and Sather [MOSS96] each support iterators whose use and implementation are both convenient; the `yield` statement of JMatch was inspired by CLU. None of these languages have pattern matching.

Pizza also extends Java by allowing a class to be implemented as an algebraic datatypes and by supporting ML-style pattern matching [OW97]. Because the datatype is not exposed outside the class, Pizza does not permit abstract pattern matching. Forax and Roussel have also proposed a Java extension for simple pattern matching based on reflection [FR99].

Ernst et al. [EKC98] have developed predicate dispatching, another way to add pattern matching to an object-oriented language. In their language, boolean formulas control the dispatch mechanism, which supports encoding some pattern-matching idioms although deep pattern matching is not supported. This approach is complementary to JMatch, in which object dispatch is orthogonal to pattern matching. Their language has limited predicate abstractions that can implement a single new view of an object, but unlike JMatch, it does not unify predicates and methods. The predicates may not be recursive or iterative and do not support modal abstraction or invertible computation.

6 Conclusions

JMatch extends Java with the ability to describe modal abstractions: abstractions that can be invoked in multiple different modes, or directions of computation. Modal abstractions can result in simpler code specifications and more readable code through the use of pattern matching. These modal abstractions can be implemented using invertible boolean formulas that directly describe the relation that the abstraction computes. In its forward mode, this relation is a function; in its backward modes it may be one-to-many or many-to-many. JMatch provides mechanisms for conveniently exploring this multiplicity. JMatch is backwards compatible with Java, but provides expressive new features that make certain kinds of programs simpler and clearer. While for some such programs, using a domain-specific language would be the right choice, having more features in a general-purpose programming language is handy because a single language can be used when building large systems that cross several domains.

A prototype of the JMatch compiler has been released for public experimentation, and improvements to this implementation are continuing.

There are several important directions in which the JMatch language could be usefully extended. An exhaustiveness analysis for switch statements and `else` disjunctions would make it easier to reason about program correctness. Automatic elimination of tests that are redundant in a particular mode might improve performance. And support for iterators with removal would be useful.

Acknowledgments. The authors would like to thank Brandon Bray and Grant Wang for many useful discussions on the design of JMatch and some early implementation work as well. Greg Morrisett and Jim O'Toole also made several useful suggestions. Nate Nystrom supported the implementation of JMatch on Polyglot. Readers of this paper whose advice improved the presentation include Kavita Bala, Michael Clarkson, Dan Grossman, Nate Nystrom, and Andrei Sabelfeld.

References

[ABPS98] Krzysztof R. Apt, Jacob Brunekreef, Vincent Partington, and Andrea Schaerf. Alma-0: An imperative language that supports declarative programming. *ACM Transactions on Programming Languages and Systems*, 20(5):1014–1066, September 1998.

[BC93] F. W. Burton and R. D. Cameron. Pattern matching with abstract data types. *Journal of Functional Programming*, 3(2):171–190, 1993.

[CL00] K. Claessen and P. Ljungl. Typed logical variables in Haskell. In *Haskell Workshop 2000*, 2000.

[CLR90] Thomas A. Cormen, Charles E. Leiserson, and Ronald L. Rivest. *Introduction to Algorithms*. MIT Press, 1990.

[Con63]   Melvin E. Conway. Design of a separable transition-diagram compiler. *Communications of the ACM*, 6(7):396–408, 1963.

[EKC98]   Michael Ernst, Craig Kaplan, and Craig Chambers. Predicate dispatching: A unified theory of dispatch. In *12th European Conference on Object-Oriented Programming*, pages 186–211, Brussels, Belgium, July 1998.

[FB97]   Manuel Fähndrich and John Boyland. Statically checkable pattern abstractions. In *Proc. 2nd ACM SIGPLAN International Conference on Functional Programming (ICFP)*, pages 75–84, June 1997.

[FR99]   Remi Forax and Gilles Roussel. Recursive types and pattern matching in java. In *Proc. International Symposium on Generative and Component-Based Software Engineering (GCSE '99)*, Erfurt, Germany, September 1999. LNCS 1799.

[GHK81]   Ralph E. Griswold, David R. Hanson, and John T. Korb. Generators in ICON. *ACM Transaction on Programming Languages and Systems*, 3(2), April 1981.

[GJS96]   James Gosling, Bill Joy, and Guy Steele. *The Java Language Specification*. Addison-Wesley, August 1996. ISBN 0-201-63451-1.

[Gre87]   Steven Gregory. *Parallel Programming in PARLOG*. Addison-Wesley, 1987.

[Han97]   Michael Hanus. A unified computation model for functional and logic programming. In *Proc. 24th ACM Symp. on Principles of Programming Languages (POPL)*, pages 80–93, Paris, France, January 1997.

[HFW86]   C. T. Haynes, D. P. Friedman, and M. Wand. Obtaining coroutines from continuations. *Journal of Computer Languages*, 11(3–4):143–153, 1986.

[HJW92]   Paul Hudak, Simon Peyton Jones, and Philip Wadler. Report on the programming language Haskell. *SIGPLAN Notices*, 27(5), May 1992.

[JMG⁺02] Trevor Jim, Greg Morrisett, Dan Grossman, Michael Hicks, James Cheney, and Yanling Wang. Cyclone: A safe dialect of C. In *Proceedings of the USENIX Annual Technical Conference*, pages 275–288, Monterey, CA, June 2002. See also http://www.cs.cornell.edu/projects/cyclone.

[Jon99]   Haskell 98: A non-strict, purely functional language, February 1999. Available at http://www.haskell.org/onlinereport/.

[L⁺81]   B. Liskov et al. CLU reference manual. In Goos and Hartmanis, editors, *Lecture Notes in Computer Science*, volume 114. Springer-Verlag, Berlin, 1981.

[Llo99]   John W. Lloyd. Programming in an integrated functional and logic programming language. *Journal of Functional and Logic Programming*, 3, March 1999.

[LM02]   Jed Liu and Andrew C. Myers. JMatch: Java plus pattern matching. Technical Report TR2002-1878, Computer Science Department, Cornell University, October 2002. Software release at http://www.cs.cornell.edu/projects/jmatch.

[Mic01]   Microsoft Corporation. *Microsoft C# Language Specifications*. Microsoft Press, 2001. ISBN 0-7356-1448-2.

[MOSS96] Stephan Murer, Stephen Omohundro, David Stoutamire, and Clemens Szyperski. Iteration abstraction in Sather. *ACM Transactions on Programming Languages and Systems*, 18(1):1–15, January 1996.

[MTH90]   Robin Milner, Mads Tofte, and Robert Harper. *The Definition of Standard ML*. MIT Press, Cambridge, MA, 1990.

[NCM02]   Nathaniel Nystrom, Michael Clarkson, and Andrew C. Myers. Polyglot: An extensible compiler framework for Java. Technical Report 2002-1883, Computer Science Dept., Cornell University, 2002.

[Nel91]   Greg Nelson, editor. *Systems Programming with Modula-3*. Prentice-Hall, 1991.

[Oka98a] Chris Okasaki. *Purely Functional Data Structures*. Cambridge University Press, 1998. ISBN 0-521-63124-6.

[Oka98b] Chris Okasaki. Views for Standard ML. In *Workshop on ML*, pages 14–23, September 1998.

[OW97]   Martin Odersky and Philip Wadler. Pizza into Java: Translating theory into practice. In *Proc. 24th ACM Symp. on Principles of Programming Languages (POPL)*, pages 146–159, Paris, France, January 1997.

[PGPN96]   Pedro Palao Gostanza, Ricardo Pena, and Manuel Núñez. A new look at pattern matching in abstract data types. In *Proc. 1st ACM SIGPLAN International Conference on Functional Programming (ICFP)*, Philadelphia, PA, USA, June 1996.

[SHC96]   Zoltan Somogyi, Fergus Henderson, and Thomas Conway. The execution algorithm of Mercury: an efficient purely declarative logic programming language. *Journal of Logic Programming*, 29(1–3):17–64, October–December 1996.

[Tul00]   Mark Tullsen. First-class patterns. In *Proc. Practical Aspects of Declarative Languages, 2nd International Workshop (PADL)*, pages 1–15, 2000.

[Wad87]   Philip Wadler. Views: A way for pattern matching to cohabit with data abstraction. In *Proceedings, 14th Symposium on Principles of Programming Languages*, pages 307–312. Association for Computing Machinery, 1987.

Sequence Quantification

Peter Schachte

Department of Computer Science
The University of Melbourne
Victoria 3010
Australia

schachte@cs.mu.oz.au

Abstract. Several earlier papers have shown that bounded quantification is an expressive and comfortable addition to logic programming languages. One shortcoming of bounded quantification, however, is that it does not allow easy and efficient relation of corresponding elements of aggregations being quantified over (lockstep iteration). Bounded quantification also does not allow easy quantification over part of an aggregation, nor does it make it easy to accumulate a result over an aggregation. We generalize the concept of bounded quantification to quantification over any finite sequence, as we can use a rich family of operations on sequences to create a language facility that avoids the weaknesses mentioned above. We also propose a concrete syntax for sequence quantification in Prolog programs, which we have implemented as a source-to-source transformation.

1 Introduction

Prolog [8] has no standard construct for looping over recursive data structures or arithmetic sequences. Beginning Prolog programmers are often told that Prolog makes recursion very natural, so no looping construct is needed. While this is true, it is also true that a looping construct could make some programs clearer and more succinct. The absence of looping construct from Prolog is all the more surprising since the predicate calculus on which it is based has had two such constructs — universal and existential quantification — for more than 120 years [5].

In designing his automatic theorem proving framework, Robinson restricted his attention to clauses, proving resolution to be a sound and complete inference rule [12]. Kowalski, in proposing the paradigm of logic programming, recommended the further restriction to Horn clauses [9]. A Horn clause is a disjunction of one atom (an atomic predication) and zero or more negated atoms, though it is more commonly thought of as a conjunction of zero or more atoms (called the clause body) implying a single atom (the head). All variables in a clause are universally quantified over the whole clause. When a clause is viewed as an implication, however, variables not appearing in the clause head can be seen as existentially quantified over the clause body.

V. Dahl and P. Wadler (Eds.): PADL 2003, LNCS 2562, pp. 128–144, 2003.

Prolog, however, was quick to loosen the Horn clause restriction. A disjunction in the body of a clause is easily accomodated by replacing the disjunction with an atom invoking a newly-created predicate whose definition comprises a clause for each disjunct. Negated atoms in a clause body can be handled using negation as failure to prove [4]. These are both now standard Prolog features.

Similarly, several earlier papers have suggested adding a restricted form of universal quantification, called *bounded quantification*, to logic programming languages. Bounded quantification is a form of universal quantification where the set of values quantified over is explicitly specified, adopting a shortcut common in much mathematical writing. Instead of writing

$$\forall x \, . \, x \in s \to p(x) \quad \text{or} \quad \exists x \, . \, x \in s \wedge p(x)$$

they write

$$\forall x \in s \, . \, p(x) \quad \text{or} \quad \exists x \in s \, . \, p(x)$$

Not only is this notation more concise, it seems quite natural to specify what a variable is to range over in the same place as how it is quantified.

Sadly, Prolog systems, and the Prolog language standard, have not been quick to accept bounded quantification. The aim of the present paper, then, is to propose a generalization of bounded quantification that is simultaneously more powerful and flexible than bounded quantification, yet still efficient, convenient, and reasonably portable.

The remainder of this paper is organized as follows. Section 2 reviews the history of bounded quantification and closely related work. Section 3 introduces the concept and semantics of sequence quantification. Section 4 discusses primitive sequences and how they are defined. It also discusses how sequences can be defined in terms of other sequences, providing the power behind sequence quantification. Section 5 presents the surface syntax we use for sequence quantification, and how the user can introduce new syntactic sugar, as well as addressing the subtle issue of resolving the scoping of variables not explicitly quantified. In section 6, we discuss our implementation of this facility, including a discussion of how we generate efficient code. Finally, we present our future work and concluding remarks in sections 7 and 8.

2   Bounded Quantification

Probably the oldest form of universal quantification in logic programming was the `all/2` [11] construct of NU Prolog [16]. Using this, one could write, *e.g.*, `all [X] p(X) => q(X)` to mean $\forall x \, . \, p(x) \to q(x)$. The most common use of this would be in what amounts to a restricted kind of bounded quantification: to check that every element of a list satisfies some constraint. Implementation was in terms of nested negation: the last example would be executed as `\+ (p(X), \+ q(X))`, except that NU Prolog would execute this negation even if X was not bound (ordinarily, NU Prolog suspends execution of non-ground negations). Since the implementation is in terms of negation, this effectively means that the `all` construct could only perform tests, and could not bind variables.

In the earliest paper we have found to discuss bounded quantification in English, Voronkov [18] gives a model-theoretical, least fixed point, and procedural semantics for typed logic programming with bounded quantification. In addition to supporting $\forall X \in S . p(X)$ and $\exists X \in S . p(X)$ where S is a list and X ranges over the elements of that list, he also defines $\forall X \sqsubseteq S . p(X)$ and $\exists X \sqsubseteq S . p(X)$ where X ranges over the tails of the list S. Voronkov also presents a translation from logic programs with bounded quantification to ordinary logic programs.

Barklund and Bevemyr [3] discuss bounded quantification in the context of arrays in Prolog. For this, they are more interested in quantifying over integer ranges, to be used as array indices, than lists. Thus rather than quantifying over forms such as $X \in S$, they quantify over $L \leq I < H$ forms, specifying that I ranges from L up to but not including H. Their focus is also practical: they have implemented their approach by extending the LUTHER WAM emulator with specialized features for bounded quantification. By quantifying over array indices, they are able to relate corresponding elements of two different arrays. This is a significant step forward, but it does not allow them to conveniently or efficiently relate array elements with elements of other structures, for example list or tree members. Another advance of this work is the inclusion of aggregation operators. In addition to quantifying over an integer range, they also allow computing the sum or product of an expression over such a range. They discuss numerous other such useful aggregations operators, but do not go so far as to suggest a general framework for defining them. They also observe that it may be possible to parallelize the execution of bounded quantifications, since the indices may be handled independently. Barklund and Hill [2] propose making a similar extension to Göedel.

Apt [1] gives many compelling example programs showing the power of bounded quantification in logic programming as well as constraint logic programming. Like Voronkov, he prefers typed logic programming.

The OPL language [7] provides a `forall` quantifier allowing iteration over integer ranges and enumerations, and allows the order of iteration to be explicitly specified. It also allows only some values, determined by an explicit test, to be iterated over. Additionally, it provides built in aggregations to compute the sum, product, minimum and maximum of a set of values. It does not appear to provide any facility for allowing iteration over any other domain, nor for lockstep iteration.

The Logical Loops package of the ECL^iPS^e system [14], developed independently of the present work, provides a facility similar similar to bounded quantification, although it eschews that label. Logical loops provide a number of iteration primitives, which can be combined to allow general lockstep iteration. One of the iteration primitives is much like our own aggregation facility (see Section 4.3), and allows fully general aggregation. In fact, this one primitive subsumes the functionality of all the other iteration primitives.

However, logical loops does not allow new iteration primitives to be defined; one must fall back on the less convenient general primitive. Nor does the package provide a primitive to iterate over part of a structure. Although the general iteration primitive can accommodate this, the author admits the technique is "rather unnatural." Finally, logical loops always commit to the fewest possible iterations. It is not possible for a logical loop to generate the list it is to iterate over or the upper bound on an arithmetic iteration, as it will commit to loop termination as early as possible.

3 Sequence Quantification

Our approach diverges from these by generalizing what data structures we can quantify over. Where the earlier works only allow quantification over integer ranges and lists, we wish to allow quantification over any *sequence* of values the user cares to define. Our belief is that a single, simple universal quantification operation, together with the ability to define new kinds of sequences to iterate over, provides a much more powerful facility than a larger set of quantification and aggregation operations limited in the constructs they quantify or aggregate over. The power and flexibility of this approach approaches that of iteration constructs in imperative languages, such as `for`, `while`, and `do` loops, without losing logic programming's declarative character. Similarly, it provides most of what is provided by the usual set of higher order functions in modern functional languages (see, *e.g.*, [17]).

The basic form of sequence quantification is much as for bounded quantification:

$$\texttt{forall } variable \texttt{ in } sequence \texttt{ do } goal$$

where *goal* is any Prolog goal, *variable* is a Prolog variable or term, and sequence is a term representing a sequence of values. (The actual syntax is slightly more general than this to allow for some syntactic sugar, as discussed in Section 5.)

We specify the semantics of sequence quantifications by translations similar to those of Voronkov [18], as shown in table 1. This translation differs from

Table 1. Definition of quantifiers and sequence membership

Formula	Translation and extra clauses
$\exists y \, . \, F$	$p(vars(F)\backslash\{y\})$ with clause:
	$p(vars(F)\backslash\{y\}) \leftarrow F$
$x \in s$	$p(x,s)$ with clauses:
	$p(x,s) \leftarrow next(s,x,s')$
	$p(x,s) \leftarrow next(s,x',s') \wedge p(x,s')$
$\forall y \in s \, . \, F$	$p(vars(F)\backslash\{y,s\},s)$ with clauses:
	$p(vars(F)\backslash\{y,s\},s) \leftarrow empty(s)$
	$p(vars(F)\backslash\{y,s\},s) \leftarrow next(s,y,s') \wedge F \wedge p(vars(F)\backslash\{y,s\},s')$

Voronkov's in that we specify the semantics of ∃ generally, not only for bounded quantifications, and we specify the semantics of ∈ outside the context of a quantification. The definition of ∈ is essentially the standard Prolog `member/2` predicate, generalized to work on sequences. Our definition of universal quantification is similar to Voronkov's, but is generalized to work on any sort of sequence.

4   Sequences

A sequence is an ordered collection of terms, possibly with repetition. For our purposes, a sequence is characterized by two predicates: $empty(s)$ holds if s is an empty sequence, and $next(s, e, t)$ holds if e is the first element of sequence s, and t is the remainder of sequence s after e. We implement these in Prolog as predicates `sequence_empty/1` and `sequence_next/3`. These predicates may be defined by anyone,[1] meaning that users of the package can define their own sequences to quantify over; they are not restricted to the sequences already supported by the implementation.

4.1   Primitive Sequences

The most obvious kinds of sequences are lists and arithmetic sequences. These are defined as follows:

```
sequence_empty(list([])).
sequence_next(list([H|T]), H, list(T)).

sequence_empty(Low..High) :-
    High is Low-1.
sequence_next(Low..High, Low, Next..High) :-
    ( nonvar(High) -> Low =< High ; true ),
    Next is Low + 1.
```

Note the `list/1` wrapper around the list sequence. All sequences must have a distinguished wrapper indicating what kind of sequence they are. This permits sequences to be produced as well as consumed by quantifications. The `nonvar` test in the final clause ensures that when the upper limit on an integer range is available at run time, it will be used to ensure iteration does not exceed the limit, but when no limit is supplied, iteration can proceed indefinitely.

Many other types of sequences are possible. For example, the following clauses define `inorder(Tree)` as the sequence of the elements of `Tree` traversed inorder. We assume `empty` denotes the empty tree, and `tree(L,Label,R)` denotes a tree with root label `Label` and left and right subtrees `L` and `R` respectively.

```
sequence_empty(inorder(empty, [])).
```

---

[1] Here we make use of standard Prolog's `multifile` declaration, allowing users to define these predicates with clauses in any number of files.

```
sequence_next(inorder(tree(L,Label,R),Stack), First, Rest) :-
    sequence_next(inorder(L,[Label-R|Stack]), First, Rest).
sequence_next(inorder(empty,[First-R|Stack]), First,
            inorder(R,Stack)).
```

Similar definitions could be written for preorder and postorder traversal.

4.2   Sequence Operations

The power of sequence quantification becomes apparent when one considers the many ways sequences can be modified and combined.

One important facility that is not naturally supported by bounded quantification is lockstep iteration, *i.e.*, parallel quantification over two sequences. For example, we might wish to specify that a relation R holds between the corresponding elements of l and m. Given a function zip that maps two sequences of the same length to a sequence of pairs of their corresponding elements, we could express this as: $\forall \langle x, y \rangle \in zip(l, m) . R(x, y)$ Note that this approach is very similar to that taken by the Python language in providing its lockstep iteration facility [20].

Of course, logic programming does not have functions (at least Prolog does not), so to use this technique we would need to write something like:

```
zip(L, M, Pairs),
    forall X-Y in Pairs do r(X,Y)
```

This unfortunately creates a separate list of pairs, wasting time and space. This shortcoming could be solved through deforestation [19], however this is not a common feature of Prolog compilers.

Our approach is instead to define a new kind of sequence constructed from two other sequences. This can be done by extending the definitions of sequence_empty/1 and sequence_next/3:

```
sequence_empty((A,B)) :-
    sequence_empty(A),
    sequence_empty(B).

sequence_next((A,B), (A1,A2), (Ar,Br)) :-
    sequence_next(A, A1, Ar),
    sequence_next(B, B2, Br).
```

This allows us to write

```
forall (X,Y) in (L,M) do r(X,Y)
```

Note that this approach requires no deforestation for optimization; a much simpler program optimization, as discussed in section 6, can remove the unnecessary term constructions.

Functional programmers will recognize this relation as similar to the standard *map* function, which applies a function to each element of a list, collecting the results into a list. There are several differences, however. Firstly, the sequence quantification approach works on sequence of any sort, not just lists. Secondly, it generalizes to arbitrary numbers of sequences. We could as easily have written

```
forall (X,Y,Z) in (L,M,N) do r(X,Y,Z)
```

to specify that r/3 relates corresponding elements of 3 sequences.

Sequence quantification also retains logic programming's relational character: it can be used to compute any of the sequences from any others, as long as the body of the quantification (the part after the **do**) can work in that mode. In the latter example, L, M, and/or N can be produced by this quantification, providing the first, second, and/or third argument of r/3 can be output.

Voronkov [18] also defines quantification over tails of lists using the syntax $\forall T \sqsubseteq L \dots$. We can achieve this effect by defining sequence operator *tails* which can be defined by:

```
sequence_empty(empty).

sequence_next(tails(S), S, Rest) :-
    (   sequence_next(S, _, Sr) ->
        Rest = tails(Sr)
    ;   Rest = empty
    ).
```

This allows us to define an ordered list similarly to Voronkov:

```
ordered([]).
ordered([_]).
ordered(L) :-
        forall Tail in tails(L) do
            (   Tail=[X,Y|_] ->
                    X=<Y
            ;   true
            ).
```

A better definition of this predicate will be presented in section 5.

Another operation we can perform on sequences is selecting only part of a sequence. For example, we can define a sequence filter: a sequence of the elements of another sequence with the elements not satisfying a specified filter predicate removed.

```
sequence_empty(when(S,F)) :-
    (   sequence_empty(S)
    ;   sequence_next(S, S1, Sr),
        \+ call(F, S1),
        sequence_empty(when(Sr,F))
    ).
```

```
sequence_next(when(S,F), N, Rest) :-
    sequence_next(S, S1, Sr),
    (   call(F, S1) ->
        N = S1,
        Rest = when(Sr,F)
    ;   sequence_next(when(Sr,F), N, Rest)
    ).
```

This can be used, for example, to count the positive elements of a sequence:

```
forall _ in (when(list(L),<(0)), 1..Count) do true
```

Here we specify that there are the same number of elements in `1..Count` as in `when(List,<(0))`. Note that the predicate `<(0)` will be given one more argument which will come last. Thus it specifies that zero is less than that argument.

Another useful sequence operator is `while`; this is similar to `when`, except that the sequence terminates once the first element not satisfying the given predicate is found. This can be used to simulate a *while* loop. For example,

```
forall (X,Y) in (while(inorder(Tree), >=(100)), list(list))
    do X = Y
```

will bind List to a list of the elements of Tree up to 100, stopping accumulation when the first element larger than 100 is found. Similarly, the `once` sequence operator specifies that the initial part of the sequence whose elements do not satisfy the specified test should be dropped, with all the remaining elements taken.

4.3   Accumulation

One common use of looping constructs in conventional programming languages is to accumulate a result. Barklund and Bevemyr propose a fixed set of accumulating quantifiers including `sum`, `product`, `min` and `max`. Thus far, sequence quantification only permits corresponding elements of sequences to be related, whereas accumulation requires elements to be related to previous elements of the sequence. We achieve this by introducing an accumulation sequence, which is a sequence of pairs, where the first element of each pair is equal to the second element of the previous pair. This is the only constraint on such a sequence, which we define as:

```
sequence_empty(thread(X,X)).

sequence_next(thread(Init,Final), (Init,Next),
              thread(Next,Final)).
```

We use such a sequence to accumulate by relating the two elements of the pair. We defer examples of accumulation to Section 5, where we introduce some syntactic sugar to make accumulations more attractive.

4.4 Scoping

One interesting question arises: how should variables not explicitly quantified be handled? For example, what does a goal like

```
forall X in L do p(X,Y)
```

mean? Is Y scoped to the p(X,Y) goal or to the whole clause? In the former case, it means $\forall x \in l \,.\, \exists y \,.\, p(x,y)$ whereas in the latter it means $\exists y \,.\, \forall x \in l \,.\, p(x,y)$.

Unfortunately, no single answer to this question seems intuitive in all cases. If the goal had instead been

```
Y=42, forall X in L do p(X,Y)
```

then it seems clear the intended scope of Y would be the whole clause. However, for the goal

```
forall X in L do (p(X,Y), q(Y))
```

the most natural reading would be that Y should be scoped inside the forall construct (i.e., this query should not require that Y be the same for all Xs).

Therefore we adopt the strategy used in the Mercury language[6]: a variable appearing only inside a forall construct is existentially quantified inside the universal quantification, while other variables are existentially quantified over the whole clause body. When this does not achieve the desired effect, explicit existential quantification can be used to specify the desired scoping of certain variables. However, this is rarely necessary as the default behavior is almost always what the user intends and expects.

Compare this, for example, to the behavior of Prolog's setof/3 and bagof/3 predicates, which implicitly scope all variables not appearing in the template (first) argument to the whole clause. Thus the anonymous variable in the goal

```
setof(X, p(X,_), List)
```

is scoped wider than the setof goal, resulting in unintended behavior in this case. To scope the anonymous variable inside the setof goal, it must be rewritten as

```
setof(X, Y^p(X,Y), List)
```

Experience shows that this often cause confusion for inexperienced Prolog programmers.

Conversely, the logical loops package [14] implicitly scopes all variables appearing in a loop to the inside of the loop. A variable appearing both outside and inside a loop is considered to be two distinct variables, unless a param form is added to the loop to indicate that the variable is to be scoped outside the loop. This, too, seems likely to cause confusion.

The disadvantage of our approach is that it can cause problems in some cases when a sequence quantification is used as a parameter to a higher order predicate. However, it should be noted that sequence quantification is intended to replace most uses of higher order code, and that explicit quantification can always be used to specify the intended scoping.

5 Syntactic Sugar

For a practical implementation of sequence quantification as a Prolog extension, we believe it is important to provide a syntax which is intuitive and palatable. In this, we have followed the spirit of the CLISP package included as part of the INTERLISP language [13], with an emphasis on extensibility.

Firstly, we generalize the *Template* in *Sequence* form to allow other ways to specify the generation of a sequence of bindings for a template. This is accomplished by allowing users to define clauses for the `sequence_generator/3` predicate. When a goal of the form `forall` *Generator* `do` *Goal* is found,

$$\texttt{sequence\_generator}\,(\textit{Generator},\textit{Template},\textit{Sequence})$$

is called, and the quantification is then treated as if it had been `forall` *Template* in *Sequence* `do` *Goal*.

This facility is used to provide some (hopefully!) more intuitive ways to write quantifications. Of course, these are only optional syntactic sugar; the syntax given earlier continues to work.

One example is the `as` operator. This allows each variable to be given together with the sequence it is quantified over, rather than requiring all the quantified variables to be bundled together and all the sequences to be bundled together. The clause:

```
sequence_generator(G1 as G2, (T1,T2), (S1,S2)) :-
    generate_sequence(G1, T1, S1),
    generate_sequence(G2, T2, S2).
```

together with an operator declaration for `as`, allows us to write:

```
forall X in list(L) as (S0,S) in thread(0,Sum) do S is S0 + X.
```

instead of

```
forall (X,S0,S) in (list(L),thread(0,Sum)) do S is S0 + X.
```

Note that `generate_sequence/3` just ensures that its first argument is not a variable, and then calls `sequence_generator/3`.

Another syntactic embellishment is provided by:

```
sequence_generator((Init->V0->V->Final),
          (V0,V), thread(Init,Final)).
```

This provides an alternative syntax for `thread` sequences introduced in Section 4.3 that presents the current and next variables for a thread between the initial and final values, allowing us instead to code the previous example as

```
forall X in list(L) as (0->S0->S->Sum) do S is S0 + X.
```

Intuitively, this says that we accumulate a value beginning with 0 and winding up with Sum, and at each iteration S0 is the previous value and S is the next one. That is, Sum is the sum of the elements of list L.

Note that there is no requirement for there to be any relationship between the current and next variables in an accumulation, only that S be determined. For example, we could better define the ordered predicate of section 4.2 as follows:

```
ordered(Seq) :-
    (   sequence_empty(Seq) ->
            true
    ;   sequence_next(Seq, First, Rest),
        forall E in Rest as (First->Prev->This->_) do
            (   E >= Prev,
                This = E
            )
    ).
```

Procedurally, this "initializes" Prev to the first element of Seq, and runs over the rest of the sequence verifying that each element is larger than Prev, and setting the value of Prev for the next iteration to the current element. This is similar to the code one might write in an imperative language, yet is entirely declarative.

Note that sequence generators can be used anywhere in the program, not only inside universal quantifications. When not immediately preceded by forall, they are considered to be in an existential context, and specify membership in the sequence. For example, a goal

```
X in list(L) as N in 1.._
```

would specify that X is an element of L and N is the position of X in that list.

6   Implementation

We have a Prolog implementation of sequence quantification built on the common term_expansion/2 Prolog extension. As each clause is compiled, it is scanned for explicit universal and existential quantifications. When such a goal is found, it is replaced by a call to a newly created predicate, plus the definition of that predicate.

The generated predicates are quite close to the form shown in table 1. A universal quantification of the form

```
forall T in S do body
```

would initially be translated to a goal

```
'forall i'(S)
```

where forall i is defined as:

```
'forall i'(S0) :-
    (   sequence_empty(S0)
    ;   sequence_next(S0, T, S)
        body,
        'forall i'(S)
    ).
```

Note that this code is entirely declarative if the *body* is. In particular, no cuts or if-then-else constructs are used to prevent backtracking. Thus a quantification may be used in any mode that the *body* and `sequence_next` and `sequence_empty` definitions will support. For example,

```
forall _ in list(L) as _ in 1..Length
```

will work to check that the length of L is `Length`, or to determine the length of list L, or to generate a list of length `Length`, or even to backtrack over longer and longer lists.

Several steps are taken to improve the efficiency of the generated code, the goal being to produce code as close as possible to the efficiency of the code an experienced Prolog programmer would write for this purpose. Firstly, users may specify improved code to generate for the empty and next predicates for particular kinds of sequences. This is done by providing clauses for the user-extensible predicates `empty_specialization/5` and `next_specialization/7`. These are certainly more complex than simply providing clauses for `sequence_empty/1` and `sequence_next/3`, but they are manageable. For example, to optimize the handling of list sequences, using L=[] and L=[H|T] in place of `sequence_empty(L)` and `sequence_next(L,H,T)`, these clauses suffice:

```
empty_specialization(list(L), _, L=[], Clauses, Clauses).
next_specialization(list(L), _, H, list(T), L=[H|T],
            Clauses, Clauses).
```

In some cases, a sequence may be more efficiently handled if it is first transformed into another form of sequence. For example, the definition of `sequence_empty/1` for integer range sequences is:

```
sequence_empty(Low..High) :- High is Low-1.
```

This requires an arithmetic computation to be done for each iteration. We could define a more efficient integer range as:

```
sequence_empty(intseq(H,H)).
sequence_next(intseq(L,H), L1, intseq(L1,H)) :-
    ( (integer(H) -> L<H ; true),
    L1 is L+1.
```

But this is less intuitive since, *e.g.*, `intseq(1,10)` specifies the sequence *2..10*.

In such cases, users can supply a clause for the `sequence_specification/7` predicate which specifies a goal to execute before beginning iteration, a goal to execute at the end, and an alternative sequence to use. For example

```
sequence_specification((L..H), _, intseq(L1,H),
                (L1 is L-1), true, Cl, Cl).
```

would substitute the sequence `intseq(L1,H)` for `L..H`, and insert the goal `L1 is L-1` before the call to the generated iteration predicate.

To make the job of writing this optimization code easier for those defining new sequences (and keen on achieving the highest performance), the translation performs a fairly simple-minded code specialization pass on the generated code. This pass looks for Prolog built in predicates that can be executed at compile time and replaces them with unifications achieving the same result. Furthermore, it executes unifications at compile time when they would unify a variable or atomic term with the first occurrence of a variable. In general, unifications should not be executed at compile time, since doing so may bind a variable used before a commit (cut or if-then-else) or in an impure operation, such as assert or input/output, changing the program behavior. It may also generate many occurrences of a large term where only one existed in a unification.

The most important optimization performed is in the generation of looping predicates. Rather than repeatedly taking apart and building sequence terms, the generated code passes the needed information in separate arguments. This is done by computing the most specific generalization of the head of the generated predicate and the call, and extracting its variables. Similarly, we compute the most specific generalization of each recursive call with the clause head.

Finally, we analyze the generated clause to see if one of its arguments is unified with a term with a distinct principal functor in each arm of the disjunction, and before any impure goal. If such an argument is identified, it is moved to the first argument position, and the disjunction is split into separate clauses, to take advantage of the first argument indexing supported by most Prolog implementations.

The resulting code is quite efficient. For the goal

```
forall _ in list(L) as _ in 1..N
```

which states that the length of list L is N, the generated code is `'forall 2'(L, 0, N)` where `'forall 2'/3` is defined by:

```
'forall 2'([], A, B) :-
    A=B.
'forall 2'([A|B], C, D) :-
    (   integer(D)
    ->  C<D
    ;   true
    ),
    E is C+1,
    'forall 2'(B, E, D).
```

The goal

```
forall E in list(L)
     as _ in 1..Count
     as (0->S0->S->Sum)
          do S is S0+E
```

which sums and counts the elements of a list, is translated to: 'forall 3'(L, 0, Count, 0, Sum), with:

```
'forall 3'([], A, B, C, D) :-
    A=B,
    D=C.
'forall 3'([A|B], C, D, E, F) :-
    (   integer(D)
    ->  C<D
    ;   true
    ),
    G is C+1,
    H is E+A,
    'forall 3'(B, G, D, H, F).
```

Finally, the goal

```
forall I in 1..10 do (write(I),nl)
```

translates to 'forall 5'(0) with:

```
'forall 5'(A) :-
    (   A=10
    ;   A<10,
        B is A+1,
        write(B),
        nl,
        'forall 5'(B)
    ).
```

7 Future Work

Currently, adding an optimization for a new kind of sequence, as described in section 6, is more difficult than it should be. We are investigating abstractions that would allow simple definition of sequences that would automatically be optimized.

There is always scope for further improvement to the specializer. It should be possible to execute more unifications at compile time when one of the terms to be unified is the first occurrence of a variable occurring only once or twice in the clause. After performing the unification and removing the goal, the term will appear at most once. Also it should be possible to unify a subsequent occurrence of a term if no impure operation has been performed since the first occurrence.

A more important optimization would be to avoid repeating a goal in multiple arms of a disjunction. In some cases, `sequence_empty`/1 may invoke the negation of `sequence_next`. In such cases, the iteration predicate will call `sequence_next` twice. It would be much more efficient to generate an if-then-else calling `sequence_next` once in the condition.

Finally, the design and implementation of a reasonably complete — but not overwhelming — set of sequence operators remains to be done. Fortunately, any operators omitted from the package can be supplied by the user without much difficulty.

We expect to release this package to the public under a suitable free or open source software license when it is completed. It will be available from

`http://www.cs.mu.oz.au/~schachte/software/`

8   Conclusions

We have described a new quantification formalism for logic programming which provides a logical facility allowing explicit iteration over any sort of sequence the user can define, as well as looping over multiple sequences in a coordinated manner, and arbitrary kinds of aggregations and accumulations. All of these things are done quite naturally using various kinds of sequences, and cannot in general be done with bounded quantification. Users can define their own kinds of sequences, including sequences defined in terms of other sequences. This facility has been implemented as a Prolog source to source translation.

Comparing the expressiveness of this facility with looping constructs of imperative languages, or with higher order operations in functional languages is quite difficult, inevitably leading one to compare apples with oranges, or to declaring all formalisms Turing equivalent. Still, since the primitive building block of this facility is simply the definition of a sequence of values, and since imperative looping constructs must loop over a sequence of values of the variables of the loop, it seems sequence quantification should be able to capture, however naturally or unnaturally, any iteration supported by imperative looping constructs. By providing the ability to define new kinds of sequences, and a facility for specifying syntactic sugar for them, we believe it should be possible to capture any iteration in a fairly natural way. Furthermore, due to the declarative semantics of the translation, all sequence quantifications have a declarative reading, providing the quantified goals and sequence definition do.

Comparison with higher order functions in functional languages is more interesting. Sequence quantification provides many of the facilities of modern functional languages. As mentioned earlier, the , sequence operator (as in the syntactically sugared version) provides a generalized version of the standard higher order `map` function. The `when`, `while`, and `once` sequence operators are closely related to Haskell's `filter`, `takewhile` and `dropwhile` functions, respectively.

The **thread** sequence provides the functionality of **foldl**. However, due to the general way sequences can be composed to allow mapping over any number and any kind of sequences, in combination with folding, filtering, taking and dropping. We also benefit from Prolog's relational notation to allow any, and any number, of those sequences to be outputs. Also, since a single step of iteration is taken as the primitive building block of sequence quantification, rather than traversing a whole list, sophisticated deforestation transformations are not necessary to produce good code; a simpler local optimization is sufficient.

Note also that while Prolog does not provide any lazy evaluation, since sequences are defined to execute **sequence_next** each time the next element of the sequence is needed, sequences behave like a crude sort of lazy evaluation, computing the next element only on demand.

Of course, looping constructs have a much longer history in the imperative programming literature than in logic or functional programming. The oldest generalized approach to defining looping constructs we are aware of was proposed by Liskov and Guttag [10] in the context of the CLU language. They distinguish three kinds of abstractions: procedural abstraction, data abstraction, and iteration abstraction. Iterators in CLU are rather similar to our sequence concept, except that they are procedural, while sequences are declarative. One important difference is that iterators are defined by procedures that loop, **yield**ing sequences elements as they are found. Thus using iterators appears to be a form of coroutining. This makes defining iterators easier than defining sequences, since iterators can use local data to store state, while implementors of sequences must store state explicitly. Iterators can be defined in terms of other iterators, much as we allow sequences to be defined in terms of other sequences.

More recently, iterators have gained prominence in object oriented programming, particularly due to their appearance in the C++ Standard Template Library.[15] C++ iterators are more like sequences than CLU's iterators, as they are not defined by a loop **yield**ing values, but rather by a class with methods to get the "current" value and advance to the next value. Sequences are similar, except that their primitive operations are checking for emptiness and getting the next element and remainder sequence. Since C++ has all the facilities of an imperative language, and since iterators are used by explicitly asking for the next value, it does not need to define iterators in terms of other iterators. However, that is possible, should it be desired.

References

1. Krzysztof R. Apt. Arrays, bounded quantification and iteration in logic and constraint logic programming. *Science of Computer Programming*, 26(1–3):133–148, 1996.
2. J. Barklund and P. Hill. Extending godel for expressing restricted quantifications and arrays. Technical Report 102, UPMAIL, Uppsala University, Box 311, S-751 05, Sweden, 1995. Available from
   http://citeseer.nj.nec.com/barklund95extending.html.

3. Jonas Barklund and Johan Bevemyr. Prolog with arrays and bounded quantifications. In A. Voronkov, editor, *Proceedings of the 4th International Conference on Logic Programming and Automated Reasoning (LPAR'93)*, volume 698 of *LNAI*, pages 28–39, St. Petersburg, Russia, July 1993. Springer Verlag.
4. Keith Clark. Negation as failure. In H. Gallaire and J. Minker, editors, *Logic and Databases*, pages 293–322. Plenum Press, 1978.
5. Gottlob Frege. *Begriffsschrift, eine der Arithmetischen Nachgebildete Formelsprache des Reinen Denkens*. Halle, 1879. English translation in *From Frege to Gödel, a Source Book in Mathematical Logic* (J. van Heijenoort, Editor), Harvard University Press, Cambridge, 1967, pp. 1–82.
6. Fergus Henderson, Thomas Conway, Zoltan Somogyi, David Jeffery, Peter Schachte, Simon Taylor, and Chris Speirs. The Mercury language reference manual. Available from <http://www.cs.mu.oz.au/mercury/>, 2000.
7. Pascal Van Hentenryck. *The OPL Optimization Programming Language*. MIT Press, 1999.
8. ISO. *Standard for the Programming Language Prolog*. ISO/IEC, 1995.
9. Robert A. Kowalski. Predicate logic as a programming language. In *Proceedings of IFIP 4*, pages 569–574, Amsterdam, 1974. North Holland.
10. Barbara Liskov and John Guttag. *Abstraction and Specification in Program Developement*. MIT Press, Cambridge, Mass., 1986.
11. Lee Naish. Negation and quantifiers in NU-Prolog. In Ehud Shapiro, editor, *Proceedings of the Third International Conference on Lo gic Programming*, pages 624–634, London, England, July 1986.
12. J. Alan Robinson. A machine-oriented logic based on the resolution principle. *Journal of the ACM*, 12(1):23–41, January 1965.
13. M. Sanella. *InterLISP Reference Manual*. Xerox PARC, Palo Alto, CA, October 1983.
14. Joachim Schimpf. Logical loops. In Peter J. Stuckey, editor, *Logic Programming*, volume 2401 of *Lecture Notes in Computer Science*, pages 224–238. Springer-Verlag, July 29–August 1 2002.
15. B. Stroustrup. *The C++ Programming Language*. Addison-Wesley, Reading, Mass., 3 edition, 1997.
16. James Thom and Justin Zobel. NU-Prolog reference manual, version 1.0. Technical Report 86/10, Department of Computer Science, University of Melbourne, Melbourne, Australia, 1986.
17. Simon Thompson. *The Craft of Functional Programming*. Addison-Wesley, second edition, 1999.
18. Andrei Voronkov. Logic programming with bounded quantification. In Andrei Voronkov, editor, *Logic Programming—Proc. Second Russian Conf. on Logic Programming*, number 592 in Lecture Notes in Computer Science, pages 486–514. Springer-Verlag, Berlin, 1992.
19. Philip Wadler. Deforestation: transforming programs to eliminate trees. *Theoretical Computer Science*, 73:231–248, 1990.
20. Barry A. Warsaw. Lockstep iteration. Python Enhancement Proposal, 2000. available from http://python.sourceforge.net/peps/pep-0201.html.

Roll: A Language for Specifying Die-Rolls

Torben Mogensen

DIKU
University of Copenhagen
Universitetsparken 1
DK2100 Copenhagen O, Denmark
Phone: +45 35321404   Fax: +45 35321401
torbenm@diku.dk

Abstract. Role-playing games (RPG's) use a variety of methods for rolling dice to add randomness to the game. In the simplest form, a small number of identical dice are rolled and added, but more advanced forms involve cumulative re-rolling of 6's, doubling the value of doubles, removing the lowest or highest result or counting the number of dice that are below a threshold, and many other weird and wonderful modifications.

While die-roll programs and net-based die-roll servers exist, they can usually only handle the simplest form of die-rolls. This paper describes **Roll**, a simple functional language for defining how dice are rolled. Such definitions are then used to emulate die-rolls or make probability calculations.

We describe two different semantics for **Roll**: One that corresponds to randomly rolling the dice and one for calculating the probability distribution. We discuss implementation issues regarding the latter.

1   Introduction

Dice, in one form or another, have probably been used for games for as long as games have existed. The earliest form of dice is *knuckle-bones*, small bones that may be painted on one or more sides. These have, for example, been used in the Egyptian game Senet [6]. Six-sided dice are probably derived from knuckle-bones and examples from 600BC or older have been found [1]. In modern times, six-sided dice are ubiquitous and are used in many games, either pure dice-games like Craps or Yahtzee or as randomizers for board games like Monopoly or Snakes and Ladders.

Role-playing games are known for their use of polyhedral dice based on the platonic solids [2]. 4000 year old neolithic carved stone polyhedra have been found [3], but whether they have been used for games is anybody's guess. The first modern game to use polyhedral dice was (probably) the role-playing game Dungeons and Dragons from 1974.

Even with a finite selection of dice, there is no limit to the number of ways they can be rolled, and dozens of different method have, indeed, been used in published games. Some methods are very simple (just roll one die and compare the value to a threshold) while others are quite complex and may involve rolling several different dice or keep rolling dice until a certain condition holds.

V. Dahl and P. Wadler (Eds.): PADL 2003, LNCS 2562, pp. 145–159, 2003.
© Springer-Verlag Berlin Heidelberg 2003

Most people have a fair idea of the probability of the different outcomes of a single die roll, but it gets increasingly more difficult to predict the outcome when the die-roll mechanisms get more complicated.

A player of a game will benefit from knowing, at least roughly, what his chances of succeeding at a certain task are, and knowing the probability of each possible die-roll result is certainly central to that. But it is even more important for a game designer to know how his chosen die-roll mechanism behaves statistically, as failure to do so can lead to a mechanism that behaves against the intention of the designer in certain situations.

However, few gamers and game designers have sufficient knowledge of statistics to calculate probability distribution of all but the simplest die-rolls. There have been examples where a published game has been modified in the second edition because the die-roll method turned out to be flawed. [4] describes such a case.

The present paper describes a tool that can help these by providing a notation, called **Roll** for describing die-roll methods and a program that can simulate die-rolling and calculate probability distribution of methods described in this notation.

We start, in section 2, by giving an overview of **Roll** and show some examples of how to specify die-rolls in the notation. In section 3, we provide two different denotational semantics for **Roll**: One for simulating single random die-rolls and one for calculating the probability distribution of a roll. In section 7, we briefly describe the implementation of **Roll** and then we round off with a short conclusion.

2   Overview of Roll

Roll assumes all die-rolls result in either a single integer value or an unordered collection of such values. A single value is equivalent to a collection of one value, which we will call a *singleton collection*.

A die-roll definition is an expression that use numbers and operators to create simple die-rolls and combine these into more complex die-rolls or modify die-rolls according to certain conditions.

2.1   Simple Die-Rolling

Following the usual RPG convention, a single die is specified by a "d" followed by a number indicating the number of faces on the die. So, for example, a six-sided die is specified as "d6". An n-sided die is assumed to yield the values from 1 to n with equal probability. The number after a "d" can be any expression with an integer value greater than 0, so, for example, "d d6" rolls a d6 to find which type of dice (from d1 to d6) is rolled.

Rolling a certain number of dice is specified by prefixing the die-specifier by a number using the operator "#", so 5 six-sided dice are specified as, e.g., "5#d6". This deviates slightly from the RPG convention that doesn't use any operator between the number and the die. Furthermore, "5#d6" produces a *collection* of 5 dice instead of adding the values of 5 dice.

To get the sum of 5 six-sided dice, you write "sum5#d6".

You can add, subtract, multiply and divide (using integer division) dice or numbers using the usual arithmetic operators (+, -, * and /).

2.2   Operations on Collections

The collections used in **Roll** don't consider ordering of the values – so a collection of the values 1 and 2 is the same as a collection of the values 2 and 1. Furthermore, a single value is considered as a singleton collection and *vice versa*.

The operator "#" can be prefixed by any expression that evaluates to a singleton collection (with non-negative value) and followed by any die-roll expression, so you can, for example, write "d4#d6" to specify a collection of 1 to 4 six-sided dice or "10#(sum 5#d6)" to specify a collection of ten values, each obtained by adding 5 six-sided dice. If you write "3#4#d6", it is read as "3#(4#d6)" and produces a collection with a total of 12 six-sided dice by combining 3 size-4 collections. In general, if what follows the "#" operator is something that produces a collection, these are combined to a single collection. In other words, you can't have a collection of collections, as these will always be collapsed to a single collection.

Combination of two collections is done by the "@" operator. As an example, "3#d6 @ 3#d8" combines a collection of 3 six-sided dice with a collection of 3 eight-sided dice.

The operator "count" counts the number of dice in a collection. This, normally, isn't useful unless combined with a *filter* that removes elements that don't obey a specified condition. For example, the expression "count =6 10#d6" rolls 10 six-sided dice and uses the filter "=6" to remove the dice that aren't equal to 6 and then count these. You can also filter by "<", ">", "<=" or ">=", so, for example, "count <4 10#d6" counts the number of dice that are less than 4. The number after the comparison operator can be any integer-valued expression, so you can write, e.g., "count <d6 10#d6" that rolls a die and counts how many of the 10 next dice that are less than this.

You can also take the n least or the n largest values from a collection using the operators "least" and "largest". For example, "largest 1 least 2 3#d6" finds the largest of the two smallest of three dice, *i.e.*, the middle (or median) value. If there are less than n values in the collection, all elements are returned.

2.3   Value Definitions, Conditionals, *etc.*

If you, for example, write "d6*d6" you get the product of two independently rolled dice. If you want to square the value of a single die, you have to store the roll of one die in a variable and use the variable twice. This can be done by a local definition of the form "let x = d6 in x*x" which defines x to be the value of a single die and then multiplies that value by itself. Any expression can be used after the equality sign and after "in".

You can make a conditional choice between two rolls using an if-then-else construction. The form of this is if e_1 then e_2 else e_3. If e_1 is a non-empty collection, e_2 is evaluated, otherwise, e_3 is evaluated. This is most often used in combination with a filter, *e.g.*, "if =x y then x+y else largest 1 (x@y)" to take the largest of two dice but let doubles count double.

Another construction that is sometimes useful is the "foreach" construction. It applies the same method to all values in a collection and combines the result to a new collection. For example, you can add 1 to all members of a collection c by writing "foreach x in c do x+1".

The "dotdot" construction, produces a range of integer values. "1..6", for example, is the collection of all integers between 1 and 6 (inclusive). You can use any integer-producing expressions instead of the constants in the above, for example write d4..d10 to get the range of values between the result of rolling a d4 and the result of rolling a d10. If the first value is larger than the second (*e.g.*, "7..3"), the empty collection is produced.

2.4   Repeated Die-Rolls

Sometimes, a die-roll involves repeating rolls until a certain condition occurs. A game may, for example, define that you roll and add 3 six-sided dice, but for all sixes rolled, one more die is added. If any of these dice are also sixes, yet more dice are added, and so on. Thus, there is no *a priori* bound on the number of dice rolled.

To allow such rolls, **Roll** allows conditionally repeated die-rolls. We show this first by an example. The above-described 3d6 with re-rolls on sixes can be described by

```
sum (let x=3#d6 in repeat ((count =6 x)#d6))
```

We first roll 3 dice, binding the result to x. We then repeat an expression that rolls a number of dice equal to the number of sixes in x, producing in each step a new x, until that new x becomes empty. Finally, we combine all the x's and add up the dice.

The semantics of the `repeat` construct is that the variable after the `let` keyword is bound to the value v_0 of the expression after the = sign. Then the expression after the keyword `repeat` is evaluated to yield a new value v_1. This is then bound to the variable and the expression is re-evaluated to yield a new value v_2, and so on, until the value of the expression becomes the empty collection. At this point, all the values are combined to a single collection $(v_0 @ v_1 @ \ldots @ v_n)$. If the value of the initial expression is the empty collection, the repetition stops immediately with the empty collection as a result.

In the example above, let us assume 3#d6 evaluates to the collection 2 6 6. This is bound to x and the expression in the body of the repeat construct is evaluated to a collection of 2 #d6, let us say 4 6. The variable x is now bound to this collection and the body is reevaluated to a single die, say 3. The variable x is now rebound to the new collection and the expression, finally, yields the empty collection. We now combine the collections 2 6 6 @ 4 6 @ 3 to 2 3 4 6 6 6.

3   Syntax of Roll

To keep the size of the semantic descriptions down, we model only a subset of **Roll**. The syntax of the modeled subset of **Roll** is described in Figure 1. The remaining cases can be added to the semantic descriptions with little problem (except size).

We will, in section 4, describe the semantics of making a single random die-roll and, in section 5, we will describe the semantics of calculating the probability distribution of a die-roll method.

$$Exp \rightarrow \textbf{number}$$
$$| \quad \textbf{variable}$$
$$| \quad \textbf{d } Exp$$
$$| \quad Exp \; + \; Exp$$
$$| \quad Exp \; \texttt{@} \; Exp$$
$$| \quad Exp \; \# \; Exp$$
$$| \quad \textbf{sum } Exp$$
$$| \quad \textbf{count } Exp$$
$$| \quad \textbf{least } Exp \; Exp$$
$$| \quad < Exp \; Exp$$
$$| \quad \textbf{let variable} = Exp \textbf{ in } Exp$$
$$| \quad \textbf{let variable} = Exp \textbf{ in repeat } Exp$$

Fig. 1. Syntax of a subset of **Roll**.

4 Single-Roll Semantics

We will first describe the semantics of **Roll** in terms of doing a single random die-roll as described by the **Roll** die-roll definition.

4.1 Domains

As mentioned in section 2, a roll describes a collection of integer values, so this is the value domain of **Roll**. To be precise, a collection is a *multi-set* or *bag* of integers, so, like sets, the order of elements is irrelevant but, unlike sets, the number of times an element occurs is significant. Mathematically, a collection is a mapping from integers (elements) to non-negative integers (the number of times the element occurs). A collection can have only a finite number of elements, so we require the mapping to have finite support, *i.e.*, that only a finite number of elements map to nonzero numbers:

$$\mathcal{C} = \{c \in \mathbb{Z} \rightarrow \mathbb{N}_0 \mid \exists n_-, n_+ \in \mathbb{Z} : \forall m \in \mathbb{Z}(m < n_- \vee m > n_+) \Rightarrow c(m) = 0\}$$

We define the following notation and operations:

- $\{\}$ is the empty collection, i.e., $\{\} \, n = 0$ for all integers n.
- $\{n_1, \ldots, n_k\}$ is the collection consisting of the numbers $n_1, \ldots, n_k$. The elements are mentioned in ascending order and as many times as they occur in the collection. Example: $\{1, 2, 2, 4\}$.
- $c_1 \texttt{@} c_2$ is the union of collections c_1 and c_2, defined by $(c_1 \texttt{@} c_2) \, n = c_1(n) + c_2(n)$ for all integers n.
- We define a subset ordering on $\mathcal{C}$ by $c_1 \subseteq c_2$ iff $\exists c_3 \in \mathcal{C}$, $c_2 = c_1 \texttt{@} c_3$. Note that the choice of c_3 is unique.
- If $c_1 \subseteq c_2$, we define $c_2 - c_1$ to be the unique c_3 such that $c_2 = c_1 \texttt{@} c_3$.

To describe randomness, we assume we have a source of random numbers. A random source σ is modeled as real number in the range $\mathcal{S} = [0, 1[$, *i.e.*, the half-open interval from 0 to 1. We will use this to produce uniformly distributed random integers, assuming that the initial source is uniformly distributed over all possible sources. The source can be considered an arithmetic encoding of a sequence of numbers. See also section 6.

We also need a mapping $\rho \in Env = V \to C$ from variables to collections, where V is the set of variables.

The `repeat` construct can cause nontermination, so we will use lifted domains, *i.e.*, domains extended with a bottom element $\bot$. We use the standard flat ordering: $\bot \sqsubseteq x$, for all elements x from the original (unlifted) domain.

Functions with lifted domains are ordered point-wisely: $f_1 \sqsubseteq f_2 \Leftrightarrow f_1(x) \sqsubseteq f_2(x)$ for all arguments x. The bottom element in a partial function domain is, hence, the function that maps all elements to $\bot$.

4.2   The Semantic Rules

We are now ready to describe the single-roll semantics of **Roll**, shown in Figure 2. The main semantic function $\mathcal{P}$ takes an expression, an environment, and a source and produces a collection and a new source. Since there can be nontermination, we lift the result domain. We use a *where* construction in the semantic rules. This is strict, so if an expression in the *where* clause doesn't terminate (*i.e.*, yields $\bot$), then the entire expression yields $\bot$. Furthermore, many of the *where* clauses assume (by pattern-matching) that a value is singleton collection. If this is not the case, the result is undefined. Note that this undefinedness is different from $\bot$. We do not model undefinedness explicitly.

Some comments:

- In the rule for d, we use the standard method for extracting a number and a new source from a source represented as a real number in the interval $[0, 1[$: We multiply the source by the range m. The fractional part of the result is the new source and the integral part is the random number. Since this is in the range $0 \cdots (m - 1)$, we add 1 to get a result between 1 and m.
- The rules for #, sum, least use a calculated n as the last index into an enumeration, which is returned as result. If $n = 0$, the resulting collection is empty. If $n < 0$, it is undefined.
- The rules for least and < exploit that the notation for enumerated collections requires the elements to be listed in nondecreasing order.
- The rule for `repeat` uses a fixed-point operator to define a recursive function F. We use *where* clauses to make sure F (and f) always get non-$\bot$ arguments. A nonterminating `repeat` will yield $\bot$, though.

5   Probability Semantics

Alternatively, **Roll** can be used to calculate the probability distribution of die-roll. A probability distribution is a mapping from collections of integers to probabilities (real numbers between 0 and 1), such that the sum of all the probabilities is 1. However, since we have a possibility of nontermination, we use *partial probability distributions*, where the sum is between 0 and 1. Intuitively, the gap up to 1.0 is the chance/risk of nontermination or undefined behaviour.

$$\mathcal{R} \; : \; Exp \to Env \to \mathcal{S} \to (\mathcal{C} \times \mathcal{S})_\perp$$

$$\mathcal{R}[\![n]\!]\rho\sigma \; = \; (\{n\}, \sigma)$$

$$\mathcal{R}[\![x]\!]\rho\sigma \; = \; (\{\rho\, x\}, \sigma)$$

$$\mathcal{R}[\![\mathtt{d}\, E]\!]\rho\sigma = (\{n\}, \sigma'')$$
$$\quad where \; (\{m\}, \sigma') = \mathcal{R}[\![E]\!]\rho\sigma \; , \;\; undefined \; if \; m < 1$$
$$\qquad\qquad\quad n \qquad\quad = 1 + \lfloor m \cdot \sigma' \rfloor$$
$$\qquad\qquad\quad \sigma'' \qquad\quad = (m \cdot \sigma') - \lfloor m \cdot \sigma' \rfloor$$

$$\mathcal{R}[\![E_1 \; + \; E_2]\!]\rho\sigma = (\{m + n\}, \sigma'')$$
$$\quad where \; (\{m\}, \sigma') = \mathcal{R}[\![E_1]\!]\rho\sigma$$
$$\qquad\qquad\;\; (\{n\}, \sigma'') = \mathcal{R}[\![E_2]\!]\rho\sigma'$$

$$\mathcal{R}[\![E_1 \; @ \; E_2]\!]\rho\sigma = (c_1 @ c_2, \sigma'')$$
$$\quad where \; (c_1, \sigma') \; = \mathcal{R}[\![E_1]\!]\rho\sigma$$
$$\qquad\qquad\;\; (c_2, \sigma'') = \mathcal{R}[\![E_2]\!]\rho\sigma'$$

$$\mathcal{R}[\![E_1 \; \# \; E_2]\!]\rho\sigma = (c_1 @ \cdots @ c_n, \sigma_n)$$
$$\quad where \; (\{n\}, \sigma_0) = \mathcal{R}[\![E_1]\!]\rho\sigma$$
$$\qquad\qquad\;\; (c_i, \sigma_i) \;\; = \mathcal{R}[\![E_2]\!]\rho\sigma_{i-1} \; , \;\; i \in \{1 \ldots n\}$$

$$\mathcal{R}[\![\mathtt{sum}\, E]\!]\rho\sigma = (\{m_1 + \cdots + m_n\}, \sigma')$$
$$\quad where \; (\{m_1, \ldots, m_n\}, \sigma') = \mathcal{R}[\![E_1]\!]\rho\sigma$$

$$\mathcal{R}[\![\mathtt{count}\, E]\!]\rho\sigma = (\{n\}, \sigma')$$
$$\quad where \; (\{m_1, \ldots, m_n\}, \sigma') = \mathcal{R}[\![E_1]\!]\rho\sigma$$

$$\mathcal{R}[\![\mathtt{least}\, E_1\, E_2]\!]\rho\sigma = (\{m_1, \ldots, m_{min(n,k)}\}, \sigma'')$$
$$\quad where \; (\{n\}, \sigma') \qquad\quad = \mathcal{R}[\![E_1]\!]\rho\sigma$$
$$\qquad\qquad\;\; (\{m_1, \ldots, m_k\}, \sigma'') = \mathcal{R}[\![E_2]\!]\rho\sigma'$$

$$\mathcal{R}[\![< E_1\, E_2]\!]\rho\sigma = \begin{cases} (\{\}, \sigma'') & if \; l = 0 \vee n \le m_1 \\ (\{m_1, \ldots, m_l\}, \sigma'') & if \; l > 0 \wedge m_l < n \\ (\{m_1, \ldots, m_k\}, \sigma'') & if \; m_k < n \wedge n \le m_{k+1} \end{cases}$$
$$\quad where \; (\{n\}, \sigma') \qquad\qquad\qquad\qquad = \mathcal{R}[\![E_1]\!]\rho\sigma$$
$$\qquad\qquad\;\; (\{m_1, \ldots, m_k, m_{k+1}, \ldots, m_l\}, \sigma'') = \mathcal{R}[\![E_2]\!]\rho\sigma'$$

$$\mathcal{R}[\![\mathtt{let}\, x = E_1\, \mathtt{in}\, E_2]\!]\rho\sigma = \mathcal{R}[\![E_2]\!]\rho[x \mapsto c_1]\sigma'$$
$$\quad where \; (c_1, \sigma') = \mathcal{R}[\![E_1]\!]\rho\sigma$$

$$\mathcal{R}[\![\mathtt{let}\, x = E_1\, \mathtt{in}\, \mathtt{repeat}\, E_2]\!]\rho\sigma = F(\mathcal{R}[\![E_1]\!]\rho\sigma)$$
$$\quad where \; F = \mathbf{fix}\, \lambda f. \lambda(c, \sigma). \begin{cases} (c, \sigma) & if \; c = \{\} \\ (c @ c_2, \sigma_2) & if \; c \ne \{\} \\ \qquad where \; (c_1, \sigma_1) = \mathcal{R}[\![E_2]\!]\rho[x \mapsto c]\sigma \\ \qquad\qquad\;\;\; (c_2, \sigma_2) = f(c_1, \sigma_1) \end{cases}$$

Fig. 2. Single-roll semantics for **Roll**.

We use the domain $\mathcal{D}$ for partial probability distributions and define a partial ordering on it:

$$\mathcal{D} = \{d \in \mathcal{C} \to [0, 1] \mid 0 \le (\textstyle\sum_{c \in \mathcal{C}} d(c)) \le 1\}$$
$$d_1 \sqsubseteq d_2 \Leftrightarrow \forall c \in \mathcal{C} : d_1\, c \le d_2\, c$$

Note that the least distribution according to the partial ordering maps all collections to 0. The intuitive meaning of this is that nontermination is the only possible result.

We combine probability distributions by a weighted sum

$$\sum_{i \in I} (p_i \cdot d_i) \quad where \quad \sum_{i \in I} p_i = 1.0$$

The meaning of the weighted sum is defined by the equation

$$\left(\sum_{i \in I} (p_i \cdot d_i) \right)(c) = \sum_{i \in I} (p_i \cdot d_1(c))$$

For any collection c, we use $\|c\|$ to denote the probability distribution that has c as certainty, *i.e.*, $\|c\|(c) = 1.0$ and $\|c\|(c') = 0.0$ if $c \neq c'$. We pronounce $\|c\|$ as "definitely c".

Environments still bind variables to collections, so these are unchanged from before.

The probability semantics is described in Figure 3. Some comments on the probability semantics:

- In many rules, we sum over the legal range of a value. Sometimes, this is the positive integers, other times it is non-negative integers, all integers or all collections.
- $\mathcal{D}$ is not a lifted domain, so the *where* clauses are not strict over $\mathcal{D}$.
- Where undefinedness is caused by a collection not being a singleton or an element not being positive etc., the undefined cases are not counted. This means that undefinedness as well as nontermination can contribute to a sum less than 1.0.
- In the rule for repeat, the fixed-point is well-defined, as it is trivial to see that the function is continuous over the point-wise extension of the ordering on $\mathcal{D}$ to functions that return $\mathcal{D}$.

5.1   Average and Spread

If a die-roll method always produces singleton collections(i.e., integers), it is meaningful and useful to consider the average and the spread (also called standard deviation) of the results. The average of a distribution d is

$$average(d) = \sum_{n \in \mathbb{Z}} n * d(\{n\})$$

The spread is the square root of the variance:

$$spread(d) = \sqrt{\left(\sum_{n \in \mathbb{Z}} n^2 * d(\{n\}) \right) - (average(d))^2}$$

6   Relating the Semantics

Intuitively, the single-roll semantics and the probability semantics are related, but exactly how? It is only through the source of random numbers that the single-roll semantics can be related to probability, so the following is a suitable statement relating the two semantics:

$$\forall c \in \mathcal{C}, \forall \rho \in (V \to \mathcal{C}) : (\mathcal{P}[\![e]\!]\rho)(c) = \int_0^1 \|c\|(\pi_1(\mathcal{R}[\![e]\!]\rho\sigma)) \, d\sigma$$

$$\mathcal{P} \; : \; Exp \to Env \to \mathcal{D}$$

$$\mathcal{P}[\![n]\!]\rho \; = \; \|n\|$$

$$\mathcal{P}[\![x]\!]\rho \; = \; \|\rho\,x\|$$

$$\mathcal{P}[\![\mathtt{d}\,E]\!]\rho = \sum_{n\in\mathbb{IN}}(d(\{n\}) \cdot \sum_{i=1}^{n} \tfrac{1}{n} \cdot \|i\|)$$
$$\text{where } d = \mathcal{P}[\![E]\!]\rho$$

$$\mathcal{P}[\![E_1 + E_2]\!]\rho = \sum_{m,n\in\mathbb{Z}}((d_1(\{m\}) \cdot d_2(\{n\})) \cdot \|\{m+n\}\|)$$
$$\text{where } d_1 = \mathcal{P}[\![E_1]\!]\rho$$
$$d_2 = \mathcal{P}[\![E_2]\!]\rho$$

$$\mathcal{P}[\![E_1 @ E_2]\!]\rho = \sum_{c_1,c_2\in\mathcal{C}}(d_1(c_1) \cdot d_2(c_2)) \cdot \|c_1 @ c_2\|$$
$$\text{where } d_1 = \mathcal{P}[\![E_1]\!]\rho$$
$$d_2 = \mathcal{P}[\![E_2]\!]\rho$$

$$\mathcal{P}[\![E_1 \# E_2]\!]\rho = \sum_{n\in\mathbb{IN}_0}(d_1(\{n\}) \cdot (f\,n))$$
$$\text{where } d_1 \quad = \mathcal{P}[\![E_1]\!]\rho$$
$$d_2 \quad = \mathcal{P}[\![E_2]\!]\rho$$
$$f\,0 \quad = \|\{\}\|$$
$$f\,(n+1) = \sum_{c_1,c_2\in\mathcal{C}}(d_2(c_1) \cdot (f\,n)(c_2)) \cdot \|c_1 @ c_2\|$$

$$\mathcal{P}[\![\mathtt{sum}\,E]\!]\rho = \sum_{c\in\mathcal{C}} d(c) \cdot \|\{sum\,c\}\|$$
$$\text{where } d \qquad\qquad = \mathcal{P}[\![E]\!]\rho$$
$$sum\,\{\} \qquad\quad = 0$$
$$sum\,\{m_1,\ldots,m_n\} = m_1 + \cdots + m_n$$

$$\mathcal{P}[\![\mathtt{count}\,E]\!]\rho = \sum_{c\in\mathcal{C}} d(c) \cdot \|\{count\,c\}\|$$
$$\text{where } d \qquad\qquad = \mathcal{P}[\![E]\!]\rho$$
$$count\,\{\} \qquad\quad = 0$$
$$count\,\{m_1,\ldots,m_n\} = n$$

$$\mathcal{P}[\![\mathtt{least}\,E_1\,E_2]\!]\rho = \sum_{n\in\mathbb{IN}_0}\sum_{c\in\mathcal{C}}(d_1(\{n\}) \cdot d_2(c)) \cdot \|least\,n\,c\|$$
$$\text{where } d_1 \qquad\qquad = \mathcal{P}[\![E_1]\!]\rho$$
$$d_2 \qquad\qquad = \mathcal{P}[\![E_2]\!]\rho$$
$$least\,n\,\{m_1,\ldots,m_k\} = \{m_1,\ldots,m_k\} \text{ if } k \le n$$
$$least\,n\,\{m_1,\ldots,m_k\} = \{m_1,\ldots,m_n\} \text{ if } k > n$$

$$\mathcal{P}[\![< E_1\,E_1]\!]\rho = \sum_{n\in\mathbb{IN}_0}\sum_{c\in\mathcal{C}}(d_1(\{n\}) \cdot d_2(c)) \cdot \|less\,n\,c\|$$
$$\text{where } d_1 \qquad\qquad\qquad = \mathcal{P}[\![E_1]\!]\rho$$
$$d_2 \qquad\qquad\qquad = \mathcal{P}[\![E_2]\!]\rho$$
$$less\,n\,\{m_1,\ldots,m_l\} \qquad = \{\} \qquad\qquad\quad \text{if } l=0 \vee n \le m_1$$
$$less\,n\,\{m_1,\ldots,m_l\} \qquad = \{m_1,\ldots,m_l\} \text{ if } l>0 \wedge m_l < n$$
$$less\,n\,\{m_1,\ldots,m_k,m_{k+1},\ldots,m_l\} = \{m_1,\ldots,m_k\} \text{ if } m_k < n \wedge n \le m_{k+1}$$

$$\mathcal{P}[\![\mathtt{let}\,x = E_1\,\mathtt{in}\,E_2]\!]\rho = \sum_{c\in\mathcal{C}} d(c) \cdot \mathcal{P}[\![E_2]\!]\rho[x \mapsto c]$$
$$\text{where } d = \mathcal{P}[\![E_1]\!]\rho$$

$$\mathcal{P}[\![\mathtt{let}\,x = E_1\,\mathtt{in}\,\mathtt{repeat}\,E_2]\!]\rho = \sum_{c\in\mathcal{C}} d_1(c) \cdot (F\,c)$$
$$\text{where } d_1 = \mathcal{P}[\![E_1]\!]\rho$$

$$F = \mathbf{fix}\,\lambda f.\lambda c_1.\lambda c_2.\begin{cases} 1.0 & \text{if } c_1 = c_2 = \{\} \\ 0.0 & \text{if } c_1 \not\subseteq c_2 \\ \sum_{c\in\mathcal{C}} d_2(c) \cdot f(c)(c_2 - c_1) & \text{if } c_1 \ne \{\} \wedge c_1 \subseteq c_2 \\ & \text{where } d_2 = \mathcal{P}[\![E_2]\!]\rho[x \mapsto c_1] \end{cases}$$

Fig. 3. Probability semantics

A complication of this equation is that the source of random numbers is threaded through the single-roll semantics in a way that makes the source for one subexpression depend on the result of another. What we need to do is to make a suitable definition of what it means for a source of random numbers to be uniform and then prove that any σ' in the single-roll semantics is uniformly distributed provided the initial σ is uniformly distributed. This will allow us to treat each σ' independently.

We define that a function $f : S \to S$ is uniform if, for all functions $F : S \to [0, 1]$, $\int_0^1 F(f(\sigma))d\sigma = \int_0^1 F(\sigma)d\sigma$. If we can prove that $\lambda\sigma.\pi_2(\mathcal{R}[\![e]\!]\rho\sigma)$ is uniform for any e and ρ, and we have $\sigma' = \mathcal{R}[\![e]\!]\rho\sigma$, then the above definition allows us to replace an integral over σ' with an integral over σ.

We can show some properties of uniform functions:

- If f and g are uniform, then $(f \circ g)$ is also uniform. Proof:

$$\int_0^1 F((f \circ g)(\sigma))d\sigma = \int_0^1 F(f(g(\sigma)))d\sigma$$
$$= \int_0^1 (F \circ f)(g(\sigma))d\sigma = \int_0^1 (F \circ f)(\sigma)d\sigma$$
$$= \int_0^1 F(f(\sigma))d\sigma = \int_0^1 F(\sigma)d\sigma$$

- For any $n \in \mathrm{IN}$, the function $\lambda\sigma.(n \cdot \sigma) - \lfloor n \cdot \sigma \rfloor$ is uniform. Proof:

$$\int_0^1 F((n \cdot \sigma) - \lfloor n \cdot \sigma \rfloor)\,d\sigma$$
$$= \sum_{i=0}^n \int_0^{\frac{1}{n}} F((n \cdot (\sigma + \tfrac{i}{n})) - \lfloor n \cdot (\sigma + \tfrac{i}{n}) \rfloor)\,d\sigma$$
$$= \sum_{i=0}^n \int_0^{\frac{1}{n}} F(n \cdot \sigma + i - \lfloor n \cdot \sigma + i \rfloor)\,d\sigma$$
$$= \sum_{i=0}^n \int_0^{\frac{1}{n}} F((n \cdot \sigma) - \lfloor n \cdot \sigma \rfloor)\,d\sigma$$
$$= n \cdot \int_0^{\frac{1}{n}} F((n \cdot \sigma) - \lfloor n \cdot \sigma \rfloor)\,d\sigma$$
$$= n \cdot \int_0^{\frac{1}{n}} F(n \cdot \sigma)\,d\sigma \quad \text{as } n \cdot \sigma < 1 \text{ for } \sigma < \tfrac{1}{n}$$
$$= \int_0^1 F(\sigma)\,d\sigma$$

This is almost enough to prove that all σ' in the semantics are uniform. Only the rule for `repeat` does not follow trivially. It may be difficult to prove uniformity for this rule (and it may not even be true). Furthermore, the suggested idea may not be the right way to approach the proof, so we leave a proof relating the two semantics as future work.

7   Implementation

The language has been implemented in Standard ML, using the Moscow ML implementation. Both the single-roll semantics and the probability semantics have been implemented.

The implementation of the single-roll semantics is very close to the formal semantics, just replacing the threaded random-number source by a pseudo-random-number generator (PRNG) that uses a global variable for the seed, and using sorted lists instead of finite maps to represent collections.

The implementation of the probability semantics is more interesting. For a given definition, it should print out the probability distribution for the defined die-roll method.

Since these distributions can have infinite support, we can't always do this. It is the repeat construction that can cause infinite support, so as long as we omit this, we can enumerate the collections that have nonzero probability and the probability for each of these. If we limit the number of iterations for repeat, we can keep using finite enumerations, so this is what we do. Section 8 will discuss an alternative to this choice.

The higher the limit on iterations is, the closer the computed distribution will be to the exact distribution. Hence, a high limit is good. The time to calculate the distribution can, however, increase dramatically with the number of iterations, so we have chosen to let the number be a parameter to the program, so the user can chose a trade-off between speed and precision.

The first prototype implementation represented distributions as sorted lists of collections with probabilities. This makes it fairly straight-forward to implement the required operations. It can, however, take extremely long time to calculate the distribution for some fairly simple definitions. As an example, consider the definition sum 10#d10. To calculate the distribution (which has support in the range 10 to 100), we first need to calculate all 92378 possible collections of 10 d10, add each up and, finally, combine the results to a single distribution. Instead, we could calculate the equivalent of d10+(d10+(d10+(···))), to a depth of 9 additions. The innermost (d10+d10) enumerates 55 collections of two d10 and adds the pairs to make a distribution with a support in 2...20. Adding the next d10 only looks at the 190 combinations of a d10 and a number in the range 2...20, and gives a new distribution with support 3...30, and so on until the last steps looks at the 820 ways of combining a d10 with a value in the range 9...90. The total number of steps is around 4000. This should not just be compared to the 92378 collections from above, since these collections have to be added up and the number of times each result occurs must be counted. The total is about a million steps, so the total enumeration is several hundred times slower than the alternative method.

The property we exploited here is that $sum(c_1 @ c_2) = (sum\ c_1) + (sum\ c_2)$. We can generalize this type of property in the following way:

Definition 1. *A function* $f : C \rightarrow C$ *is* linear, *iff for all collections* $c_1, c_2 : f(c_1 @ c_2) = (f\ c_1) @ (f\ c_2)$.

Note that a linear function must map the empty collection to the empty collection.

Definition 2. *A function* $f : C \rightarrow C$ *is* semi-linear, *iff there exists a function* $g : C \rightarrow C$ *and a value* i, *such that* $g(\{\}) = i$ *and for all values* v, $g(v, i) = g(i, v) = v$ *and for all collections* $c_1, c_2 : f(c_1 @ c_2) = g(f\ c_1, f\ c_2)$.

Filters (*e.g.*, <7) are linear. The sum and count operators are semi-linear with $g(x, y) = x + y$ and $i = 0$. The operator least n is semi-linear with $g(x, y) = least\ n\ (x @ y)$ and $i = \{\}$.

In order to exploit linear and semi-linear functions, we must delay the application of @ as long as possible and let $n \# d$ be treated as $d @ \cdots @ d$ with $n - 1$ delayed @'s. We do this by defining a data type for distributions:

$$\mathcal{D} = \|\mathcal{C}\|\ |\ (\mathcal{D} @ \mathcal{D})\ |\ (choose\ ]0, 1[\ \mathcal{D}\ \mathcal{D})$$

For a collection c, $\|c\|$ represents the distribution that has the value c with probability 1. The probability distribution function for $d_1@d_2$ is defined by $(d_1@d_2)c = \sum_{c_1 \subseteq c} d_1(c_1) \cdot d_2(c-c_1)$. The probability distribution function for *choose* is defined by $(choose\ p\ d_1\ d_2)c = p \cdot d_1(c) + (1.0-p) \cdot d_2(c)$. Note that $]0,1[$ is the open interval from 0 to 1. We don't include the endpoints, as no choice is necessary if $p = 0$ or $p = 1$.

We can now extend a linear function f to operate on this structure as well as on collections:

$$\begin{aligned}
f(\|c\|) &= \|f(c)\| \\
f(d_1@d_2) &= f(d_1)@f(d_2) \\
f(choose\ p\ d_1\ d_2) &= choose\ p\ f(d_1)\ f(d_2)
\end{aligned}$$

Semi-linear functions are somewhat more complex. We extend a semi-linear function f and its corresponding function g in the following way:

$$\begin{aligned}
f(\|c\|) &= \|f(c)\| \\
f(d_1@d_2) &= g(f(d_1), f(d_2)) \\
f(choose\ p\ d_1\ d_2) &= choose\ p\ f(d_1)\ f(d_2)
\end{aligned}$$

$$\begin{aligned}
g(\|c_1\|, \|c_2\|) &= \|g(c_1, c_2)\| \\
g(c_1, choose\ p\ c_2\ c_3) &= choose\ p\ g(c_1, c_2)\ g(c_1, c_3) \\
g(choose\ p\ c_1\ c_2, c_3) &= choose\ p\ g(c_1, c_3)\ g(c_2, c_3)
\end{aligned}$$

While linear functions are applied to arguments whose combined size is linear in the size of the data structure, semi-linear functions can in the worst case be applied to arguments with combined exponential size. It will, however, not be any worse than if the data structure was first flattened to a series of choices of collections before applying f to each collection. If all applications of a semi-linear function f and its related function g return a value of constant size, the combined size of arguments to f and g will be linear in the size of the data structure. This is, for example, the case for the sum and count operations, where the values are integers.

For operations that are neither linear nor semi-linear, we flatten the data structure to a right-associated choice of collections before applying the operator to each collection. We keep the list of choices sorted and combine choices of identical elements.

We also flatten the data structure when evaluating the binding of a let or repeat construction, as variables are bound to individual collections rather than to distributions.

As mentioned, we limit repetition to a user-specified cutoff. Additionally, we use simple memoization to avoid recomputing the body of the repeat construct for identical values and cutoffs.

The implementation doesn't model nontermination: Since repeat is bounded, the implementation will always terminate. Unlike in the probability semantics, applying an operator that requires a (positive) number to something that isn't a (positive) number causes an error message, even if this occurs with a probability that is less than 1. As such, the implementation of the probability semantics can be used as a kind of type check: If the probability semantics doesn't make an error message, no single roll can make such an error. The probability semantics ignores erroneous cases: The possibility of such just makes the probabilities add up to less than 1.

7.1   Obtaining the Implementation

The implementation can be obtained from the authors web page:
http://www.diku.dk/~torbenm/Dice.zip

The package contains the sources of the implementation and a manual with installation instructions and a more detailed description of the language.

8   What Could Be Done Differently?

We have chosen to let all values in **Roll** be collections, but at times we require these to be singletons. An alternative would be to have two different types – integers and collections – and let some constructions (*e.g.*, d n) return integers while other constructions (*e.g.*, $n\#e$) return collections. A subtype ordering could allow integers where collections are expected and a cast operator can test if a collection is a singleton and coerce it to an integer if true. We wouldn't get rid of all run-time testing, though, as some operations require positive or non-negative integers.

While this solution would be more elegant from a semantic viewpoint, it may make the language harder to grasp for nonprogrammers (who are the intended audience). Hence, we have chosen the dynamically typed approach.

The implementation of the probability semantics produces a distribution by enumerating all possible values and the probability for each. An alternative is to do it more like the semantics and produce a function from collections to probabilities. Given a single collection, this function would analyse the definition and calculate the probability of arriving at this value. This approach can give more accurate probabilities for definitions containing `repeat`. For example, the current semantics needs to limit the number of rerolls in a definition like

```
sum let x=3#d6 in repeat (count <4 x)#d6
```

and hence only compute an approximation. A function that needs to compute the chance of obtaining, for example, the value 42 can keep track of partial sums and stop when this exceeds 42, and hence calculate an exact probability.

Not all single probabilities can in this way be calculated exactly in finite time, though. If we modify the above definition to

```
sum <2 let x=3#d6 in repeat (count <4 x)#d6
```

no finite cutoff will yield precise information even for a single value. The single-value approach will also require considerably more time to compute a complete distribution, so it should only be used as a supplement to the current method, if at all.

9   Related Work

A 10 year old newsgroup posting [7] describes an idea for a language for expressing die rolls. The meat of the idea is evident from the following extract:

```
Die language:
 In this descriptive language, the lower case letters represent
 parameters which are discussed in the definition of the term.

=_dfun_  summation of the scores of dfun into 1 number
S(_dfun_) same as equals, summation of values of _dfun_

D(_range_) generates a random number within _range_, inclusive.

x(_dfun_) generates x occurrences of _dfun_, keeping each occurrence
  separate from the others (see examples below).

B(b,_dfun_) keep the best b occurrences of _dfun_, discarding the rest

L(l,_dfun_) keep the least l occurrences of _dfun_, discarding the rest

*,/  multiply/divide per left to right rules
+,-  add/subtract per left to right rules
```

It can be seen that this language has equivalents to sum, d, #, least, largest and arithmetic operators from **Roll**. It lacks the more advanced features of filters and repeated rolls, though. There is no indication that the language was ever implemented. Also, its stated intention was only to make a specified number of rolls according to the definition, not to calculate probabilities.

In [5], an extension of the lambda calculus with probabilistic choice is discussed, and a monad-based semantics is shown. By instantiating the monad in different ways, sampling, probabilities and support can be calculated. While the language is different, the approach to sampling and calculating probability distributions is similar to what we have done. The stochastic lambda calculus (being typed) lacks recursion, so the issue of nontermination doesn't come up. The authors also note that calculating product spaces (the equivalent of @) can take disproportionate time and discuss a way of translating expressions into what they call *measure terms*, which keep the parts of a product space separate as long as possible. The method is more general than the method we used in the implementation of **Roll**, but it is also considerably more complicated.

10   Conclusion

Roll is a flexible and powerful tool for defining die-rolls and should be able to specify almost any die-roll method, even methods involving unbounded rerolling. Simple methods are very easy to describe and even moderately complex methods can be described in one line of text.

The prototype implementation has been released to the game design community (through the mailing list rpg-create@yahoogroups.com and the newsgroup rec.games.design) and has generated some interest, including from a major producer of role-playing games.

Correspondence with the latter has shown a shortcoming with the current implementation: At present, the program shows the distribution of a roll with fixed parameters for such things as the number of dice and treshold values. However, in order to explore a design space, the game designers would like to see a table where the probability of certain outcomes is shown for a variety of design choices, *e.g.*, as a two-dimensional table that cross-indexes the number of dice with a treshold value to find the probability of getting at least a certain result. This problem is probably best handled by adding a formatting/scripting language on top of **Roll** instead of extending the core language, so future work will address the design of such.

Acknowledgements. Thanks to Niels H. Christensen for pointing me to [7] and to Andrzej Filinski for discussions about the semantic domains.

References

1. Stewart Culin. Dominoes: a form of dice.
   http://www.ahs.uwaterloo.ca/
   ~museum/Archive/Culin/Dice1893/formof.html.
2. George Hart. The five platonic solids.
   http://www.georgehart.com/virtual-polyhedra/platonic-info.html.
3. George Hart. Neolithic carved stone polyhedra.
   http://www.georgehart.com/virtual-polyhedra/neolithic.html.
4. Torben Æ. Mogensen. Fid 223: Analysis of die-roll methods.
   http://www.rpg.net/news+reviews/columns/fiddly18jun02.html, 2002.
5. Norman Ramsey and Avi Pfeffer. Stochastic lambda calculus and monads of probability distributions. In *POPL'02*, pages 154–164. ACM, 2002.
6. Mark T. Rigby. A selection of ancient egyptian games.
   http://homepage.powerup.com.au/~ancient/museum11.htm.
7. Coyt D. Watters. Dice equation language.
   http://groups.google.com/groups
   ?selm=1992Jun12.131256.25628%40magnus.acs.ohio-state.edu, 1992.

Reconstructing the Evolutionary History of Indo-European Languages Using Answer Set Programming

Esra Erdem[1], Vladimir Lifschitz[2], Luay Nakhleh[2], and Donald Ringe[3]

[1] Department of Computer Science
University of Toronto, Toronto, ON M5S 3H5, Canada
[2] Department of Computer Sciences
University of Texas at Austin, Austin, TX 78712, USA
[3] Department of Linguistics
University of Pennsylvania, Philadelphia, PA 19104, USA

Abstract. The evolutionary history of languages can be modeled as a tree, called a phylogeny, where the leaves represent the extant languages, the internal vertices represent the ancestral languages, and the edges represent the genetic relations between the languages. Languages not only inherit characteristics from their ancestors but also sometimes borrow them from other languages. Such borrowings can be represented by additional non-tree edges. This paper addresses the problem of computing a small number of additional edges that turn a phylogeny into a "perfect phylogenetic network". To solve this problem, we use answer set programming, which represents a given computational problem as a logic program whose answer sets correspond to solutions. Using the answer set solver SMODELS, with some heuristics and optimization techniques, we have generated a few conjectures regarding the evolution of Indo-European languages.

1 Introduction

The evolutionary history of languages can be modeled as a tree, called a "phylogeny" (or an "evolutionary tree"), where the leaves represent the extant languages, the internal vertices represent the ancestral languages, and the edges represent the "genetic" relations between the languages. For instance, when we say "French and Italian are both descendants of Latin" we refer to such a tree where French and Italian are denoted by leaves, and Latin is denoted by an internal vertex that is a common ancestor of these two leaves.

Reconstructing phylogenies for various language families is a major endeavor in historical linguistics, but is also of interest to archaeologists, human geneticists, and physical anthropologists. For instance, an accurate reconstruction of the evolutionary history of certain languages can help us answer questions about human migrations, the time that certain artifacts were developed, when ancient people began to use horses in agriculture [4,5,11,15].

V. Dahl and P. Wadler (Eds.): PADL 2003, LNCS 2562, pp. 160–176, 2003.
© Springer-Verlag Berlin Heidelberg 2003

Languages not only inherit characteristics from their ancestors but also sometimes borrow them from other languages. In such cases, trees are not a fully adequate model of evolution. Nakhleh *et al.* [7] make this idea precise by defining "perfect phylogenetic networks." They start with a phylogeny built automatically from a dataset describing characteristics of Indo-European languages, and show how some perfect phylogenetic networks can be obtained from it by adding a small number of new edges.

This paper addresses the same computational problem—computing a small set of additional edges that turn a given phylogeny into a perfect phylogenetic network. To solve this problem, we use answer set programming [6,8,3]—a new form of declarative programming based on "answer sets" (or stable models) [1,2]. The idea of answer set programming is to represent a computational problem as a logic program whose answer sets correspond to solutions to the given problem. There are systems specifically designed to compute the answer sets of a logic program. These systems are called answer set solvers. For instance, SMODELS [12] is one of the answer set solvers that are currently available. In the main part of this paper, we assume that the reader has some familiarity with the input language of SMODELS.

In the following, we will first describe the problem mathematically (Section 2) and then formalize it in the language of SMODELS (Section 3). Useful heuristics and optimization techniques will be discussed in Sections 4–6. After that, we will describe the dataset we used to find some explanations to the evolutionary history of the Indo-European languages and present the explanations computed by SMODELS (Section 7). Proofs of theorems can be found in the full version of this paper available at http://www.cs.toronto.edu/~esra/papers/ie.pdf.

2   Problem Description

We describe the problem of computing perfect phylogenetic networks built on a given phylogeny as a graph problem. Therefore, we first introduce some definitions related to graphs.

Recall that a *directed graph (digraph)* is an ordered pair (V, E) where V is a set and E is a binary relation on V. In a digraph (V, E), the elements of V are called *vertices*, and the elements E are called the *edges* of the digraph.

In a digraph, we say that the edge (u, v) is *incident from u* and is *incident into v*. The *out-degree* of a vertex is the number of edges incident from it, and the *in-degree* of a vertex is the number of edges incident into it.

In a digraph (V, E), a *path* from a vertex u to a vertex u' is a sequence $v_0, v_1, \ldots, v_k$ of vertices such that $u = v_0$ and $u' = v_k$, and $(v_{i-1}, v_i) \in E$ for $1 \leq i \leq k$. If there is a path from a vertex u to a vertex v then we say that v is *reachable from u*. If V' is a subset of V, and there exists a path from u to v whose vertices belong to V' then we say that v is *reachable from u in V'*.

A *rooted tree* is a digraph with a vertex of in-degree 0, called the *root*, such that every vertex different from the root has in-degree 1 and is reachable from the root. In a rooted tree, a vertex of out-degree 0 is called a *leaf.*

A digraph (V', E') is a *subgraph* of a digraph (V, E) if $V' \subseteq V$ and $E' \subseteq E$.

A *phylogeny* is a triple of the form (V, E, f) where (V, E) is a finite rooted tree and f is a function from $L \times I$ to S, where L is the set of leaves of (V, E), and I, S are finite sets.

We are interested in the problem of turning a phylogeny into a perfect phylogenetic network by adding at most k bidirectional edges. Formally, the problem is defined as follows:

Input: A phylogeny (V, E, f), with $f : L \times I \to S$; a nonnegative integer k.

Output: a function $g : V \times I \to S$ and a symmetric irreflexive binary relation N on V such that

(i) $g|_{L \times I} = f$,
(ii) for all $i \in I$ and $s \in S$, if $V_{is} = \{u \in V : g(u, i) = s\}$ is not empty then
      $(V, E \cup N)$ has a subgraph with the set V_{is} of vertices that is a rooted tree,
(iii) for every edge $(u, v) \in E$, u is not reachable from v in $(V, E \cup N)$,
(iv) the cardinality of N is at most $2k$.

If (V, E, N, g) satisfies conditions (i)–(iii) then we say that it is a *perfect (phylogenetic) network built on* (V, E, f). The problem described above is essentially the *Minimum Increment to Perfect Phylogenetic Network (MIPPN)* problem — an important computational problem posed in [7]. In place of (iv), MIPPN as defined in that paper includes a minimality condition.

Intuitively, the edges of the phylogeny (V, E, f) show the "genetic" relations between languages; each leaf of this phylogeny corresponds to an extant language; the internal vertices represent ancestral languages. The languages are identified by a set of specific observable discrete characteristics, called "(qualitative) characters" (such as grammatical features, unusual sound changes, and cognate classes for different meanings). For every extant language, function f maps every character to a "state"; we say that the leaves of the tree (V, E) are "labeled" by f. Function g extends f to ancestral languages (condition (i)).

Languages can affect each other by transmitting some linguistic properties due to contact. These contacts are not represented on the given phylogeny. They correspond to the elements of N in a perfect network (V, E, N, g) built on (V, E, f). A perfect network explains how every state of every character evolved from its original occurrence in some "root" language (condition (ii)). Languages cannot borrow characteristics from their descendants (condition (iii)). We are only interested in the perfect networks where the number of postulated borrowings is small (condition (iv)), because inheritance of characteristics of a language from its ancestors is far more probable than acquiring them through borrowing. In the case of the phylogeny of Indo-European languages discussed in Section 7 the fact that a small number of edges is sufficient was established in a preliminary analysis done by Tandy Warnow and Donald Ringe.

For instance, consider the phylogeny presented in Figure 1(a) that is reconstructed for 4 extant languages A, B, C, D. There is one character, i.e., $|I| = 1$, and there are two states ($S = \{0, 1\}$). The leaves of the phylogeny are labeled: $f(A, 1) = f(C, 1) = 0$ and $f(B, 1) = f(D, 1) = 1$. A perfect network built on this

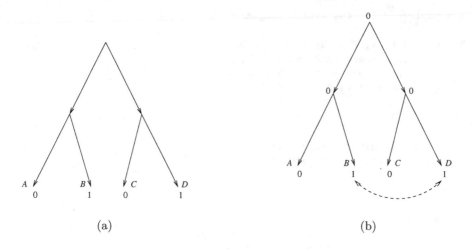

(a)   (b)

Fig. 1. A phylogeny (a), and a perfect network (b) built on it with $N = \{(B, D), (D, B)\}$.

phylogeny is presented in Figure 1(b). The new bidirectional edge is added to make the vertices labeled 1 connected via a rooted tree, i.e., to satisfy condition (ii).

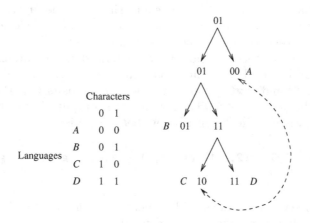

Fig. 2. A perfect network.

Another example, with two characters ($I = \{0, 1\}$) and two states ($S = \{0, 1\}$), is presented in Figure 2. The new edge is added to make the vertices labeled 0 at Character 1 connected via a rooted tree.

The phylogeny of Indo-European languages described in Section 7 below is a tree with 24 leaves, 370 characters, and 74 states.

```
% a phylogeny for the extant languages A, B, C, D:

% denote A by 1, B by 2, C by 3, D by 4,
%          the parent of A and B by 5,
%          the parent of C and D by 6,
%          the root by 0.

vertex(0..6).

edge(0,5). edge(0,6). edge(5,1).
edge(5,2). edge(6,3). edge(6,4).

state(0;1).

character(0).

f(1,0,0). f(2,0,1). f(3,0,0). f(4,0,1).
```

Fig. 3. Input file describing the phylogeny of Figure 1.

3   Presenting the Problem to SMODELS

A phylogeny is defined by the "domain predicates"[1] vertex(X), edge(X,Y), state(S), character(C), f(X,C,S) (expressing that the function f maps the leaf X and the character C to the state S). For instance, the phylogeny of Figure 1 is described to SMODELS by the file presented in Figure 3.[2]

The solutions of the problem are characterized by the atoms of the form g(X,C,S) (expressing that the function g maps the vertex X and the character C to the state S) and new(X,Y) (expressing that the pairs (X,Y) and (Y,X) are elements of the set N; X < Y). For instance, the output of SMODELS describing the solution presented in Figure 1(b) (with $I = \{0\}$) is:

```
g(0,0,0) g(1,0,0) g(2,0,1) g(3,0,0) g(4,0,1) g(5,0,0) g(6,0,0)
new(2,4)
```

First we describe conditions on the labeling g of the vertices. According to (i), g coincides with f where the latter is defined:

```
g(X,C,S) :- f(X,C,S).
```

---

[1] Intuitively, the domain predicates are the predicates that are used to find all possible variable bindings during grounding. See [13, Definition 8, page 7] for a definition of a domain predicate.

[2] In this file, the expression vertex(0..6). has the same meaning as vertex(0). ... vertex(6).; the expression state(0;1). has the same meaning as state(0). state(1). [14].

Every internal vertex should be labeled by exactly one state for each character:[3]

```
1 {g(X,C,S): state(S)} 1 :-
       vertex(X), not leaf(X), character(C).
```

Then, we add at most k pairs of edges between the vertices of this phylogeny:

```
{new(X,Y): vertex(X;Y): X < Y} maxE.
```

(maxE represents the value of k).

However, due to (iii), we cannot add such a pair between two vertices if adding it will create a cycle that includes at least one edge of the given phylogeny. To express this condition, we first define the extended set of edges $E \cup N$ by the rules

```
an_edge(X,Y) :- edge(X,Y).
an_edge(X,Y) :- new(X,Y), vertex(X;Y).
an_edge(X,Y) :- new(Y,X), vertex(X;Y).
```

Then we define the binary predicate directed_path as the transitive closure of an_edge, and impose the constraint

```
:- directed_path(X,Y), edge(Y,X).                          (*)
```

Finally, we need to make sure that (ii) holds. For that we use the following proposition:

Proposition 1 *For any finite digraph (V, E), and any set $V' \subseteq V$, the following conditions are equivalent:*

(a) there exists a subgraph of (V, E) with the set V' of vertices that is a rooted tree,

(b) there exists a vertex $v \in V'$ such that every vertex in V' is reachable from v in V'.

This fact shows that condition (ii) in the statement of the MIPPN problem can be equivalently expressed as follows:

(ii') for all $i \in I$ and $s \in S$, if $V_{is} = \{u \in V : g(u, i) = s\}$ is not empty then there exists a vertex v in V_{is} such that every vertex in V_{is} is reachable from v in V_{is}.

We consider pairs (i, s) for which some vertex is labeled by state s at character i, so that V_{is} is not empty. After picking an element v of V_{is}, and defining reachability of vertices in V_{is} from v by the predicate reachable, we express (ii') by the constraint

---

[3] In this rule, for every internal vertex X and for every character C, the expression
1 {g(X,C,S): state(S)} 1 describes a set of atoms of the form g(X,C,S) where S is a state whose cardinality is at least 1 and at most 1. Such expressions are called "cardinality constraints" [9, page 5].

```
:- g(X,C,S), not reachable(X,C,S), character(C),
   state(S), vertex(X).
```

The answer sets for the program described above correspond to the solutions of the MIPPN problem. We will call it "the basic program."

We can use SMODELS with the basic program to solve small instances of the MIPPN problem. Larger data sets, such as the one described in Section 7, require the use of some heuristics and optimization techniques. Some of these techniques are not complete, that is, do not allow us, generally, to find all solutions. We will discuss them in the following sections.

4   Preprocessing

Sometimes the MIPPN problem for a given phylogeny can be simplified by making its set I of characters smaller. If (V, E, N, g) is a perfect network built on a phylogeny (V, E, f) then, for any subset J of I, $(V, E, N, g|_{V \times J})$ is obviously a perfect network built on $(V, E, f|_{L \times J})$. Proposition 2 below shows, for some special choice of J, that every perfect network built on $(V, E, f|_{L \times J})$ can be extended to a network built on (V, E, f).

Consider a phylogeny (V, E, f), with $f : L \times I \to S$. We say that a character $j \in I$ is *inessential* if there exists a perfect network $(V, E, \emptyset, g)$ built on $(V, E, f|_{L \times \{j\}})$. For instance, in the phylogeny of Figure 2, the first of the two characters is inessential. In the phylogeny of Indo-European languages described in Section 7, 352 characters out of 370 are inessential.

Proposition 2 *Let (V, E, f) be a phylogeny, with $f : L \times I \to S$, and let I' be the set of its inessential characters. There exists a function $g' : V \times I' \to S$ such that, for every perfect network (V, E, N, g) built on $(V, E, f|_{L \times (I \setminus I')})$, $(V, E, N, g \cup g')$ is a perfect network built on (V, E, f).*

This theorem shows that the sets N in solutions to the MIPPN problem for a phylogeny (V, E, f) are identical to the sets N in the solutions to the same problem for the smaller phylogeny $(V, E, f|_{L \times (I \setminus I')})$ (although the functions g in these solutions are, generally, different).

Another way to make a given phylogeny smaller is to check whether it has an internal vertex v such that all leaves descending from v are labeled in the same way. In Figure 4, for instance, this condition holds for the common parent of $A1$ and $A2$. If such a vertex v is found, then we remove all its descendants from the tree, so that v turns into a leaf. The labeling of v in the reduced phylogeny (V', E', f') is the same as the common labeling of the descendants of v in the given phylogeny. For instance, this process turns Figure 4 into the phylogeny of Figure 2. This process is similar to how [7] collapses the given phylogeny to a smaller one.

In our work on the phylogeny of Indo-European languages with 24 leaves, we repeated this process, along with other preprocessing steps, several times, and reduced the given tree to a tree with 13 leaves.

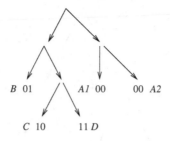

Fig. 4. A phylogeny.

Every solution to the MIPPN problem for the pruned phylogeny can be extended to a solution for the original phylogeny:

Proposition 3 *Let (V, E, f) be a phylogeny, with $f : L \times I \rightarrow S$, and (V', E', f') be the phylogeny obtained from it as described above. Let (V', E', N, g') be a perfect network built on (V', E', f'). Then there exists a function g from $V \times I$ to S with $g|_{V' \times I} = g'$ such that (V, E, N, g) is a perfect network built on (V, E, f).*

However this preprocessing is not complete, i.e., there may be a solution to the MIPPN problem such that its set N of new edges will not be found after pruning vertices. For instance, the perfect network built on the phylogeny of Figure 4 in which new edges connect C with $A1$ and with $A2$ will not be generated after $A1$ and $A2$ are removed from the tree.

5   Partial Perfect Networks and Essential States

The basic program (Section 3) can be improved using "partial" perfect phylogenetic networks—a generalization of the "total" version of this concept defined in Section 2.

Let (V, E, f) be a phylogeny, with $f : L \times I \rightarrow S$. A *partial perfect (phylogenetic) network* built on this phylogeny is a quadruple of the form (V, E, N, g), where N is a symmetric irreflexive binary relation on V, and g is a partial mapping of $V \times I$ to S such that the domain of g contains $L \times I$, and conditions (i)–(iii) from Section 2 are satisfied. For instance, a partial perfect network built on the phylogeny of Figure 1 can be defined by

$$N = \{(A, C), (C, A), (B, D), (D, B)\}, \ g = f$$

(Figure 5).

Every partial perfect network can be extended to a perfect network:

Proposition 4 *Let (V, E, f) be a phylogeny, with $f : L \times I \rightarrow S$. For any partial perfect network (V, E, N, g) built on this phylogeny there exists an extension g' of g to $V \times I$ such that (V, E, N, g') is a perfect network built on the same phylogeny.*

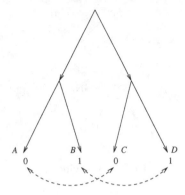

Fig. 5. A partial perfect network built on the phylogeny of Figure 1 with $N = \{(A,C),(C,A),(B,D),(D,B)\}$, $g = f$.

Proposition 5 below shows, on the other hand, that every perfect network can be obtained by extending a partial perfect network satisfying a certain condition, expressed in terms of "essential states." Let (V, E, f) be a phylogeny, with $f : L \times I \to S$. We say that a state $s \in S$ is *essential* with respect to a character $j \in I$ if there exist two different leaves l_1 and l_2 in L such that $f(l_1, j) = f(l_2, j) = s$. For instance, in the phylogeny of Figure 6(a), State 3 is essential, and States 1 and 2 are not. There is no need to use inessential states to label internal vertices:

Proposition 5 *Let (V, E, f) be a phylogeny, with $f : L \times I \to S$. For any perfect network (V, E, N, g') built on this phylogeny there exists a partial mapping g of $V \times I$ to S such that*

- *(V,E,N,g) is a partial perfect network built on the same phylogeny,*
- *g' is an extension of g to $V \times I$, and*
- *$g(v, i)$ is essential with respect to i whenever $v \notin L$.*

For instance, if (V, E, N, g') is the perfect network of Figure 6(a), then the partial perfect network of Figure 6(b) satisfies the conditions of this theorem as (V, E, N, g). In this partial perfect network, inessential states 1 and 2 are not used for labeling internal vertices.

Propositions 4 and 5 show that the problem of computing a perfect network built on a given phylogeny is closely related to the problem of computing a partial perfect network (V, E, N, g) built on this phylogeny such that $g(v, i)$ is essential with respect to i for every internal vertex v and every character i. The sets N in the solutions to this modification of the problem are identical to the sets N in the solutions to the original problem (although the functions g are, generally, different).

For instance, in the phylogeny of Indo-European languages described in Section 7, the range of f for Character 39 contains 11 elements from S, and only 3 of them are essential. When we consider essential states and want to find a

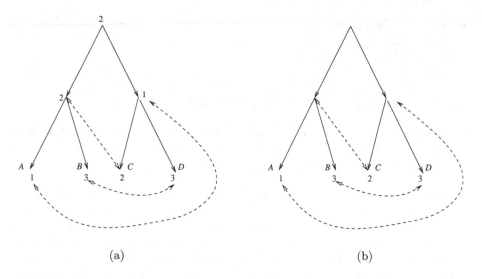

Fig. 6. A perfect network (a), and a partial perfect network (b) obtained from it via Proposition 5.

partial network built on the given phylogeny for this character, the computation time reduces from 16 seconds to 5 seconds.

To adapt the basic program (Section 3) to the modification of the problem described above, we replace

```
1 {g(X,C,S): state(S)} 1 :-
        vertex(X), not leaf(X), character(C).
```

with the rule

```
{g(X,C,S): essential_state(C,S)} 1 :-
        vertex(X), not leaf(X), character(C).
```

where `essential_state` is defined by the rule

```
essential_state(C,S) :- f(X,C,S), character(C),
        f(X1,C,S), X != X1, vertex(X;X1).
```

6   A Divide-and-Conquer Strategy

Recall that a perfect network built on a phylogeny (V, E, f) is a quadruple (V, E, N, g) satisfying conditions (i)–(iii) from Section 2. If (V, E, N, g) satisfies the first two of these conditions, we will call it an *almost perfect network*.

The divide-and-conquer approach we use is based on the following fact: if, for each $j \in I$, (V, E, N_j, g_j) is an almost perfect network built on $(V, E, f|_{V \times \{j\}})$ then $(V, E, \bigcup_j N_j, \bigcup_j g_j)$ is an almost perfect network built on (V, E, f). In view of this fact, solutions to the MIPPN problem can be generated by finding such networks (V, E, N_j, g_j) for all characters j and checking that $(V, E, \bigcup_j N_j, \bigcup_j g_j)$ satisfies conditions (iii) and (iv).

Proposition 6 below shows that this process can generate every *minimal* solution—every network (V, E, N, g) in which the set N of new edges cannot be replaced by its proper subset without violating condition (ii).

Proposition 6 *Let (V, E, N, g) be a minimal almost perfect network built on (V, E, f). For every $j \in I$, there exists a minimal almost perfect network $(V, E, N_j, g|_{V \times \{j\}})$ built on $(V, E, f|_{L \times \{j\}})$ such that $\bigcup_{j \in I} N_j = N$.*

To compute almost perfect networks (V, E, N_j, g_j) for each character j, we use the basic program without the definition of `directed_path` and without constraint (*). We can find all such networks using the `compute all {}` statement of SMODELS. However, there may be more than one such network with the same set N of new edges where the labelings g of the vertices differ; we are only interested in solutions with different sets of new edges. For this reason, we wrote a script that calls SMODELS repeatedly to compute one value of N at a time. To ensure that every next N_j computed by SMODELS is different from the sets computed so far, we add appropriate constraints to the program at every iteration. For instance, if the first call to SMODELS produces `new(1,2)`, `new(3,4)` then the constraint

```
:- new(1,2), new(3,4).
```

will be added to the program when SMODELS is called for the second time, so that SMODELS will now compute an answer set that does not contain {`new(1,2)`, `new(3,4)`}. To compute all minimal almost perfect networks with at most $2k$ new edges, we start with `maxE=0` and increment `maxE` by 1 until it reaches k.

The verification of conditions (iii) and (iv) for the networks $(V, E, \bigcup_j N_j, \bigcup_j g_j)$ generated from the almost perfect networks (V, E, N_j, g_j) is performed by SMODELS programs.

This divide-and-conquer strategy can be extended to partial networks (Section 5) in a straightforward way.

7   The Evolutionary History of the Indo-European Languages

We have applied the computational methods described above to the phylogeny of Indo-European languages that was generated automatically [10] on the basis of a dataset assembled by Donald Ringe and Ann Taylor, who are specialists in Indo-European historical linguistics, with the advice of other specialist colleagues. Figure 7 shows the tree (V, E) of this phylogeny. Its leaves correspond to the following 24 Indo-European languages: Hittite (HI), Luvian (LU), Lycian (LY), Tocharian A (TA), Tocharian B (TB), Vedic (VE), Avestan (AV), Old Persian (PE), Classical Armenian (AR), Ancient Greek (GK), Latin (LA), Oscan (OS),

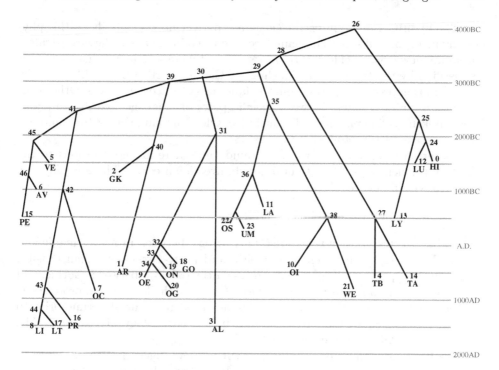

Fig. 7. The phylogeny obtained from the Indo-European dataset.

Umbrian (UM), Gothic (GO), Old Norse (ON), Old English (OE), Old High German (OG), Old Irish (OI), Welsh (WE), Old Church Slavonic (OC), Old Prussian (PR), Lithuanian (LI), Latvian (LT), and Albanian (AL). All these languages are "historic," that is, recorded, and the position of every leaf vertex against the time line in Figure 7 corresponds to the earliest period at which there is substantial attestation of the corresponding language.

The internal vertices of this tree represent "prehistoric" languages, or "protolanguages," which were reconstructed by comparison of their descendants. For instance, Vertex 38 is proto-Celtic, reconstructed by comparison of Old Irish and Welsh. The position of every internal vertex against the time line corresponds to the time period when the corresponding protolanguage split up into daughter languages, each spoken by a different speech community.

There are 370 characters in this phylogeny.[4] Out of 370 characters, 22 are phonological characters encoding regular sound changes that have occurred in the prehistory of various languages, 15 are morphological characters encoding details of inflection (or, in one case, word formation), and 333 are lexical characters defined by meanings on a basic word list.

---

[4] We disregard the 20 characters that take into account multiple character coding and parallel development.

The SMODELS program used to generate perfect networks built on this phylogeny incorporated several domain-specific constraints. One of these constraints prohibits new edges incident with Vertex 24 and its descendants; this constraint is justified by the fact that the labelings of the leaves HI, LU and LY are "disjoint," in their essential parts, from the labelings of the other leaves. Other constraints prohibit contacts between specific pairs of languages which, we know, were spoken at different times. For instance, Old Prussian (Vertex 16) could not be in contact with proto-Celtic (Vertex 38).

Under these constraints, we have found that there are no solutions to the MIPPN problem with fewer than 5 new bidirectional edges. There is only one solution with 5 new edges:

- (32,38) (38,40) (32,43) (18,34) (7,44) .

According to this solution there are 5 borrowings: between proto-Germanic and proto-Celtic (32,38), between proto-Celtic and proto-Greco-Armenian (38,40), between and proto-Germanic and proto-Baltic (32,43), between Gothic and proto-West-Germanic (18,34), and between Old Church Slavonic and proto-East-Baltic (7,44). Each of these contacts is understood to occur at a time prior to the dates assigned to the two languages in the chronology of Figure 7. The approximate times of these contacts are shown in Figure 8.

We have also computed 52 solutions with 6 new edges; 8 of these solutions do not include any borrowings that would be historically implausible:

- (32,38) (31,36) (27,41) (32,43) (18,34) (7,44)
- (32,38) (31,36) (35,40) (32,43) (18,34) (7,44)
- (32,38) (31,36) (36,40) (32,43) (18,34) (7,44)
- (32,38) (31,36) (27,42) (32,43) (18,34) (7,44)
- (32,38) (31,36) (31,40) (32,43) (18,34) (7,44)
- (32,38) (31,36) (27,45) (32,43) (18,34) (7,44)
- (7,27) (32,38) (38,40) (32,42) (18,34) (7,44)
- (32,38) (38,40) (3,7) (32,42) (18,34) (7,44)

In addition to the phylogeny of Figure 7, we considered its modification in which additional internal vertices are introduced—one vertex in the middle of every edge. This extension reflects the possibility of ancestral languages not represented in the original phylogeny, and it was used as the starting point in the work reported in [7]. The calculations described in that paper are limited to the case when new edges are inserted between additional vertices only. To facilitate comparison with that work, we included the same restriction in our program.

For the modified problem, we have computed 11 solutions with 5 new edges; we found among them 3 solutions historically plausible:

- (47,65) (51,64) (51,56) (65,68) (57,60)
- (47,65) (52,56) (52,64) (65,68) (57,60)
- (51,61) (51,56) (56,66) (65,68) (57,60)

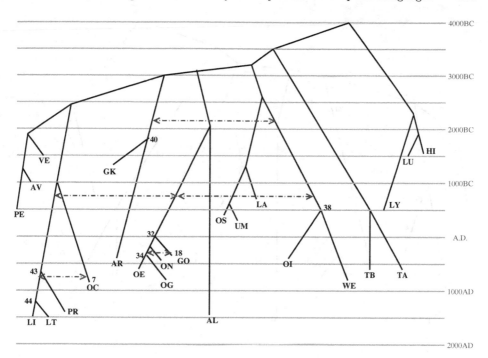

Fig. 8. Contacts between Indo-European languages according to the 5-edge solution.

For instance, the first solution is presented in Figure 9. Note that the last solution is very close to the 5-edge solution for the phylogeny of Figure 7.

In [7], the authors excluded Characters 116 and 292 from the original list of qualitative characters. As a result, their dataset included 16 essential characters, and not 18 as ours. Accordingly, the problem they arrived at is smaller than the one that we obtained after preprocessing.

They compute 15 perfect phylogenetic networks, with 3 additional edges, of which these two are plausible:

- (47,65) (51,64) (51,56)
- (47,65) (52,56) (52,64)

The first of these solutions is presented in Figure 3 of [7].

These two solutions can be obtained from our first two solutions using the following proposition:

Proposition 7 *Let $(V, E, \cup_j N_j, \cup_j g_j)$ be a minimal perfect network built on (V, E, f) where, for each $j \in I$, (V, E, N_j, g_j) is a minimal perfect network built on $(V, E, f|_{L \times \{j\}})$. Let k be an element of I such that, for every $i \in I$ different from k, $N_i \cap N_k$ is empty. Then $(V, E, \cup_{j \neq k} N_j, \cup_{j \neq k} g_j)$ is a minimal perfect network built on $(V, E, f|_{L \times (I \setminus \{k\})})$.*

In our first two solutions, for Character 116, $N_{116} = \{(57, 60)\}$, and, for every $j \neq 116$, $N_{116} \cap N_j$ is empty. Similarly, for Character 116, $N_{292} = \{(65, 68)\}$,

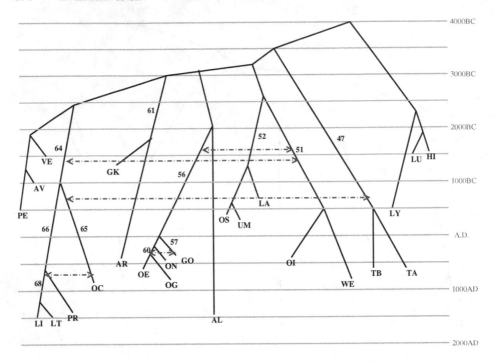

Fig. 9. The phylogeny of Figure 7 with additional vertices.

and, for every $j \neq 292$, $N_{292} \cap N_j$ is empty. Therefore, using the proposition above twice, we can obtain the first solution of [7] presented above.

Conversely our first 2 solutions can be obtained from the 2 solutions from [7] using the following fact:

If, for each $j \in I$, (V, E, N_j, g_j) is an almost perfect network built on $(V, E, f|_{V \times \{j\}})$ then $(V, E, \bigcup_j N_j, \bigcup_j g_j)$ is an almost perfect network built on (V, E, f).

To sum up, the collection of conjectures about the evolutionary history of Indo-European languages generated in our experiments is different from what is found in [7] in two ways. First, we looked for the perfect networks built on the phylogeny of Figure 7 without additional vertices, and found several historically plausible solutions. Second, we considered 18 characters, including Characters 116 and 292.

8   Conclusion

The Minimum Increment to Perfect Phylogenetic Network problem discussed in this paper is a combinatorial search problem well suited to the use of answer set programming. But the basic SMODELS program for the MIPPN problem will produce solutions reasonably fast only if the given phylogeny is small. Several ideas helped us adapt this program to a large phylogeny of Indo-European languages.

One idea is to make the given phylogeny smaller by removing its inessential characters and some of its vertices. This kind of preprocessing is somewhat similar to reducing every language group to a single vertex in [7]. The difference is that our preprocessing is domain-independent—it is defined for any phylogeny. Second, there is no need to use inessential states for labeling the internal vertices of the tree. Finally, a divide-and-conquer strategy allowed us to replace a single run of SMODELS by a series of invocations that solve subproblems of the given problem.

The input program included some domain-specific information about the impossibility of contacts between languages spoken at different times. These constraints helped us further reduce the computation time. Even so, computing the results reported in this paper involved thousands of calls to SMODELS and took more than a week of CPU time. In spite of the presence of several constraints of this kind, most perfect networks computed by our program turned out to be impossible or implausible for historical reasons. To weed out unacceptable solutions, we had to analyze each solution carefully on the basis of the conclusions of earlier research in historical linguistics.

Acknowledgments. We are grateful to Tandy Warnow for useful discussions related to the subject of this paper, and to Selim Erdoğan for comments on a preliminary version. The first two authors were partially supported by the National Science Foundation under grant IIS-9732744 and by Texas Higher Education Coordinating Board under grant 003658-0322-2001.

References

1. Michael Gelfond and Vladimir Lifschitz. The stable model semantics for logic programming. In Robert Kowalski and Kenneth Bowen, editors, *Logic Programming: Proc. Fifth Int'l Conf. and Symp.*, pages 1070–1080, 1988.
2. Michael Gelfond and Vladimir Lifschitz. Logic programs with classical negation. In David Warren and Peter Szeredi, editors, *Logic Programming: Proc. Seventh Int'l Conf.*, pages 579–597, 1990.
3. Vladimir Lifschitz. Answer set programming and plan generation. *Artificial Intelligence*, 138:39–54, 2002.
4. V.H. Mair, editor. *The Bronze Age and Early Iron Age Peoples of Eastern Central Asia*. Institute for the Study of Man, Washington, 1998.
5. J.P. Mallory. *In Search of the Indo-Europeans*. Thames and Hudson, London, 1989.
6. Victor Marek and Mirosław Truszczyński. Stable models and an alternative logic programming paradigm. In *The Logic Programming Paradigm: a 25-Year Perspective*, pages 375–398. Springer Verlag, 1999.
7. L. Nakhleh, D. Ringe, and T. Warnow. Perfect phylogenetic networks: A new methodology for reconstructing the evolutionary history of natural languages. Unpublished manuscript, 2002.
8. Ilkka Niemelä. Logic programs with stable model semantics as a constraint programming paradigm. *Annals of Mathematics and Artificial Intelligence*, 25:241–273, 1999.

9. Ilkka Niemelä and Patrik Simons. Extending the Smodel system with cardinality and weight constraints. In Jack Minker, editor, *Logic-Based Artificial Intelligence.* Kluwer, 2000.
10. D. Ringe, T. Warnow, and A. Taylor. Indo-European and computational cladistics. *Transactions of the Philological Society*, 100(1):59–129, 2002.
11. R.G. Roberts, R. Jones, and M.A. Smith. Thermoluminescence dating of a 50,000-year-old human occupation site in Northern Australia. *Science*, 345:153–156, 1990.
12. Patrik Simons, Ilkka Niemelä, and Timo Soininen. Extending and implementing the stable model semantics. *Artificial Intelligence*, 138:181–234, 2002.
13. Tommi Syrjänen. Omega-restricted logic programs. In *Proceedings of the 6th International Conference on Logic Programming and Nonmonotonic Reasoning (LP-NMR)*, 2001.
14. Tommi Syrjänen. Lparse 1.0 user's manual,[5] 2002.
15. J.P. White and J.F. O'Connell. *A Prehistory of Australia, New Guinea, and Sahul.* Academic Press, New York, 1982.

---

[5] http://www.tcs.hut.fi/software/smodels/lparse.ps .

Multi-agent Reactive Systems

Prahladavaradan Sampath[*]

p.sampath@bcs.org.uk

Abstract. We present a formalism for programming complex multi-agent reactive systems in a structured manner. The motivation behind this work is to obtain a simple semantic framework for such reactive systems. The approach followed is to build upon a timed extension of concurrent constraint programs that have been used to present an elegant declarative framework for reactive systems.

Timed concurrent constraint (TCC) programs are extended with the primitives for defining and manipulating *ambients* that contain TCC programs. The extension is simple and conservative, in the sense that TCC programs are a subset of the new formalism – Mobile Timed Concurrent Constraints (MTCC).

1 Introduction

Reactive systems are those that continuously interact with their environment asynchronously; i.e. where the environment is unable to wait for a response from the system. Reactive systems are generally applicable to automatic process control and monitoring. They are also very useful in specifying and implementing systems such as communication protocols where various timing considerations need to be satisfied.

A number of formalisms have been presented in the literature for reactive systems. These include the languages LUSTRE, ESTEREL, and SIGNAL [HCP91, BB91,GB86,Ber98]. These formalisms have been quite successful in specifying, reasoning with, and implementing reasonably complex reactive systems; however they do not model systems that consist of a number of reactive sub-components that dynamically interact with each other and the environment. An example of this type of system can be seen in the telecommunications arena, where sophisticated telephony applications involve controlling a number of individual calls distributed across different switches, and where the interactions between the calls changes dynamically.

In this paper we present a formalism for modelling a system consisting of a number of reactive sub-components, that dynamically interact with each other and the environment. Our technique is based on extending an existing formalism for specifying reactive systems – Timed Concurrent Constraints – with a formalism for capturing the dynamic configuration of the reactive sub-components –

---

[*] TRDDC Pune, India from Nov 2002

Part of this work was carried out while the author was employed at Teamphone.com

V. Dahl and P. Wadler (Eds.): PADL 2003, LNCS 2562, pp. 177–193, 2003.

the Ambient Calculus. One of the major motivations for using Timed Concurrent Constraints (TCC) over other formalisms is the very simple and elegant semantic model presented in [SJG94b] for TCC. The concepts introduced by the Ambient Calculus to model the multi-agent nature of systems are orthogonal to the concepts in TCC, and the combination of the two gives an elegant model for multi-agent reactive systems.

In the rest of the paper, we first outline the TCC approach to reactive programming, followed by an overview of the Ambient Calculus. We then present the syntax and semantics of Mobile Timed Concurrent Constraints (MTCC), which combines aspects of TCC and Ambient Calculus. We then present some motivating examples of the use of MTCC to model multi-agent reactive systems. We conclude the paper with some pointers for future work.

Related Work. There is limited published research in trying to model multi-agent reactive systems. [RR00,BRS93] come closest presenting extensions to ESTEREL for multiple agents communicating asynchronously; but the notion of *mobility* is not modelled. A related effort is the modelling of higher-order Signal [TN98], where mobility can be modelled as signals that are themselves agents.

From the perspective of concurrent constraints, [GP00] presents a multi-agent concurrent constraint system, consisting of *computational spaces* arranged in a hierarchy of locations; mobility is modelled by allowing *closures* to migrate to named locations.

Another interesting approach for integrating time into a process calculus is [BH00] which presents a timed extension of the π-calculus.

2   Timed Concurrent Constraints

Concurrent Constraints is a computational paradigm where the notion of the *value-store*, that forms the basis of imperative languages, is replaced with the notion of a *constraint-store*; i.e. computation *constrains* instead of *assigns* values to locations in the store. Correspondingly, the notions of "read" and "write" are replaced by notions of "ask" and "tell" that query the information in the store, and *monotonically refine* the information in the store respectively. Concurrent constraint programs consist of a number of *agents* that interact concurrently with the store. An agent can either add a constraint to the store (*tell*) or suspend until there is sufficient information in the store to entail a given constraint (*ask*).

Formally, a constraint system, $\mathcal{C}$, consists of a set of tokens with a minimal first-order structure – variables, substitution, and existential quantification – equipped with an *entailment* relation, $\vdash_e$. Examples of constraint systems include Herbrand underlying logic programs where the variables range over finite trees and tokens indicate equality of trees; and Gentzen [SJG94a] where variables range over a set of names, and the tokens are the names themselves. The entailment relation in Gentzen is very simple:

$$\Gamma \vdash_e c \Longleftrightarrow c \in \Gamma$$

$$A, B ::= \quad c \qquad\qquad\qquad\qquad\qquad \text{(Tell)}$$

$$\mid \textbf{if } c \textbf{ then } A \qquad\qquad\qquad \text{(Positive Ask)}$$

$$\mid \textbf{if } c \textbf{ else next } A \qquad\qquad \text{(Timed Negative Ask)}$$

$$\mid \textbf{skip} \qquad\qquad\qquad\qquad\qquad \text{(Skip)}$$

$$\mid \textbf{next } A \qquad\qquad\qquad\qquad \text{(Unit Delay)}$$

$$\mid A \parallel B \qquad\qquad\qquad \text{(Parallel Composition)}$$

$$\mid \textbf{new } X \textbf{ in } A \qquad\qquad\qquad \text{(Hiding)}$$

$$\mid \textbf{abort} \qquad\qquad\qquad\qquad \text{(Abort)}$$

Fig. 1. Syntax for TCC

The tokens (names) in Gentzen can be interpreted as the *signals* of reactive systems. Because of its simplicity, we will consider the Gentzen constraint system as the underlying constraint system for the formalisms presented in the rest of the paper.

Timed concurrent constraints (TCC) extend the concurrent constraint paradigm with the notion of time-steps. TCC was first proposed in [SJG94b, SJG94a] where it was used to give an elegant model for reactive programs. The basic idea behind TCC is to consider each step of reaction with the environment as a concurrent constraint program, and to provide language primitives that *extend* the behaviour of a concurrent constraint program over time. In this paper, we use TCC to refer to both the model and the programming language as presented in [SJG94b].

Execution of a concurrent constraint program consists of executing all the agents concurrently, and adding information to the store, until the agents can no longer add any further information to the store – the program is said to have reached a *quiescent* state. The execution of a TCC programs now consists of a sequence of time-steps where each time-step is the execution of a concurrent constraint program to quiescence. The underlying model for TCC programs is therefore a set of traces, where each trace is a sequence of the quiescent states of the program.

The combinators for TCC programs can be classified into the base concurrent constraint combinators: Tell, Positive Ask, Parallel Composition, and Abort; and timed combinators: Timed Negative Ask, and Unit Delay. The abstract syntax for the TCC language is given in Figure 1. In the abstract syntax we have assumed that variables (X) range over signals in the underlying Gentzen constraint system. The operational, denotational and logical semantics for TCC is presented in [SJG94b]. In this section we will outline the operational semantics of TCC.

The operational semantics of TCC programs is given using two binary transition relations, $\rightarrow$ and $\rhd$. The $\rightarrow$ transition describes transitions within a time-step, and the $\rhd$ relation describes a transition from one time-step to another.

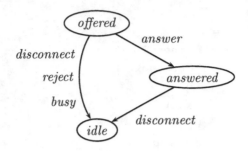

Fig. 2. Call States and transitions

Tell. This agent imposes a given constraint on the store.

Positive Ask. This agent checks if a given constraint, c, is entailed by the store, if so it evolves to a agent A, otherwise it blocks until the constraint, c is entailed.

Negative Ask. This agent checks if a given constraint is entailed by the current time-step after reaching quiescence. If the constraint is not entailed, then it evolves into the agent A in the *next* time step.[1]

Skip. skip is the agent that does nothing at every time instant.

Unit Delay. This agent acts as **skip** in the current time-step, and evolves into the agent A in the next time-step.

Parallel composition. This combinator executes both the agents, A and B, in parallel.

Hiding. This combinator generates a new name (constraint), and binds it to the variable X in the agent A.

Abort. abort is the agent that instantaneously causes all interactions with the environment to cease.

It is also possible to define other constructs based on the model for TCC, such as *extended waits*, *watch-dogs*, *suspension-activation* and *multi-form time* etc. In the rest of the paper we will make use of these constructs and refer the reader to [SJG94a] for a more detailed presentation of TCC.

Example 1 (Modelling a phone-call in TCC). As an example of the use of TCC we model a simplified call in TCC. A call can be in one of three states; *offered*, *answered* and *idle*. The transitions between the states are governed by the events *busy*, *reject*, *answer*, and *disconnect*. The state transitions can be visualised as in Figure 2.

In the syntax of TCC, a call can be represented as follows

> Call =   **watching** {*answer,reject,busy,disconnect*} **do** (**always** *offered*)
>
>   ‖ **whenever** *answer* **do** (**next** AnsweredCall)
>
>   ‖ **whenever** {*reject, busy,disconnect*} **do next** (**always** *idle*)

---

[1] Note that since negative information is only acted upon in a future time-step, the detection of negative information is stable – in particular, the paradoxes of other synchronous approaches are side-stepped.

AnsweredCall = **watching** *disconnect* **do** (**always** *answered*)

|| **whenever** *disconnect* **do next** (**always** *idle*)

Here, we have used the watchdog construct **watching**, which executes some agent watching for a condition to be satisfied. If the watchdog condition is satisfied, the agent is terminated from the *next* time-step. The converse of this behaviour is exhibited by the **whenever** construct, which waits till a condition is satisfied to start the execution of an agent. We refer the reader to [SJG94b] for a formal definition and semantics of these constructs.

The example basically asserts the *offered* state till one of the events *answer*, *busy*, *reject*, *disconnect* are observed, at which stage a state transition takes place. If the event is either *busy*, or *reject*, then a transition is made to the *idle* state. Otherwise, if the *answer* event occurs, the Call agent evolves into AnsweredCall in the next time step. A similar explanation can be given for the AnsweredCall agent.

Because of the simplicity of our model, we can use the same TCC program to model both an *incoming* and an *outgoing* call. In Example 4, we will present an example of call control, exhibiting both these aspects of a call.

3 Ambient Calculus

The ambient calculus was introduced in [CG98,CG00b] to model mobility of agent based systems. The central concept of the ambient calculus is that of an *ambient*, which captures the notion of a *container* within which computation takes place. Each ambient can itself contain other ambients to form an hierarchy of ambients. The ambient calculus then provides mechanisms to manipulate the containers as a whole; for example by *moving* an ambient, *opening* an ambient, *creating* new ambients etc. The essence of the ambient calculus is the manipulation of *computational spaces*; it does not specify any restriction on the computation that can be contained within these spaces.

The ambient calculus has been used in the literature to study a wide range of aspects of mobile computation. Named ambients and the associated capabilities have also been used to study the security aspects of mobile computation [Car00]. The ambient calculus can be equipped with an equational theory [GC99], which allows reasoning about the behaviour of ambients. A technique for describing and reasoning about the temporal properties of the ambient calculus has been presented in [CG00a]; this enables us to reason about the dynamic evolution of the structure of the ambients.

The syntax of the ambient calculus is presented in Figure 3. We have only considered a limited form of the ambient calculus without replication, and the prefixing operation. We have taken some liberties with the syntax to make it closer to the syntax of TCC. The actions of the ambient calculus are represented using *capabilities*. As we mentioned before, each ambient is named, and manipulating an ambient requires the name of the ambient; this is reflected in the fact that each of the capabilities (**in**, **out**, and **open**) are parametrised with a

$$P, Q ::= \textbf{skip} \qquad \qquad \text{(Inactivity)}$$
$$| \textbf{ new } X \textbf{ in } P \qquad \text{(Restriction)}$$
$$| P \parallel Q \qquad \qquad \text{(Composition)}$$
$$| n[P] \qquad \qquad \text{(Ambient)}$$
$$| M \qquad \qquad \text{(Action)}$$

where the actions (M) are defined as

$$M ::= \textbf{in } n \qquad \qquad \text{(Can enter } n)$$
$$| \textbf{ out } n \qquad \qquad \text{(Can exit } n)$$
$$| \textbf{ open } n \qquad \qquad \text{(Can open } n)$$

Fig. 3. Syntax of the ambient calculus

$$(n[\textbf{in } m \parallel P] \parallel m[Q]) \triangleright (m[n[P] \parallel Q]) \qquad \qquad (\textbf{in } \text{capability})$$
$$(m[n[\textbf{out } m \parallel P] \parallel Q]) \triangleright (n[P] \parallel m[Q]) \qquad \qquad (\textbf{out } \text{capability})$$
$$(\textbf{open } m \parallel m[P] \parallel Q) \triangleright (P \parallel Q) \qquad \qquad (\textbf{open } \text{capability})$$

Fig. 4. Semantics of the ambient calculus

name. The set of capabilities presented here are quite minimal; it is possible to extend this set of capabilities to introduce concepts that are specific to a particular application of the ambient calculus. We use such a capability (**connect**) in Example 5.

The semantics of the ambient calculus is given by a binary transition relation, $\triangleright$, that describes the evolution of ambients. We have presented the rules pertaining to capabilities in Figure 4.

Example 2. As a simple example, we consider an ambient calculus program that exemplifies the idiom of *boot-strapping*. An ambient m that represents a simple program, spawns off another program Complex, representing complex behaviour. Once this is done, the ambient m transfers itself into the ambient of the complex program.

$$\text{Bootstrap} = m[\textbf{new } X \textbf{ in } (\textbf{in } X \parallel X[\text{Complex} \parallel \textbf{out } m])]$$
$$\triangleright m[\textbf{in } n \parallel n[\text{Complex} \parallel \textbf{out } m]] \qquad \qquad (\text{where } n \text{ is fresh})$$
$$\triangleright m[\textbf{in } n] \parallel n[\text{Complex}] \qquad \qquad (\text{by the } \textbf{out } \text{capability})$$
$$\triangleright n[\text{Complex} \parallel m[\,]] \qquad \qquad (\text{by the } \textbf{in } \text{capability})$$

Note that the use of a fresh name for the name of the complex ambient would disallow any other ambient from entering the complex ambient — this is a form of access-control.

4   Mobile Timed Concurrent Constraints

We extend the TCC paradigm of computation by introducing ambient structure. We consider each ambient as *containing* a TCC program that evolves within the ambient. The evolution of the ambient structure can then model the mobility and coordination of individual reactive computations. The resulting formalism, which we call Mobile Timed Concurrent Constraints (MTCC), is capable of expressing reactive behaviour where a number of reactive sub-components interact with each other and the environment in a coordinated manner. In effect, each reactive sub-component can be seen as a single agent, and the entire program can be seen as representing the global (distributed) behaviour of a multi-agent system.

One of the criteria in the design of MTCC was to keep the reactive aspects and the coordination aspects orthogonal to each other. This would not only simplify the resulting formalism, but could allow the formal techniques for reasoning with TCC programs, and ambient calculus programs, applicable to MTCC. Another criteria for the design was to make the MTCC formalism a conservative extension of the TCC formalism, both syntactically and semantically; i.e. every TCC program should remain a valid MTCC program and the semantic model for TCC programs should be a special case of the semantic model for MTCC programs.

One of the first issues we come across when integrating ambients into TCC is the issue of *names*. The approach we follow in this paper is to identify the names of ambients with the signals (names) of TCC. Creation of a new ambient can be achieved by a *tell*; i.e. we assert the existence of an ambient.

Syntax. The syntax for MTCC is presented in Figure 5. The terms of MTCC are the terms in the *free-algebra* generated by the grammar rules in Figure 5.

Example 3 (Examples of MTCC terms). Note that every term of the ambient calculus is a term in MTCC. For example, the following term is a pure ambient calculus term.

$$m[\, n[\, A\,] \parallel n[\, B\,]\,]$$

Note that the ambient m contains two ambients, named n. This is a legal term and is allowed by MTCC. Every term of TCC is also a valid term of MTCC. For example, the terms, Call, and AnsweredCall defined in Example 1 are also terms of MTCC. Below, we give an example of a term that combines aspects of both TCC and the ambient calculus

$$m[\, n[\, \mathbf{open}\ p\,] \parallel \mathbf{if}\ n\ \mathbf{then}\ (\mathbf{next}\ (\mathbf{open}\ n) \parallel p[\ ])\,]$$

$$
\begin{array}{llr}
A, B ::= & c & \text{(Tell)} \\
& \mid c[A] & \text{(Ambient)} \\
& \mid \textbf{if } c \textbf{ then } A & \text{(Positive Ask)} \\
& \mid \textbf{if } c \textbf{ else next } A & \text{(Negative Ask)} \\
& \mid \textbf{skip} & \text{(Skip)} \\
& \mid \textbf{next } A & \text{(Unit Delay)} \\
& \mid A \parallel B & \text{(Parallel Composition)} \\
& \mid \textbf{new } X \textbf{ in } A & \text{(Hiding)} \\
& \mid \textbf{abort} & \text{(Abort)} \\
& \mid M & \text{(Action)}
\end{array}
$$

where the actions (M) are defined as

$$
\begin{array}{llr}
M ::= & \textbf{in } n & \text{(Can enter } n) \\
& \mid \textbf{out } n & \text{(Can exit } n) \\
& \mid \textbf{open } n & \text{(Can open } n)
\end{array}
$$

Fig. 5. Syntax for MTCC

Semantics. Recall that the semantic model for TCC presented in Section 2, models TCC programs as sets of sequences of quiescent states. In the case of MTCC the model can be extended to be sets of sequences of trees of quiescent states; i.e. each time-step of an MTCC program can be modelled as a tree of quiescent states. The tree structure reflects the structure of the ambient component of the program for that time-step, and the quiescent states represent the reactive components of the program for that time-step. We refer to this intuitive model of MTCC programs in the rest of the paper[2].

First we note that an MTCC program exhibits the hierarchical structure of an ambient calculus term: it can be viewed as a labelled tree where the nodes of the tree are labelled and represent an ambient. The nodes contain a multi-set of MTCC agents. Parallel composition of MTCC agents in an ambient is represented by multi-set union. The top level node is labelled with the unique label τ representing the top-level ambient. We refer to this hierarchical structure as a *configuration*.

We assume that each node in the configuration is labelled with an unique label, and therefore it is possible to refer to any node in the tree using a sequence of labels starting with τ. We refer to such sequences of labels with the Greek alphabet ϕ. Given a configuration, Γ, we use $\sigma_\Gamma(\phi)$ to refer to the sub-multiset of

---

[2] The denotational model of MTCC is actually based on this intuitive picture, however we defer the presentation of the denotational model to a future paper (cf. Section 6).

tokens and ambient names in the node ϕ of a configuration. Note that the labels mentioned above are not the same as the names of the ambients. This is because following the ambient calculus, MTCC permits the presence of multiple ambients with the same name at the same level (cf. Example 3). Therefore, ambient names cannot be used to uniquely identify a node in the configuration.

The operational semantics for MTCC is presented as an extension of the binary transition relations for TCC (cf. Section 2). The inter-step transition relation, $\triangleright$, is extended so that it captures the evolution of the ambient structure of the configuration in addition to the temporal constructs of TCC. The transition relations, $\rightarrow$ and $\triangleright$ are parametrised by the context, ϕ, within a configuration: $\rightarrow_\phi$ captures the transformation on an agent at node ϕ within a time-step; and $\triangleright_\phi$ captures the transformation of an agent at node ϕ between time-steps.

Execution of a MTCC program now consists of alternating *maximal* sequences of $\triangleright$ and $\rightarrow$, starting with a *maximal* sequence of $\rightarrow$ steps. The sequences are maximal in the sense that no further execution steps are possible; in the case of $\rightarrow$, quiescence has been reached; and in the case of $\triangleright$ a *normal form* has been reached.

Tell. The effect of a simple tell constraint is to assert the constraint in the context of a node in the configuration. There is no other operational step associated with this construct. Note that the constraint is only asserted for a single time-step – it is not persistent across time-steps.

Ambient. The assertion of an ambient $m[A]$, results in the creation of a new node in the configuration below the current node, containing the multi-set of agents corresponding to A. The constraint m is also asserted in the current node.

Unlike a simple tell constraint, an ambient is persistent across time-steps. Given an ambient $m[A]$ in the configuration, it will persist in the configuration unless specified otherwise by the operational semantics (cf. semantics for **abort**, and capabilities below). This behaviour is implicit in the operational semantics by the fact that we specify the transitions in the context of the nodes of configurations, whose tree structure is assumed to persist into the next step, unless specified otherwise.

Positive Ask. Consider the agent **if** c **then** A. In the context of a node ϕ of a configuration Γ, this agent evolves into A if the constraint c is satisfied.

$$\frac{\sigma_\Gamma(\phi) \vdash c}{\textbf{if } c \textbf{ then } A \rightarrow_\phi A} \qquad \text{(Positive Ask 1)}$$

If, on quiescence the constraint c is not satisfied, the agent evolves into **skip** in the next time-step

$$\textbf{if } c \textbf{ then } A \triangleright_\phi \textbf{skip} \qquad \text{(Positive Ask 2)}$$

Negative Ask. Consider the agent **if** c **else next** A. In the context of a node ϕ of a configuration Γ, this agent evolves into **skip** if the constraint c is satisfied.

$$\frac{\sigma_\Gamma(\phi) \vdash c}{\textbf{if } c \textbf{ else next } A \rightarrow_\phi \textbf{skip}} \qquad \text{(Negative Ask 1)}$$

otherwise, if c is not satisfied on quiescence of the node ϕ (i.e. no more $\rightarrow$ steps are possible), the agent A is executed in the node ϕ of the configuration in the *next* time step.

$$\textbf{if } c \textbf{ else next } A \rhd_\phi A \qquad\qquad \text{(Negative Ask 2)}$$

Unit Delay. The agent **next** A has no effect in the current time step. It executes the agent A in the next time step.

$$\textbf{next } A \rhd_\phi A \qquad\qquad \text{(Unit Delay)}$$

Skip. The agent **skip** is the agent that does nothing at a time instant. Operationally, **skip** has no effect.

$$\Delta \parallel \textbf{skip} \rightarrow_\phi \Delta \qquad\qquad \text{(Skip)}$$

Abort. The agent **abort** is the agent that instantaneously *halts* the program executing at a node. It stops all interaction with the environment

$$\Delta \parallel \textbf{abort} \rightarrow_\phi \textbf{abort} \qquad\qquad \text{(Abort 1)}$$
$$\textbf{abort} \nrightarrow_\phi \qquad\qquad \text{(Abort 2)}$$

If an ambient contains the **abort** agent, then it evolves into **skip** in the next time-step. Intuitively, an ambient is active only as long as it contains an active agent that can interact with the environment

$$m[\,\textbf{abort}\,] \rhd_\phi \textbf{skip} \qquad\qquad \text{(Abort 3)}$$

New Name. The agent **new** X **in** A, generates a *fresh* name, n, that is not currently used and binds it to the variable X; i.e. substitutes all free occurrence of X in A with n.

$$\frac{n \text{ is fresh}}{\textbf{new } X \textbf{ in } A \rightarrow_\phi A[n/X]} \qquad\qquad \text{(New Name)}$$

Capabilities. The capabilities of MTCC are given an operational semantics that is essentially the same as their semantics in the ambient calculus.

$$(n[\,\textbf{in } m \parallel P\,] \parallel m[Q]) \rhd_\phi (m[\,n[P\,] \parallel Q\,]) \qquad\qquad \text{(In Capability)}$$
$$(m[\,n[\,\textbf{out } m \parallel P\,] \parallel Q\,]) \rhd_\phi (n[P\,] \parallel m[Q]) \qquad\qquad \text{(Out Capability)}$$
$$(\textbf{open } m \parallel m[P\,] \parallel Q) \rhd_\phi (P \parallel Q) \qquad\qquad \text{(Open Capability)}$$

Similar to ambients, the capabilities of MTCC persist across time-steps until they are consumed.

$$\textbf{in } m \rhd_\phi \textbf{in } m$$
$$\textbf{out } m \rhd_\phi \textbf{out } m$$
$$\textbf{open } m \rhd_\phi \textbf{open } m$$

In the presentation given above, we have modelled capabilities as *agent combinators*; an alternative semantics would be to consider capabilities as being constraints. The capabilities can be viewed as *first-order* or *predicate* constraints. This would involve extending the underlying constraint system beyond the Gentzen constraint system, to include *first-order* constraints. In this case the capability constraints would have the same behaviour as any other constraint. In particular, they would not persist across time-steps. An advantage of this approach would be to unify the presentation of constraints and capabilities; which would in turn simplify the denotational model of MTCC.

We note from the operational semantics that we could dispense with the simple *tell* construct. For all effective purposes, the term $m[\textbf{abort}]$ has the same behaviour as the term m; i.e. we have the the equation

$$m[\textbf{abort}] = m$$

Intuitively, an ambient containing an agent that cannot interact with the environment, and cannot be observed, is equivalent to a signal. This equation can also be validated by the denotational model of MTCC that we have alluded to earlier.

It is easy to see that the operational semantics presented above is a conservative extension of the operational semantics of TCC. The significant change is that the transitions are now specified in the context of a node in the configuration. The other significant change from TCC is that the presence of ambients and ambient evolution has introduced non-determinism into the transition relations. The non-determinism is however confined to the $\triangleright_\phi$ transition that specifies the evolution of the ambient structure.

An extension to the language that might be useful in practice would be to extend the *ask* constructs to allow querying constraints within named ambients. Syntactically, this extension would amount to allow querying constraints of the form $m.n.p$, i.e. a sequence of names. Semantically, such an *ask* would succeed if the current node contained an ambient with name m, that in turn contained an ambient with name n, where the constraint p is asserted.

Given a sequence of node labels in a configuration, ϕ', let $\alpha(\phi')$ be the sequence of ambient names corresponding to the nodes in the configuration. We represent the concatenation of sequences ϕ, and ϕ' as $\phi.\phi'$. The operational semantics for the extended *ask* construct can be given as

$$\frac{\exists \phi' \bullet \alpha(\phi') = \psi \wedge \sigma_\Gamma(\phi.\phi') \vdash a}{\textbf{if } \psi.a \textbf{ then } A \rightarrow_\phi A} \qquad \text{(Positive Ask 1)}$$

$$\textbf{if } \psi.a \textbf{ then } A \triangleright_\phi \textbf{skip} \qquad \text{(Positive Ask 2)}$$

$$\frac{\exists \phi' \bullet \alpha(\phi') = \psi \wedge \sigma_\Gamma(\phi.\phi') \vdash a}{\textbf{if } \psi.a \textbf{ else next } A \rightarrow_\phi \textbf{skip}} \qquad \text{(Negative Ask 1)}$$

$$\textbf{if } \psi.a \textbf{ else next } A \triangleright_\phi A \qquad \text{(Negative Ask 2)}$$

The corresponding extension for a *tell*, $\psi.a$, asserts the signal a in every ambient accessible from the current node by following the sequence of names, ψ; i.e. in the context ϕ of the configuration:

$$\forall \phi' \bullet \alpha(\phi') = \psi \Rightarrow \sigma_\Gamma(\phi.\phi') \vdash a$$

Note that according to this definition, the *tell*, $\psi.a$, has no effect if there are no ambients accessible by the sequence of labels ψ.

Note that the extended *ask*, and *tell* constructs imply *instantaneous* communication of information between an inner ambient and an outer ambient that contains it. In the absence of such an extended constructs, the information would have to be encapsulated in another ambient representing a *message* that would then carry the information between the inner ambient to the outer ambient – such techniques have been explored in the literature on ambients for modelling access-control issues [Car00].

5   Examples

In this section we present two motivating examples for the use of MTCC. The first example is from the telecommunications arena; we build upon the simple call model presented in Example 1 to show how we can use MTCC to express reactive control of multiple calls. The second example is taken from multi-agent systems, where we model the distributed state of a multi-agent exploratory system.

Example 4 (Reactive control of calls). One of the motivations for the work in this paper was to model complex reactive systems, consisting of a number of interacting reactive components. One such system is a telephone switch, that has to handle incoming calls, make outgoing calls if necessary, and connect the two together.

We model such a situation, albeit in a considerably simplified form. Let us consider a telephone switch as being an ambient with the name *switch*. The switch interacts with the environment by receiving and making calls.

Initially, let us assume that the switch has no ongoing calls, i.e. it is idle. This situation can be modelled as:

$$switch[\,\mathsf{HandleIncoming}\,]$$

where HandleIncoming is the behaviour of the switch for handling incoming calls, which we will define later.

An incoming call could be signalled to the switch by asserting a signal, *incoming*. Another technique for signalling an incoming call would be to assert an *ambient* with the name *incoming*; this has the advantage of encapsulating the reactive nature of the call within an ambient. This situation can be represented as

$$switch[\,\mathsf{HandleIncoming} \parallel incoming[\,\mathsf{SimpleCall}\,]\,]$$

where SimpleCall is the MTCC program modelling a simple call (cf. Example 1).

The program to handle incoming calls can now be modelled as the MTCC program:

HandleIncoming = **watching** *connected* **do always** *searching*

    ‖ **whenever** *incoming* **do** InitiateOutgoing

    ‖ **whenever** *outgoing.answered* **do** *incoming.answer*

    ‖ **whenever** *outgoing.answered* **do** (**connect** *incoming outgoing*)

    ‖ **whenever** *outgoing.answered* **do next always** *connected*

    ‖ **whenever** *incoming.idle* **do** *outgoing.disconnect*

where

InitiateOutgoing = **watching** *outgoing.idle* **do** *outgoing*[*SimpleCall*]

This program basically has two states: *searching*, and *connected*. The initial state is *searching*. The agent

whenever *incoming* **do** InitiateOutgoing

waits for an incoming call, and on receiving an incoming call, spawns off an outgoing call. The outgoing call is itself spawned off by asserting an ambient with the name *outgoing*. Note that this ambient is *deleted* once it becomes *idle* — this is achieved by the agent

watching *outgoing.idle* **do** *outgoing*[*SimpleCall*]

If the outgoing call is answered, then the incoming call is also answered, and the incoming and outgoing calls are *connected* to each other. This is achieved by the agents:

whenever *outgoing.answered* **do** *incoming.answer*

whenever *outgoing.answered* **do connect** *incoming outgoing*

We have used the ambient capability **connect** *incoming outgoing* to model the action of connecting the speech-paths of two calls together — it is a domain-specific capability.

Finally, if the incoming call is disconnected, the outgoing call is also disconnected. This is expressed by the agent:

whenever *incoming.idle* **do** *outgoing.disconnect*

This example models a very simplistic scenario, but it gives the flavour of the power of MTCC to model multi-agent systems. This example can be extended in a number of ways; for example, it is possible to model call-transfer between switches, by moving the ambient corresponding to a call from one switch (ambient) to another. It is also possible to model different procedures for handling calls as different ambients, and dynamically change the way in which a call is handled by the switch by moving the call between these *call-handling* ambients. Due to a lack of space, we leave an exploration of these possibilities to a future paper.

Example 5 (Multi-agent explorer). The second example that we present is a variation of an example presented quite often in the literature, about an agent exploring some terrain. The behaviour of the agent is quite simple: if it can go left, it moves to the left; if it can move to the right, it moves to the right; if neither, it stops. We can express this agent as follows:

$$\text{Explore} = \mathbf{if}\ canmoveleft\ \mathbf{then}\ left[\mathbf{out}\ explorer]$$
$$\|\ \mathbf{if}\ canmoveright\ \mathbf{then}\ right[\mathbf{out}\ explorer]$$
$$\|\ stop[\mathbf{out}\ explorer]$$
$$\text{Explorer} = explorer[\text{Movement}\ \|\ \mathbf{always}\ \text{Explore}]$$
$$\text{Movement} = \mathbf{always}\ (\mathbf{in}\ left\ \|\ \mathbf{in}\ right\ \|\ \mathbf{in}\ stop\ \|\ \mathbf{out}\ stop)$$
$$\text{System} = \text{Explorer}$$

Basically, every location that the explorer reaches is modelled by an ambient, starting with the top-level ambient of System. The explorer is also modelled by an ambient with the name *explorer*. The ability to move left or right is controlled by the signals *canmoveleft*, and *canmoveright*, which we assume are asserted by the environment. The definition Explore, captures the act of exploring: if the explorer can move to the left, an ambient is created with the label *left*, which then moves out of the *explorer* ambient; and similarly if the explorer can move right. At every step of the exploration, it is also possible for the explorer to stop, which is captured by the *stop* ambient.

At every step of the exploration, the explorer can move left or right, stop by moving into the *stop* ambient, or start again by moving out of the *stop* ambient. These capabilities are available at every time-step to the explorer as expressed by Movement. The non-determinism of the exploration is captured by the evolution of the ambient structure that is non-deterministic by nature.

This example presents a very elegant technique for expressing exploration. With MTCC, we can go further and introduce multiple agents into the framework. For example, a component of the explorer, could be an agent of the form

$$\text{Detail} = \mathbf{always}\ (\mathbf{if}\ detail\ \mathbf{then}\ \mathbf{new}\ X\ \mathbf{in}\ (X[\mathbf{out}\ explorer\ \|\ \text{ExploreDetail}]))$$

Basically, if detailed exploration of a particular location is required, a sub-agent can be spawned off that performs detailed exploration, while the explorer continues. Note that the sub-agent is created with a fresh name, and first moves out of the *explorer* ambient.

This example can be further enhanced to include details such as *markers* that the explorer can leave at each location to indicate the direction in which it has moved. This information can then be accessed by the sub-agents to re-join the main explorer when they have finished their task. We leave a further exploration of this design space to a future paper.

6   Conclusion and Future Work

In this paper we have presented an extension of a reactive programming language to allow for the expression of multi-agent reactive systems. The extension is achieved by incorporating notions from the ambient calculus into a reactive language, TCC. The main thesis of this paper is that the issues of reactive programming and multi-agent systems are orthogonal to each other. This has been demonstrated by the orthogonal combination of the features of the ambient calculus and TCC.

We have presented the syntax and operational semantics of the language Mobile Timed Concurrent Constraints (MTCC). Both the syntax and semantics of MTCC, can be seen as a conservative extension of the semantics for TCC, and the ambient calculus. We have also hinted at a denotational model for MTCC that can be expressed as a conservative extension of the denotational model of TCC as presented in [SJG94b].

We have also presented some motivating examples that demonstrate the expressive power of MTCC. The examples take commonly used examples in the literature of single-agent systems and extends them modularly to incorporate multi-agent features. The example of a telephone switch demonstrates a simple technique for expressing reactive control of reactive sub-agents, while keeping the definition of the sub-agents simple. The second example that we present of an exploratory agent makes more essential use of the ambient structure. This example shows how a multi-agent reactive system can be expressed in MTCC, by combining reactive computation, and multi-agent interaction in the same formalism.

By its very nature, this paper raises more questions than it answers. We outline below some of the more obvious areas for further work

Denotational Model. We have hinted earlier that the denotational model of MTCC, can be viewed as an extension of the denotational model of TCC: the denotational model of MTCC can be seen as a set of traces where each element in the trace is a *tree* of quiescent states of TCC. However, some work is required in presenting this denotational model in a compositional manner. The main difficulty is in expressing the evolution of the ambient structure in a compositional manner.

Another interesting question is whether the evolution of a single agent, i.e. a sequence of quiescent states, can be identified from the sequence of trees of quiescent states. This question could possibly addressed by a compositional expression of the semantics of MTCC.

Programming with MTCC. The combination of ambients with reactive programs, opens up a huge range of possibilities for programming. A number of interesting programming idioms can be expressed by this combination. For example, it might be possible to express *boot-strapping* of reactive program using the boot-strap idiom of ambients (cf. Example 2).

Reasoning with MTCC. One of the main motivations behind this work was to obtain a simple and elegant semantic model for multi-agent reactive computation. Having a simple model, will allow us to develop effective techniques for reasoning about multi-agent systems. An interesting exercise would be to develop a *logic* for reasoning with MTCC, following [SJG96], where a logic is presented for an extension of TCC, Timed Default Concurrent Constraints.

Both TCC, and ambient calculus come equipped with some tools for reasoning. It is hoped that the orthogonal combination of these two formalisms will allow us to carry over some of the work already done for TCC, and ambient calculus, to be carried over to reasoning about MTCC programs.

Compiling MTCC. Ultimately, MTCC, is a reactive programming language. The driving force behind high-level reactive languages such as ESTEREL, LUSTRE, and SIGNAL, has been to derive a *compilation* of programs written in these languages into finite state automatons, that can then be incorporated into low-level code for reactive controllers. The finite state automaton also allows the validation of various real-time timing constraints of the reactive controllers. Such a *compilation* technique needs to be investigated for MTCC.

References

[BB91]   G. Berry and A. Benveniste. The synchronous approach to reactive and real-time systems. In *Procedings of the IEEE*, volume 79, 1991.

[Ber98]   Gérard Berry. The foundations of ESTEREL. In G Plotkin, C Stirling, and M Tofte, editors, *Proof, Language and Interaction: Essays in Honour of Robin Milner*. MIT Press, 1998.

[BH00]   Martin Berger and Kohei Honda. The two-phase commit protocol in an extended π-calculus. In Luca Aceto and Björn Victor, editors, *Proceedings of the 7th International Workshop on Expressiveness in Concurrency, EXPRESS '00*, August 2000.

[BRS93]   G. Berry, S. Ramesh, and R. K. Shyamasundar. Communicating reactive processes. In *Conference Record of the Twentieth Annual ACM SIGPLAN-SIGACT Symposium on Principles of Programming Languages*, pages 85–98, Charleston, South Carolina, 1993.

[Car00]   Luca Cardelli. Mobility and security. In Friedrich L Bauer and Ralf SteinBrüggen, editors, *Foundations of Secure Computation*, NATO Science Series, pages 3–37. IOS Press, Marktoberdorf, Germany, 2000.

[CG98]   Luca Cardelli and Andrew D Gordon. Mobile ambients. In *Foundations of Software Science and Computation Structures*, volume 1378 of *Lecture Notes in Computer Science*, pages 140–155. Springer-Verlag, 1998.

[CG00a]   Luca Cardelli and Andrew D Gordon. Anytime, anywhere. modal logics for mobile ambients. In *Proceedings of the 27th ACM Symposium on Principles of Programming Languages*, pages 365–377, 2000.

[CG00b]   Luca Cardelli and Andrew D Gordon. Mobile ambients. *Theoretical Computer Science*, 240(1):177–213, June 2000.

[GB86]   P. Le Guernic and A. Benveniste. Real time, synchronous, data-flow programming: the language SIGNAL and its mathematical semantics. Technical Report # 533, INRIA, June 1986.

[GC99]   Andrew D Gordon and Luca Cardelli. Equational properties of mobile ambients. In Wolfgang Thomas, editor, *Proceedings of Foundations of Software Science and Computational Structures, Second International Conference, FOSSACS'99*, volume 1578 of *LNCS*, pages 212–226. Springer, March 1999.

[GP00]   David Gilbert and Catuscia Palamidessi. Concurrent constraint program-
            ming with process mobility. In John Lloyd et al., editor, *Proceedings of the
            Conference on Computational Logic - CL 2000*, Lecture Notes in Artificial
            Intelligence, pages 463–477. Springer-Verlag, 2000.

[HCP91]   N Halbwachs, P Caspi, and D Pilaud. The synchronous programming lan-
            guage LUSTRE. In *Proceedings of the IEEE, Special Issue on Another Look
            at Real Time Systems*. September 1991.

[RR00]   Basant Rajan and R.K.Shyamsundar. Multiclock esterel: An asynchronous
            framework for asynchronous design. In *International Parallel and Dis-
            tributed Processing Symposium*, Cancun, Mexico, May 2000.

[Sam02]   Prahladavaradan Sampath.   Modelling multi-agent reactive systems
            (poster). In Peter J. Stuckey, editor, *ICLP*, volume 2401 of *Lecture Notes
            in Computer Science*, page 476. Springer, 2002.

[SJG94a]   Vijay Saraswat, Radha Jagadeesan, and Vineet Gupta.   Programming
            in timed concurrent constraint languages.   In B.Mayoh, E.Tyugu, and
            J.Penjam, editors, *Constraint Programming*, NATO Advanced Science In-
            stitute Series, Series F: Computer and System Sciences. 1994.

[SJG94b]   Vijay A Saraswat, Radha Jagadeesan, and Vineet Gupta. Foundations of
            timed concurrent constraint programming. In *Proceedings of the Ninth An-
            nual IEEE Symposium on Logic in Computer Science*. Paris, France, 1994.

[SJG96]   Vijay Saraswat, Radha Jagadeesan, and Vineet Gupta. Timed default con-
            current constraint programming. *Journal of Symbolic Computation*, 11,
            1996.

[TN98]   Jean-Pierre Talpin and David Nowak. A Synchronous Semantics of Higher-
            Order Processes for Modeling Reconfigurable Reactive Systems. In *Proceed-
            ings of the 18th International Conference on Foundations of Software Tech-
            nology and Theoretical Computer Science (FST&TCS'98)*, volume 1530 of
            Lecture Notes in Computer Science, pages 78–89. Springer-Verlag, Decem-
            ber 1998.

ACTILOG: An Agent Activation Language

Jacinto A. Dávila

Centro de Simulación y Modelos (CESIMO)
Universidad de Los Andes. Mérida. Venezuela
jacinto@ula.ve
http://cesimo.ing.ula.ve/~jacinto
FAX: +58 274 2402811

Abstract. ACTILOG is a language to write generalized **condition** → **action** activation rules. We propose it as an alternative and a complement to OPENLOG [6], another agent logic programming language for an abductive reasoner. We want to show how implications (conditional goals) can be used to state integrity contraints for an agent. These integrity contraints describe conditions under which the agent's goals must be reduced to plans that can be executed. For instance, a rule such as **if** A **then** B, will indicate to the agent that whenever it can prove that A is the case, it then should pursue goal B. B is normally the description of a task that must be reduced to a set of low-level, primitive actions that the agent can execute.

1 Introduction

ACTILOG is a language to write generalized **condition** → **action** activation rules. We propose it as an alternative and a complement to OPENLOG [6], another agent logic programming language for an abductive reasoner. The design is such that any semantics for abductive logic programs could be taken as the basic semantics for the programming languages ACTILOG and OPENLOG. In this way, we build upon existing formalizations of abductive reasoning and abductive logic programming[10].

Our objectives are similar to those of the IMPACT project [8] and their **taps** (Temporal Agent Programs), i.e. to program agents using the most expressive knowledge representation. However, instead of pursuing a characterization of the model-theoretic semantics, we have aimed first towards the description of the reasoning mechanisms based on abduction.

In previous work [4], [6], we suggested that the process of *activation of goals* in an agent could be understood as the derivation of unconditional goals from integrity contraints. Here, we want to show how implications (conditional goals) can be used to state integrity contraints for an agent. These integrity contraints describe conditions under which the agent's goals must be reduced to plans that can be executed. For instance, a rule such as **if** A **then** B, will indicate to the agent that whenever it can prove that A is the case, it then should pursue goal B. B is normally the description of a task that must be reduced to a set of low-level, primitive actions that the agent can execute.

V. Dahl and P. Wadler (Eds.): PADL 2003, LNCS 2562, pp. 194–207, 2003.

ACTILOG is similar to other well-known *production-rule* languages (such as OPS5 [3]). A first difference with respect to previous work is that ACTILOG, as OPENLOG [6], relies on a general purpose representation of actions and events (i.e. a logic of actions) in the form of background theories. Temporal and common-sense reasoning about initiation and termination of properties is, as we have seen, possible within this framework.

A second important difference (with respect OPS5, in particular) is that ACTILOG is an *object-level* language[1]. It does not include syntactic constructs like **goal G** or **plan P**. These characterizations are provided by the architecture of the agent [11].

ACTILOG is intended as a language to write declarative sentences stating the relations between observations and subsequent actions to be performed in response to those observations. These sentences are regarded as *integrity constraints* for the behaviour of the agent, in close analogy to integrity constraints for information stored in a database. All the control devices required to interpret and verify integrity contraints are provided by the proof procedure that characterizes the reasoning mechanism of the agent [4], [9].

The enriched syntax of ACTILOG (with respect to languages that allow simple implications with atomic heads) supports the arrangement of the activating conditions so as to minimize redundant processing. The head of an implication can be almost any logical sentence (including implications) and thus it is possible to write, not only sentences of the form: $(A \leftarrow B) \leftarrow C$, but also sentences such as $((A \leftarrow B) \land (C \leftarrow D)) \leftarrow E)$, where E is a condition shared by both nested implications. This captures some of the functionalities of the RETE algorithm which has been used to improve the efficiency of the OPS5 platform (.ibid).

The following two sections describe ACTILOG in detail. Afterwards, We compare the language with OPENLOG and discuss the advantages of each.

2   Syntax of ACTILOG

The syntax of ACTILOG is presented in table 1 in a variant of the BNF form. The conventions to read the table are the same as in normal BNF. Notably, C* represents zero or more occurrence of the category symbol C. As in OPENLOG, ACTILOG's syntax is open so that the programmer can include fluent and action names into the language. Actually, all the lower level syntactic categories, including boolean fluents, are borrowed from [6].

The top-most syntactic category is $UNIT$. A "unit" in ACTILOG gathers a set of activation rules (defined by ACT_Rule) related to a particular task. Below (in fig. 1), we give an example of ACTILOG encoding by translating the instructions for an elevator controller.

Another important category in the syntax is *Quants*. It stands for the sub-expression in an ACT_rule that specifies which variables are existentially and universally quantified.

Variables for which quantification is not indicated are assumed as universally quantified and their scope of quantification is the whole activation unit. This

---

[1] As it is the case with OPENLOG.

Table 1. Syntax of ACTILOG

ACTILOG Language: Syntax		
Unit	::= *Set* **to** *TaskName*	*Activation Unit*
Set	::= *Act_Rule* (**and** *Set*)*	*Activation Set*
Act_Rule	::= *Quants* **if** *Body* **then** *Head*	*Basic Activation Rule*
Quants	::= *One_Quant**	*Quantifiers*
One_Quant	::= ∃*Var*	*One Quantifier*
	| ∀*Var*	
Body	::= *Condition* (**and** *Body*)*	*Body of an IC*
Head	::= *Disjunct* (**or** *Head*)*	*Head of an IC*
Disjunct	::= *Set*	
	| *Task*	
	| **false**	
Condition	::= *Func$_{fluent}$* **at** *Term*	*Conditions*
	| *Task*	
	| **not** *Condition*	
	| *Query*	*Tests on "rigid" information*
Task	::= *TaskName Schedule*	*Task descriptions*
Schedule	::= *Schedule* **and** *Schedule*	*Schedules*
	| **at** *Term* | **before** *Term*	
	| **after** *Term* | **starting at** *Term*	
	| **finishing at** *Term*	
	| **starting before** *Term*	
	| **finishing before** *Term*	
	| **starting after** *Term*	
	| **finishing after** *Term*	
TaskName	::= *Func$_{action}$* | *Func$_{proc}$*	*Action names*
	| *TaskName* (**;** *TaskName*)*	
	| *TaskName* (**par** *TaskName*)*	
Func$_{action}$	::= ...	*As in OPENLOG*
Func$_{proc}$	::= ...	*As in OPENLOG*
Func$_{fluent}$	::= ...	*As in OPENLOG*
Func$_{boolean}$	::= ...	*As in OPENLOG*
Term	::= *Ind* | *Var*	*As in OPENLOG*
Ind	::= ...	*As in OPENLOG*
Var	::= ...	*As in OPENLOG*

means that the scope of the variable so *implicitly* quantified *will include the scope of quantification of the other variables*. This aspect must be emphasized because it implies that existentially quantified variables will depend on those implicitly quantified variables for *skolemization*, as shown in example 1:.

Example 1. Consider the ACTILOG rule:

```
exists T1 if on(N) at T and T lt T1 then serve(N) at T1
```

It should be read as: $\forall N \ \forall T \ \exists T1(serve(N, T1) \leftarrow on(N, T) \wedge T < T1)$.

So, in clausal form one would write: $serve(N, f(N,T)) \leftarrow on(N,T) \wedge T < f(N,T)$, where $f(N,T)$ is a skolem function.

Thus, the syntax of ACTILOG takes it beyond the realm of Horn clauses extended with negation. One can now have existentially quantified variables in the *head* of the clause. The implications of this are discussed in the following section.

The other syntactic categories are better understood by the translation of the rules into integrity constraints involving the predicates $holds(P,T)$ and $done(A, T_o, T_f)$. This is the purpose of tables 3, 4 and 5 in the following sections. Before that, however, we include the semantics specification of OPENLOG for easy reference.

2.1   The Semantics of OPENLOG Revisited

As in [6], the basic semantics of OPENLOG is shown in table[2] 2 by means of the predicate $done$[3]. That is, we employ a indirect mechanism: the definition of a predicate, to state the semantic. Basically, it is a mapping from our languages into normal logic programs. Thus, OPENLOG code inherits existing semantics for logic programs, including, we presume, those semantics for *positive* **taps** [8].

Recall that the definition of *done* can also function as an interpreter for the language. Declaratively, $done(A, T_o, T_f)$ reads "an action of type A is started at T_o and completed at T_f". One of the innovations in OPENLOG was that between any two actions in a sequence it is always possible to "insert" a third event without disrupting the semantics of the programming language. Axiom [DN02] formalizes this possibility. This is what we mean by plans (derived from OPENLOG programs) as *being open to updates* from the execution environment.

The definition of semantics in table 2 needs to be completed with a "base case" clause for the predicate *done* and the definition of *holds*. These two elements are part of the semantics, but they are also the key elements of a *background theory*, a theory of change that, as we have shown in [6,4], can be based on the Situation Calculus [14] or the Event Calculus [12].

ACTILOG also allows for *composite task names*, using the operators ";" and "**par**" (and we could also add "**+**"). The idea is to borrow part of the definition of *done* in table 2 to deal with these. However, for the sake of simplicity we omit these operators in the semantics of ACTILOG.

3   The Semantics of ACTILOG

It must be evident at this stage that OPENLOG and, now ACTILOG, are no more than "syntactic sugar" for logic (traditional logic programming in the case of OPENLOG). The exercise of defining these languages is important, however, because it helps to clarify what logical concepts are involved in programming an agent.

---

[2] PROLOG-like syntax is being used.

[3] The definitions of other predicates are also required but are not problematic.

Table 2. The Semantics of OPENLOG and ACTILOG

OPENLOG – ACTILOG : Semantics and interpreter		
$done(Pr, T_o, T_f)$	$\leftarrow$ **proc** Pr **begin** C **end** $\\ \wedge\ done(C, T_o, T_f)$	**[DN01]**
$done((C_1\ ;\ C_2), T_o, T_f)$	$\leftarrow\ done(C_1, T_o, T_1) \wedge\ T_1 < T_2 \\ \wedge\ done(C_2, T_2, T_f)$	**[DN02]**
$done((C_1\ \textbf{par}\ C_2), \\ \qquad T_o, T_f)$	$\leftarrow\ done(C_1, T_o, T_1)\ \wedge\ done(C_2, T_o, T_f) \\ \qquad \wedge\ T_1\ \leq\ T_f \\ \vee\ done(C_1, T_o, T_f)\ \wedge\ done(C_2, T_o, T_1) \\ \qquad \wedge\ T_1\ <\ T_f$	**[DN03]**
$done((C_1 + C_2), T_o, T_f)$	$\leftarrow\ done(C_1, T_o, T_f)\ \wedge\ done(C_2, T_o, T_f)$	**[DN04]**
$done((\textbf{if}\ E\ \textbf{then}\ C_1), \\ \qquad T_o, T_f)$	$\leftarrow\ holdsAt(E, T_o)\ \wedge\ done(C_1, T_o, T_f) \\ \vee\ \neg holdsAt(E, T_o)\ \wedge\ T_o = T_f$	**[DN05]**
$done((\textbf{if}\ E\ \textbf{then}\ C_1 \\ \qquad \textbf{else}\ C_2), T_o, T_f)$	$\leftarrow\ holdsAt(E, T_o)\ \wedge\ done(C_1, T_o, T_f) \\ \vee\ \neg holdsAt(E, T_o)\ \wedge\ done(C_2, T_o, T_f)$	**[DN06]**
$done((\textbf{while} \\ \qquad \exists L\ (E_b(L) \\ \qquad \textbf{do}\ B(L))), \\ \qquad T_o, T_f)$	$\leftarrow\ (\neg\exists L\ holdsAt(E_b(L), T_o) \\ \qquad \wedge\ T_o\ =\ T_f) \\ \vee\ (holdsAt(E_b(L'), T_o) \\ \qquad \wedge\ done(B(L'), T_o, T_1) \\ \qquad \wedge\ T_o < T_1 \\ \qquad \wedge\ done((\textbf{while} \\ \qquad\qquad \exists L\ (E_b(L)\ \textbf{do}\ B(L))\ ), T_1, T_f))$	**[DN07]**
$done((\textbf{begin}\ C\ \textbf{end}), \\ \qquad T_o, T_f)$	$\leftarrow\ done(C, T_o, T_f)$	**[DN08]**
$done(\textbf{nil}, T_o, T_o)$		**[DN09]**
$holdsAt(\textbf{and}(X, Y), T)$	$\leftarrow\ holdsAt(X, T)\ \wedge\ holdsAt(Y, T)$	**[DN10]**
$holdsAt(\textbf{or}(X, Y), T)$	$\leftarrow\ holdsAt(X, T)\ \vee\ holdsAt(Y, T)$	**[DN11]**
$holdsAt(\textbf{not}(X), T)$	$\leftarrow\ \neg holdsAt(X, T)$	**[DN12]**
$holdsAt(X, T)$	$\leftarrow\ nonrigid(X)\ \wedge\ holds(X, T)$	**[DN13]**
$holdsAt(Q, T)$	$\leftarrow\ rigid(Q)\ \wedge\ Q$	**[DN14]**
$nonrigid(X)$	$\leftarrow\ isfluent(X)$	**[DN15]**
$rigid(X)$	$\leftarrow\ \neg isfluent(X)$	**[DN16]**

Thus, as with OPENLOG, to understand the meaning of any ACTILOG unit, one must restore it to its underlying logical form. Unlike OPENLOG programs however, an ACTILOG unit cannot be transformed into a normal logic program, without losing expressiveness. This is due to the fact that existential quantification is highly restricted in logic programs. We must use a richer form of logic that admits explicit quantification of variables and a more complex sentence structure.

Nevertheless, this is not a problem in our system because it is based on the **iff** abductive proof procedure[9], **iff**PP, which can accommodate a more general structure for implications (conditional goals). However, a few functionalities must be added to the specification of **iff**PP to support the agent programming language. The inference rules of the proof procedure remain the same except for **splitting of implications** and **case analysis**, which must now include a new set of conditions for their application. This rule is not applied if there are universally quantified variables in the head of an implication. The reason for this, which also applies to the rule of *case analysis* is analogous to the reason for skolemization and is better explained by example 2, a follow-up to example 1:

Example 2. Suppose that we split:

$$\forall N \ \forall T \ \exists T1((serve(N, T1) \wedge T < T1) \leftarrow on(N, T)) \tag{1}$$

We will end up with:

$$\forall N \ \forall T \ \exists T1((serve(N, T1) \wedge T < T1) \vee (\textbf{false} \leftarrow on(N, T))) \tag{2}$$

The reason not to split the sentence in this example is that the first disjunct in the resulting sentence ($serve(N, T1)$) cannot be incorporated into the unconditional goals (as it should be), because it involves the universally quantified variable N. If one insists on doing so, the proof procedure will treat N as existentially quantified. Note that whether this yields incorrect answers depends on the rest of the formalization (in particular on the definition of $serve$).

However, it remains a problem that the system is losing the *dependency between existential and universal quantification*. One can see this by looking back at the clausal form of the sentence in the example 2: $serve(N, f(N, T)) \leftarrow on(N, T) \wedge T < f(N, T)$, which after splitting leaves $serve(N, f(N, T))$ as a separate disjunct. The value of the second argument of $serve$ is *determined*, not only by N but also by T.

Of course, nothing has been lost if one keeps the dependency by appealing to the skolem function ($f(N, T)$). However, this would imply significant modifications to the proof procedure. The use of skolemization has been attempted before (see Denecker and De Schreye's SLDNFA [7] for a system similar to **iff**PP, but that uses skolemization) and it has proved to be cumbersome and inefficient.

However, one can reach a proper compromise with the following strategy: The proof procedure will preserve the dependencies between variables in the implications and will be **banned** from splitting (or doing case analysis) on any implication the head of which contains variables with **active dependencies**.

The concept of **active dependency** is simple. The dependency between $T1$ and N and T above is active if N and T, in that implication, have not been assigned known constant values. For instance, when, by propagation of $on(3, 1)$, the implication above becomes $\exists T1(serve(3, T1) \leftarrow 1 < T1)$ then this can safely be handled by splitting because $T1$ is now as defined as it can be by skolemization ($T1 = f(3, 1)$).

Observe that, for this strategy, the only extension required in **iff**PP is a list of "dependencies" between variables in the implications. A list which could be built by straightforward parsing of the quantifiers in the original integrity constraints. To make the process easier, we restrict the quantifiers in the ACTILOG rules to appear as shown in table 1.

All this explained, we can now show how to transform ACTILOG units into sets of integrity contraints for agent programming. The procedure is described by a normal (meta-)logic program in tables 3, 4 and 5. To simplify the presentation the syntax of the logic programs is slightly relaxed. "{}" represents both empty categories in ACTILOG and empty formulae. The predicate *append*/3 has the usual interpretation.

Table 3. Translating ACTILOG rules into Integrity Constraints (Part 1)

ACTILOG translation into Integrity Constraints

$rewrite\_activa\_ic(Set$ **to** $TaskName, IC)$
    $\leftarrow transform(Set, IC)$ **[RW – ACTI]**

$transform(QVars\ FRule$ **and** $RestRules,$
        $NQVars(NewFRule \wedge NRestRules))$
    $\leftarrow transform(\{\}\ FRule, QVarsFR\ (NewFRule))$
   $\wedge\ transform(\{\}\ RestRules, QVarsRest\ (NRestRules))$
   $\wedge\ transform\_quantifiers(QVars, QVars')$
   $append(QVarsFR, QVarsRest, QVarTemp)$
   $append(QVars', QVarTemp, NQVars)$ **[TRSET]**

$transform(QVars$ **if** $Body$ **then** $Head,$
        $NQVars(NewHead \leftarrow NewBody))$
    $\leftarrow transform(\{\}\ Body, \{\}\ NewBody)$
   $\wedge\ transform(QVars\ Head, NQVars\ (NewHead))$ **[TRRULE]**

$transform(\{\}\ Condition$ **and** $RestConds,$
        $\{\}(holds(P,T) \wedge NRestCond))$
    $\leftarrow Condition = P$ **at** T
   $\wedge\ is\_fluent(P)$
   $transform(\{\}\ RestCond, \{\}\ (NRestCond))$ **[TRCOND – FL]**

4 OPENLOG versus ACTILOG

OPENLOG and ACTILOG **are not** exactly alternative solutions for the same problem. We need a mechanism for the activation of goals in an agent. ACTILOG

Table 4. Translating ACTILOG rules into Integrity Constraints (Part 2)

ACTILOG translation into Integrity Constraints

$transform(\{\} \ Condition \ \textbf{and} \ RestConds,$
$\qquad \{\}(done(Name, T_1, T_2) \wedge LogSched \wedge NewRC))$
$\quad \leftarrow Condition = Name \ Schedule$
$\quad \wedge \ actionname(Name)$
$\quad \wedge \ transform\_schedule(T_1, T_2, Schedule, LogSched)$
$\quad \wedge \ transform(\{\} \ RestConds, \{\} \ (NewRC))$ **[TRCOND – ACT]**

$transform(\{\} \ \textbf{not} \ Condition, \{\}\neg(NewCond))$
$\quad \leftarrow transform(\{\} \ Condition, \{\} \ (NewCond))$ **[TRCOND – NOT]**

$transform(QVars \ Disjunct \ \textbf{or} \ RestDisj,$
$\qquad NQVars(NewDisj \vee NewRD))$
$\quad \leftarrow transform(\{\} \ Disjunct, Vars1 \ (NewDis))$
$\quad \wedge \ transform(\{\} \ RestDisj, ReVars \ (NewRD))$
$\quad \wedge \ transform\_quantifiers(QVars, LogQVars)$
$\quad append(Vars1, ReVars, QVarTemp)$
$\quad append(LogQVars, QVarTemp, NQVars)$ **[TRHEAD – OR]**

$transform(QVars \ Task,$
$\qquad NQVars(LogSched \wedge done(TaskName, T_1, T_2)))$
$\quad \leftarrow Task = TaskName \ Schedule$
$\quad \wedge \ transform\_schedule(T_1, T_2, Schedule, LogSched)$
$\quad \wedge \ transform\_quantifiers(QVars, QVars')$
$\quad append(QVars', \{\exists T_1 \ \exists T_2\}, NQVars)$ **[TRHEAD – ACT]**

allows the triggering of tasks at anytime, even if the task itself is defined by OPENLOG procedures. In the examples above *serve* could be defined by an OPENLOG procedure, but we will still need the aforementioned ACTILOG rule to activate the goal.

If we do not allow for activation of goals (i.e. we do not want to use AC-TILOG, only OPENLOG), the agent would have to have one, top-most main goal from which all the possible activities of the agent are derived. This is the solution in GOLOG[13]. Ours is closer to the *forward-chaining-like solution* in the **taps**[8], without the overhead of model-theoretic computations.

ACTILOG rules contribute to keep the agent *open* to its environment (as we show below). Thus, the programmer will normally have to use ACTILOG and OPENLOG to program the agent.

The ACTILOG rule in figure 1 provides a solution for an simple *reactive* elevator-controller agent.

Table 5. Translating ACTILOG rules into Integrity Constraints (Part 3)

ACTILOG translation into Integrity Constraints	
$transform\_quantifiers(\{\}, \{\})$	[**TRQU1**]
$transform\_quantifiers(\textbf{exists } V \, RestQV, \exists V \, RestQV')$	
$\quad \leftarrow var(V) \wedge transform\_quantifiers(RestQV, RestQV')$	[**TRQU2**]
$transform\_schedule(T_o, T_f, \textbf{at } T, T \textbf{ le } T_o \wedge T \textbf{ lt } T_f)$	[**TRSCH1**]
$transform\_schedule(T_o, T_f, \textbf{before } T, T_o \textbf{ lt } T \wedge T_f \textbf{ le } T)$	[**TRSCH2**]
$transform\_schedule(T_o, T_f, \textbf{after } T, T \textbf{ le } T_o \wedge T \textbf{ lt } T_f)$	[**TRSCH3**]
$transform\_schedule(T_o, T_f, \textbf{starting at } T, T_o \textbf{ eq } T \wedge T_f \textbf{ lt } T)$	[**TRSCH4**]
$transform\_schedule(T_o, T_f, \textbf{finishing at } T, T_o \textbf{ lt } T \wedge T_f \textbf{ eq } T)$	[**TRSCH5**]
$transform\_schedule(T_o, T_f, \textbf{starting before } T, T_o \textbf{ lt } T)$	[**TRSCH6**]
$transform\_schedule(T_o, T_f, \textbf{finishing before } T, T_f \textbf{ lt } T)$	[**TRSCH7**]
$transform\_schedule(T_o, T_f, \textbf{starting after } T, T \textbf{ lt } T_o)$	[**TRSCH8**]
$transform\_schedule(T_o, T_f, \textbf{finishing after } T, T \textbf{ le } T_f)$	[**TRSCH9**]

```
if currentfloor(M) at T and on(N) at T then (
        if M eq N then open par turnoff(N); close after T
    and if M lt N then addone(M,Nx); up(Nx) after T
    and if N lt M then subone(M,Nx); down(Nx) after T )
```

Fig. 1. ACTILOG rule for a simple elevator controller

Observe that an ACTILOG "unit" will have neither recursive call, nor **while** statements. The iterative reasoning is generated by the architecture of the agent, i.e. by the *cycl*ing in which the whole system is engaged (as explained in [11]).

An ACTILOG unit is more *open* to the environment than a OPENLOG procedure because *cycle* will check the environment on each iteration and new information will be constantly arriving. There is less interaction with the environment when one has a **while** statement in a OPENLOG procedure which is being unfolded. By using **while**, one is introducing an iterative process in addition to (and without the benefits of interaction with the environment of) the iterative process generated by *cycle*. It is like having a loop within a loop, with the inconvenience that the "included-loop" (the *demo* predicate in [11] processing the **while** statement) is not forced to check the environment on every iteration, as *cycle* is.

Notice that this is the case even if **while** statements can be interrupted to assimilate inputs. To achieve the same number of "tests" on the environment per unit of time, one would have to to force the program processing the **while** to suspend processing after each iteration. In ACTILOG, *cycle* defines the only iterative mechanism. No "loops within loops" can affect the interaction with the environment.

In addition, ACTILOG units can support "planning ahead". Actions will be promoted from the head of implications to *the bag of abducibles* and, after that, they will be "firing" implications and triggering subsequent actions.

There still is one more advantage in ACTILOG due to the fact the we are using the **iff** abductive proof procedure. Plans generated from ACTILOG rules, in contrast to those obtained from OPENLOG procedures, *can be made to contain a minimal set of abduced steps.* The checking of preconditions can be done in the body of the implications, where abduction is not allowed by the proof procedure. This form of precondition testing blurs the distinction between triggering conditions and proper preconditions of actions. However, by using ACTILOG only, we will not have to inhibit the abductive process to cater for "over-generation of abducibles". The problem is explained in [6].

Thus, OPENLOG and ACTILOG, in the context of abductive logic programs, *could be* alternative solutions for the same problem (i.e. both could be used to generate the same behaviour in the agent) if OPENLOG is accompanied by a mechanism to inhibit abduction. All these advantages suggest that ACTILOG is a more expressive programming framework than OPENLOG and, perhaps, that integrity constraints are equality related to traditional logic programs.

There are however, points in favour of using OPENLOG as the programming language (or even better, a combination of OPENLOG and ACTILOG. We followed this approach in the prototype).

The first advantage comes from Software Engineering. For complex tasks and domains, the set of integrity contraints can be very large and difficult to arrange as one "unit". In those circumstances, a more "modular" approach, for instance with procedures in OPENLOG, could be more advisable.

The second advantage is related to the first but is more subtle. In OPENLOG procedures, the ultimate goal being pursued can always be inferred from the code of the procedures. For instance, in the elevator example, once $on(3, 1)$ triggers the goal $1 < T_1 \wedge serve(3, 1, T_1)$, the goal $serve(3, T_2, T_1) \wedge 1 < T_2$ can be inferred from the other literals involved. These literals are part of the agent's goals while the agent is trying to achieve "serving the third floor by T_1". Thus, having information about which higher goal the agent is aiming to (and how much is still to be done to achieve it) in a partial plan is easier in OPENLOG.

This kind of information can be particularly useful when the system is using heuristics to guide its search process and when it is trying to decide on the importance or urgency of its goals.

But even this can be done, to some extend, in ACTILOG, although by appealing to an extra-logical resource. In the first category in table 1, a *Unit* could be characterized by a *Set* and a *TaskName* (*Unit* ::= *Set* **to** *TaskName*), where *TaskName* indicates the ultimate goal at which the integrity contraints in *Set* are aiming.

This is an extra-logical device because *TaskName* is lost in the translation of ACTILOG rules into integrity contraints that define their semantics. However, if one maintains this "label" attached to the ACTILOG unit, one could identify the tasks that have been triggered and reason about their state of planning and execution.

Of course, this is not the only way of knowing about pending tasks. One could also use "state encoding", as described by Allen [1]: within the language, one would introduce the fluent $serving(N, T)$, initiated by the observation $on(N, T)$, and this would be enough for the agent to know which the on-going tasks are.

One last remark about ACTILOG and the activation of goals. Observe that, from the perspective of a reactive agent, *there may be no need* to remember which higher goal the agent is planning and acting for. For instance, in the case of the elevator controller, the agent does not need to remember $serve(3, T)$, activated by $on(3, T')$ for some $T' < T$.

If the signal stays on "outside in the environment", the agent will be able to realize that the task is still pending if it fails to reach its higher goal ($serve(3, T)$ in this case) with the first (re-)actions. It is as if the agent is using the "world as its own model" [2] and so, representations (memory) of inputs and goals (such as records of the signals and the triggered tasks) will not be necessary. In a "cooperating" environment like that, an agent needs fewer deliberative resources in order to be efficient and effective. We are exploiting this possibility in the implementation.

The following section discuss the logic of activation of goals with one example to illustrate how the reactive nature of integrity constraints can be combined with planning.

5   Activation of Goals for Planning

The purpose of activating a goal is to have the agent plan actions to achieve it. As we discussed above, sometimes the environment is such that the agent does not need to plan. In those cases, reactivity becomes more important in producing sensible behaviour, and then simple integrity constraint or ACTILOG rules are sufficient to generate that behaviour.

However, the "reactive" use of integrity constraints to activate goals could be a source of inadequate or improper behaviour. This could be the case, for instance, if the agent continues executing a plan that it has devised to achieve an "activated" goal, even though the "activating" conditions have ceased to hold.

To illustrate this, let us use the context of the following example. Imagine that the goal:

$$\exists T_1 \ \exists T2 \ (0 < T_1 \ \wedge \ serve(2, T_1, T_2) \ ) \tag{3}$$

has been activated from the implication:

$$\exists T_1 \ \exists T2 \ (T < T_1 \ \wedge \ serve(N, T_1, T_2) \leftarrow \ obs(on(N), T) \ ) \tag{4}$$

by the input: $obs(on(2), 0)$

Also imagine that half-way through the execution of the corresponding plan, the signal at floor 2 is turned off. The agent observes this, because it has interrupted its reasoning to try the first action of the plan, and the information about the new status of the signal arrives as "feedback".

It would be incorrect[4] for the elevator to keep executing this plan as its motivating condition (that the signal was "on" and the floor ought to be served) has vanished.

The problem is that the elevator (executing an OPENLOG "serve" procedure and with the integrity constraint 4 above) has no means of deducing that the plan is now unnecessary and must be abandoned, until it actually tries the *turnoff* action (which will fail because the signal is not "on").

We can solve this problem in several ways with our agent architecture. We discuss one general[5] and one specific solution below.

A general solution is to include this version of the axiom [DNEC0] which includes an explicit test of all the preconditions of all the primitive actions, like this:

$$done(A, T_o, T_f) \leftarrow primitive(A) \land preconds(A, T_o)$$
$$\land T_o \leq T_f \land do(A, T_o, T_f) \qquad \textbf{[DNEC0']}$$

The axiom [DNEC0'] would allow for the "clipped" constraint to be produced and used by the planner to falsify the plan. If the agent completes that plan up to the point where the preconditions of *turnoff* are reasoned about, it will "realize" (before trying to execute it) that the action *turnoff(2)* is going to fail (precisely because the elevator assumes that the signal will not be "on" at that floor). This is the reason to drop the plan.

Notice that we are assuming here that either some action of the plan has been executed or the planner has access to some mechanism to handle inequalities and time-constraints involving the current time. As we said in that section, this inequality-handling mechanism could be combined with a mechanism to evaluate agent's action preferences. One could also maintain an explicit record of the goal that has been activated and its activating condition as "contextual" information.

That "general" solution to the problem of activating conditions that ceased to hold (leaving "triggered" plans *without justification for their execution*) could be expected to be inefficient. This is because the planner needs to "complete" the plan up to the point where the constraints on the preconditions of the actions are made explicit (e.g. the constraint **false** $\leftarrow clipped(0, on(2), T_3)$ must be derived by the planner, before it can be used to test whether the precondition persists).

One could improve the efficiency of the planner by providing a more precise and informative integrity constraint to activate the "serve" goal. This would be a specific solution because it uses knowledge specific to the problem. For instance, after introducing a new abducible predicate[6] *serving*, the constraints:

---

[4] With respect to an idealised model of perfect rationality with no resource constraints for reasoning.

[5] General solution for those cases when the "motivating" condition (e.g. *on(2)* above) is also the precondition of some action in the plan (as in the case of *turnoff(2)* above).

[6] This means that the *bag of abduced atoms* will contain $\{do, =, <, obs, serving\}$. The introduction of *serving* could be regarded as an instance of "state-encoding" as discussed by Allen in [1] and also mentioned in the previous section.

$$\exists T_1 \; \exists T_2 \; (\; (T < T_1 \; \wedge \; serving(N,T,T_2) \; \wedge \; serve(N,T_1,T_2) \;)$$
$$\leftarrow \; obs(on(N),T) \;)$$
$$\wedge \; (\mathbf{false} \leftarrow \; (serving(N,T_3,T_4) \; \wedge \; do(S, turnoff(N), T_0, T_f)$$
$$\wedge \; S \neq self \; \wedge \; T_3 \leq T_0 \; \wedge \; T_f \leq T_4 \;) \;)$$

will have any plan to achieve the goal $serve(N,T_1,T_2)$ falsified, if an event that switches the signal off (presumably other agent doing it) is observed before the plan is executed by *this* agent[7]

Thus, integrity constraints do support some basic, rational behaviour in a multi-agent, dynamic environment. Whether they can be extended to cater for more complex cases of coordination and cooperative behaviour requires further investigation.

6   Conclusions and Further Work

This article and the previous one [6] have presented a family of extended logic programming languages to program an agent. The characteristic common to all these languages is that their sentences have an unambiguous translation into subsets of first order logic. In the case of OPENLOG, the translation has a more restrictive output, yielding *normal logic programs*. In the case of ACTILOG the translation is into a form that supports sentences formalizing integrity contraints, that can be used to guide the process of activation of goals in the agent. Both programming languages have an operational semantics closely related to the specification of the abductive proof procedure [9].

OPENLOG is a logic programming language that can be used to write procedural code which can be combined with a declarative specification of a problem domain (a background theory). ACTILOG complements that language by providing for integrity constraint and activation rules for the agent. However, ACTILOG can also be used to state integrity constraints as an alternative representation of procedural descriptions.

We plan to complete the family of language to program agents, with means to represent agent preferences and priorities. We will also offer this family of programming languages in a platform to simulate multi-agents systems [5].

Acknowledgments. This work has been partially funded by Fonacit-CDCHT-University of Los Andes, projects I-524-95-02-AA, I-667-99-02-B and S1-2000000819.

References

1. James F. Allen, *Temporal reasoning and planning*, Reasoning About Plans (J. F. Allen, H. Kautz, R. Pelavin, and J. Tenenberg, eds.), Morgan Kauffmann Publishers, Inc., San Mateo, California, 1991, ISBN 1-55860-137-6.

---

[7] Here we also assume that there is a mechanism to deduce that the turning off of the signal does occur after the instant when the goal is activated ($T_3 \leq T_0$) and before the plan is completed ($T_f \leq T_4$).

2. Rodney Brooks, *Intelligence without representation*, Artificial Intelligence (1991), 139–159.
3. Lee Brownston, *Programming expert systems in ops5*, Addison-Wesley Inc., USA, 1985.
4. Jacinto Dávila, *Agents in logic programming*, Ph.D. thesis, Imperial College, London, UK, 1997.
5. Jacinto Dávila and Mayerlin Uzcátegui, *Galatea: A multi-agent simulation platform*, The best of AMSE (C. Berger-Vachon and A.M. Gil lafuente, eds.), http://www.amse-modelling.org/Periodical_AMSE.html, AMSE, Barcelona, Spain, 2000.
6. Jacinto A. Dávila, *Openlog: A logic programming language based on abduction*, Lecture Notes in Computer Science (Proceedings of PPDP'99. París,France) Gopalan, Nadathur (Ed.). Springer. ISBN 3-540-66540-4. **1702** (1999).
7. M. Denecker and D. De Schreye, *Sldnfa: an abductive procedure for normal abductive programs*, Proc. International Conference and Symposium on Logic Programming (1992), 686–700.
8. Jürgen Dix, Sarit Kraus, and V.S Subrahmanian, *Temporal agent programs*, Artificial Intelligence (2001), no. 127, 87–135.
9. T.H Fung and R. Kowalski, *The iff proof procedure for abductive logic programming*, Journal of Logic Programming (1997).
10. A. C. Kakas, R. Kowalski, and F. Toni, *Handbook of logic in artificial intelligence and logic programming 5*, ch. The Role of Abduction in Logic Programming, pp. 235–324, Oxford University Press, 1998.
11. R Kowalski and F. Sadri, *From logic programming towards multi-agent systems*, Annals of Mathematics and Artificial Intelligence **25** (1999), 391–419.
12. Robert Kowalski and Marek Sergot, *A logic-based calculus of events*, New Generation Computing **4** (1986), 67–95.
13. H. Levesque, R. Reiter, Y. Lespérance, L. Fangzhen, and R. B. Scherl, *Golog: A logic programming language for dynamic domains*, (1995), (Also at http://www.cs.toronto.edu/~cogrobo/).
14. J. McCarthy and P. Hayes, *Some philosophical problems from the standpoint of artificial intelligence*, Machine Intelligence **4** (1969), 463–502.

Logic Programs for Querying Inconsistent Databases

Pablo Barceló[1] and Leopoldo Bertossi[2]

[1] University of Toronto
Department of Computer Science
Toronto, Canada. `pablo@cs.toronto.edu`
[2] Carleton University
School of Computer Science
Ottawa, Canada.
`bertossi@scs.carleton.ca`

Abstract. Consistent answers from a relational database that violates a given set of integrity constraints (ICs) are characterized as ordinary answers that can be obtained from every minimally repaired version of the database (a repair). Repairs can be specified and interpreted as the stable models of a simple disjunctive normal logic program with database predicates extended with appropriate annotation arguments. In consequence, consistent query answers can be obtained by running a query program in combination with the repair program under the cautious or skeptical stable model semantics. In this paper we show how to write repair programs for universal and referential ICs; we establish their correctness and show how to run them on top of the *DLV* system.

1 Introduction

Integrity constraints (ICs) capture the semantics of a relational database, establishing its correspondence with the application domain that the database is modeling. However, it is not unusual for a database instance to become inconsistent with respect to a given, intended set of ICs. This could happen due to different factors, being one of them the integration of several data sources. The integration of consistent databases may easily lead to an inconsistent integrated database.

A natural problem in databases consists in retrieving answers to queries that are "consistent" with the given ICs, even when the database as a whole does not satisfy those ICs. Very likely "most" of the data is still consistent. The notion of consistent answer to a first order (FO) query was defined in [2], where also a computational mechanism for obtaining consistent answers was presented. Intuitively speaking, a ground tuple $\bar{t}$ to a first order query $Q(\bar{x})$ is *consistent* in a, possibly inconsistent, relational database instance DB if it is an (ordinary) answer to $Q(\bar{x})$ in every minimal repair of DB, i.e. in every database instance over the same schema and domain that differs from DB by a minimal (under set inclusion) set of inserted or deleted tuples.

Computing consistent query answers is a natural problem in DBs. Apart from applications in data integration [10], we also foresee interesting applications in

V. Dahl and P. Wadler (Eds.): PADL 2003, LNCS 2562, pp. 208–222, 2003.
© Springer-Verlag Berlin Heidelberg 2003

the context of intelligent information systems, where a particular user might impose his/her particular view of the semantics of the database by querying the database through his/her user ICs, that are not necessarily maintained by the DB central administration. This user could specify his/her own constraints as queries are posed, by means of a new, extra SQL statement or a new option in the usual menu for interacting with the DB.

The mechanism presented in [2] for consistent query answering (CQA) has some limitations in terms of the ICs and queries it can handle. In [4], a more general methodology based on logic programs with a stable model semantics was introduced. More general queries could be considered, but ICs were restricted to be "binary", i.e. universal with at most two database literals (plus built-ins). Independently, a similar methodology based on logic programs for CQA wrt arbitrary universal ICs was presented in [23].

For CQA we need to deal with all the repairs of a database, but hopefully in a compact, succinct manner, without having to compute all of them explicitly. Actually, the database repairs corresponds to just an auxiliary conceptual notion used to characterize what is relevant to us, the consistent answers. In consequence, a natural approach consists in providing a manageable logical specification of the class of database repairs, that treats them as a whole. The specification must include information about the database and the ICs.

In this paper we show how to specify the database repairs by means of simple classical disjunctive normal programs with a stable model semantics. The database predicates in these programs contain annotations as extra arguments. In their turn, the annotations are inspired by the theories written in annotated predicate logic that specify database repairs as presented in [3,8]. Nevertheless, the programs are classical, as opposed to annotated or paraconsistent logic programs [11,25]. The *coherent* stable models of the program turn out to correspond to the database repairs. The logic programs introduced in [4,23] to specify database repairs may contain an exponential number of rules depending on the number of database literals appearing in the ICs. However, the programs presented here contain only a linear number of rules.

With this approach we reach two goals. The first goal consists in obtaining a computable specification of all the possible minimal sets of changes required to restore the consistency of a theory corresponding to the positive information explicitly stored in a relational database. However, we are not interested in computing database repairs, neither in repairing in any way the inconsistent database. Actually, the main, second goal consists in providing a general computational mechanism to obtain the consistent answers to a first order query. They can be obtained by "running" the combination of the repair program and a query program under the skeptical stable model semantics that sanctions as true what is true of every stable model. The less a logic programming implementation explicitly computes all stable models in order to answer a query, the better. We have experimented with *DLV*, an implementation of the disjunctive stable model semantics [19].

The methodology presented here works for arbitrary first order queries and arbitrary universal ICs, what considerable extends the cases that could be handled in [2,4,3]. We also show how to apply the methodology in the presence of referential integrity constraints [1].

2   Preliminaries

2.1   Database Repairs and Consistent Answers

We consider a fixed relational database schema $\Sigma = (D, P, B)$, consisting of a fixed, possibly infinite, database domain $D = \{c_1, c_2, ...\}$, a fixed set of database predicates $P = \{p_1, \ldots, p_n\}$ with fixed arities, and a fixed set of built-in predicates $B = \{e_1, \ldots, e_m\}$. This schema determines a first order language $\mathcal{L}(\Sigma)$.

A database instance over Σ is a finite collection DB of facts of the form $p(c_1, ..., c_n)$, where p is a predicate in P and $c_1, ..., c_n$ are constants in D. A built-in predicate has a fixed and the same extension in every database instance, not subject to any changes.

An *integrity constraint* (IC) is an implicitly quantified clause of the form

$$\bigvee_{i=1}^{n} \neg p_i(\bar{t}_i) \vee \bigvee_{j=1}^{m} q_j(\bar{s}_j) \vee \varphi, \tag{1}$$

where, p_i and q_j are predicates in P, $\bar{t}_i, \bar{s}_j$ are tuples containing constants and variables, and φ is a formula containing predicates in B only.

We will assume that DB and IC, separately, are consistent theories. Nevertheless, it may be the case that $DB \cup IC$ is inconsistent. Equivalently, if we associate in the natural way to DB a first order structure, also denoted with DB, i.e. by applying the closed world assumption (CWA) that makes false any ground atom not explicitly appearing in the set of atoms DB, it may happen that DB, as a structure, does not satisfy the IC. We denote with $DB \models_\Sigma IC$ the fact that the database satisfies IC. In this case we say that DB is consistent wrt IC; otherwise we say DB is inconsistent.

As in [2], we define that the *distance* between two database instances DB_1 and DB_2 is their symmetric difference $\Delta(DB_1, DB_2) = (DB_1 - DB_2) \cup (DB_2 - DB_1)$.

Now, given database instances DB, possibly inconsistent wrt IC, we say that the instance DB' is a *repair* of DB iff $DB' \models_\Sigma IC$ and $\Delta(DB, DB')$ is minimal under set inclusion in the class of instances that satisfy IC [2], that is, there is no instance DB'' such that $DB'' \models_\Sigma IC$ and $\Delta(DB, DB'') \subsetneq \Delta(DB, DB')$.

Example 1. Consider the relational schema $Book(author, name, publYear)$ and a database instance $DB = \{Book(kafka, metamorph, 1915), Book(kafka, metamorph, 1919)\}$. We also have the functional dependency [1] $FD: author, name \rightarrow publYear$, that can be expressed by $IC: \neg Book(x, y, z) \vee \neg Book(x, y, w) \vee z = w$.

DB is inconsistent with respect to IC. The original instance has two possible repairs, namely $DB_1 = \{Book(kafka, metamorph, 1915)\}$ and $DB_2 = \{Book(kafka, metamorph, 1919)\}$.   □

Let DB be a database instance, possibly not satisfying a set IC of integrity constraints. Given a query $Q(\bar{x})$ to DB, we say that a tuple of constants $\bar{t}$ is a *consistent answer* [2], denoted $DB \models_c Q(\bar{t})$, if for every repair DB' of DB, $DB' \models_\Sigma Q(\bar{t})$. If Q is a closed formula, i.e. a sentence, then *true* is a *consistent answer* to Q, denoted $DB \models_c Q$, if for every repair DB' of DB, $DB' \models_\Sigma Q$.

Example 2. (example 1 continued) Query Q_1: $Book(kafka, metamorph, 1915)$ does not have *true* as a consistent answer, because it is not true in every repair. Query $Q_2(y)$: $\exists x \exists z Book(x, y, z)$ has $y = metamorph$ as a consistent answer. Query $Q_3(x)$: $\exists z Book(x, metamorph, z)$ has $x = kafka$ as a consistent answer. $\Box$

Notice that repairs are obtained by insertion/deletion of whole relational tuples, and we do not specify a preference for any particular kind of repairs. Repairs are just used to characterize the consistent answers.

Annotated Predicate Calculus was introduced in [24]. It constitutes a non classical logic where classical inconsistencies may be accommodated without trivializing reasoning. Its syntax is similar to that of classical logic, except for the fact that atoms are annotated with values drawn from a truth-values lattice. In [3], in order to embed the database and the ICs into a single consistent theory, a particular lattice was introduced. It contains the four usual truth values: $\mathbf{t}, \mathbf{f}$ (classical true and false), $\top$ (inconsistent), $\bot$ (unknown) plus $\mathbf{t_c}$, $\mathbf{t_d}$, $\mathbf{f_d}$, $\mathbf{f_c}$, $\mathbf{t_a}$, $\mathbf{f_a}$. It was also shown that there is a one to one correspondence between some minimal models of the annotated theory and the repairs of the inconsistent database for universal ICs. This was extended to existential ICs in [8].

The values $\mathbf{t_c}$, $\mathbf{f_c}$ are used to annotate what is needed for constraint satisfaction: If the IC is written in disjunctive normal form, positive, resp. negative, literals are annotated with $\mathbf{t_c}$, resp. $\mathbf{f_c}$. The values $\mathbf{t_d}$ and $\mathbf{f_d}$ represent the truth values according to the original database: An atom in (outside) the DB is annotated with $\mathbf{t_d}$ ($\mathbf{f_d}$). Finally, $\mathbf{t_a}$ and $\mathbf{f_a}$ are considered *advisory* truth values, to solve conflicts between the original database and the ICs, that have to be satisfied by the former. Conflicts are always solved in favor of the ICs, as only the database instance can be changed to restore consistency. That is, $lub(\mathbf{t_d}, \mathbf{f_c}) = \mathbf{f_a}$, meaning that in case an atom is true at the data level, but false at the IC level, it will get the derived annotation $\mathbf{f_a}$, expressing that it is advised to make it false, i.e. to delete it from the database. Similarly, $lub(\mathbf{f_d}, \mathbf{t_c}) = \mathbf{t_a}$ is an indication that the literal which receives the annotation $\mathbf{t_a}$ must be inserted into the database.

In this paper, instead of explicitly using a lattice, the annotations will be new constants in the language, to be used in an extra argument introduced in the database atoms. The rules 3. in Definition 1 will capture the relationships between the annotations we described above.

3   Logic Programming Specification of Repairs

In this section we will consider ICs of the form (1). Our aim is to specify database repairs using classical first order logic programs. However, those programs will be suggested by the non classical annotated theory. In order to accommodate annotations in this classical framework, we replace each predicate $p(\bar{x}) \in P$ by a new predicate $p(\bar{x}, \cdot)$, with an extra argument for annotations. This defines a new FO language, $\mathcal{L}(\Sigma)^{an}$, for annotated $\mathcal{L}(\Sigma)$.

Definition 1. *The repair logic program, $\Pi(DB, IC)$, for DB and IC, is written with predicates from $\mathcal{L}(\Sigma)^{an}$ and contains the following clauses:*

1. *For every atom $p(\bar{a}) \in DB$, $\Pi(DB, IC)$ contains the fact $p(\bar{a}, t_d)$.*
2. *For every predicate $p \in P$, $\Pi(DB, IC)$ contains the clauses:*

$$p(\bar{x}, t^\star) \leftarrow p(\bar{x}, t_d). \qquad p(\bar{x}, t^\star) \leftarrow p(\bar{x}, t_a).$$
$$p(\bar{x}, f^\star) \leftarrow p(\bar{x}, f_a). \qquad p(\bar{x}, f^\star) \leftarrow \text{ not } p(\bar{x}, t_d).,$$

   where $t^\star, f^\star$ are new, auxiliary elements in the domain of annotations.
3. *For every constraint of the form (1), $\Pi(DB, IC)$ contains the clause:*

$$\bigvee_{i=1}^{n} p_i(\bar{t}_i, f_a) \vee \bigvee_{j=1}^{m} q_j(\bar{s}_j, t_a) \quad \longleftarrow \quad \bigwedge_{i=1}^{n} p_i(\bar{t}_i, t^\star) \wedge \bigwedge_{j=1}^{m} q_j(\bar{s}_j, f^\star) \wedge \bar{\varphi},$$

   where $\bar{\varphi}$ represents the negation of φ. □

Intuitively, the clauses in 3. say that when the IC is violated (the body), then DB has to be repaired according to one of the alternatives shown in the head. Since there may be interactions between constraints, these single repairing steps may not be enough to restore the consistency of DB. We have to make sure that the repairing process continues and stabilizes in a state where all the ICs hold. This is the role of the clauses in 2. containing the new annotations $t^\star$, that groups together those atoms annotated with t_d and t_a, and $f^\star$, that does the same with f_d and f_a. Notice that the annotations $t^\star$, $f^\star$, obtained through the combined effect of rules 2. and 3., can be fed back into rules 3. until consistency is restored. This possibility is what allows us to have just one program rule for each IC.

Example 3 shows the interaction of a functional dependency and an inclusion dependency. When atoms are deleted in order to satisfy the functional dependency, the inclusion dependency could be violated, and in a second step it should be repaired. At that second step, the annotations $t^\star$ and $f^\star$, computed at the first step where the functional dependency was repaired, will detect the violation of the inclusion dependency and trigger the corresponding repairing process.

Example 3. (example 1 continued) We extend the schema with the table *Eurbook(author, name, publYear)*, for European books. Now, DB also contains the literal *Eurbook(kafka, metamorph, 1919)*}. If in addition to the ICs we had before, we consider the set inclusion dependency $\forall xyz\, (Eurbook(x, y, z) \rightarrow Book(x, y, z))$, we obtain the following program $\Pi(DB, IC)$:

1. $EurBook(kafka, metamorph, 1919, t_d). \qquad Book(kafka, metamorph, 1919, t_d).$
$Book(kafka, metamorph, 1915, t_d).$

2. $Book(x, y, z, t^\star) \leftarrow Book(x, y, z, t_d). \qquad Book(x, y, z, t^\star) \leftarrow Book(x, y, z, t_a).$
$Book(x, y, z, f^\star) \leftarrow Book(x, y, z, f_a). \qquad Book(x, y, z, f^\star) \leftarrow \text{ not } Book(x, y, z, t_d).$
$Eurbook(x, y, z, t^\star) \leftarrow Eurbook(x, y, z, t_d).$
$Eurbook(x, y, z, t^\star) \leftarrow Eurbook(x, y, z, t_a).$

$Eurbook(x, y, z, \mathbf{f}^\star) \leftarrow Eurbook(x, y, z, \mathbf{f_a})$.
$Eurbook(x, y, z, \mathbf{f}^\star) \leftarrow not\ Eurbook(x, y, z, \mathbf{t_d})$.

3. $Book(x, y, z, \mathbf{f_a}) \vee Book(x, y, w, \mathbf{f_a}) \leftarrow Book(x, y, z, \mathbf{t}^\star), Book(x, y, w, \mathbf{t}^\star),$
$$z \neq w.$$
$Eurbook(x, y, z, \mathbf{f_a}) \vee Book(x, y, z, \mathbf{t_a}) \leftarrow Eurbook(x, y, z, \mathbf{t}^\star), Book(x, y, z, \mathbf{f}^\star).$

□

For our programs, that contain negation as failure, we will consider the stable models semantics. A model $\mathcal{M}$ is a stable model of a disjunctive program P iff it is a minimal model of $P^{\mathcal{M}}$, where $P^{\mathcal{M}} = \{A_1 \vee \cdots \vee A_n \leftarrow B_1, \cdots, B_m \mid A_1 \vee \cdots \vee A_n \leftarrow B_1, \cdots, B_m, not\ C_1, \cdots, not\ C_k$ is a ground instance of a clause in P and $\mathcal{M} \not\models C_i$ for $1 \leq i \leq k\}$ [20,21].

Definition 2. *A Herbrand model $\mathcal{M}$ is* coherent *if it does not contain both* $p(\bar{a}, \mathbf{t_a})$ *and* $p(\bar{a}, \mathbf{f_a})$. □

Example 4. (example 3 continued) The coherent stable models of the program presented in Example 3 are:

$\mathcal{M}_1 = \{Book(kafka, metamorph, 1919, \mathbf{t_d}),\ Book(kafka, metamorph, 1919, \mathbf{t}^\star),$
$Book(kafka, metamorph, 1915, \mathbf{t_d}),\ Book(kafka, metamorph, 1915, \mathbf{t}^\star),$
$Book(kafka, metamorph, 1915, \mathbf{f_a}),\ Book(kafka, metamorph, 1915, \mathbf{f}^\star),$
$Eurbook(kafka, metamorph, 1919, \mathbf{t_d}),\ Eurbook(kafka, metamorph, 1919, \mathbf{t}^\star)\};$

$\mathcal{M}_2 = \{Book(kafka, metamorph, 1919, \mathbf{t_d}),\ Book(kafka, metamorph, 1919, \mathbf{t}^\star),$
$Book(kafka, metamorph, 1919, \mathbf{f_a}),\ Book(kafka, metamorph, 1919, \mathbf{f}^\star),$
$Book(kafka, metamorph, 1915, \mathbf{t_d}),\ Book(kafka, metamorph, 1915, \mathbf{t}^\star),$
$Eurbook(kafka, metamorph, 1919, \mathbf{t_d}),\ Eurbook(kafka, metamorph, 1919, \mathbf{t}^\star),$
$Eurbook(kafka, metamorph, 1919, \mathbf{f_a}),\ Eurbook(kafka, metamorph, 1919, \mathbf{f}^\star)\}.$ □

The stable models of the program will include the database contents with its original annotations ($\mathbf{t_d}$). Every time there is an atom in a model annotated with $\mathbf{t_d}$ or $\mathbf{t_a}$, it will appear annotated with $\mathbf{t}^\star$. From these models we should be able to "read" database repairs. Every stable model of the logic program has to be interpreted. In order to do this, we introduce two new annotations, $\mathbf{t}^{\star\star}, \mathbf{f}^{\star\star}$, in the last arguments. The first one groups together those atoms annotated with $\mathbf{t_a}$ and those annotated with $\mathbf{t_d}$, but not $\mathbf{f_a}$. Intuitively, they correspond to those annotated with $\mathbf{t}$ in the models of $\mathcal{T}(DB, IC)$. A similar role plays the other new annotation wrt the "false" annotations. These new annotations will simplify the expression of the queries to be posed to the program. Without them, instead of simply asking $p(\bar{x}, \mathbf{t}^{\star\star})$ (for the tuples in p in a repair), we would have to ask for $p(\bar{x}, \mathbf{t_a}) \vee (p(\bar{x}, \mathbf{t_d}) \wedge \neg p(\bar{x}, \mathbf{f_a}))$. The interpreted models can be easily obtained by adding new rules.

Definition 3. *The interpretation program $\Pi^\star(DB, IC)$ extends $\Pi(DB, IC)$ with the following rules:*

$p(\bar{a}, \mathbf{f}^{\star\star}) \leftarrow p(\bar{a}, \mathbf{f_a}).$ $p(\bar{a}, \mathbf{f}^{\star\star}) \leftarrow not\ p(\bar{a}, \mathbf{t_d}), not\ p(\bar{a}, \mathbf{t_a}).$
$p(\bar{a}, \mathbf{t}^{\star\star}) \leftarrow p(\bar{a}, \mathbf{t_a}).$ $p(\bar{a}, \mathbf{t}^{\star\star}) \leftarrow p(\bar{a}, \mathbf{t_d}), not\ p(\bar{a}, \mathbf{f_a}).$ □

Example 5. (example 4 continued) The coherent stable models of the interpretation program extend

$\mathcal{M}_1$ with $\{Eurbook(kafka, metamorph, 1919, \mathbf{t}^{\star\star}),$
    $Book(kafka, metamorph, 1919, \mathbf{t}^{\star\star}), Book(kafka, metamorph, 1915, \mathbf{f}^{\star\star})\};$

$\mathcal{M}_2$ with $\{Eurbook(kafka, metamorph, 1919, \mathbf{f}^{\star\star}),$
    $Book(kafka, metamorph, 1919, \mathbf{f}^{\star\star}), Book(kafka, metamorph, 1915, \mathbf{t}^{\star\star})\}.$ □

From an interpretation model we can obtain a database instance.

Definition 4. *Let $\mathcal{M}$ be a coherent stable model of program $\Pi^\star(DB, IC)$. The database associated to $\mathcal{M}$ is $DB_\mathcal{M} = \{p(\bar{a}) \mid p(\bar{a}, \mathbf{t}^{\star\star}) \in \mathcal{M}\}$.* □

Theorem 1 establishes the one-to-one correspondence between coherent stable models of the program and the repairs of the original instance.

Theorem 1. *If $\mathcal{M}$ is a coherent stable model of $\Pi^\star(DB, IC)$, and $DB_\mathcal{M}$ is finite, then $DB_\mathcal{M}$ is a repair of DB with respect to IC. Furthermore, the repairs obtained in this way are all the repairs of DB.* □

Example 6. (example 5 continued) The following database instances obtained from Definition 4 are the repairs of DB:

$DB_{\mathcal{M}_1} = \{Eurbook(kafka, metamorph, 1919), \ Book(kafka, metamorph, 1919)\},$
$DB_{\mathcal{M}_2} = \{Book(kafka, metamorph, 1915)\}.$ □

3.1   The Query Program

Given a first order query Q, we want the consistent answers from DB. In consequence, we need those atoms that are simultaneously true of Q in every stable model of the program $\Pi(DB, IC)$. They are obtained through the query $Q^{\star\star}$, obtained from Q by replacing, for $p \in P$, every positive literal $p(\bar{s})$ by $p(\bar{s}, \mathbf{t}^{\star\star})$ and every negative literal $\neg p(\bar{s})$ by $p(\bar{s}, \mathbf{f}^{\star\star})$. Now $Q^{\star\star}$ can be transformed into a query program $\Pi(Q^{\star\star})$ by a standard transformation [27,1]. This query program will be run in combination with $\Pi^\star(DB, IC)$.

Example 7. For the query $Q(y) : \exists z Book(kafka, y, z)$, we generate $Q^{\star\star}(y) : \exists z Book(kafka, y, z, \mathbf{t}^{\star\star})$, that is transformed into the query program clause $Answer(y) \leftarrow Book(kafka, y, z, \mathbf{t}^{\star\star})$. □

4   Computing from the Program

The database repairs could be computed using an implementation of the disjunctive stable models semantics like DLV [19], that also supports denial constraints as studied in [12]. In this way we are able to prune out the models that are not coherent, imposing for every predicate p the constraint $\leftarrow p(\bar{x}, \mathbf{t_a}), p(\bar{x}, \mathbf{f_a})$.

Example 8. Consider the database instance $\{p(a)\}$ that is inconsistent wrt the set inclusion dependency $\forall x \ (p(x) \rightarrow q(x))$. The program $\Pi^\star(DB, IC)$ contains the following clauses:

1. Database contents: $p(a, \mathbf{t_d})$.
2. Rules for the closed world assumption:

   $p(x, \mathbf{f^\star}) \leftarrow \ not \ p(x, \mathbf{t_d})$. $q(x, \mathbf{f^\star}) \leftarrow \ not \ q(x, \mathbf{t_d})$.
3. Annotation rules:

   $p(x, \mathbf{f^\star}) \leftarrow p(x, \mathbf{f_a})$. $p(x, \mathbf{t^\star}) \leftarrow p(x, \mathbf{t_a})$. $p(x, \mathbf{t^\star}) \leftarrow p(x, \mathbf{t_d})$.
   $q(x, \mathbf{f^\star}) \leftarrow q(x, \mathbf{f_a})$. $q(x, \mathbf{t^\star}) \leftarrow q(x, \mathbf{t_a})$. $q(x, \mathbf{t^\star}) \leftarrow q(x, \mathbf{t_d})$.
4. Rule for the IC: $p(x, \mathbf{f_a}) \vee q(x, \mathbf{t_a}) \leftarrow p(x, \mathbf{t^\star}), q(x, \mathbf{f^\star})$.
5. Denial constraints for coherence

   $\leftarrow p(\bar{x}, \mathbf{t_a}), p(\bar{x}, \mathbf{f_a})$. $\leftarrow q(\bar{x}, \mathbf{t_a}), q(\bar{x}, \mathbf{f_a})$.
6. Interpretation rules:

   $p(x, \mathbf{t^{\star\star}}) \leftarrow p(x, \mathbf{t_a})$. $p(x, \mathbf{t^{\star\star}}) \leftarrow p(x, \mathbf{t_d}), \ not \ p(x, \mathbf{f_a})$.
   $p(x, \mathbf{f^{\star\star}}) \leftarrow p(x, \mathbf{f_a})$. $p(x, \mathbf{f^{\star\star}}) \leftarrow \ not \ p(x, \mathbf{t_d}), \ not \ p(x, \mathbf{t_a})$.
   $q(x, \mathbf{t^{\star\star}}) \leftarrow q(x, \mathbf{t_a})$. $q(x, \mathbf{t^{\star\star}}) \leftarrow q(x, \mathbf{t_d}), \ not \ q(x, \mathbf{f_a})$.
   $q(x, \mathbf{f^{\star\star}}) \leftarrow q(x, \mathbf{f_a})$. $q(x, \mathbf{f^{\star\star}}) \leftarrow \ not \ q(x, \mathbf{t_d}), \ not \ q(x, \mathbf{t_a})$.

Running program $\Pi^\star(DB, IC)$ with *DLV* we obtain two stable models:

$\mathcal{M}_1 = \{p(a, \mathbf{t_d}), p(a, \mathbf{t^\star}), q(a, \mathbf{f^\star}), q(a, \mathbf{t_a}), p(a, \mathbf{t^{\star\star}}), q(a, \mathbf{t^\star}), q(a, \mathbf{t^{\star\star}})\}$,

$\mathcal{M}_2 = \{p(a, \mathbf{t_d}), p(a, \mathbf{t^\star}), p(a, \mathbf{f^\star})), q(a, \mathbf{f^\star}), p(a, \mathbf{f^{\star\star}}), q(a, \mathbf{f^{\star\star}}), p(a, \mathbf{f_a})\}$.

The first model says, through its atom $q(a, \mathbf{t^{\star\star}})$, that $q(a)$ has to be inserted in the database. The second one, through its atom $p(a, \mathbf{f^{\star\star}})$, that $p(a)$ has to be deleted.   □

The coherence denial constraints did not play any role in the previous example, we obtain exactly the same model with or without them. The reason is that we have only one IC; in consequence, only one step is needed to obtain a repair of the database. There is no way to obtain an incoherent stable model due to the application of the rules 1. and 2. in Example 8 in a second repair step.

Example 9. (example 8 continued) Let us now add an extra set inclusion dependency, $\forall x \ (q(x) \rightarrow r(x))$, keeping the same instance. One repair is obtained by inserting $q(a)$, what causes the insertion of $r(a)$. The program is as before, but with the additional rules

$r(x, \mathbf{f^\star}) \leftarrow \ not \ r(x, \mathbf{t_d})$. $r(x, \mathbf{f^\star}) \leftarrow r(x, \mathbf{f_a})$. $r(x, \mathbf{t^\star}) \leftarrow r(x, \mathbf{t_a})$.
$r(X, \mathbf{t^\star}) \ \leftarrow \ r(X, \mathbf{t_d})$. $r(x, \mathbf{t^{\star\star}}) \ \leftarrow \ r(x, \mathbf{t_a})$. $r(x, \mathbf{t^{\star\star}}) \ \leftarrow$
$r(x, \mathbf{t_d}), not \ r(x, \mathbf{f_a})$.
$r(x, \mathbf{f^{\star\star}}) \leftarrow r(x, \mathbf{f_a})$. $r(x, \mathbf{f^{\star\star}}) \leftarrow \ not \ r(x, \mathbf{t_d}), \ not \ r(x, \mathbf{t_a})$.
$q(x, \mathbf{f_a}) \vee r(x, \mathbf{t_a}) \leftarrow q(x, \mathbf{t^\star}), r(x, \mathbf{f^\star})$. $\leftarrow r(x, \mathbf{t_a}), r(x, \mathbf{f_a})$.

If we run the program we obtain the expected models, one that deletes $p(a)$, and a second one that inserts both $q(a)$ and $r(a)$. However, if we omit the coherence denial constraints, more precisely the one for table q, we obtain a third model, namely $\{p(a, \mathbf{t_d}), p(a, \mathbf{t^*}), q(a, \mathbf{f^*}), r(a, \mathbf{f^*}), q(a, \mathbf{f_a}), q(a, \mathbf{t_a}), p(a, \mathbf{t^{**}}),$ $q(a, \mathbf{t^*}), q(a, \mathbf{t^{**}}), q(a, \mathbf{f^{**}}), r(a, \mathbf{f^{**}})$, that is not coherent, because it contains both $q(a, \mathbf{f_a})$ and $q(a, \mathbf{t_a})$, and cannot be interpreted as a repair of the original database.   □

Notice that the programs with annotations obtained are very simple in terms of their dependency on the ICs. As mentioned before, consistent answers can be obtained "running" a query program together with the repair program $\Pi^*(DB, IC)$, under the skeptical stable model semantics, that sanctions as true what is true of all stable models.

5   Programs with Referential ICs

So far the repair programs have been for universal ICs. Now we also want to consider referential ICs (RICs) of the form $p(\bar{x}) \rightarrow \exists y(q(\bar{x}', y))$, where $\bar{x}' \subseteq \bar{x}$. It is assumed that the variables range over an underlying database domain D, that does not include the value *null*, nevertheless, a RIC can be repaired by insertion of the null value, say $q(\bar{a}, null)$, or by cascaded deletion. If the repair is by introduction of *null*, it is expected that this change will not propagate through other ICs, e.g. a set inclusion dependency like $\forall \bar{x}(q(\bar{x}', y) \rightarrow r(\bar{x}', y))$. The program should not detect such inconsistency wrt this IC. This can be easily avoided at the program level by appropriately qualifying the values of variables in the disjunctive repair clause for the other ICs, like the set inclusion IC above. The program $\Pi^*(DB, IC)$ is then extended with the following formulas:

$$p(\bar{x}, \mathbf{f_a}) \vee q(\bar{x}', null, \mathbf{t_a}) \leftarrow p(\bar{x}, \mathbf{t^*}), \; not \; aux(\bar{x}'), \; not \; q(\bar{x}', null, \mathbf{t_d}). \quad (2)$$
$$aux(\bar{x}') \leftarrow q(\bar{x}', y, \mathbf{t_d}), \; not \; q(\bar{x}', y, \mathbf{f_a}). \quad (3)$$
$$aux(\bar{x}') \leftarrow q(\bar{x}', y, \mathbf{t_a}). \quad (4)$$

Intuitively, clauses (3) and (4) detect if the formula $\exists y(q(\bar{a}', y){:}\mathbf{t} \vee q(\bar{a}', y){:}\mathbf{t_a}))$ is satisfied by the model. If this is not the case, and $p(\bar{a}, \mathbf{t^*})$ belongs to the model, and $q(\bar{a}', null)$ is not in the original instance, i.e. there is a violation of the RIC, then, according to rule (2), the repair is done either by deleting $p(\bar{a})$ or inserting $q(\bar{a}', null)$.

Example 10. Consider the database instance $\{p(\bar{a})\}$ and the following set of ICs: $p(x) \rightarrow \exists y q(x, y)$, $q(x, y) \rightarrow r(x, y)$. The program $\Pi^*(DB, IC)$ is written in *DLV* as follows (ts, tss, ta, etc. stand for $\mathbf{t^*}, \mathbf{t^{**}}, \mathbf{t_a}$, etc.):

Database contents

```
domd(a).     d(a,td).     p(X,td) :- d(X,td), domd(X).
```

Rules for CWA

```
p(X,fs) :- domd(X), not p(X,td).
q(X,Y,fs) :- domd(X), domd(Y), not q(X,Y,td).
r(X,Y,fs) :-  not r(X,Y,td), domd(X), domd(Y).
```

Annotation rules
```
p(X,fs) :- p(X,fa), domd(X).     p(X,ts) :- p(X,ta), domd(X).
p(X,ts):- p(X,td), domd(X).
q(X,Y,fs) :- q(X,Y,fa), domd(X), domd(Y).
q(X,Y,ts) :- q(X,Y,ta), domd(X), domd(Y).
q(X,Y,ts) :- q(X,Y,td), domd(X), domd(Y).
r(X,Y,fs) :- r(X,Y,fa), domd(X), domd(Y).
r(X,Y,ts) :- r(X,Y,ta), domd(X), domd(Y).
r(X,Y,ts) :- r(X,Y,td), domd(X), domd(Y).
```

Rules for the ICs
```
aux(X) :- q(X,Y,td), not q(X,Y,fa), domd(X), domd(Y).
aux(X) :- q(X,Y,ta), domd(X), domd(Y).
p(X,fa) v q(X,null,ta) :- p(X,ts), not aux(x), not q(X,null,td), domd(X).
q(X,Y,fa) v r(X,Y,ta) :- q(X,Y,ts), r(X,Y,fs), domd(X), domd(Y).
```

Interpretation rules
```
p(X,tss) :- p(X,ta), domd(X). p(X,tss) :- p(X,td), not p(X,fa), domd(X).
p(X,fss) :- p(X,fa), domd(X). p(X,fss) :- domd(X), not p(X,td), not p(X,ta).
q(X,Y,tss) :- q(X,Y,ta), domd(X),domd(Y).
q(X,Y,tss) :- q(X,Y,td), not q(X,Y,fa), domd(X), domd(Y).
q(X,Y,fss) :- q(X,Y,fa), domd(X), domd(Y).
q(X,Y,fss) :- not q(X,Y,td), not q(X,Y,ta), domd(X), domd(Y).
r(X,Y,tss) :- r(X,Y,ta), domd(X),domd(Y).
r(X,Y,tss) :- r(X,Y,td), not q(X,Y,fa), domd(X), domd(Y).
r(X,Y,fss) :- r(X,Y,fa), domd(X), domd(Y).
r(X,Y,fss) :- not r(X,Y,td), not r(X,Y,ta), domd(X), domd(Y).
```

Rules for interpreting null values
```
q(X,null,tss) :- q(X,null,ta).
q(X,null,tss) :- q(X,null,td), not q(X,null,fa).
r(X,null,tss) :- r(X,null,ta).
r(X,null,tss) :- r(X,null,td), not r(X,null,fa).
```

Denial constraints
```
:- p(X,ta), p(X,fa).   :- q(X,Y,ta), q(X,Y,fa).   :-r(X,Y,ta),r(X,Y,fa).
```

The models obtained are:

```
{domd(a), d(a,td), p(a,td), p(a,ts), p(a,fs), p(a,fss), p(a,fa),
        q(a,a,fs), r(a,a,fs), q(a,a,fss), r(a,a,fss)}

{domd(a), d(a,td), p(a,td), p(a,ts), p(a,tss), q(a,null,ta),
        q(a,a,fs), r(a,a,fs), q(a,a,fss), r(a,a,fss), q(a,null,tss)},
```

corresponding to the database instances $\emptyset$ and $\{p(a),\ q(a, null)\}$. The program does not consider the inclusion dependency $q(x, y) \rightarrow r(x, y)$ to be violated by the insertion of the tuple $q(a, null)$. If the fact $q(a, null)$ is added to the instance. Then, the clauses `e(a,null,td). q(X,null,td) :- e(X,null,td), domd(X).` are part of the program. In this case, the program considers that the instance $\{p(a),\ q(a, null)\}$ does not violate the RIC, what is reflected through its only model

```
{domd(a), d(a,td), e(a,null,td), p(a,td), p(a,ts), q(a,null,td), p(a,tss),
  q(a,a,fs), r(a,a,fs), q(a,a,fss), r(a,a,fss), q(a,null,tss)}.
```

□

If we want to impose the policy of repairing the violation of a RIC just by deleting tuples, then, rule (2) should be changed by

$$p(\bar{x}, \mathbf{f_a}) \leftarrow p(\bar{x}, \mathbf{t}^\star), \ \ not \ aux(\bar{x}'), \ \ not \ q(\bar{x}', null, \mathbf{t_d}),$$

saying that if the RIC is violated, then the fact $p(\bar{a})$ that produces such violation must be deleted.

Notice that in this section we have been departing from the definition of repair given in section 2, in the sense that repairs now are obtained by deletion of tuples or insertion of null values only, the usual ways to maintain RICs. However, if the instance is $\{p(\bar{a})\}$ and IC contains only $p(\bar{x}) \to \exists y q(\bar{x}, y)$, then $\{p(\bar{a}), q(\bar{a}, b)\}$, with $b \in D$, will not be obtained as a repair, because it will not be captured by the program.

If we insist in keeping the original definition of repair, i.e. allowing $\{p(\bar{a}), q(\bar{a}, b)\}$ to be a repair for every element $b \in D$, clause (2) could be replaced by:

$$p(\bar{x}, \mathbf{f_a}) \vee q(\bar{x}', y, \mathbf{t_a}) \leftarrow p(\bar{x}, \mathbf{t}^\star), \ \ not \ aux(\bar{x}'), \ \ not \ q(\bar{x}', null, \mathbf{t_d}), choice(\bar{x}', y). \tag{5}$$

where $choice(\bar{X}, \bar{Y})$ is the static non-deterministic choice operator [22] that selects one value for attribute tuple $\bar{Y}$ for each value of the attribute tuple $\bar{X}$. In equation (5), $choice(\bar{x}', y)$ selects one value from the domain. Then, this rule forces the one to one correspondence between stable models and repairs.

6   Conclusions

We have presented a general treatment of consistent query answering for first order queries and ICs. In doing so, we have also shown how to specify database repairs by means of classical disjunctive logic programs with stable model semantics. Those programs have annotations as new arguments. In consequence, consistent query answers can be obtained by "running" a query program together with the specification program. Finally, we showed how to run the programs using the DLV system. Our treatment of referential ICs considerably extends what has been sketched in [4,23].

The problem of consistent query answering was explicitly presented in [2], where also the notions of repair and consistent answer were formally defined. In addition, a methodology for consistent query answering based on a rewriting of the original query was developed (and further investigated and implemented in [13]). Basically, if we want the consistent answers to a FO query expressed in, say SQL2, a new query in SQL2 can be computed, such that its usual answers from the database are the consistent answers to the original query. That methodology has a polynomial data complexity, and that is the reason why it works for some restricted classes of FO ICs and queries, basically for non existentially quantified conjunctive queries [1]. Actually, in [14] it is shown that the problem of CQA is coNP-complete for simple functional dependencies and existential queries. Furthermore, in [8], the problem of CQA is formulated as a problem of non-monotonic reasoning, more precisely of minimal entailment, whose complexity, even in the propositional case, can be Π_2^P-complete [17].

Under those circumstances, it makes sense to apply techniques from logic programming, given its success in formalizing and implementing complex nommonotonic reasoning tasks [7]. The problem then is to come up with the best logic programming specification and the best way to use them, so that the computational complexity involved does not go beyond the theoretical lower bound. Consistent query answering from relational databases is a new and natural application domain for logic programs, and answer set programming, in particular.

6.1 Implementation Issues

Implementation and applications are important directions of research. The logic programming environment will interact with a DBMS, where the inconsistent DB will be stored. As much of the computation as possible should be pushed into the DBMS instead of doing it at the logic programming level. Furthermore, whenever possible, materialization of negative (absent) data should be avoided.

The problem of developing query evaluation mechanisms from disjunctive logic programs that are guided by the query, most likely containing free variables and then expecting a set of answers, like magic sets [1], deserves more attention from the logic programming and database communities. The current alternative relies on finding those ground query atoms that belong to all the stable models once they have been computed via a ground instantiation of the original program. In [18] intelligent grounding strategies for pruning in advance the instantiated program have been explored and incorporated into *DLV*. It would be interesting to explore to what extent the program can be pruned from irrelevant rules and subgoals using information obtained by querying the database.

As shown in [6], there are classes of ICs for which the intersection of the stable models of the repair program coincides with the well-founded semantics, which can be computed more efficiently than the stable model semantics. It could be possible to take advantage of this efficient "core" computation for consistent query answering if ways of modularizing or splitting the whole computation into a core part and a query specific part are found. Such cases were identified in [5] for FDs and aggregation queries.

The logic programs could be optimized in several senses. In some cases, the resulting programs turn out to be "head cycle free" (HCF) [9]. Basically, a program is HCF if there are no cycles in the associated graph that shows an arrow from a predicate p to a predicate q if there is a rule where q appears in the disjunction in the head and p appears positive in the body. Example 8 shows a HCF program.

HCF programs can be transformed into non disjunctive normal programs, that have better complexity properties [26]. Such transformations can be justified or discarded on the basis of a careful analysis of the intrinsic complexity of consistent query answering [14]. If the original program can be transformed into a normal program, then also other efficient implementations could be used for query evaluation, e.g. *XSB* [29], that has been already successfully applied in the context of consistent query answering via query transformation, with non-existentially quantified conjunctive queries [13].

6.2   Related Work

In [23], a general methodology based on disjunctive logic programs with stable model semantics is used for specifying database repairs wrt universal ICs. In their approach, preferences between repairs can be specified. The program is given through a schema for rule generation.

Independently, in [4] a specification of database repairs for binary universal ICs by means of disjunctive logic programs with a stable model semantics was presented. Those programs contained both "triggering" rules and "stabilizing" rules. The former trigger local, one-step, changes, and the latter stabilize the chain of local changes in a state where all the ICs hold. The same rules, among others, are generated by the schema in [23].

The programs presented here also work for the whole class of universal ICs, but they are much simpler and shorter than those presented in [23,4]. Actually, the schema presented in [23] and the extended methodology sketched in [4], both generate an exponential number of rules in terms of the number of ICs and literals in them. Instead, in the present work, due to the simplicity of the program, that takes full advantage of the relationship between the annotations, a linear number of rules is generated.

There are several similarities between our approach to consistency handling and those followed by the belief revision/update community. Database repairs coincide with revised models defined by Winslett in [30]. The treatment in [30] is mainly propositional, but a preliminary extension to first order knowledge bases can be found in [15]. Those papers concentrate on the computation of the models of the revised theory, i.e., the repairs in our case, but not on query answering. Comparing our framework with that of belief revision, we have an empty domain theory, one model: the database instance, and a revision by a set of ICs. The revision of a database instance by the ICs produces new database instances, the repairs of the original database.

Nevertheless, our motivation and starting point are quite different from those of belief revision. We are not interested in computing the repairs *per se*, but in answering queries, hopefully using the original database as much as possible, possibly posing a modified query. If this is not possible, we look for methodologies for representing and querying simultaneously and implicitly all the repairs of the database. Furthermore, we work in a fully first-order framework.

Another approach to database repairs based on logic programming semantics consists of the *revision programs* [28]. The rules in those programs explicitly declare how to enforce the satisfaction of an integrity constraint, rather than explicitly stating the ICs, e.g. $in(a) \leftarrow in(a_1), \ldots, in(a_k), out(b_1), \ldots, out(b_m)$ has the intended procedural meaning of inserting the database atom a whenever $a_1, \ldots, a_k$ are in the database, but not $b_1, \ldots, b_m$. Also a declarative, stable model semantics is given to revision programs. Preferences for certain kinds of repair actions can be captured by declaring the corresponding rules in program and omitting rules that could lead to other forms of repairs.

In [11,25] paraconsistent and annotated logic programs, with non classical semantics, are introduced. However, in [16] some transformation methodologies for paraconsistent logic programs [11] are shown that allow assigning to them extensions of classical semantics. Our programs have a stable model semantics.

Acknowledgments.   Work funded by DIPUC, FONDECYT Grant 1000593, Carleton University Start-Up Grant 9364-01, NSERC Grant 250279-02. We are grateful to Alberto Mendelzon, Marcelo Arenas, and Nicola Leone for useful conversations.

References

1. Abiteboul, S.; Hull, R. and Vianu, V. "Foundations of Databases". Addison-Wesley, 1995.
2. Arenas, M.; Bertossi, L. and Chomicki, J. "Consistent Query Answers in Inconsistent Databases". In *Proc. ACM Symposium on Principles of Database Systems (ACM PODS'99)*, 1999, pp. 68–79.
3. Arenas, M.; Bertossi, L. and Kifer, M. "Applications of Annotated Predicate Calculus to Querying Inconsistent Databases". In *'Computational Logic - CL2000' Stream: 6th International Conference on Rules and Objects in Databases (DOOD'2000)*. Springer Lecture Notes in Artificial Intelligence 1861, 2000, pp. 926–941.
4. Arenas, M.; Bertossi, L. and Chomicki, J. "Specifying and Querying Database Repairs using Logic Programs with Exceptions". In *Flexible Query Answering Systems. Recent Developments*, H.L. Larsen, J. Kacprzyk, S. Zadrozny, H. Christiansen (eds.), Springer, 2000, pp. 27–41.
5. Arenas, M.; Bertossi, L. and Chomicki, J. Scalar Aggregation in FD-Inconsistent Databases. In *Database Theory - ICDT 2001*, Springer, LNCS 1973, 2001, pp. 39–53.
6. Arenas, M.; Bertossi, L. and Chomicki, J. Answer Sets for Consistent Query Answers. Submitted in 2001. (CoRR paper cs.DB/0207094)
7. Baral, Ch. Knowledge Representation, Reasoning and Declarative Problem Solving with Answer Sets. Cambridge University Press. To appear.
8. Barcelo, P. and Bertossi, L. Repairing Databases with Annotated Predicate Logic. In *Proc. Nineth International Workshop on Non-Monotonic Reasoning (NMR'2002), Special session: Changing and Integrating Information: From Theory to Practice*, S. Benferhat and E. Giunchiglia (eds.), 2002, pp. 160–170.
9. Ben-Eliyahu, R. and Dechter, R. "Propositional Semantics for Disjunctive Logic Programs". *Annals of Mathematics in Artificial Intelligence*, 1994, 12:53–87.
10. Bertossi, L., Chomicki, J., Cortes, A. and Gutierrez, C. "Consistent Answers from Integrated Data Sources". In 'Flexible Query Answering Systems', Proc. of the 5th International Conference, FQAS 2002. T. Andreasen, A. Motro, H. Christiansen, H. L. Larsen (eds.). Springer LNAI 2522, 2002, pp. 71–85.
11. Blair, H.A. and Subrahmanian, V.S. "Paraconsistent Logic Programming". *Theoretical Computer Science*, 1989, 68:135–154.
12. Buccafurri, F.; Leone, N. and Rullo, P. "Enhancing Disjunctive Datalog by Constraints". *IEEE Transactions on Knowledge and Data Engineering*, 2000, 12(5):845–860.
13. Celle, A. and Bertossi, L. "Querying Inconsistent Databases: Algorithms and Implementation". In 'Computational Logic - CL 2000', J. Lloyd et al. (eds.). Stream: 6th International Conference on Rules and Objects in Databases (DOOD'2000). Springer Lecture Notes in Artificial Intelligence 1861, 2000, pp. 942–956.
14. Chomicki, J. and Marcinkowski, J. "On the Computational Complexity of Consistent Query Answers". Submitted in 2002 (CoRR paper cs.DB/0204010).

15. Chou, T. and Winslett, M. A Model-Based Belief Revision System. *Journal of Automated Reasoning*, 1994, 12:157–208.

16. Damasio, C. V. and Pereira, L.M. "A Survey on Paraconsistent Semantics for Extended Logic Programas". In *Handbook of Defeasible Reasoning and Uncertainty Management Systems*, Vol. 2, D.M. Gabbay and Ph. Smets (eds.), Kluwer Academic Publishers, 1998, pp. 241–320.

17. Eiter, T. and Gottlob, G. Propositional Circumscription and Extended Closed World Assumption are Π_2^p-complete. Theoretical Computer Science, 1993, 114, pp. 231–245.

18. Eiter, T., Leone, N., Mateis, C., Pfeifer, G. and Scarcello, F. "A Deductive System for Non-Monotonic Reasoning". Proc. LPNMR'97, Springer LNAI 1265, 1997, pp. 364–375.

19. Eiter, T.; Faber, W.; Leone, N. and Pfeifer, G. "Declarative Problem-Solving in DLV". In *Logic-Based Artificial Intelligence*, J. Minker (ed.), Kluwer, 2000, pp. 79–103.

20. Gelfond, M. and Lifschitz, V. "The Stable Model Semantics for Logic Programming". In *Logic Programming, Proceedings of the Fifth International Conference and Symposium*, R. A. Kowalski and K. A. Bowen (eds.), MIT Press, 1988, pp. 1070–1080.

21. Gelfond, M. and Lifschitz, V. "Classical Negation in Logic Programs and Disjunctive Databases". *New Generation Computing*, 1991, 9:365–385.

22. Giannotti, F.; Greco, S.; Sacca, D. and Zaniolo, C. Programming with Nondeterminism in Deductive Databases. *Annals of Mathematics and Artificial Intelligence*, 1997, 19(3–4).

23. Greco, G.; Greco, S. and Zumpano, E. "A Logic Programming Approach to the Integration, Repairing and Querying of Inconsistent Databases". In *Proc. 17th International Conference on Logic Programming, ICLP'01*, Ph. Codognet (ed.), LNCS 2237, Springer, 2001, pp. 348–364.

24. Kifer, M. and Lozinskii, E.L. "A Logic for Reasoning with Inconsistency". *Journal of Automated reasoning*, 1992, 9(2):179–215.

25. Kifer, M. and Subrahmanian, V.S. "Theory of Generalized Annotated Logic Programming and its Applications". *Journal of Logic Programming*, 1992, 12(4):335–368.

26. Leone, N.; Rullo, P. and Scarcello, F. Disjunctive Stable Models: Unfounded Sets, Fixpoint Semantics, and Computation. *Information and Computation*, 1997, 135(2):69–112.

27. Lloyd, J.W. "Foundations of Logic Programming". Springer Verlag, 1987.

28. Marek, V.W. and Truszczynski, M. "Revision Programming". *Theoretical Computer Science*, 1998, 190(2):241–277.

29. Sagonas, K.F.; Swift, T. and Warren, D.S. XSB as an Efficient Deductive Database Engine. In *Proc. of the 1994 ACM SIGMOD International Conference on Management of Data*, ACM Press, 1994, pp. 442–453.

30. Winslett, M. Reasoning about Action using a Possible Models Approach. In *Proc. Seventh National Conference on Artificial Intelligence (AAAI'88)*, 1988, pp. 89–93.

A CLP-Based Tool for Computer Aided Generation and Solving of Maths Exercises*

Ana Paula Tomás and José Paulo Leal

DCC-FC & LIACC, Universidade do Porto, Portugal
{apt,zp}@ncc.up.pt

Abstract. We propose an interesting application of Constraint Logic Programming to automatic generation and explanation of mathematics exercises. A particular topic in mathematics is considered to investigate and illustrate the advantages of using the CLP paradigm. The goal is to develop software components that make the formulation and explanation of exercises easier. We describe exercises by grammars which enables us to get specialized forms almost for free, by imposing further conditions through constraints. To define the grammars we concentrate on the solving procedures that are taught instead of trying to abstract an exercise template from a sample of similar exercises. Prototype programs indicate that Constraint Logic Programming frameworks may be adequate to implement such a tool. These languages have the right expressiveness to encode control on the system in an elegant and declarative way.

1 Introduction

This paper proposes an application of Constraint Logic Programming (CLP) in education, namely to automatic generation of mathematics exercises for students. The ultimate goal of the project is to develop an intelligent tutoring tool for mathematics that integrates software components to make the formulation and explanation of exercises easier.

1.1 The Motivation

Though not all students have high mathematical skills, one of the reasons for the lack of success in mathematics is that too often students merely memorize how to solve some exercises, instead of trying to understand fundamental concepts and results. Hence, a possible drawback of classical textbooks and some existing online course-ware and exercise systems is that the proposed problems are quite pre-defined, either fixed or at best randomly generated instances of the same problem template [3,5].

Rather than to reproduce the classical textbooks, advances in the computer technology and the Internet should be exploited to develop really interactive and

---

* Work partially supported by funds granted to LIACC through *Programa de Finan-ciamento Plurianual, Fundação para a Ciência e Tecnologia* and *Programa POSI*.

V. Dahl and P. Wadler (Eds.): PADL 2003, LNCS 2562, pp. 223–240, 2003.

re-usable contents. Sophisticated web-based learning environments are emerging, that include interactive textbooks projects with user-adaptive contents [15] and that support exploratory learning through communication with (commercial) mathematical systems [3,15].

Some systems, as *Geometer's Sketchpad* [6], *Maple* [11] and *Mathematica* [13], just to name a few, are indeed often used as tools for explorations [8,16], enabling the students to try their own examples. Some already offer web access to their applications. The focus of this paper is not on problem solving in the broader sense of exploration, but rather on the repetitive drills students have to do for consolidation of concepts and practice of algebraic procedures. For constructive learning to be effective, students need self-confidence and also basic knowledge.

Web-based systems for computer aided training and/or assessment, with authoring facilities for teachers to create question files are spread over the web (e.g. [1,5,9,10,15]). Non-negligible effort is required from teachers to generate problem instances that are not immediately recognized as simple variants of a few basic expressions. For all the on-line systems we have come to, the exercises are not generic enough and the user can almost anticipate the form of the next instance of the problem, after a while. The situation is illustrated by Fig. 1. The

$-\dfrac{4}{\lvert 4y+1 \rvert}$	$-\dfrac{1}{(3y+4)^3}$	$-5\,\left\lvert \sqrt{-y-1} \right\rvert - 5$
$-\dfrac{4}{\lvert -y-1 \rvert}$	$\dfrac{2}{(-5y+2)^2}$	$2\,\left\lvert \sqrt[3]{y-2} \right\rvert - 5$
$\dfrac{a}{\lvert by+c \rvert}$	$\dfrac{a}{(by+c)^n}$	$a\,\sqrt[n]{\lvert by+c \rvert} + d$

Fig. 1. Abstracting types of expressions from samples

ability to generate several distinct types of expressions automatically, in addition to as many instances of the same basic type of expression as wanted, is surely an advantage of our approach. Another unusual, and therefore distinguishing, feature is that we are not simply using samples of problems, say samples of expressions, to find the possible types, as Fig. 1 may wrongly suggest. As we shall see, the focus will mainly be on the analysis of solving procedures. For example, if a solving procedure for cubic equations (i.e., for $ax^3 + bx^2 + cx + d = 0$) could be used, we would take it into account to characterize generic exercises. Then, students' actual background may be somehow encoded by further constraining the form of the instances of problem templates that the computer will generate.

1.2   The Main Ideas of This Approach

When a student is using mathematical software for exploratory learning, it is reasonable that the system may output *don't know* or rather complicate formulas as an answer. This is not acceptable when the system is *asking* the student to solve a problem that it has automatically generated. Both the computer and the student (if he/she has learned the topic in assessment) must know how to solve the exercise. For instance, the system shall not produce an ad-hoc polynomial of degree greater than three and ask the student to find its roots. Indeed, it is known that there exist no generic algorithm to solve that. In contrast, there are algorithms to compute the *rational* roots of any polynomial with rational coefficients, which, nevertheless students may not have learned. The fundamental ideas in our approach are:

- To abstract and represent the forms of the exercises that may be solved by the procedures that students are taught at different levels of education.
- To support additional (user-defined) constraints on problem instances to control the difficulty and adequacy of the exercises for a certain curriculum, stage or user.
- To have some knowledge about the solutions to the generated exercises so that they may be of pedagogical interest (i.e.: Are the numbers arising in intermediate computations awkward? How many steps are required to achieve a solution? How simple is the solution?)
- To implement the solving procedures so that the computer may either output a concise explanation (that may help students get familiar with mathematical language) or, at least, show the solving steps.

This strategy is fairly the same teachers follow to formulate basic problems in some context. Thus, to design a system based in this approach, it is needed expertise in the field and some interdisciplinary collaboration may be important.

Other works have implicit a similar idea [17,18], although they seem not to be taking enough advantage of that to achieve generality and reduce the burden of writing the on-line exercises sheets. Sangwin [17] addresses how to generate exercises that get students to construct instances of mathematical objects with some properties. How to reduce teachers' effort to prepare questions is not considered at all and, moreover, it is assumed that they have some expertise in writing computer programs. Indeed, it is examined an application of an authoring system for computer aided assessment [9], that ultimately uses *Maple* to process the exercises but that counts on the teacher to program them and in some situations their grade scheme. This is quite different from what we have in mind.

Our approach has many different potentialities that include user-adaptiveness, easy definition of several curricula, and possible integration in intelligent tutoring systems.

On the limits of this approach. Although not all topics taught in mathematics at high school allow such an automatic treatment, a large number does.

Many of the questions that students have to work out in mathematics courses may successfully be solved by algebraic procedures. Some procedures are crucial to different problems. As we noted above, we do not address problem solving in the broader sense of exploration, but the repetitive drills students do for consolidation of concepts. In general, more elaborate problems that require higher level mathematical skills or reasoning, such as theorem proving, cannot be generated in a similar way. Theoretical limitations make evident that in such cases the best is likely to follow the most traditional approach: to create and use a database of pre-defined problems and solutions.

1.3   Particular Application Domains

Software applications that automatically generate exercises are highly domain dependent. Some deep understanding of the topics in assessment is needed. This work focussed on a particular problem in Calculus, namely the analysis of sign variation, zeros and domain of real-valued functions. Its interest goes largely beyond the problem itself. Indeed, it has several applications that include the study of intervals where a function is monotonic, the study of concavity and convexity for twice differentiable functions, sketching their graphs, and even the study of continuity. The difficulties this problem raises help illustrate the main ideas of the approach.

1.4   The Available Prototype

Demomath - a prototype of the proposed system - was implemented as a web application, and is available at `http://www.ncc.up.pt/~apt/demomath.html`. Using Demomath in a web browser the teacher/user can fill in a sequence of forms to define user constraints, select an exercise type and produce a set of exercises formated either in PDF, PS or HTML.

Fig. 2 shows the architecture of the system: modules are represented as strong rectangles, interface forms are represented as dashed rectangles, data flow is represented as solid arrows, control flow is represented as dotted arrows, files are represented standard by file icons.

The two main modules are written in Prolog and act as filters: the expression generator processes a user constraints file and produces an expressions and types file; the exercise generator and solver processes this last file and produces an exercises and solutions file. This last module is the core of the system and makes use of several libraries that handle arithmetics, set operations, symbolic constraints (to solve inequations, disequations and equations) and LATEX files.

The control module is responsible for managing user interaction: it receives data from HTML forms, produces the user constraints files and launches the execution of the main modules. During the interaction, this module binds intermediate data files (kept in the server side) with each of the users accessing the system simultaneously. The control module communicates with an HTTP server using the CGI protocol and was written in Tcl scripting language.

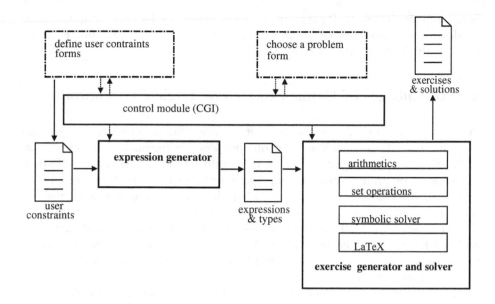

Fig. 2. The prototype's architecture

Displaying Mathematical Expressions. To illustrate potentialities of the program, we have written some predicates to convert the internal representations of mathematical expressions and solutions to LATEX. This allowed us to pretty print mathematical expressions. LATEX files can be easily typeset to produce HTML, PS and PDF files.

Another possibility, that we considered at start and may further investigate, amounts to use a prototype viewer/editor of MathML documents [14], written to Tcl/Tk by P. Vasconcelos (some more details may be found in [21]). We would like to obviate the need for students to learn a special syntax just for typing and reading formulas on the computer, unlike *WebMathematica* [13] and *AIM* [9], for example.

1.5   The Rest of the Paper

This paper reports on the results achieved so far that support our decision to proceed with the project. In the rest of the paper we first argue about advantages of using CLP to develop the work in comparison to, for instance, computer algebra systems as *Maple*. For that, we analyze an example that concerns one of the programs developed in *Maple*. In Section 3, we present the grammar we have defined to characterize expressions in our application domain, giving examples that show the kind of expressions tackled. A vast sample of examples from some high school textbooks is covered by this grammar although it shall still be extended to include other basic functions (such as, the trigonometric ones). Then, relevant aspects of our prototype implementation are described in

Sections 4 and 5. The CLP programs that were developed for this prototype may be downloaded from the Demomath site. New versions may be made available because the implementation is not stable yet.

2   Advantages of Using Constraint Logic Programming

Whereas powerful computer algebra systems are quite adequate for exploratory learning, they do not work well for our purpose. In particular, our experience with *Maple* has shown that the algebraic simplifications it does are troublesome. Additional constraints must be imposed on the expressions that arise in the exercises, to avoid inconsistencies in explanations. For instance, it is not possible to pretty print $3(x^2 + 5)$ in *Maple* since it will naturally yield $3x^2 + 15$. By a similar reason, we would better not ask the student to find the domain of a rational function defined by $f(x) = (x-1)^2/(x-1)$, because that expression would be printed as $f(x) = x - 1$, and hence 1 belongs to domain of the latter but not of the former one.

This points to a more fundamental problem, that is the need for full control of the tutoring system, to be able to produce explanations. Logic Programming based languages offer natural support for implementing symbolic representations and to do symbolic manipulations. Declarativeness is of help to specify the form of the expressions and of the problem templates. Moreover, for some problems in mathematics, we have to do exact computations and present the results in simplified forms. For that purpose, constraint logic programming solvers for rationals are of help, whereas the current ones for CLP(R) are less adequate. Nevertheless, they also act as black-boxes, which may not allow to fully control the tutor. Being incomplete solvers, that delay nonlinear constraints, they may not be used to compute the solutions even if we did not want to show the solving steps. Therefore, we need to implement symbolic processing of algebraic expressions and of constraints both to provide exact representations of solutions and explanations.

As we mentioned already, to achieve re-usability, the application shall be well parametrized to easily cater for different curricula or user-defined constraints. CLP seems to offer the right expressiveness to encode this kind of control in an elegant way through constraints. In this application, the optimization facilities of the CLP systems are not utilized, but rather the consistency checking and constraint propagation mechanisms. Different domains are needed, which cause some difficulties. It is still not easy to share variables between different solvers in a natural way. Furthermore, similar built-in constraints have different semantics and usage modes for different platforms, rendering the code non-portable (e.g., the finite domain constraint `element`).

CLP also plays an important role while giving natural support to tackle representations of problem templates defined by symbolic type schemes with constrained domain variables.

2.1   Some Experiments Using a Computer Algebra System

In some preliminary experiments we have used *Maple* to design worksheets to present some specific topic in mathematics. Besides some concise notes on the addressed issue, such *Maple* worksheets typically include pointers to other ones where the end-user student may find randomly generated examples and exercises to work on.

Example 1. Fig. 3 contains output from one of our *Maple* programs, that explains the determination of the domain of rational functions. Some typesetting has been done to spare space.

```
> domains(true);
FIND THE DOMAIN OF THE FUNCTION f DEFINED BY
```

$$f(x) = \frac{(8x^2 + 14x - 15)(2x + 1)}{(4x^6 - x^5 - 5x^4)(3x^2 - 17x + 10)^2}$$

```
SOLUTION: Being f a rational function, it is defined for all real
numbers except the zeros of the denominator of its expression. We
have
```

$$(4x^6 - x^5 - 5x^4)(3x^2 - 17x + 10)^2 = 0$$

```
if and only if 4x⁶ - x⁵ - 5x⁴ = 0 or (3x² - 17x + 10)² = 0.
As concerns 4x⁶ - x⁵ - 5x⁴ = 0, we have
```

$$4x^6 - x^5 - 5x^4 = 0 \iff x^4(4x^2 - x - 5) = 0$$
$$\iff x = 0 \lor 4x^2 - x - 5 = 0$$

```
To solve 4x²-x-5 = 0, we apply the solving formula for polynomial
equations of degree 2, the roots being -1 and 5/4.
As concerns (3x² - 17x + 10)² = 0, we have
```

$$(3x^2 - 17x + 10)^2 = 0 \iff 3x^2 - 17x + 10 = 0$$

```
To solve 3x² - 17x + 10  =  0, we apply the solving formula for
polynomial equations of degree 2, the roots being 2/3 and 5.
We conclude that all real numbers are in the domain of f, but 2/3,
0, -1, 5 and 5/4.
```

Fig. 3.   Finding the domain of a rational function. To generate $f(x)$, factors were restricted to polynomials P of degree ≤ 2, to the expansion of $x^n P$, for some n, or to powers of such expressions. This implies that the roots of the expressions in the numerator and denominator may be exactly found by an algorithm.

As other computer algebra systems, *Maple* supports polynomial expressions and thus it is easy to implement this procedure. For educational purposes, it is important to control the generated expressions, so that the exercise may have pedagogical interest. Instead of simply using the builtin *Maple* procedure to generate random polynomials, the computation of $f(x)$ was driven by the selection of the set of roots. In this way, the domain of the generated expression is known. It is important that we do not restrict roots to rational numbers, for that could mislead the student. Because of that, and to avoid awkward coefficients, we extended their range to conjugated irrational numbers. Factors with no real roots were obtained by adding appropriate constants to quadratic polynomial expressions with real roots to shift their representing parabolas upwards or downwards so that every intersection with the horizontal axis is eliminated. This illustrates the sort of mathematical expertise that our approach may require.

Further restrictions were imposed on the types of the generated functions to prevent puzzling inconsistencies in explanations, that may result from automatic simplification of expressions. In particular, we disallowed repetitions of factors (either in a product or quotient) and required that the involved polynomials just have integer coefficients. Since we would like to cover more general expressions, this does not seem the right way to proceed.

2.2   How to Write Natural Explanations?

An important point that is interesting to investigate further is how to improve the linguistic quality of output explanations. It is not immediate to obtain good explanations in natural language by annotating recursive programs. In the example in Fig. 3, almost no use was made of global context information, which renders explanations fairly repetitive and, therefore, unnatural or pedagogically poor. With traditional applications to Natural Language Processing, Logic Programming languages may be also useful to tackle the problem of writing concise mathematical explanations through the analysis of the resolution steps.

3   Using Grammars and Constraints to Define Expressions

A good abstract representation for expressions makes easier the implementation of solving procedures and the characterization of problem templates. In this section, we consider a particular topic in mathematics – introductory calculus – and introduce a representation for the expressions that define the functions. We propose a grammar that characterizes a wide range of the function expressions that may be found in high school textbooks and whose zeros may be exactly computed by an algorithm.

3.1   Finding a Grammar

In order to be able to abstract the possible forms of function expressions, we have carried out a thorough analysis of Portuguese textbooks in mathematics for the latest years (i.e., levels 10 to 12). To design the grammar, we focused on the solving procedures that are taught, instead of on the form of the sampling exercises, which does not seem to be a common practice.

For prototyping, the trigonometric, exponential and logarithmic functions have been left out. Generic functions are built from polynomial functions, the absolute value function $x \rightarrow |x|$, and the power and radix functions $x \rightarrow x^n$ and $x \rightarrow \sqrt[n]{x}$, possibly using composition, addition, product and quotient operations. Composition is the main operation, being denoted by $\circ$. For example, we may see the expressions in Fig. 1 as

$$\frac{a}{|by + c|} \qquad (k/(abs \circ p_1))(y)$$

$$\frac{a}{(by + c)^n} \qquad (k/(pow_n \circ p_1))(y)$$

$$a\sqrt[n]{|by + c|} + d \qquad (p_1 \circ rad_n \circ abs \circ q_1))(y)$$

where q_1 and p_1 are linear functions (i.e., defined by polynomials of degree 1), k denotes a constant function, and abs, rad_n, pow_n the absolute value, radix and power functions, respectively.

To find the grammar we have tried to identify expressions for which the computation of the domain and zeros may just involve the solving procedures for linear or quadratic equations ($ax + b = 0$ or $ax^2 + bx + c = 0$), or equations of the form $aX^n + b = 0$, $a\sqrt[n]{X} + b = 0$, $X^n \pm Y^n = 0$, $\sqrt[n]{X} \pm \sqrt[n]{Y} = 0$, for $n \geq 2$, or $X/Y \pm Z/T = 0$, with $degree(XT) \leq 2$ and $degree(YZ) \leq 2$, or even some case-based reasoning to get rid of the absolute value operators. It is important to observe that if we are able to compute the zeros of a given expression X, we are also able to find the zeros of X^n, $\sqrt[n]{X}$ and $|X|$. The same may be said of XY and X/Y when we are able to compute the zeros of X and Y.

Three functions have also been defined as basic, namely $x \rightarrow ax^{2n} + bx^n + c$, $x \rightarrow ax^{n+1} + bx^n$ and $x \rightarrow ax^{n+2} + bx^{n+1} + cx^n$. The last ones result from the expansion of $x^n P$, for a polynomial P of degree 1 or 2. We denote them by $\mathtt{expand}(x, n, P)$. Equations that involve these kind of expressions are solved by factoring them first. The other one is called $bisqr$, and $ax^{2n} + bx^n + c = 0$ is seen as $a(x^n)^2 + b(x^n) + c = 0$ and solved as a quadratic equation.

The grammar is shown in Fig. 4. We use $(\mathtt{k*})^? \mathtt{rad}(basic_{12}, N)$ as an abbreviation for $\mathtt{k*rad}(basic_{12}, N)$ or $\mathtt{rad}(basic_{12}, N)$. Here, $*$ means product. We note that by writing, for instance, $(\mathtt{k*})^? \mathtt{rad}(basic_{12}, N) + (\mathtt{k*})^? \mathtt{rad}(basic_{12}, N)$ we really want to restrict N to be the same for both subterms, so that the grammar is not context-free (meaning that, the language it defines is not a context-free language).

In the grammar, some categories have names that are indexed by 1, 2 or 12, because they result from the $basic$ category when we restrict the degree to be 1, 2, or any of these two. As for $vquot_{12k}$ and $quot_{12k}$ the idea is that the numerator and denominator have degrees 1, 2, or 0. To avoid defining more grammar rules, the abbreviated notations $pol_1(T)$, $ipol_2(T)$ and $ipol_1(T)$ were introduced. For instance, $ipol_2(\mathtt{pow}(\mathtt{x}, N))$ rewrites to $\mathtt{pol}(\mathtt{pow}(\mathtt{x}, N), [a, b, c])$ by applying the rule (scheme) for $ipol_2(T)$.

$$
\begin{aligned}
function &\longrightarrow (\texttt{k*})^? prodfact \mid (\texttt{k*})^? divexpr \\
prodfact &\longrightarrow factor \mid prodsexpr \\
divexpr &\longrightarrow prodfact/prodfact \mid \texttt{k}/prodfact \mid prodfact/\texttt{k} \\
&\longrightarrow \texttt{pow}(divexpr, N) \mid \texttt{rad}(divexpr, N) \mid \texttt{abs}(divexpr) \\
prodexpr &\longrightarrow factor*factor \mid factor*prodexpr \\
&\longrightarrow \texttt{pow}(prodsexpr, N) \mid \texttt{rad}(prodsexpr, N) \mid \texttt{abs}(prodsexpr) \\
factor &\longrightarrow sumexpr \mid vxip \mid basic \\
sumexpr &\longrightarrow \texttt{abs}(sumexpr) \mid \texttt{pow}(sumexpr, N) \mid \texttt{rad}(sumexpr, N) \mid bsum \\
bsum &\longrightarrow ipol_1(vquot_{12k}) \\
&\longrightarrow (\texttt{k*})^? \texttt{rad}(basic_{12}, N) + (\texttt{k*})^? \texttt{rad}(basic_{12}, N) \\
&\longrightarrow (\texttt{k*})^? \texttt{pow}(basic_{12}, N) + (\texttt{k*})^? \texttt{pow}(basic_{12}, N) \\
&\longrightarrow (\texttt{k*})^? \texttt{pow}(basic_{12}, N) + (\texttt{k*})^? \texttt{pow}(basic_1, 2N) \\
&\longrightarrow (\texttt{k*})^? \texttt{rad}(basic_{12}, 2N) + (\texttt{k*})^? \texttt{rad}(basic_1, N) \\
&\longrightarrow (\texttt{k*})^? \texttt{rad}(2, basic_{12}) + (\texttt{k*})^? basic_1 \\
&\longrightarrow (\texttt{k*})^? \texttt{pow}(2, basic_1) + (\texttt{k*})^? basic_{12} \\
&\longrightarrow (\texttt{k*})^? basic_{12} + (\texttt{k*})^? basic_{12} \\
&\longrightarrow (\texttt{k*})^? quot_{12k} + (\texttt{k*})^? basic_{12}, \text{ subject to } \textbf{Condition} \\
&\longrightarrow (\texttt{k*})^? quot_{12k} + (\texttt{k*})^? quot_{12k}, \text{ subject to } \textbf{Condition} \\
vquot_{12k} &\longrightarrow \texttt{pow}(vquot_{12k}, N) \mid \texttt{rad}(vquot_{12k}, N) \mid quot_{12k} \\
quot_{12k} &\longrightarrow \texttt{k}/basic_{12} \mid basic_{12}/\texttt{k} \mid basic_{12}/basic_{12} \mid \texttt{abs}(quot_{12k}) \\
basic_{12} &\longrightarrow basic_1 \mid basic_2 \\
basic_2 &\longrightarrow fpol_1(\texttt{abs}(basic_2)) \mid ipol_2(\texttt{x}) \mid \texttt{expand}(1, \texttt{x}, ipol_1(\texttt{x})) \\
&\longrightarrow basic_1*basic_1 \mid fpol_1(\texttt{pow}(2, basic_1)) \mid \texttt{pow}(2, basic_1) \\
&\longrightarrow \texttt{abs}(basic_2) \\
basic_1 &\longrightarrow \texttt{abs}(basic_1) \mid fpol_1(\texttt{abs}(basic_1)) \mid fpol_1(\texttt{x}) \\
basic &\longrightarrow ipol_2(\texttt{x}) \mid \texttt{expand}(1, \texttt{x}, ipol_1(\texttt{x})) \mid bisqr \mid fbasic \\
&\longrightarrow fpol_1(fbasic) \mid fpol_1(\texttt{x}) \\
fbasic &\longrightarrow \texttt{abs}(basic) \mid \texttt{pow}(basic, N) \mid \texttt{rad}(basic, N), N \geq 2 \\
vxip &\longrightarrow xip \mid \texttt{k}*vxip \mid \texttt{abs}(vxip) \mid \texttt{pow}(vxip, N) \mid \texttt{rad}(vxip, N), N \geq 2 \\
xip &\longrightarrow \texttt{expand}(N, \texttt{x}, ipol_2(\texttt{x})) \mid \texttt{expand}(N+1, \texttt{x}, ipol_1(\texttt{x})), \; N \geq 1 \\
bisqr &\longrightarrow ipol_2(\texttt{pow}(\texttt{x}, N)), \; N \geq 2 \\
fpol_1(T) &\longrightarrow \texttt{pol}(T, [a, b]), \; a \neq 0 \\
ipol_2(T) &\longrightarrow \texttt{pol}(T, [a, b, c]), \; abc \neq 0 \\
ipol_1(T) &\longrightarrow \texttt{pol}(T, [a, b]), \; ab \neq 0 \\
\texttt{x} &\longrightarrow variable \\
\texttt{k} &\longrightarrow constant
\end{aligned}
$$

Condition: Being either of the form $(\texttt{k*})^? A/B + (\texttt{k*})^? C$ with $degree(BC) \leq 2$ or of the form $(\texttt{k*})^? A/B + (\texttt{k*})^? C/D$ with $degree(AD) \leq 2$ and $degree(BC) \leq 2$.

Fig. 4. Describing functions that may appear in exercises and whose zeros can be found by an algorithm.

It is interesting to observe that $pol_1(T)$ plays a central role. In particular, instead of seeing, for instance, $2|x+5| + 3$ as the sum of two functions, we view it as a composition, $\texttt{pol}(\texttt{abs}(\texttt{pol}(x, [1,5])), [2,3])$. This is quite helpful to simplify the implementation of solving procedures. Sums increase complexity.

Example 2. It may be checked that

$$\frac{(8x^2 + 14x - 15)(2x + 1)}{(4x^6 - x^5 - 5x^4)(3x^2 - 17x + 10)^2}$$

is of the form

$$\frac{\texttt{pol}(x, [8,14,-15]) * \texttt{pol}(x, [2,1])}{\texttt{expand}(4, x, \texttt{pol}(x, [4,-1,5])) * \texttt{pow}(\texttt{pol}(x, [3,-17,10]),2\ )}$$

And, we may also conclude that e.g., $2\,|2y + 4| - 4\,|3y - 3| + 5$ belongs to *bsum* (i.e., basic sum expression), since it is given by

$$\texttt{pol}(\texttt{abs}(\texttt{pol}(y, [2,4])), [2,0]) + \texttt{pol}(\texttt{abs}(\texttt{pol}(y, [3,-3])), [-4,5])$$

To solve equations involving *sum expressions* one may need to know how to solve $X^n \pm Y^n = 0$, $\sqrt[n]{X} \pm \sqrt[n]{Y} = 0$, for $n \geq 2$, or $X/Y \pm Z/T = 0$, with $degree(XT) \leq 2$ and $degree(YZ) \leq 2$. We notice that, in general we would not be able to solve the first two if instead of 0 we had a non-null constant k, which would render the generic problem undecidable.

3.2   Introducing Types

We want to generate expressions that share a similar pattern and also to generate distinct patterns. We introduce *types* to represent distinct patterns. For example,

$$\frac{a}{|by + c|} \quad \text{and} \quad \frac{a}{(by + c)^n}$$

would be of types k / abs o p1 o x and k / pow(n) o p1 o x. Fig. 5 shows the expressions that correspond to basic types. Types k and x are omitted. They denote the constant functions and the identity function. In the middle, we see

Type	*Expression*	*Pretty − printed*
p1 o *TypeT*	$\texttt{pol}(T, [a, b])$	$aT + b$
p2 o *TypeT*	$\texttt{pol}(T, [a, b, c])$	$aT^2 + bT + c$
xip$(1, N)$	$\texttt{expand}(N, \texttt{x}, \texttt{pol}(\texttt{x}, [a, b]))$	$ax^{N+1} + bx^N$
xip$(2, N)$	$\texttt{expand}(N, \texttt{x}, \texttt{pol}(\texttt{x}, [a, b, c]))$	$ax^{N+2} + bx^{N+1} + cx^N$
pow(N) o *TypeT*	$\texttt{pow}(T, N)$	T^N
rad(N) o *TypeT*	$\texttt{rad}(T, N)$	$\sqrt[N]{T}$
abs o *TypeT*	$\texttt{abs}(T)$	$|T|$
p2 o pow(N) o x	$\texttt{pol}(\texttt{pow}(\texttt{x},N), [a, b, c])$	$ax^{2N} + bx^N + c$
instead of bisqr(N)		

Fig. 5. Internal representations and output expressions.

the symbolic representations for expressions used in the programs. Some types (e.g., pow(2) o p1 o x) may be seen as instances of a *type scheme with finite domain variables*. These variables represent the exponents and, hence, may be constrained. Thus, for example,

$$\left(-2\frac{-2y-1}{-3y+4}+3\right)^7$$

that belongs to the grammar category *sumexpr*, is characterized by

pow(_) o ip(1) o (p1 o x/p1 o x)

and, more specifically by, pow(7) o ip(1) o (p1 o x/p1 o x). Here, ip(1) and p1 replace $ipol_1$ and pol_1, respectively. Patterns correspond actually to the general types, which are the ones the generator produces first. Although the variable that occurs in the expression is y, its type does not capture that. Because types identify patterns, the variable (i.e. x, y, z ...) in the expression is not relevant to its type.

4   Generating Exercises in a CLP System

CLP languages are quite convenient to constrain the exercises by imposing constraints on some variables of the problems' generator. In this way, constraints are useful to control the difficulty and adequacy of the exercises for a certain curriculum, stage or user. In order to test these ideas, we have developed a prototype of a generator for expressions, that runs in SICStus Prolog [20] and uses CLP(FD) [2]. For instance, examples/6 yields NumbInst exercises of each type for some given specifications.

```
examples(File,Degree,RateMin,RateMax,X,NumbInst) :-
  tell(File), define_counters(CountTypes),
  constrs(CountTypes,urestr_function), % user-defined constraints
  def_infinity(OpMax),  CountOps #>= 0, CountOps #=< OpMax,
  Rate in RateMin..RateMax,  indomain(Rate),
  function(Type,Degree,Rate,CountTypes,CountOps), % finds a type
  CountExerc in 1..NumbInst, indomain(CountExerc),
  expression(Type,X,Expr),  % finds an expression
  write(Type), nl, write(Expr), nl, nl,
  fail.
examples(_,_,_,_,_,_) :- told.
```

E.g., if we launch examples(probs2,2,9,12,y,1), the system writes expressions in the variable y, of degree 2 and difficulty level in 9..12 to the file probs2, one expression per type. The output looks like this.

```
abs o p1 o abs o xip(1,1)
abs(pol(abs(expand(1,y,pol(y,[-5,-3])))),[-3,1]))
```

```
pow(2)o p1 o x+p1 o x
pow(pol(y,[-4,-1]),2)+pol(y,[2,4])
```

The difficulty rate may be settled by the user who is given permission to assign a rate to each type. The overall rate of an exercise is then the sum of such rates. Different and more sophisticated criteria shall be investigated.

The expressions of a given *degree* evaluate to polynomials of that degree when simplified to get rid of abs and pow, and shall not contain quotients and radicals. For the latter, the degree is undefined. The previous expressions have degree 2, as wanted.

It is quite impressive how quickly the program may obtain a huge number of expressions. Throughout this section, it is assumed that the reader is familiar with CLP systems, and in particular with CLP(FD) (for an introduction and some references, see e.g. [12]). We note that the finite domain constraint solver is mainly used to do *consistency checking* and *to propagate constraints* on the exponents and on the number of occurrences of some combinations of particular function types.

4.1 Finding Type Schemes for Expressions

In general, the grammar rules were implemented by predicates of the form

$$category(\text{Type},\text{Degree},\text{Rate},\text{CountTypes},\text{CountOps})$$

the main one, function/5, appeared already in examples/6.

$$\text{function}(\text{Type},\text{Degree},\text{Rate},\text{CountTypes},\text{CountOps})$$

The parameters Degree, Rate, CountTypes, CountOps are used to constrain the resulting scheme Type. This allows to impose constraints to control the difficulty level or form of the generated expressions and to tackle user-defined constraints.

Rate. The domain variable Rate gives some control on the application of each of the clauses that define a predicate. It must be either instantiated or have an upper bound when function/5 is called. This is important also to guarantee that the generation terminates. User-defined rates are assigned through user_rate/2 to the primitive functions (i.e., to p2, abs, rad(_), pow(_), xip(_,_), bisqr(_)) and to particular sub-expressions (as for example, sums of radicals, quotients and products). The overall rate is then the sum of such rates, as we mentioned before.

Since the teacher/user is not supposed to know CLP to be able to constrain the generator, an user-friendly interface was developed to help illustrate current functionalities of the prototype. For the moment, very simple constraints may be stated using this interface. We would like to achieve high flexibility and expressiveness, but keep the parameterization task simple. It is not easy to decide the form of constraints the interface shall support.

Type Counters. The parameter `CountTypes` is a list of finite domain variables, each one giving the number of occurrences of a given type. These types include the primitive constructs but also more general information as, for instance, `prodstype`, `divstype` and `sum`. The latter is related to the expressions identified by *sumtype* in the grammar. The idea is that the user may define constraints on the values of the counters in `CountTypes`. These constraints may involve a single variable (e.g., to specify its domain) or any subset of them. Calls to `constrs/2` result in imposing the user-defined constraints on `CountTypes` for the category identified by `urestr_name`. Thus, for example, to state that the number of `abs`, `bisqr(_)`, `pow(_)` and `rad(_)` shall not exceed four and that there shall be at least one `abs` and one `bisqr(_)`, we may write,

```
elements([abs,bisqr(_),pow(_),rad(_)],CountTypes,Vars),
sum(Vars, #=<, 4),
elements([abs,bisqr(_)],CountTypes,[Abs,BSqr]),
Abs #>=1, BSqr #>= 1
```

An integer is associated to each construct by a predicate `type_index/2`, so that we may then use the built-in constraint `element` to implement `elements/3`.

Counting Operations. The number of operations (i.e., compositions, sums, products and quotients) may be also limited, for which the domain variable `CountOps` is used. This parameter is also used to partially filter out symmetries in the type schemes through the propagation of constraints on the number of operators. Indeed, `abs o p1 o x + abs o p2 o x` and `abs o p2 o x + abs o p1 o x` may be viewed as the same type, because `+` is commutative.

Illustrating the Generation of Type Schemes. To provide some further intuition on the available implementation, we give the code of a predicate that partially defines the grammar category *vxip*.

```
vxnptype(xip(I,N),G,Rate,Ts,0) :-
   rate(xip(I,N),Rate),  G #>= 3,
   sum(Ts,#=,1), incr_restr(xip(I,N),Ts),
   degree(xip(I,N),G).
vxnptype(T o Tc,G,Rate,Ts,Ops) :-  npftype(T),
   rate_restr(T,Rate,[RateC]),
   types_restr(T,Ts,[TsC]),
   ops_restr(Ops,1,[OpsC]),
   degree(T,Gt),  Gc #>= 1, G #= Gt*Gc,
   ctype_(T,Tc), vxnptype(Tc,Gc,RateC,TsC,OpsC).
```

In the implementation, we distinguished the basic constructs for the grammar categories *basic* and *vxip* as polynomial or non-polynomial functions, `npftype/1` defines the latter.

```
npftype(abs).    npftype(rad(_)).    npftype(pow(_)).
```

The functions to which a basic function may be applied (i.e., composed with) are defined by `ctype_/2`, the relevant clauses for `vxnptype/5` being

```
ctype_(T,xip(_,_)) :- npftype(T).
ctype_(T,Tc o _) :- npftype(T),(pftype(Tc);(npftype(Tc),T \= Tc)).
```

The predicates `rate_restr/3`, `types_restr/3`, and `ops_restr/3` increment the counters, and consistently update the list of variables for recursive calls. This implementation is not taking full advantage of CLP because it follows a strategy that is still closer to generate-and-test than to constrain-and-generate. Whereas in this implementation we are propagating information only on counters, we could have defined other domain variables to identify the constructs that are applicable at each derivation step. In SICStus, such patterns shall be encoded by integers, since finite domain variables must take integer values. A more effective pruning could then be achieved. This improvement will be the focus of future implementations.

4.2   Finding Particular Expressions

Instances of the expressions of a given `Type` may be obtained by calling

$$\text{expression(Type,X,Expr)}$$

For each type scheme, we may generate several expressions of that type by repeated calls to `expression/3`. The coefficients are first created as finite domain variables whose range may be constrained by the user. A particular expression is obtained by labeling the domain variables that represent coefficients and exponents. Variations of the same example, in which the coefficients and exponents may change, can be easily found by forcing backtracking.

The predicate `function/5` generates a type scheme that may contain domain variables (representing exponents) with some attached constraints. Now, instead of saving all these constraints on the exponents for later usage, we would rather either save a particular instance of the type scheme or some pre-defined number of expressions that conform the type scheme. Different algorithms may be implemented to define `expression/3`, which may be even specialized to the particular problem we have in mind.

One possibility was described in Example 1, but we may also simply compute coefficients at random, though within a given range of pedagogical interest. Another possibility could be to use the program to generate several exercises which would later be filtered out, in view of the special application.

When only partial consistency is enforced, we have to guarantee that the (random) labeling process eventually stops, when no solution exists (that is, when no coefficients and exponents may be found). The program currently implements committed-choice, disallowing backtracking to the random numbers generator when a feasible value is found to the variable that is being labeled. In this way, the program may fail to find a solution even if one exists. This problem is not specific of CLP and other strategies could be devised to overcome it.

The type scheme plays a crucial role not only in the generation phase but also to render the implementation of problem solvers easier. We are mainly using CLP(FD) to generate expressions, which then naturally have integer coefficients. We have also made some simple experiments with other constraint programming domains, namely CLP(R), to define and tackle some conditions on the final expressions. However, the preliminary results had almost no interest for educational purpose. Further experiments could be done.

If a not too elaborate algorithm is implemented to generate expressions, then, an advantage of using a CLP framework is that `expression/3` may be used both to generate an expression `Expr` given its type scheme `Type`, or to generate a type for the given expression. This means that the predicates we have implemented to solve constraints, may still be used to solve user-defined problems of the same kind, provided the type of the expression is found.

5   Solving Problems in CLP

We have mainly addressed the computation of roots and of domains of functions which involves solving linear and non-linear constraints. As we mentioned earlier this is a fundamental problem in Calculus, with applications to several other problems. In general, we need symbolic processing of algebraic expressions to provide *an exact representation* of solutions. Indeed, CLP(Q) [7] could be used for finding the solutions, but expressions should have degree 1 and not involve the `abs` construct, so that they would be quite elementary.

5.1   Limited Support of Irrationals

To handle irrational numbers we have implemented a simple arithmetic package, that supports irrational numbers of the special forms $r_0 \sqrt[n]{r_1}$, $r_0 + r_1 \sqrt[n]{r_2}$ and $r_0 \sqrt[n]{r_1 + r_2 \sqrt[m]{r_3}}$, where the r_i's stand for rational numbers. For educational purposes, we do not need to support full generality. Some of these forms are already too sophisticated and awkward for the common intended users. We introduced some normal form $\sqrt[n]{r_1}$ so that the system would reduce, for instance, $\sqrt[3]{-40}$ to $-2\sqrt[3]{5}$, $\sqrt[6]{4}$ to $\sqrt[3]{2}$, $\sqrt{\frac{1}{2}}$ to $\frac{\sqrt{2}}{2}$, $\sqrt[3]{\frac{1}{2}}$ to $\frac{\sqrt[3]{4}}{2}$. When high exponents occur, the numbers may exponentially grow if we apply the latter transformation, so that we shall likely revise that in future versions of the programs. The arithmetic package makes limited usage of CLP(R) and CLP(Q). Irrational numbers are evaluated to floating point to simplify the implementation of the ordering predicates (i.e., of `geq`, `lt`, ...). As regards the CLP(Q) solver, it is used to perform exact computations involving rationals.

5.2   Implementing Symbolic Solving of Constraints

To solve problems that require finding the domain of a function, the system needs to exactly solve disequations and disjunctions, and also non-linear constraints. These kind of constraints are not fully solved by CLP(Q) and CLP(R) solvers, being often delayed. Furthermore, we would like to be able to provide explanations of the solving steps. For both these reasons, the CLP(Q) solver, acting as a black-box, cannot be utilized to discard symbolic manipulation of constraints, even when no irrationals are involved.

We have partially implemented a solver for constraints that may involve any of the relational operators $=$, $\neq$, $<$, $>$, $\geq$ and $\leq$. The solutions are given by a *set in normal form* that is an ordered list as, for example

```
[a(-infty),f(8),i(12),i(17),f(1000),a(1002), a(1002),a(infty)]
```

which means $]-\infty, 8] \cup \{12, 17\} \cup [1000, 1002[\cup]1002, \infty[$. It represents a union of intervals and of sets of isolated points, $a(X)$ and $f(X)$ stand for *open* and *closed* at X, respectively, and $i(X)$ says that X is an isolated point. We have also implemented a package to perform the traditional operations on sets to handle such symbolic representations.

These programs can be run both in Yap [4] and SICStus Prolog, since only the CLP(Q) and CLP(R) modules are used.

6   Conclusions

This paper presents an interesting application of Constraint Logic Programming (CLP) in education, namely to automatic generation of mathematics exercises for students. We have focused on a particular topic in mathematics, and investigate the usage of CLP to develop software components that make the formulation and explanation of exercises easier.

Instead of considering a sample of similar exercises to abstract an exercise template, we propose to concentrate on the analysis of the solving procedures that are taught. The interesting point is that we then may get specialized forms of the exercises almost for free, by adding further restrictions through constraints.

Prototype programs using CLP show that these platforms have the right expressiveness to encode control on the system in an elegant way. The main drawback is that we cannot take complete advantage of CLP solvers to reduce the implementation effort. Indeed, we need to handle symbolic representations of some types of irrational numbers. Moreover, we also need symbolic processing of constraints, for example, to be able to find the domain of a function or to provide explanations. Since the system must have great control on the solving procedure to be able to explain the solving steps, we think we would not benefit if we used other languages and platforms to implement the system.

We shall consider the integration in Ganesh [10], although, so far, this distributed learning environment has been mainly used for Computer Science topics, with an emphasis on automatic grading and correction of students exercises.

Thanks. To anonymous referees and Inês Dutra for constructive comments.

References

1. Bryc, W., Pelikan, S.: Online Exercises System. Univ. of Cincinnati, US (1996)
2. Carlsson, M., Ottosson, G., Carlson, B.: An Open-Ended Finite Domain Constraint Solver. In Proceedings of PLILP'97, LNCS 1292. Springer-Verlag, (1997) 191–206
3. Cohen, A. M., Cuypers, H., Sterk, H.: *Algebra Interactive*, Springer-Verlag (1999)
4. Damas, L., Santos Costa, V., Reis, R., Azevedo, R.: YAP User's Guide and Reference Manual. Univ. Porto (1998) http://www.ncc.up.pt/~vsc/YAP
5. Gang, X.: WIMS – An Interactive Mathematics Server. J. Online Mathematics and its Applications, 1, MAA (2001) http://wims.unice.fr
6. Geometer Sketchpad, Key Curriculum Press. http://www.keypress.com/
7. Holzbaur, C.: OFAI clp(q,r) Manual, Edition 1.3.3. Austrian Research Institute for Artificial Intelligence, Vienna, TR-95-09 (1995)
8. Kent, P.: Computer-Assisted Problem Posing in Undergraduate Mathematics. Institute of Education, Univ. of London (1996) http://metric.ma.ic.ac.uk
9. Klai, S., Kolokolnikov, T., Van der Bergh, N.: Using Maple and the web to grade mathematics tests. Int. Workshop on Advanced Technologies, Palmerston North, New Zealand (2000) http://allserv.rug.ac.be/~nvdbergh/aim/docs
10. Leal, J. P., Moreira, N.: Using matching for automatic assessment in computer science learning environments. In: Proceedings of Web-based Learning Environments Conference (2000) http://www.ncc.up.pt/~zp/ganesh
11. Maple, Waterloo Maple Corporate. http://www.maplesoft.com
12. Marriott, K., and Stuckey, P.: Programming with Constraints – An Introduction. The MIT Press (1998)
13. Mathematica, Wolfram Research Inc. http://www.wolfram.com/
14. Mathematical Markup Language (MathML) Version 2.0. W3C Recomendation (2001) http://www.w3.org/Math/
15. Melis, E. et al.: ActiveMath: A Generic and Adaptive Web-Based Learning Environment. Int. J. Artificial Intelligence in Education, 12(4) (2001) 385–407 http://www.activemath.org/
16. Moore, L., Smith, D. et al.: Connected Curriculum Project CCP. Duke University (2001) http://www.math.duke.edu/education/ccp
17. Sangwin, C.J.: New opportunities for encouraging higher level mathematical learning by creative use of emerging computer aided assessment. Univ. of Birmingham, UK (2002)
18. Moura Santos, A., Santos, P. A., Dionísio F. M., Duarte P.: CAL – A System for generating multiple choice questions and delivering them by Internet. In: Proc. of the Workshop on Electronic Media in Mathematics, Coimbra, Portugal (2001)
19. Schrönert, M. et al.: GAP – Groups, Algorithms, and Programming. Lehrstuhl D für Mathematik, Rheinisch Westfälische Tecnhische Hochschule, Germany (1995)
20. SICStus Prolog User Manual Release 3.8.6. SICS, Sweden (2001) http://www.sics.se/isl/sicstus.html
21. Tomás, A. P., Vasconcelos, P.: Generating Mathematics Exercises by Computer. Internal Report DCC-2001-6, DCC - FC & LIACC, University of Porto. Presented at Workshop CSOR'01, Porto (2001)
22. WeBWorK. University of Rochester (2001) http://webwork.math.rochester.edu

A Logical Framework for Modelling eMAS

Pierangelo Dell'Acqua[1,2] and Luís Moniz Pereira[2]

[1] Department of Science and Technology - ITN
Linköping University, Norrköping, Sweden
`pier@itn.liu.se`

[2] Centro de Inteligência Artificial - CENTRIA
Departamento de Informática, Faculdade de Ciências e Tecnologia
Universidade Nova de Lisboa, 2829-516 Caparica, Portugal
`lmp@di.fct.unl.pt`

Abstract. We investigate how to explicitly represent organizational structures in epistemic multi-agent systems (eMAS). We introduce a logical framework $\mathcal{F}$ suitable for representing organizational structures for epistemic agents, and provide its declarative and procedural semantics. We show how a number of organizational structures can be represented in $\mathcal{F}$ and discuss their properties.

1 Motivation

In previous papers [6,8,9] we presented a logical formalization of a framework for multi-agent systems where we embedded a flexible and powerful kind of epistemic agent. In fact, these agents are rational, reactive, abductive, able to prefer and they can update the knowledge base of other agents (including their own). The knowledge state of each agent is represented by an abductive logic program in which it is possible to express rules, integrity constraints, active rules, and priorities among rules. This allows the agents to reason, to react to the environment, to prefer among several alternatives, to update both beliefs and reactions, and to abduce hypotheses to explain observations. There we presented a declarative semantics for this kind of agent. In [1] we provided a syntactical transformation that is at the basis for a proof procedure for updating and preferring in agents, and in [7] we presented a framework for handling the communication among epistemic agents asynchronously.

Within the multi-agent system framework proposed in [8] we can represent coalitions of agents, groups, teams implicitly based on the internal mental states of the members. It is advocated, especially in open multi-agent systems (cf. [3, 11,16]), that there is a need to make the organizational elements as well as the formalization of the agent interactions of a multi-agent system externally visible rather than being embedded in the mental state of each agent, i.e., it is desired to explicitly represent the organizational structure and the agent interactions.

Organizational structures and rules are required to provide control over the member agents with respect to their actions and interactions. Castelfranchi [4]

V. Dahl and P. Wadler (Eds.): PADL 2003, LNCS 2562, pp. 241–255, 2003.
© Springer-Verlag Berlin Heidelberg 2003

argues that social order is a major problem in multi-agent systems. The idea of a total control and a technical prevention against chaos, conflicts and deception in computers is unrealistic and even self-defeating in some cases, e.g. in the building up of trust. He states that there is some illusion in Computer Science about solving this problem by rigid formalization and rules, constraining infra-structures, security devices, etc. and there is skepticism or irritation towards more soft and social approaches, that leave more room to spontaneous emergence, or to decentralized control, or to normative "stuff" which is not externally imposed but internally managed by the agents. He claims that the most effective solution to this problem is social modelling and that it should leave some flexibility and try to deal with emergent and spontaneous form of organizational building (that is, decentralized and autonomous social control). The problem with this approach is that of modelling the feedback from the global results to the local/individual layer.

Zambonelli [15] states that modelling and engineering interactions in complex and open multi-agent systems cannot simply rely on the agent capabilities for communicating and of acting according to the expectations of each agent of the system. Rather, there is a need for concepts like "organizational rules", "social laws" and "active environments". For the effective engineering of multi-agent systems, high-level, inter-agent concepts, language extensions, and abstractions must be defined to explicitly model the organization, the society in which agents operate, and the associated organizational laws.

In this paper, with the above purpose in mind, we elaborate over the approach proposed in [8], and usher in the more flexible notion of weighted directed acyclic graphs (WDAGs), generalizing the notion of DAGs presented in [12], and permitting us to address the issues at hand by assigning a measure of strength to the knowledge sharing relationships represented by the edges. We introduce a logical framework $\mathcal{F}$, provide its declarative semantics, and sketch its procedural semantics in some detail. We next show how several organizational structures in multi-agent systems (eMAS) for epistemic agents can indeed be explicitly represented in $\mathcal{F}$. $\mathcal{F}$ having a formal semantics enables us to study and prove properties of eMAS structures.

2   Background

To represent negative information in logic programs, we need a language that allows default negation $not\ A$ not only in premises of rules but also in their heads[1]. By a *generalized logic program* P over a language $\mathcal{L}$ we mean a finite or infinite set of propositional rules r of the form $L_0 \leftarrow L_1 \wedge \ldots \wedge L_n$, where each L_i is a literal (i.e. an atom A or its default negation $not\ A$). It is convenient to syntactically represent generalized logic programs as propositional Horn theories. In particular, we represent default negation $not\ A$ as a propositional variable.

---

[1] For further motivation and intuitive reading of logic programs with default negations in the heads see [2].

If r is a rule, by $head(r)$ we mean L_0, and by $body(r)$ we mean $L_1 \wedge \ldots \wedge L_n$. If $head(r) = A$ (resp. $head(r) = not\, A$) then $not\, head(r) = not\, A$ (resp. $not\, head(r) = A$). By a (2-valued) *interpretation* M of $\mathcal{L}$ we mean any set of literals from $\mathcal{L}$ that satisfies the condition that for any atom A, precisely one of the literals A or $not\, A$ belongs to M. Given an interpretation M, we define $M^+ = \{A : A \in M\}$ and $M^- = \{not\, A : not\, A \in M\}$. Following established tradition, wherever convenient we omit the default atoms when describing interpretations and models. We say that a (2-valued) interpretation M of $\mathcal{L}$ is a stable model of a generalized logic program P if $M = least(P \cup M^-)$. The class of generalized logic programs can be viewed as a special case of yet broader classes of programs, introduced earlier in [14], and, for the special case of normal programs, their semantics coincides with the stable models semantics [10].

3   Weighted Directed Acyclic Graphs

A *directed graph* $D = (V, E)$ is a pair comprised of a finite set V of *vertices* and a finite set E of ordered pairs (v, w) called *edges*, where v and w are vertices in V. The vertex v is the *initial vertex* of the edge and w the *terminal vertex*. The *in-valency* of a vertex v is the number of edges with v as their terminal vertex. The *out-valency* of a vertex v is the number of edges with v as their initial vertex. A *source* is a vertex with in-valency 0 and a *sink* a vertex with out-valency 0. A weighted directed graph is a directed graph in which a positive real number has been assigned to each edge. A *weighted directed graph* is a tuple (V, E, w) where V is a set of vertices, E a set of edges and $w : E \to \mathbb{R}^+$ a function mapping the edges in E to positive real numbers in $\mathbb{R}^+$. A *path* in a directed graph is a sequence of consecutive edges in the graph that begins at an initial vertex and ends at a terminal vertex. If there exists a path from a vertex v_1 to a vertex v_2 we write $v_1 \prec v_2$, otherwise $v_1 \nprec v_2$. We write $v_1 \preceq v_2$ if $v_1 \prec v_2$ or $v_1 = v_2$. We write $v_1 \npreceq v_2$ if $v_1 \nprec v_2$ and $v_1 \neq v_2$. Sometime to make explicit the vertices occurring in a path $v_1 \prec v_n$ with $1 < n$ we write the sequence $v_1, v_2, \ldots, v_n$ of all vertices occurring in it. A *cycle* is a path in which the initial vertex of the path is also the terminal vertex.

Definition 1 (WDAG). *A weighted directed acyclic graph (WDAG) is a weighted directed graph that does not contain any cycles.*

Definition 2 (Path dominance). *Let $D = (V, E, w)$ be a WDAG and $a_1 \prec a_n$ ($1 < n$) a path with vertices $a_1, a_2, \ldots, a_n$. Then $a_1 \prec a_n$ is a dominant path iff there exists no other path $b_1, b_2, \ldots, b_m$ ($1 < m$) such that $b_1 = a_1$, $b_m = a_n$ and there exist i, j with $1 < i \leq n, 1 < j \leq m$ such that $a_i = b_j$ and $w((a_{i-1}, a_i)) < w((b_{j-1}, b_j))$.*

Example 1. Let $D = (V, E, w)$ be a WDAG, where $V = \{v_1, v_2, v_3, v_4\}$, E consists of the edges: $e_1 = (v_2, v_1)$, $e_2 = (v_3, v_2)$, $e_3 = (v_3, v_1)$, $e_4 = (v_2, v_4)$ and

$e_5 = (v_4, v_1)$. Let $w(e_1) = 0.4$, $w(e_2) = 0.8$, $w(e_4) = 0.3$ and $w(e_3) = w(e_5) = 0.6$. Then, there exist two paths from v_3 to v_1 that are dominant: the path v_3, v_1 and the path v_3, v_2, v_4, v_1.

Definition 3 (Prevalence wrt. a vertex a_n). *Let $D = (V, E, w)$ be a WDAG and $a_1 \prec a_n$ a dominant path with vertices $a_1, a_2, \dots, a_n$. Then, every vertex a_i prevails a_1 wrt. a_n, for every $1 < i \le n$. If in addition there exists a path $b_1 \prec a_i$ with vertices $b_1, \dots, b_m, a_i$ ($1 \le m$), for some $1 < i \le n$, and $w((a_{i-1}, a_i)) < w((b_m, a_i))$, then every vertex b_j prevails a_1 wrt. a_n, for every $1 \le j \le m$.*

In the following, we write $v_2 \underset{s}{\triangleleft} v_1$ to indicate that v_1 prevails v_2 wrt. s.

Example 2. Let $D = (V, E, w)$ where $V = \{v_1, v_2, v_3, v_4, v_5, v_6\}$, E consists of the following edges $e_1 = (v_2, v_1)$, $e_2 = (v_3, v_2)$, $e_3 = (v_4, v_2)$, $e_4 = (v_5, v_1)$ and $e_5 = (v_6, v_5)$. Let $w(e_1) = 0.5$, $w(e_2) = w(e_3) = 0.8$, $w(e_4) = 0.6$ and $w(e_5) = 0.2$. Then, for instance, the following prevalences hold: $v_4 \underset{v_1}{\triangleleft} v_1$, $v_2 \underset{v_1}{\triangleleft} v_1$, $v_6 \underset{v_1}{\triangleleft} v_5$, $v_2 \underset{v_1}{\triangleleft} v_5$ and $v_4 \underset{v_1}{\triangleleft} v_6$.

Example 3. Let $D = (V, E, w)$ where $V = \{v_1, v_2, v_3, v_4\}$, E consists of the following edges $e_1 = (v_2, v_1)$, $e_2 = (v_3, v_2)$, $e_3 = (v_4, v_1)$ and $e_4 = (v_4, v_3)$. Let $w(e_1) = 0.2$, $w(e_2) = 0.3$, $w(e_3) = 0.4$ and $w(e_4) = 0.2$. The following prevalences holds: $v_3 \underset{v_1}{\triangleleft} v_1$, $v_4 \underset{v_1}{\triangleleft} v_1$, $v_2 \underset{v_1}{\triangleleft} v_4$ and $v_3 \underset{v_1}{\triangleleft} v_4$. The vertex v_3 does not prevail v_4 since the unique dominant path from v_4 to v_1 is v_4, v_1.

The next notion allows us to connect vertices of distinct WDAGs.

Definition 4 (Link). *Let $D_1 = (V_1, E_1, w_1)$ and $D_2 = (V_2, E_2, w_2)$ be WDAGs. A link from D_1 to D_2 is an ordered pair (v_1, v_2) whose initial vertex v_1 belongs to V_1 and terminal vertex v_2 belongs to V_2.*

To simplify the notation, in the remaining of the paper we assume that each vertex in a WDAG has a unique name, that is, given two arbitrary WDAGs D_1 and D_2 we assume that $V_1 \cap V_2 = \{\}$.

Definition 5 (WDAGs joining). *Let $D = \{D_1, \dots, D_n\}$ be a set of WDAGs, L a set of links over D and $w_L : L \to \mathbb{R}^+$ a function. Assume that $D_i = (V_i, E_i, w_i)$ for every $1 \le i \le n$. The joining of the WDAGs in D w.r.t. L and w_L, written as $\sqcup(D, L, w_L)$, is the WDAG (V, E, w) where:*

$$V = \bigcup_{1 \le i \le n} V_i \qquad E = \bigcup_{1 \le i \le n} E_i \cup L \qquad and \qquad w(e) = \begin{cases} w_i(e) & if\ e \in E_i \\ w_L(e) & if\ e \in L \end{cases}$$

Example 4. Let $D = \{D_1, D_2\}$, where $D_1 = (\{a_1, a_2, a_3\}, \{(a_1, a_2), (a_2, a_3)\}, w_1)$ and $D_2 = (\{b_1, b_2, b_3\}, \{(b_1, b_3), (b_2, b_3)\}, w_2)$. Let $L = \{(a_2, b_1), (b_2, a_3)\}$ and w_L a weight function over L. Then $(a_1, a_2), (a_2, b_1), (b_1, b_3)$ is a path $a_1 \prec b_3$ over $\sqcup(D, L, w_L)$.

4   Logic Framework

In this section we present a logical framework suitable to formalize organizational structures for epistemic agents. We start by defining the notion of generalized logic programs indexed by WDAGs. The next definition extends the original definition of MDLP (presented in [12,13]) to take into consideration WDAGs.

Definition 6 (Multi-dimensional Dynamic Logic Program). *Let $\mathcal{L}$ be a propositional language. A Multi-dimensional Dynamic Logic Program (MDLP), $\mathcal{P}$, is a pair $(\mathcal{P}_D, D)$, where $D = (V, E, w)$ is a WDAG and $\mathcal{P}_D = \{P_v : v \in V\}$ is a set of generalized logic programs over the language $\mathcal{L}$ indexed by the vertices $v \in V$. We call* states *such vertices of D. For simplicity, we often leave the language $\mathcal{L}$ implicit.*

To characterize the models of $\mathcal{P}$ at any given state we will keep to the basic intuition of logic program updates, whereby an interpretation is a stable model of the update of a program P by a program U iff it is a stable model of a program consisting of the rules of U together with a subset of the rules of P comprised by those that are not rejected (do not carry over by inertia) due to their being overridden by the updating program U. With the introduction of WDAGs to index programs, a program may have more than a single ancestor. This has to be dealt with, the desired intuition being that a program $P_v \in \mathcal{P}_D$ can be used to reject rules of any program $P_u \in \mathcal{P}_D$ if v prevails u. Moreover, if an atom A is not defined in any program P_u in $\mathcal{P}_D$ ancestor of P_v, then its negation *not A* is assumed by default in P_v.

Definition 7 (Stable Models of MDLP at state s). *Let $\mathcal{P} = (\mathcal{P}_D, D)$ be a MDLP where $\mathcal{P}_D = \{P_v : v \in V\}$ and $D = (V, E, w)$. Let s be a state in V. An interpretation M is a* stable model *of $\mathcal{P}$ at state s iff*

$$M = least(O \cup Default(O, M)) \text{ where:}$$

$$Q = \bigcup_{v \preceq s} P_v$$

$$Reject(s, M) = \{r \in P_{v_2} : \exists r' \in P_{v_1} head(r) = not\ head(r'), M \vDash body(r'),$$
$$\text{and } v_2 \underset{s}{\vartriangleleft} v_1\}$$

$$O = Q - Reject(s, M)$$

$$Default(O, M) = \{not\ A : \nexists r \in O, head(r) = A \text{ and } M \vDash body(r)\}.$$

Intuitively, the set $Reject(s, M)$ contains those rules belonging to a program indexed by a state v_2 that are overridden by the head of another rule with true body in state v_1 such that v_1 prevails v_2 wrt. s. Q contains all rules of all programs that are indexed by a state along all paths to state s, i.e. all rules that are potentially relevant to determine the semantics at state s. The set $Default(O, M)$ contains default negations *not A* of all unsupported atoms A, i.e., those atoms A for which there is no rule in O (i.e. the non-rejected rules of Q) whose body is true in M.

Example 5. Let $\mathcal{P} = (\mathcal{P}_D, D)$ be a MDLP where $D = (V, E, w)$, $V = \{v_1, v_2, v_3\}$. E consists of $e_1 = (v_1, v_3)$ and $e_2 = (v_2, v_3)$. Let $\mathcal{P}_D = \{P_1, P_2, P_3\}$ with $P_1 = \{a\}$, $P_2 = \{not\, a\}$ and $P_3 = \{\}$. If $w(e_1) = w(e_2)$, then there exists no stable model M of $\mathcal{P}$ at state v_3. In fact, $Q = \{a, not\, a\}$ and $Reject(s, M) = \{\}$, $Default(O, M) = \{\}$, for any interpretation M. Thus, there exists no model M such that $M = least(O)$. If instead $w(e_1) > w(e_2)$, then there exists a unique stable model $M = \{a\}$ of $\mathcal{P}$ at state v_3. In fact, $Reject(s, M) = \{not\, a\}$ as $v_2 \underset{v_3}{\lhd} v_1$, $Default(O, M) = \{\}$ and $M = least(\{a\})$.

Example 6. Let $\mathcal{P} = (\mathcal{P}_D, D)$ be a MDLP where $D = (V, E, w)$, $V = \{v_1, v_2, v_3, v_4\}$. E consists of $e_1 = (v_2, v_1)$, $e_2 = (v_3, v_1)$ and $e_3 = (v_4, v_3)$, and $w(e_1) = 0.7$, $w(e_2) = 0.4$ and $w(e_3) = 0.2$. Let $\mathcal{P}_D = \{P_1, P_2, P_3, P_4\}$ with $P_1 = \{b\}$, $P_2 = \{a\}$, $P_3 = \{not\, a, d \leftarrow a \wedge b\}$ and $P_4 = \{not\, b\}$. The stable model of $\mathcal{P}$ at state v_1 is $\{a, b, d\}$. In fact, as it holds that $v_4 \underset{v_1}{\lhd} v_1$ and $v_3 \underset{v_1}{\lhd} v_2$, we have that $Reject(s, M) = \{not\, a, not\, b\}$ and $Default(O, M) = \{\}$.

We can now introduce the logical framework $\mathcal{F}$ and its declarative semantics. The idea of the approach is to formalize epistemic agents by MDLPs and to organize them into structures by means of $\mathcal{F}$.

Definition 8 (Logical Framework $\mathcal{F}$). *The logical framework $\mathcal{F}$ is a tuple $(\mathcal{A}, L, w_L)$ where $\mathcal{A} = \{\mathcal{P}_1, \ldots, \mathcal{P}_n\}$ is a set of MDLPs $\mathcal{P}_i = (\mathcal{P}_{D_i}, D_i)$, L is a set of links over the D_is and $w_L : L \to \mathbb{R}^+$ is a function.*

Definition 9 (Joined MDLP). *Let $\mathcal{F} = (\mathcal{A}, L, w_L)$ be a logical framework. Assume that $\mathcal{A} = \{\mathcal{P}_1, \ldots, \mathcal{P}_n\}$ and each $\mathcal{P}_i = (\mathcal{P}_{D_i}, D_i)$ for $1 \leq i \leq n$. The joined MDLP induced by $\mathcal{F}$, if it is a WDAG, is $\mathcal{P} = (\mathcal{P}_D, D)$ where $D = (V, E, w)$ is $\sqcup(\{D_1, \ldots, D_n\}, L, w_L)$ and $\mathcal{P}_D = \{P_v : v \in V$ and $P_v \in \bigcup_{1 \leq i \leq n} \mathcal{P}_{D_i}\}$.*

Definition 10 (Stable Models of $\mathcal{F}$ at state s). *Let $\mathcal{F} = (\mathcal{A}, L, w_L)$ be a logical framework, s be a state and $\mathcal{P}$ the joined MDLP induced by $\mathcal{F}$. An interpretation M is a stable model of $\mathcal{F}$ at state s iff M is a stable model of $\mathcal{P}$ at state s.*

5   Syntactic Transformation for WDAGs

By Def. 10, to have a proof procedure for the logical framework $\mathcal{F}$ we need a proof procedure for MDLPs. This can be achieved via a syntactical transformation that, given a multi-dimensional logic program $\mathcal{P}$, produces a generalized logic program whose stable models coincide with the stable models of $\mathcal{P}$. Thus this transformation provides the grounds for implementing $\mathcal{F}$.

The transformation is established based on the proven correct syntactical transformation for the original definition of MDLP over DAGs given in [12]. The original contains transformation among others the following two axioms.

- *Inheritance rules:* $A_v \leftarrow A_u \wedge not\ reject(A_u)$

  for all atoms A and edges (u, v). It states that an atom A is true in a state v if it is true in any ancestor state u and it is not rejected, i.e., forced to be false.

- *Rejection rules:* $reject(A_u) \leftarrow A_{P_v}^-$

  for all atoms A and all vertices u, v such that $u \prec v$. The rejection rules say that if an atom A is false (represented by A^-) in the program P_v, then it rejects inheritance of any true atom A of any ancestor u.

To generate a transformation for MDLPs based on a WDAG $D = (V, E, w)$, we can explicitly represent the edges in E by $edge(u, v, x)$ for all edges $(u, v) \in E$ whose weight is x, and the prevalence relation $u \vartriangleleft v$ by $prevail(u, v)$. Then, we can substitute the axioms above with:

- *Inheritance rules*:* $A_v \leftarrow A_u \wedge not\ reject(A_u) \wedge edge(u, v, x)$

  for all atoms A. It states that an atom A is true in a state v if it is true in a state u, it is not rejected, and there exists an edge x between u and v.

- *Rejection rules*:* $reject(A_u) \leftarrow A_{P_v}^- \wedge prevail(u, v)$

  for all atoms A. The rejection rules say that if an atom A is false in the program P_v and v prevails over some a vertex u, then the rule rejects inheritance of any true atom A at vertex u.

6   Modelling Organizational Structures

Typically, agents operate in the context of multi-agent systems. Some of these systems can be understood as a computational society whose role is to allow its members to coexist in a shared environment and to pursue their goals. Several attempts to define organizational structures for agents have been proposed, e.g., coalitions, groups, teams and institutions. In this section we show how a number of organizational structures can be formalized within the proposed logical framework, and discuss some of their properties. The idea is to formalize both agents and organizational structures via MDLPs and to glue them together via $\mathcal{F}$. We assume that the WDAG of the MDLP of each agent is equipped with a sink[2] v, with an empty program P_v associated with it, indicating where the semantics of the agent can be determined. v is called the *inspection point* of the agent. Following Davidsson [5], agent societies can be categorized with respect to the following properties: *openness*, the possibility for agents to join the society without any restriction; *flexibility*, the degree to which agents are restricted in their behavior by the society; *stability*, predictability of the consequences of actions, and *trustfulness*, the extent to which the owners of the agents trust the society.

---

[2] A vertex with out-valency 0.

6.1 Groups

A *group* is a system of agents that are constrained in their mutual interactions. A group can be formalized in $\mathcal{F}$ in a flexible way: the behavior of the agents in the group can be restricted by the group itself to different degrees depending on its purpose. The formalization of the group supports also trustfulness. In fact, restricting the behavior of the members of the group with norms and regulations may enhance the degree of trust vis-à-vis the group.

Fig. 1 depicts a group of three agents: A, B and C. (The oval in the picture represents the group.) Suppose that A is the leader of the group.

We want to formalize a situation where B must operate (strictly) in accordance with A, while C has a certain degree of freedom. In this scenario, B and C are secretaries to A and both believe that it is not their duty to answer phone calls. In contrast, A believes that one of the duties of a secretary is indeed to answer the phone. This situation can be formalized as follows.

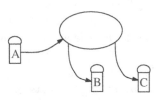

Fig. 1. Group of agents

We let $\mathcal{P}_A$, $\mathcal{P}_B$ and $\mathcal{P}_C$ be the MDLPs of the agents A, B and C, and $\mathcal{P}_G$ be the MDLP of the group. Let $\mathcal{P}_A = (\mathcal{P}_{D_A}, D_A)$ where $D_A = (\{v_1\}, \{\}, w_A)$ and $P_{v_1} = \{answerPhone \leftarrow secretary \wedge phoneRing\}$. Let $\mathcal{P}_B = (\mathcal{P}_{D_B}, D_B)$ where $D_B = (\{v_3, v_4\}, \{(v_4, v_3)\}, w_B)$, $w_B((v_4, v_3)) = 0.6$, $P_{v_3} = \{\}$ and $P_{v_4} = \{phoneRing, secretary, not\ answerPhone\}$. Let $\mathcal{P}_C = (\mathcal{P}_{D_C}, D_C)$ where $D_C = (\{v_5, v_6\}, \{(v_6, v_5)\}, w_C)$, $w_C((v_6, v_5)) = 0.6$, $P_{v_6} = P_{v_4}$ and $P_{v_5} = P_{v_3}$. Let $\mathcal{P}_G = (\mathcal{P}_{D_G}, D_G)$ where $D_G = (\{v_2\}, \{\}, w_G)$ and $P_{v_2} = \{\}$.

$\mathcal{F} = (\mathcal{A}, L, w_L)$ where $\mathcal{A} = \{\mathcal{P}_A, \mathcal{P}_B, \mathcal{P}_C, \mathcal{P}_G\}$, $L = \{(v_1, v_2), (v_2, v_3), (v_2, v_5)\}$ and $w_L((v_1, v_2)) = 0.5$, $w_L((v_2, v_3)) = 0.7$ and $w_L((v_2, v_5)) = 0.5$.

Let v_3 and v_5 be the inspection points of the agents B and C, respectively. Then, according to the declarative semantics of $\mathcal{F}$, B will answer the phone, while C will not do it. In fact, the semantics of B, whose model is determined at its inspection point v_3, is $M_{v_3} = \{phoneRing, secretary, answerPhone\}$, while the semantics of C is $M_{v_5} = \{phoneRing, secretary, not\ answerPhone\}$. Although the theories of B and C are the same, their models are different

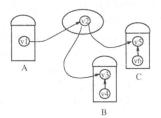

Fig. 2. Group of agents

because the edges (v_2, v_3) and (v_2, v_5) have different weights. M_{v_3} is a stable model of the joined MDLP $\mathcal{P}$ induced by $\mathcal{F}$ at state v_3 since we have that:

$$M_{v_3} = least(O \cup Default(O, M_{v_3}))\ \text{where:}$$
$$Q = \{phoneRing, secretary, not\ answerPhone,$$
$$answerPhone \leftarrow secretary \wedge phoneRing\}$$

$$Reject(v_3, M_{v_3}) = \{not\ answerPhone\} \text{ since } v_4 \triangleleft_{v_3} v_1$$

$$O = Q - Reject(v_3, M_{v_3})$$

$$Default(O, M_{v_3}) = \{\}.$$

Consequently, by Def. 10 it holds that M_{v_3} is a stable model of $\mathcal{F}$ at state v_3 (the inspection point of B).

6.2 Bi-directional Information Exchange between a Group and Its Members

A different situation occurs when the exchange of information between the group and its members is bi-directional. That is, an agent makes part of its information available to the group when it joins it. This situation occurs, for example, in systems whose functioning requires different areas of expertise.

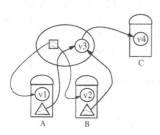

Suppose that each agent in the group has its own area of expertise. When an agent joins a group, the agent receives the information made available from the group, and in turn makes its area of expertise available it. Fig. 3 depicts a group of three agents A, B and C. The group provides part of its information (i.e., the part of its WDAG depicted by the box in the oval) to both A and B. They in turn make available to the group the part of their WDAGs

Fig. 3. Bi-directional exchange of information

depicted by the corresponding triangles. Finally, a third agent C has visibility over the part of the information made available to the group by the other two agents.

6.3 Groups with Roles

$\mathcal{F}$ can be used to formalize groups whose members have an associated role. In this context a role can be understood as a system of prescribed behavior. We are not concerned here how the agent's mental state (represented by its MDLP) is influenced by the social context in which the agent is situated. Fig. 4 depicts a group with three agents. The role of agent C dominates the role of agent B which in turn dominates the role

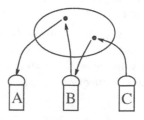

Fig. 4. Group with roles

of agent A. Note that this formalization of the group does not guarantee trustfulness. That is, an agent may not respect the prevalence of another agent with a superior role. This occurs for instance in the following example.

Consider the group in Fig. 4 where C prevails over B which in turn prevails over A.

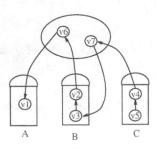

Fig. 5. Abuse of roles

We let $\mathcal{P}_A$, $\mathcal{P}_B$ and $\mathcal{P}_C$ be the MDLPs of the agents A, B and C, and $\mathcal{P}_G$ be the MDLP of the group.

Let $\mathcal{P}_A = (\mathcal{P}_{D_A}, D_A)$ where $D_A = (\{v_1\}, \{\}, w_A)$ and $P_{v_1} = \{\}$. Let $\mathcal{P}_B = (\mathcal{P}_{D_B}, D_B)$ where $D_B = (\{v_2, v_3\}, \{(v_3, v_2)\}, w_B)$, $w_B((v_3, v_2)) = 0.3$, $P_{v_2} = \{\}$ and $P_{v_3} = \{b, not\, a\}$. Let $\mathcal{P}_C = (\mathcal{P}_{D_C}, D_C)$ where $D_C = (\{v_4, v_5\}, \{(v_5, v_4)\}, w_C)$, $w_C((v_5, v_4)) = 0.3$, $P_{v_4} = \{\}$ and $P_{v_5} = \{a \leftarrow b\}$. Let $\mathcal{P}_G = (\mathcal{P}_{D_G}, D_G)$ where $D_G = (\{v_6, v_7\}, \{\}, w_G)$ and $P_{v_6} = P_{v_7} = \{\}$.

Let $\mathcal{F} = (\mathcal{A}, L, w_L)$ where $\mathcal{A} = \{\mathcal{P}_A, \mathcal{P}_B, \mathcal{P}_C, \mathcal{P}_G\}$, $L = \{(v_4, v_7), (v_7, v_3), (v_2, v_6), (v_6, v_1)\}$ and $w_L((v_i, v_j)) = 0.5$, for every $(v_i, v_j) \in \mathcal{L}$.

The intended model of B at state v_2 is $M = \{a, b\}$ because the knowledge of C is intended to override the knowledge of B. Agent B instead overrides the knowledge of C (due to the edge from v_7 to v_3). Thus, the unique stable model of A (i.e., the stable model of $\mathcal{F}$ at state v_1) is $M_{v_1} = \{b, not\, a\}$.

Note that this problem could be easily solved by removing the edge (v_7, v_3) from $\mathcal{F}$ and by adding the edge (v_7, v_2) with sufficiently high weight to overcome the weight of (v_3, v_2). However, not always the group can guarantee that each member will respect the other agent's roles. This may happen when agents are able to self-modify their WDAGs.

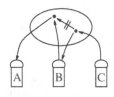

Fig. 6. Enforcing prevalence

To solve this problem we need to enforce a prevalence within the WDAG of the formalization of the group. Specifically, we need to add an edge (v_7, v_6) with high weight (i.e., the edge with double marks in Fig. 6) with the aim of making the new edge prevail over the edge (v_2, v_6) coming out from B. In this way the path $v_4 \prec v_6$ via v_7 will be a dominant path and consequently $v_3 \vartriangleleft_{v_6} v_5$.

However, this solution, by enforcing the prevalence of vertices at the group level, would give less autonomy to the group's members. In general, nevertheless, it may increase the stability of the system. The study of the various options, and their connection to other problems, is earmarked for future work.

6.4   Groups with Equal Roles

Our approach caters for the possibility of capturing the equivalent interdependency of agents in a group (that is, when two or more agents reciprocally influence one another). This implies that contradicting rules in the two agents simply reject one another. (An alternative semantics could instead introduce the disjoint availability of each rule in distinct stable models.)

Consider a group with two agents A and B having equal roles. Let $\mathcal{P}_A$ and $\mathcal{P}_B$ be the MDLPs of the agents A and B, and $\mathcal{P}_G$ be the MDLP of the group.

Let $\mathcal{P}_A = (\mathcal{P}_{D_A}, D_A)$ where $D_A = (\{v_4, v_5\}, \{(v_5, v_4)\}, w_A)$, $w_A((v_5, v_4)) = 0.1$ and $P_{v_5} = \{a, c\}$. Let $\mathcal{P}_B = (\mathcal{P}_{D_B}, D_B)$ where $D_B = (\{v_6, v_7\}, \{(v_7, v_6)\}, w_B)$, $w_B((v_7, v_6)) = 0.1$ and $P_{v_7} = \{b, not\,a \leftarrow b \wedge c\}$.

Let $\mathcal{P}_G = (\mathcal{P}_{D_G}, D_G)$ where $D_G = (\{v_1, v_2, v_3\}, \{(v_2, v_1), (v_3, v_1)\}, w_G)$ and $w_G((v_2, v_1)) = w_G((v_3, v_1)) = 0.1$.

Let $\mathcal{F} = (\mathcal{A}, L, w_L)$ where $\mathcal{A} = \{\mathcal{P}_A, \mathcal{P}_B, \mathcal{P}_G\}$, $L = \{(v_4, v_2), (v_4, v_3), (v_6, v_2), (v_6, v_3)\}$ and $w_L((v_4, v_2)) = w_L((v_6, v_3)) = 0.4$ and $w_L((v_4, v_3)) = w_L((v_6, v_2)) = 0.1$.

Then, the unique stable model of $\mathcal{F}$ at state v_1 is $M = \{b, c\}$. In fact, the inspection points v_4 and v_6 of A and B have both two dominant paths to v_1, and consequently it holds that $v_5 \triangleleft_{v_1} v_7$ and $v_7 \triangleleft_{v_1} v_5$. This means that the rules in v_5 and v_7 reject one another.

6.5   Institutions

An institution is a system of agents having a legal standing. The following example illustrates the use of an institution to enforce norms and regulations over the behavior of an agent A. To this aim, we formalize the environment where A is situated via a

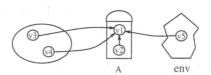

Fig. 7. Institution

MDLP named *env*, and extend the language $\mathcal{L}$ to contain integrity constraints and active rules. (For a more detailed presentation of such a language see [8].)

Informally, an *integrity constraint* is a rule of the form *false* $\leftarrow L_1 \wedge \ldots \wedge L_n$ where every L_i $(1 \leq i \leq n)$ is a literal. Integrity constraints are rules that enforce some condition over the state, and therefore always take the form of denials, without loss of generality, in a 2-valued semantics.

An *active rule* is a rule of the form $L_1 \wedge \ldots \wedge L_n \Rightarrow Z$, where every L_i $(1 \leq i \leq n)$ is a literal and Z is a project. Active rules are rules that can modify the current state, to produce a new state updated with the project, when triggered. If the body $L_1 \wedge \ldots \wedge L_n$ of the active rule is satisfied, then the project (fluent) Z can be selected and executed. Z can take the form $do(action)$ to indicate the project of the agent to execute *action* on the environment.

Consider a scenario where the agent A formalizes the theory of a driver, and the institution I formalizes norms and regulations about driving in a certain country. We let $\mathcal{P}_A$, $\mathcal{P}_I$ and $\mathcal{P}_{env}$ be the MDLPs of agent A, the institution I and the environment.

Let $\mathcal{P}_A = (\mathcal{P}_{D_A}, D_A)$ where $D_A = (\{v_1, v_2\}, \{(v_2, v_1)\}, w_A)$, $w_A((v_2, v_1)) = 0.7$, $P_{v_1} = \{\}$ and

$$P_{v_2} = \left\{ \begin{array}{r} \textit{false} \leftarrow \textit{drive} \wedge \textit{do}(\textit{usePhone}) \\ \textit{not lowSpeed} \leftarrow \textit{late} \\ \textit{currentSpeed}(100) \leftarrow \\ \textit{drive} \leftarrow \\ \\ \textit{currentSpeed}(S) \wedge \textit{speedLimit}(L) \wedge S > L \Rightarrow \textit{do}(\textit{decreaseSpeed}) \\ \textit{lowSpeed} \wedge \textit{currentSpeed}(S) \wedge S > 90 \Rightarrow \textit{do}(\textit{decreaseSpeed}) \\ \textit{phoneRing} \Rightarrow \textit{do}(\textit{usePhone}) \end{array} \right\}$$

The first rule in P_{v_2}, for example, is an integrity constraint stating that it is not possible to drive and to use the phone contemporarily (this holds for example in Portugal). The first active rule says that if the current speed S is greater than the speed limit L, then the speed must be decreased (i.e., A executes the project to decrease its speed). Let v_1 be the inspection point of A. Note that if we determine the (only) stable model of A in isolation from the context $\mathcal{F}$ (where A is situated), then the integrity constraint prevents A to use the phone when driving.

Let $\mathcal{P}_I = (\mathcal{P}_{D_I}, D_I)$ where $D_I = (\{v_3, v_4\}, \{\}, w_I)$ and

$$P_{v_3} = \left\{ \begin{array}{r} \textit{not false} \leftarrow \textit{drive} \wedge \textit{do}(\textit{usePhone}) \\ \textit{speedLimit}(110) \leftarrow \end{array} \right\}$$

$$P_{v_4} = \{\, \textit{lowSpeed} \leftarrow \textit{traffic} \,\}$$

This institution formalizes the norms of a certain country that must be obeyed when A is driving in that country. It is natural that A has its own rules for driving, but when it enters another country it must respect the regulations of that country. P_{v_3} contains an integrity constraint (with a default atom in its head) stating that it is not forbidden to drive and to use the phone. The institution contains also the speed limit of the country (these rules hold for example in Sweden). The institution may also contain norms of behavior that are not strict, rather they are advised for safety reasons, like to lower the speed in case of traffic. The idea is that we would like to enforce the norms that are strict within the institution, while letting the driver free to decide about the merely suggested rules.

Let $\mathcal{P}_{env} = (\mathcal{P}_{D_{env}}, D_{env})$ where $D_{env} = (\{v_5\}, \{\}, w_{env})$ and

$$P_{v_5} = \left\{ \begin{array}{r} \textit{traffic} \leftarrow \\ \textit{late} \leftarrow \\ \textit{phoneRing} \leftarrow \end{array} \right\}$$

Let $\mathcal{F} = (\mathcal{A}, L, w_L)$ where $\mathcal{A} = \{\mathcal{P}_A, \mathcal{P}_I, \mathcal{P}_{env}\}$, $L = \{(v_3, v_1), (v_4, v_1), (v_5, v_1)\}$ and $w_L((v_3, v_1)) = 0.9$, $w_L((v_4, v_1)) = 0.5$ and $w_L((v_5, v_1)) = 1$.

To enforce the norms of the institution, $\mathcal{F}$ associates a high weight to the edge (v_3, v_1) and a low weight to (v_4, v_1) since v_4 contains the suggested rules.

$\mathcal{F}$ associates the maximum weight to the environment. The stable model of A is $M_{v_1} = \{$ *traffic*, *late*, *phoneRing*, *speedLimit*(110), *drive*, *currentSpeed*(100), *do* (*usePhone*)$\}$. Note that M_{v_1} does not contain *do*(*decreaseSpeed*).

To provide a legal standing to the institution, we may add a new vertex v_6 to the environment with the aim to maintain the history of all the projects executed by A, through updates to it. Then we can add a new agent B to the institution whose job is to control the environment and the projects executed. As soon as A executes a non-legal project, B can detect it and in response take a suitable action.

6.6   Agent Societies

More complex organizational structures can be formalized in $\mathcal{F}$, e.g., group of groups. In principle, there is no restriction on the membership of agents in groups: an agent can belong to several groups provided that the joined MDLP induced by $\mathcal{F}$ does not contain any cycle. We can then empower agents with communication abilities so that they can have multiple means of interaction amongst each other, and make the knowledge of the agents updatable and self-evolvable to incorporate new incoming information along the lines outlined in [8]. All these ingredients assembled into a single eMAS architecture will allow us to engineer configurable agent societies where the agents can self-organize themselves with respect to their goals, and self-evolve. In this way, the overall "emerging" structure will be flexible and dynamic.

6.7   Agent Societies Based on Voting

The presented framework builds on the notion of prevalence of vertices. However, other notions of prevalence can be accommodated within it. To do so it is necessary to incorporate these new notions both at the semantical level, that is to modify the definition of $Reject(s, M)$ in Def. 7, and at the syntactical level, that is to modify the *rejection rules*.

An interesting notion that can be incorporated is to represent agent societies based on voting. The idea is to engineer societies where, although each agent has a role which drives its behavior, we can provide some degree of freedom to the agents as a whole. One possibility in this direction is to incorporate a *voting system* in the society. The voting system can be based on the incoming edges of a certain node. Thus rules can be rejected because they are outweighed or outvoted, e.g., by opting for the best positive or negative average, or even for none. A receiving node, once it weighs the incoming edges, "commits" to the ones not rejected by the voting. A weighed voting can be employed to resolve multiple (or simply paired) contradictions. More sophisticated weighing schemes, including the introduction of (outgoing) rule weights, and their combination with the (incoming) edge weights shall be the subject of future research.

7   Concluding Remarks

We have shown a logical framework that allows us to model structures of epistemic agents. In Section 3 we have introduced the notion of WDAG that extends DAGs to associate weights to every edge of the graph, and in Section 4 we have presented the logical framework $\mathcal{F}$ with the corresponding declarative semantics. Its procedural semantics has been sketched in Section 5. Having the framework $\mathcal{F}$ a formal semantics will allow us to study and prove the properties of eMAS structures. For simplicity, this paper focuses only on the agent structures, rather than on the agent theories. Therefore, we haven't considered the dynamic aspects of the agent knowledge like, for example, when an agent updates its knowledge to incorporate new incoming information (via updates). These aspects are discussed in [8].

Another interesting direction for future work is to represent the logical framework $\mathcal{F}$ within the theory of the agent members of the group. That is, we can code the graph structure of the agents and the links among them into the theory of the agents themselves. Doing so will empower the agents with the ability to reason about and to modify the structure of their own graph together with the general group structure comprising the other agents. At the level of each single agent, declaratively expressing the graph structure enables that agent to reason over it in a declarative way. At the level of the group structure, this ability will permit the managing of open societies where agents can enter/leave the society. This in fact can be achieved by updating the graph structure representing the group by adding/removing vertices and edges. Therefore, encoding the links of $\mathcal{F}$ within the language of the agents makes $\mathcal{F}$ updatable to capture the dynamic aspects of the system, i.e., of the open society.

A further interesting extension is to investigate how to represent agent societies based on voting.

Acknowledgements. L. M. Pereira acknowledges the support of POCTI project 40958 "FLUX - FleXible Logical Updates" and P. Dell'Acqua a Research Grant by the *Stiftelsen Lars Hiertas Minne*.

References

1. J. J. Alferes, P. Dell'Acqua, and L. M. Pereira. A compilation of updates plus preferences. In S. Flesca, S. Greco, N. Leone, and G. Ianni, editors, *Logics in Artificial Intelligence, Proc. 8th European Conf. (JELIA02)*, LNAI 2424, pages 62–73. Springer, 2002.
2. J. J. Alferes, J. A. Leite, L. M. Pereira, H. Przymusinska, and T. C. Przymusinski. Dynamic updates of non-monotonic knowledge bases. *The J. of Logic Programming*, 45(1-3):43–70, 2000. A short version titled *Dynamic Logic Programming* appeared in A. Cohn and L. Schubert (eds.), *KR'98*, Morgan Kaufmann.
3. A. Artikis and G. Pitt. A formal model of open agent societies. Proc. of Autonomous Agents, 2001.

4. C. Castelfranchi. Engineering Social Order. In Andrea Omicini, Robert Tolksdorf, and Franco Zambonelli, editors, *Engineering Societies in the Agents World. 1st Int. Workshop ESAW 2000. Revised Papers*, LNAI 1972, pages 1–18, Berlin, 2000. Springer-Verlag.

5. P. Davidsson. Categories of artificial societies. In A. Omicini, P. Petta, and R. Tolksdorf, editors, *Engineering Societies in the Agents' World (ESAW 2001)*, LNAI 2203, pages 1–9. Springer-Verlag, 2001.

6. P. Dell'Acqua, J. A. Leite, and L. M. Pereira. Evolving multi-agent viewpoints - an architecture. In P. Brazdil and A. Jorge, editors, *Progress in Artificial Intelligence, 10th Portuguese Int. Conf. on Artificial Intelligence (EPIA'01)*, LNAI 2258, pages 169–182. Springer-Verlag, 2001.

7. P. Dell'Acqua, U. Nilsson, and L. M. Pereira. A logic based asynchronous multi-agent system. Computational Logic in Multi-Agent Systems (CLIMA02). Electronic Notes in Theoretical Computer Science (ENTCS), Vol. 70, Issue 5, 2002.

8. P. Dell'Acqua and L. M. Pereira. Preferring and updating in abductive multi-agent systems. In A. Omicini, P. Petta, and R. Tolksdorf, editors, *Engineering Societies in the Agents' World (ESAW 2001)*, LNAI 2203, pages 57–73. Springer-Verlag, 2001.

9. P. Dell'Acqua and L. M. Pereira. Preferring and updating in logic-based agents. In: Web-Knowledge Management and Decision Support. Selected Papers from the 14th Int. Conf. on Applications of Prolog (INAP), Tokyo, 2001. To appear in LNAI, 2001.

10. M. Gelfond and V. Lifschitz. The stable model semantics for logic programming. In R. Kowalski and K. A. Bowen, editors, *ICLP'88*, pages 1070–1080. MIT Press, 1988.

11. N. R. Jennings. On agent-based software engineering. *Artificial Intelligence*, 117:277–296, 2000.

12. J. A. Leite, J. J. Alferes, and L. M. Pereira. Multi-dimensional dynamic logic programming. In F. Sadri and K. Satoh, editors, *Procs. of the CL-2000 Workshop on Computational Logic in Multi-Agent Systems (CLIMA'00)*, pages 17–26, 2000.

13. J. A. Leite, J. J. Alferes, and L. M. Pereira. Multi-dimensional dynamic knowledge representation. In T. Eiter, W. Faber, and M. Truszczynski, editors, *Procs. of the Sixth Int. Conf. on Logic Programming and Nonmonotonic Reasoning (LP-NMR'01)*, LNAI 2173, pages 365–378. Springer, 2001.

14. V. Lifschitz and T. Woo. Answer sets in general non-monotonic reasoning (preliminary report). In B. Nebel, C. Rich, and W. Swartout, editors, *KR'92*. Morgan-Kaufmann, 1992.

15. F. Zambonelli. Abstractions and infrastructures for the design and development of mobile agent organizations. In M. J. Wooldridge, G. Weiß, and P. Ciancarini, editors, *Agent-Oriented Software Engineering II, Second International Workshop, AOSE 2001*, LNCS 2222, pages 245–262, Berlin, 2001. Springer-Verlag.

16. F. Zambonelli, N. R. Jennings, and M. Wooldridge. Organisational abstractions for the analysis and design of multi-agent systems. In P. Ciancarini and M. Wooldridge, editors, *Agent-Oriented Software Engineering*, LNCS 1957, pages 127–141, Berlin, 2001. Springer-Verlag.

SXSLT: Manipulation Language for XML

Oleg Kiselyov[1] and Shriram Krishnamurthi[2]

[1] FNMOC oleg@okmij.org
[2] Brown University sk@cs.brown.edu

Abstract. The growing use of XML languages has spurred the demand for means to transform XML documents. Many XML transformation systems are, however, limited in their expressive power, and fail to provide a useful collection of combinators for several tasks.

This paper describes SXSLT, a practical, higher-order, concise, expressive and readable declarative XML transformation language. The language is a head-first rewriting system over abstract XML syntax trees, implemented as a library extension of Scheme. SXSLT features local scoping of re-writing "templates", first-class stylesheets, flexible traversal strategies, the ability to re-traverse the original or the transformed trees. The language can emulate XSLT in whole or in part, in a more coherent and expressive manner. By virtue of being a Scheme library, SXSLT is seamlessly integrated with Scheme.

We illustrate the power of SXSLT with several examples abstracted from practical projects. We and other people have used SXSLT for over two years for real-life projects, ranging from authoring of static and dynamic Web pages to content-distribution engines. Our experience and user comments show that SXSLT is expressive and easy to use. We argue that this outcome is a consequence of SXSLT providing right abstractions for XML transformations, of being higher-order, declarative and extensible.

Keywords: XML, SXML, XSLT, tree traversal, Scheme.

1 Introduction

So far, the official (W3C) XML transformation language XSLT [19] has not proven very satisfactory. The problem is not XSLT's being a functional language — it is XSLT not being functional enough [15]. XML practitioners often cite the following drawbacks of the language:

Poor syntax. Large XSLT programs are so verbose that they become unreadable. XML turns out a poor notation for a programming language [2]

Missing nuts-and-bolts. "While the designers probably left 'generic' functionality out of the spec on the grounds that XSLT was never intended to be a general-purpose programming language, they failed to realize that even simple document transformations often require a little nuts-and-bolts programming. Leaving out the nuts and bolts made XSLT a half-broken language." [15]

V. Dahl and P. Wadler (Eds.): PADL 2003, LNCS 2562, pp. 256–272, 2003.

Low order. XSLT templates are not first class. A transformed document or its part cannot easily be re-transformed [15]

Closed system. XSLT is designed as a closed system. Extensions to operate with other languages exist, but are notably unwieldy [5].

In this paper, we present a practical XML transformation language that is free from the above drawbacks. This language, SXSLT, is more expressive than XSLT and is also simpler and more coherent. SXSLT is a *higher-order* pure functional transformation language based on flexible tree traversals. The language is implemented as a library in a pure functional subset of Scheme. The choice of core constructions and the illustration of their expressiveness is one contribution of this paper.

SXSLT has been used in real-life, commercial, educational and government environments. One example is an aviation weather query tool [7] for operational users and small plane pilots equipped with a handheld and a wireless receiver. Another example is generating an XML manifest file required for cataloging a weather data markup format in the U.S. Department of Defense's XML repository. Manual creation of such a file is unfeasible [8]. A Census Scope web site authored with SXSLT was highlighted in *Yahoo Pick!* on May 30, 2002. The authors of that site, whom we have not met nor corresponded with, publicly commented on how "extraordinarily easy" the project was [1]. Finally, this very paper has been composed in an abstract XML syntax (SXML) and then converted to LATEX by an appropriate SXSLT transformation. SXSLT is in the public domain and available from a SourceForge repository [16].

SXSLT is characterized by the following features:

– XSLT and SXSLT both assume that the source XML document has been parsed into a tree form. They both transform the tree as instructed by a stylesheet. The result should be pretty-printed afterwards. A transformer of a re-writing rule (a "template") in SXSLT is a ordinary Scheme procedure, often a lambda-expression.

– SXSLT is a head-first re-writing system similar to Scheme macros. This fact makes it trivial to see when a rewriting rule applies. In XSLT, understanding when a template is triggered is a complex problem, requiring evaluating XPath expressions, computing priorities and keeping track of import orders. Unlike macros, SXSLT offers: (i) wildcard re-writing rules and transformers for text strings; (ii) the choice of applicative or normal transformation orders, even within the same stylesheet; (iii) local scoping of "templates"; (iv) repeated traversals of the source document.

– Like XSLT, SXSLT can scan the source document repeatedly; the traversal order can however be controlled by the user. Unlike XSLT 1.0, the result of the traversal can itself be traversed and manipulated, by the same or a different stylesheet.

– In an XSLT stylesheet the set of effective templates can be altered at runtime only by explicitly changing modes. In SXSLT, we can amend or replace the current stylesheet indirectly (via local scoping) or directly. The latter feature is reminiscent of expansion-passing macros.

We believe the combination of the above features is unique and powerful. We must stress that these features are not heaped up indiscriminately, but are induced by a compact core of tree traversal combinators and first class transformers. In its essence XSLT, too, implements a very simple mechanism of iterating over the document and of dispatching based on predicates. This simplicity is however covered by layers of extensions, such as modes and priorities. The examples in later sections of the paper show that SXSLT's technique of implicit and explicit switching of stylesheets subsumes the modes. In SXSLT, transformation templates become first class, which expands the expressiveness to a large degree. A user of SXSLT can easily re-transform the source or the output trees and hence "invoke a template" or an entire stylesheet, without any need for additional syntactic sugar.

SXSLT is seamlessly integrated with Scheme: re-writing transformers are ordinary Scheme functions, which may invoke other Scheme procedures. Traversal combinators are also Scheme functions. This integration of SXSLT with the mature general purpose programming language is especially important in the context of Web services, which require a deeper relation between manipulating the incoming XML document and performing the requested service.

We must stress that SXSLT transformation stylesheets are ordinary Scheme data structures: S-expressions. The ability of a transformation language to manipulate its own transformation rules was considered important by the designers of XSLT. The XML notation was meant to enable such a reflection. XSLT however fell short: matching, selections, string and arithmetic operations are expressed in XPath, in a syntax markedly different from that of XML, and from XSLT in particular. XML notation for the rest of XSLT made the language terribly verbose. In contrast, SXSLT is both reflective and comprehensible. The fact that an SXSLT transformer is a Scheme function generally limits the reflective power. The selection criterion of a SXSLT transformation rule, however, is always open to reflection. In contrast, the non-XML syntax of an action trigger in XSLT inhibits reflection.

The bulk of this paper introduces SXSLT on three expository examples. The examples meant to exhibit the salient features of SXSLT and to compare SXSLT and XSLT in expressiveness, while avoiding the deluge of minute details present in real-world projects. This paper cannot illustrate however all SXSLT features. In particular, the use of XPath-conformant expressions in SXSLT will not be covered. All the examples were inspired by XSLT samples found in literature. The first example gives a general feel for SXSLT and exhibits local scoping of re-writing transformers. The example in Section 3 highlights the higher order of SXSLT and its treatment of XML Namespaces. We show how the higher functional order of SXSLT has made a context-sensitive transformation concise. Section 4 elaborates an example of a multi-stage transformation with several stylesheets. We emphasize the ability to invoke stylesheets and to emulate XSLT's modes. The final two sections discuss the related work and conclude. Appendix A formally specifies SXML and SXSLT and shows an implementation of the SXSLT engine.

2   Example 1: Context-Sensitive Character Substitutions

The present section gives a general illustration of SXSLT. We describe a traversal combinator pre-post-order, first-class transformers, wildcard re-writing rules, and local scoping of the rules.

As the illustrating example we chose the conversion of XML documents into LATEX for further typesetting and publishing. The example is of clear practical relevance: indeed, we use its full version to produce this paper. The conversion has to preserve and appropriately translate the marked-up structure. We should also translate between character encodings: XML and LATEX have different sets of "bad" characters and different rules for escaping them. Furthermore, the escaping rules depend on the context. More precisely, we want to transform <tag>text</tag> into a LATEX environment \begin{tag}text\end{tag}, <p>text</p> into text followed by an empty line, and <br/> into \\. The text, the content of an XML element, may contain characters such as $, %, and { that must generally be escaped in LATEX , the verbatim markup being an exception.

A simplified version of our example, without the context dependency of character encoding rules, was elaborated by Moertel [15]. We deliberately built on his example so to compare our SXSLT solution with the XSLT code in his article. Even though Moertel solves a notably simpler problem, his XSLT code is voluminous.

The first step of an XML transformation is parsing a source document into an abstract syntax tree (AST). SXSLT uses an abstract syntax called SXML [10], which is also a realization of the XML Information set in the form of Lisp's S-expressions. An input XML document to translate into LATEX will look in SXML similar to the following:

```
(document (quotation "citation line 1" (br) "another line"))
```

An SXML expression is indeed a tree of proper nodes and text strings. Proper SXML nodes are S-expressions formed from a *tag* (a Scheme symbol) followed by the list of child nodes. The SXML specification [10] describes in great detail the syntax of SXML nodes: element, attribute, namespace declaration, processing instruction, and other nodes. We can use any XML parser to convert the source document into this format.

Just like XSLT, SXSLT turns an AST of the source document into an AST of the result. The latter, when written out, is the transformed (in our case, LATEX) document. Figure 1 presents the translation function and auxiliary procedures. An auxiliary procedure make-char-quotator, a higher-order generator of character-replacement functions, is elided. That code is available from the SXSLT distribution. The transformation task is carried out by a traversal combinator pre-post-order, which is invoked with the source SXML expression and a transformation stylesheet. The stylesheet is a list of re-writing rules, which associate SXML node tags (as keys) with the corresponding transformation procedures. We often call the latter handlers. Recall that an SXML node tag is the head of an S-expression that represents the node. The stylesheet is therefore not unlike a macro environment of Scheme, which associates syntactic keywords with macro transformers. Both SXSLT and macro transformers are ordinary Scheme procedures, which often use quasiquotation. Given a source S-expression, the pre-post-order combinator visits its nodes, looks up node tags in the supplied stylesheet and applies the corresponding transformers to the nodes. Therefore, pre-post-order is similar to Scheme's macro-expander. There are important differences however. By default, the combinator pre-post-order traverses the source expression in post-order. Given an SXML node (`tag child-node ...`) the combinator first visits `child-nodes`, then looks up a re-writing rule for the `tag` in the stylesheet, and applies the corresponding handler to the *transformed children*. Such a re-writing regimen is appropriate for our task. The combinator pre-post-order can carry out other transformation strategies, which will be demonstrated in the later sections. The complete specification of the pre-post-order function and its implementation are given in Appendix A.

Figure 1 shows that the SXML->LaTeX translation is indeed rather uniform. We turn text strings into escaped text strings and proper SXML nodes into the corresponding LaTeX environments. SXSLT stylesheets may contain wildcard rules `*text*` and `*default*`, which facilitate such a generic processing. A `*default*` re-writing rule applies when no other rule does. A `*text*` transformer handles SXML character data nodes.

We have to make an exception for `verbatim` nodes in the source SXML document. Such nodes are translated into an `alltt` LaTeX environment to set off literal text. The `alltt` environment has a different set of characters to be escaped. Therefore, we have to alter our normal handling of text strings. The pre-post-order traversal combinator supports such a switching of node handlers, through scoping. An association between a node tag and its handler in a stylesheet may optionally include a "local stylesheet," which extends the current stylesheet during the traversal of node's children. The rule for a `verbatim` node, Fig. 1, takes advantage of this facility. Therefore, whenever pre-post-order visits a `verbatim` node, it shadows the default text transformer with the local one. The latter is responsible for special encoding of character data within the node. Altering the transformation environment through scoping appears more intuitive than that through XSLT modes.

The present paper is a production version of our example. The master file [11] contains the source of this paper in SXML and the stylesheet to transform the source into the LaTeX format.

3   Example 2: Context-Sensitive Term Generation

XSLT offers good tools for XML transformations, and acceptable string processing facilities. Leaving out seemingly luxurious features such as higher-order functions, however, has proven to cripple the language: "The really bad thing is that the designers of XSLT made the language free of side effects but then failed to include fundamental support for basic functional programming idioms. Without such support, many trivial tasks become hell." [15]

```
(define (generate-TEX Content)

  (pre-post-order Content
    ; The stylesheet, the initial environment.
   '(
     (*default* . ,(lambda (tag . elems)
                     (in-tex-env tag '() elems)))

     (*text* . ,(lambda (trigger str)
                  (if (string? str) (string->goodTeX str) str)))
     (p
      . ,(lambda (tag . elems)
           (list elems nl nl)))

     (br . ,(lambda (tag)
              (list "\\\\ ")))

     (verbatim  ; set off pieces of code: one or several lines
       ((*text* . ; Different quotation rules apply here
          ,(let ((string->goodTeX-in-verbatim
                   (make-char-quotator
                     '((#\~ . "\\textasciitilde{}")
                       (#\{ . "\\{")
                       (#\} . "\\}")
                       (#\\ .
                          "{\\begin{math}\\backslash\\end{math}}")))))
              (lambda (trigger str)
                (if (string? str)
                    (string->goodTeX-in-verbatim str) str))
                ))
       . ,(lambda (tag . lines)
            (in-tex-env "alltt" '()
                    (map (lambda (line) (list "      " line nl))
                         lines)))))
     )))

; Quotator for bad characters in the document's body
(define string->goodTeX
  (make-char-quotator
    '((#\# . "\\#") (#\$ . "\\$") (#\% . "\\%") (#\& . "\\&")
      (#\~ . "\\textasciitilde{}") (#\_ . "\\_") (#\^ . "\\\^")
      (#\\ . "$\\backslash$") (#\{ . "\\{") (#\} . "\\}"))))

; Place the 'body' within the LaTeX environment named 'tex-env-name'
(define (in-tex-env tex-env-name options body)
  (list "\\begin{" tex-env-name "}" options nl
        body
        "\\end{" tex-env-name "}" nl))
```

Fig. 1. The SXML->TeX converter and auxiliary functions. nl is a string of the newline character. The make-char-quotator procedure takes a list of (char . string) pairs and returns a quotation procedure. The latter checks to see if its argument string contains any instance of a character that needs to be encoded. If the argument string is "clean", it is returned unchanged. Otherwise, the quotation procedure will return a list of string fragments. The input string will be broken at the places where the special characters occur. The special character will be replaced by the corresponding encoding string.

The example in this section emphasizes how higher-order transformers in SXSLT elegantly solve a class of frequently arising problems: transforming an XML document so that different occurrences of an element yield different results depending on that element's ancestors, siblings, or descendants. We also high-light the treatment of XML Namespaces. Our example is an extended version of generating rudimentary English phrases from a database. The original problem was used in [13] to demonstrate XT3D: Given a database of purchase records, the goal is to create a purchase summary such that multiple purchases are sep-arated by commas, except for the last two, which are separated by the word "and". Two examples of the input and generated terms are given on Fig. 2. The transformation involves the restructuring of the original markup and the inser-tion of item delimiters: commas and "and". We also add to the top-level `text` element an attribute `count` with the count of the descendant `text` elements.

```
<db:purchase
  xmlns:db='http://internal.com/db'>        <out:text
  <html:p                                        xmlns:out='http://internal.com/out'
    xmlns:html=                    ⟹           xmlns:acc=
      'http://www.w3c.org/HTML/'>                'http://internal.com/accounting'
  4 tinkers</html:p>                           acc:count='0'>4 tinkers</out:text>
</db:purchase>

                                             <out:text
<db:purchase                                    xmlns:out='http://internal.com/out'
  xmlns:db='http://internal.com/db'             xmlns:acc=
    xmlns:html=                                   'http://internal.com/accounting'
      'http://www.w3c.org/HTML/'>             acc:count='3'>4 tinkers,
    <html:p>4 tinkers</html:p>     ⟹            <out:text>5 tailors,
    <html:p>5 tailors</html:p>                     <out:text>2 soldiers and
    <html:p>2 soldiers</html:p>                      <out:text>1 spy</out:text>
    <html:p>1 spy</html:p>                        </out:text>
</db:purchase>                                  </out:text>
                                             </out:text>
```

Fig. 2. Sample XML purchase records and the corresponding generated phrases.

As before, the first step of the transformation is parsing of an XML document into an abstract syntax tree form, SXML. The sample input and generated terms from Fig. 2 have the SXML form shown on Fig. 3.

```
(http://internal.com/db:purchase  ⟹  (out:text (@ (acc:count 0)) "4 tinkers"))
  (h:p "4 tinkers"))
(http://internal.com/db:purchase      (out:text (@ (acc:count 3))
  (h:p "4 tinkers")                      "4 tinkers,"
  (h:p "5 tailors")            ⟹        (out:text "5 tailors,"
  (h:p "2 soldiers")                      (out:text "2 soldiers and"
  (h:p "1 spy"))                            (out:text "1 spy"))))
```

Fig. 3. The sample SXML terms before and after the purchase-records-to-phrases translation.

The figure demonstrates that SXML tags are *extended* XML names, made of a local name and a Namespace URIs parts [20]. SXML tags are also Scheme symbols, with a space-efficient internal representation as mere references into a symbol table. A user may still wish to assign a short *namespace-id* for a long Namespace URI. We have indeed done so on Fig. 3: we assigned the namespace-id

h for the HTML namespace URI. The namespace-ids are not to be confused with
XML Namespace prefixes. The former uniquely identify Namespace URIs, and
are chosen by the author of the stylesheet rather than by the author of the source
document. The subject of namespaces in SXML is thoroughly discussed in [10].
We must emphasize that both simple and extended XML names are represented
in SXML as atomic Scheme symbols. They only differ in appearance: symbols
representing extended XML names are spelt with a colon character.

Figure 4 presents the translation function, `convert-db`. The latter takes an
SXML expression, such as the one in the left column of Fig. 3, and yields the
corresponding expression in the right column. The translation function is again
an invocation of the pre-post-order traversal combinator. The combinator receives the source SXML expression and the translation stylesheet with three
transformation rules. Of a particular interest is the rule for a `h:p` element. Its
transformer is of a higher order: it rewrites an `h:p` element into a procedure.
The latter takes a `count` argument and the variable number of arguments that
must be procedures of the same kind. The transformer for the `purchase` element starts the domino effect of applying these procedures to the list of their
followers. This sequence of (implicitly context-passing) applications is the reason
the transformation of a `h:p` element turns out to be dependent on the element's
siblings.

The stylesheet code on Fig. 4 is complete. It is instructive to compare the
stylesheet with the equivalent XSLT code ([13], Fig. 4). The latter code (which
does not generate the attribute `count`) occupies the better half of a page in
a two-column layout and contains 31 elements, with numerous selections and
mathematical operations.

```
(define (convert-db doc)
  (pre-post-order doc
   ; the conversion stylesheet
   '((h:p . ,(lambda (tag str)
       (lambda (count . args)  ; count can be #f:
         (let ((att-list       ;   don't generate the attr
                (if count '((@ (acc:count ,count))) '())))
           (match-case args
             (() '(out:text ,@att-list ,str))
             ((?arg)
              '(out:text ,@att-list
                ,(string-append str " and")
                ,(arg #f)))
             ((?arg . ?rest)
              '(out:text ,@att-list ,(string-append str ",")
                ,(apply arg (cons #f rest))))))))))

     (http://internal.com/db:purchase . ,(lambda (tag . procs)
       (if (null? procs) '()
           (apply (car procs)
                  (cons (length (cdr procs)) (cdr procs))))))
     (*text* . ,(lambda (trigger str) str)))))
```

Fig. 4. SXSLT transformation that implements translation on Fig. 3.

To obtain the final result as the one shown in the right-hand column of Fig. 2, we need to pretty-print the transformed tree. Curiously, SXML-to-XML conversion is also a SXSLT transformation task. The SXML specification (itself authored in SXML) and the SXSLT distribution give several examples of this straightforward transformation.

4   Example 3: Recursively Reorganizing Punctuation

Our third example, which highlights recursive, reflexive transformations with several stylesheets, was suggested by David Durand, a member of Brown University's Scholarly Technology Group (STG). The STG has done extensive work on real-world SGML and XML documents with rich markup; the problem here is abstracted from one of their applications. Durand's example requires a transformer that moves punctuation inside a tag:

```
Click <a href='url'>here</a>! ==> Click <a href='url'>here!</a>
```

Even in this simple formulation, an XSLT solution is extremely unwieldy [3].

This transformation, to be truly useful, should account for several important particular cases. For example, we should not move the punctuation inside an XML element in the following context:

```
<br></br>;scheme comment
```

Furthermore, we may need to exempt an element from receiving adjacent punctuation, for instance, in

```
<p>For more details, see
    the paper <cite>Krishnamurthi2001</cite>.</p>
```

The content of the `cite` element is typically a bibliographic key, so it is not appropriate to add any punctuation to it. Finally, we do want to move punctuation recursively: given

```
<p>This <strong><em>needs punctuating</em></strong>!</p>
```

we would like to see the exclamation mark inside the innermost appropriate element (`<em>` in our case).

Suppose we begin with the following sample document:

```
<div><p>some text
        <strong><em>needs punctuating</em></strong>!</p>
<br></br>. This is a <cite>citation</cite>.
Move <a href='url'>period around</a>.text</div>
```

We assume that `cite` elements are barriers to inward punctuation movement. We define the punctuation character set as:

```
(define punctuation '(#\. #\, #\? #\! #\; #\:))
```

Again we start by parsing the sample document into SXML (using the SSAX parser [9]):

```
(*TOP* (div (p "some text "
              (strong (em "needs punctuating")) "!")
            (br)
            ".\nThis is a "
            (cite "citation")
            ". Move "
            (a (@ (href "url")) "period around")
            ".text"))
```

Our pull-in transformation works in two alternating phases. The first phase is a classification, which identifies the punctuation and the nodes that can receive punctuation. The identified nodes are wrapped in annotating elements. That is, if an SXML node is a string that starts with a punctuation character, we break the string and return the punctuation and the remainder wrapped into an identifying SXML element: (*move-me* punctuation-char-string orig-string-with-punctuation-removed). Other string SXML nodes are returned unannotated. If an SXML node is an element node, we check whether the node has no children or has been blacklisted from receiving punctuation. If so, we return the node unchanged. Otherwise, we annotate it by wrapping it in an SXML element (*can-accept* original-node).

The second phase, which performs the actual transformation, examines the result of the classification. When we see a (*can-accept* original-node) immediately followed by a (*move-me* punctuation-char-string string) node, we move the punctuation inside the original-node. We then apply the algorithm recursively to the children of the node.

While the description of the algorithm is fairly simple, it calls for a pre-order traversal. This is because nodes must examine their neighbors before they examine their children, and must modify the traversal of their children based on what they find adjacent. Fig. 5 presents the classification stylesheet and Fig. 6 that for transformation. Both stylesheets instruct the pre-post-order traversal combinator to navigate pre-order. This is the most appropriate strategy since the pull-in algorithm appears to require a hybrid traversal strategy based on breadth-first search.

The classification stylesheet is the only place that specifies, in a clear declarative manner, which elements can or cannot accept punctuation. The transformation stylesheet is generic. We should point out that the the *default* handler on Fig. 6 first transforms element children with a different, classification, stylesheet. The handler then re-processes that transformation's result. This fact highlights the advantages of SXSLT over XSLT. Because a node handler may recursively invoke the traversal function and pass it an arbitrary stylesheet, there is no need to introduce modes and to clutter the syntax and the semantics of the transformation language. Because the traversal combinator is a ordinary function, we can easily capture the result of a stylesheet transformation for further manipulation. Such an operation in XSLT 1.0 is immensely unwieldy [15].

```
; The identity function for use in a SXSLT stylesheet
(define sxslt-id (lambda x x))

(define classify-ss
  '((*text*
     . ,(lambda (trigger str)
          (cond
            ((equal? str "") str)
            ((memv (string-ref str 0) punctuation)
             (list '*move-me*
                   (string (string-ref str 0))
                   (substring str 1 (string-length str))))
            (else str))))

    ; the following nodes never accept the punctuation
    (@ *preorder* . ,sxslt-id)  ; an attribute node
    (cite *preorder* . ,sxslt-id)

    (*default*
     *preorder*
     . ,(lambda (tag . elems)
          (cond
            ((null? elems) (cons tag elems)) ; no children, won't accept
            ((match-tree '((@ . _)) elems '()) ; no children but attributes
             (cons tag elems))                 ; ... won't accept
            (else
             (list '*can-accept*
                   (cons tag elems)))))
    )
  ))
```

Fig. 5. A stylesheet for the pre-post-order function to convert an SXML tree into an annotated tree. The latter identifies strings of punctuation characters and nodes that can accept the punctuation.

The transformed SXML tree looks as follows:

```
(div (p "some text "
        (strong (em "needs punctuating" "!") "")
        "")
     (br)
     ".\nThis is a "
     (cite "citation")
     ". Move "
     (a (@ (href "url")) "period around" ".")
     "text")
```

which, converted to XML, reads as

```
<div><p>some text
        <strong><em>needs punctuating!</em></strong></p><br/>.
This is a <cite>citation</cite>.
Move <a href="url">period around.</a>text</div>
```

```
(define transform-ss
  '(
    (*text* . ,(lambda (trigger str) str))

    (@ *preorder* . ,sxslt-id)  ; Don't mess with the attributes

    (*move-me*                  ; remove the wrapper
     *preorder*
     . ,(lambda (trigger str1 str2)
          (string-append str1 str2)))

    (*can-accept*               ; remove the wrapper and transform
     *preorder*                 ; the node (recursively)
     . ,(lambda (trigger node)
          (pre-post-order node transform-ss)))

    (*default*
     *preorder*
     . ,(lambda (tag . elems)
          (cons tag
            (pre-post-order
             (let loop ((classified (pre-post-order elems classify-ss)))
               (cond
                 ((null? classified) classified)
                 ; check to see if a *can-accept* node is followed
                 ; by a *move-me* node
                 ((match-tree '((*can-accept* _node)
                                (*move-me*  _punctuation _str)
                                . _rest)
                              classified
                              '())
                  =>
                  (match-bind (node punctuation str rest)
                    (cons (append node (list punctuation))
                          (cons str (loop rest)))))
                 (else
                  (cons (car classified) (loop (cdr classified)))))
               ))
             transform-ss)
          )))))
```

Fig. 6. The transformation stylesheet.

5   Related Work

The most venerable related work on applying functional programming to markup
is probably DSSSL, a Document Style Semantics and Specification Language [4].
DSSSL did not, however, survive the switch from SGML to XML. One of the
major differences between SXML transformations and DSSSL are more flexible
traversal strategies of SXSLT and flexible switching of stylesheets.

XT3D, introduced in [13], is a declarative XML transformation language
based on transformation-by-example. This language is intentionally very different from XSLT: XT3D is far more intuitive and designed for inexperienced users.
In contrast, the present paper is oriented towards power users, who need all the
expressive and transformation power of W3C standards and even more.

One common way to specify graph traversals and transformations is by combining node accessors by combinators. Wallace and Runciman [17] [18] have
developed a combinator library that serves as an extensible domain-specific lan-

guage for transforming a subset of XML. SXML supports all of XML, including processing instructions and XML Namespaces. In addition, the combinator approach is less intuitive for specifying generic transformations with exceptions (i.e., where the set of excepted nodes depends on the traversal context).

XDuce [6] employs a powerful notion of regular expression types to capture XML values. It employs a powerful notion of subtyping, as well as union types, to support the rich set of patterns that programmers might write to match against evolving and semi-structured data. Its pattern-matching machinery is also strictly more powerful than that of languages like ML, while providing the benefits of static typing. In contrast to SXML, however, XDuce effectively forces programmers to write transformations as interpreters. Furthermore, the current XDuce language appears to be rather limited, without support for higher-order functions and hence traversal strategies, which are critical in many realistic transformation contexts.

It is possible to specify traversals more concisely than we do. The Demeter project revolves around a notion of "traversal strategies" [14], whereby a programmer writes a regular expression-based path through an object graph, and Demeter generates the appropriate traversal code. While this is extremely useful for processing XML trees (and even graphs), Demeter's programming language support remains weak. It currently runs atop C++ and Java, which have limited means to cleanly express higher-order behavior. Worse, Demeter currently computes entirely through side-effects, making it a poor fit for many XML transformation tasks, which have a highly functional flavor.

6   Conclusion and Future Work

This paper has described SXSLT, an XML manipulation language. The language is a Scheme library that realizes a head-first re-writing system over trees representing XML Information set. SXSLT has been used in practice for over two years by us and other users. The examples elaborated in this paper have been abstracted from real-life projects. In our and other users' experience, SXSLT is expressive and easy to use. The elaborated examples indicate that such a positive experience is the consequence of SXSLT being a domain-specific declarative layer over a general-purpose functional language. The layer implements right abstractions and patterns of XML transformations: (i) abstract XML syntax trees, (ii) pre- and post-order traversals of abstract syntax trees, (iii) transformation environments (stylesheets), (iv) dispatch to re-writing transformers based on node names, (v) wildcard transformation rules, (vi) local scoping of re-writing rules. The base language, Scheme, gives us mature syntax, first-class and higher-order transformers and traversal combinators, extensibility, and "nuts-and-bolts."

We identify several directions for future work. First, we would like to improve the expressiveness of the system. The current traversals do not automatically pass the context (as fold does). While we have not needed this for our applications so far, their value is becoming increasingly clear. We therefore hope to put more emphasis on building stronger traversal strategies. Second, we have not discussed transformations that more closely resemble database queries followed by rewriting; for such transformations, it remains open to combine our approach with a database query optimizer. Finally, many aspects of SXSLT can be expressed in a powerful macro system such as McMicMac [12], which commutes with program-processing tools such as type inference engines; this is one useful path for recovering type information.

SXML transformations often make multiple selections from one or more XML documents. It is possible to perform such queries with an SXSLT stylesheet that rewrites the document tree into the one that contains the desired selection. Using transformations to implement queries is inefficient, however, and reflects a mismatch of abstractions. For these situations, our library includes a query language called SXPath [16]. SXPath is, of course, a reflection of the W3C's XPath query language [21] into Scheme. Comparing SXPath with the Consortium's more advanced declarative language, XQuery [22], is a task for future work.

Acknowledgments. We would like to thank Philip Wadler for comments and invaluable advice, and the anonymous reviewers for many helpful suggestions. This work has been supported in part by the National Science Foundation under grants ESI-0010064 and ITR-0218973, the National Research Council Research Associateship Program, Naval Postgraduate School, and the Fleet Numerical Meteorology and Oceanography Center.

References

1. Abresch, B.: for those keeping score... A message on the PLT-Scheme mailing list. May 30, 2002
   http://www.cs.utah.edu/plt/mailarch/plt-scheme-2002/msg00998.html
2. Bosworth, A.: Programming Paradox. XML Magazine, February 2002
   http://www.fawcette.com/xmlmag/2002_02/magazine/departments/endtag/
3. Durand, D.: private communication. May 22, 2002
4. ISO/IEC. Information technology, Processing Languages, Document Style Semantics and Specification Languages (dsssl). Technical Report 10179 :1996(E), ISO (1996)
5. Fuchs, M.: SOXT: Building the XSL Family of Languages. The Eleventh International World Wide Web Conference. Proc. Alternate Paper Tracks (2002)
   http://www2002.org/CDROM/alternate/417/index.html
6. Hosoya, H., Pierce, B.C.: Regular expression pattern matching for XML. In The 25th Annual ACM SIGPLAN-SIGACT Symposium on Principles of Programming Languages (2001) 67-80
7. Kiselyov, O.: Aviation total weather and SIGMET advisory queries. June 12, 2000
   http://zowie.metnet.navy.mil/cgi-bin/oleg/get-advisories
   http://zowie.metnet.navy.mil/~dhuff/pqa/FNMOC.html
8. Kiselyov, O.: SXML as a normalized database. April 17, 2001
   http://pobox.com/~oleg/ftp/Scheme/xml.html#SXML-as-database
9. Kiselyov, O.: A better XML parser through functional programming. In: Lecture Notes in Computer Science, Vol. 2257. Springer-Verlag, Berlin Heidelberg New York (2002) 209-224

10. Kiselyov, O.: SXML Specification. Revision 2.5. August 9, 2002
    http://pobox.com/~oleg/ftp/Scheme/SXML.html
11. Kiselyov, O., Krishnamurthi, S.: SXSLT: Manipulation Language for XML. Master
    SXML file. http://pobox.com/~oleg/ftp/Scheme/SXSLT.scm
12. Krishnamurthi, S., Felleisen, M., Duba, B.F.: From Macros to Reusable Generative
    Programming. In: Lecture Notes in Computer Science, Vol. 1799. Springer-Verlag,
    Berlin Heidelberg New York (1999) 105-120
13. Krishnamurthi, S., Gray, K.E., Graunke, P.T.: Transformation-by-Example for
    XML. Practical Aspects of Declarative Languages (2000)
14. Lieberherr, K.L., Patt-Shamir, B.: Traversals of Object Structures: Specification
    and Efficient Implementation. Technical Report NU-CCS-97-15, College of Com-
    puter Science, Northeastern University, Boston, MA (1997)
15. Moertel, T.: XSLT, Perl, Haskell, & a word on language design. Posted on
    kuro5hin.org on January 15, 2002
    http://www.kuro5hin.org/story/2002/1/15/1562/95011
16. S-exp-based XML parsing/query/conversion. http://ssax.sourceforge.net/
17. Wallace, M., Runciman, C.: Haskell and XML: generic combinators or type-based
    translation? Proc. the fourth ACM SIGPLAN international conference on Func-
    tional programming (1999) 148 -159
18. Wallace, M., Runciman, C.: HaXml - 1.07b (2002)
    http://www.cs.york.ac.uk/fp/HaXml/
19. World Wide Web Consortium. XSL Transformations (XSLT). Version 1.0. W3C
    Recommendation November 16, 1999 http://www.w3.org/TR/xslt
20. World Wide Web Consortium. Namespaces in XML. W3C Recommendation. Jan-
    uary 14, 1999 http://www.w3.org/TR/REC-xml-names/
21. World Wide Web Consortium. XML Path Language (XPath). Version 1.0. W3C
    Recommendation. November 16, 1999 http://www.w3.org/TR/xpath
22. World Wide Web Consortium. XQuery 1.0: An XML Query Language. W3C Work-
    ing Draft. August 16, 2002 http://www.w3.org/TR/xquery/

Appendix A: SXSLT Specification and Implementation

SXSLT is a higher-order pure functional transformation language based on flexible tree traversals. The tree in question is usually an SXML tree [10], which
is an abstract syntax tree of an XML document. In SXML, character data are
represented as Scheme strings. XML markup — elements, processing instructions, attribute lists — are uniformly represented by a Scheme list. The head of
such a list, which is always a Scheme identifier, names the markup. For an XML
element, the corresponding SXML list starts with element's expanded name, optionally followed by lists of attributes and of effective namespaces. The rest of
the SXML list is an ordered sequence of element's children — character data,
processing instructions, and other elements.

Since SXML data is essentially a tree structure, the SXML grammar can
be presented as a set of two mutually-recursive datatypes, Node and Nodelist,
where the latter is a list of Nodes:

⟨Node⟩ ::= (⟨name⟩ . ⟨Nodelist⟩) | "text string"

⟨Nodelist⟩ ::= (⟨Node⟩ ⟨Node⟩*)
⟨name⟩ ::= ⟨LocalName⟩ | ⟨ExpandedName⟩ | @ |
TOP | *PI* | *COMMENT* | *ENTITY* |
NAMESPACES | @@

The SXML Specification [10] gives more detail.

The SXSLT language is implemented as a library in a pure functional subset of Scheme. At the core of this library is a function `pre-post-order`, which takes an SXML tree and and a stylesheet, and returns a transformed tree: `pre-post-order::` ⟨tree⟩ x ⟨bindings⟩ -> ⟨tree⟩.

The stylesheet, ⟨bindings⟩, is a list of ⟨binding⟩s of the following structure:

⟨tree⟩ ::= ⟨Node⟩ | ⟨Nodelist⟩
⟨bindings⟩ ::= (⟨binding⟩ ⟨binding⟩*)
⟨binding⟩ ::= (⟨trigger-symbol⟩ *preorder* .
⟨handler⟩) | (⟨trigger-symbol⟩
⟨new-bindings⟩? . ⟨handler⟩)
⟨trigger-symbol⟩ ::= ⟨name⟩ | *text* | *default*
⟨new-bindings⟩ ::= ⟨bindings⟩

and the ⟨handler⟩ is a procedure ⟨trigger-symbol⟩ x ⟨tree⟩ -> ⟨tree⟩.

The function pre-post-order traverses a ⟨tree⟩, which is either a ⟨Node⟩ or a ⟨Nodelist⟩. For each ⟨Node⟩ of the form (⟨name⟩ ⟨Node⟩*) the function looks up an association with the given ⟨name⟩ among its ⟨bindings⟩. When pre-post-order fails to find the association, it tries to locate a *default* binding. It is an error if the latter attempt fails as well.

Having found a binding, the function pre-post-order first checks whether the binding is of the form (⟨trigger-symbol⟩ *preorder* . ⟨handler⟩). If the found binding prescribes a pre-order traversal, the handler is 'applied' to the current node. Otherwise, the pre-post-order function first calls itself recursively for each child of the current node, with ⟨new-bindings⟩ prepended to the current bindings. The result of these calls is passed to the ⟨handler⟩, along with the head of the current ⟨Node⟩. To be more precise, the handler is applied to the head of the current node and its processed children. The result of the handler, which should also be a ⟨tree⟩, becomes a ⟨Node⟩ of the transformed tree. If the current ⟨Node⟩ is a text string, a special binding with a symbol *text* is looked up.

The ⟨new-bindings⟩ that appears in (⟨trigger-symbol⟩ ⟨new-bindings⟩ . ⟨handler⟩) has the same form as ⟨bindings⟩. The ⟨new-bindings⟩ is a local stylesheet. It takes effect only when traversing the children of a particular node (whose name is the ⟨trigger-symbol⟩). The bindings of ⟨new-bindings⟩ override the bindings from the "parent" stylesheet.

Fig. 7 provides an implementation of `pre-post-order` that satisfies the above specification.

```
(define (pre-post-order tree bindings)
  (cond
   ((nodeset? tree)
    (map (lambda (a-tree) (pre-post-order a-tree bindings)) tree))
   ((not (pair? tree))
    (let ((trigger '*text*))
      (cond
       ((or (assq trigger bindings) (assq '*default* bindings)) =>
        (lambda (binding)
          ((if (procedure? (cdr binding)) (cdr binding) (cddr binding))
           trigger tree)))
       (else
        (error "Unknown binding for " trigger " and no default")))
      ))
   (else
    (let ((trigger (car tree)))
      (cond
       ((or (assq trigger bindings) (assq '*default* bindings)) =>
        (lambda (binding)
          (if (and (pair? (cdr binding)) (eq? '*preorder* (cadr binding)))
              (apply (cddr binding) tree)
              (apply
               (if (procedure? (cdr binding)) (cdr binding) (cddr binding))
               (cons trigger
                     (pre-post-order (cdr tree)
                                     (if (pair? (cdr binding))
                                         (append (cadr binding) bindings)
                                         bindings)))))))
       (else
        (error "Unknown binding for " trigger " and no default")))))))
```

Fig. 7. The function **pre-post-order**: the core function of SXSLT

Type-Based XML Processing in Logic Programming

Jorge Coelho[1] and Mário Florido[2]

[1] Instituto Superior de Engenharia do Porto
Porto, Portugal
jcoelho@dei.isep.ipp.pt
[2] University of Porto, DCC-FC & LIACC
Porto, Portugal
amf@ncc.up.pt

Abstract. In this paper we propose a type-based framework for using logic programming for XML processing. We transform XML documents into terms and DTDs into regular types. We implemented a standard type inference algorithm for logic programs and use the types corresponding to the DTDs as additional type declarations for logic programs for XML processing. Due to the correctness of the type inference this makes it possible to use logic programs as an implicitly typed processing language for XML with static type (in this case DTDs) validation. As far as we know this is the first work adding type validation at compile time to the use of logic programming for XML processing.

1 Introduction

In this paper, we present the design and implementation of a statically typed logic programming language specialized for XML processing[1]. One of the nice features of XML is the static typing of documents provided by DTDs or XML Schema. Some programming languages go beyond types for documents and provide static type checking for programs for XML processing. One example is the functional language XDuce [9].

In this paper we present an *implicitly typed* version of *pure Prolog* and apply it to the domain of XML processing. The approach used is the following:

- we translate XML elements and documents to Prolog terms whose syntax is specified by a DTD;
- we translate DTDs to *regular types* [6]. Regular types are the most used type language for typing logic programs [13,24,23,7,6,8,11];
- we use implicitly typed *pure Prolog* clauses as rules for expressing element and data transformations;

---

[1] The framework described in this paper is available on the WWW at
http://www.dei.isep.ipp.pt/~jcoelho/x-prolog/

V. Dahl and P. Wadler (Eds.): PADL 2003, LNCS 2562, pp. 273–285, 2003.

- we implemented a type inference module which, given a predicate which relates two or more terms representing XML documents checks at compile time if the predicate is *well-typed* (i.e. if the transformation defined by the predicate respects the DTDs of the XML documents involved)

The novel feature of our framework is the use of regular type inference for logic programming to guarantee type safety at compile time. This feature points out the similarities between DTDs and *regular types* for logic programming. We now give a simple example of the kind of translations involved in our work.

Given the XML document

```
<teachers>
    <name>Jorge Coelho</name>
    <office>403</office>
    <email>jcoelho@isep.ipp.pt</email>
    <name>Mario Florido</name>
    <office>202</office>
</teachers>
```

and the DTD

```
<!ELEMENT teachers (name,office,email?)*>
<!ELEMENT name #PCDATA>
<!ELEMENT office #PCDATA>
<!ELEMENT email #PCDATA>
```

our program builds the pure Prolog term

```
teachers([(name(''Jorge Coelho''),
          office(''403''),
          email(''jcoelho@isep.ipp.pt'')),
          (name(''Mario Florido''),
          office(''202''))])
```

and the regular type

$$\tau_1 \rightarrow \{teachers(\tau_2)\}$$
$$\tau_2 \rightarrow \{nil, .(\tau_3, \tau_2)\}$$
$$\tau_3 \rightarrow \{\tau_4, \tau_5\}$$
$$\tau_4 \rightarrow \{(name(string), office(string), email(string))\}$$
$$\tau_5 \rightarrow \{(name(string), office(string))\}$$

We follow Dart and Zobel ([6]) in the syntax of regular types. A *regular type* is defined by a set of type rules of the form $\tau \rightarrow T$ where τ is a type symbol and T a set of type terms. The rule $\tau \rightarrow T$ should be read as τ is defined by any member of T. Note that T represents a union of types. In the previous example τ_2 is the usual type for a list of elements of type τ_3 (as usual in logic programming, we use the functor . for the list constructor). Note that τ_3 is τ_4 or τ_5. This disjunction comes from the optional operator ? in the corresponding DTD.

In this paper, we assume that the reader is familiar with XML ([22]) and logic programming [10]. We start in Section 2 with a brief overview of XML. Then, in Section 3, we present the translation from XML to Prolog terms. In Section 4 we show the relation between DTDs and regular types. In Section 5 we present an example of the use of pure Prolog for XML transformation. We then give an overview of the implementation and then we present the related work. Finally, we conclude and outline the future work.

2   XML

XML is a meta-language useful to describe domain specific languages for structured documents. Besides its use in the publishing industry XML is now the standard interchange format for data produced by different applications. An XML document is basically a tree structure. There are two basic types of content in a document: elements and plain text. An element consists of a start tag and an end tag which may enclose any sequence of other content. Elements can be nested to any depth and an XML document consists of a single top-level element (the root of the tree) containing other nested elements. For example, the next XML document could be used by a specific address book application:

```
<addressbook>
   <name>John</name>
   <address>London</address>
   <phone>
      <home>12345678</home>
      <mobile>87654321</mobile>
   </phone>
   <email>john@mailserver.uk</email>
   <name>Rita</name>
   <address>Copacabana</address>
   <address>Rio de Janeiro</address>
   <phone>
      <home>12457834</home>
   </phone>
</addressbook>
```

2.1   Document Type Definition (DTD)

A powerful feature of XML is the possibility to create a Document Type Definition, that is, a way to define rules that determine the validity of a document. The example bellow shows a DTD for the address book:

```
<!ELEMENT addressbook (name,address+,phone?,email?)*>
<!ELEMENT name, (#PCDATA)>
```

```
<!ELEMENT address (#PCDATA)>
<!ELEMENT phone (home,mobile*)>
<!ELEMENT email (#PCDATA)>
<!ELEMENT home (#PCDATA)>
<!ELEMENT mobile (#PCDATA)>
```

This DTD tells that this kind of address book has the root element < address-book > and four sub elements <name> <address> <phone> and <email>. It also tells that the <name></name> tags must exist, the <address></address> tags must appear at least once and may appear several times (in a sequence of address lines). The <phone></phone> and <email></email> tags are optional and each phone element may have zero or more <mobile></mobile> tags.

Although it is not mandatory to have a DTD when we conceive a XML document, it is a good idea. We can use validating parsers or other mechanisms that use the DTD to check for document consistency.

3   XML in Prolog

This paper is about processing XML using *pure Prolog*. By *pure Prolog* we mean *Prolog* [16] restricted to definite Horn clauses (see [10] for standard definitions in the area of logic programming). *Pure Prolog* inherits from logic programming the notion of *term*, which is especially suitable to deal with tree-structured data such as XML.

3.1   Translating XML to Prolog Terms

A XML document can be seen as a variable free (ground) term. This ground term is composed by a main functor (the root tag) and zero or more arguments. For example, consider the following simple XML file, describing an address book:

```
<addressbook>
    <name>Fran\c{c}ois</name>
    <address>Paris</address>
    <phone>135680864</phone>
    <name>Frank</name>
    <address>New York</address>
    <email>frank@mailserver.com</email>
</addressbook>
```

One equivalent Prolog term is:

```
addressbook(
    name('Fran\c{c}ois'),
    address('Paris'),
    phone('135680864'),
    name('Frank'),
    address('New York'),
    email('frank@mailserver.com'))
```

In our implementation, the structure of the term is determined by the DTD associated with the XML document. Note that the same document, when it is validated by different DTDs, can give rise to different terms.

In our framework, we can include the attributes in the term as a list. If the previous address book had some kind of attribute, such as:

```
    ...
        <address>Paris</address>
        <phone type='office'>135680864</phone>
    ...
```

The corresponding term is:

```
        addressbook([],
            name([],'Fran\c{c}ois'),
            address([],'Paris'),
            phone([attribute('type','office')],'135680864'),
            name([],'Frank'),
            address([],'New York'),
            email([],'frank@mailserver.com'))
```

Since attributes do not play a relevant role in our work, we ignore them in future examples.

4   DTD as Regular Types

In this section, we describe the relationship between Document Type Definition (DTD) and Regular Types. We use the Dart-Zobel definition for Regular Types [6].

4.1   Regular Types

The next definitions and examples introduce briefly the notion of Regular Types along the lines presented in [6].

Definition 41 *Assuming an infinite set of* type symbols, *a* type term *is defined as follows:*

1. *A constant symbol is a type term* $(a, b, c, ...)$.
2. *A variable is a type term* $(x, y, ...)$.
3. *A type symbol is a type term* $(\alpha, \beta, ...)$
4. *If f is an n-ary function symbol and each τ_i is a type term, $f(\tau_1, ..., \tau_n)$ is a type term.*

Example 41 *Let a be a constant symbol, α a type symbol and x a variable. The expressions a, α, x and $f(a, \alpha, x)$ are type terms. If the expression is variable free, we call it a* pure type term. *The expressions a, α and $f(\alpha, g(\beta), c)$ are pure type terms.*

Definition 42 *A type rule is an expression of the form* $\alpha \to \Upsilon$ *where* α *is a type symbol (represents types) and* Υ *is a set of pure type terms. We will use* T *to represent a set of type rules.*

Sets of type rules are *regular term grammars* [18].

Example 42 *Let* α *and* β *be type symbols,* $\alpha \to \{a, b\}$ *and* $\beta \to \{nil, tree (\beta, \alpha, \beta)\}$ *are type rules.*

Definition 43 *A type symbol* α *is defined by a set of type rules* T *if there exists a type rule* $\alpha \to \Upsilon \in T$.

We make some assumptions:

1. The constant symbols are partitioned in non-empty subsets, called *base types*. Some examples are, *string*, *int*, and *number*.
2. The existence of μ, the universal type, and ϕ representing the empty type.
3. Each type symbol occurring in a set of type rules T is either μ, ϕ, a base type symbol, or a type symbol defined in T, and each type symbol defined in T has exactly one defining rule in T.

Definition 44 *Regular types are defined as the class of types that can be specified by sets of type rules (or alternatively by regular term grammars).*

Example 43 *Let* α_i *bet the type of the* i^{th} *argument of append. The predicate append is defined as follows:*

$append(nil, L, L).$
$append(.(X, RX), Y, .(X, RZ)) :- append(RX, Y, RZ).$

Regular types for $\alpha_1, \alpha_2, \alpha_3$ *are*

$$\alpha_1 \to \{nil, .(\mu, \alpha_1)\}$$
$$\alpha_2 \to \{\mu\}$$
$$\alpha_3 \to \{\alpha_2, .(\mu, \alpha_3)\}$$

4.2   DTDs as Regular Types

So far, we have considered translation from XML to *Prolog terms*. In our framework *regular types* statically type the logic programming language considered. Thus DTDs can be viewed as type declarations for the terms corresponding to the XML documents in the general logic program for XML processing. We now give some examples of the translation from DTDs to the type language considered. Figure 1 shows an example DTD for recipes. Figure 2 shows the corresponding regular types.

```
<!ELEMENT recipe (title, author,description?, ingredients, instructions?)>
<!ELEMENT title (#PCDATA)>
<!ELEMENT author (name,email?)>
<!ELEMENT name (#PCDATA)>
<!ELEMENT email (#PCDATA)>
<!ELEMENT description (#PCDATA)>
<!ELEMENT ingredients (item*)>
<!ELEMENT item (qtd,ingredient)>
<!ELEMENT qtd (#PCDATA)>
<!ELEMENT ingredient (#PCDATA)>
<!ELEMENT instructions (step+)>
<!ELEMENT step (#PCDATA)>
```

Fig. 1. A DTD for recipes

$$
\begin{aligned}
\tau_1 \;\to\; &\{\mathrm{recipe}(\tau_2, \tau_3, \tau_6, \tau_7, \tau_{12}), \\
&\;\mathrm{recipe}(\tau_2, \tau_3, \tau_7, \tau_{12}), \\
&\;\mathrm{recipe}(\tau_2, \tau_3, \tau_7), \\
&\;\mathrm{recipe}(\tau_2, \tau_3, \tau_6, \tau_7)\} \\
\tau_2 \;\to\; &\{\mathrm{title}(\mathrm{string})\} \\
\tau_3 \;\to\; &\{\mathrm{author}(\tau_4,\tau_5), \mathrm{author}(\tau_4)\} \\
\tau_4 \;\to\; &\{\mathrm{name}(\mathrm{string})\} \\
\tau_5 \;\to\; &\{\mathrm{email}(\mathrm{string})\} \\
\tau_6 \;\to\; &\{\mathrm{description}(\mathrm{string})\} \\
\tau_7 \;\to\; &\{\mathrm{ingredients}(\tau_8)\} \\
\tau_8 \;\to\; &\{\mathrm{nil}, .(\tau_9, \tau_8)\} \\
\tau_9 \;\to\; &\{\mathrm{item}(\tau_{10},\tau_{11})\} \\
\tau_{10} \;\to\; &\{\mathrm{qtd}(\mathrm{string})\} \\
\tau_{11} \;\to\; &\{\mathrm{ingredient}(\mathrm{string})\} \\
\tau_{12} \;\to\; &\{\mathrm{instructions}(\tau_{13})\} \\
\tau_{13} \;\to\; &\{.(\tau_{14}, nil), .(\tau_{14}, \tau_{13})\} \\
\tau_{14} \;\to\; &\{\mathrm{step}(\mathrm{string})\}
\end{aligned}
$$

Fig. 2. Regular types for the receipts DTD

The type rule for a tag is defined by a type symbol and a set of disjoint types for the tag body. A simple element, without any subelements, is a ground term. When a tag has one or more optional subelements, the rule must include a set of ground terms that represent all the possible subelements combinations. When a tag must include at least one element, we represent its rule by a list of at least one element (for instance τ_{13} represents step+). When a tag must have zero or more elements, we represent it by a list of elements of its type (for instance τ_8 represents item*). When a tag has optional elements, they are all listed in the type rule.

In figure 3 we define a function $\mathcal{T}$, which translates DTDs to regular types:

$$
\begin{aligned}
\mathcal{T}(\texttt{<!ELEMENT } e \texttt{ (\#PCDATA) >}) \quad &= \tau_e \to \{e(string)\} \\
\mathcal{T}(\texttt{<!ELEMENT } e \texttt{ EMPTY >}) \quad &= \tau_e \to \{e\} \\
\mathcal{T}(\texttt{<!ELEMENT } e \texttt{ ANY >}) \quad &= \tau_e \to \{e(\mu)\} \\
\mathcal{T}(\texttt{<!ELEMENT } e\ (e_1,\ldots,e_n) \texttt{ >}) \quad &= \tau_e \to \{e(\tau_{e_1},\ldots,\tau_{e_n})\}, \text{ where} \\
&\quad \mathcal{T}(\texttt{<!ELEMENT } e_i \texttt{ >}) = \tau_{e_i} \to \Upsilon_{e_i}, \\
&\quad \text{for } 1 \le i \le n \\
\mathcal{T}(\texttt{<!ELEMENT } e\ e_1\texttt{* >}) \quad &= \tau_e \to \{nil, .(\tau_{e_1}, \tau_e)\}, \text{where} \\
&\quad \mathcal{T}(\texttt{<!ELEMENT } e_1 \texttt{ >}) = \tau_{e_1} \to \Upsilon_{e_1} \\
\mathcal{T}(\texttt{<!ELEMENT } e\ e_1\texttt{+ >}) \quad &= \tau_e \to \{.(\tau_{e_1}, nil), .(\tau_{e_1}, \tau_e)\}, \text{where} \\
&\quad \mathcal{T}(\texttt{<!ELEMENT } e_1 \texttt{ >}) = \tau_{e_1} \to \Upsilon_{e_1} \\
\mathcal{T}(\texttt{<!ELEMENT } e\ (e_1|\ldots|e_n) \texttt{ >}) \quad &= \tau_e \to \{\tau_{e_1}, \ldots, \tau_{e_n}\}, \text{where} \\
&\quad \mathcal{T}(\texttt{<!ELEMENT } e_i \texttt{ >}) = \tau_{e_i} \to \Upsilon_{e_i}, \\
&\quad \text{for } 1 \le i \le n \\
\mathcal{T}(\texttt{<!ELEMENT } e\ (e_1,\ldots,e_i?,\ldots,e_n)) &= \tau_e \to \{e(\tau_{e_1},\ldots,\tau_{e_{i-1}},\tau_{e_{i+1}},\ldots,\tau_{e_n}), \\
&\quad\quad e(\tau_{e_1},\ldots,\tau_{e_{i-1}},\tau_{e_i},\tau_{e_{i+1}},\ldots,\tau_{e_n})\}, \\
&\quad \text{where} \\
&\quad \mathcal{T}(\texttt{<!ELEMENT } e_i \texttt{ >}) = \tau_{e_i} \to \Upsilon_{e_i}, \\
&\quad \text{for } 1 \le i \le n
\end{aligned}
$$

Fig. 3. DTD translation rules

5   Processing XML in Pure Prolog

With terms representing XML documents, it is now easy to make pure Prolog programs for processing those terms. For example, given the input DTD:

```
<!ELEMENT addressbook1 (name,country,email?)*>
<!ELEMENT name (#PCDATA)>
<!ELEMENT country (#PCDATA)>
<!ELEMENT email (#PCDATA)>
```

And given the output DTD:

```
<!ELEMENT addressbook2 (name,email)*>
<!ELEMENT name (#PCDATA)>
<!ELEMENT email (#PCDATA)>
```

We can easily make a program to translate a document valid for the input DTD to a new document valid for the output DTD. The next example translates an address book with triples (name, country, email) to a second address book of pairs (name, email). We omit the XML to term and term to XML translations for the sake of clarity.

```
process1(addressbook1(X),addressbook2(Y)):-
       process2(X,Y).

process2([],[]).

process2([name(X),country(Y),email(Z)|R1],[name(X),email(Z)|R2]):-
       process2(R1,R2).

process2([name(X),country(Y)|R1],R2):-
       process2(R1,R2).
```

If the program does not produce an output valid with respect to the output DTD, for example:

```
...
process2([],[]).

process2([name(X),country(Y),email(Z)|R1],[name(X),phone(Z)|R2]):-
       process2(R1,R2).

process2([name(X),country(Y)|R1],R2):-
       process2(R1,R2).
```

the type checking module outputs a type error.

6   Implementation

Our implementation has four main parts:

1. Translating XML documents to terms;
2. Translating the DTDs to regular types;
3. Type checking of the *pure Prolog* program used to process XML;
4. Translating the resulting Prolog term to an XML document.

This implementation relies on a toolkit of basic components for processing XML in Prolog (for instance a parser). These supporting components are implemented using existing libraries for SWI Prolog [14]. Type inference for Prolog programs is based on Zobel algorithm ([25], [11]).

7   Discussion and Related Work

7.1   XML and Logic Programming

XML processing in logic programming was the topic of a recent paper of Bry and Shaffert [4] where it was defined an untyped rule-based transformation language based on logic programming. Previous work on the representation of XML using a term language inspired in logic programming was presented in [5], [3] and [2].

The kind of terms used to represent XML in our work follows the representation presented in [2]. In [3] it was presented a term language with *flexible terms*, where the depth of an element may not be fixed. These terms are suitable to express the complex subterm dependencies used for processing XML data. Adapting our work to use *flexible terms* would mean defining new type inference algorithms and we think that this can be a promising line of future work.

All these previous work did not deal with type inference for the transformation languages. As far as we know, our work is the first one dealing with statically type validation in the context of logic programming for XML processing.

Several approaches, referring to *semantic web* [21], adapt techniques from logic programming to XML. Even though connections between our work and *semantic web* are not immediately perceived, it would be a useful investigation whether results from the former can be transfered to the later.

7.2   XML and Functional Programming

Our work was inspired by previous work on the use of functional programming languages for processing XML such as XDuce [9] and HaXml [20]. In XDuce types were denoted by *regular expression types*, a natural generalization of DTDs. Transformation of DTDs to types of Haskell was done in [20], where type checking was done by the Haskell type system itself.

The differences from our approach are in the programming paradigm used (functional *versus* logic) and in the type inference systems. In fact, type inference for logic programming is substantially different from type inference for functional languages due to specific characteristics of the logic paradigm such as built-in unification and the use of the logic variable.

Another difference from XDuce is the representation of XML. We use terms (finite trees) to represent XML documents. XDuce terms are sequences. This difference in the view of XML data leads to significant differences in the processing stage. For example, consider the following DTDs:

```
<!ELEMENT a ((b,b?)*)>
<!ELEMENT b EMPTY>
```

and

```
<!ELEMENT a (b*)>
<!ELEMENT b EMPTY>
```

In our approach the two DTDs don't validate the same set of terms representing XML documents. For example the document:

```
<a>
    <b></b>
    <b></b>
</a>
```

is translated to $a([(b, b)])$ when one uses the first DTD and to $a([b, b])$ when one uses the second DTD. The regular types corresponding to the DTDs are different and in fact they are not equivalent because they type different kinds of terms. In XDuce the elements of every type are sequences, thus the document in the example corresponds to the same value $a[b, b]$. Then XDuce type system can correctly prove that the types corresponding to the DTDs are equivalent.

We could have reached the same conclusion without changing our type inference system if our initial choice to represent XML was lists of elements. In this case both documents would have been translated to the same Prolog term $a([b, b])$ and the regular types corresponding to the DTDs would be:

$$\tau_a \to \{a(\tau_1)\}$$
$$\tau_1 \to \{nil, .(\tau_b, .(\tau_b, \tau_1)), .(\tau_b, \tau_1)\}$$
$$\tau_b \to \{b\}$$

and:

$$\tau_a \to \{a(\tau_1)\}$$
$$\tau_1 \to \{nil, .(\tau_b, \tau_1)\}$$
$$\tau_b \to \{b\}$$

Then our type system would correctly prove that the types are equivalent (using Zobel *subset* algorithm [25] in the two directions).

This difference is due to a design decision: to translate XML to lists (which correspond to the original view of XML documents) or to finite trees (arbitrary Prolog terms) which is more natural in the logic programming paradigm. We chose the second option because terms are the basic Prolog data-structure. It would be interesting to implement both representations and to compare the final results.

7.3   Type Checking of XML

Type checking for XML was the subject of several previous papers. Milo, Suciu and Vianu studied the type checking problem using *tree transducers* in [12]. This work was extended to deal with data values in [1]. A good presentation on type checking for XML can be found in [17]. Standard languages used to denote types in the previous context were based on extensions of *regular tree languages*. The types we use in our framework correspond to *regular tree languages*.

8   Conclusion and Future Work

In this paper we use standard type inference for logic programming to get static validation of logic programs for XML transformation given their DTDs. There is plenty of scope for further work, in several directions:

1. *Efficiency*: our type inference implementation is based directly on the algorithm described in Zobel thesis [25]. This algorithm is suitable for a first implementation of *regular type* inference for logic programming because it relies on basic operations on *regular types* such as *intersection, comparison* and *unification*, which clarify several important concepts related to the type language. It can also be implemented in an efficient way using tabulation. We are now improving the efficiency of our implementation using efficient tabulation techniques for logic programming.

2. *Expressiveness*: More expressive languages for the validation of XML are now proposed (for instance [15]). The study of type languages which enable the use of those more expressive frameworks, deserves a careful research.

3. *Explicitly typed languages*: our framework relies on an implicitly typed logic programming language. The features proposed by our framework can be easily adapted for explicitly typed logic programming languages (such as *Mercury* [19]) by translating DTDs to types in the host language.

Acknowledgements. Work partially supported by funds granted to *LIACC* through the *Programa de Financiamento Plurianual, Fundação para a Ciência e Tecnologia* and *Programa POSI*.

References

1. Noga Alon, Tova Milo, Frank Neven, Dan Suciu, and Victor Vianu. XML with data values: Typechecking revisited. In *PODS*, 2001.
2. H. Boley. Relationships between logic programming and XML. In *Proc. 14th Workshop Logische Programmierung*, 2000.
3. Fran ois Bry and Norbert Eisinger. Data modeling with markup languages: A logic programming perspective. In *15th Workshop on Logic Programming and Constraint Systems, WLP 2000, Berlin*, 2000.
4. Fran ois Bry and Sebastian Schaffert. Towards a declarative query and transformation language for XML and semistructured data: simulation unification. In *Proc. of the 2002 International Conference on Logic Programming*, 2002.
5. D. Cabeza and M. Hermenegildo. Distributed WWW Programming using Ciao-Prolog and the PiLLoW Library. *Theory and Practice of Logic Programming*, 1(3):251–282, May 2001.
6. P. Dart and J. Zobel. A regular type language for logic programs. In Frank Pfenning, editor, *Types in Logic Programming*. The MIT Press, 1992.
7. M. Florido and L. Damas. Types as theories. In *Proc. of post-conference workshop on Proofs and Types, Joint International Conference and Symposium on Logic Programming*, 1992.
8. J.P. Gallagher and D.A. de Waal. Fast and precise regular approximation of logic programs. In *Proceedings of the Eleventh International Conference on Logic Programming*, 1993.
9. Haruo Hosoya and Benjamin Pierce. Xduce: A typed XML processing language. In *Third International Workshop on the Web and Databases (WebDB2000)*, volume 1997 of *Lecture Notes in Computer Science*, 2000.
10. J. W. Lloyd. *Foundations of Logic Programming*. Springer-Verlag, second edition, 1987.

11. Lunjin Lu. On Dart-Zobel algorithm for testing regular type inclusion. In *SIG-PLAN Notices Volume 36*, 2001.
12. T. Milo, D. Suciu, and V. Vianu. Typechecking for XML transformers. In *ACM Symposium on Principles of Database Systems*, 2000.
13. P. Mishra. Towards a theory of types in Prolog. In *Proc. of the 1984 International Symposium on Logic Programming*, 1984.
14. SWI Prolog. http://www.swi-prolog.org/.
15. XML Schema. http://www.w3.org/XML/Schema/, 2000.
16. Leon Sterling and Ehud Shapiro. *The Art of Prolog, 2nd edition.* The MIT Press, 1994.
17. Dan Suciu. Typechecking for semistructured data. In *International Workshop on Database Programming*, 2001.
18. J.W. Thatcher. *Tree automata: An informal survey.* Prentice-Hall, 1973.
19. The Mercury Programming Language. http://www.cs.mu.oz.au/research/mercury/.
20. Malcom Wallace and Colin Runciman. Haskell and XML: Generic combinators or type-based translation? In *International Conference on Functional Programming*, 1999.
21. Semantic Web. http://www.w3.org/2001/sw/, 1999.
22. Extensible Markup Language (XML). http://www.w3.org/XML/.
23. E. Yardeni and E. Shapiro. A type system for logic programs. In *The Journal of Logic Programming*, 1990.
24. Justin Zobel. Derivation of polymorphic types for prolog programs. In *Proc. of the 1987 International Conference on Logic Programming*, pages 817–838, 1987.
25. Justin Zobel. *Analysis of Logic Programs.* PhD thesis, Department of Computer Science, University of Melbourne, 1990.

WAM Local Analysis

Michel Ferreira and Luís Damas

DCC-FC & LIACC, University of Porto,
Rua do Campo Alegre, 823 - 4150 Porto, Portugal
{michel,luis}@ncc.up.pt

Abstract. The abstract interpretation framework has been used mainly in the *global* analysis of programs. Most often also, this interpretation is applied to the source Prolog program. In this paper we present an abstract interpretation of more *local* nature, and applied to the intermediate code (WAM). The purpose of obtaining a more efficient specialized version of the program remains the same as in global analysis approaches. Our specialization is multiple, meaning that we generate a different version for each entry pattern detected by analysis. This poly-variant unfolding of predicates allows the local (predicate level) analysis to propagate inter-procedurally relevant information. Besides time and complexity reduction of local versus global analysis, our approach is suited for *goal-independent* specialization, and for the partial selection of predicates to specialize. The evaluation of this more general specialization of programs in a full compiler shows that it is an alternative to global and goal-dependent methods.

Keywords: Prolog Compilation, Abstract Interpretation, Multiple Specialization.

1 Introduction

The major problem in compiling efficiently Prolog programs is the declarative style in which its predicates are written. The substitution of a procedural description of *how* by a declarative description of *what*, leads programmers to generalize in the design of the predicates of their programs. And for those general predicates, which are often multi-directional and type independent, it is difficult to generate efficient compiled implementations.

One good solution is to correct the over-generalization of the programming style by *analyzing* the predicates and the interaction between them in the context of the current program. The idea is to extract the missing procedural information from a pseudo-execution of the program. This is normally done by *abstract interpretation* [5], which basically consists in executing the program over a simplified abstract domain and treating recursion by fix-points.

Traditional specialization of a predicate is *single-specialization*, in which all the information derived by program analysis is combined in a unique implementation of the predicate. Another approach is *multiple-specialization* [23,11, 17,16,12], where several implementations (versions) are generated for a single

V. Dahl and P. Wadler (Eds.): PADL 2003, LNCS 2562, pp. 286–303, 2003.

predicate, each one specialized in a particular use of it. This approach suits the multi-directionality of Prolog, with different versions for different directions.

Global analysis of Prolog programs based on abstract interpretation, both for single and multiple specialization has not become an usual compiler technique. This is because of its large complexity and because it is not suited for real programs compilation, as it does not scale well. When the number of predicates of a program becomes large, considering all the possible interactions between them easily becomes too complex.

In this paper we show how we can replace a program level analysis by a predicate level analysis. Instead of a global program analysis we analyze locally each predicate. Through multiple specialization, where we generate a different version for each entry pattern detected by local analysis, we are able to propagate inter-procedurally relevant information. The most useful part is the fact that, because predicates are analyzed individually, we can select just a number of predicates to perform analysis and multiple specialization on a goal-independent basis. This approach is evaluated in a full Prolog compiler implemented over the wamcc [4] Prolog-to-C system, and yields good results.

The remaining of this paper is organized as follows: in the next section we present our analysis of the WAM code, describe the abstract domain and the abstract meaning of WAM instructions; section 3 shows how the multiple versions of predicates are generated and how the specialization can be goal-independent; section 4 shows how efficient multiple specialization of large programs is possible while keeping code size and compilation time reasonable; section 5 presents the evaluation of the system. We end with some conclusions.

2   WAM Analysis

The traditional approach in the process of *analysis+code specialization* of Prolog programs is to abstractly interpret the source code of the Prolog program in order to derive the intended information. This information is then used in the generation of the low-level code. As WAM instructions are too general to profit from the analysis information, new low-level abstract machines are used, or extensions to the original WAM are done.

Another approach which aims to speed-up the analysis process is known as *abstract compilation* [10]. Instead of interpreting the Prolog source code it is compiled to produce the intended analysis information upon execution.

In both approaches though, there is a clear separation between program analysis and program specialization, i.e. between the process of deriving the needed information and the process of using that information in the specialized implementation of the program.

We use another approach, *WAM analysis*, as illustrated in Figure 1.

Instead of analyzing the source Prolog code we analyze the intermediate WAM code. The generation of the specialized code is made during the analysis.

There are two previous experiences with abstract interpretation of the intermediate code, one in the context of the WAM, by Tan & Lin [19], and one in

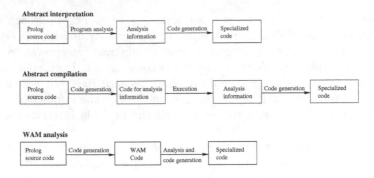

Fig. 1. Analysis approaches

the context of the VAM (Vienna Abstract Machine [15]), by Krall & Berger [14]. See [7] for a discussion of source-level versus low-level abstract interpretation.

A clear point in favor of low-level abstract interpretation is that what is *explicit* is easier to analyze than what is *implicit*. For example, determining if a variable has to be *trailed* or not has been one goal of Prolog analyses [20]. This trailing operation is directly connected to the creation and elimination of choice-points. In Prolog code this creation and elimination is implicit, but in WAM code it is explicit, through instructions `try_me_else(L)` and `retry_me_else(L)`.

To derive optimizing information from each predicate and to produce the specialized code, we have re-defined the meaning of each WAM instruction. We refer to this re-interpretation as *abstract emulation*.

In the abstract emulation of WAM instructions there is no heap, no environment stack and no trail. WAM instructions act over a single structure that we call *Status*. This *Status* is a local structure, i.e. it has a predicate level existence and is never passed within inter-procedural calls.

Besides changing the *Status* structure, WAM instructions have another effect: they output a new unfolded WAM instruction belonging to the specialized implementation of the predicate being analyzed. In the end of the abstract emulation the specialized code has all been generated.

2.1   The Unfolded WAM

Systems like Parma [21] or Aquarius [22] use, in their compilation process, an abstract machine which is more low-level than the WAM. We define new WAM instructions, which are special cases of a generic WAM instruction.

The single specialization approaches of system like Parma and Aquarius, where the specialization of a predicate is goal-dependent and determined by a particular set of calling patterns, are suited for the development of very low-level abstract machines. The single version generated should be as specialized as possible, and this is achieved by using very low-level abstract instructions, where every possible optimization can be implemented.

The scenario on a multiple specialization implementation, particularly in its goal-independent perspective, is different. Compromises between overall code size and particular versions efficiency have to be done. On a goal-independent perspective the set of specialized versions of a predicate should cover every possible calling pattern. Clearly, optimal low-level implementation of each version would lead to an enormous amount of versions.

In the unfolded WAM we divide each WAM instruction in its most important special cases. For instance, a `unify_x_variable(X_i)` only has two cases depending on the unification mode and thus gives rise to two instructions, `unify_x_variable_read(X_i)` and `unify_x_variable_write(X_i)`. More interesting are the cases where the argument type influences the implementation of the instruction. For instance, the implementation of `get_integer(N,A_i)` can be specialized if register A_i is known to be dereferenced or not. Knowledge about the dereferenced tag of A_i is also useful, as implementation is different if it is a *var* tag, an *int* tag or any other. Finally, when A_i has tag *var* implementation can also be specialized depending if such variable is older or newer than the last choice-point created. In Aquarius, for instance, these simplifications are obtained by using the low-level BAM instructions which include deref, trail and low-level comparison instructions. In our system the WAM instruction set is extended with three new instructions which specialize the generic `get_integer(N,A_i)` instruction.

2.2   The Abstract Domain

Attempting to analyze a program by simulating its execution for all possible inputs is, in general, unsolvable. Abstract interpretation solves this problem by mapping the concrete values into abstract descriptions. Analysis is then carried out over this abstract domain, which normally forms a complete lattice, that is, a set of values where a partial ordering ($\sqsubseteq$) and the least upper bound ($\sqcup$) and the greatest lower bound ($\sqcap$) are defined for any subset, and which includes top ($\top$) and bottom ($\bot$) elements.

Our domain captures the relevant information for WAM code optimization, namely, mode, functor type, dereferencing and trailing information about WAM registers. It is described as follows.

- *any* represents the set of all terms, the top element ($\top$) of the abstract domain.
- *nv* and *nv_{ndrf}* represent all non-variable terms and all non-variable terms not needing a dereferencing operation.
- *cst* and *cst_{ndrf}* represent the set of atomic terms, excluding integers and the nil atom.
- *int* and *int_{ndrf}* represent the set of integer terms.
- *nil* and *nil_{ndrf}* represent the nil atom.
- *struct*$(f/n, \alpha_1, ..., \alpha_n)$ and *struct_{ndrf}*$(f/n, \alpha_1, ..., \alpha_n)$ represent the set of all structure terms with functor f/n and with each argument of type $\alpha_i (1 \leq i \leq n)$ in the abstract domain.

- $lst(\alpha_1, \alpha_2)$ and $lst_{ndrf}(\alpha_1, \alpha_2)$ represent structure terms with functor $'.'/2$, α_1 in the abstract domain and α_2 with type $lst(\alpha_1, \alpha_2)$ or $lst_{ndrf}(\alpha_1, \alpha_2)$ or nil or nil_{ndrf}.
- lst_or_nil and $lst_{ndrf}\_or\_nil_{ndrf}$ represent the least upper bound of the above types lst and nil. These elements are important because $lists$ (functor $./2$) and nil often appear in the same argument of the clauses of a predicate.

For variable types we add extra information about trailing:

- v^{ntr} and v^{ntr}_{ndrf} represent all variables not needing trailing.
- v and v_{ndrf} represent all variables that have to be trailed.
- $impossible$ represents the set of impossible terms, the bottom element ($\bot$) of the abstract domain.

2.3 Widening of Complex Types

The domain described above is not finite because of the possible infinite *term-depth* of the abstract types *struct* and *lst*. To guarantee analysis termination we could make the domain finite by restricting the term-depth to a fix value, loosing precision when analysis encounters terms whose depth is larger than this value. This is known as *depth-k abstraction* [18] and is commonly used in analysis frameworks [21,19,13]. Depth-k abstractions normally represent the principal functor of a term complete with descriptions for its subterms. Subterm descriptions are given to the depth of a predetermined constant bound k.

In our system we implement a different approach. We restrict the types of the domain only when calling a predicate. This way we have a possibly infinite precision within a predicate, which allows us to extract as much as there is local information, and we guarantee termination by simplifying types across predicates boundaries. This can be seen has having two domains: a local domain used intra-procedurally and a simpler finite global domain used inter-procedurally.

In the simplification of compound types *lst* and *struct* we reduce the terms considering only the principal functor and ignoring the sub-terms. This implies a larger loss in precision than what usually is present on other analysis frameworks. As we will see shortly, we specialize predicates in a number of versions determined by calling patterns that are described by the types of the arguments of the call. Simplifying these types reduces the number of versions generated, which is the main motivation in this simplification.

To improve precision it is possible to augment the abstract domain with more informative descriptions of compound types. For instance, some structures which appear often in Prolog programs, like *list of integers* and *list of constants*, allow useful optimizations if the abstract domain can represent them across predicates boundaries. For instance, the type $lst_{ndrf}(int_{ndrf}, lst_{ndrf}(int_{ndrf}, nil_{ndrf}))$ is simplified to $lst_{ndrf}\_of\_int_{ndrf}$, while $lst_{ndrf}(v_{ndrf}, nil_{ndrf})$ simplifies to lst_{ndrf}.

This approach can result in relevant precision losses. Consider for example the following program:

:- $p([1,X],[X,1])$, $q(X)$.

$p(X,X)$.

The pattern to $p/2$ is $(lst_{ndrf}(int_{ndrf}, lst_{ndrf}(v_{ndrf}^{ntr}, nil_{ndrf})), lst_{ndrf}(v_{ndrf}^{ntr}, lst_{ndrf}(int_{ndrf}, nil_{ndrf})))$. The abstract unification can derive that X will exit $p/2$ with type int_{ndrf}, and $q/1$ can be specialized for such pattern. If however when calling $p/2$ we simplify types $(lst_{ndrf}(int_{ndrf}, lst_{ndrf}(v_{ndrf}^{ntr}, nil_{ndrf}))$ and $lst_{ndrf}(v_{ndrf}^{ntr}, lst_{ndrf}(int_{ndrf}, nil_{ndrf}))$ to lst_{ndrf} then nothing will be known about the type of variable X when calling $q/1$.

This lost of precision is acceptable from the point of view of our analyzer. As we will show, our focus is much more centered on goal-independent and local analysis than in goal-dependent and global analysis, and clearly clause $p(X,X)$ gives very few of such local and goal-independent information.

2.4   Abstract Meaning of WAM Instructions

We assume in this section that the reader is familiar with the concrete meaning of WAM instructions. For a detailed explanation of the WAM execution model and its instruction set see Ait-Kaci tutorial [1].

As we have said, in its abstract emulation WAM instructions have two effects: they produce changes in the local *Status* structure and they output a new *unfolded* WAM instruction. It is important to note that there is no global structure, such as the *Heap*, where WAM instructions from distinct predicates interact. It is this absence that allows us to qualify our analysis as local.

In their concrete meaning WAM instructions construct terms on the heap from their textual form. In this process a number of temporary and permanent (variable) *registers* X1, Y1, etc, are used to save pieces of terms yet to be processed or a variable that may occur later in the term or in another goal. As in the abstract emulation we do not have an heap and because locally (within a predicate) we need to keep (abstract) term representations, we use the WAM temporary and permanent registers to save these abstract terms. To avoid temporary registers being overwritten by an optimized register allocation [3] this allocation is not performed in the first WAM generation.

The simplest WAM instructions are *put* instructions. They load argument registers in the goals of a clause. We define the abstract meaning of instructions $\texttt{put\_y\_variable}(Y_i, A_j)$, $\texttt{put\_x\_value}(X_i, A_j)$ and $\texttt{put\_list}(A_i)$ as follows:

$$\texttt{put\_y\_variable}(Y_i, A_j) \equiv AddStatus(Status, Y_i \leftarrow v\_ndrf\_ntr)$$
$$AddStatus(Status, A_j \leftarrow Y_i)$$
$$AbstractEmulate(NextInst, Status) \rightarrow outcode_1$$
$$outcode \rightarrow \texttt{put\_y\_variable}(Y_i, A_j), outcode_1$$

$$\texttt{put\_x\_value}(X_i, A_j) \equiv AddStatus(Status, A_j \leftarrow X_i)$$
$$AbstractEmulate(NextInst, Status) \rightarrow outcode_1$$
$$outcode \rightarrow \texttt{put\_x\_value}(X_i, A_j), outcode_1$$

$$\texttt{put\_list}(A_i) \equiv AddStatus(Status, SMode \leftarrow write(i))$$
$$AddStatus(Status, A_i \leftarrow lst\_ndrf(\_,\_))$$
$$AbstractEmulate(NextInst, Status) \rightarrow outcode_1$$
$$outcode \rightarrow \texttt{put\_list}(A_i), outcode_1$$

Every *put* instruction generates an identical instruction as output, because no optimizations can be performed. They simply add some information to the *Status* structure, like aliasing between variables, unification mode or a register's type. Note that put_list(A_i) builds and stores the abstract term in register A_i instead of in the heap. Subsequent unify instructions will work on these register and not on the heap.[1]

An essential operation of a large number of WAM instructions is unification. This unification will have a correspondent *abstract unification*. Concrete unification unifies concrete terms. Abstract unification unifies elements of the abstract domain. The procedure $AbsUnify(T1, T2, Status)$ abstractly unifies terms $T1$ and $T2$, using information from the current *Status* and produces a new status with $T1$ and $T2$ unified. Here are some examples of abstract unification:

- $AbsUnify(X_1, int, [X_1 \leftarrow any]) = [X_1 \leftarrow int]$
- $AbsUnify(X_1, lst(int, X_2), [X_1 \leftarrow any, X_2 \leftarrow v]) = [X_1 \leftarrow lst(int, X_2), X_2 \leftarrow any]$
- $AbsUnify(X_1, X_2, [X_1 \leftarrow v_{ndrf}, X_2 \leftarrow v_{ndrf}]) = [X_1 \leftarrow v, X_2 \leftarrow v, alias(X_1, X_2)]$

WAM instructions get and unify perform unification. The abstract meaning of get_x_value(X_i, A_j) and unify_y_variable(Y_i) is defined as follows:

$$
\begin{aligned}
\text{get\_x\_value}(X_i, A_j) \quad &\equiv TypeX_i \leftarrow ReadStatus(X_i, Status) \\
&TypeA_j \leftarrow ReadStatus(A_j, Status) \\
&if(Status \leftarrow AbsUnify(TypeX_i, TypeA_j, Status)) \\
&\quad TypeA_j \leftarrow ReadStatus(A_j, Status) \\
&\quad if(Arg(j)) AddStatus(Status, Exit(j) \leftarrow TypeA_j \\
&\quad AbstractEmulate(NextInst, Status) \rightarrow outcode_1 \\
&\quad outcode \rightarrow \text{get\_x\_value\_}TypeX_i\_TypeA_j(X_i, A_j), \\
&\quad\quad outcode_1 \\
&else\ outcode \rightarrow \text{fail\_f} \\
\text{unify\_y\_variable}(Y_i) &\equiv AddStatus(Status, Y_i \leftarrow v\_ndrf\_ntr) \\
&SMode \leftarrow ReadSMode(Status) \\
&if SMode = read(j, S) \\
&\quad Status \leftarrow AbsUnify(Y_i, X_j, Status) \\
&\quad AbstractEmulate(NextInst, Status) \rightarrow outcode_1 \\
&\quad outcode \rightarrow \text{unify\_y\_variable\_read}(Y_i), outcode_1 \\
&if SMode = write(j) \\
&\quad Status \leftarrow WriteType(X_j, Y_i) \\
&\quad AbstractEmulate(NextInst, Status) \rightarrow outcode_1 \\
&\quad out \rightarrow \text{unify\_y\_variable\_write}(Y_i), outcode_1
\end{aligned}
$$

The get instructions, if used for head arguments, also save on the *Status* exit information, to be used for the updating of the exit extension table when finishing the analysis of the current predicate.

Choice-point management instructions, try_me_else(L), retry_me_else(L) and trust_me_else_fail, will act over the *Status* structure modifying only the trailing condition of registers of type *var*. Recall that a variable only has to be trailed if it is older than the last choice-point. Instructions try_me_else(L)

---

[1] The unification mode kept on the *Status* also saves the number (i) of the register being unified ($SMode \leftarrow write(i)$)

and `retry_me_else(L)` create choice-points, and thus *var* type registers of the current *Status* *will* have to be trailed after this choice-point creation. The abstract meaning of these two instructions promotes the no trailing variable types of the current *Status* to the correspondent have-to-be-trailed variable types. A `trust_me_else_fail` instruction does not create a choice-point in its concrete execution and therefore does not imply such type promotion.

The tracking of choice-point creation cannot be done just locally, but has also to propagate inter-procedurally the creation of choice-points. The exit types extension table saves for each predicate if it creates or not choice-points, and the affected registers of the local *Status* of the calling predicate are updated by checking this value after a `call` instruction. The abstract meaning of these instructions is the following:

$$\texttt{try\_mo\_oloo}(L) \quad \equiv \forall_i\, V_i = X_i \vee V_i = Y_i$$
$$TypeV_i \leftarrow ReadStatus(V_i, Status)$$
$$if(TypeV_i = v_{ndrf}^{ntr})\, AddStatus(Status, V_i \leftarrow v_{ndrf})$$
$$if(TypeV_i = v^{ntr})\, AddStatus(Status, V_i \leftarrow v)$$
$$AddStatus(Status, choicepoint \leftarrow true)$$
$$AbstractEmulate(NextInst, Status) \rightarrow outcode_1$$
$$outcode \rightarrow \texttt{try\_me\_else}(L), outcode_1$$

$$\texttt{retry\_me\_else}(L) \quad \equiv \forall_i\, V_i = X_i \vee V_i = Y_i$$
$$TypeV_i \leftarrow ReadStatus(V_i, Status)$$
$$if(TypeV_i = v_{ndrf}^{ntr})\, AddStatus(Status, V_i \leftarrow v_{ndrf})$$
$$if(TypeV_i = v^{ntr})\, AddStatus(Status, V_i \leftarrow v)$$
$$AddStatus(Status, choicepoint \leftarrow true)$$
$$AbstractEmulate(NextInst, Status) \rightarrow outcode_1$$
$$outcode \rightarrow \texttt{retry\_me\_else}(L), outcode_1$$

$$\texttt{trust\_me\_else\_fail} \equiv AbstractEmulate(NextInst, Status) \rightarrow outcode_1$$
$$outcode \rightarrow \texttt{trust\_me\_else\_fail}, outcode_1$$

3   Multiply Specializing Predicates

In the previous section we did not define the abstract meaning of control instructions. They are `call`, `execute` and `proceed`. We define them now and show how the different versions of a predicate are generated in its multiple specialization.

Our specialization strategy is to generate a new version of a predicate for each distinct activation pattern, whether or not they allow new optimizations.

When encountering a `call` or `execute` instruction, the *Status* structure is consulted to build the activation pattern. If code has not yet been generated for that pattern then the WAM code for that predicate is searched, selecting only the clauses that match the activation pattern, and it is analyzed. Control is transfered to the called predicate, where analysis further continues resulting in the respective specialized code being outputed.

Upon return from the called predicate the *Status* structure of the predicate being analyzed has to be updated, namely the unbound permanent variables passed on the arguments of the called predicate. This update is done using the exit type information of the predicate, saved on the exit types extension table.

The abstract meaning of the `call(P)` instructions is as follows:

$$\texttt{call}(P) \equiv P' \leftarrow BuildCallingPattern(Status)$$
$$WamAnalyze(P')$$
$$ExitP' \leftarrow ReadExitTypes(P')$$
$$UpdateStatus(Status, ExitP')$$
$$AbstractEmulate(NextInst, Status) \rightarrow outcode_1$$
$$outcode \rightarrow \texttt{call}(P'), outcode_1$$

A `proceed` instruction ends the execution of a predicate. Its abstract meaning simply updates the Exit extension table. The head exit pattern is calculated from the *Status* structure and the least upper bound of this pattern and the previous exit pattern is calculated and the extension table updated. More formally, the abstract meaning of `proceed` when predicate P is being analyzed is:

$$\texttt{proceed} \equiv ExitP \leftarrow CalculateHeadExitPattern(Status)$$
$$ExitP' \leftarrow ReadExitTypes(P)$$
$$ExitP'' \leftarrow lub(ExitP, ExitP')$$
$$UpdateExitExtensionTable(P, ExitP'')$$
$$outcode \rightarrow \texttt{proceed}$$

A `execute` instruction performs last-call optimization. It is equivalent to a `call` followed by a `proceed`.

3.1 Goal-Independent Specialization

The specialized versions of a predicate are created for detected entry patterns. These entry patterns will initialize the local *Status* and are a major source of information to the specialized implementation of each version of a predicate. WAM instructions add some more information because of their specialized unification primitives, defined for each type of term ($\texttt{get\_const}(c, A_i)$, $\texttt{get\_list}(A_i)$, $\texttt{unify\_x\_variable}(X_i)$, etc). When specialization uses entry patterns information and is initialized by user defined entry points, it is said to be *goal-dependent*.

The question is if our WAM analysis process can also guide a more useful *goal-independent* specialization, i.e. without using entry patterns knowledge but only the information collected from WAM instructions.

The idea is to propagate forward the information from some WAM instructions, by *unfolding* the remaining code in a number of possible success types for that instruction. The instructions where we perform this propagation and unfolding are `get_list`, `get_structure` and `switch_on_term`.

Consider the `append/3` predicate of Figure 2. Code for `append/3` has three conditional instructions, `switch_on_term()`, `get_list(1)` and `get_list(3)`.

Because of $\texttt{put\_x\_variable}(X_3, A_3)$ in `$exe_1` code, the pattern built on the `execute` instruction will have type v_{ndrf}^{ntr} on the third argument. This information is useful for the $\texttt{get\_list}(A_3)$ of `append/3` code. In particular, it sets mode to *write* and the $\texttt{unify\_x\_variable}(A_3)$ executed in this mode re-assigns register A_3 to v_{ndrf}^{ntr}. The pattern built on the next `execute` instruction will continue to have v_{ndrf}^{ntr} on the third argument. This is a valuable information.

But what happens if we do not know the entry pattern, because no entry point is used, when analyzing `append/3`? The third argument has type *any* and the $\texttt{get\_list}(A_3)$ cannot be specialized and the unification mode is unknown in the $\texttt{unify\_x\_variable}(A_3)$ instruction. No valuable information here.

```
:- append([1,2],[3],R).

append([],L,L).
append([H|T],L,[H|R]) :- append(T,L,R).
```

```
$exe_1/0: allocate(1)                    $append/3: switch_on_term(1,2,4,fail)
          get_y_bc_reg(0)                           label(1)
          put_list(1)                               try_me_else(3)
          unify_integer(2)                          label(2)
          unify_nil                                 get_nil(0)
          put_list(0)                               get_x_value(1,2)
          unify_integer(1)                          proceed
          unify_x_value(1)                          label(3)
          put_list(1)                               trust_me_else_fail
          unify_integer(3)                          label(4)
          unify_nil                                 get_list(0)
          put_x_variable(2,2)                       unify_x_variable(3)
          call(append/3)                            unify_x_variable(0)
          cut_y(0)                                  get_list(2)
          deallocate                                unify_x_value(3)
          proceed                                   unify_x_variable(2)
                                                    execute(append,3)
```

Fig. 2. The append program

The idea is that if `get_list`(A_3) succeeds then A_3 can have only type *var* or type *list*. We can then create two *Status*, one where A_3 has type *var* and one where A_3 has type *list*, and analyze the remaining code in each situation. The output code will be a `switch_on_list`(A_3) responsible for testing A_3 and jumping accordingly, followed by the output code from the two situations analyzed.

The same propagation of test information can be done in the `switch_on_term` instruction. In the current case, this instruction succeeds if the first argument has type *var*, *const* or *list*. Three *Status* are then created and analysis proceeds exploring the three situations, generating the code shown in Figure 3.

Note that in the code of Figure 3 append/3 is called with four distinct entry patterns. WAM analysis of this code will create the four versions and analyze each one using the entry patterns knowledge. Although this information is used the specialization remains goal-independent because of the generic start.

We now define the abstract meaning of `get_list`(A_i) for the subpart where A_i has type *any*:

$$\texttt{get\_list}(A_i) \equiv TypeA_i \leftarrow ReadStatus(A_i, Status)$$

$$...$$
$$if(TypeA_i = any)$$
$$\quad Status_1 \leftarrow Status$$
$$\quad AddStatus(Status, SMode \leftarrow read(i,1))$$
$$\quad AddStatus(Status, A_i \leftarrow lst(H,T))$$
$$\quad if(Arg(i))AddStatus(Status, Exit(i) \leftarrow lst(H,T))$$
$$\quad AbstractEmulate(NextInst, Status) \rightarrow outcode_1$$
$$\quad AddStatus(Status_1, SMode \leftarrow write(i))$$
$$\quad AddStatus(Status_1, A_i \leftarrow lst(H,T))$$
$$\quad if(Arg(i))AddStatus(Status, Exit(i) \leftarrow lst(H,T))$$
$$\quad AbstractEmulate(NextInst, Status_1) \rightarrow outcode_2$$
$$\quad outcode \rightarrow \texttt{switch\_on\_list}(A_i, L_1, L_2),$$
$$\quad\quad \texttt{label}(L_1), outcode_1, \texttt{label}(L_2), outcode_2$$

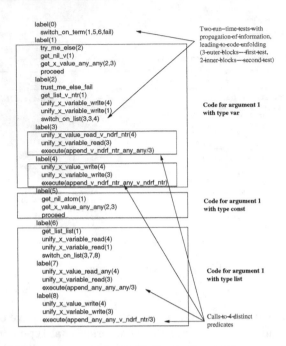

Fig. 3. The unfolded WAM code for `append_a_a_a/3`

The `switch_on_list`(A_i, L_1, L_2) instruction behaves as a `get_list`(A_i) but propagates forward through a two-way branch the result of the runtime test.

3.2 WAM Analysis Cycle

A single pass over the WAM code is not sufficient to generate the final multiply specialized code. This is because exit types will change during analyses and such changes will lead to the derivation of new entry patterns. The WAM analysis process has to iterate until a fix-point is reached. As the abstract domain is finite and forms a complete lattice this fix-point clearly exists [6].

4 Controlling Code Expansion

The code expansion in a multiple specialization compiler can be quite large, because the code of each predicate is multiplied by a number of versions. This number of versions is a function of the arity of the predicate and of the analysis domain complexity. If d is the number of elements and a is the arity of the predicate, then, in the worst possible case, the number of versions generated for a predicate will be d^a.

This is a wildly pessimistic number of versions as, due to the structure of the domain, only a pathological predicate could achieve such a variety of activation patterns. It is, though, an indicator of the order of growth of a multiple specialization implementation, revealing its exponential nature.

In order to make a multiple specialization strategy feasible for real-size programs it is necessary to use a strong selection criteria of the predicates to be multiply specialized. In real-size programs only the most critical predicates of a program must be multiply specialized, performing partial multiple specialization instead of total multiple specialization. Further more, not every version of a particular predicate that is generated is relevant for the overall performance of the program. A process of generating the optimal set of versions for a particular predicate is also determinant for the success of a multiple specialization implementation.

We base our selection of predicates to unfold on the results of a (goal-dependent) profiler implemented at the WAM level. Prior to specialization programs are profiled, and the most important predicates are selected to be multiply specialized.

As expected the time distribution per predicate follows a pattern that is adequate for partial selection, as execution time is concentrated on just few predicates. Figure 4 represents the time/predicate distribution for chat_parser, where the x axis represent the predicates ordered descendently by execution time, and the y axis represent the accumulative percentage of execution time. It follows a logarithmic pattern - on the 10 most important predicates more than 50% of the time is present, and chat_parser has over 150 predicates.

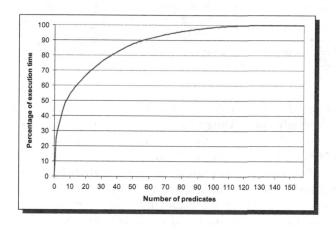

Fig. 4. Time/predicate distribution for chat_parser.pl

Note that profiling implies executing, and thus the selection of predicates is goal-dependent, though the subsequent specialization is goal-independent. This situation is acceptable, as the structure of the program is more or less independent of the input it receives, and goal-independent profilings are very difficult to obtain. See [8] for our approach in goal-independent selection of predicates.

5   Performance Evaluation

Table 1 shows the percentage of time spent per *percentage of the number of pred-icates* for the 17 benchmarks considered. We have used 10 measuring points from 10% to 100%, in order to reach a meaningful average information. 10% means the 10% most important predicates, and so on. This allows reaching a meaningful average information, considering the size differences of the benchmarks.

Table 1. Percentage of execution time for varying percentages of most relevant predicates

Program(Number of Predicates	10%	20%	30%	40%	50%	60%	70%	80%	90%	100%
qsort(1)	36.5	73.3	73.3	95.8	95.8	95.8	99.8	99.8	100	100
query(2)	35.4	35.4	69.0	69.0	84.8	99.5	99.5	100	100	100
derive(2)	86.2	86.2	89.7	93.1	96.1	96.1	98.8	99.9	99.9	100
zebra(2)	52.6	52.6	79.0	96.4	100	100	100	100	100	100
serialise(2)	49.6	73.5	73.5	85.8	91.3	96.4	99.5	99.5	99.8	100
mu(2)	26.0	50.7	71.0	84.2	91.4	91.4	96.0	99.6	100	100
fast_mu(2)	56.1	80.8	91.4	97.2	98.8	98.8	99.2	99.6	99.8	100
crypt(2)	57.9	89.8	94.6	97.7	98.5	99.2	99.6	99.9	100	100
meta_qsort(3)	41.0	75.4	83.8	89.5	97.6	100	100	100	100	100
queens_8(3)	42.6	57.6	70.0	80.2	99.2	100	100	100	100	100
nreverse(3)	91.2	99.8	99.9	100	100	100	100	100	100	100
prover(3)	60.0	74.2	93.3	96.4	99.5	99.7	99.9	99.9	100	100
browse(4)	95.0	99.0	99.5	99.7	99.9	99.9	100	100	100	100
boyer(6)	87.0	97.8	99.4	99.8	100	100	100	100	100	100
sdda(9)	76.0	89.0	95.7	98.8	99.8	100	100	100	100	100
nand(16)	65.2	83.9	90.2	94.3	97.7	99.5	99.9	100	100	100
chat_parser(32)	62.4	77.2	86.2	92.1	95.7	99.4	99.4	99.9	100	100
Average	60.0	76.2	85.9	92.4	96.8	98.6	99.5	99.8	100	100

On average 60% of the total execution time is concentrated on 10% of the predicates. Multiply specializing this part of the program can significantly im-prove the overall efficiency. Multiple specialization could be taken further, and applied to 20% of the predicates that, on average, account for 76% of the exe-cution time. If performance is critical and the program being considered is not large we could select the 30% most important predicates, where 86% of the total execution time is present. Further than that only marginal improvements would be achieved, or the code growth could even introduce some slow-downs due to caching problems.

Notice that the results in Table 1 show an increasing trend as the programs become larger. Considering the last 3 programs which have more than 40 pred-icates, the percentage of the time on 20% of the predicates is on average 83.4%. Considering the first 7 programs (less than 10 predicates), this percentage is 64.6%.

We have selected to multiply specialize 20% of the predicates of each bench-mark. This means 1 predicate for *qsort*, the smallest program, and 32 predicates for *chat_parser*, the largest one. In terms of execution time, this means an interval from 50.7% for *mu* to 99.8% for *nreverse*.

5.1   Execution Time

Table 2 compares the results of our system (*u*-WAM) with the `wamcc` basic system, in terms of execution speed. This is the fundamental comparison, as the C targeting is equivalent in both systems, and the results obtained give an accurate measure of the benefits of multiple specialization. In this table we also include the results obtained in the SICStus Prolog 3.8.4 compiler [2], using compiled emulated code and compiled native code. This Prolog system, developed at the SICS (Swedish Institute of Computer Science), is currently the most well known Prolog compiler and is widely used as a benchmark for Prolog implementations.

For each of the 17 benchmarks Table 2 presents the best execution time from a series of ten runs. We show the execution time in seconds for the `wamcc` system, and the speed-up or slowdown obtained by the other systems. The timings were measured running the benchmarks on a Sun Ultra Sparc 248 Mhz with 256MB of RAM, as the Sparc architecture is the only for which SICStus can generate native code. The C code generated by `wamcc` and *u*-WAM has been compiled using `gcc 2.8.1` with the `-O2` option.

Table 2. Execution times of `wamcc`, *u*-WAM and SICStus

Program(Number of Predicates)	wamcc 2.22	*u*-WAM	Sicstus 3.8.4 Emulated	Native
qsort(1)	0.120	1.44	0.92	3.61
query(2)	0.070	1.31	0.64	1.39
derive(2)	0.110	1.67	0.92	3.32
zebra(2)	0.030	1.25	1.00	1.04
serialise(2)	0.190	1.46	1.12	3.45
mu(2)	0.730	1.24	0.95	2.52
fast_mu(2)	0.770	1.42	0.83	2.11
crypt(2)	0.380	1.83	0.57	1.47
meta_qsort(3)	0.580	1.54	0.63	2.41
queens_8(3)	0.100	1.39	0.91	2.92
nreverse (3)	0.170	1.81	1.13	5.58
prover(3)	0.150	1.36	0.83	3.13
browse(4)	0.550	1.61	0.74	2.84
boyer(6)	0.440	1.81	0.80	2.44
sdda(9)	0.080	1.42	1.33	2.15
nand(16)	3.110	1.49	0.92	2.10
chat_parser(32)	1.410	1.51	0.87	2.41
Average speedup		1.50	0.89	2.59

The average speedup of *u*-WAM over `wamcc` is of 1.5. The `wamcc` system is somewhere between SICStus emulated and SICStus native, and the speedup obtained in *u*-WAM importantly reduces the difference with respect to SICStus native. In some benchmarks, like *query*, *zebra* and *crypt*, the performance of *u*-WAM is even better than or equal to native SICStus. Furthermore, *u*-WAM compiled programs are as portable as SICStus programs compiled to emulated code, over which *u*-WAM has a speedup of almost 2.

These results have also to be interpreted based on the percentage of the execution time that is being improved. The 20% of the predicates of each benchmark mean in execution time an interval from 50.7% for *mu* to 99.8% for *nreverse*. For instance, the *chat_parser* benchmark in the comparison between *u*-WAM and wamcc obtains a global speed-up of 1.51, translating a real speedup greater than 1.7 for the 77% improved.

Specialization is also goal-independent. This means that any predicate of the program can be an entry point, including the predicates selected for multiple specialization, for which we have to generate a most-general-version. This goal independence is clearly not necessary for the benchmark programs, where it always exists a directive working as the single entry point in the program. Specializing in a goal-dependent manner would obviously increase performance, as less versions would be generated and the code would be more compact. Furthermore , the activation pattern of the goal of the directive may be lost in the calling path to the multiply specialized versions, if a non-specialized predicate is called in between. Clearly, a goal-dependent and total specialization of the predicates of each benchmark yields better results than the partial, goal-independent specialization results presented in Table 2.

The *zebra* benchmark yields the worst result, with a speedup of just 22%. This program performs heavy search through the *member/2* predicate, spending 25% of the total execution time in the management of choice-points. This choice-point creation is not improved on the specialization of this program, and no gains are obtained on this percentage. The specialized versions for *member/2* that are used during execution have bounded types on the arguments, $member\_struct_{ndrf}\_list_{ndrf}/2$ and $member\_struct_{ndrf}\_any/2$, and read mode unification profits less from specialization. The other multiply specialized predicate, *next_to/3*, is more efficiently specialized, but is less time relevant than *member/2*.

Most of the predicates which are multiply specialized are simple recursive predicates. This allows good results in partial multiple specialization, because *Status* information is not lost in the partial process, as it is passed from the entry calling pattern of the current predicate to the goal called in its body. This happens, for instance, in the *deriv* benchmark, where the predicate *d/3*, which recursively defines differentiation rules, gives rise to the recursive specialized version $d\_nv_{ndrf}\_cst_{ndrf}\_v_{ndrf}/3$.

The *nreverse* program also obtains very good speed-ups. First, the 3 predicates multiply specialized represent over 99% of the total execution time. Second, the crucial predicate of these 3 predicates is *append/3*, which gives rise to a specialized version, $append\_any\_any\_v_{ndrf}^{ntr}/3$ that invariantly calls itself, repeatedly profiting from the simplified unification of a dereferenced variable, not needing trailing, with a list.

Programs which use predicates in multiple directions are the ones which profit more from multiple specialization. In the *chat_parser* benchmark for instance, this poly-variant use appears in the *terminal/5* predicate. This predicate is called in some clauses with the first argument bound to a constant, and sometimes with the first argument unbound. Multiple specialization creates two versions for these cases. Furthermore, this *terminal/5* predicate is called 22 times in the program, and is the most time relevant predicate, representing 25% of the total execution time of the program, which has 158 predicates.

Before ending this subsection on execution speedup, we refer the results obtained for the total specialization of a number of small benchmarks, generating just goal-dependent code. All the predicates of the program are specialized assuming that the only entry point is the directive existing in the benchmark. As a result, the specialized versions that are generated correspond to all the calling patterns detected in the execution which starts with the declared entry point. Starting with a concrete calling pattern eliminates much more versions than if we start with the most-general-pattern. In goal-independent specialization, we have to abstractly execute every predicate that is to be multiply specialized starting with its most-general-pattern. In goal-dependent specialization we only generate versions for the calling patterns reached in the execution path starting from the single entry point.

Using such specialization on *qsort*, *query*, *queens_8*, *nreverse* and *browse*, improves the speedup to 2.61 times over wamcc. As our system is still a prototype, we can only apply total multiple specialization to few small programs. Even in a robust implementation, total multiple specialization will be impossible because of the code growth issue. Also, goal-dependent specialization is not so interesting for real applications, since they often require separate modules compilation. The speed obtained is only interesting in the comparison with the SICStus system: the complexity difference between the *u*-WAM system and SICStus is enormeous, and yet *u*-WAM can be as efficient as native SICStus, while being as portable as emulated SICStus.

5.2 Code Size and Compilation Time

Table 3 compares the code size and the compilation time of wamcc and *u*-WAM. We present the (stripped) size of the object files generated by the C compiler (.o files) in Kbytes. Compilation time includes the generation of WAM or *u*-WAM code, C emission, gcc compilation of the C file and linking. By far, the major part of this time is due to the gcc compilation of the C file.

On average the object file size increases 1.57 times. In three programs, *qsort*, *nand* and *chat_parser*, this increase is greater than 2 times. The increase is directly related to the number of versions created for the predicates multiply specialized. This number of versions depends in part of the arity of these predicates. As programs become larger, this arity tends to grow. For *nand* and *chat_parser*, the two largest programs of the benchmark set, the average arity of the predicates multiply specialized is 5.1 and 5.9, respectively, which is substancially higher than the average for the other 14 programs, 2.6. The single multiply specialized predicate for *qsort*, *partition/4*, is a 4-arity predicate, leading to a large code growth on this small program. Code growth is limited by the fact that specialized versions have a smaller code than that of generic predicates. The code growth factor of 1.57 for a multiple specialization of 20% of the program clearly shows that partial multiple specialization is mandatory, as total specialization of programs would lead to an unbearable code explosion. Furthermore, the rate

Table 3. Comparing code size and compilation time of `wamcc` and u-WAM

	wamcc 2.22		u-WAM	
Program	Object Size	Compile Time	Object Size	Compile Time
qsort	14.5	1.452	29.8	3.123
query	33.9	2.508	40.6	3.191
derive	19.8	1.440	30.9	2.429
zebra	19.6	1.296	28.5	2.240
serialise	24.3	1.476	38.1	2.496
mu	17.7	1.428	23.6	2.164
fast_mu	19.7	1.752	26.1	2.393
crypt	26.0	2.244	30.6	2.806
meta_qsort	32.8	2.700	38.9	3.567
queens_8	17.2	1.356	26.1	2.393
nreverse	17.6	1.296	23.2	1.824
prover	38.9	2.964	65.2	5.125
browse	33.7	3.168	60.4	6.330
boyer	125.8	10.476	148.4	13.608
sdda	67.7	5.340	122.6	11.242
nand	202.9	30.240	453.2	71.243
chat_parser	378.0	39.048	839.9	99.024
Average increase			**1.57**	**1.72**

of code growth is not linear on the percentage of the program specialized, as higher percentages lead to higher interactions between the predicates multiply specialized, that result in the derivation of more calling patterns.

The compilation time increases 1.72 on average. The `gcc` compiler and its optimization phase, are responsible for more than 90% of this compilation time. If we compile without optimization, the time is reduced to 1/3. The `gcc` optimization phase time is influenced essentially by the size of the C functions compiled. The `wamcc` C codification method gives rise to as many functions as there are goals in the body of a clause, and this size remains similar in the u-WAM code, which explains the linear growth between code size and compilation time.

6   Conclusions

Our WAM analysis is not purely local. Although each predicate, existing or created, is analyzed locally, its creation is global (depends on another predicate). Even within the predicate level analysis, some global information is used - the exit patterns information. This is not essential information for analysis, it just improves precision. In [9] the exit type analysis was done previously and independently of the entry patterns, in an half-way solution.

The most useful part of our analysis is the fact that predicates are analyzed individually and we can thus independently multiply specialize a subset of the program.

Part of the good results obtained are due to the fact that the most relevant predicates are, almost always, recursive predicates. Therefore entry patterns are not lost due to a non multiply specialized middle predicate. The results could be improved by a more intelligent selection of predicates, that considers non time relevant predicates that can derive, through their specialization, entry patterns for the time relevant predicates.

References

1. Hassan Aït-Kaci. *Warren's Abstract Machine — A Tutorial Reconstruction*. MIT Press, 1991.
2. Mats Carlsson. Internals of Sicstus Prolog version 0.6. Internal Report, Gigalips Project, November 1987.
3. Mats Carlsson. *Design and Implementation of an OR-Parallel Prolog Engine*. SICS Dissertation Series 02, The Royal Institute of Technology, 1990.
4. Philippe Codognet and Daniel Diaz. wamcc: Compiling Prolog to C. In Leon Sterling, editor, *Proc. of the 12th International Conference on Logic Programming*, pages 317–332, Cambridge, June 13–18 1995. MIT Press.
5. P. Cousot and R. Cousot. Abstract interpretation: A unified lattice model for static analysis of programs by construction or approximation of fixpoints. In *Proc. of SPPL'77*, pages 238–252, Los Angeles, California, 1977.
6. P. Cousot and R. Cousot. Abstract interpretation and application to logic programs. *The Journal of Logic Programming*, 13(1, 2, 3 and 4):103–179, 1992.
7. S. K. Debray. Abstract Interpretation and Low-Level Code Optimization. In *Proc. of PEPM'95*, pages 111–121. ACM Press, June 1995.
8. M. Ferreira. *Advanced Specialization Techniques for the Compilation of Declarative Languages* . PhD thesis, Universidade do Porto, April 2002.
9. M. Ferreira and L. Damas. Multiple specialization of WAM code. *Proc. of PADL'99,LNCS*, 1551:243–258, 1999.
10. M. Hermenegildo, R. Warren, and S. K. Debray. Global Flow Analysis as a Practical Compilation Tool. *JLP*, 13(4):349–367, August 1992.
11. D. Jacobs, A. Langen, and W. Winsborough. Multiple specialization of logic programs with run-time tests. *Proc. of ICLP'90*, pages 717–731, June 1990.
12. A. Kelly, A. Macdonald, K. Marriott, P. Stuckey, and R. Yap. Effectiveness of optimizing compilation for CLP(R). *Proc. of JICSLP'96*, pages 37–51, 1996.
13. A. King and P. Soper. Depth-k sharing and freeness. In *Proc. of the ICLP'94*, pages 553–568. The MIT Press, 1994.
14. A. Krall and T. Berger. The VAM_{AI} - an abstract machine for incremental global dataflow analysis of Prolog. In *ICLP'95 Post-Conference Workshop on Abstract Interpretation of Logic Languages*, pages 80–91, Tokyo, 1995.
15. A. Krall and U. Neumerkel. The Vienna Abstract Machine. In *Proc. of PLIP'90*, number 456 in LNCS, pages 121–135. Sweeden, Springer-Verlag, 1990.
16. Thomas Lindgren. Polyvariant detection of uninitialized arguments of Prolog predicates. *Journal of Logic Programming*, 28(3):217–229, September 1996.
17. G. Puebla and M. Hermenegildo. Implementation of Multiple Specialization in Logic Programs. In *Proc. of PEPM'95*, pages 77–87. ACM Press, June 1995.
18. Taisuke Sato and Hisao Tamaki. Enumeration of success patterns in logic programs. *Theoretical Computer Science*, 34(1–2):227–240, November 1984.
19. J. Tan and I. Lin. Compiling dataflow analysis of logic programs. In *Proc. of PLDI'92*, pages 106–115, San Francisco, California, 1992. SIGPLAN.
20. A. Taylor. Removal of Dereferencing and Trailing in Prolog Compilation. In *Proc. of ICLP'89*, pages 48–60, Lisbon, 1989. The MIT Press.
21. A. Taylor. *High Performance Prolog Implementation*. PhD thesis, University of Sydney, June 1991.
22. P. Van Roy. *Can Logic Programming Execute as Fast as Imperative Programming?* PhD thesis, University of California at Berkeley, November 1990.
23. W. H. Winsborough. Path-dependent reachability analysis for multiple specialization. In *Proc. of NACLP'89*. "MIT Press", 1989.

Garbage Collection Algorithms for Java–Based Prolog Engines

Qinan Zhou and Paul Tarau

University of North Texas, Denton, TX 76203, USA

Abstract. Implementing a Prolog Runtime System in a language like Java, which provides its own automated memory management and safety features (like built-in index checking and array initialization) requires a consistent approach to memory management based on a simple ultimate goal: minimizing total memory management time (the sum of Java's own and ours). Based on our experience with Jinni 2002 - a Java based compiled Prolog system, we analyze the existing garbage collection algorithms and propose new optimizations. In particular, we aim to have a garbage collector with least extra helper memory space yet with reasonably fast speed. Efforts are made in reducing both time and space overhead for the mark–sweep–compact algorithm. We suggest an in-place compaction algorithm and provide its implementation. As the Prolog engine uses dynamic arrays for its stacks, the impact of Java's garbage collector on the system becomes a key factor. In this context, we measure and optimize the performance of the garbage collector with the overall memory management scheme in mind.

Keywords: Implementation of Prolog, Garbage collection algorithms in the context of multiple memory managers

1 Introduction

Automatic dynamic memory allocation and reclamation has been a clear trend in new language implementations. As a program executes, it allocates memory to hold data from time to time. When some of the data such as those of localized scope have already been used and will never be used again, they are referred to as garbage. In programming languages with garbage collection, the system must be able to identify the data objects that are no longer reachable from any path of pointer trace and reclaim the occupied memory space.

Different algorithms for garbage collection have been proposed since McCarthy's work in the early 1960's [6]. Reference counting, mark–and–sweep, copying collection and generational garbage collection are among the most prominent. Each algorithm has its own advantages and disadvantages. The original mark–and–sweep algorithm is known to make several traversals of an array whose size is proportional to the entire heap. While copying collection reduces the size of the traversal, it can cause loss of segment ordering and disrupt locality of reference. Although some disadvantages are inherent to sliding algorithms, others can be minimized by clever implementation techniques, such as using a bitmap

V. Dahl and P. Wadler (Eds.): PADL 2003, LNCS 2562, pp. 304–319, 2003.

for marking bits [7]. The discussion of efficiency of garbage collection algorithms must also be placed in the context of the actual implementation of the programming language – by taking into account the following new elements: the implementation language itself might be subject to garbage collection; dynamic arrays and other "amortized" low cost data structures may be used.

2 Garbage Collection Algorithms in the Context of Jinni

Jinni 2002 is a Java based compiled Prolog system available as an online demo at http://www.binnetcorp.com/Jinni. One feature of Jinni is its ability to expand and shrink the heap at runtime. Expansion of the heap occurs when it runs out of space in building a term on the heap. Shrinking may occur when the top of the heap is reset. If the active heap is one fourth of the total heap space, then heap shrinks. Expansion of the heap is a natural way of dealing with insufficient memory space for two reasons. First, because Jinni uses Java arrays it is possible for Jinni to run out of heap space. Such an expansion is useful for another reason: Jinni doesn't check the availability of heap space when building terms on the heap. At the time it finds there is not enough storage to allocate on the heap, it is too late for the system to retreat – it will only crash if no more space is provided. Heap is implemented as an integer array, where the contents of the array can represent a constant, a pointer to another heap location, or a structure. Each index of the array represents the address of that location. During heap expansion, the current heap space is doubled. This is achieved by Java's fast C–based array copy. In this paper, the doubled heap is called the upper heap, and the original heap is called the lower heap.

Even though Java has its own garbage collector, Jinni's heap can still run out of space in program execution. Memory management is a necessity at Jinni's level in such a multi-layered system, considering total available memory resources granted for use by Jinni is largely determined by the underlying Java Virtual Machine. Moreover, Jinni's own usage of memory is determined by program constructs that it supports and is transparent to the virtual machine. So it is very difficult and impractical for Java Virtual Machine to share the responsibility of garbage collection with Jinni. In the implementation of a garbage collector for Jinni, the underlying Java Virtual Machine provides a layer of protection of resources but also poses challenges because it increases the complexity of the software as a whole and any implementation needs to take the Java Virtual Machine into account. Another challenge facing Jinni's garbage collector is when collector should be called. Jinni's heap expansion is triggered by an exception that needs instant handling. Implementation wise, this is simpler than keeping a margin to get to a safe point where garbage collection can be invoked. Calling garbage collector at heap expansion is a good choice because we have a better control of executing collector and potentially can make better use of the expanded heap. Our goal in developing the garbage collector for Jinni is to minimize both the time and space complexity in the algorithm within the context of this Java–based Prolog engine, and to make the best use of the feature of heap expansion. Each garbage collection algorithm has its pros and cons, but clever ways have been proposed to combine the advantages of those algorithms. Previous research work has demonstrated that a copying collector can achieve both linear time to the size of useful data and preservation of segment ordering [3]. But because of Jinni's feature of expansion of heap, the saving from a copying collector is offset by Java's copying of the heap and initialization of the expanded heap. Thus, for Jinni even a copying collector still needs to pay the price of heap doubling, which defeats the complexity advantage of a copying collector. For that reason, we have implemented the original mark–and–sweep algorithm and proposed optimizations for compaction of the heap. Performance studies on the time spent on garbage collection and its relative proportion to the runtime are conducted.

Among the implemented garbage collectors for Jinni, some components share common characteristics:

1. The objects in the root set are taken from the argument registers, the saved registers in the choice points and the heap cell at index 0.
2. The marking phase of the algorithm is similar in different implementations. A non–recursive depth–first search is used with the help of an explicitly declared stack. The stack is referred to as the border set, which contains the marked objects whose children may or may not have been marked. It is the boundary between marked objects whose children have also been marked and objects that have not been marked. Any objects that are reachable from the root set should also be reachable from the border set. Each marked object is pushed and popped into the border set exactly once [17].

Algorithm 1 Marking with non–recursive depth–first search

$B \leftarrow Borderset$
while B is not empty **do**
  $r \leftarrow B.pop()$
  if r is variable **then**
    if r is not marked **then**
      mark r as a live object
      $v \leftarrow dereference(r)$
      if v is a variable **then**
        $B.push()$
      else if v is a compound term **then**
        for i=1 to arity of v **do**
          if (r+i) is unmarked **then**
            $B.push(r + i)$
          end if
        end for
      end if
    end if
  end if
end while

---

3. After the heap has been garbage collected, the argument registers, registers in the choice points and the registers on the trail stack all need to be updated. It is possible that the registers in the trail are already pointing to dead objects by the time they need to be updated. Thus those registers themselves are not included in the root set. If the values in the trail registers are not marked as live, they are updated as pointing to the heap index 0 because heap cell at index 0 is not used by the running program and can be a valid value to indicate the unusefulness of that cell.

2.1   A Simple Multi–pass Sliding Garbage Collection Algorithm

We first implemented a simple multi–pass mark–and–sweep algorithm in Jinni. Instead of using the tag associated with each cell as a marker, we use a separate Boolean array to record the marked cell information. Initially, the Boolean array is as big as the active heap itself, with each index corresponding to the index of the heap. Whenever a live cell is found, we set the Boolean value corresponding to that cell as true. After marking is finished we are left with an array of Boolean values that stores information about the location of live cells. The algorithm requires three passes of the heap – the first one traverses the entire active heap and finds the live objects that correspond to the indices in the Boolean array. At the time garbage collection is called, the heap has already been doubled. Therefore we make use of the doubled heap area by copying the marked cells to upper heap and set the forward links from the old cells to the copied new cells for all data types. This step is equivalent to adding the unmarked cells to a list of free nodes in the traditional sweeping phase. By copying the marked cells to the upper heap, however, we eliminate the disadvantage of the fragmentation. Variables in the new cells still point to the old objects, so we need an additional pass to redirect the new variables to point to where they should be by following the pointers stored in the old cells. At this stage, the upper heap contains the relocated and updated live cells. Finally the cells on the upper heap are slid back to the lower heap and the heap top is reset.

In this algorithm, we make one pass of the entire heap, and two additional passes of the marked cells. It has time complexity of $O(n)$, n being the size of the active heap. The worst case is when most of the heap is populated with live cells, then it is close to making three passes of the entire heap. The Boolean array created for the marking phase has size proportional to the entire heap. To ensure fast lookup, the Boolean array constitutes one–to–one mapping with the cells on the heap. That array is used solely for marking which cell is a live object so it is not needed later in the sweeping phase. Although the array is set to NULL after the first pass of the heap is completed, there is no guarantee that the memory space occupied by this array is freed immediately. This is because it is not clear to us whether Java's own garbage collector will reclaim the space at that point.

2.2   An Optimized Two–Pass Algorithm

The traditional mark-sweep–compact algorithm is easy to understand and implement. However, it also has the disadvantages of creating overhead in terms of both time and space. It would be more desirable to make fewer passes of the heap and use less extra space. Obviously the algorithm described above has a few places that can be optimized.

One pass of the marked objects can be saved if we have another separate array to store the forwarding pointers. A separate integer array can be created which stores the updated addresses of all the marked objects. Such an array would be as large as the entire active heap to make updating the pointers constant time.

A major difference between the optimized two–pass algorithm and the previous multi–pass algorithm is the usage of the upper heap. With the help of an allocation array, the lower heap is untouched during the first pass in the sweep – the forwarding pointers are recorded on the allocation array while the upper heap is used temporarily to store the locations of marked objects. The second sweep therefore traverses the marked objects only based on the information in the upper heap. So this algorithm incorporates an update–before–copy policy. In contrast, the multi–pass algorithm suggested previously applies an update–after–copy policy. In the previous algorithm the marked live objects are copied to the upper heap first and then updated, so they need to be slid back to the old heap space.

2.3   One–Pass Optimized Algorithm

The previous two algorithms, although traversing the heap different number of times, share some features in common:

1. Both of them use the upper heap. Multi–pass compaction uses the upper heap to temporarily store the copied objects and use the lower heap for forwarding purposes. Two–pass compaction uses the upper heap for no purposes other than storing the copied objects (without updating forwarding pointers). In both algorithms, the upper heap is used only to the extent of the marked objects, so most of the doubled heap space is still in an unused state because a) the marked objects are not always as many as the whole heap. In some extreme cases, the live objects only take up 10 % or less of the heap space. b) Only a very small amount of the doubled space is used for building the terms that would otherwise not fit the original heap.

2. A marked Boolean array is used in the marking process to record the marked cell indices. Implementation–wise, it is not most efficient to use a Boolean array in Java for the purpose of marking. Theoretically one bit to store such information for one cell is sufficient. But even bit arrays take up additional memory space noticeably when the heap becomes large. Another solution is to use the expanded upper heap for the purpose of marking. The upper heap should provide enough space to hold all the marking information because the heap space is just doubled before garbage collection. All that's needed

is to add an offset to the heap index which is marked live. The offset value can be obtained by finding the top of the heap at the used heap space. As a matter of fact, the upper heap space can be used both for marking and pointer updating purposes. The only challenge is to differentiate between the liveness mark and the updated index. This leads to most efficient use of the dynamic heap and the doubled space in garbage collection, because mark–and–sweep now doesn't incur extra space in Jinni.

3. Although the second algorithm makes one pass fewer than the first one, it is still not optimal because an additional loop adds the overhead of setting up loop counters and initializing registers for the compiler. It is thus desirable to combine the two traverses of the heap into a single pass.

In the next algorithm that we propose for sweep–and–compact phase, we do in fact make use of the upper heap both for the purpose of marking and updating forwarding pointers. In addition, we combine the two processes into a single traversal of the active heap. As in previous cases, the heap is divided into two parts: the lower and the upper heap. The lower heap ranges from 0 to where the current heap top points to, which represents the active heap in use. The upper heap starts from one cell above the used heap to the maximum size allowed for the heap. This portion is a result of heap expansion. The upper heap contains an updated "image" of the lower heap after marking and updating. During the marking phase, all the live cells are marked -1 in the upper heap. The reason to mark it as -1 is to not confuse it later with forwarding pointers, since no forwarding pointers will contain -1. Marking with -1 is safe also because no cell can have an actual value of -1. Doubling of the heap space initializes the upper heap cell to 0, so live cells are necessarily non–zero in the upper heap.

To compact all the live cells in a single pass, it is necessary to update the pointers in the cells in place – i.e. updating should happen at the time compaction takes place. Two situations can occur in this phase. A cell can refer to another with either higher or lower index. In the case of referring to lower-indexed cell, updating the pointers poses no difficulty because the new index of the cell pointed to is already recorded on the upper heap – all it needs to do is to refer to the upper heap and get the updated index. If a cell is referring to another one with higher heap index, then the pointer cannot be updated right away until the cell pointed to is encountered.

In Fig.1 which represents a hypothetical heap structure, cell 18 contains a reference to cell 26. Since the new address of cell 26 is not known yet, a mechanism to defer the update until necessary is incorporated. The content in the location corresponding to 26 in the upper heap is replaced with the updated index of cell 18 (Since 26 is on the reachability graph, the location should be already marked as -1). When cell 26 is ready to be copied, its content in the upper heap is first checked. In this case we know it contains a forwarding pointer from the new location of cell 18 on the old heap. At this moment the new index for cell 26 can be computed and previous references to that cell can be updated.

Another situation may arise when multiple cells all refer to the same cell in the higher heap index. Based upon the mechanism just described, it is technically

---

Algorithm 2 One–pass compaction of the heap

---

int dest ← 0
OFFSET ← *heap.getUsed()*
for *i* ← 0 to *OFFSET* **do**
  if heap[i] is live or is a forwarding pointer **then**
    ref ← *i*
    val ← *dereference(ref)*
    if val is a variable **then**
      if val < ref **then**
        val ← *heap[OFFSET + val]*
      else if val > ref **then**
        set new ref on the upper heap
      else
        heap[OFFSET + val] ← *dest*
      end if
    else
      val ← *dest*
    end if
    if heap[OFFSET+i]>0 **then**
      update forwarding pointers
    end if
    heap[OFFSET + i] ← *dest*
    heap[dest] ← *val*
    increment dest
  end if
end for

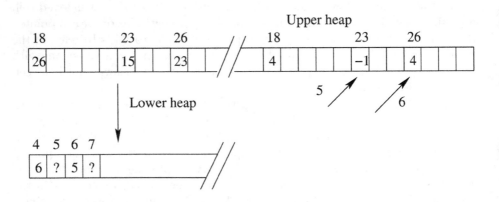

Fig. 1. The hypothetical upper and lower heap

impossible to store multiple heap locations in one place. To solve this problem, reference chaining is used.

As illustrated in Fig.2, heap cells 18, 20 and 23 all refer to heap cell 26 originally. Since three different cells refer to the same heap location, cell 20 is encountered before the new index of cell 26 can be updated for cell 18. At this stage, a reference chain is created by replacing the content of cell 18 at the new location with the updated heap index of cell 20 and making cell 20 point to cell 26. Such a chain is extended until cell 26, when the end of the traversal is reached. Heap contents at the previous locations no longer directly refer to the cell as they used to before updating – they must instead go through a reference chain. After cell 26 is reached, it goes back to cell 18 and traces the reference chain to update all the cells to point to the new location of cell 26. Now that we have covered reference in both situations, we will be able to compact the marked cells and update the references at the same time. Compaction of the cells also happens in the lower heap. Once a cell is moved to the next available index, whatever is left in that index is overwritten later. Data integrity would be preserved because there is no danger of overwriting the content of that heap index. The content there has already been copied and compacted to lower heap index if that cell is determined to be live.

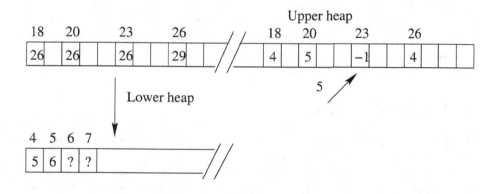

Fig. 2. The hypothetical upper and lower heap with multiple forwarding pointers pointing to one heap location

One observation of the heap requires a slight modification of the management of the dynamic allocation. Since this algorithm must use the full upper heap for both marking and updating purposes, the upper heap needs to be made at least as large as the lower heap. If the heap is doubled due to lack of space to build terms, it becomes possible that even after doubling the upper heap is ten to hundreds of cells fewer than the lower heap. This is undesirable because if the cells at the end of the lower heap are determined to be live, then there is no place to mark these cells on the upper heap – which calls for another expansion.

However, another expansion is costly at this stage, because the expanded heap is used only temporarily but then must shrink again. In addition, after each expansion, the next expansion would take twice as much time as the previous one since the number of cells to copy is doubled. To solve this problem, expansion of the heap always doubles the current space plus a constant number of cells. This constant is set to 8192 in the actual implementation, which is a generous value for what is needed during the expansion time and garbage collection time. This always happens within one clause to be executed and usually one clause cannot consume more heap than its own size as a term. This makes the expanded heap much less likely to be short of space for marking and updating. In the actual implementation, a check of available space is also inserted before the marking phase.

3 Implementation

For Jinni, we implemented three versions of garbage collector, all of which are mark–sweep–compact algorithm with different number of passes of the entire heap and different requirement for extra helper space. The garbage collector is wrapped in a separate class file called JinniGC.java. A call to garbage collector is invoked in the Machine.java. This call in turn creates an object of JinniGC and calls the collect() method of the object. The collect() method wraps all phases of garbage collector. In different phases of garbage collection, we inserted statements that print out the statistics of the runtime system. This is to help us evaluate the overall performance of the algorithms and in the context of memory management in Jinni.

4 Empirical Evaluation

When evaluating these algorithms, we measured their performance in relation with the total runtime of the Prolog system.

Theoretically, mark–sweep–compact is not newly proposed algorithm. In these implementations we make it specifically suitable for our Prolog system. We tested a wide range of benchmark programs on these implementations: allperms.pl(permutation benchmark with findall), boyer.pl(Boyer benchmark), choice.pl(choice–intensive ECRC benchmark), tsp.pl(traveling salesman benchmark), qsort(quick sort benchmark), tak.pl(tak benchmark), maxlist.pl(maximun value of a list benchmark), bfmeta.pl(breadth first metainterpreter). A separate program bm.pl combines all the above testing programs as one.

It is worth pointing out that some Prolog programs are written specifically for testing the garbage collector. Program gc.pl, for instance is one that continues to generate useless data during its execution.

For performance measurement, these same programs are run on the different implementations. Performance is measured on a cluster of Pentium II 800MHz PCs running Debian Linux. In particular, we measured the time consumption of garbage collection, the expand/shrink operation of the dynamic heap and total runtime of the Prolog engine for the benchmarks in 10 separate batches, each representing an average of 10 experiments. This is a valid approach because we want to measure how much time is spent on garbage collection and related operations in comparison with the total execution time. A comparison of such measurement is illustrated in Table 1.

Table 1. Comparison of time spent on Garbage collection and Expand/Shrink (E/S). Time is measured in milliseconds.

No.	One–pass sweep			Multi–pass sweep		
	GC time	E/S time	total	GC time	E/S time	total
1	8746	16305	154059	9471	14026	151661
2	8756	16014	154490	9456	14162	153477
3	8740	16214	156690	9466	14193	151931
4	8741	15984	152345	9463	14207	149997
5	8766	16242	152225	9446	14068	150304
6	8739	16110	151779	9424	13731	150261
7	8744	16284	153288	9905	13694	149856
8	8737	16303	151631	9451	14215	150045
9	8766	16040	158502	9458	13994	154409
10	8749	16158	151383	9441	14067	149922

The time spent on garbage collection and expand/shrink is measured both in the one–pass and multi–pass algorithm. On average the time spent on GC in the one–pass algorithm is 8 % less than the multi–pass compaction. The time spent on expanding and shrinking heap space is 15 % more in the one–pass compaction. This can be caused by two reasons: 1) one–pass algorithm, when expanding the heap, already more than doubles the heap by a constant number of cells. 2) Even when heap is more than doubled, some programs still need more upper heap area for marking – which causes the heap to be expanded again. In spite of that, it is interesting to note the increased performance in the actual time it spends on collecting the heap space.

Because bm.pl wraps all the programs, it is hard to tell by the table above which program is making a difference between the two implementations. We thus measured each benchmark separately and recorded the number of times garbage collector is called and the time it spent collecting garbage in each program. Each cell in Table 2 is represented as the total time of garbage collection with the number of calls to the garbage collection in the parenthesis.

As is shown in Table 2, most programs take less time in garbage collection in the one–pass algorithm than the others. It takes progressively more time to collect garbage when the number of passes of the heap increases. The code statements in the program enable us to see a breakdown of the time spent on each call of garbage collection.

Table 2. Time spent on garbage collection for selected programs

Program	One–pass (ms)	Two–pass (ms)	Multi–pass (ms)
boyer	1420(34)	1519(34)	1690(34)
tsp	411(3)	475(3)	495(3)
tak	1325(172)	1095(172)	1105(172)
allperms	2029(8)	2239(8)	2587(8)
bfmeta	17(2)	20(2)	47(2)
choice	4459(5)	4303(5)	4692(5)
maxlist	174(2)	216(2)	331(2)
qsort	41(2)	50(2)	44(2)

Program allperms.pl is a permutation benchmark. Subtables 1, 2 and 3 in Table 3 record the heap usage, reclaimed memory space and garbage collection time for one–pass, two–pass and multi–pass algorithms, respectively. Garbage collector is called 8 times in each implementation. In the first four calls, it is obvious that a pattern of heap space usage exists. After each garbage collection, the number of heap cells is doubled because the number of live cells doubles, and the garbage collected in each collection is also doubled. In the third garbage collection, the one–pass compaction appears to be faster than the other two, especially than the multi–pass compaction because it does less work in the compaction phase as a whole. This suggests that one–pass of the heap could save time on sweeping when the number of live objects gets large, as shown in Fig.3.

Table 3. Statistics of allperms.pl for various implementations

allperms.pl one–pass implementation								
	1st	2nd	3rd	4th	5th	6th	7th	8th
Heap	65538	139265	286734	581634	65555	139277	286739	581640
Reclaimed	23690	33496	55874	127047	23644	33476	55873	127069
Freed	97416	180951	350772	716869	97353	180919	350766	716885
Time (ms)	56	129	280	549	53	128	290	551
allperms.pl two–pass implementation								
Heap	65538	131075	262147	524291	65555	131074	262157	524294
Reclaimed	23690	32236	47769	112258	23644	32214	47770	112258
Freed	89224	163305	309910	636543	89161	163284	309901	636540
Time (ms)	58	128	318	601	55	129	317	600
allperms.pl multi–pass implementation								
Heap	65538	131074	262146	524290	65555	131073	262156	524293
Reclaimed	23691	32236	47769	112258	23645	32214	47770	112258
Freed	89225	163306	309911	636544	89162	163285	309902	636541
Time (ms)	73	163	353	676	69	162	353	687

In another example, the program maxlist.pl displays an extreme pattern of heap usage. As shown in Table 4 and Fig.4 for the one–pass compaction, the

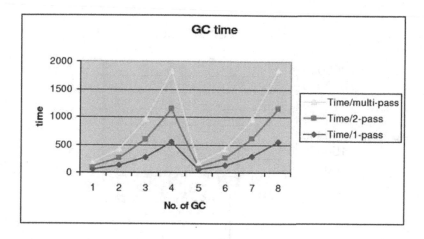

Fig. 3. Garbage collection time of allperms.pl in different implementations. Time axis is scaled to display difference among three collections.

Table 4. Statistics of maxlist.pl for all three implementations

	One–pass		Two–pass		Multi–pass	
	1st	2nd	1st	2nd	1st	2nd
Heap	65538	139266	65538	131073	65538	131075
Reclaimed	72	0	72	0	73	0
Freed	73798	147454	65606	393215	65607	393213
Time (ms)	78	175	84	217	95	235

second garbage collection shows that all the cells on the heap are live data – no data is collected from the heap. Also shown in the comparison is the difference of the freed cells in the second invocation of garbage collection across three implementations. The number of freed cells almost tripled in the two–pass and multi–pass compaction phase due to an additional expansion. That expansion was necessary because the number of live cells is greater than the free space in the upper heap and the upper heap should at least be able to outnumber the live cells in those two algorithms. The same expansion was unnecessary for the one–pass algorithm because the heap was already more than doubled in the first place. Interestingly, however, for two–pass and multi–pass algorithms, it is unnecessary to more than double the heap space in each heap expansion because most of the time garbage collection only uses a small portion of the heap. Overdoubling would only waste more space. This suggests that it is good to more than double the heap in the one–pass implementation, because the entire upper heap is in use to save extra space. From Table 4, although the heap space is doubled between every garbage collection, the heap may have been shrunken and then re–expanded.

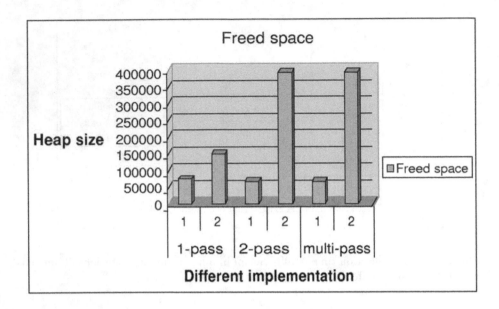

Fig. 4. Heap space wasted in extreme situations

A comparison of garbage collection efficiency needs to take into account additional features of the programming language that implements a garbage collector. It is true that a copying collector is proportional to the size of the live data, but in the Jinni system, the price of time complexity of a simple mark–sweep–compact is already paid by doubling of the heap space. This makes mark–sweep–compact theoretically as good as copying collection, because the expansion of the heap already copies everything (including garbage) on the heap, and this expansion offsets the advantage of the copying collection. If the heap was not made dynamic – thus unable to expand or shrink when needed, then Java's own array boundary check would throw an exception and in turn stop the machine. However, the amount and frequency of the heap shrinking is interesting to observe. Obviously the less frequently it shrinks, the less frequently it needs to be re–expanded. This is especially helpful for the runtime system such as the one in running the allperms.pl program, when the amount of live data and total amount of data grow progressively.

Among the three compaction methods introduced in the paper, although there is difference in running time, the time spent on garbage collection doesn't exceed 10 % of the total execution time. This shows that the cost of memory management in Jinni is dominated by dynamic heap management but not GC. Combining this data with previous measuring of time and space consumption, it suggests that our algorithms for garbage collection and the compaction phase of mark–and–sweep have served our initial goal, while keeping themselves simpler for implementation than a copying collector.

5   Future Work

An adaptive algorithm was recently suggested [17], where it selects different marking strategies depending on the number of live objects. Based on their measurement, marking with sorting when the live cells are significantly less than the active heap takes much less time than marking without sorting. Such sorting enables the sweep phase to take time proportional to the live data instead of the entire heap. This scheme is thus partially dependent on the particular memory usage of a program. However, a user might need to run programs that all generate a lot of garbage or that don't generate much garbage (at least above the threshold where it decides to not sort). It is hard and unreasonable to predict what kind of programs or their memory usage pattern will be run on a particular Prolog engine. Thus a fundamental improvement of the mark–sweep–compact collector would be to minimize the sweeping of dead objects in all situations. Generational garbage collector is successful in this sense because it only chooses to collect part of the heap anytime when there is a difference in generation. Such an algorithm is independent on the program that runs on the abstract machine. Thus the algorithm in itself is consistent across all the programs.

When analyzing the heap usage pattern for particular Prolog programs, it is interesting to notice the specific heap usage patterns each program displays. Some programs, such as boyer.pl and gc.pl use a particular region of the heap consistently during runtime. In boyer.pl, the front of the heap is saturated with live objects during runtime, whereas other areas are less populated with live data as the first few hundred/thousand heap locations. It becomes obvious that it is unnecessary to loop through those live·data again without even moving them to a different location. Based on this observation, an algorithm that takes advantage of the heap usage can be designed to only collect the region with most garbage. It still requires marking, however, to find out the pattern of heap usage. But marking live objects itself is a cheap operation compared with the sweeping process. Such a scheme marks the live data as general mark–and–sweep algorithm does. The heap can be divided into areas of blocks of cells and the number of marked cells in each block is polled. If the number exceeds a threshold then data objects in that particular block need not be collected because most of the data are useful objects. Otherwise the data objects are swept and compacted. It doesn't make a specific choice of what algorithm or policy to use under different heap usage patterns and is thus not dependent on specific programs for the algorithm to work. Before such a scheme can be implemented, it must answer similar questions a generational garbage collector needs to: it has to make sure all pointers are updated correctly via a certain mechanism, both for the collected and uncollected blocks. Other implementation details to be solved for this scheme are to avoid fragmentation between blocks and use least extra space, if any.

6   Conclusion

Based on the evaluation shown above, we are able to see the difference among the three compaction algorithms. One–pass algorithm uses the least amount of space and also displays advantage in collection time when the heap becomes large. A similar algorithm was proposed in the 1970's [18], except in that algorithm updating the pointers need to be performed from both ends of the heap one at a time, which effectively increases the number of traversals of the heap. Slightly more than doubling the heap also avoids the need to redouble the heap during garbage collection especially when the whole heap is populated with live cells. More than doubling is not necessarily good in multi–pass and two–pass compaction because the upper heap is partially used most of the time in those algorithms. It is thus an overkill for the heap to be more than doubled in those cases.

Jinni's dynamically–allocated heap serves as a good mechanism for memory management. The expanded heap in our one–pass algorithm is solely used for marking and updating the pointer references thus to avoid any other extra memory space usage. This expansion also keeps the machine from crashing because at the time heap overflow exception is caught, the machine is not ready for garbage collection yet but cannot retreat either. In this sense, heap expansion has served multiple purposes both for the Prolog runtime system and for garbage collection. In conclusion, we have made the best use of the dynamic heap to waste the least amount of space in garbage collection, and the one–pass algorithm achieves our initial goal of minimizing the space overhead while maintaining a speed overhead at least as good as the traditional mark–sweep–compact algorithm.

Acknowledgements. The authors wish to thank Jeff Barrett for his participation in the discussions and his help in proofreading this paper.

References

[1] Sterling,Leon, Ehud Shapiro. "The Art of Prolog." *The MIT Press.* 1999.

[2] Appleby, Karen, Mats Carlsson, Seif Haridi, Dan Sahlin. "Garbage Collection for Prolog Based on WAM." *Communications of the ACM.* 31(6):719–741, 1998.

[3] Demoen,Bart, Geert Engels, Paul Tarau. "Segment Order Preserving Copying Garbage Collection for WAM Based Prolog." *Proceedings of the 1996 ACM Symposium on Applied Computing.* 380–386,1996.

[4] Zorn, Benjamin. "Comparing mark-and-sweep and Stop-and-copy Garbage Collection." *Communications of ACM* 1990

[5] Cheney, C.J. "A nonrecursive list compacting algorithm." *Communications of the ACM* 13(11) 677–678, 1970

[6] McCarthy, John. "Recursive functions for symbolic expressions and their computations by machine, part I." *Communications of the ACM* 3(4) 184–195, 1960

[7] Wilson, Paul. "Uniprocessor Garbage Collection Techniques." *Proceedings of the 1992 International Workshop on Memory Management.* 1992.

[8] Appel, Andrew. "Simple Generational Garbage Collection and Fast Allocation." *Software – Practice and Experience.* 19(2) 171–183, 1989.

[9] Cohen, Jacques. "Garbage Collection of Linked Data Structure." *Computing Surveys* 13(3) 341–367, 1981.

[10] Bevemyr, Johan, Thomas Lindgren. "A Simple and Efficient Copying Garbage Collector for Prolog." *Lecture Notes on Computer Science* 1994.

[11] Lieberman, Henry, Carl Hewitt. "A real-time garbage collector based on the life-times of objects." *Communications of the ACM* 26(6): 419–429, 1983

[12] Greenblatt, Richard. "The LISP machine." *Interactive Programming Environments* McCraw Hill, 1984.

[13] Courts, Robert. "Improving locality of reference in a garbage-collecting memory management system." *Communications of the ACM* 31(9):1128–1138. 1988

[14] Ungar, David. "Generation scavenging: A non–disruptive high–performance storage reclamation algorithm." *ACM SIGSOFT/SIGPLAN Software Engineering Symposium on Practical Software Development Environments* 157–167, 1984.

[15] Ungar, David, Frank Jackson. "Tenuring policies for generation–based storage reclamation." *ACM SIGPLAN Conference on Object Oriented Programming System, Languages and Application* 1988

[16] Ait-Kaci, H. "Warren's Abstract Machine: A tutorial Reconstruction." *The MIT Press* 1999

[17] Sahlin, Dan, Y.C.Chung, S.M.Moon, K.Ebcioglu. "Reducing sweep time for a nearly empty heap." *Symposium on Principles of Programming Languages* 378–389, 2000

[18] Morris, F.Lockwood. "A Time– and Space– Efficient Garbage Compaction Algorithm" *Communications of the ACM* 21(8):662–665. 1978

[19] Tarau, Paul. " Inference and Computation Mobility with Jinni." *The Logic Programming Paradigm: a 25 Year Perspective* 33–48, 1999

[20] Tarau, Paul, Veronica Dahl. "High-Level Networking with Mobile Code and First Order AND-Continuations." *Theory and Practice of Logic Programming* 1(1), March 2001. Cambridge University Press.

[21] Tyagi, Satyam, Paul Tarau. "Multicast Protocols for Jinni Agents." *Proceedings of CL2000 Workshop on Parallelism and Implementation Technology for (Constraint) Logic Programming* London, UK, June 2000.

[22] Tarau, Paul. "Intelligent Mobile Agent Programming at the Intersection of Java and Prolog." *Proceedings of The Fourth International Conference on The Practical Application of Intelligent Agents and Multi-Agents* 109–123, London, U.K., 1999.

[23] Tarau, Paul, Ulrich Neumerkel. "A Novel Term Compression Scheme and Data Representation in the BinWAM." *Proceedings of Programming Language Implementation and Logic Programming, Lecture Notes in Computer Science* 844, 73–87.September 1994.

Solving Combinatorial Problems with a Constraint Functional Logic Language

Antonio J. Fernández[1], Teresa Hortalá-González[2], and Fernando Sáenz-Pérez[2]

[1] Depto. de Lenguajes y Ciencias de la Computación, Universidad de Málaga,
Spain[* * *]
[2] Depto. de Sistemas Informáticos y Programación Universidad Complutense de
Madrid, Spain[†]
afdez@lcc.uma.es, {teresa,fernan}@sip.ucm.es

Abstract. This paper describes a proposal to incorporate finite domain constraints in a functional logic system. The proposal integrates functions, higher-order patterns, partial applications, non-determinism, logical variables, currying, types, lazyness, domain variables, constraints and finite domain propagators.

The paper also presents TOY(FD), an extension of the functional logic language TOY that provides FD constraints, and shows, by examples, that TOY(FD) combines the power of constraint logic programming with the higher-order characteristics of functional logic programming.

Keywords: Constraints, Functional Logic Programming, Finite Domains.

1 Introduction

Constraint logic programming (CLP) emerged recently to increase both the expressiveness and efficiency of logic programming (LP) [8]. The basic idea in CLP consists of replacing the classical LP unification by constraint solving on a given computation domain. Among the domains for CLP, the finite domain (FD) [11] is one of the most and best studied since it is a suitable framework for solving discrete constraint satisfaction problems.

Unfortunately, literature lacks proposals to integrate FD constraints in functional programming (FP). This seems to be caused by the relational nature of FD constraints that do not fit well in FP. To overcome this limitation we consider a functional logic programming (FLP) setting [7] and integrate FD constraints in the FLP language TOY [9] giving rise to CFLP(FD) (i.e., constraint functional logic programming over finite domains).

This paper describes, to our knowledge, the first FLP system that completely incorporates FD constraints. The main contribution then is to show how

* * * Fernández was partially supported by the projects TIC2001-2705-C03-02 and TIC2002-04498-C05-02 funded by the Spanish Ministry of Science and Technology.
† Hortalá-González and Fernando Sáenz-Pérez were supported by the Spanish project PR 48/01-9901 funded by UCM.

V. Dahl and P. Wadler (Eds.): PADL 2003, LNCS 2562, pp. 320–338, 2003.

to apply FD constraints to a functional logic language. We believe that our proposal has many advantages and considerable potential since it benefits from both the logical and functional settings and the constraint framework, by first taking functions, higher-order patterns, partial applications, non-determinism, logical variables, currying, function composition, types and lazy evaluation from functional logic programming, and, second, domain variables, constraints and efficient propagators from finite domain constraint programming.

The paper is structured as follows. Section 2 presents a formalization for CFLP(FD). Section 3 describes briefly TOY(FD), an implementation of a CFLP(FD) system, whereas Section 4 shows several examples of programming in TOY(FD). Then, Section 5 discusses some related work and, Section 6 develops a performance comparison with related systems. Finally, the paper ends with some indications for further research and some conclusions.

2   CFLP(FD) Programs

This section presents, by following the formalization given in [6], the basics about syntax, type discipline, and declarative semantics of CFLP(FD) programs.

2.1   CFLP(FD) Fundamental Concepts

Types and Signatures: We assume a countable set $TVar$ of *type variables* α, β, ... and a countable ranked alphabet $TC = \bigcup_{n \in \mathbb{N}} TC^n$ of *type constructors* $C \in TC^n$. Types $\tau \in Type$ have the syntax

$$\tau ::= \alpha \quad | \ C \ \tau_1 \ldots \tau_n \quad | \ \tau \to \tau' \ | \ (\tau_1, \ldots, \tau_n)$$

By convention, $C \ \overline{\tau}_n$ abbreviates $C \ \tau_1 \ldots \tau_n$, "$\to$" associates to the right, $\overline{\tau}_n \to \tau$ abbreviates $\tau_1 \to \cdots \to \tau_n \to \tau$, and the set of type variables occurring in τ is written $tvar(\tau)$. A type without any occurrence of "$\to$" is called a *datatype*. The type $(\tau_1, \ldots, \tau_n)$ is intended to denote n-tuples. FD variables are integer variables. A *signature* over TC is a triple $\Sigma = \langle TC, \ DC, \ FS \rangle$, where $DC = \bigcup_{n \in \mathbb{N}} DC^n$ and $FS = \bigcup_{n \in \mathbb{N}} FS^n$ are ranked sets of *data constructors* resp. *defined function symbols*. Each n-ary $c \in DC^n$ comes with a principal type declaration $c :: \overline{\tau}_n \to C \ \overline{\alpha}_k$, where $n, k \geq 0, \alpha_1, \ldots, \alpha_k$ are pairwise different, τ_i are datatypes, and $tvar(\tau_i) \subseteq \{\alpha_1, \ldots, \alpha_k\}$ for all $1 \leq i \leq n$. Also, every n-ary $f \in FS^n$ comes with a principal type declaration $f :: \overline{\tau}_n \to \tau$, where τ_i, τ are arbitrary types. In practice, each CFLP(FD) program P has a signature which corresponds to the type declarations occurring in P. For any signature Σ, we write $\Sigma_\perp$ for the result of extending Σ with a new data constructor $\perp :: \alpha$, intended to represent an undefined value that belongs to every type. As notational conventions, we use $c \in DC$, $f, g \in FS$ and $h \in DC \cup FS$.

FD constraints: A *FD constraint* is a primitive function declared with type either

Table 1. Datatypes for FD Constraints

data labelType = ff | ffc | leftmost | mini | maxi | step | enum | bisect | up
| down | all | toMinimize int | toMaximize int | assumptions int
data statistics = resumptions | entailments | prunings | backtracks | constraints
data reasoning = value | domains | range
data options = on reasoning | complete bool
data typeprecedence = d (int,int,int)
data newOptions = precedences [typeprecedence] | path_consistency bool
| static_sets bool | edge_finder bool | decomposition bool

Table 2. Some FD Constraints in TOY(FD)

RELATIONAL	ARITHMETICAL
(#>) :: int → int → bool	(#*) :: int → int → int
(#<) :: int → int → bool	(#/) :: int → int → int
(#>=) :: int → int → bool	(#+) :: int → int → int
(#<=) :: int → int → bool	(#−) :: int → int → int
(# =) :: int → int → bool	sum :: [int] → (int → int → bool) → int → bool
(#\=) :: int → int → bool	scalar_product :: [int] → [int]
	→ (int → int → bool) → int → bool

COMBINATORIAL	
assignment :: [int] → [int] → bool	all_different :: [int] → bool
circuit :: [int] → bool	all_different' :: [int] → [options] → bool
circuit' :: [int] → [int] → bool	serialized :: [int] → [int] → bool
all_distinct :: [int] → bool	serialized' :: [int] → [int] → [newOptions] → bool
all_distinct' :: [int]→[options]→bool	cumulative :: [int] → [int] → [int] → int → bool
exactly :: int → [int] → int → bool	cumulative' :: [int] → [int] → [int] → int
element :: int → [int] → int → bool	→ [newOptions] → bool
	count :: int → [int] → (int → int → bool)
	→ int → bool

MEMBERSHIP
domain :: [int] → int → int → bool

ENUMERATION	STATISTICS
labeling :: [labelType]→[int]→bool	fd_statistics :: statistics → int → bool
indomain :: int → bool	fd_statistics' :: bool

- int → int → int to transform pairs of FD variables into FD variables, or
- $\overline{\tau}_n$ → bool such that for all τ_i in $\overline{\tau}_n$, $\tau_i \in Type_{FD}$ and $Type_{FD} \subset Type$ is

$$Type_{FD} = \{ \text{ int}, [\text{int}], [\text{labelType}], \text{statistics},$$
$$(\text{int} \rightarrow \text{int} \rightarrow \text{bool}), [\text{options}], [\text{newOptions}] \}.$$

int is a predefined type for integers, and [τ] is the type 'list of τ'. The datatypes labelType, statistics, options and newOptions are predefined types and their complete definitions are shown in Table 1.

Some FD constraints supported in our language are shown in Table 2. Examples of the first sort of constraints are the arithmetic functions #+, #−, #∗ and #/. Examples of the second sort of constraints are the relations #<, and #> as well as the functions all_distinct'/2, and labeling/2.

In the rest of the section, $FS_{FD} \subset FS^n$ denotes the set of FD constraints that return a Boolean value.

In CFLP(FD), functions (e.g., constraints) are first-class citizens, which means that a function can appear in any place where a data can. As a direct consequence, a FD constraint may appear as an argument (or even as a result) of another function or constraint. The functions managing other functions are called *higher-order (HO) functions*. As examples of HO constraints, look at the FD constraints sum/3, scalar_product/4 and count/4 in Table 2. These constraints accept a FD constraint of type int → int → bool (e.g., #<, or #>) as argument.

Expressions and Patterns: In the sequel, we always assume a given signature Σ, often not made explicit in the notation. Assuming a countable set Var of (data) variables $X, Y, \ldots$ disjoint from $TVar$ and Σ, *partial expressions* $e \in Exp_\perp$ have the syntax

$$e ::= \perp \mid X \mid h \mid e\, e' \mid (e_1,\, \ldots,\, e_n)$$

where $X \in Var$, $h \in DC \cup FS$. Expressions of the form $e\, e'$ stand for the application of expression e (playing as a function) to expression e' (playing as an argument), while expressions $(e_1, \ldots, e_n)$ represent tuples with n components. As usual, we assume that application associates to the left and thus $e_0\, e_1 \ldots\, e_n$ abbreviates $(\ldots (e_0\ e_1) \ldots)\ e_n$. The set of data variables occurring in e is written $var(e)$.

An expression e is called *linear* iff every $X \in var(e)$ has one single occurrence in e. An expression e is in *head normal form* iff e is a variable X or has the form $c(\bar{e}_n)$ for some data constructor $c \in DC^n$ $(n \geq 0)$ and some n-tuple of expressions $\bar{e}_n = (e_1,\, \ldots,\, e_n)$ where e_i is in head normal form.

Partial patterns $t \in Pat_\perp \subset Exp_\perp$ are built as

$$t ::= \perp \mid X \mid c\, t_1 \ldots t_m \mid f\, t_1 \ldots t_m$$

where $X \in Var$, $c \in DC^k$, $0 \leq m \leq k$, $f \in FS^n$, $0 \leq m < n$ and $t_i \in Pat_\perp$ for all $1 \leq i \leq m$. They represent *approximations* of the values of expressions. Partial patterns of the form $f\, t_1 \ldots t_m$ with $f \in FS^n$ and $m < n$ serve as a convenient representation of functions as values [6]; therefore functions becoming first-class citizens of the language. Expressions and patterns without any occurrence of $\perp$ are called *total*. The sets of total expressions and patterns are denoted, respectively, by Exp and Pat. Actually, the symbol $\perp$ never occurs in a program's text.

Substitutions: A *substitution* is a mapping $\theta : Var \to Pat$ with a unique extension $\hat{\theta} : Exp \to Exp$, which is also denoted as θ. As usual, $\theta = \{X_1 \mapsto t_1, \ldots, X_n \mapsto t_n\}$ stands for the substitution with domain $\{X_1, \ldots, X_n\}$ which satisfies $\theta(X_i) = t_i$ for all $1 \leq i \leq n$. *Subst* denotes the set of all variable substitutions.

Up to this point we have considered *data substitutions*. *Type substitutions* can be defined similarly, as mappings $\theta_t : TVar \to Type$ with a unique extension $\hat{\theta}_t :$ $Type \to Type$, also denoted θ_t. *TSubst* denotes the set of all type substitutions.

Finite Domains: A *finite domain* (FD) is a mapping $\delta : Var \to \wp(Integer)$ (as usual $\wp(C)$ denotes the powerset of the set C), with a unique extension $\hat{\delta} : Exp \to Exp$, which will be denoted also as δ, and *Integer* is the set of integers. We use $\delta = \{X_1 \in d_1, \ldots, X_n \in d_n\}$, which stands for the FD with domain $\{X_1, \ldots, X_n\}$ and satisfies $\delta(X_i) = d_i$ for all $1 \leq i \leq n$, where $d_i \subseteq Integer$.

By convention, if δ is either a FD or a substitution we write $e\delta$ instead of $\delta(e)$, and $\delta\sigma$ for the composition of δ and σ s.t. $e(\delta\sigma) = (e\delta)\sigma$ for any e.

2.2   Well-Typedness

Inspired by Milner's type system we now introduce the notion of well-typed expression. We define a *type environment* as any set T of type assumptions $X :: \tau$ for data variables s.t. T does not include two different assumptions for the same variable. The *domain* $dom(T)$ of a type environment is the set of all data variables that occur in T. For any variable $X \in dom(T)$, the unique type τ s.t. $(X :: \tau) \in T$ is denoted as $T(X)$. The notation $(h :: \tau) \in_{var} \Sigma$ is used to indicate that Σ includes the type declaration $h :: \tau$ up to a renaming of type variables. *Type judgements* $(\Sigma, T) \vdash_{WT} e :: \tau$ are derived by means of the following *type inference* rules:

VR $(\Sigma, T) \vdash_{WT} X :: \tau$, if $T(X) = \tau$.
ID $(\Sigma, T) \vdash_{WT} h :: \tau\sigma_t$, if $(h :: \tau) \in_{var} \Sigma_\perp$, $\sigma_t \in TSubst$.
AP $(\Sigma, T) \vdash_{WT} (e\ e_1) :: \tau$, if $(\Sigma, T) \vdash_{WT} e :: (\tau_1 \to \tau)$, $(\Sigma, T) \vdash_{WT} e_1 :: \tau_1$,
    for some $\tau_1 \in Type$.
TP $(\Sigma, T) \vdash_{WT} (e_1, \ldots, e_n) :: (\tau_1, \ldots, \tau_n)$, if $\forall i \in \{1, \ldots, n\} : (\Sigma, T) \vdash_{WT} e_i :: \tau_i$.

An expression $e \in Exp_\perp$ is called *well-typed* iff there exist some *type environment* T and some type τ, s.t. the *type judgement* $T \vdash_{WT} e :: \tau$ can be derived. Expressions that admit more than one type are called *polymorphic*. A well-typed expression always admits a so-called *principal type* (PT) that is more general than any other. A pattern whose PT determines the PTs of its subpatterns is called *transparent*.

A *well-typed CFLP(FD) program* P is a set of *well-typed defining rules* for the function symbols in its signature. Defining rules for $f \in FS^n$ with principal type declaration $f :: \overline{\tau}_n \to \tau$ have the form

$$(R) \quad \underbrace{f\ t_1\ \ldots\ t_n}_{\text{left hand side}} = \underbrace{r}_{\text{right hand side}} \Leftarrow \underbrace{C}_{\text{Condition}}$$

and must satisfy the following requirements:

1. $t_1 \ldots t_n$ is a linear sequence of transparent patterns and r is an expression.
2. The *condition* C is a sequence of *conditions* $C_1, \ldots, C_k$, where each C_i can be either a *joinability statement* of the form $e == e'$, or a *disequality statement* of the form $e /= e'$, with $e, e' \in Exp$, or a Boolean function g of the form $g \, e_1 \ldots e_m$, with $e_i \in Exp$ and $g \in FS^m$ (of course, perhaps $g \in FS_{FD}$).
3. There exists some type environment T with domain $var(R)$ which well-types the defining rule in the following sense:
   a) For all $1 \le i \le n$: $(\Sigma, T) \vdash_{WT} t_i :: \tau_i$.
   b) $(\Sigma, T) \vdash_{WT} r :: \tau$.
   c) For each $(e == e') \in C$, $\exists \mu \in Type$ s.t. $(\Sigma, T) \vdash_{WT} e :: \mu :: e'$.
   d) For each $(e /= e') \in C$, $\exists \mu \in Type$ s.t. $(\Sigma, T) \vdash_{WT} e :: \mu :: e'$.
   e) For each $(g \, e_1 \ldots e_m) \in C$, where $g :: \tau_1 \to \ldots \to \tau_m \to \texttt{bool}$, $(\Sigma, T) \vdash_{WT} e_i :: \tau_i$, and $\tau_i \in Type$, for all $1 \le i \le m$.

Here, $(\Sigma, T) \vdash_{WT} a :: \tau$, $(\Sigma, T) \vdash_{WT} b :: \tau$ denotes $(\Sigma, T) \vdash_{WT} a :: \tau :: b$.

Informally, the intended meaning of a program rule as (R) above is that a call to a function f can be reduced to r whenever the actual parameters match the patterns t_i, and both the joinability conditions, the disequality conditions and the Boolean functions (including the FD constraints) are satisfied. A condition $e == e'$ is satisfied by evaluating e and e' to some common total pattern. Predicates are viewed as a particular kind of functions, with type $p :: \overline{\tau}_n \to \texttt{bool}$. As a syntactic facility, we can use *clauses* as a shorthand for defining rules whose right-hand side is *true*. This allows to write Prolog-like predicate definitions; each clause $p \, t_1 \ldots t_n : - C_1, \ldots, C_k$ abbreviates a defining rule of the form $p \, t_1 \ldots t_n = true \Leftarrow C_1, \ldots, C_k$.

A *well-typed goal* G has the same form as a well-typed expression and must satisfy the admissibility requirements but regarding the empty set of variables.

In general, a CFLP(FD) system is expected to *solve* goals, returning a set of 4-tuples $\langle E, \sigma, C, \delta \rangle$ as a computed answer where $E \in Exp$ is a TOY expression, $\sigma \subseteq Subst$ is the set of variable substitutions, C is a set of disequality constraints, and δ is the set of pruned finite domains.

3   TOY(FD): A CFLP(FD) Implementation

This section describes briefly part of TOY(FD), our CFLP(FD) implementation that extends the TOY system [9] to deal with FD constraints.

Table 2 shows some FD constraints provided by TOY(FD). Among others, TOY(FD) supports equality and disequality constraints, well-known global constraints (e.g., `all_different`/1), a membership constraint (i.e., `domain`/3) and enumeration constraints (e.g., `labeling`/2) with a number of options to reactivate the search process when no more constraint propagation is possible.

TOY(FD) also provides a set of constraints (not shown in Table 2), called *reflection constraints*, that allow to recover information about constrained FD variables and their associated domains during the solving of a goal (e.g., the reflection constraints `fd_min`, `fd_max` :: `int` $\to$ `int` applied to a FD variable return respectively the minimum and maximum value of this FD variable in its current domain). For reasons of space, we do not describe all the constraints in detail and encourage the interested reader to visit the link proposed in [4] for a more detailed explanation (this link also shows several examples of TOY(FD) programs).

TOY(FD) is implemented on top of Sicstus Prolog 3.8.4 and uses the FD constraint solver of SICStus [2]. FD constraints are integrated in TOY(FD) as functions and evaluated internally by using mainly two predicates: hnf(E,H), which specifies that H is one of the possible results of narrowing the expression E into head normal form, and solve/1, which checks the satisfiability of constraints (of rules and goals) previously to the evaluation of a given rule. This predicate is, basically, defined as follows[1]:

(1) $\texttt{solve}((\varphi,\varphi'))$ $:- \texttt{solve}(\varphi), \texttt{solve}(\varphi').$

(2) $\texttt{solve}(\texttt{L} == \texttt{R})$ $:- \texttt{hnf}(\texttt{L},\texttt{L}'), \texttt{hnf}(\texttt{R},\texttt{R}'), \texttt{equal}(\texttt{L}',\texttt{R}').$

(3) $\texttt{solve}(\texttt{L} /= \texttt{R})$ $:- \texttt{hnf}(\texttt{L},\texttt{L}'), \texttt{hnf}(\texttt{R},\texttt{R}'), \texttt{notequal}(\texttt{L}',\texttt{R}').$

(4) $\texttt{solve}(\texttt{L}\#\Diamond\ \texttt{R})$ $:- \texttt{hnf}(\texttt{L},\texttt{L}'), \texttt{hnf}(\texttt{R},\texttt{R}'), \{\texttt{L}'\#\Diamond\texttt{R}'\}.$
         where $\Diamond \in \{<, <=, >, >=, =, \backslash=\}.$

(5) $\texttt{solve}(\texttt{C A}_1 \ldots \texttt{A}_n) :- \texttt{hnf}(\texttt{A}_1,\texttt{A}_1'), \ldots, \texttt{hnf}(\texttt{A}_n,\texttt{A}_n'), \{\texttt{C}(\texttt{A}_1', \ldots, \texttt{A}_n')\}.$
         where C is any constraint returning a Boolean.

The interaction with SICStus FD constraint solver is reflected in the two last clauses: every time a FD constraint appears, the solver is eventually invoked with a goal $\{G\}$ where G is the translation of the FD constraint from TOY(FD) to SICStus Prolog. The expressions have to be 'simplified' in order to allow the solver to solve the constraint. By simplifying we mean computing the head normal forms (hnf) of both expressions.

4 Programming in TOY(FD)

Any CLP(FD)-program can be straightforwardly translated into a CFLP(FD)-program. As example, Section 4.1 shows the TOY (FD) code to solve the classical arithmetic puzzle "send+more=money". We do not insist more on this matter, but prefer to concentrate on the extra capabilities of the language and illustrate some of them by means of a more interesting example developed in Section 4.2.

4.1 An Introductory TOY(FD) Example

Below, a TOY(FD) program to solve the classical arithmetic puzzle "send more money" is shown. TOY(FD) allows to use infix constraint operators such as #> to build the expression X #> Y, which is understood as #> X Y. The signature of the program can be easily inferred from the type declarations included in its text. The intended meaning of the functions should be clear from their names, definitions and Tables 1 and 2.

---

[1] The code does not correspond exactly to the implementation, which is the result of many transformations and optimizations.

```
smm :: int -> int -> int -> int -> int -> int -> int -> int
          -> [labelType] -> bool
smm S E N D M O R Y Label :- domain [S,E,N,D,M,O,R,Y] 0 9,
          S #> 0, M #> 0,
          all_different [S,E,N,D,M,O,R,Y],
                        1000#*S #+ 100#*E #+ 10#*N #+ D
                  #+ 1000#*M #+ 100#*O #+ 10#*R #+ E
          #=  10000#*M #+ 1000#*O #+ 100#*N #+ 10#*E #+ Y,
          labeling Label [S,E,N,D,M,O,R,Y]
```

4.2   A Hardware Design Problem

A more interesting example comes from the hardware area. In this setting, many constrained optimization problems arise in the design of both sequential and combinational circuits as well as the interconnection routing between components. Constraint programming has been shown to effectively attack these problems. In particular, the interconnection routing problem (one of the major tasks in the physical design of very large scale integration - VLSI - circuits) have been solved with constraint logic programming [13].

For the sake of conciseness and clarity, we focus on a constraint combinational hardware problem at the logical level but adding constraints about the physical factors the circuit has to meet. This problem will show some of the nice features of TOY for specifying issues such as behavior, topology and physical factors.

Our problem can be stated as follows. Given a set of gates and modules, a switching function, and the problem parameters maximum circuit area, power dissipation, cost, and delay (dynamic behavior), the problem consists of finding possible topologies based on the given gates and modules so that a switching function and constraint physical factors are met. In order to have a manageable example, we restrict ourselves to the logical gates NOT, AND, and OR. We also consider circuits with three inputs and one output, and the physical factors aforementioned. We suppose also the following problem parameters:

Gate	Area	Power	Cost	Delay
NOT	1	1	1	1
AND	2	2	1	1
OR	2	2	2	2

In the sequel we will introduce the problem by first considering the features TOY offers for specifying logical circuits, what are its weaknesses, and how they can effectively be solved with the integration of constraints in TOY(FD).

Example 1. FLP Simple Circuits. With this example we show the FLP approach that can be followed for specifying the problem stated above. We use patterns to provide an *intensional* representation of functions. The alias behavior is used for representing the type bool → bool → bool → bool. Functions of this type are intended to represent simple circuits which receive three Boolean inputs and return a Boolean output. Given the Boolean functions not, and, and or defined elsewhere, we specify three-input, one-output simple circuits as follows.

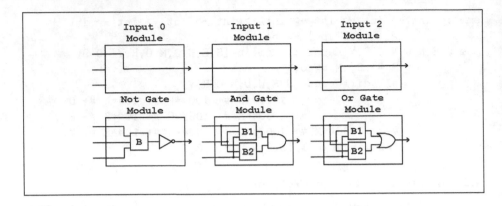

Fig. 1. Basic Modules.

```
i0,i1,i2 :: behavior        notGate :: behavior -> behavior
i0 I2 I1 I0 = I0            notGate B I2 I1 I0 = not (B I2 I1 I0)
i1 I2 I1 I0 = I1
i2 I2 I1 I0 = I2
```

```
andGate, orGate :: behavior -> behavior -> behavior
andGate B1 B2 I2 I1 I0 = and (B1 I2 I1 I0) (B2 I2 I1 I0)
orGate B1 B2 I2 I1 I0 = or (B1 I2 I1 I0) (B2 I2 I1 I0)
```

Functions i0, i1, and i2 represent inputs to the circuits, that is, the minimal circuit which just copies one of the inputs to the output. (In fact, this can be thought as a fixed multiplexer - selector.) They are combinatorial modules as depicted in Figure 1. The function notGate outputs a Boolean value which is the result of applying the NOT gate to the output of a circuit of three inputs. In turn, functions andGate and orGate output a Boolean value which is the result of applying the AND and OR gates, respectively, to the outputs of three inputs-circuits (see Figure 1).

These functions can be used in a higher-order fashion just to generate or match topologies. In particular, the higher-order functions notGate, andGate and orGate take behaviors as parameters and build new behaviors, corresponding to the logical gates NOT, AND and OR. For instance, the multiplexer depicted in Figure 2 can be represented by the following pattern:

```
orGate (andGate i0 (notGate i2)) (andGate i1 i2).
```

This first-class citizen higher-order pattern can be used for many purposes. For instance, it can be compared to another pattern or it can be applied to actual values for its inputs in order to compute the circuit output. So, with the previous pattern, the goal:

```
P == orGate (andGate i0 (notGate i2)) (andGate i1 i2),
P true false true == O
```

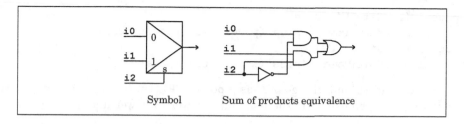

Fig. 2. Two-Input Multiplexer Circuit.

is evaluated to **true** and produces the substitution **O == false**. The rules that define the behavior can be used to generate circuits, which can be restricted to satisfy some conditions. If we use the standard arithmetics, we could define the following set of rules for computing or limiting the power dissipation.

```
power :: behavior -> int
power i0 = 0
power i1 = 0
power i2 = 0
power (notGate C) = notGatePower + (power C)
power (andGate C1 C2) = andGatePower + (power C1) + (power C2)
power (orGate C1 C2) = orGatePower + (power C1) + (power C2)
```

Then, we can submit the goal **power B == P, P < maxPower** (provided the function **maxPower** acts as a problem parameter that returns just the maximum power allowed for the circuit) in which the function **power** is used as a behavior generator[2]. As outcome, we get several solutions ($\langle$i0, {P==0}, {}, {}$\rangle$, $\langle$i1, {P==0}, {}, {}$\rangle$, $\langle$i2, {P==0}, {}, {}$\rangle$, $\langle$not i0, {P==1}, {}, {}$\rangle$, ..., $\langle$not (not i0), {P==2}, {}, {}$\rangle$, ... Declaratively, it is fine; but our operational semantics requires a head normal form for the application of the arithmetic operand **+**. This implies that we reach no more solutions beyond $\langle$ not (... (not i0) ...), maxPower, {}, {}$\rangle$ because the application of the fourth rule of **power** yields to an infinite computation. This drawback is solved by recursing to Peano's arithmetics, that is:

```
data nat = z | s nat                    plus :: nat -> nat -> nat
                                        plus z Y = Y
power' :: behavior -> nat               plus (s X) Y = s (plus X Y)
power' i0 = z
power' i1 = z                           less :: nat -> nat -> bool
power' i2 = z                           less z (s X) = true
power' (notGate C) =                    less (s X) (s Y) = less X Y
    plus notGatePower (power' C)
```

---

[2] Equivalently and more concisely, **power B < maxPower** could be submitted, but doing so we make the power unobservable.

```
power' (andGate C1 C2) =
    plus andGatePower (plus (power' C1) (power' C2))
power' (orGate C1 C2) =
    plus orGatePower  (plus (power' C1) (power' C2))
```

So, we can submit the goal less (power' P) (s (s (s z))), where we have written down explicitly the maximum power (3 power units).

With the second approach we get a more awkward representation due to the use of successor arithmetics. The first approach to express this problem is indeed more declarative than the second one, but we get non-termination. FD constraints can be profitably applied to the representation of this problem as we show in the next example.

Example 2. CFLP(FD) Simple Circuits
As for any constraint problem, modelling can be started by identifying the FD constraint variables. Recalling the problem specification, circuit limitations refer to area, power dissipation, cost, and delay. Provided we can choose finite units to represent these factors, we choose them as problem variables. A circuit can therefore be represented by the 4-tuple state ⟨area, power, cost, delay⟩. The idea to formulate the problem consists of attaching this state to an ongoing circuit so that state variables reflect the current state of the circuit *during* its generation. By contrast with the first example, we do not "generate" and then "test", but we "test" when "generating", so that we can find failure in advance. A domain variable has a domain attached indicating the set of possible assignments to the variable. This domain can be reduced during the computation. Since domain variables are constrained by limiting factors, during the generation of the circuit a domain may become empty. This event prunes the search space avoiding to explore a branch known to yield no solution. Let's firstly focus on the area factor. The following function generates a circuit characterized by its state variables.

```
type area, power, cost, delay = int
type state = (area, power, cost, delay)
type circuit = (behavior, state)
genCir :: state -> circuit
genCir (A, P, C, D) = (i0, (A, P, C, D))
genCir (A, P, C, D) = (i1, (A, P, C, D))
genCir (A, P, C, D) = (i2, (A, P, C, D))
genCir (A, P, C, D) = (notGate B, (A, P, C, D)) <==
            domain [A] ((fd_min A) + notGateArea) (fd_max A),
            genCir (A, P, C, D) == (B, (A, P, C, D))
genCir (A, P, C, D) = (andGate B1 B2, (A, P, C, D)) <==
            domain [A] ((fd_min A) + andGateArea) (fd_max A),
            genCir (A, P, C, D) == (B1, (A, P, C, D)),
            genCir (A, P, C, D) == (B2, (A, P, C, D))
genCir (A, P, C, D) = (orGate B1 B2, (A, P, C, D)) <==
            domain [A] ((fd_min A) + orGateArea)  (fd_max A),
```

```
genCir (A, P, C, D) == (B1, (A, P, C, D)),
genCir (A, P, C, D) == (B2, (A, P, C, D))
```

The function genCir has an argument to hold the circuit state and returns a circuit characterized by a behavior and a state. (Note that we can avoid the use of the state tuple as a parameter, since it is included in the result.) The template of this function is like the previous example. The difference lies in that we perform domain pruning during circuit generation with the membership constraint domain, so that each time a rule is selected, the domain variable representing area is reduced in the size of the gate selected by the operational mechanism. For instance, the circuit area domain is reduced in a number of notGateArea when the rule for notGate has been selected. For domain reduction we use the reflection functions fd_min and fd_max. This approach allows us to submit the following goal:

```
domain [Area] 0 maxArea,
genCir (Area, Power, Cost, Delay) == Circuit
```

which initially sets the possible range of area between 0 and the problem parameter area expressed by the function maxArea, and then generates a Circuit. Recall that testing is performed during search space exploration, so that termination is ensured because the add operation is monotonic. The mechanism which allows this "test" when "generating" is the set of propagators, which are concurrent processes that are triggered whenever a domain variable is changed (pruned). The state variable delay is more involved since one cannot simply add the delay of each function at each generation step. The delay of a circuit is related to the maximum number of levels an input signal has to traverse until it reaches the output. This is to say that we cannot use a single domain variable for describing the delay. Therefore, considering a module with several inputs, we must compute the delay at its output by computing the maximum delays from its inputs and adding the module delay. So, we use new fresh variables for the inputs of a module being generated and assign the maximum delay to the output delay. This solution is depicted in the following function:

```
genCirDelay :: state -> delay -> circuit
genCirDelay (A, P, C, D) Dout = (i0, (A, P, C, D))
genCirDelay (A, P, C, D) Dout = (i1, (A, P, C, D))
genCirDelay (A, P, C, D) Dout = (i2, (A, P, C, D))
genCirDelay (A, P, C, D) Dout = (notGate B, (A, P, C, D)) <==
  domain [Dout] ((fd_min Dout) + notGateDelay) (fd_max Dout),
  genCirDelay (A, P, C, D) Dout == (B, (A, P, C, D))
genCirDelay (A, P, C, D) Dout = (andGate B1 B2, (A, P, C, D)) <==
  domain [Din1, Din2] ((fd_min Dout) + andGateDelay)(fd_max Dout),
  genCirDelay (A, P, C, D) Din1 == (B1, (A, P, C, D)),
  genCirDelay (A, P, C, D) Din2 == (B2, (A, P, C, D)),
  domain [Dout] (maximum (fd_min Din1)(fd_min Din2)) (fd_max Dout)
genCirDelay (A, P, C, D) Dout = (orGate B1 B2, (A, P, C, D)) <==
  domain [Din1, Din2] ((fd_min Dout) + orGateDelay) (fd_max Dout),
```

```
genCirDelay (A, P, C, D) Din1 == (B1, (A, P, C, D)),
genCirDelay (A, P, C, D) Din2 == (B2, (A, P, C, D)),
domain [Dout] (maximum (fd_min Din1)(fd_min Din2)) (fd_max Dout)
```

Observing the rules for the AND and OR gates, we can see two new fresh domain variables for representing the delay in their inputs. These new variables are constrained to have the domain of the delay in the output but pruned with the delay of the corresponding gate. After the circuits connected to the inputs had been generated, the domain of the output delay is pruned with the maximum of the input module delays. Note that although the maximum is computed *after* the input modules had been generated, the information in the given output delay has been propagated to the input delay domains so that whenever an input delay domain becomes empty, the search branch is no longer searched and another alternative is tried. Putting together the constraints about area, power dissipation, cost, and delay is straightforward, since they are orthogonal factors that can be handled in the same way. In addition to the constraints shown, we can further constrain the circuit generation with other factors as fan-in, fan-out, and switching function enforcement, to name a few. Then, we could submit the following goal:

```
domain [A] 0 maxArea, domain [P] 0 maxPower,
domain [C] 0 maxCost, domain [D] 0 maxDelay,
genCir (A,P,C,D) == (B, S),   switchF B == sw
```

where `switchF` can be defined as the switching function that returns the result of a behavior B for all its input combinations, and `sw` is the function that returns the intended result (`sw` is referred as a problem parameter, as well as `maxArea`, `maxPower`, `maxCost`, and `maxDelay`).

```
data functionality = [bool]
switchF :: behavior -> functionality
switchF Behavior = [Out1,Out2,Out3,Out4,Out5,Out6,Out7,Out8] <==
      (Behavior false false false) == Out1,
      (Behavior false false true)  == Out2,
      (Behavior false true  false) == Out3,
      (Behavior false true true)   == Out4,
      (Behavior true  false false) == Out5,
      (Behavior true  false true)  == Out6,
      (Behavior true  true  false) == Out7,
      (Behavior true  true  true)  == Out8
```

Then, to generate a NOR circuit with `maxArea`, `maxPower`, `maxCost` and `maxDelay` equal 6, we could submit the following goal:

```
domain [A, P, C, D] 0  6, genCir (A,P,C,D) == (B, S),
switchF B == [true,false,false,false,false,false,false,false]
```

This goal has 24 possible answers, 4 of them are:

(1) ⟨true,{B == (notGate (orGate i0 (orGate i1 i2)))}, S == (_A,
_B,

   _C, _D)}, { },{_A ∈ 5..6, _B ∈ 5..6, _C ∈ 5..6, _D ∈ 5..6}⟩.
(2) ⟨true,{B == (notGate (orGate (orGate i2 i1) i0)), S == (_A,
_B,

   _C, _D)}, { }, {_A ∈ 5..6, _B ∈ 5..6, _C ∈ 5..6, _D ∈ 5..6}⟩.
(3) ⟨true,{B == (andGate (notGate i0) (notGate (orGate i1 i2)))},
      S == (6, 6, _A, _B)}, { }, {_A ∈ 5..6, _B ∈ 4..6}⟩.
(4) ⟨true,{B == (andGate (notGate (orGate i2 i1)) (notGate i0))},
      S == (6, 6, _A, _B)}, { }, {_A ∈ 5..6, _B ∈ 4..6}⟩.

5   Related Work

[1] described an implementation of the FLP language Curry to enable the use
of existing constraint solvers. As far as we know, our implementation is the first
complete FLP system that includes truly solving on FD constraints although,
recently, we have known about the existence of an (unpublished) implementation
(called PAKCS) of the Curry language that supports (a small set of) FD constraints [3]. Specifically, PAKCS provides the following constraints: a set of arithmetic operations { #*, #+, . . . , }, a membership constraint, an *all_different/1*
constraint and an enumeration constraint that just provides naïve labeling.

   Also, it is well-known that CLP(FD) is a successful declarative instance of
CP and thus is strongly-related to our work. In fact, CLP(FD) is an instance of
CFLP(FD) as any CLP(FD)-program can be straightforwardly translated into
a CFLP(FD)-program. Observe that CFLP(FD) provides the main characteristics of CLP(FD), i.e., FD constraint solving, non-determinism, logical variables
and relational form. Of course this determines initially a wide range of applications for our language. But CFLP(FD) is more than CLP(FD). Throughout
the paper we have highlighted, by example, some CFLP(FD) features not existing in CLP(FD). Particularly, Example 2 shows that CFLP(FD) provides functions, higher-order patterns, partial applications, combination of relational and
functional notation, and types. This leads to an alternative way of expressing
problems to that provided by CLP(FD). Moreover, there are additional features
existing in CFLP(FD) and not presented in CLP(FD) that have not been discussed so far as it is not the issue here and will be discussed in a further paper
(currently under preparation). As an example we can cite the *lazy evaluation* of
goals in which the arguments may be partially evaluated or evaluated just when
they are necessary. Lazy evaluation opens new possibilities for FD constraint
solving. For instance, CFLP(FD) enables the management of infinite lists of FD
constraints.

Example 3. Consider the following function that generates an infinite list of FD
variables constrained in the interval [0,N-1] for some integer N.

```
generateFD :: int -> [int]
generateFD N = [X | generateFD N] <== domain [X] 0 (N-1)
```

Consider also the polymorphic predefined function `take:: int -> [A] -> [A]` such that `take N L` returns a list containing the first `N` elements of the list `L`. Then the goal

`take 3 (generateFD 10) == List`

does not terminate with classical constraint solving as it tries to evaluate first the second argument yielding to an infinite list; however, a lazy evaluation generates just the first 3 elements of the list returning thus a correct answer.

In addition, our proposal can be considered in the context of multi-paradigm constraint programming, i.e., to combine CP with several paradigms in one setting. In this line, one decade ago, [10] presented an idea to combine characteristics of CLP, functional and concurrent languages and it was implemented in the language Oz. Despite Oz generalizes the CLP(FD) and concurrent constraint programming paradigms, it is very different to TOY(FD) as functional programming and constraints are not integrated. Moreover, instead of the typical LP approach of left-right first-depth, search strategies in Oz are encoded in *search procedures* to explore the search space.

There are also other declarative CP systems such as the algebraic CP languages (OPL [12], AMPL [5]). However, we think that our approach is far more declarative mainly since, first, those systems are not general-purpose programming languages, and, second, they do not benefit neither from complex terms and patterns nor from non-determinism.

6   Comparative Work

In this section we compare the performance of TOY(FD) with respect to related systems. One is PAKCS (cited in Section 5) that claims to be an efficient implementation. In the comparison we used the *Curry2Prolog* compiler, which is the most efficient implementation of Curry inside PAKCS. In addition, we also compared the performance of TOY(FD) with the FD constraint library of the efficient and well-known system SICStus Prolog (version 3.8.4).

Labeling. FD constraint solving can be seen as a combination of constraint propagation and labeling. Here, we consider two labelings, the naïve labeling (i.e., choose the leftmost variable of a list and then select the smallest value in its domain) and the *first fail* labeling (i.e., choose the variable with the smallest domain). The naïve labeling assures that both variable and value ordering are the same for all the systems and hence in many ways, although less efficient, is better for comparing the different systems when only one solution is required.

The Benchmarks. We have used a set of five classical benchmarks [11]: **send-more** (a cryptoarithmethic problem with 8 variables ranging over $\{0, \dots, 9\}$), one linear equation and 36 disequations; **equation 10** and **equation 20** (systems of 10 and 20 linear equations respectively with 7 variables ranging over

Table 3. Performance Results for First Solution Search and Naïve Labeling.

Benchmark	SICStus	TOY(FD)	PAKCS	$\frac{TOY(FD)}{SICStus}$	$\frac{PAKCS}{SICStus}$	$\frac{PAKCS}{TOY(FD)}$
sendmore	10	10	40	1.00	4.00	4.00
equation10	20	70	80	3.50	4.00	1.14
equation20	30	130	160	4.33	5.33	1.23
queens (8)	10	20	30	2.00	3.00	1.50
queens (16)	1180	1220	4430	1.03	3.75	3.63
queens (20)	26430	31390	129510	1.18	4.90	4.12
queens (24)	57100	64770	326090	1.13	5.71	5.03
queens (30)	??	??	??	(?)	(?)	(?)
magic (64)	790	890	N	1.12	∞	∞
magic (100)	2270	2300	N	1.01	∞	∞
magic (150)	5840	5990	N	1.02	∞	∞
magic (200)	11450	11920	N	1.04	∞	∞
magic (300)	31280	34200	N	1.09	∞	∞

Table 4. Performance Results for First Solution Search and *First Fail* Labeling.

Benchmark	SICStus	TOY(FD)	$\frac{TOY(FD)}{SICStus}$	$\frac{SICStus(n)}{SICStus(f)}$	$\frac{TOY(FD)(n)}{TOY(FD)(f)}$
sendmore	5	5	1.00	2.00	2.00
equation10	10	50	5.00	2.00	1.40
equation20	20	110	5.50	1.50	1.18
queens (8)	10	15	1.50	1.00	1.33
queens (16)	40	50	1.25	29.50	24.40
queens (20)	80	160	2.00	330.37	196.18
queens (24)	70	90	1.28	815.71	719.66
queens (30)	130	660	5.07	∞	∞
magic (64)	320	330	1.03	2.46	2.69
magic (100)	640	690	1.07	3.54	3.33
magic (150)	1500	1510	1.00	3.89	3.96
magic (200)	2510	2620	1.04	4.56	4.54
magic (300)	6090	6180	1.01	5.13	5.53

$\{0, \ldots, 10\}$); **queens (N)** (place N queens on a $N \times N$ chessboard such that no queen attacks each other) and **magic sequences (N)** (calculate a sequence of N numbers such that each of them is the number of occurrences in the series of its position in the sequence).

Results. All the benchmarks were tested on the same SPARCstation under SunOs 5.8. Due to space limitations we only provide the results for first solution search. Table 3 shows the results using naïve labeling. The meaning for the columns is as follows. The first column gives the name of the benchmark used in the comparison. The next three columns show the running (elapsed) time (measured in milliseconds) to find the first answer for each system. The fourth and fifth columns indicate the slow-down of TOY(FD) and PACKS with respect to SICStus. The last column shows the slow-down of the PAKCS with respect to our implementation.

Table 4 shows similar results but using first fail labeling. Observe that PAKCS is not included as it only provides naïve labeling (which is not very useful in practice as it is well-known). The meaning for the columns is as follows. The three first columns are as in Table 3. The fourth column indicates the slow-down of TOY(FD) with respect to SICStus. The last two columns show the slow-down of the solution using naïve labeling (n) with respect to the solution using first fail labeling (f).

In these tables, all numbers represent the average of a number of runs. The symbol ?? means that a solution was not received in a reasonable time and (?) indicates a non-determined value. The symbol **N** in the PAKCS column means that we could not formulate that benchmark because of insufficient provision for constraints. Particularly, the classical formulation of the magic sequence problem requires to use reified constraints in the form $X = Y \Leftrightarrow B$ with B being a (Boolean) FD variable. In these cases, when a problem cannot be expressed in PAKCS, the symbol ∞ is used in the average columns. All the benchmarks are available in [4].

7   Conclusions

We have presented CFLP(FD), a functional logic programming approach to FD constraint solving, which may be profitably applied to solve real-life problems. FD constraints are defined as functions and thus integrated naturally on FLP languages. Due to its functional component, CFLP(FD) provides better tools, when compared to CLP(FD), for a productive declarative programming. Due to the use of constraints, the expressivity and capabilities of this approach are clearly superior to those of both the functional and purely CP approaches.

We have described a formal language for CFLP(FD) and shown, by example, the benefits of integrating FLP and FD. For the execution mechanism of the language, we have seamlessly integrated constraint solving into a sophisticated, state-of-the-art execution mechanism for lazy narrowing. Our implementation, TOY(FD), translates CFLP(FD)-programs into Prolog-programs in a system equipped with a constraint solver. TOY(FD) provides a reasonably-complete set of FD constraints (including an acceptable number of practical options for labeling) and is fairly efficient as, in general, it is around two and five times faster than another CFLP(FD) implementation to come and also behaves closely to that of SICStus that means that the wrapping of SICStus by TOY does not increase significantly the computation time. The exception is in the solving of linear equations on which it is about three and five times slower. The reason seems to be in the process previous to the FD solver invocation that transforms the expressions in head normal form. This process produces an overhead when expressions (such as those for linear equations) involve a high number of arguments and sub-expressions.

We have also discussed briefly the advantages of CFLP(FD) wrt. CLP(FD). One of them is that CFLP(FD) enables to solve all the CLP(FD) applications as well as another problems closer to the functional setting. Moreover, the integration of FD constraints into the FLP paradigm provides extra advantages not existing in CLP(FD) such as types, higher-order computations, partial applications on constraints, functional notation and lazy evaluation among others.

In addition, we claim that our approach can be extended to other kind of interesting constraint systems, such as non-linear real constraints, constraints over sets, or Boolean constraints, to name a few.

References

1. S. Antoy and M. Hanus. Compiling multi-paradigm declarative programs into prolog. In H. Kirchner and C. Ringeissen, editors, *3rd International Workshop on Frontiers of Combining Systems*, number 1794 in LNCS, pages 171–185. Springer-Verlag, 2000.
2. M. Carlsson, G. Ottosson, and B. Carlson. An pen-ended finite domain constraint solver. In U. Montanari and F. Rossi, editors, *9th International Symposium on Programming Languages: Implementations, Logics und Programs (PLILP'97)*, number 1292 in LNCS, pages 191–206, Southampton, UK, 1997. Springer-Verlag.
3. M. Hanus (editor). Pakcs 1.4.0, user manual. The Portland Aachen Kiel Curry System. Available from
   http://www.informatik.uni-kiel.de/~pakcs/, 2002.
4. A.J. Fernández, T. Hortalá-González, and F. Sáenz-Pérez. TOY(FD): User manual, latest Version. Available at
   http://www.lcc.uma.es/~afdez/cflpfd/, 2002.
5. R. Fourer, D.M. Gay, and B.W. Kernighan. Ampl: A modeling language for mathematical programming. Scientific Press, 1993.
6. J.C. González-Moreno, M.T. Hortalá-González, and M. Rodríguez-Artalejo. Polymorphic types in functional logic programming. In Aart Middeldorp and Taisuke Sato, editors, *4th International Symposium on Functional und Logic Programming (FLOPS'99)*, number 1722 in LNCS, pages 1–20, Tsukuba, Japan, November 1999. Springer-Verlag. There is special issue of the Journal of Functional and Logic Programming, 2001. See http://danae.uni-muenster.de/lehre/kuchen/JFLP.
7. M. Hanus. The integration of functions into logic programming: A survey. *The Journal of Logic Programming*, 19–20:583–628, 1994. Special issue: Ten Years of Logic Programming.
8. J. Jaffar and M. Maher. Constraint logic programming: a survey. *The Journal of Logic Programming*, 19–20:503–581, 1994.
9. F.J. López-Fraguas and J. Sánchez-Hernández. TOY: A multiparadigm declarative system. In P. Narendran and M. Rusinowitch, editors, *10th International Conference on Rewriting Techniques und Applications*, number 1631 in LNCS, pages 244–247, Trento, Italy, 1999. Springer-Verlag. The system and further documentation including programming examples is available at http://babel.dacya.ucm.es/toy and http://titan.sip.ucm.es/toy.
10. G. Smolka. The Oz programming model. In Jan Van Leeuwen, editor, *Computer Science Today*, number 1000 in LNCS, pages 324–343, Berlin, 1995. Springer-Verlag.

11. P. Van Hentenryck. *Constraint satisfaction in logic programming*. The MIT Press, Cambridge, MA, 1989.
12. P. Van Hentenryck. *The OPL optimization programming language*. The MIT Press, Cambridge, MA, 1999.
13. N-F. Zhou. Channel Routing with Constraint Logic Programming and Delay. In *9th International Conference on Industrial Applications of Artificial Intelligence*, pages 217–231. Gordon and Breach Science Publishers, 1996.

Logic Programs as Compact Denotations*

Patricia M. Hill[1] and Fausto Spoto[2]

[1] School of Computing, University of Leeds, UK
hill@comp.leeds.ac.uk
[2] Dipartimento di Informatica
Strada Le Grazie, 15, Ca' Vignal, 37134 Verona, Italy
spoto@sci.univr.it
Ph.: +39 0458027076   Fax: +39 0458027068

Abstract. This paper shows how logic programs can be used to implement the transition functions of denotational abstract interpretation. The logic variables express regularity in the abstract behaviour of commands. The technique is applied here to sign, class and escape analysis for object-oriented programs. We show that the time and space costs using logic programs are smaller than those of a ground relational representation. Moreover, we show that, in the case of sign analysis, our technique requires less memory and has an efficiency comparable to that of an implementation based on binary decision diagrams.

1 Introduction

The use of denotational semantics as the basis for abstract interpretation [5] is appealing since it leads to clean, compositional static analyses. In that context, the abstract denotation (the *transition* or *transfer function*) of a piece of code is a function from the abstract properties of its input to those of its output. Provided the domain of abstract properties is finite, this relational approach can be naively implemented through a *ground* relational database. However, as such a domain can be very large, the traditional way to implement these relations is by means of a more compact representation based on *binary decision diagrams* (*bdd's*) [3]; a bdd denotes a propositional formula that defines the input/output relation determined by the abstract denotation. In logic, general rules are defined by non-ground formulas and, in particular, ground relational databases can be defined very compactly by (non-ground) logic programs. Thus, in this paper, we investigate (both theoretically and experimentally) a *non-ground* representation, implemented as a logic program, for the abstract denotation of a piece of code. In this representation, the logic variables are used to provide a compact and efficient implementation of dependencies between the abstract input and the abstract output of the code. For instance, for any variable that is not used by a given command, the abstract value just has to be copied from its abstract input to its abstract output, at least for a large class of static analyses. Similarly, an

---

* This work has been funded by the MURST grant "Abstract Interpretation, type systems and control-flow analysis" and the EPSRC grant GR/R53401.

V. Dahl and P. Wadler (Eds.): PADL 2003, LNCS 2562, pp. 339–356, 2003.

assignment statement copies the abstract value of the right hand side to the abstract value of the left hand side. Dependencies like these can be naturally represented by non-ground clauses of a logic program. We plug this non-ground representation inside a fixpoint static analyser for object-oriented programs. The fixpoint computation is stopped by a two-stage equivalence test on denotations: first variance (*i.e.*, equality up to variable renaming) and then, if variance fails, explicit model comparison.

The first contribution of this paper is to describe a methodology for non-ground analysis using three different static analyses to illustrate the approach:

- *Sign analysis*. This approximates integer variables by their sign using the domain defined in [20]. This is described in more detail in the next section.
- *Class analysis* for object-oriented programs. This overapproximates the set of classes which an expression can have at run-time at a given program point. Indeed, an expression can have every type (class) compatible with its declared type, although only some of them actually arise at run-time. The class analyses here are those formalised in [13] by abstract interpretation and are derived from the ideas in [1], [6] and [18], respectively. *Rapid type analysis* [1] provides just one set of classes which approximates all the classes instantiated up to a given program point. The *dataflow analysis* of [6] is more precise since it approximates every program variable with a set of possible classes. It is described in more detail in the next section. Although more precise than [1], [6] does not provide any approximation for the fields of the objects. This is instead the main feature of the *constraint analysis* in [18].
- *Escape analysis* for object-oriented programs [2]. This determines which dynamically created objects will not *escape* from their creating method. This information allows one to allocate these objects to the stack instead of the heap. Compared to heap allocation, stack allocation reduces the garbage collection overhead at run-time. Moreover, in the case of object-oriented languages such as Java, a knowledge of those objects that cannot escape the methods of their creating threads can be used to remove unnecessary synchronisations when the objects are accessed. We use here the escape analysis for object-oriented languages defined in [10], which collects the set of *creation points* of the objects reachable at a given program point.

The second contribution is an experimental comparison of our technique (the use of non-ground logic programs) with two other techniques: one based on the naive ground representation through ground logic programs, and one based on a highly-optimised bdd library [15]. The results show that an analyser based on the non-ground technique uses much less memory and is often many orders of magnitude faster than the ground logic program implementation. More importantly, it is comparable, *w.r.t.* efficiency, to the bdd implementation that however requires a large amount of memory to attain that efficiency (the bdd implementation of sign analysis is due to Aurélie Lagasse). Note that we are considering different *implementations* of the same abstract domains. The precision of the analyses does not change, whether we use ground, non-ground or bdd-based implementations.

The paper is organised as follows. In the next section we motivate the rest of the paper using sign and class analysis. Section 3 introduces our notation and terminology. Section 4 presents the framework of analysis. Section 5 defines the compact representation of the abstract denotations using (non-ground) logic programs. Section 6 shows how these compact representations may be composed. Section 7 describes the implementation and summarises our experimental results. Section 8 discusses related work and concludes the paper. A longer version of the paper (with proofs) is available at www.sci.univr.it/~spoto/papers.html.

2   Some Motivating Examples

Consider the problem of the *sign analysis* of a program. Assuming there is a set of types that includes the type *int*, sign analysis tries to determine the sign (positive or negative) of the variables of type *int*. We use here the domain $\{*, +, -, u\}$ which is similar to that defined in [20]. The set $\{*, +, -, u\}$ is partially ordered by $\preceq$, which is the minimal reflexive relation such that $+ \preceq u$ and $- \preceq u$. Suppose $V = \{v_1, \ldots, v_\ell\}$ is a set of variables of interest and that τ is a *type environment* i.e., a map which assigns a type to each element of V. Then we define a domain

$$S_\tau = \{\mathsf{empty}\} \cup \left\{ \varsigma : V \mapsto \{*, +, -, u\} \,\middle|\, \begin{matrix} \text{for all } v \in V : \\ \varsigma(v) = * \text{ iff } \tau(v) \neq int \end{matrix} \right\}. \tag{1}$$

The idea underlying the domain S_τ is that the variables of type *int* are approximated by $+$ if they are positive or zero, they are approximated by $-$ if they are negative and by u if their sign is unknown. The other variables are approximated by a don't care mark $*$. The element empty represents the empty set of states.

The set S_τ is partially ordered w.r.t. $\sqsubseteq$ where $\mathsf{empty} \sqsubseteq s$ for every $s \in S_\tau$ and $\varsigma_1 \sqsubseteq \varsigma_2$ if $\varsigma_1(v_i) \preceq \varsigma_2(v_i)$ for all i, $1 \leq i \leq \ell$. An element $\varsigma \in S_\tau \setminus \{\mathsf{empty}\}$ is represented by $[x_1, \ldots, x_\ell]$, where v_i is the ith variable in lexicographical order in $\{v_1, \ldots, v_\ell\}$ and $\varsigma(v_i) = x_i$ for every $i = 1, \ldots, \ell$.

2.1   Representing Abstract Denotations

Consider the following program, written in a pseudo-syntax for a simple imperative object-oriented language *i.e.*, Pascal functions with objects, fields and virtual calls.

```
foo(a:int,c:int):int {
  let b:int in {
    ... a:=b; ...
  }
}
```

The denotation of the assignment a:=b w.r.t. sign information is a (*transition*) function from the abstract sign properties of the variables before the assignment to those of the variables after it. Since only the variables a, b, c and out are addressable at that program point (we assume that the special variable out holds the return value of the function) and they all have type int, that denotation is a function $f : S_\tau \mapsto S_\tau$ (with $\tau = [\mathsf{a} \mapsto int, \mathsf{b} \mapsto int, \mathsf{c} \mapsto int, \mathsf{out} \mapsto int]$) which can be represented as

$$
\begin{array}{ll}
\texttt{empty} \to \texttt{empty} & \\
[+,+,+,+] \to [+,+,+,+] & [+,+,+,-] \to [+,+,+,-] \\
[+,+,-,+] \to [+,+,-,+] & [+,+,-,-] \to [+,+,-,-] \\
[+,-,+,+] \to [-,-,+,+] & [+,-,+,-] \to [-,-,+,-] \\
[+,-,-,+] \to [-,-,-,+] & \cdots
\end{array}
\tag{2}
$$

Note that f is not explicitly specified for the elements of S_τ binding some variables to u. This is because these values can be recovered from those provided above [14,17,20] (see Definition 1 in Section 4). For instance, $f([+, u, +, +]) = f([+,+,+,+]) \sqcup f([+,-,+,+]) = [+,+,+,+] \sqcup [-,-,+,+] = [u, u, +, +]$.

Mapping (2) can be naturally seen as a ground logic program stating an input/output relationship $i.e.$,

$$
\begin{array}{l}
\texttt{io}(\texttt{empty}, \texttt{empty}). \\
\texttt{io}([+,+,+,+],[+,+,+,+]). \\
\texttt{io}([+,+,+,-],[+,+,+,-]). \\
\cdots
\end{array}
$$

This simple representation is not practical as its size grows exponentially with the number of program variables. Note that the same would happen if we used a domain which collects the set of definitely positive and that of definitely negative variables, since we might still have to consider an exponential number of input configurations for a given command.

However, there is some regularity in (2); namely, f does not change the values of b, c and out; and the input value of b always becomes the output value of a. We can therefore represent f, by $using$ $logical$ $variables$ corresponding to the original program variables, as

$$
\texttt{empty} \to \texttt{empty} \qquad [\mathsf{A}, \mathsf{B}, \mathsf{C}, \mathsf{Out}] \to [\mathsf{B}, \mathsf{B}, \mathsf{C}, \mathsf{Out}].
\tag{3}
$$

This representation is smaller than (2) and grows linearly with the number of program variables. It can be seen as isomorphic to the logic program:

$$
\texttt{io}(\texttt{empty}, \texttt{empty}). \qquad \texttt{io}([\mathsf{A}, \mathsf{B}, \mathsf{C}, \mathsf{Out}], [\mathsf{B}, \mathsf{B}, \mathsf{C}, \mathsf{Out}]).
\tag{4}
$$

From now on, the notation in (3) denotes the corresponding program in (4).

Consider now the program:

```
foo(a:int,c:int):int {
  let b:int in {
    ... a:=b-1; ...
  }
}
```

```
swap(a:array of int,i:int,j:int):array of int {
  let temp:int in {
    temp:=a[i]; a[i]:=a[j]; a[j]:=temp; out:=a;
  }
}

nested(a:array of int,b:array of int,n:int):int {
  out:=0;
  let i:int in {
    n:=n-1;
    while (i <= n) do
      let j:int in
        while (j <= n) do {
          out:=out+a[i]*b[j]; a:=swap(a,i,n);
          b:=swap(b,j,n); out:=out+nested(a,b,n);
          a:=swap(a,i,n); b:=swap(b,j,n);
        }
  }
}
```

nested : $[\text{a} \mapsto int, \text{b} \mapsto int, \text{n} \mapsto int] \to [\text{out} \mapsto int]$

$$empty \to empty$$
$$[+,+,+] \to [+] \quad [+,+,-] \to [+] \quad [+,-,+] \to [u] \quad [+,-,-] \to [+]$$
$$[-,+,+] \to [u] \quad [-,+,-] \to [+] \quad [-,-,+] \to [+] \quad [-,-,-] \to [+]$$

$$empty \to empty \quad [A,B,-] \to [+]$$
$$[+,+,+] \to [+] \quad [-,-,+] \to [+] \quad [-,+,+] \to [u] \quad [+,-,+] \to [u]$$

Fig. 1. The program **nested** and its ground and non-ground sign analysis.

The denotation of the assignment a:=b-1 can be represented by the program:

$$empty \to empty$$
$$[\text{A}, -, \text{C}, \text{Out}] \to [-, -, \text{C}, \text{Out}] \tag{5}$$
$$[\text{A}, +, \text{C}, \text{Out}] \to [\text{u}, +, \text{C}, \text{Out}].$$

Although (5) is slightly more complex than (3), it is more compact than an exhaustive representation and its size grows linearly with the number of variables.

2.2   Sign Analysis of Imperative Programs

As explained in Subsection 2.1, logic programs can be used to represent compactly the abstract denotation of a piece of code. This feature can be used by a static analyser based on denotational semantics. Figure 1 shows the program **nested** with its sign analysis. This analysis is first computed by using the domain S_τ in (1) implemented through ground dependencies (arrays of integers are treated as if they were a single integer *i.e.*, their sign is the least upper bound

```
class a {              class b extends a {      class main {
  f:int;                 g:int;                   clone(x:a):a {
  next:a;                                            if x=null then out:=null;
                         clone():b {                 else {
  clone():a {              out:=new(b);                out:=x.clone();
    out:=new(a);           out.f:=this.f;              out.next:=
    out.f:=this.f;         out.g:=this.g;                this.clone(x.next);
  }                      }                          }
}                      }                          } }
```

main.clone: $[\text{this} \mapsto \text{main}, x \mapsto a] \to [\text{out} \mapsto a]$

  empty → empty $[[\text{main}], []] \to [[]]$ $[[\text{main}], [a]] \to [[a]]$ $[[\text{main}], [b]] \to [[b]]$

a.clone: $[\text{this} \mapsto a] \to [\text{out} \mapsto a]$

      empty → empty $[[a]] \to [[a]]$ $[[b]] \to [[a]]$

b.clone: $[\text{this} \mapsto b] \to [\text{out} \mapsto b]$

          empty → empty $[[b]] \to [[b]]$

Fig. 2. Classes a, b and main and the ground class analysis of their clone methods.

of the signs of their elements) and then through a compact representation which uses logic variables. The result is the same with both analyses, but variables provide a more compact representation. Moreover, computing the ground dependencies required 118.732 seconds and 13453432 Prolog atoms in the stack of our machine, while computing their compact representation only 0.564 seconds and just 56390 atoms (Figure 7). This definitely justifies our investigation.

2.3 Class Analysis of Object-Oriented Programs

Figure 2 shows three simple classes written in an object-oriented language and their class analysis through the domain in [6], as formalised in [13]. That abstract domain contains a bottom element empty, which represents the empty set of states, and lists of sets of classes, one for every variable of interest. For instance, if the type environment which describes the variables of interest is $\tau = [\text{this} \mapsto \text{main}, x \mapsto a]$, then the abstract element $[[\text{main}], [b]]$ represents the set of states where this is bound to an object of class main and x is bound to an object of class b (which is legal since b is a subclass of a, see Figure 2).

The result of the analysis in Figure 2 shows that the method clone of the class main always returns an object of the same class as its x parameter. The same analysis, performed through a non-ground implementation of the same domain, yields the same results except for the denotation of the method clone of the class a, which is now

$$\text{empty} \to \text{empty} \qquad\qquad [[C]] \to [[a]]$$

Note that also the denotation of the method `clone` of the class `main` could be compacted by using a logic variable, but our analyser lost the regularity which that denotation contains. Nevertheless, the non-ground analysis, compared to the ground one, is performed in 0.07 seconds instead of 11.377 and requires to keep in memory 11527 Prolog atoms instead of 2293636 (Figure 8).

We conclude that a major increase in the efficiency of the analysis is achieved through a non-ground representation although the final results of the analyses could be further compacted. This is because the partial computations of the analyser are significantly enhanced by the non-ground representation. A further boost in performance could be achieved by recovering some regularity which is lost during the analysis. This aspect has, however, to be investigated further.

3   Preliminaries

The $(co\text{-})domain$ of a function f is $\mathsf{dom}(f)$ $(\mathsf{cd}(f))$. A total (partial) function is denoted by $\mapsto$ $(\rightarrow)$. We denote by $[v_1 \mapsto t_1, \dots, v_n \mapsto t_n]$ a function f whose domain is $\{v_1, \dots, v_n\}$ and such that $f(v_i) = t_i$ for $i = 1, \dots, n$. An *update* of f is denoted by $f[w_1 \mapsto d_1, \dots, w_m \mapsto d_m]$, where the domain of f may be enlarged.

A pair $\langle C, \leq \rangle$ is a *poset* if $\leq$ is reflexive, transitive and antisymmetric on C. A poset is a *complete lattice* when *least upper bounds* (lub) and *greatest lower bounds* (glb) always exist. In abstract interpretation [5], a *Galois connection* between two posets $\langle C, \leq \rangle$ and $\langle A, \preceq \rangle$ (the *concrete* and the *abstract* domain) is a pair of monotonic maps $\alpha : C \mapsto A$ and $\gamma : A \mapsto C$ such that $\gamma\alpha$ is extensive $(\gamma\alpha(c) \geq c)$ and $\alpha\gamma$ is reductive $(\alpha\gamma(a) \leq a)$.

Given a finite set of variables *Vars* and a set of function symbols Σ with associated arity, the set of *terms* over *Vars* and Σ is the smallest set containing *Vars* and the application of every $f \in \Sigma$ to as many terms as the arity of f requires. A *substitution* is a map from a finite set of variables to terms. If t is a term and σ a substitution, we denote by $t\sigma$ the *application* of σ to t. The partial ordering on terms (up to variable renaming) is defined as $t_1 \leq t_2$ if there exists a substitution σ such that $t_1 = t_2\sigma$. The partial ordering on substitutions is defined as $\theta_1 \leq \theta_2$ if there exists a substitution σ such that $\theta_1 = \theta_2\sigma$.

4   The Framework of Analysis

Our framework is not bound to any particular programming paradigm, although all our examples are for an imperative object-oriented language. In general, however, all we require is that the (concrete or abstract) denotation (*semantics*) of a program P is defined as the fixpoint of a transformer of denotations T_P. This T_P is itself defined as the sequential *composition* of *basic* denotations. For instance, in the case of logic programs, the basic denotations are the denotations of the (concrete or abstract) built-in's and substitutions. In the case of imperative programs, the basic denotations are the denotations of every (concrete or abstract) single command or bytecode. In order to simplify the presentation, we assume that there is a lexicographically ordered set of *program variables* and a finite set of *types*. The only predefine type is *int*. All other types are programmer-defined classes. We recall from Section 2 that a *type environment* τ is a map which assigns a type to the variables in its domain. From now on, τ will silently stand for a type environment.

We suppose that there is a set C_τ of the concrete *states* of the computation for the variables described by τ. The exact nature of these states is irrelevant for this paper. They might be substitutions in the case of logic programs, or pairs of environment and memory in the case of an imperative language [13]. We assume that there is a generic abstract domain $\langle D_\tau, \sqsubseteq \rangle$ with no infinite descending chains, related to $\langle \wp(C_\tau), \subseteq \rangle$ through a Galois connection. We are interested in those elements in D_τ which convey some information that cannot be constructed by merging the information coveyed by the strictly smaller elements.

Definition 1. *We say that $d \in D_\tau$ is (γ-)union-reducible if $\gamma_\tau(d) = \cup\{\gamma_\tau(d') \mid d' \sqsubset d\}$. Otherwise, d is* union-irreducible. *The set of the union-(ir)reducible elements of D_τ is denoted by* $\mathsf{ur}(D_\tau)$ *(*$\mathsf{ui}(D_\tau)$*).*

Example 1. Consider the domain S_τ in (1). Then

$$\mathsf{ui}(S_\tau) = \{\mathsf{empty}\} \cup \{\varsigma \in S_\tau \setminus \{\mathsf{empty}\} \mid \varsigma(v) \neq u \text{ for every } v \in \mathsf{dom}(\tau)\} \ .$$

Let $\mathsf{dom}(\tau) = \{v_1, \dots, v_\ell\}$. It can be shown that the variables abstracted into u actually stand for the disjunction of $+$ and $-$ (for the concretisation map γ_τ^S, see [20]). Namely, for every $\varsigma \in S_\tau \setminus \{\mathsf{empty}\}$ we have

$$\gamma_\tau^S(\varsigma) = \bigcup \left\{ \gamma_\tau^S([s_1, \dots, s_\ell]) \ \middle| \ \begin{matrix} s_i \in \{+, -, *\} \\ s_i \preceq \varsigma(v_i) \text{ for } 1 \leq i \leq \ell \end{matrix} \right\} \cup \gamma_\tau^S(\mathsf{empty}) \ .$$

If $\varsigma \in \mathsf{ur}(S_\tau)$, then there exists some $1 \leq j \leq \ell$ such that $\varsigma(v_j) = u$. Thus, in this case, we have $\gamma_\tau^S(\varsigma) = \cup\{\gamma_\tau^S(\varsigma') \mid \varsigma' \sqsubset \varsigma\}$.

The next result shows that the concretisation map is uniquely identified by the union-irreducible elements of the domain.

Proposition 1. *Let $d \in \mathsf{ur}(D_\tau)$. Then $\gamma_\tau(d) = \cup\{\gamma_\tau(d') \mid d' \in \mathsf{ui}(D_\tau), \ d' \sqsubset d\}$.*

We are interested in functions that can be identified by their restriction to the union-irreducible elements. Such functions do not introduce imprecision in the approximation of the union-reducible elements and, in practice, only the union-irreducible elements are *meaningful* to represent the functions.

Definition 2. *Let $n \geq 1$ and $a \in D_{\tau_1} \times \dots \times D_{\tau_n} \mapsto D_\tau$. We say that a is* ui-induced *if for every $(d_1, \dots, d_n) \in D_{\tau_1} \times \dots \times D_{\tau_n}$ such that there exists j, $1 \leq j \leq n$, with $d_j \in \mathsf{ur}(D_{\tau_j})$, we have*

$$a(d_1, \dots, d_n) = \sqcup\{a(d_1, \dots, d', \dots, d_n) \mid d' \in \mathsf{ui}(D_{\tau_j}) \text{ and } d' \sqsubset d_j\} \ .$$

$[op] : \mathbb{D}_\tau^{\tau_1, \cdots, \tau_n}$, with $op : (C_{\tau_1} \times \cdots \times C_{\tau_n}) \mapsto C_\tau$

$\circ : \left(\mathbb{D}_{\tau'}^{\tau_1, \cdots, \tau_n} \times \mathbb{D}_{\tau_1}^\tau \times \cdots \times \mathbb{D}_{\tau_n}^\tau \right) \mapsto \mathbb{D}_{\tau'}^\tau$ (infix)

$[op](d_1, \ldots, d_n) = \alpha_\tau \left(op(\gamma_{\tau_1}(d_1), \ldots, \gamma_{\tau_n}(d_n)) \right)$

$$(T \circ (T_1, \ldots, T_n))(d) = \begin{cases} T(T_1(d), \ldots, T_n(d)) & d \in \mathsf{ui}(D_\tau) \\ \bigsqcup \{ T(T_1(d'), \ldots, T_n(d')) \mid d' \in \mathsf{ui}(D_\tau) \text{ and } d' \sqsubset d \} & \text{otherwise.} \end{cases}$$

Fig. 3. Signature and implementation of the operations on denotations.

Example 2. Let $\tau = [\mathsf{v} \mapsto int, \mathsf{w} \mapsto int]$ and consider the domain S_τ in (1). The map $a : D_\tau \mapsto D_\tau$ defined as

$$a(\mathsf{empty}) = [+, +] \quad a([+, +]) = [+, u] \quad a([+, -]) = [+, +] \quad a([+, u]) = [+, u]$$
$$a([-, +]) = [-, +] \quad a([-, -]) = \mathsf{empty} \quad a([-, u]) = [u, +]$$
$$a([u, +]) = [+, u] \quad a([u, -]) = [+, -] \quad a([u, u]) = [u, u] \quad (6)$$

is not ui-induced, since $\{ s \in S_\tau \mid s \sqsubset [u, +] \} = \{ \mathsf{empty}, [+, +], [-, +] \}$ and $a(\mathsf{empty}) \sqcup a([+, +]) \sqcup a([-, +]) = [u, u]$, but $a([u, +]) \neq [u, u]$. A ui-induced map is obtained by replacing line (6) with

$$a([u, +]) = [u, u] \qquad a([u, -]) = [+, +] \qquad a([u, u]) = [u, u] . \qquad (7)$$

The monotonic maps over $\wp(C)$ are approximated by *abstract* denotations.

Definition 3. *Let* $n \geq 1$. *The set* $\mathbb{D}_\tau^{\tau_1, \cdots, \tau_n}$ *of the (abstract)* $(\tau_1, \ldots, \tau_n, \tau)$-*denotations consists of the monotonic and* ui-*induced maps in* $D_{\tau_1} \times \cdots \times D_{\tau_n} \mapsto D_\tau$. *It is a complete lattice w.r.t. the pointwise extension of* $\sqsubseteq$.

Example 3. Neither map a of Example 2 nor that obtained from a by replacing (6) by (7) are (τ, τ)-denotations. This is because $\mathsf{empty} \sqsubseteq [-, +]$ but $a(\mathsf{empty}) \not\sqsubseteq a([-, +])$. Hence a is not monotonic. Instead, the map $b : D_\tau \mapsto D_\tau$ defined as

$$b(\mathsf{empty}) = \mathsf{empty} \quad b([+, +]) = [+, u] \quad b([+, -]) = [+, +] \quad b([+, u]) = [-, u]$$
$$b([-, +]) = [-, +] \quad b([-, -]) = \mathsf{empty} \quad b([-, u]) = [-, +]$$
$$b([u, +]) = [u, u] \quad b([u, -]) = [+, +] \quad b([u, u]) = [u, u] \quad (8)$$

is both monotonic and ui-induced and, hence, a (τ, τ)-denotation. As line (8) is induced by the previous ones, it is *superfluous* (i.e., ignored in an implementation).

Figure 3 defines the abstract denotation of every basic operation op by using its best approximation $\alpha op \gamma$ and also defines the composition of abstract denotations. We have proved that the operations in Figure 3 are well-defined *i.e.*, they compute monotonic and ui-induced maps (Definition 3).

Example 4. Consider the abstract domain S_τ in (1) where $\tau = [\mathsf{v} \mapsto int, \mathsf{w} \mapsto int]$. The denotation of the operation $\mathsf{w} := \mathsf{v}$ on the concrete domain is approximated by the following denotation on S_τ

$$a(\mathsf{empty}) = \mathsf{empty} \quad a([+,+]) = [+,+] \quad a([+,-]) = [+,+] \quad a([+,u]) = [+,+]$$
$$a([-,+]) = [-,-] \quad a([-,-]) = [-,-] \quad a([-,u]) = [-,-]$$
$$a([u,+]) = [u,u] \quad a([u,-]) = [u,u] \quad a([u,u]) = [u,u] .$$

The concrete operation **if** $\mathsf{v} \geq 0$ **then**, which checks whether v is positive, and otherwise diverges, is approximated by the following denotation on S_τ

$$b(\mathsf{empty}) = \mathsf{empty} \quad b([+,+]) = [+,+] \quad b([+,-]) = [+,-] \quad b([+,u]) = [+,u]$$
$$b([-,+]) = \mathsf{empty} \quad b([-,-]) = \mathsf{empty} \quad b([-,u]) = \mathsf{empty}$$
$$b([u,+]) = [+,+] \quad b([u,-]) = [+,-] \quad b([u,u]) = [+,u] .$$

Observe that a and b are monotonic and ui-induced maps, hence $a, b \in \mathbb{D}_\tau^\tau$.

5 Logic Programs as Compact Denotations

In Section 2 we have illustrated how logic programs may be used to represent abstract denotations (Definition 3) in a compact way. We detail here this representation.

Definition 4. *We assume that there is a finite set of variables Vars which can be used to build terms. Let D be a set of ground terms. Let every $d \in D_\tau$ be represented by a term in D where d and its representation are used interchangeably. Let $D_\tau^* \supseteq D$ denote a set of terms with variables in Vars and such that $\{d^* \in D_\tau^* \mid vars(d^*) = \varnothing\} = D_\tau$.*

We generalise the concept of union-irreducibility and union-reducibility given in Definition 1 to non-ground terms.

Definition 5. *A (possibly non-ground) term $d^* \in D_\tau^*$ is* union-irreducible *if it has an instance $d \in \mathsf{ui}(D_\tau)$. Otherwise, it is* union-reducible. *The set of the union-irreducible elements in D_τ^* is denoted by $\mathsf{ui}(D_\tau^*)$.*

Example 5. Consider the domain S_τ in (1). We have already introduced the ground terms empty and $[x_1, \ldots, x_\ell]$ ($x_i \in \{*, +, -, \mathsf{u}\}$) to represent its elements. Let $\mathsf{dom}(\tau) = \{v_1, \ldots, v_\ell\}$. We define

$$S_\tau^* = \{\mathsf{empty}\} \cup \left\{ [x_1, \ldots, x_\ell] \,\middle|\, \begin{array}{l} \text{for } i = 1, \ldots, \ell, \, x_i \in \{*, +, -, \mathsf{u}\} \cup Vars \\ \text{and } x_i = * \text{ iff } \tau(v_i) \neq int \end{array} \right\}. \quad (9)$$

If $\tau = [\mathsf{a} \mapsto int, \mathsf{b} \mapsto int, \mathsf{c} \mapsto int, \mathsf{d} \mapsto int]$, the set S_τ^* contains the non-ground union-irreducible terms $[+, -, \mathsf{X}, \mathsf{Y}]$ and $[+, -, \mathsf{X}, \mathsf{X}]$, as well as the non-ground union-reducible terms $[+, \mathsf{u}, \mathsf{X}, \mathsf{Y}]$ and $[+, \mathsf{u}, \mathsf{X}, \mathsf{X}]$.

A *non-ground representation* is defined by D_τ^* and a set of substitutions Λ.

Definition 6. *Let Λ be a set of substitutions with variables in Vars and closed by composition and let Λ^g denote its* grounding subset *on Vars i.e., the set of ground instances of Λ with domain in Vars. Let $\xi^\Lambda(X) = \{X\sigma \mid \sigma \in \Lambda^g\}$ for every syntactic object X (terms, clauses, programs). Let Typenv denote a set of type environments. Then we say that the pair $\langle\{D_\tau^* \mid \tau \in Typenv\}, \Lambda\rangle$ is a* non-ground *representation and Λ is* legal *if the pair satisfies the following conditions:*

1. *if $d^* \in D_\tau^*$ and $\sigma \in \Lambda$ then $d^*\sigma \in D_\tau^*$ (D_τ^* is closed w.r.t. application of substitutions in Λ),*
2. *if $d^* \in \mathsf{ui}(D_\tau^*)$ then $\xi^\Lambda(d^*) = \{d \in \mathsf{ui}(D_\tau) \mid d \le d^*\}$ (union-irreducibility cannot be lost).*

Example 6. Consider the domain S_τ^* in (9). A set of legal substitutions for a term in S_τ^* is $\{\sigma \mid \forall v \in Vars : \sigma(v) \in Vars \cup \{+, -, *\}\}$ i.e., we do not allow variables to be bound to u. This is because a set of legal substitutions must not lose union-irreducibility (point 2 of Definition 6).

From now on, we write ξ for ξ^Λ and assume that $\langle\{D_\tau^* \mid \tau \in Typenv\}, \Lambda\rangle$ is given.

By using a non-ground representation (Definition 6) we can write clauses that represent more-compactly the ui-induced maps.

Definition 7. *Let $n \ge 1$. A $(\tau_1, \dots, \tau_n, \tau)$-compact clause is $l_1, \dots, l_n \to r$, with $l_i \in \mathsf{ui}(D_{\tau_i}^*)$ for $i = 1, \dots, n$, $r \in D_\tau^*$ and $vars(r) \subseteq \cup\{vars(l_i) \mid i = 1, \dots, n\}$. We say that $l_1, \dots, l_n$ are its* inputs *and that r is its* output*. The meaning of a set t of $(\tau_1, \dots, \tau_n, \tau)$-compact clauses is the unique ui-induced map $\bar{t} : D_{\tau_1} \times \cdots \times D_{\tau_n} \mapsto D_\tau$ such that, for every $L \in \mathsf{ui}(D_{\tau_1}) \times \cdots \times \mathsf{ui}(D_{\tau_n})$,*

$$\bar{t}(L) = \sqcup\{r\theta \mid L' \to r \in t, \ \theta \in \Lambda^g \text{ and } L'\theta = L\} \ .$$

Example 7. If $\tau = [\mathsf{a} \mapsto int, \mathsf{b} \mapsto int, \mathsf{c} \mapsto int, \mathsf{out} \mapsto int]$ then

$$c_1 = (\mathsf{empty} \to [+, +, \mathsf{u}, -])$$
$$c_2 = ([+, -, \mathsf{X}, \mathsf{Y}] \to [\mathsf{u}, \mathsf{Y}, +, +])$$
$$c_3 = ([+, \mathsf{X}, +, +] \to [+, -, \mathsf{X}, \mathsf{u}])$$

are (τ, τ)-compact clauses. The meaning of $\{c_1, c_2, c_3\}$ is the unique ui-induced map $\overline{\{c_1, c_2, c_3\}} : S_\tau \mapsto S_\tau$ such that

$$
\begin{array}{lll}
\mathsf{empty} \to [+, +, \mathsf{u}, -] & [+, +, +, +] \to [+, -, +, \mathsf{u}] & [+, +, +, -] \to \mathsf{empty} \\
[+, +, -, +] \to \mathsf{empty} & [+, +, -, -] \to \mathsf{empty} & [+, -, +, +] \to [\mathsf{u}, \mathsf{u}, \mathsf{u}, \mathsf{u}] \\
[+, -, +, -] \to [\mathsf{u}, -, +, +] & [+, -, -, +] \to [-, +, +, +] & [+, -, -, -] \to [\mathsf{u}, -, +, +] \\
[-, +, +, +] \to \mathsf{empty} & [-, +, +, -] \to \mathsf{empty} & [-, +, -, +] \to \mathsf{empty} \\
[-, +, -, -] \to \mathsf{empty} & [-, -, +, +] \to \mathsf{empty} & [-, -, +, -] \to \mathsf{empty} \\
[-, -, -, +] \to \mathsf{empty} & [-, -, -, -] \to \mathsf{empty} &
\end{array}
$$

Note that both c_2 and c_3 contribute to determine the output for the input $[+, -, +, +]$. Moreover, note that $\overline{\{c_1, c_2, c_3\}}$ is not monotonic. Hence, it is *not* a (τ, τ)-denotation (Definition 3).

As Example 7 shows, the meaning of a set of compact clauses is not necessarily a denotation because it can lack monotonicity (Definition 3). Thus Definition 8 requires monotonicity to guarantee that the meaning of a set of compact clauses is a denotation (Proposition 2). It also requires that sets of compact clauses have exhaustive and non-overlapping inputs, defining a *normal form* which keeps the sets of compact clauses small.

Definition 8. *Let $n, m \geq 1$. The set $\mathbb{CD}_\tau^{\tau_1, \ldots, \tau_n}$ of the $(\tau_1, \ldots, \tau_n, \tau)$-compact denotations is formed by those sets $\{L_1 \to r_1, \ldots, L_m \to r_m\}$ of $(\tau_1, \ldots, \tau_n, \tau)$-compact clauses such that*

i) $\cup\{\xi(L_i) \mid 1 \leq i \leq m\} = \mathsf{ui}(D_{\tau_1}) \times \cdots \times \mathsf{ui}(D_{\tau_n})$ (exhaustivity),
ii) $\underline{\xi(L_j) \cap \xi(L_k) = \varnothing}$ for $1 \leq j, k \leq m$, $j \neq k$ (non-overlapping),
iii) $\{L_1 \to r_1, \ldots, L_m \to r_m\}$ is monotonic (monotonicity).

Example 8. The set of compact clauses $\{c_1, c_2, c_3\}$ of Example 7 does not satisfy any of the conditions of Definition 8. Instead, the set of compact clauses (5) in Subsection 2.2 satisfies those conditions. Hence, it is a (τ, τ)-compact denotation.

Proposition 2. *Let $n \geq 1$ and $t \in \mathbb{CD}_\tau^{\tau_1, \ldots, \tau_n}$. We have $\bar{t} \in \mathbb{D}_\tau^{\tau_1, \ldots, \tau_n}$.*

The next result provides an explicit definition of the meaning of a compact denotation, also for union-reducible inputs (compare with Definition 7).

Proposition 3. *Let $n \geq 1$, $t \in \mathbb{CD}_\tau^{\tau_1, \ldots, \tau_n}$ and $L \in D_{\tau_1} \times \cdots \times D_{\tau_n}$. We have $\bar{t}(L) = \sqcup\{r\theta \mid L' \to r \in t, \ \theta \in \Lambda^g, \ L'\theta \sqsubseteq L\}$.*

Now that we have a notion of compact denotations $\mathbb{CD}$, we need operations which mimic over $\mathbb{CD}$ what the operations in Figure 3 do over $\mathbb{D}$. For the operations $[op]$, we assume that an explicit compact denotation for every op is given. Note that such compact denotations always exist, since we can use ground representations (Figure 3) as degenerate cases of compact denotations. However, we should try to use logic variables as much as possible, in order to better exploit the capabilities of our non-ground representation.

Example 9. Consider the operations given in Example 4. A non-degenerate compact denotation for $[op]$, where $op = (\mathtt{w} := \mathtt{v})$, is $\{\mathtt{empty} \to \mathtt{empty}, [\mathtt{V}, \mathtt{W}] \to [\mathtt{V}, \mathtt{V}]\}$. A non-degenerate compact denotation for $[op]$, where $op = \mathtt{if}\ \mathtt{v} \geq 0\ \mathtt{then}$, is $\{\mathtt{empty} \to \mathtt{empty}, [+, \mathtt{W}] \to [+, \mathtt{W}], [-, \mathtt{W}] \to \mathtt{empty}\}$. A correct composition operation over $\mathbb{CD}$ is described in the next section.

6   Composition of Compact Denotations

In this section, we define an operation $\circ^*$ which composes compact denotations, and show that it exactly mimics what $\circ$ does over denotations (Figure 3). We consider only the simpler case when $n = 1$. For the general case, see the longer version of the paper available on-line. All the examples will be for the domain S_τ^* in (9).

Figure 4 collects the operations that an abstract domain must implement in order to define $\circ^*$ and, more generally, an analyser. We discuss them in this section as soon as they are needed. We start from `domain_entails`. A call `domain_entails(`τ`,A,B)` computes all possible ways for making A entail B.

Example 10. Let $\tau = [\mathtt{a} \mapsto int, \mathtt{b} \mapsto int]$. An implementation of `domain_entails` is such that `domain_entails(`τ`,[X,-],[+,u])` succeeds and binds X to +, while `domain_entails(`τ`,[+,X],[+,u])` succeeds first binding X to + and then to -. `domain_entails(`τ`,[+,+],[+,u])` succeeds. `domain_entails(`τ`,[+,-],[+,+])` fails. Note that we do not allow X to be bound to u (Example 6).

We define now a *pre-composition* • which, although it correctly mimics ∘, is not closed on $\mathbb{CD}$ (Example 11).

Definition 9. *Let* $t_1 \in \mathbb{CD}_{\tau'}^{\tau_1}$ *and* $t_2 \in \mathbb{CD}_{\tau_1}^{\tau}$ *be renamed apart. We define the* compact pre-composition $t_1 \bullet t_2 \in \mathbb{CD}_{\tau'}^{\tau}$ *as*

$$t_1 \bullet t_2 = \left\{ (l_2 \to r_1)\theta \,\middle|\, \begin{array}{l} l_2 \to r_2 \in t_2,\ l_1 \to r_1 \in t_1 \\ \mathtt{domain\_entails}(\tau_1, l_1, r_2)\ computes\ \theta \end{array} \right\}.$$

Example 11. Using Definition 9, we will compute

$$
\begin{array}{cc}
\mathtt{empty} \to \mathtt{empty} & \mathtt{empty} \to \mathtt{empty} \\
[\mathtt{B},+] \to [-] \quad [\mathtt{B},-] \to [+] & \bullet \quad [\mathtt{A},+] \to [-,\mathtt{u}] \quad [\mathtt{A},-] \to [+,+]
\end{array}
$$

$$=$$

$$
\mathtt{empty} \to \mathtt{empty} \quad [\mathtt{A},+] \to [-] \quad [\mathtt{A},+] \to [+] \quad [\mathtt{A},-] \to [-] . \tag{10}
$$

To see this, consider every clause on the right. We start with `empty` → `empty`. Its output is entailed only by the input of the clause `empty` → `empty` on the left. Folding those clauses we obtain the clause `empty` → `empty` itself. Consider next the clause $[\mathtt{A},+] \to [-,\mathtt{u}]$. Its output $[-,\mathtt{u}]$ is entailed by the inputs $[\mathtt{B},+]$ and $[\mathtt{B},-]$ of two clauses on the left if we bind B to −. This results in *two* clauses $[\mathtt{A},+] \to [-]$ and $[\mathtt{A},+] \to [+]$. Finally, consider the clause $[\mathtt{A},-] \to [+,+]$, whose output is entailed by the input $[\mathtt{B},+]$ of a clause on the left if we bind B to +. This results in the clause $[\mathtt{A},-] \to [-]$. Note that (10) is not a compact denotation, since condition (ii) of Definition 8 is not satisfied (there are overlapping inputs).

We have proved that condition (ii) is the only property of Definition 8 which is not preserved by •. We can make condition (ii) hold through a *normalisation* procedure which, without changing their meaning, transforms a set of clauses to a set whose inputs are disjoint. It iteratively splits two overlapping but distinct inputs into their intersection and their two differences. When no such inputs exist anymore, ⊔ is applied to the outputs corresponding to the same input. Hence this `make_disjunctive` procedure can be defined through the `domain_intersect_ui`, `domain_subtract_ui` and `domain_lub` operations specified in Figure 4. The interested reader can find its definition inside our implementation (Section 7).

Example 12. If we apply `make_disjunctive` to the set (10), we just have to compute the ⊔ of the two outputs for the same input $[\mathtt{A},+]$. We obtain the compact denotation $\{\mathtt{empty} \to \mathtt{empty}, [\mathtt{A},+] \to [\mathtt{u}], [\mathtt{A},-] \to [-]\}$.

We can now define the counterpart of ∘ over $\mathbb{CD}$. We have proved that it is correct and optimal and preserves all three conditions of Definition 8.

Operation	Semantics
domain_entails(τ,A,B) with A, B $\in D_\tau^*$	computes $\theta_1,\dots,\theta_n \in \Lambda$ such that $\{\sigma \in \Lambda^g \mid A\sigma \sqsubseteq B\sigma\}$ $= \{\sigma \in \Lambda^g \mid \sigma \le \theta_i \text{ with } 1 \le i \le n\}$
domain_intersect_ui(τ,A,B) with A, B $\in$ ui(D_τ^*)	computes $\theta_1,\dots,\theta_n \in \Lambda$ such that for every $\sigma \in \Lambda^g$ we have $A\theta_i\sigma = B\theta_i\sigma$ and $\xi(A) \cap \xi(B) = \cup_{i=1,\dots,n}\xi(A\theta_i)$
domain_subtract_ui(τ,A,B) with A, B $\in$ ui(D_τ^*) and $\xi(A) \cap \xi(B) \ne \varnothing$	computes $\theta_1,\dots,\theta_n \in \Lambda$ such that $\cup_{i=1,\dots,n}\xi(A\theta_i) = \xi(A) \setminus \xi(B)$
domain_lub(τ,A,B,L) with A, B $\in D_\tau^*$	computes $\theta_1,\dots,\theta_n \in \Lambda$ such that $\cup_{i=1,\dots,n}\xi(A\theta_i) = \xi(A)$, $\cup_{i=1,\dots,n}\xi(B\theta_i) = \xi(B)$ and for every $i = 1,\dots,n$ and $\sigma \in \Lambda^g$ we have $L\theta_i\sigma = A\theta_i\sigma \sqcup_{D_\tau} B\theta_i\sigma$
domain_bottom(τ_{in},τ_{out},B)	computes B $\in A_{\tau_{in},\tau_{out}}^*$ s.t. $\xi(B) = \perp_{A_{\tau_{in},\tau_{out}}}$
domain_the_same(τ_{in},τ_{out},A,B)	checks if $\xi(A) = \xi(B)$, with A, B $\in A_{\tau_{in},\tau_{out}}^*$

Fig. 4. Domain-specific operations.

Definition 10. *In the hypotheses of Definition 9, we define the abstract composition as* $t_1 \circ^* t_2 = \text{make\_disjunctive}(t_1 \bullet t_2)$.

Example 13. Proceeding as in Example 11, we have

$$\begin{array}{cc}\text{empty} \to \text{empty} & [A,+] \to [+] \\ [+,-] \to [-] & [-,-] \to [+]\end{array} \bullet \begin{array}{cc}\text{empty} \to \text{empty} \\ [X] \to [X,u]\end{array} = \begin{array}{cc}\text{empty} \to \text{empty} & [X] \to [+] \\ [+] \to [-] & [-] \to [+]\end{array}.$$

The input of $[X] \to [+]$ overlaps with that of both $[+] \to [-]$ and $[-] \to [+]$. The call domain_intersect_ui(τ,[X],[+]) binds X to + while the call domain_subtract_ui(τ,[X],[+]) binds X to -. The two clauses $[X] \to [+]$ and $[+] \to [-]$ can hence be split and we obtain the set of clauses $\{\text{empty} \to \text{empty}, [+] \to [+], [+] \to [-], [-] \to [+]\}$. After the domain_lub operation we obtain the compact denotation $\{\text{empty} \to \text{empty}, [+] \to [u], [-] \to [+]\}$.

The operation domain_bottom in Figure 4 is used to start the fixpoint computation and domain_the_same to stop it. This last operation can be implemented by a two-stage test. It first checks for variance of logic programs. If they are not variant of each other, a more expensive model equivalence test is applied.

7   Implementation

LOOP (Localised for Object-Oriented Programs) [19] is a generic analyser for our simple object-oriented programs. LOOP is an implementation in Prolog of the watchpoint semantics of [20] extended to deal with object-oriented features through the operations of [13].The structure of LOOP is given in Figure 5.

The highest-level module **analyser** implements a fixpoint engine for a denotational semantics in terms of the operations in **semantic** (for instructions, conditionals, loops). Those operations are themselves compiled in terms of calls to **combinators**, a module which implements the operations of Figure 3. The module **typenv** implements the type environments (Section 2). The module **aux** implements auxiliary and logging functions. External modules must contain the abstract syntax of the code of the program to be analysed as well as the abstract domains and their operations. Note that LOOP can perform both an abstract interpretation and a combination of abstract compilation [9] and partial evaluation of the program. The result is the same in both cases, but abstract compilation is in general cheaper in time and space and is the one used in our experiments. The analysis

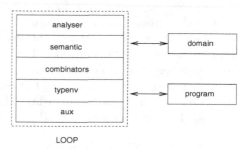

Fig. 5. The structure of LOOP.

analysis	reference	ground	non-ground	bdd's
sign analysis	Equation (1)	signs	signs_vars	signs_bdd
rapid type (*i.e.*, class) analysis	[1,13]	rt	rt_vars	
dataflow class analysis	[6,13]	df	df_vars	
constraint class analysis	[18,13]	ps	ps_vars	
escape analysis	[10]	e	e_vars	

Fig. 6. The abstract domains implemented for our LOOP analyser.

Bmrk	#w	signs		signs_vars		signs_bdd small		and large	
		time	space	time	space	time	space	time	space
fib	0	1.683	348291	0.049	7658	0.047	1000	0.026	1000000
fib	3	2.186	478132	0.119	15896	0.111	1000	0.064	1000000
fib	6	2.234	493412	0.147	20771	0.131	1000	0.091	1000000
nested	0	118.732	13453432	0.564	56390	0.758	1000	0.195	1000000
nested	7	119.004	13671816	0.859	145752	1.659	1000	0.484	1000000
nested	13	120.012	13852568	1.149	230778	3.281	1000	0.916	1000000
arith	0	108.578	13617292	0.163	26242	0.364	1000	0.114	1000000
arith	7	108.993	13654012	0.181	32238	0.393	1000	0.136	1000000
arith	14	109.453	13730012	0.198	38485	0.481	1000	0.168	1000000

Fig. 7. Time and space required for sign analysis.

computed by LOOP is automatically *focused* on a set of program points deemed *of interest* for the analysis. Those program points are called *watchpoints* [20]. In general, the cost of the analysis depends on the number of watchpoints #w. If #w = 0, just an input/output analysis of the program is performed.

We have implemented in Prolog five abstract analyses (domains) for LOOP, with both a ground and a non-ground representation. We have also implemented sign analysis by using bdd's [3], normally viewed as the most efficient way for representing abstract denotations. Figure 6 shows those domains. We use Prolog lists to represent sets of classes or sets of creation points. The domain signs_bdd is implemented in C++, by using the BuDDy library for bdd's [15]. Our experiments have been performed by using SICStus Prolog version 3.8.5 on a Pentium III 736 Mhz machine with 256 Mbytes of RAM.

Bmrk	#w	rt		rt_vars		df		df_vars		ps		ps_vars	
		time	space	time	space	time	space	time	space	time	space	time	space
inv	0	0.048	16608	0.016	5556	0.431	94363	0.032	6823	0.460	105601	0.032	7619
inv	2	0.051	17946	0.020	6894	0.441	98637	0.034	8077	0.464	110381	0.034	9031
inv	4	0.058	18906	0.022	7854	0.444	101745	0.035	8879	0.472	113857	0.035	9933
clone	0	0.071	22951	0.042	11563	11.377	2293636	0.070	11527	283.687	29282466	0.162	25307
clone	6	0.095	27805	0.055	16417	11.450	2320420	0.078	18935	284.624	29393040	0.165	47855
clone	11	0.125	40457	0.079	26650	15.297	3149401	0.296	78574	376.172	39337617	0.495	240844
figures	0	2.791	696952	1.106	216494	0.934	166487	0.092	26099	3.574	844796	0.237	53094
figures	9	2.881	739802	1.128	259344	0.971	177605	0.106	32497	3.651	891134	0.250	70796
figures	17	2.956	776338	1.193	295880	1.071	188949	0.132	37938	3.717	936542	0.255	85612

Fig. 8. Time and space required for class analysis.

For sign analysis, we use three benchmarks: fib, the Fibonacci procedure; nested, the program in Figure 1; and arith which implements some arbitrary precision arithmetic operations. For class and escape analysis we use three benchmarks: inv, a procedure that changes from a to b and back the class of a variable. It does it twice through two calls, inside a while loop, to a virtual function; clone (Figure 2), which implements a generic cloning of a list by means of a virtual call to the clone method of the elements of the list; and figures which implements geometric figures with a generic method for rotating them.

Figure 7 compares time (in seconds) and space (amount of data structures built during the analysis) costs of the signs and signs_vars analyses. It can be seen that the analysis scales with the number of watch-points. Figures 8 and 9 do the same for the three domains for class analysis and the domain for escape analysis summarised in Figure 6, respectively. These show that X_vars is always more efficient than X and gains up to three orders of magnitude in time and space

Bmrk	#w	e		e_vars	
		time	space	time	space
inv	0	0.421	12722	0.205	7930
inv	2	0.432	14060	0.217	9268
inv	4	0.442	15020	0.227	10228
clone	0	0.867	15398	0.556	10872
clone	6	1.122	24680	0.745	19102
clone	11	1.166	31800	0.789	26222
figures	0	6.588	142880	4.179	88280
figures	9	6.725	161564	4.336	110588
figures	17	6.894	181208	4.491	133520

Fig. 9. Escape analysis.

(for instance, the case of the analyses ps and ps_vars for the benchmark clone). The cost in space of the analyses i.e., the number of data structures built, is independent of the choice of the language used to implement LOOP, indicating that their time cost is also probably unrelated to this choice.

Figure 7 also compares our compact representation of the domain for sign analysis in (1) with the other implementation we have built through a highly-optimised library for bdd's [15]. We have run the test with two different initial numbers of bdd nodes and cache size. These are suggested by the authors of [15] for "small" and "large" examples, respectively. Figure 7 shows that a compact representation through logic programs has an efficiency comparable with that of an implementation based on bdd's and consumes much less memory space. The more efficient results in the column headed *large* were obtained by considering the sign analysis of programs no more than thirty lines long as a "large" example, making the maximal amount of memory available to the bdd library, and by disabling the garbage collection of bdd nodes. W.r.t. space, Figure 7 reports the number of Prolog atoms, for `signs_vars`, and of bdd nodes, for `signs_bdd`. Those units can be considered the same, since they are related by a small constant.

8 Related Work and Conclusion

Non-ground logic programs have been used for the static analysis of both functional and logic programs. In the case of ML, they have been used to model type dependencies [11,16], but only a single clause (a single type dependency) was used. In the case of logic programs they have been used for type analysis [4,12]. Non-ground terms have been used also for mode and structure analysis of logic programs [7]. The application of non-ground terms or clauses to the abstract interpretation of other programming paradigms has not before been studied. In [8], non-ground constraints have been used for set-based static analysis, which is not based on abstract interpretation. There, dependencies between variables cannot be expressed. Moreover, since constraints have a *flat* structure, the (abstract) values of variables in different instantiations of the same procedure or in different program points are indistinguishable. This paper has introduced the notion of union-reducibility (Definition 1), which is new. In [14,17], a notion of (component-)additivity is used to limit the number of iterations to obtain a fixpoint. Union-irreducibility, as defined here, might force the analyser to consider more inputs in a denotation than additivity, but allows one to represent more precisely non-additive denotations.

Compared to bdd's [3], there are several advantages in using our technique.

- Logic programs are closer to the specification since denotations are immediately recognisable as logic programs (*i.e.*, sets of input/output arrows), while a bdd uses a formula to code the denotation.
- The symbolic capability of logic programs helps the programming task. For instance, we do not need to *code* sets of classes or escape contexts through binary digits, but we can use logic programming lists.
- Our technique just requires the unification procedure and not the whole machinery of logic programming (resolution, backtracking). Section 7 shows that only a relatively small amount of memory is needed, with efficiency similar to that obtained with a bdd library which requires a large statically allocated space for the bdd nodes and the cache (Figure 7). This makes our technique ideal when memory is a concern, for instance inside a smart card.

References

1. D. F. Bacon and P. F. Sweeney. Fast Static Analysis of C++ Virtual Function Calls. In *Proc. of OOPSLA'96*, volume 31(10) of *ACM SIGPLAN Notices*, pages 324–341, New York, 1996. ACM Press.
2. B. Blanchet. Escape Analysis for Object Oriented Languages. Application to Java^{TM}. In *OOPSLA'99*, volume 34(10) of *SIGPLAN Notices*, pages 20–34, 1999.
3. R. E. Bryant. Graph-Based Algorithms for Boolean Function Manipulation. *IEEE Transactions on Computers*, 35(8):677–691, 1986.
4. M. Codish and B. Demoen. Deriving Polymorphic Type Dependencies for Logic Programs Using Multiple Incarnations of Prop. In B. Le Charlier, editor, *Proc. SAS*, volume 864 of *LNCS*, pages 281–296. Springer-Verlag, 1994.
5. P. Cousot and R. Cousot. Abstract Interpretation: A Unified Lattice Model for Static Analysis of Programs by Construction or Approximation of Fixpoints. In *Proc. of POPL'77*, pages 238–252, 1977.
6. A. Diwan, J. E. B. Moss, and K. S. McKinley. Simple and Effective Analysis of Statically Typed Object-Oriented Programs. In *Proc. of OOPSLA'96*, volume 31(10) of *ACM SIGPLAN Notices*, pages 292–305, New York, 1996. ACM Press.
7. J. Gallagher, D. Boulanger, and H. Saglam. Practical Model-Based Static Analysis for Definite Logic Programs. In J. W. Lloyd, editor, *Proc. of the Int. Logic Programming Symp., ILPS'95*, pages 351–365, Portland, Oregon, 1995. MIT Press.
8. N. Heintze and J. Jaffar. Set Constraints and Set-Based Analysis. In A. Borning, editor, *Proc. of Principles and Practice of Constraint Programming*, volume 874 of *LNCS*, pages 281–298. Springer-Verlag, 1994.
9. M. Hermenegildo, W. Warren, and S.K. Debray. Global Flow Analysis as a Practical Compilation Tool. *Journal of Logic Programming*, 13(2 & 3):349–366, 1992.
10. P. M. Hill and F. Spoto. A Foundation of Escape Analysis. In H. Kirchner and C. Ringeissen, editors, *Proc. of AMAST'02*, volume 2422 of *LNCS*, pages 380–395, St. Gilles les Bains, La Réunion island, France, September 2002. Springer-Verlag.
11. R. Hindley. The Principal Type-Scheme of an Object in Combinatory Logic. *Trans. Amer. Math. Soc.*, 146:29–60, 1969.
12. J. M. Howe and A. King. Implementing Groundness Analysis with Definite Boolean Functions. In G. Smolka, editor, *ESOP 2000*, volume 1782 of *LNCS*, pages 200–214, Berlin, Germany, 2000. Springer-Verlag.
13. T. Jensen and F. Spoto. Class Analysis of Object-Oriented Programs through Abstract Interpretation. In F. Honsell and M. Miculan, editors, *Proceedings of FOSSACS 2001*, volume 2030 of *LNCS*, pages 261–275. Springer-Verlag, 2001.
14. J. Köller and M. Mohnen. A New Class of Function for Abstract Interpretation. In A. Cortesi and G. Filé, editors, *Proc. of the Static Analysis Symposium, SAS'99*, volume 1694 of *LNCS*, pages 248–263, Venice, Italy, 1999. Springer-Verlag.
15. J. Lind-Nielsen. BuDDy - A Binary Decision Diagram Package. Available at www.itu.dk/research/buddy/.
16. R. Milner. A Theory of Type Polymorphism in Programming. *Journal of Computer and Systems Sciences*, 17-3:348–375, 1978.
17. H. R. Nielson and F. Nielson. Bounded Fixed Point Iteration. In *Proc. of POPL'92*, pages 71–82. ACM Press, 1992.
18. J. Palsberg and M. I. Schwartzbach. Object-Oriented Type Inference. In *Proc. OOPSLA'91*, volume 26(11) of *ACM SIGPLAN Notices*, pages 146–161, 1991.
19. F. Spoto. The LOOP Analyser. www.sci.univr.it/~spoto/loop/.
20. F. Spoto. Watchpoint Semantics: A Tool for Compositional and Focussed Static Analyses. In P. Cousot, editor, *Proc. of SAS'01*, LNCS. Springer-Verlag, 2001.

A *Strafunski* Application Letter

Ralf Lämmel[1,2] and Joost Visser[1,3]

[1] CWI, Kruislaan 413, NL-1098 SJ Amsterdam
[2] Vrije Universiteit, De Boelelaan 1081a, NL-1081 HV Amsterdam
[3] Software Improvement Group, Kruislaan 419, NL-1098 SJ Amsterdam
(Ralf.Laemmel|Joost.Visser)@cwi.nl
http://www.cwi.nl/~(ralf|jvisser)/

Abstract. *Strafunski* is a Haskell-centred software bundle for implementing language processing components — most notably program analyses and transformations. Typical application areas include program optimisation, refactoring, software metrics, software re- and reverse engineering.

Strafunski started out as generic programming library complemented by generative tool support to address the concern of *generic traversal* over typed representations of parse trees in a scalable manner. Meanwhile, *Strafunski* also encompasses means of *integrating external components* such as parsers, pretty printers, and graph visualisation tools.

In a selection of case studies, we demonstrate that typed functional programming in Haskell, augmented with *Strafunski*'s support for generic traversal and external components, is very appropriate for the development of practical language processors. In particular, we discuss using Haskell for Cobol reverse engineering, Java code metrics, and Haskell re-engineering.

Keywords: *Strafunski*, Program transformation, Program analysis, Language processing, Generic traversal, External components, Interchange formats, Functional programming

1 Haskell Meets Cobol

Consider the following software reverse engineering problem in the context of re-documentation of Cobol software. Given a Cobol program, we want to synthesise and view the so-called *perform graph*. It is called 'perform graph' because of Cobol's verb PERFORM for procedure invocation. Such a graph helps maintenance programmers to understand the control flow of Cobol programs of non-trivial size: typical Cobol programs are about 1500 lines, but individual programs of 25,000 lines are not uncommon. A perform graph contains nodes for each procedure, and edges for each procedure invocation. The perform graph of a simple Cobol program is shown in Fig. 1. Roughly, a perform graph is computed as follows:

1. Find all PERFORMs to reconstruct what labelled code blocks represent procedures.
2. Reconstruct the main procedure of the program by a kind of control-flow analysis.
3. Find all PERFORMs per procedure to determine outgoing procedure invocations.

V. Dahl and P. Wadler (Eds.): PADL 2003, LNCS 2562, pp. 357–375, 2003.

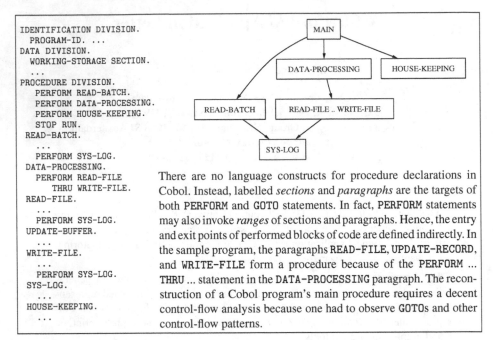

```
IDENTIFICATION DIVISION.
  PROGRAM-ID. ...
DATA DIVISION.
  WORKING-STORAGE SECTION.
  ...
PROCEDURE DIVISION.
  PERFORM READ-BATCH.
  PERFORM DATA-PROCESSING.
  PERFORM HOUSE-KEEPING.
  STOP RUN.
READ-BATCH.
  ...
  PERFORM SYS-LOG.
DATA-PROCESSING.
  PERFORM READ-FILE
    THRU WRITE-FILE.
READ-FILE.
  ...
  PERFORM SYS-LOG.
UPDATE-BUFFER.
  ...
WRITE-FILE.
  ...
  PERFORM SYS-LOG.
SYS-LOG.
  ...
HOUSE-KEEPING.
  ...
```

There are no language constructs for procedure declarations in Cobol. Instead, labelled *sections* and *paragraphs* are the targets of both PERFORM and GOTO statements. In fact, PERFORM statements may also invoke *ranges* of sections and paragraphs. Hence, the entry and exit points of performed blocks of code are defined indirectly. In the sample program, the paragraphs READ-FILE, UPDATE-RECORD, and WRITE-FILE form a procedure because of the PERFORM ... THRU ... statement in the DATA-PROCESSING paragraph. The reconstruction of a Cobol program's main procedure requires a decent control-flow analysis because one had to observe GOTOs and other control-flow patterns.

Fig. 1. A Cobol program and the corresponding perform graph.

In addition to the specific problem of defining precisely how to compute a perform graph, there are more general complications that surround the implementation of a perform-graph extractor in a practical setting. These include the extraordinary size of the Cobol language, the proliferation of its dialects, the size of the typical code base to be processed, and the realities of limited budgets and time frames.

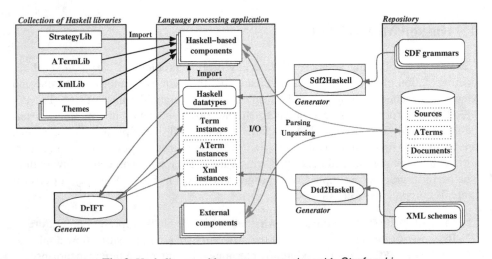

Fig. 2. Haskell-centred language processing with *Strafunski*.

In this paper, we report on using *typed functional programming in Haskell* to implement problems like the one above. Haskell seems to be suited for language processing: meta-programs in Haskell operate on representations of object-programs based on algebraic datatypes. However, in the typical textbook approach, two bits are missing, namely support for generic traversal, and integration of external components:

Generic traversal. We must be able to employ generic programming techniques. That is, we want to deal generically with all language constructs that are not immediately relevant to our problem. As for the discussed perform-graph extractor, we do not want to take all of the several hundred syntactic elements of Cobol into account, but only PERFORMs and code blocks. Also, every time a new dialect or language cocktail pops up (think of embedded SQL or CICS, in-house preprocessors, OO Cobol), we want to adapt the tool with minimal effort.

External components. We must be able to integrate external components on the basis of suitable interchange formats. As for the perform-graph extractor, we want to reuse an existing Cobol parser. Note that the development of an industrial-strength Cobol parser from scratch takes at least a few months, and choosing the right parsing technology is crucial for scalability. Other typical external components are graph visualisers, browsers, pretty printers, and databases.

The Haskell-centred software bundle *Strafunski*[1] addresses these two concerns as illustrated in Fig. 2. The block labelled 'language processing application' emphasises that Haskell-based and external components coexist in an application. The components communicate on the basis of the interchange formats XML and ATerms [2], or they access a repository with source programs and XML documents. Haskell-based components take advantage of generic programming with 'functional strategies' [12,11,8] based on *Strafunski*'s Haskell library *StrategyLib*. Functional strategies are generic functions that can traverse into terms of any type while mixing type-specific and uniform behaviour. Here we assume that algebraic datatypes serve for the typed representation of parse trees. Strategic programming in Haskell relies on supportive code per term type. The corresponding instances of a *Term* class can be generated using the *DrIFT* preprocessing technology [17]. The algebraic datatypes might be derived from XML schemas (or DTDs) and syntax definitions in SDF [5]; see the generators *Sdf2Haskell* and *Dtd2Haskell*. There are further Haskell libraries: *XmlLib* for XML document processing (contributed by HaXML [16]) and *ATermLib* for data interchange. *DrIFT* is also used to generate *XML* instances and *ATerm* instances needed as mediators between Haskell terms and the interchange formats. The collection of libraries also encompasses themes for language processing such as name analyses and refactorings [9].

Road-map. This application letter reports on the use of the *Strafunski* bundle for the implementation of language processing tools. We discuss three case studies: reverse engineering (Sec. 4), software metrics (Sec 5), and re-engineering (Sec. 6). The object languages involved are Cobol, Java, and Haskell, respectively. Before we embark on

---

[1] *Strafunski* home page: http://www.cs.vu.nl/Strafunski/ — Stra refers to strategies, fun refers to functional programming, and their harmonious composition is a homage to the music of Igor Stravinsky.

full_td:
Process all nodes.

once_td:
Process one subtree.

stop_td:
Descend into failing subtrees.

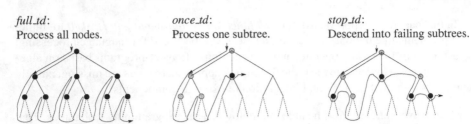

Typically, a traversal scheme takes one argument strategy for node processing. The above schemes all stick to a top-down, left-to-right order of node processing but they vary as for the coverage of nodes (indicated by bullets; black nodes denote success; dashed nodes denote failure). In the case of *full_td*, node processing is assumed to succeed for all nodes while success and failure behaviour controls descent for *once_td* and *stop_td*.

Fig. 3. Full traversal vs. single-hit traversal vs. cut-off traversal.

the case studies, we explain *Strafunski*'s two contributions to language processing in Haskell: generic traversal (Sec. 2) and external components (Sec. 3).

2 Generic Traversal

Strategic programming. The key idea underlying the *Strafunski*-style of generic programming is to view traversals as a kind of generic functions that can traverse into terms while mixing uniform and type-specific behaviour. In [12], we defined *functional strategies* accordingly. Strategies are composed via *function combinators*. *Strafunski* supports 'strategic programming' via the library *StrategyLib* of reusable strategy combinators, and the *DrIFT* generator for supportive code for user-supplied Haskell datatypes. Recall that the Haskell datatypes are typically generated from SDF grammars or XML DTDs. Hence, functional strategies allow us to process parse trees and XML documents in both *typed-based* and *generic* manner. By contrast, the HaXML [16] combinator library for generic XML processing is DTD-unaware.

Strategy combinators. We qualify combinators by a postfix TP vs. TU for 'type preservation' or 'type unification' resp. to point out if they deal with transformation or analysis. The originality of strategic programming arises from the following concepts:

- Update strategies by type-specific cases (denoted by `adhocTP` and `adhocTU`).
- One-layer traversal that acts on immediate subterms (e.g., `allTU` for reduction).

Using strategy update, ingredients for actual traversals can be composed. Using one-layer traversal combinators, all kinds of traversal schemes can be assembled as recursive functions (see [8] for the design space). Three frequently used schemes are illustrated in Fig. 3. The first one can be defined as follows for the TU case:

```
full_tdTU s x =
    (s x) 'mappend' (allTU mappend mempty (full_tdTU s) x)
```

This reads as "apply s to the term x, and then recurse into `all` immediate subterms of x while combining the intermediate results with the binary operation `mappend` of

```
-- Synthesis of the traversal
findPerforms = applyTU ( full_tdTU  step)
  where step = constTU [] 'adhocTU' matchPerform
```

```
-- Type-specific case
matchPerform (Perform Nothing _ _ _ _ ) = return []
matchPerform (Perform (Just (Perform_procedure p thru)) _ _ _ _)
  = return [(procedure_name2string p,
             case thru of
               Nothing -> Nothing
               (Just (Through_label _ p')) -> Just (procedure_name2string p'))]
```

The function `findPerforms` performs a pattern match according to `matchPerform` all over the place, and it accumulates the identified invocations as a list using the `full_tdTU` traversal scheme. The function `matchPerform` extracts the referenced labels from a given `PERFORM` statement. The first equation covers an 'inline' `PERFORM` statement which does not refer to any label. Hence, the empty list `[]` is returned. The second equation deals with `PERFORM`s that actually invoke labelled code blocks. There is an extra `case` discrimination for the optional end label (see patterns `Nothing` and `Just ...`). So it returns a singleton list with a pair of the type (`String`, `Maybe String`) corresponding to the start label and an optional end label.

Fig. 4. Find all `PERFORM`s in Cobol program.

a monoid using the 'unit' `mempty` as initial value". Assembling traversal schemes is actually a rather rare activity. Mostly, one reuses schemes defined in *StrategyLib*.

Traversal design. The most frequently used *design patterns* for strategic programming [11] are to define 'rewrite steps' and to synthesise actual 'traversals'. A *type-specific* rewrite step is a monomorphic function that cares about problem-specific patterns. One obtains a *generic* rewrite step by 'lifting' one or more type-specific rewrite steps to the strategy level. That is, the steps are used to update a default strategy (recall `adhocTP` and `adhocTU`). An actual traversal is synthesised by simply passing a (generic) rewrite step as a parameter to the suitable traversal scheme. This is illustrated in the following Haskell code skeleton:

$$\text{traversal term} = \text{apply} (\text{scheme step}) \text{ term}$$
$$\textbf{where } \text{step} = \text{default 'adhoc' } mono_1 \cdots \text{'adhoc' } mono_n$$

Here, *apply* is a place holder for an explicit application combinator `applyTP` or `applyTU` (needed for technical reasons). The place holder *scheme* can be resolved to a traversal scheme such as `full_tdTU` from above. The infix operator *adhoc* is a place holder for either `adhocTP` or `adhocTU`. The $mono_1, \ldots, mono_n$ are type-specific rewrite steps. Common *defaults* are the following:

- the identity strategy `idTP`,
- a constant strategy of the form `constTU` u, or
- the always failing strategy `failTP` or `failTU`.

In Fig. 4, the code skeleton is illustrated for our running example of a Cobol perform-graph extractor. The shown *traversal* `findPerforms` implements the first step of the extraction process: it collects all procedure invocations via the `full_tdTU` scheme.

The generic rewrite *step* returns the empty list by *default* (cf. constTU []), and the single type-specific rewrite step matchPerform destructs actual PERFORM statements to retrieve the relevant labels. To summarise, this very concise and adaptive style of programming effectively focuses on the patterns that are relevant for a given problem.

```
-- The abstract syntax of ATerms
data ATerm = AAppl String [ATerm]      -- Application
           | AList [ATerm]             -- Lists
           | AInt Integer              -- Integers
           deriving (Read,Show,Eq,Ord)

-- Mediation between ATerms and algebraic datatypes
class ATermConvertible t where
  toATerm   :: t -> ATerm
  fromATerm :: ATerm -> t
```

While ATerms are suitable for import, export, run-time representation, and external storage, they are not directly suited for programming on syntaxes or formats because of the lack of typing. Due to the provisions of the *Strafunski* architecture, one can turn terms of any algebraic datatype into an ATerm (cf. member toATerm) and vice versa (cf. member fromATerm).

Fig. 5. ATerm support in Haskell.

3   External Components

Complementary interchange formats. The *Strafunski* architecture features integration of external components on the basis of the interchange formats XML and ATerms. For short, the low-level ATerm format is particularly suited for the integration of language processing components, whereas XML is favoured when we deal with application-specific data models (say, import / export formats). For XML, we rely on the type-based translation facilities of HaXML [16]. Given an XML document type definition (DTD), the HaXML tool *Dtd2Haskell* generates a corresponding system of Haskell datatypes, and instances of the *XmlContent* class. These instances, in combination with the HaXML library *XmlLib*, allow translation of terms over the generated datatypes to XML documents that adhere to the input DTD, and vice versa. The ATerm format for annotated terms [2] is a very simple, untyped interchange format that was designed specifically for component-based development of language tools. It is used in other language processing environments, too [1,6]. The ATerm format supports data compression through maximal subterm sharing. The *Strafunski* architecture features two elements for ATerm support. Firstly, the Haskell ATerm library *ATermLib* provides a datatype for the representation of ATerms together with a class *ATermConvertible* for conversion between ATerms and algebraic datatypes (see Fig. 5). Secondly, the *DrIFT* preprocessor can be used to generate instances of the *ATermConvertible* class for any given Haskell datatype.

Parser integration. A typical kind of external components that we need to integrate with Haskell components are *parsers*. In the *Strafunski* architecture, we provide support

```
-- SDF grammar fragment dealing with code blocks in Cobol
Paragraphs Section-with-header*              -> Sections {cons("Sections")}
Section-header "." Paragraphs                -> Headed-section {cons("Headed-section")}
Section-name "SECTION" Priority-number? -> Section-header {cons("Section-header")}
Sentence* Paragraph*                         -> Paragraphs {cons("Paragraphs")}
Paragraph-1                                  -> Paragraph {cons("Paragraph-1")}
Altered-goto                                 -> Paragraph {cons("Altered-goto")}
Paragraph-name "." Sentence*                 -> Paragraph-1 {cons("Paragraph-11")}
Paragraph-name "." "GO" "TO"? "."            -> Altered-goto {cons("Altered-goto1")}
Statement-list "."+                          -> Sentence {cons("Sentence")}

-- Haskell counterpart (generated algebraic datatypes)
data Sections       = Sections Paragraphs [Headed_section]
data Headed_section = Section_with_header Section_header Paragraphs
data Section_header = Section_header Section_name (Maybe Priority_number)
data Paragraphs     = Paragraphs [Sentence] [Paragraph]
data Paragraph      = Paragraph_1 Paragraph_1
                    | Altered_goto Altered_goto
data Paragraph_1    = Paragraph_11 Paragraph_name [Sentence]
data Altered_goto   = Altered_goto1 Paragraph_name (Maybe ())
data Sentence       = Sentence Statement_list [()]
```

The derivation of algebraic datatypes from context-free grammars (EBNF, YACC, SDF, etc.) is largely straightforward. The above snippets illustrate the following techniques. The alternative productions that define a nonterminal amount to the different constructors of an algebraic datatype. Constructor annotations (`cons(...)`) in the grammar are used as proposals for constructor names in the algebraic datatypes. There are direct mappings for EBNF operators +, *, ? in Haskell, namely the `List` and the `Maybe` datatype. Keywords can be omitted from the algebraic representation.

Fig. 6. Fragment of the *VS COBOL II* grammar [10] and its Haskell counterpart.

for one specific syntax definition formalism, namely SDF [5]. This is a suitable candidate for extending the capabilities of an otherwise Haskell-centred architecture for language processing. Firstly, SDF provides a very general grammar format. Secondly, SDF is supported by powerful parsing technology, namely (scannerless) generalised LR parsing with an implementation that matured inside the Meta-Environment [1]. Thirdly, we have access to an SDF-based grammar base[2] with grammars for several languages. Fourthly, SDF is supported by the Grammar Deployment Kit[3] (GDK) [7]. This kit can generate parsers for different parsing technologies, e.g., for YACC with backtracking [13], C-based combinator parsing as supported by GDK itself, generalised LR parsing, and Haskell-based combinator parsing.

In the *Strafunski* architecture, the tool *Sdf2Haskell* supports the derivation of algebraic Haskell datatypes from an SDF grammar. For a Cobol fragment, this correspondence is illustrated in Fig. 6. We assume that the external parsers emit parse trees in the ATerm format. Then, Haskell components can read in the parse trees relying on the *ATermConvertible* instances for the Haskell datatypes that correspond to the grammar. We dwell upon the fact that parser reuse is crucial by referring to Cobol again. A plain Cobol grammar has about 1000 productions (assuming EBNF operators for lists and optionals), not talking about extensions for SQL, CICS and others. Just this size rules out a manual approach to parser development – using maybe Haskell parser combinators. In fact, implementing a Cobol grammar specification is a challenge for any technology.

---

[2] http://www.program-transformation.org/gb/
[3] http://gdk.sourceforge.net/

```
 1   main = do prg        <- parseCobol              -- Parsing
 2              dotGraph <- toPerformGraph prg        -- Graph synthesis
 3              putStrLn dotGraph                     -- Output
 4
 5   toPerformGraph prg
 6   = do name     <- getProgramName prg
 7        procs    <- findPerforms prg                -- see Fig. 4
 8        main     <- findMain prg
 9        perproc <- findPerformsPerProc procs prg
10        inmain  <- findPerformsInMain main
11        return (mkGraph (name++" Perform Graph") (perproc++inmain))
```

We obtain the parse tree of the Cobol source program by the invocation of the external parser
and converting its untyped ATerm output into a heterogeneously typed Haskell representation of
the parse tree (line 1). The perform-graph generation synthesises the perform graph as a valid
input string for the visualisation tool based on a simple API (line 2). The perform graph is then
just written to the stdout (line 3). The actual synthesis of the perform graph consists of a number
of steps (lines 6–11) as outlined on the paper's first page. The steps are arranged in a monadic
do-sequence to be prepared for aspects such as I/O, failure or debugging.

Fig. 7. Top-level program structure of the perform-graph extractor for Cobol.

To implement a scalable Cobol parser, one needs to resolve grammar conflicts or ambi-
guities, provide provision for error recovery and parse tree construction, and tweak for
non-context-free constructs and performance.

4   Case Study I: Cobol Reverse Engineering

We complete our running example of a perform-graph extractor for Cobol. Its top-level
functionality is shown in Fig. 7. We already described the approach to reusing an external
Cobol parser, and the implementation of the first step in the synthesis of the perform
graph, that is, to extract all PERFORMs. We will skip over the second step, that is, the
identification of the main procedure of a Cobol program. Below we work out the third
step, namely the identification of PERFORMs per procedure. In addition to this traversal
functionality, we will also explain the integration of a graph visualisation tool.

Find all PERFORMs per procedure. The simple traversal findPerforms (recall Fig. 4)
provided us with the nodes in the perform graph. We shall now identify the edges in
the graph, that is, we need to determine the outgoing procedure invocations for each
previously identified procedure. The implementation of this idea is complicated by the
fact that we need to deal with procedures *spanned* over several paragraphs or sections
as triggered by PERFORM . . . THRU . . . statements. We basically have to look up intervals
from lists of paragraphs and sections according to the identified procedure labels. Once
we retrieved a relevant code block, we apply the simply traversal findPerforms to find
all PERFORMs in the block. The corresponding piece of traversal functionality is found
in Fig. 8.

Graph visualisation. We integrate the dot tool as an external component for graph
visualisation. We simply export the synthesised perform graph in the dot input format.
We use a rather direct approach, that is, the corresponding API maps the given nodes

```
1   findPerformsPerProc procs = applyTU ( full_tdTU  step)
2     where
3      step = constTU []  'adhocTU'  matchParagraph  'adhocTU'  matchParagraphList
4                         'adhocTU'  matchSection    'adhocTU'  matchSectionList
5
6      matchParagraph (Paragraph_11 pname sentences)
7        = do name <- return $ paragraph_name2string pname
8             singletonBlock name sentences
9
10     matchParagraphList (paragraphs::[Paragraph])
11       = do results <- mapM (rangeInParagraphs paragraphs) procs
12            return (concat results)
13
14     matchSection     ... = ... -- omitted for brevity
15     matchSectionList ... = ... -- omitted for brevity
16
17     singletonBlock name block
18       = if (name,Nothing) 'elem' procs
19          then scanBlock name block else return []
20
21     scanBlock name block
22       = do procs  <-  findPerforms  block -- Find all PERFORMs in code block
23            node   <- return $ mkProcedure name
24            edges  <- return $ map (mkPerform name) procs
25            return (node:edges)
26
27     rangeInParagraphs _ (_, Nothing) = return [] -- no range but a singleton block
28     rangeInParagraphs paragraphs (start, Just end)
29       = let spanned = fromto ((==) start . getParagraphName)
30                              ((==) end   . getParagraphName)
31                              paragraphs
32          in scanBlock (mkRangeName start end) spanned
```

The traversal `findPerformsPerProc` employs the `full_tdTU` traversal scheme (line 1), and it exhibits type specific behaviour for paragraphs, sections, and lists thereof (lines 3–4). Given a single paragraph (see `matchParagraph`; lines 6–8), we investigate whether it constitutes a procedure (see `singletonBlock`; lines 17–19). In case it is, we scan this block for edges in the perform graph (see `scanBlock`; lines 21–25). The type-specific case for *lists* of paragraphs (see `matchParagraphList`; lines 10–12) maps over `procs` (line 11) to check for every element if it happens to refer to a range of paragraphs in the given list (see `rangeInParagraphs`; lines 27–32). To this end, we attempt to split up the list using the labels at hand as boundaries. Here we assume a helper `fromto` to select an interval of a list via predicates (used in line 29; definition omitted). Once we retrieved a code block consisting of a number of paragraphs, we invoke `scanBlock` (line 32) to scan this block for edges in the perform graph.

Fig. 8. Find PERFORMs per Cobol procedure.

```
mkGraph name ascii      = "digraph "++(quote name)++" {\n"++(concat ascii)++"}\n"
mkProcedure p           = (quote p)++" [ shape=box ]\n"
mkPerform f (t,Nothing) = (quote f)++" -> "++(quote t)++"\n"
mkPerform f (t,Just t') = (quote f)++" -> "++(quote (mkRangeName t t'))++"\n"
mkRangeName t t'        = t ++ ".." ++ t'
```

`mkGraph` completes the ASCII content of a `dot` graph (i.e., a list of strings for nodes and edges) into a complete `dot` input with the given `name`; `mkProcedure` and `mkPerform` derive the nodes and edges in ASCII from procedure names and PERFORM labels; `mkRangeName` builds an ASCII representation for labels in a PERFORM ... THRU ... statement.

Fig. 9. API for `dot`-file generation from Cobol perform graphs.

(i.e., procedures) and edges (i.e., invocations) to plain strings adhering to the dot input format. The API is included in Fig. 9. This approach is very lightweight. Recall Fig. 1 where we illustrated the visual output of the extractor. In more demanding contexts, APIs preferably synthesise a public or opaque intermediate representation as opposed to plain strings. This adds type safety, and it enables subsequent processing of the intermediate representation.

```
-- Relevant Java statement syntax in SDF
LabelledStatement                           -> Statement {cons("LabelledStatement")}
ClassDeclaration                            -> Statement {cons("ClassDeclaration")}
StatementWithoutTrailingSubstatement -> Statement {cons("WithoutTrailing")}
Block           -> StatementWithoutTrailingSubstatement {cons("Block")}
EmptyStatement -> StatementWithoutTrailingSubstatement {cons("EmptyStatement")}
";"                     -> EmptyStatement     {cons("semicolon")}
Identifier ":" Statement -> LabelledStatement {cons("colon")}

-- Counting statements; not counting certain constructors
1  statementCounter :: Term t => t -> Int
2  statementCounter = runIdentity . applyTU (full_tdTU step)
3  where
4    step = constTU 0 'adhocTU' statement 'adhocTU' localVarDec
5    statement s = case s of
6      (WithoutTrailing (EmptyStatement _)) -> return 0
7      (WithoutTrailing (Block _))          -> return 0
8      (LabelledStatement _)                -> return 0
9      (ClassDeclaration _)                 -> return 0
10     _                                    -> return 1
11
12    localVarDec (_::LocalVariableDeclaration) = return 1
```

The type of the `statementCounter` (line 1) points out that this traversal can be applied to any term type `t`, and that the result type is an `Integer`. The statement count is computed by performing a `full_tdTU` traversal with one 'tick' per statement. We do not count empty statements (`return` 0 in line 6). We also do not let a block statement, a labelled statement or a class declaration statement contribute to the statement count (lines 7–9), but only the statement(s) nested inside them. The catch-all case for `statement` 'ticks' for all other statements (`return` 1 in line 10). Finally, we want local variable declarations to contribute to the count, and hence an extra type-specific case for the traversal is needed (line 12).

Fig. 10. Counting Java statements.

5   Case Study II: Java Code Metrics

In this section we discuss the implementation of the calculation of metrics for Java applications on the basis of source code. Such metrics are useful for determining volume and quality of Java code as required for the estimation of maintenance costs. We discuss the implementation of three metrics:

- *Statement count*: the number of statements.
- *Cyclometric complexity*: the number of conditionals (McCabe).
- *Nesting depth*: the maximal depth of nested conditionals.

We want to compute these metrics not only for an entire Java application, but also per method and per class or interface. Furthermore, we want to export the computed metrics in XML format for further processing. As in the case of Cobol, we employ an external parser component. Indeed, Java's grammar is available in the SDF grammar base.

```
 1  mcCabeIndex :: Term t => t -> Int
 2  mcCabeIndex = unJust . applyTU (full_tdTU step)
 3    where
 4    step = ifTU isConditional        -- potentially failing strategy
 5                (const (constTU 1)) -- 'then' branch; value consumer
 6                (constTU 0)          -- 'else' branch
 7
 8  isConditional
 9   = failTU -- resolves to: const mzero = const Nothing
10         'adhocTU' (\(_::IfThenStatement)      -> return ())
11         'adhocTU' (\(_::IfThenElseStatement) -> return ())
12         'adhocTU' (\(_::WhileStatement)      -> return ())
13         'adhocTU' (\(_::ForStatement)        -> return ())
14         'adhocTU' (\(_::TryStatement)        -> return ())
```

In Java, the statements that contribute to the cyclometric complexity are not only conditionals and loops, but also the *try* statement associated to the exception handling mechanism. Recognition of a relevant statement is modelled via success and failure of the helper strategy isConditional (lines 8–14). Note that only types are matched but not patterns (see the type annotations '::'in lines 10–14). This is because of the particular format of the Java grammar that defines nonterminals for several statement forms. In the rewrite step for the full traversal (lines 4–6), success and failure behaviour is mapped to 1 vs. 0 by using a strategy combinator ifTU.

Fig. 11. Computing cyclometric complexity.

```
   -- Java metrics via instantiation of generic metrics
   nestingDepth :: Term t => t -> Int
   nestingDepth = unJust . applyTU (depthWith isConditional)

   -- Generic algorithm for depth of nesting
 1  depthWith s
 2   = recurse 'passTU'       -- Sequential composition
 3       \depth_subterms ->
 4          let max_subterms = maximum (0:depth_subterms)
 5          in (ifTU s
 6                    (const (constTU (max_subterms + 1)))
 7                    (constTU max_subterms))
 8    where
 9    recurse = allTU (++) [] (depthWith s 'passTU' \depth -> constTU [depth])
```

Generic depth calculation works as follows. We first compute a list of depths for the various subterms (line 2) by recursing into them. The helper recurse does not employ any recursive traversal scheme, but we use *Strafunski*'s basic one-layer traversal combinator allTU (line 9) to apply the strategy for depth calculation to all *immediate* subterms. This setup for recursion leads to the needed awareness of nesting. From the list of depths, we compute the maximum depth (line 4), and then we complete this maximum to take the current term into account. If the recogniser succeeds for the term at hand, then we add 1 to the maximum (lines 5–7).

Fig. 12. Computing nesting depth of conditionals.

```
<!DOCTYPE javaMetrics [
  <!ELEMENT javaMetrics (compilationunitMetric*) >
  <!ELEMENT compilationunitMetric (interfaceMetric | classMetric)* >
    <!ATTLIST compilationunitMetric name CDATA #REQUIRED>
  <!ELEMENT interfaceMetric EMPTY >
    <!ATTLIST interfaceMetric name        CDATA #REQUIRED
                              methodCount CDATA #REQUIRED
                              fieldCount  CDATA #REQUIRED>
  <!ELEMENT classMetric (methodMetric | classMetric)* >
    <!ATTLIST classMetric name       CDATA #REQUIRED
                          fieldCount CDATA #REQUIRED>
  <!ELEMENT methodMetric (classMetric)* >
    <!ATTLIST methodMetric name           CDATA #REQUIRED
                           statementCount CDATA #REQUIRED
                           mcCabe         CDATA #REQUIRED
                           nestingDepth   CDATA #REQUIRED>
]>
```

The structure of Java metrics documents roughly follows the syntactical structure of Java itself, but in a highly condensed manner. The attributes of the document elements contain the names of these elements and the values of various metrics.

Fig. 13. A DTD for Java metrics documents.

```
1   extractClassMetrics :: ClassDeclaration -> Maybe ClassMetric
2   extractClassMetrics (Class1 _ name extends implements body)
3    = do nestedClassMetrics <- mapM extractClassMetrics (getNestedClasses body)
4        methodMetrics      <- mapM extractMethodMetrics (getMethods body)
5        return $ ClassMetric
6                    ClassMetric_Attrs {
7                      classMetricName       = str2cdata name,
8                      classMetricFieldCount = int2cdata (length (getFields body)) }
9                    ((map ClassMetric_ClassMetric nestedClassMetrics)++
10                    (map ClassMetric_MethodMetric methodMetrics))
11
12  extractMethodMetrics :: MethodDeclaration -> Maybe MethodMetric
13  extractMethodMetrics (MethodHeader_MethodBody header body)
14   = do name              <- getMethodName header
15       statCount          <- statementCounter body
16       mcCabe             <- mcCabeIndex body
17       nestingDepth       <- nestingDepth body
18       nestedClasses      <- collectNestedClasses body
19       nestedClassMetrics <- mapM extractClassMetrics nestedClasses
20       return $ MethodMetric
21                   MethodMetric_Attrs {
22                     methodMetricName           = str2cdata name,
23                     methodMetricStatementCount = int2cdata statCount,
24                     methodMetricMcCabe         = int2cdata mcCabe,
25                     methodMetricNestingDepth   = int2cdata nestingDepth }
26                   nestedClassMetrics
27     where
28      collectNestedClasses = applyTU (stop_tdTU getClassDecl)
29      getClassDecl = failTU 'adhocTU' (\(cd::ClassDeclaration) -> return [cd])
```

The traversal for computing and storing metrics is structured as five cooperating functions, one for each DTD element. For brevity, we show the most interesting ones for class metrics and for method metrics. Trivial helper functions are omitted. The shown code performs little traversal on its own but pattern matching (lines 2 and 13) and list processing (lines 3,4,9,10,19) is usually sufficient. The only exception is to look up nested classes (line 28). Here we use a traversal with *stop* because we only want to gather immediate nested classes and not the transitive closure.

Fig. 14. Computing Java metrics and storing them in XML.

Metrics computation. The number of statements in any fragment of Java code can basically be computed by counting the number of nodes of type `Statement` in the corresponding parse tree. A full traversal is appropriate. A few exceptions are in place for the sake of precise counting. Fig. 10 shows the relevant productions from the Java grammar, and the implementation of statement count. The cyclometric complexity (or McCabe index) of a fragment of Java code can again be computed by a full traversal. This time we need to count the occurrences of conditional and looping constructs in the corresponding parse tree. The implementation is shown in Fig. 11. Note that the rewrite `step` for the traversal employs a strategy `isConditional` that merely serves as a 'recogniser' of relevant constructs as opposed to 'ticking'. This is expressed by a predicate-like result type `Maybe ()`. The actual ticking is done separately on the use site of `isConditional`. This style is more suitable for the reuse of the pattern recogniser in the implementation of other metrics. Indeed, for the nesting-depth metric, the same statements are relevant as for cyclometric complexity, but the traversal behaviour is more involved. That is, we need to count levels of nesting rather than simply certain kinds of nodes. The implementation is shown in Fig. 12. The actual problem of counting levels of nesting is completely generic, and hence it is captured in a strategy combinator `depthWith` that is parameterised by a strategy for pattern recognition. The depth of a given term is the maximum of the depths of its children, possibly incremented by 1 if the term itself is relevant. Nesting depth for Java is then simply computed by passing `isConditional` to `depthWith`.

Exporting to XML. To process metrics information by external components such as viewers, report generators, code browsers, and others, we use XML as interchange format. A DTD that describes the structure of Java metric documents is shown in Fig. 13. The *Dtd2Haskell* tool generates the corresponding system of Haskell datatypes. These datatypes are then used in our Haskell component to collect the results of our metrics calculations. The implementation is shown in Fig. 14. After the metrics have been computed, we invoke the conversion provided by *Dtd2Haskell* to export the metrics to an XML document that adheres to our metrics DTD.

6 Case Study III: Haskell Re-engineering

As a third object language for language processing we selected Haskell—not so much for the size of its grammar but rather because it is a complicated language with modules, overloading, type inference, nested scopes, and higher-orderness. While the other case studies concerned *analysis* problems, the Haskell case study deals with *transformation*. Two forms of dead code elimination shall be discussed:

- Elimination of dead local declarations in nested scopes.
- Elimination of dead top-level declarations in a chased module hierarchy.

The first form is a simple 'clean-up' refactoring while the second form generalises dead code elimination to the inter-modular level of a complete application. In fact, these transformations do not just serve a purpose in software re-engineering (in the sense of code improvement). They are also valuable for application extraction in software packaging, or for optimising compilation. Our tooling for the implementations of the transformations reuse available support for Haskell parsing and pretty printing (formerly called *hsparser* or *hssource*, now part of the Haskell Core Libraries — in the haskell-src package).

```
1   elimDeadWheres :: Term t => t -> Maybe t
2   elimDeadWheres = applyTP (full_tdTP step)
3     where
4       step = idTP `adhocTP` match
5       match  (HsMatch sl fun pats rhs wheres)
6         = do (pf,pd) <- hsFreeAndDeclared pats
7              (rf,rd) <- hsFreeAndDeclared rhs
8              (df,dd) <- hsFreeAndDeclaredGroup wheres
9              wheres' <- filterM (hsDeclUsed ((df `union` rf) \\ pd)) wheres
10             return  (HsMatch sl fun pats rhs wheres')
11
12  hsDeclUsed names decl
13    = do (_,[name]) <- hsFreeAndDeclared decl
14         return $ name `elem` names
```

A full traversal is used (line 2) because declarations can be arbitrarily nested in Haskell. The rewrite step behaves like the identity function by default with a type-specific case for pattern match equations (line 4). Such equations are treated as follows (lines 5–10). We first destruct the HsMatch construct (line 5). Then, the free and declared names are determined for the various fragments in this scope (line 6 for the patterns on the left-hand side; line 7 for the expression on the right-hand side; line 8 for the local declarations). Then, we filter the declarations to only keep those that are actually used (line 9). Finally, we return the reconstructed pattern match equation with the filtered list of local declarations as the result of this rewrite step for transformation (line 10). The helper hsDeclUsed (lines 12–14) is a shorthand for determining the name defined by a declaration and performing a membership test with respect to a given set of names.

Fig. 15. Elimination of dead local declarations (meta-language = object-language = Haskell).

Elimination of dead local declarations. In the given scope of a Haskell pattern match equation, a local 'where' declaration is dead if it is neither used by the right-hand side expression, nor by other declarations in the same group of bindings. Fig. 15, specifies the corresponding transformation by a generic traversal. Note that we rely on an analysis hsFreeAndDeclared for free and declared names in a Haskell program fragment. It is needed to decide whether a given abstraction is used. We also need a variant hsFreeAndDeclaredGroup that specifically deals with groups of bindings. The needed name analysis will be explained below.

Inter-modular dead code elimination. The transformation to eliminate dead top-level declarations uses the same machinery as above, but it operates on lists of modules. We eliminate dead top-level declarations with respect to a given main module. Fig. 16, specifies the corresponding transformation. Note that there is no need for a deep term traversal because we only deal with top-level declarations of modules.

Name analysis. The notion of free and declared names as assumed above is essential for a broad class of language processing problems. Any analysis and transformation that

```
1   elimDeadTops ::      [(ModuleName,[ModuleName],HsModule)]
2                     -> Maybe [(ModuleName,[ModuleName],HsModule)]
3
4   elimDeadTops l@(h:t)                          -- h is the main module
5     = do l' <- mapM worker t >>= return . (:) h   -- elimination per module
6         if l==l' then return l else elimDeadTops l' -- fixpoint by equality
7     where
8       worker (n,i,m@(HsModule n' i' e' ds))
9         = do clients <- return $ filter (\e@(_,i'',_) -> n 'elem' i'') l
10             (imp,_) <- hsFreeAndDeclared clients
11             ds'     <- filterM (hsDeclUsed imp) ds
12             return (n,i,HsModule n' i' e' ds')
```

The elimination function operates on lists of modules which are tupled with, for convenience, the name of the module, and the imported modules (see the type in lines 1–2). The head of the list is the main module to be preserved as is. We continuously map a `worker` transformation over the chased modules (line 5) until no more top-level declarations are eliminated (line 6). The worker first determines all `clients` of the given module (line 9), that is, the modules that happen to import the given module. Then, we determine all top-level declarations used by these clients (line 10). Then, we filter away all dead top-level declarations of the given module accordingly (line 11). Finally, the module is reconstructed (line 12). The shown implementation only takes simple Haskell forms of module import into account (i.e., no selection, no re-export, and others).

Fig. 16. Inter-modular dead code elimination (meta-language = object-language = Haskell).

deals with entities in modules and possibly nested scopes needs to be aware of scopes with their declared and free names. In Fig. 17, we define such an algorithm for Haskell. In the shown fragment, we focus on the core patterns such as lambdas, variables, nested scopes. The full algorithm deals with do-statements, list comprehensions, modules, and classes in largely the same manner. Note that generic traversal allows us to skip over many constructs that do not contribute directly to the set of free or declared names.

7   Related Language Processing Setups

Let us leave the scope of functional programming (in Haskell) to compare *Strafunski* with other setups for language processing. We only discuss a few examples here while we are predominantly interested in the ways how these other approaches tackle the concerns of generic traversal and external components. This will also clarify the roots of our approach, and it will provide further evidence that functional programming in Haskell is in need of *Strafunski*'s contributions.

The ASF+SDF Meta-Environment [1]. This is an interactive environment for the development of language processing tools. The ATerm format and the SDF formalism together with supporting tools were developed in the context of this project. A form of generic traversal has recently been added to the ASF term rewriting language, which is the central implementation language. The toolbus coordination language is offered for component integration. It is founded on process algebra, and it uses the ATerm format.

XT [6]. This is a package for transformation tools, or more generally, for the development of language processors. The Stratego language for term rewriting with strategies plays a central role in XT's architecture. Stratego allows untyped generic programming. In fact, *Strafunski*'s support for functional strategies is largely inspired by Stratego, but

```
1   hsFreeAndDeclared :: Term t => t -> Maybe ([HsQName],[HsQName])
2   hsFreeAndDeclared = applyTU (stop_tdTU step)
3    where
4     step = failTU 'adhocTU' exp 'adhocTU' pat 'adhocTU' match ... 'adhocTU' decls
5
6     exp (HsVar qn)           = return ([qn],[])
7     exp (HsCon qn)           = return ([qn],[])
8     exp (HsLambda pats body) = do (pf,pd) <- hsFreeAndDeclared pats
9                                   (bf,bd) <- hsFreeAndDeclared body
10                                  return ((bf 'union' pf) \\ pd,[])
11    ...
12    exp _                    = mzero  -- fail for all other expression forms
13
14    pat (HsPVar n)           = return ([],[UnQual n])
15    pat (HsPApp qn pats)     = addFree qn (hsFreeAndDeclared pats)
16    ...
17    pat _                    = mzero  -- fail for all other forms of patterns
18
19    match (HsMatch _ n pats rhs {-where-} decls)
20     = do (pf,pd) <- hsFreeAndDeclared pats
21          (rf,rd) <- hsFreeAndDeclared rhs
22          (df,dd) <- hsFreeAndDeclared decls
23          return (pf 'union' (((rf \\ (dd 'union' [n]) 'union' df) \\ pd)), [n])
24
25    decls (ds::[HsDecl]) = do (f,d) <- hsFreeAndDeclaredGroup ds
26                             return (f \\ d,d)


    -- Elaboration for groups of bindings
    hsFreeAndDeclaredGroup ds = do names <- mapM hsFreeAndDeclared l
                                   return ( foldr union [] (map fst names),
                                            foldr union [] (map snd names) )

    -- Shorthand for adding one free name
    addFree free mfd = mfd >>= \(f,d) -> return ([free] 'union' f,d)
```

The analysis relies on a type-unifying traversal with *stop* (line 2). This is because we need to restart the traversal in a pattern-specific fashion (see the various recursive occurrences of `hsFreeAndDeclared`). There are type-specific cases for Haskell expressions, patterns (as in pattern-match equations), and groups of binding (i.e., lists of mutually recursive declarations). We omit a few cases that were needed for full Haskell. The equations for variables (line 6) and constructors (line 7) simply return the corresponding names as free. In the case of a lambda expression (line 8), we compute the free names from the free names of the body by subtracting the names that were declared (say bound) via the patterns. Note that there are no declared names that would escape from this scope. Other kinds of scope are illustrated in the functions `match` for pattern match equations (lines 19–23) and `decls` (lines 25–26) for groups of bindings.

Fig. 17. Free and declared names in Haskell program fragments.

realizes strategic programming in a statically typed higher-order functional programming context. XT also uses ATerms and SDF.

Eli [3] and Cocktail [4]. These are prominent examples of attribute grammar systems. This paradigm specifically addresses language implementation, in particular semantic analysis, and translation from context-free structure to intermediate representations. Attribute grammars on their own normally fall short when applied to transformation tasks. This has been a typical application domain for rewriting technology. The aforementioned systems support integration of external components to some extent, e.g., by allowing semantic functions to be programmed in a general purpose programming language. Several non-trivial extensions of the basic attribute grammar formalism target at genericity (say, conciseness, and reusability).

SmartTools [14]. This system supports language tool development based on two mainstream technologies, namely XML and Java. From an *abstract* syntax definition, it generates a development environment that includes a structure editor and some basic visitors that allow for generic graph traversals. SmartTools's foundation on XML makes integration of external components an easy task. If the user specifies additional syntactic sugar, a parser and a pretty printer are generated as well. In a designated simple language, the user can specify 'visitor profiles' to obtain more sophisticated visitors.

JJForester and JJTraveler [15]. This is another architecture centred around Java. JJTraveler is basically a visitor framework including a library of reusable visitors. The specific approach provides full traversal control, basically because visitors can be combined in nearly the same way as *Strafunski*'s functional strategies. JJForester provides generative tool support to derive a Java class hierarchy from a given SDF grammar, and also the interface classes to use the JJTraveler visitor framework. Hence, JJForester corresponds to *Strafunski*'s employment of *DrIFT* for the generation of *Term* instances combined with the capabilities of the generator *Sdf2Haskell*.

8   The Virtue of Functional Programming

So it is fair to say that generic traversal and external components are ubiquitous concerns in language processing. At the risk of saying the obvious, we want to argue that functional programming in Haskell has something to add when compared to other setups of language processing, that is: strong typing, higher-order functions, pattern matching, and Haskell's status of a general purpose language.

Lack of typing implies a tiresome amount of debugging when dealing with non-trivial syntaxes and formats in language processing. This is the case, for instance, for the Stratego language underlying XT [6]. Higher-orderness is basically the key to conciseness, composability, and reuse in our experience. We realise that certain readers are hard to convince but we refer to a 'benchmark' for genericity and conciseness in language processing [9]. We do not expect that the *Strafunski*-based reference solution can be outperformed by other approaches. To give an example, in a Java-based setting, one normally uses object composition, inheritance, object construction, and others to encode the combinator style of functional strategies. The merits of pattern matching in the context of language processing are obvious. The merits of a general purpose language are that the overhead for integrating external components only arises in the reuse context but not as an implication of lacking expressiveness. Also, *Strafunski* is very lightweight for this reason whereas setups that are based on attribute grammars or rewriting tend to necessitate a complete language implementation effort with all the known benefits (e.g., opportunities for designated checks and optimisations) and drawbacks (e.g., the need for a compiler, debugger, the need to deal with yet another notation, etc.).

9   Concluding Remarks

This application letter substantiates that *typed functional programming* can be made fit to develop practical language processors in an integrated, concise, and scalable manner. To this end, we have spelled out the **Strafunski** architecture for language processing. This architecture is based on Haskell augmented with libraries and generators that provide support for *generic traversal* and the *integration of external components*. We have argued that these are the two crucial bits that are missing in plain functional programming. Generic traversal is founded on the *StrategyLib* library for *functional strategies* complemented by generative tool support. Generic traversal is essential to deal with only those language constructs that are relevant to the problem at hand. The integration of external components is supported by **Strafunski**'s ATerm library, by its connectivity to SDF parser generation, and by HaXML's support for Haskell-based XML processing.

We have applied this setup in three language processing case studies: reverse engineering of Cobol systems, computation of metrics for Java systems, and re-engineering of Haskell systems. Thus, our selection of case studies covers widely used languages from various paradigms and ages, and recurring problems of diverse algorithmic nature. The case studies clearly demonstrate that generic traversal is indispensable to achieve concise, scalable, and adaptive implementations. They also also prove that our approach to the integration of external components allows Haskell to be applied to previously alien applications: think of analysing and transforming huge Cobol portfolios.

References

1. M. v. d. Brand et al. The ASF+SDF Meta-Environment: a Component-Based Language Development Environment. In R. Wilhelm, editor, *Proc. of Compiler Construction 2001 (CC 2001)*, volume 2027 of *LNCS*, pages 365–370. Springer-Verlag, 2001.
2. M. v. d. Brand, H. d. Jong, P. Klint, and P. Olivier. Efficient Annotated Terms. *Software—Practice & Experience*, 30(3):259–291, Mar. 2000.
3. R. Gray, V. Heuring, S. Levi, A. Sloane, and W. Waite. Eli: A Complete, Flexible Compiler Construction System. *Communications of the ACM 35*, pages 121–131, Feb. 1992.
4. J. Grosch and H. Emmelmann. A Tool Box for Compiler Construction. In D. Hammer, editor, *Proc. of Compiler Compilers, Third International Workshop on Compiler Construction*, volume 477 of *Lecture Notes in Computer Science*, pages 106–116, Schwerin, Germany, 22–26 Oct. 1990. Springer, 1991.
5. J. Heering, P. R. H. Hendriks, P. Klint, and J. Rekers. The syntax definition formalism SDF — Reference manual. *SIGPLAN Notices*, 24(11):43–75, 1989.
6. M. d. Jonge, E. Visser, and J. Visser. XT: a bundle of program transformation tools. In M. v. d. Brand and D. Parigot, editors, *Proc. LDTA 2001*, volume 44 of *ENTCS*. Elsevier Science, 2001.
7. J. Kort, R. Lämmel, and C. Verhoef. The Grammar Deployment Kit–System Demonstration. In M. Brand and R. Lämmel, editors, *Proc. of LDTA'02*, volume 65 of *ENTCS*. Elsevier Science, 2002.
8. R. Lämmel. The Sketch of a Polymorphic Symphony. In B. Gramlich and S. Lucas, editors, *Proc. of International Workshop on Reduction Strategies in Rewriting and Programming (WRS 2002)*, volume 70 of *ENTCS*. Elsevier Science, 2002. 21 pages.
9. R. Lämmel. Towards Generic Refactoring. In *Proc. of Third ACM SIGPLAN Workshop on Rule-Based Programming RULE 2002*, Pittsburgh, USA, 5 Oct. 2002. ACM Press. 14 pages.

10. R. Lämmel and C. Verhoef. *VS COBOL II grammar Version 1.0.3*, 1999. Available at: `http://www.cs.vu.nl/grammars/vs-cobol-ii/`.
11. R. Lämmel and J. Visser. Design Patterns for Functional Strategic Programming. In *Proc. of Third ACM SIGPLAN Workshop on Rule-Based Programming RULE 2002*, Pittsburgh, USA, 5 Oct. 2002. ACM Press. 14 pages.
12. R. Lämmel and J. Visser. Typed Combinators for Generic Traversal. In S. Krishnamurthi and C. Ramakrishnan, editors, *Proc. of PADL 2002, Portland, OR, USA*, volume 2257 of *LNCS*. Springer-Verlag, Jan. 2002.
13. V. Maslov and C. Dodd. Btyacc—backtracking yacc, 1995-2001. `http://www.siber.org/btyacc/`.
14. D. Parigot, C. Courbis, P. Degenne, A. Fau, C. Pasquier, J. Fillon, C. Held, and I. Attali. Aspect and XML-oriented Semantic Framework Generator: SmartTools. In M. v. d. Brand and R. Lämmel, editors, *Proc. LDTA 2002*, volume 65 of *ENTCS*. Elsevier Science, 2002.
15. J. Visser. Visitor Combination and Traversal Control. *ACM SIGPLAN Notices*, 36(11):270–282, Nov. 2001. OOPSLA 2001 Conference Proceedings: Object-Oriented Programming Systems, Languages, and Applications.
16. M. Wallace and C. Runciman. Haskell and XML: Generic combinators or type-based translation? *ACM SIGPLAN Notices*, 34(9):148–159, Sept. 1999. Proceedings of ICFP'99.
17. N. Winstanley. A type-sensitive preprocessor for Haskell. In *Glasgow Workshop on Functional Programming, Ullapool*, 1997.

Functional Hybrid Modeling

Henrik Nilsson, John Peterson, and Paul Hudak

Department of Computer Science, Yale University,
P.O. Box 208285 New Haven, CT 06520-8285 U.S.A.
{Henrik.Nilsson, John.C.Peterson, Paul.Hudak}@yale.edu

Abstract. The modeling and simulation of physical systems is of key importance in many areas of science and engineering, and thus can benefit from high-quality software tools. In previous research we have demonstrated how *functional programming* can form the basis of an expressive language for *causal* hybrid modeling and simulation. There is a growing realization, however, that a move toward *non-causal* modeling is necessary for coping with the ever increasing size and complexity of modeling problems. Our goal is to combine the strengths of functional programming and non-causal modeling to create a powerful, strongly typed *fully declarative modeling language* that provides modeling and simulation capabilities beyond the current state of the art. Although our work is still in its very early stages, we believe that this paper clearly articulates the need for improved modeling languages and shows how functional programming techniques can play a pivotal role in meeting this need.

1   Introduction

Modeling and simulation is playing an increasingly important role in the design, analysis, and implementation of real-world systems. In particular, whereas modeling fragments of systems in isolation was deemed sufficient in the past, considering the interaction of these fragments *as a whole* is now necessary. The resulting models are large and complex, and span multiple physical domains.

Furthermore, these models are almost invariably *hybrid*: they exhibit both continuous-time and discrete-time behaviors. For example, the modeled system may contain a digital controller, or it could be that the very structure of the modeled system changes over time. Either way, the resulting model will have a number of structural configurations, or *modes*, each described by continuous equations. In general, the total number of modes can be enormous, or even unbounded, and often cannot be predicted a priori. We refer to systems whose number of modes cannot be practically predetermined as *structurally dynamic*.

Special *modeling languages* have been developed to facilitate modeling and simulation. There are two broad language categories in this domain. *Causal* (or *block-oriented*) languages are most popular; languages such as Simulink [9] and Ptolemy II [8] represent this style of modeling. In causal modeling, the equations that represent the physics of the system must be written so that the direction of signal flow, the *causality*, is explicit. The second, but less populated, class

V. Dahl and P. Wadler (Eds.): PADL 2003, LNCS 2562, pp. 376–390, 2003.
© Springer-Verlag Berlin Heidelberg 2003

of language is *non-causal* (or *object-oriented*[1]), where the model focuses on the interconnection of the components of the system being modeled, from which causality is then inferred. Examples include Dymola [3] and Modelica [11].

The main drawback of casual languages is the need to explicitly specify the causality. This hampers modularity and reuse [2]. Non-causal languages address this problem by allowing the user to avoid committing the model itself to a specific causality: depending on how the model is being used, the appropriate causality constraints are inferred using both symbolic and numerical methods. Unfortunately, current non-causal modeling languages sacrifice generality, particularly when it comes to hybrid modeling.

There are additional weaknesses that are common to both types of language. Many languages are either untyped, or important invariants are only checked dynamically. No commercially available modeling system enforces the consistent use of physical dimensions. Also, the number of modes is usually limited, since this simplifies implementation by making it possible to generate simulation code for all modes at compile time [12].

In previous research at Yale, we have developed a framework called *functional reactive programming*, or FRP [20], which is highly suited for causal hybrid modeling. This framework is embodied in a language called *Yampa*[2] as an extension of Haskell. Yampa permits highly dynamic hybrid systems to be described clearly and concisely [14]. In addition, because the full power of a functional language is available, it exhibits a high degree of modularity, allowing reuse of components and design patterns. It also employs Haskell's polymorphic type system to ensure that signals are connected consistently, even as the system topology changes. The semantic foundations of Yampa are well defined and understood, making models expressed using Yampa suited for formal manipulation and reasoning. Yampa and its predecessors have been used in robotics simulation and control as well as a number of related domains [16,17,18].

Non-causal modeling and FRP complement each other almost perfectly. We therefore aim to integrate the core ideas of FRP with non-causal modeling to create *Hydra*, a powerful, fully declarative modeling language combining the strengths of each. If we treat causality and dynamism as two dimensions in the modeling language design space, we see that Hydra occupies a unique point:

	Static structure	Dynamic structure
Causal	Simulink	Yampa
Non-causal	Modelica	Hydra

We refer to the combined paradigm of functional programming and non-causal, hybrid modeling as *functional hybrid modeling*, or FHM. Conceptually,

---

[1] Not to be confused with object-oriented *programming* languages. Concepts like classes and inheritance may be part of an object-oriented modeling language, but methods and imperative variables are not.

[2] See http://haskell.org/yampa.

FHM can be seen as a generalization of FRP, since FRP's *functions* on signals are a special case of FHM's *relations* on signals. In its full generality, FHM, like FRP, also allows the description of structurally dynamic models.

The main contribution of this paper is that it outlines how notions appropriate for non-causal, hybrid simulation in the form of *first-class relations on signals* and *switch constructs* can be integrated into a functional language, yielding a non-causal modeling language supporting structural dynamism. It also identifies key research issues, and suggests how recent developments in the field of programming languages could be employed to address those issues.

2   Non-causal and Hybrid Modeling

We believe that both the *non-causal* and *hybrid* styles of modeling are essential to address the increasing complexity of modeled systems. Unfortunately, combining these styles is difficult. In this section, we explain non-causal modeling and its advantages. We then outline the state of the art of non-causal hybrid modeling, and identify a number of shortcomings that must be addressed.

2.1   Advantages of Non-causal Modeling

Consider the simple electrical circuit in Fig. 1(a) (adapted from [10]). We can model this circuit in a causal language such as Simulink by transforming the circuit into the *block diagram* of Fig. 1(b).

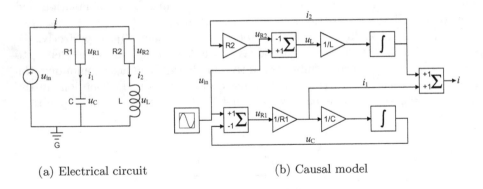

(a) Electrical circuit   (b) Causal model

Fig. 1. A simple electrical circuit and its causal model.

Mathematically, such a block diagram corresponds to a system of ordinary differential equations (ODEs) in explicit form.[3] In such an ODE, the *causality*,

---

[3] Since a system of ODEs can be written as a single ODE using vector notation, we will just write ODE and not worry about whether there are one or more equations.

i.e. the cause-and-effect relationship, is explicit: "known" quantities (inputs and state variables) are used to define "unknown" quantities (outputs and state derivatives). Hence the name causal modeling. The block diagram in Fig. 1(b) is a rendering of the following equations, where i_2 and u_C are the state variables:

$$u_{R_2} = R_2 i_2, \qquad u_L = u_{in} - u_{R_2}, \quad i_2' = \frac{u_L}{L}$$
$$u_{R_1} = u_{in} - u_C, \quad i_1 = \frac{u_{R_1}}{R_1}, \qquad u_C' = \frac{i_1}{C}$$
$$i = i_1 + i_2$$

With causal modeling, it is easy to derive the simulation code by transliterating the ODEs into a sequence of assignment statements that compute the outputs and the derivatives of the state variables for each time step. Simulation is then just a matter of stepwise numerical integration.

Unfortunately, the above equations, and consequently also the corresponding block diagram, bear little structural resemblance to the physical circuit they model. The burden of deriving the causal model rests entirely with the modeler, and is generally a difficult task. In particular, a causal model is not *compositional*: it cannot be expressed structurally as a composition of physical models of the individual components. For instance, consider a resistor. In a causal model, this component may be modeled (via Ohm's law) by one of two equations, $u = Ri$, or $i = u/R$, depending on whether the voltage needs to be computed from the current or vice versa. Thus, no single type of causal representation can capture the behavior of a resistor. Details of how the equations that define the model are to be solved dictate how the user must express the model. In practice, modeling using causal equations is quite "brittle": a small change in the physical structure of the system may have global consequences in the causality of the equations. This make it difficult to reuse components in models [2].

In contrast, non-causal modeling frees the modeler from the need to spell out the "how" of the simulation code through an explicit ODE. A non-causal model is an implicit system of differential and algebraic equations (DAE):

$$\mathbf{f}(\mathbf{x}, \mathbf{x}', \mathbf{w}, \mathbf{u}, t) = \mathbf{0}$$

where $\mathbf{x}$ is a vector of state variables, $\mathbf{w}$ is a vector of algebraic variables, $\mathbf{u}$ is a vector of inputs, and t is the time. This allows the modeler to express the model in a way that directly reflects its physical structure. Models of individual components can be *reused* without first having to adapt them according to any specific causality requirements.

For example, a non-causal model of a resistor can be formulated as follows:

$$u = v_p - v_n$$
$$i_p + i_n = 0$$
$$u = R i_p$$

where the subscripts p and n signify the positive and negative pin of the component, respectively. A non-causal model for an inductor is given by the following equations:

$$u = v_\mathrm{p} - v_\mathrm{n}$$
$$i_\mathrm{p} + i_\mathrm{n} = 0$$
$$u = L i_\mathrm{p}'$$

Note that the equations are identical to those in the resistor model, except for the last one. This is also the case for a capacitor model where the last equation would read:

$$i_\mathrm{p} = C u'$$

In the context of a composite model, such as the circuit from Fig. 1(a), the models of individual components can be reused simply by copying the equations (and renaming variables to avoid name clashes). The sub-models are then interconnected by adding connection equations according to Kirchhoff's voltage and current laws. For instance, after suitable renaming, the connection equations for the node between the resistor R_1 and the capacitor C would be:

$$v_{\mathrm{R}_1,\mathrm{n}} = v_{\mathrm{C},\mathrm{p}}$$
$$i_{\mathrm{R}_1,\mathrm{n}} + i_{\mathrm{C},\mathrm{p}} = 0$$

Good abstraction mechanisms can facilitate the mechanical aspects of copying code and creating connections, allowing the user to define component models in the form of named groups of equations and then create multiple interconnected instances by referring to the components by name. A non-causal language can also support component hierarchies, allowing the reuse of modeling knowledge in an *object-oriented* way. For example, the common aspects of the resistor, inductor and capacitor models above (the two first equations of each model) can be collected into a superclass describing what is common for two-pin components. This modeling knowledge would then be reused in the actual component models through inheritance from the common superclass. A good example of such a language is Modelica [11].

A non-causal simulation tool must undertake a substantial amount of symbolic processing to put the model into a form suitable for simulation. While there are numerical methods for integrating implicit DAEs, these methods are not suitable for solving higher-index[4] DAEs which are very common in practice. Fortunately, it is possible to automatically reduce the index of a DAE to 1 through symbolic manipulations [15], and further transformations allow the system to be put into a form which can be solved efficiently by specialized numerical methods [4,5].

2.2   The Need for Non-causal Hybrid Modeling

A *hybrid model* contains both *continuous* and *discrete* values. The continuous and discrete parts of the model interact via discrete transitions at distinct points in time. These interactions are known as *events*. In between events, the model

---

[4] The *index* of a DAE is the number of symbolic differentiations it takes to transform the system to an ODE.

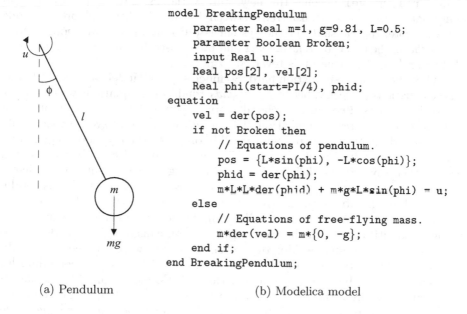

```
model BreakingPendulum
    parameter Real m=1, g=9.81, L=0.5;
    parameter Boolean Broken;
    input Real u;
    Real pos[2], vel[2];
    Real phi(start=PI/4), phid;
equation
    vel = der(pos);
    if not Broken then
        // Equations of pendulum.
        pos = {L*sin(phi), -L*cos(phi)};
        phid = der(phi);
        m*L*L*der(phid) + m*g*L*sin(phi) = u;
    else
        // Equations of free-flying mass.
        m*der(vel) = m*{0, -g};
    end if;
end BreakingPendulum;
```

(a) Pendulum   (b) Modelica model

Fig. 2. A pendulum, subject to externally applied torque and gravity.

evolves continuously: all discrete values remain fixed. Since the model may depend conditionally on the discrete values, each discrete value assignment defines a potentially unique configuration or *mode* of continuous operation.

While the simulation of pure continuous systems is relatively well understood, hybrid systems pose a number of unique challenges [12,1]. Problems include handling a large number of modes, event detection, and consistent initialization of state variables. The integration of hybrid modeling with non-causal modeling raises further problems. Indeed, current non-causal modeling languages are quite limited in their ability to express hybrid systems. Many of the limitations are related to the symbolic and numerical methods that must be used in the non-causal approach. But a more important reason is that most such systems insist on performing all symbolic manipulations *before* simulation begins [12]. Avoiding these limitations is an important part of our approach, see Sec. 4.

Since Modelica is representative of state-of-the-art, non-causal, hybrid modeling languages, we illustrate the limitations of present languages with an example from the Modelica documentation [10, pp. 31–33]. The system is a pendulum in the form of a mass m at the end of a rigid, mass-less rod, subject to gravity mg and an externally applied torque u at the point of suspension; see Fig. 2(a). Additionally, the rod could break at some point, causing the mass to fall freely.

Figure 2(b) shows a Modelica model of this system that, on the surface, looks like it achieves the desired result. Note that it has two modes, described by conditional equations. In the non-broken mode, the position `pos` and velocity `vel` of the mass are calculated from the state variables `phi` and `phid`. In the broken mode, `pos` and `vel` become the new state variables. This implies that state information has to be transferred between the non-broken and broken mode. Furthermore, the causality of the system is different in the two modes. When non-broken, the equation relating `vel` and `pos` is used to compute `vel` from `pos`. When broken, the situation is reversed.

These facts make simulation hard. So much so that Modelica does not handle these equations correctly, because it *forbids* conditional equations with dynamic conditions. Thus, `Broken` is declared to be a *parameter*, meaning that it will remain constant during simulation. Therefore the model above does not really solve the hybrid simulation problem at all! In order to actually model a pendulum that dynamically breaks at some point in time, the model must be expressed in some other way. The Modelica documentation suggests a causal, block-oriented formulation with explicit state transfer. Unsurprisingly, the result is considerably more verbose, nullifying the advantage of working in a non-causal language.

Thus we see that even quite simple examples go beyond the non-causal modeling capabilities of one of the most advanced non-causal, hybrid modeling languages currently available. Moreover, even if `Broken` were allowed to be a dynamic variable, a fundamental problem would remain: once the pendulum has broken, it cannot become whole again. However, Modelica provides no way to declaratively express the *irreversibility* of this structural change. The best that can be done is to capture this fact indirectly through a state machine model and use that to control the value of `Broken`. But this makes the resulting model harder to understand, and it is also difficult for a simulator to exploit the fact that a certain set of equations and variables cannot be used again (to save memory and computational resources) since the simulator would have to infer this fact from the state machine model.

3   Integrating Functional Programming and Non-causal Modeling

In the previous section we pointed out the advantages of non-causal modeling and the importance of hybrid modeling. We also pointed out serious shortcomings in current modeling languages with respect to these features. In this section, we describe a new way to combine non-causal and hybrid modeling techniques that addresses these issues. The two key ideas are to give first-class status to relations on signals and to provide constructs for discrete switching between relations. The result is Hydra, a declarative, semantically coherent, functional hybrid modeling language capable of representing structurally dynamic systems.

3.1   First-Class Signal Relations

A *signal* is, conceptually, a function of time. A *signal function* maps a stimulating signal onto a responding signal; i.e., a signal function is just a (causal) block in the terminology of block-oriented modeling languages. A natural mathematical description of a continuous signal function is that of an ODE in explicit form. Signal functions are first-class entities in Yampa: they have a type, they can be bound to variables, they can be passed to and returned from functions. This is the key to the tight integration of the discrete and continuous aspects of Yampa, and is what makes Yampa uniquely flexible as a language for hybrid modeling.

A function is just a special case of the more general concept of a *relation*. While functions usually are given a causal interpretation, relations are inherently non-causal. DAEs, which are at the heart of non-causal modeling, express dependences among signals without imposing a causality on the signals in the relation. Thus it is natural to view the meaning of a DAE as a non-causal *signal relation*, just as the meaning of an ODE in explicit form can be seen as a causal signal function. Since signal functions and signal relations are closely connected, this view offers a clean way of integrating non-causal modeling into an Yampa-like setting, which is the essence of Hydra.

In the following, first-class signal relations are made concrete by proposing a (tentative) system for integrating them into a polymorphically typed functional language. Signal functions are also useful, but since they are just relations with explicit causality, we need not consider them in detail in the following.

Conceptually, we define the polymorphic type of signals as $S\ \alpha = \text{Time} \to \alpha$; that is, $S\ \alpha$ is the type of a signal whose instantaneous value is of type α. However, signals only exist implicitly via signal functions and signal relations: there is no syntactic entity which has type $S\ \alpha$. We then introduce the type

$$\text{SR}\ \alpha$$

for a relation on a signal of type $S\ \alpha$. Specific relations use a more refined type. For example, for the derivative relation *der* we have the typing:

$$der :: \text{SR}\ (\text{Real, Real})$$

where :: is the typing relation. Since a signal carrying pairs is isomorphic to a pair of signals, we can understand *der* as a binary relation on two real-valued signals.

Next we need notation for defining relations. The following construct, in spirit analogous to a λ-abstraction, denotes a signal relation:

sigrel *pattern* **where** *equations*

The pattern introduces *signal variables* which at each point in time are bound to the *instantaneous* value (a "sample") of the corresponding signal. Thus, given $p :: t$, we have:

sigrel p **where** ... :: SR t

Consequently, the equations express relationships between instantaneous signal values. This resembles the standard notation for differential equations in mathematics. For example, consider $x' = f(y)$, which means that the instantaneous value of the derivative of (the signal) x at every time instant is equal to the value obtained by applying the function f to the instantaneous value of y.

We introduce two styles of equations:

$$e_1 = e_2$$
$$sr \diamond e_3$$

where e_i are expressions (possibly introducing new signal variables), and sr is an expression denoting a signal relation. We require equations to be well-typed. Given $e_i :: t_i$, this is the case iff $t_1 = t_2$ and $sr :: SR\ t_3$.

The first kind of equation requires the values of the two expressions to be equal at all points in time. For example:

$$f(x) = g(y)$$

where f and g are functions.

The second kind allows an arbitrary relation to be used to enforce a relationship between signals. The symbol $\diamond$ can be thought of as *relation application*; the result is a constraint which must hold at all times. The first kind of equation is a special case of the second in the following sense: if taking the syntactic liberty to allow $=$ to denote the identity relation $(= :: SR\ (\text{Real},\text{Real}))$, one could write $f(x) = g(x)$ as

$$= \diamond(f(x), g(x))$$

For another example, consider a differential equation like $x' = f(x, y)$. Using our notation, this equation could be written:

$$der \diamond (x, f(x, y))$$

where der is the relation relating a signal to its derivative. For convenience, a notation closer to the mathematical tradition should be supported as well:

$$\mathbf{der}(x) = f(x, y)$$

The meaning is exactly as in the first version.

We illustrate our language by modeling the electrical circuit from Fig. 1(a). The type Pin is a record type describing an electrical connection. It has fields v for voltage and i for current.[5]

$twoPin :: SR\ (\text{Pin}, \text{Pin}, \text{Voltage})$
$twoPin = \mathbf{sigrel}\ (p, n, u)\ \mathbf{where}$
$\qquad\qquad u = p.v - n.v$
$\qquad\qquad p.i + n.i = 0$

$resistor :: \text{Resistance} \to SR\ (\text{Pin}, \text{Pin})$
$resistor(r) = \mathbf{sigrel}\ (p, n)\ \mathbf{where}$
$\qquad\qquad twoPin \diamond (p, n, u)$
$\qquad\qquad r \cdot p.i = u$

$inductor :: \text{Inductance} \to SR\ (\text{Pin}, \text{Pin})$
$inductor(l) = \mathbf{sigrel}\ (p, n)\ \mathbf{where}$
$\qquad\qquad twoPin \diamond (p, n, u)$
$\qquad\qquad l \cdot \mathbf{der}(p.i) = u$

---

[5] The name Pin is perhaps a bit misleading since it just represents a pair of physical quantities, *not* a physical "pin component"; i.e., Pin is the type of *signal variables* rather than *signal relations*.

$capacitor :: \textsf{Capacitance} \to \textsf{SR (Pin, Pin)}$
$capacitor(c) = \textbf{sigrel}\ (p, n)\ \textbf{where}$
$$twoPin \diamond (p, n, u)$$
$$c \cdot \textbf{der}(u) = p.i$$

As in Modelica, the resistor, inductor and capacitor models are defined as extensions of the *twoPin* model. However, we accomplish this directly with functional abstraction rather than the Modelica class concept. With first-class relations we have a language that is both simpler and more expressive. Note how parameterized models are defined through functions *returning* relations. Since the parameters are normal function arguments, *not* signal variables, their values remain unchanged throughout the lifetime of the returned relations.[6]

To assemble these components into the full model, we will adopt a Modelica-like **connect**-notation as a convenient abbreviation for connection equations. This is syntactic sugar which is expanded to proper connection equations, i.e. equality constraints or sum-to-zero equations depending on what kind of physical quantity is being connected. We assume that a voltage source model *vSourceAC* and a ground model *ground* are available in addition to the component models defined above. Moreover, we are only interested in the total current through the circuit, and, as there are no inputs, the model thus becomes a *unary* relation:

$simpleCircuit :: \textsf{SR Current}$
$simpleCircuit = \textbf{sigrel}\ \textsf{i}\ \textbf{where}$
$$resistor(1000) \diamond (r1p, r1n)$$
$$resistor(2200) \diamond (r2p, r2n)$$
$$capacitor(0.00047) \diamond (cp, cn)$$
$$inductor(0.01) \diamond (lp, ln)$$
$$vSourceAC(12) \diamond (acp, acn)$$
$$ground \diamond gp$$
$$\textbf{connect}\ acp, r1p, r2p$$
$$\textbf{connect}\ r1n, cp$$
$$\textbf{connect}\ r2n, lp$$
$$\textbf{connect}\ acn, cn, ln, gp$$
$$i = r1p.i + r2p.i$$

3.2   Modeling Systems with Dynamic Structure

In order to describe structurally dynamic systems we need to represent an evolving structure. To this end, we introduce two Yampa-inspired switching constructs: the *recurring switch* and the *progressing switch*. The recurring switch allows repeated switching between equation groups. In contrast, the progressing switch expresses that one group of equations *first* is in force, and then, *once* the switching condition has been fulfilled, another group, thus irreversibly progressing to a new structural configuration. For either sort of switching, difficult issues such as state transfer and proper initialization have to be considered.

---

[6] Compare to Modelica's **parameter**-variables mentioned in Sec. 2.2.

We will revisit the breaking pendulum example from Sec. 2.2 to illustrate these switching constructs. To deal with initialization and state transfer, we introduce special initialization equations that are only active at the time of switching, that is, during *events*, and we allow such equations to refer to the values of signal variables just prior to the event through a special **pre**-construct devised for that purpose. The initialization equations describe the initial conditions of the DAE after a switch. Mathematically, these equations must yield an initial value for every state variable in the new continuous equations. It is important that each branch of a switch can be associated with its own initialization equations, since each such branch may introduce its proper set of state variables. Initialization equations typically state continuity assumptions, as in the case of *pos* and *vel* below.[7]

First, consider a direct transliteration of the equation part of the Modelica model using a recurring switch. The necessary initialization equations have also been added:

$$vel = \mathbf{der}(pos)$$
$$\mathbf{switch} \ broken$$
$$\quad \mathbf{when} \ False \ \mathbf{then}$$
$$\quad\quad \mathbf{init} \ phi = pi/4$$
$$\quad\quad \mathbf{init} \ phid = 0$$
$$\quad\quad pos = \{l \cdot \sin(phi), -l \cdot \cos(phi)\}$$
$$\quad\quad phid = \mathbf{der}(phi)$$
$$\quad\quad m \cdot l \cdot l \cdot \mathbf{der}(phid) + m \cdot g \cdot l \cdot \sin(phi) = u$$
$$\quad \mathbf{when} \ True \ \mathbf{then}$$
$$\quad\quad \mathbf{init} \ vel = \mathbf{pre}(vel)$$
$$\quad\quad \mathbf{init} \ pos = \mathbf{pre}(pos)$$
$$\quad\quad m \cdot \mathbf{der}(vel) = m \cdot \{0, -g\}$$

A recurring switch has one or more **when**-branches. The idea is that the equations in a **when**-branch are in force whenever the pattern after **when** (which may bind variables) matches the value of the expression after **switch**. Thus, whenever that value changes, we have an event and a switch occurs (this is similar to **case** in a functional language).

To express the fact that the pendulum cannot become whole once it has broken, we refine the model by changing to a progressing switch:

$$vel = \mathbf{der}(pos)$$
$$\mathbf{switch} \ broken$$
$$\quad \mathbf{first}$$
$$\quad\quad \ldots$$
$$\quad \mathbf{once} \ True \ \mathbf{then}$$
$$\quad\quad \ldots$$

---

[7] Since Modelica does not support hybrid models where the set of state variables changes, it does not provide any declarative constructs for relating the states across modes. However, it does provide an essentially imperative construct for reinitializing individual state variables.

A progressing switch has one **first**-branch and one or more **once**-branches. Initially, the equations in the **first**-branch are in force, but as soon as the value of the expression after **switch** matches one of the **once**-patterns, a switch occurs to the equations in the corresponding branch, after which no further switching occurs (for that particular instance of the switch).

By combining recursively-defined relations and progressing switches, it is possible to express very general sequences of structural changes over time, from simple mode transitions to making and breaking of connections between objects. A simple example of a recursively defined relation parameterized on a discrete state variable n is shown below. Initially, the relation behaves according to the equations in the **first**-branch, which may depend on n. Whenever the switching condition is fulfilled, the relation switches to a new instance of itself with the parameter n increased by one. In functional parlance, this is a form of tail call.

$$sysWithCntr :: \texttt{Int} \rightarrow \texttt{SR (Real, Real)}$$
$$sysWithCntr(n) = \textbf{sigrel } (x, y) \textbf{ where}$$
$$\textbf{switch} \ldots$$
$$\textbf{first}$$
$$\ldots$$
$$\textbf{once} \ldots \textbf{ then}$$
$$sysWithCntr(n+1) \diamond (x, y)$$

Yampa supports even more radical structural changes, including dynamic addition and deletion of objects [14]. We hope to carry over much of that functionality to Hydra as well.

4   Implementation Issues

There are a number of significant challenges that must be addressed in an implementation of a language like Hydra. The primary issues are ensuring model correctness, simulation in the presence of dynamic mode changes, and mode initialization. The static and dynamic semantics of the language must also be worked out in detail. The dynamic semantics are best described using a reference implementation as an embedding in a functional language such as Haskell. Good surface syntax is also important and can be provided through a pre-processor.

It is critical that dynamic changes in the model should should not weaken the static checking of the model, i.e. we want to ensure *compositional correctness*. Using a Haskell-like polymorphic type system, as in FRP, ensures that the system integrity is preserved. In addition we would like to find at least necessary conditions for statically ensuring that causality analysis can always be carried out, that the equations at least could have a solution, and so on, regardless of how relations are composed dynamically. An example of a necessary but not sufficient condition is that the number of equations and number of variables agree, and that each variable can be paired with one equation. Since it will be necessary to keep track of the balance between equations and variables across relation boundaries, it is natural to integrate this aspect into the type system. Similar considerations apply to the number of initialization equations and continuous state variables. Recent work on dependent types is relevant here [21]. We also aim at extending the type system to handle physical dimensions [7].

In a structurally dynamic language, it will be impossible to identify all possible operating modes and then factor them out as separate systems. We intend to generate the modes *dynamically* during simulation. In non-causal modeling, that implies that causality analysis and the prerequisite symbolic processing has to be performed whenever mode switches occur during simulation. The hybrid bond graph simulator HyBrSim has demonstrated the feasibility of this approach, and that it indeed allows some difficult cases to be handled [13]. However, HyBrSim is an *interpreted* system. Simulation is thus slowed down both by occasional symbolic processing and by the interpretive overhead. To avoid interpretive overhead, we intend to leverage recent work on run-time code generation, such as 'C [6] or Cyclone [19]. We will need to adapt the sophisticated mathematical techniques used in existing non-causal modeling languages [15,4, 5] to this setting. In part, it may be possible to do this systematically by *staging* the existing algorithms in a language like Cyclone.

Whenever a switch occurs, a new, global, "flattened" DAE has to be generated. This DAE is what governs the overall continuous system behavior until the next discrete event. It is obtained by first carrying out the necessary discrete processing. This amounts to standard functional evaluation, including evaluation of the *relational expressions* in the equations that are to be active after the switch. The evaluation of relational expression is what creates *new instances* of relations, and carrying out the instantiation dynamically when switching occurs is what enables modeling of truly structurally dynamic systems. Once the new flattened DAE has been generated, it is subjected to causality analysis and other symbolic manipulations in preparation for simulation using suitable numerical methods [15,4,5]. The result is causal simulation code (a sequence of "assignment statements"), which should be compiled dynamically for better efficiency.

The initial conditions of the (new) differential equations must be determined on transitions from one mode to another. However, arriving at consistent initial conditions is, in general, hard. Some state variables in the continuous part of the system may exhibit discontinuities at the time of switching while others will not: simply preserving the old value is not always the right solution. Structural changes could change the set of state variables, and the relationship between the new and old states may be difficult to determine. One approach is to require the modeler to provide a function that maps the old state to the new one for each possible mode transition [1]. However, the declarative formulation of non-causal models means that the simulator sometimes has a choice regarding which continuous variables should be treated as state variables. Requiring the user to provide a state mapping function is therefore not always reasonable.

A key to the success of HyBrSim is that bond graphs are based on physical notions such as energy and energy exchange, which are subject to continuity and conservation principles. We intend to generalize this idea by exploring the use of *declarations* for stating such principles, along the lines illustrated in Sec. 3.2. It may also be possible to infer continuity and conservation constraints automatically based on physical dimension types.

Nevertheless, particularly when dealing with systems with highly dynamic structure, manual intervention may be necessary. In our work on Yampa, we have developed high-level mechanisms that exploit the first-class status of signal functions to give the user fine control over state transfer across mode switches [14]. We hope to generalize these results to signal relations and a non-causal setting in Hydra.

5 Conclusions

Hybrid modeling is a domain in which the techniques of declarative programming languages have the potential to greatly advance the state of the art. The modeling community has traditionally been concerned more with the mathematics of modeling than language issues. As a result, present modeling languages do not scale in a number of ways, particularly in hybrid systems that undergo significant structural changes. Hydra uses functional programming techniques to describe dynamically changing systems in a way that preserves the non-causal structure of the system specification and allows arbitrary switching among modes, yielding expressive power beyond current non-causal modeling languages.

Although we have not completed an implementation of Hydra, this paper demonstrates our basic design approach and maps out the design landscape. We expect that further research into the links between declarative languages and hybrid modeling will produce significant advances in this field.

References

1. Paul I. Barton and Cha Kun Lee. Modeling, simulation, sensitivity analysis, and optimization of hybrid systems. Submitted to ACM Transactions on Modelling and Computer Simulation: Special Issue on Multi-Paradigm Modeling, September 2001.
2. François E. Cellier. Object-oriented modelling: Means for dealing with system complexity. In *Proceedings of the 15th Benelux Meeting on Systems and Control, Mierlo, The Netherlands*, pages 53–64, 1996.
3. Hilding Elmqvist, François E. Cellier, and Martin Otter. Object-oriented modeling of hybrid systems. In *Proceedings of ESS'93 European Simulation Symposium*, pages xxxi–xli, Delft, The Netherlands, 1993.
4. Hilding Elmqvist and Martin Otter. Methods for tearing systems of equations in object-oriented modeling. In *Proceedings of ESM'94, European Simulation Multiconference*, pages 326–332, Barcelona, Spain, June 1994.
5. Hilding Elmqvist, Martin Otter, and François E. Cellier. Inline integration: A new mixed symbolic/numeric approach. In *Proceedings of ESM'95, European Simulation Multiconference*, pages xxiii–xxxiv, Prague, Czech Republic, June 1995.
6. Dawson R. Engler, Wilson C. Hsieh, and M. Frans Kaashoek. 'C: A language for high-level, efficient, and machine-independent dynamic code generation. In *Proceedings of the 23rd ACM Symposium on Principles of Programming Languages (POPL'96)*, pages 131–144, January 1996.
7. Andrew Kennedy. *Programming Languages and Dimensions*. PhD thesis, University of Cambridge, Computer Laboratory, April 1996. Published as Technical Report No. 391.

8. Edward A. Lee. Overview of the ptolemy project. Technical memorandum UCB/ERLM01/11, Electronic Research Laboratory, University of California, Berkeley, March 2001.
9. The MathWorks, Inc. *Using Simulink Version 4*, June 2001.
10. The Modelica Association. *Modelica – A Unified Object-Oriented Language for Physical Systems Modeling: Tutorial version 1.4*, December 2000.
11. The Modelica Association. *Modelica – A Unified Object-Oriented Language for Physical Systems Modeling: Language Specification version 2.0*, July 2002.
12. Pieter J. Mosterman. An overview of hybrid simulation phenomena and their support by simulation packages. In Fritz W. Vaadrager and Jan H. van Schuppen, editors, *Hybrid Systems: Computation and Control '99*, number 1569 in Lecture Notes in Computer Science, pages 165–177, 1999.
13. Pieter J. Mosterman, Gautam Biswas, and Martin Otter. Simulation of discontinuities in physical system models based on conservation principles. In *Proceedings of SCS Summer Conference 1998*, pages 320–325, July 1998.
14. Henrik Nilsson, Antony Courtney, and John Peterson. Functional reactive programming, continued. In *Proceedings of the 2002 ACM SIGPLAN Haskell Workshop (Haskell'02)*, pages 51–64, Pittsburgh, Pennsylvania, USA, October 2002. ACM Press.
15. Constantinos C. Pantelides. The consistent initialization of differential-algebraic systems. *SIAM Journal on Scientific and Statistical Computing*, 9(2):213–231, March 1988.
16. Izzet Pembeci, Henrik Nilsson, and Greogory Hager. Functional reactive robotics: An exercise in principled integration of domain-specific languages. In *Principles and Practice of Declarative Programming (PPDP'02)*, Pittsburgh, Pennsylvania, USA, October 2002.
17. John Peterson, Greg Hager, and Paul Hudak. A language for declarative robotic programming. In *Proceedings of IEEE Conference on Robotics and Automation*, May 1999.
18. John Peterson, Paul Hudak, Alastair Reid, and Greg Hager. FVision: A declarative language for visual tracking. In *Proceedings of PADL'01: 3rd International Workshop on Practical Aspects of Declarative Languages*, pages 304–321, January 2001.
19. Frederick Smith, Dan Grossman, Greg Morrisett, Luke Hornof, and Trevor Jim. Compiling for run-time code generation. Submitted for publication to JFP SAIG.
20. Zhanyong Wan and Paul Hudak. Functional reactive programming from first principles. In *Proceedings of PLDI'01: Symposium on Programming Language Design and Implementation*, pages 242–252, June 2000.
21. Hongwei Xi and Frank Pfenning. Dependent types in practical programming. In *Proceedings of ACM SIGPLAN Symposium on Principles of Programming Languages*, pages 214–227, San Antonio, January 1999.

Lambda Goes to Hollywood*

Victor M. Gulias, Carlos Abalde, and Juan J. Sanchez

LFCIA, Department of Computer Science
University of A Coruña, SPAIN,
{gulias, carlos, juanjo}@lfcia.org,
http://www.lfcia.org

Abstract. In this paper, some experiences of using the concurrent functional language Erlang to implement a distributed video-on-demand server are presented. This server is the result of a project supported by a regional cable company, and it is intended to provide services for real users in the real world. The nature of the problem, with fuzzy and changing requirements, suggests a highly flexible and scalable architecture. The use of abstractions (functional patterns) and compositionality (both functional and concurrent composition) have been key factors to reduce the amount of time spent adapting the system to changes in requirements. Despite our initial concerns, efficiency constraints have been succesfully met.

Keywords: Functional programming, distributed computing, concurrent programming, design patterns, real-world applications

1 Introduction

A *Video-on-Demand* server is a system that provides video services to many clients which can request a video object at any time, with no pre-established temporal constraints. The main applications for such systems are movie-on-demand distribution, remote learning, interactive news, among others.

In this paper, we introduce some of our experiences designing and implementing a video-on-demand server called VoDKA (http://vodka.lfcia.org). The main novelty of this system is that it has been developed using a declarative language, the concurrent functional language Erlang [AVWW96]. To achieve the performance required to provide video services, the server needs a distributed architecture, deploying control agents on Pile-of-PC clusters (cheap distributed systems built using off-the-shelf components) all along the service network. The use of Erlang has considerably simplified the development of such distributed control system.

This server is the result of a research project partially supported by the Galician regional cable company, *R Cable y Comunicaciones de Galicia S.A.* (http://www.mundo-R.com), which intends to provide its users with streaming services, mainly broadband-quality movie-on-demand contents. Hence, we are

---

* Partially supported by CICyT TIC 2002-02859 and Xunta de Galicia PR425M

V. Dahl and P. Wadler (Eds.): PADL 2003, LNCS 2562, pp. 391–407, 2003.

talking about a real-world problem with forty-thousand potential clients. More-over, at the beginning of the project (2000), the requirements for the service were not all clearly stated, thus needing a highly flexible and scalable design.

The use of functional abstractions and compositionality, both functional and concurrent composition, have been key factors to reduce the amount of time spent adapting the system to changes in requirements. However, despite our initial concerns, efficiency constraints have been succesfully accomplished.

This paper is structured as follows: First, some background knowledge is pre-sented to introduce both the notion of video-on-demand as well as the functional programming language Erlang. Section 3 is devoted to introduce the design of VoDKA, including some observations about efficiency. Section 4 discusses some of the benefits of using a functional language in the project and, in particular, how using abstractions simplified some issues such as device heterogeneity or multi-protocol data movement. Finally, we present the conclusions.

2   Background

2.1   A Glimpse of Video-on-Demand Servers

As we said before, a *video-on-demand* (VoD) server is a system that provides video services to many clients which can request a video object at any time, with no pre-established temporal constraints. Actually, video-on-demand should be stated as *media-on-demand* because there is almost no difference with other streaming media such as audio. However, in this presentation the term VoD server is being used for streaming server in general.

VoD systems must satisfy several critical requirements, including:

- *Large storage capacity*: the system should be able to offer users a large num-ber of multimedia objects, and each media object may be large.
- *Many concurrent users*: the system should be able to handle thousands of concurrent requests, guaranteeing reasonable, and ideally predictable, re-sponse times.
- *High bandwidth*: as long as many users are receiving high bitrate media for a long time, the system should be able to deliver such aggregated bandwith.
- *Reliability*: given the nature of the application, with service times of hours (think, for instance, of a two-hour movie show), reliability is a must. That means to ship error-free code, to recover gracefully from hardware or soft-ware errors, and to provide mechanisms to incorporate new features without stopping the system.
- *Scalability*: both upwards and also downwards scalability. A simple configu-ration can be enough to attend only a few clients, but it should be possible to increase system resources as soon as new potential users arise.
- *Adaptability*: the system should adapt to the underlying topology, making an efficient use of the available network bandwidth.
- *Low cost*: Our goal is to reduce the costs involved in the whole system — hardware, software and network usage.

During the last years, many companies have been developing video-on-demand related solutions. Some of them are well suited for low bandwidth networks (*Internet*), like the popular RealNetworks RealVideo Server, based on standard real-time protocols such as RTP/RTSP [Gro96,Gro98], or Microsoft Windows Media Server, that uses proprietary protocols for video delivering. Other solutions are more focused to LAN or MAN, with high bandwidth availability. The most representative ones are Apple Darwin Streaming Server [App01], an efficient but not distributed RTP streaming server; IBM's DB2 Digital Library Video Charger [WDRW99]; Oracle Video Server [Ora98], probably the most widely used system, with a client/server architecture, but with scalability limitations; Kasenna MediaBase, that put emphasis on a modular system that separates acquisition, distribution and streaming stages; Philips WebCine Server [Phi00], an MPEG4 streaming server based on Linux; Cisco IP/TV [Cis00], a closed solution with high-level tools oriented to e-learning; and Sun's system: StorEdge Media Central [Sun99]. A detailed study of some of these solutions can be found in [SGVM00].

2.2   The Distributed Functional Language Erlang

Erlang [AVWW96] is a distributed and concurrent functional programming language developed by Ericsson for telecommunication applications. The language has no constructs inducing side effects to an implicit store with the exception of communications among threads (*processes*, in Erlang terminology). Erlang evaluates expressions eagerly as many other strict functional languages such as ML.

Values in Erlang (i.e., non-reducible expressions) range from numbers and *atoms* (symbolic constants, lower-case in Erlang syntax) to complex data structures (lists, tuples) and functional values, which are treated as first-class citizens. A function is defined by a set of equations, each stating a different set of constraints based primarily on the structure of the arguments (*pattern-matching*). Iterative control flow is carried out by using function recursion. Lists, the most important data structure in functional languages, are written [a,b,c] with [] being the empty list, and a list whose first element is X and whose rest is Xs is denoted [X|Xs]. Thus, to define a function that tests for membership in a list, we can write:

```
member(X,[])     -> false;
member(X,[X|Xs]) -> true;
member(X,[Y|Ys]) -> member(X,Ys).
```

Functions are grouped into modules, and a subset of those functions can be exported, declaring both function name and arity, to be used in other modules.

```
-module(mymodule).
-export([member/2]).
```

Hence, `mymodule:member(3, [1,2,3])` evaluates to the atom **true**, while `mymodule:member(5, [1,2,3])` reduces to **false**. In the absence of a static type system such as many modern functional languages provide, lists can contain heterogeneus values such as `[a, [], 1]`. Besides lists, Erlang programmers also can use *tuples*, similar to C structures, which are constructed in arbitrary but finite length by writing {A,B,...,C}. Lists and tuples can hold any valid Erlang value, from numbers and atoms to lists, tuples and even functional values. *Records* are also provided as useful syntactic sugar for accesing tuples by name instead of by position.

As other modern functional languages, interesting features such as higher-order functions (functional parameters or functional results), on-the-fly function creation, dynamic typing, list comprehensions, and a powerful collection of libraries which constitutes the Open Telecom Platform (OTP) that includes a distributed database, graphical interfaces, an ASN.1 compiler, a CORBA object request broker, COM and Java interfaces among others. In fact, these features make Erlang one of the notable success exceptions in real world applications [Wad98].

2.3   Concurrent Erlang

What makes Erlang different from other functional languages is its support for concurrency and distribution. With Erlang's primitives for concurrency, it resembles formal calculi such as Milner's CCS [MPW92] or Hoare's CSP [Hoa85]. The idea behind the scenes is clear: concurrent programming is far simpler in a functional language than in an imperative one because of the absence of side-effects (only process creation and communications).

A new thread is created by using the built-in primitive **spawn**. Given a module M, a function F with arity N exported from module M, and a list of arguments $[A_1, A_2, \ldots, A_N]$, the expression $\mathtt{spawn}(M, F, [A_1, A_2, \ldots, A_N])$ starts a new process to compute $M : F(A_1, A_2, \ldots, A_n)$. Once evaluated, **spawn** returns the *process identifier*, `Pid`, of the newly created lightweight process.

In order to allow interaction among processes, a couple of asynchronous message passing primitives are available:

- *Asynchronous send*:

      Pid ! Msg

  `Msg` is sent to process `Pid` without blocking the sending process. If `Pid` exists, the message is stored in `Pid`'s *mailbox*. Any valid Erlang value can be sent to other process, including complex data structures containing lists, tuples, functions, or process identifiers.

- *Mailbox pattern matching*:

      receive
          Pat₁ -> Expr₁;
          ...
          Pat_M -> Expr_M
      end

It searches the process mailbox looking for a message that matches one of the patterns $Pat_1, \ldots, Pat_M$ sequentially. If no such message exists, the process blocks until it arrives. The result is the evaluation of $Expr_i$ with the bindings carried out in Pat_i.

Using these concurrency constructs, a *server* can be defined as a recursive function that receives a request from a client and sends the response back. The *state* of the server is plumbed explicitly as a function parameter. For instance, the following code defines a process which adds Inc to the client request parameter.

```
-module(inc_server).
-export([loop/1]).

loop(Inc) ->
  receive
    {From, X} -> From ! X+Inc,
                 loop(Inc)
  end.
```

In order to create the server with *Inc=1*, we should evaluate `spawn(inc_server, loop, [1])`. Observe that, as part of the request, the client includes its own identity to receive the server response. Also, note the use of the *sequential operator*: E_1, E_2 evaluates E_1 (perhaps performing communications), discards the computed value and then evaluates E_2.

The client API can be defined as:

```
client(X) ->
  ServerPid ! {self(), X},
  receive
    Response -> Response
  end.
```

where *ServerPid* is the identity of the server process, and `self` is a built-in primitive that returns the identity of the running process.

Higher-order functions can be used to generalize the basic server pattern and to avoid the repetition of the same structure at different places. In this case, the algorithm to compute the response given a request is encapsulated into a function $F : Request \times State \rightarrow Response \times State$, delivering also the state for the next iteration.

```
-module(server).
-export([start/2, loop/2]).

start(F, State) ->
  spawn(server, loop, [F, State]).

loop(F, State) ->
  receive
    {From, Req} ->
      {Resp, NewState} = F(Req, State),
      From ! Response,
      loop(F, NewState)
  end.
```

This skeleton can be specialized then to build the aforementioned inc_server:

```
server:start(fun (X,Inc) -> {X+Inc,Inc} end, 1).
```

2.4   Distributed Erlang

The natural extension of Erlang to a distributed framework is to have processes running in more than one Erlang virtual machine (*nodes*, in Erlang terminology) possibly running at different physical nodes. In order to create a process on a remote node, spawn(*Node, M, F, Args*) should be used, adding *Node* as an extra parameter with the location for the newly created process. The nice feature is that all the concurrency constructs are semantically equivalent in this distributed framework (even though communications among remote processes are less efficient, of course).

3   The VoDKA Project

3.1   History and Goals

In 2000, a project partially supported by the cable operator *R Cable y Comunicaciones de Galicia* was started to provide VoD services to its clients all along Galicia (about forty-thousand subscribers living in the north-west of Spain, with a quite sparse distribution of population). After a brief analysis of commercial VoD products [SGVM00], it was revealed that most of them represent very expensive, closed, non-scalable and non-adaptable solutions. Therefore, the proposed goal for the project was:

  – *To build an extremely scalable, fault tolerant, multiprotocol, adaptable (to the network topology and end-user protocols) streaming server.*

  Since its foundation, our group had been working with functional programming languages such as ML or Haskell, and had also been interested in clusters built from cheap off-the-shell components [BG99]. Thus, our solution will be considering two technologies:

  – *The use of commodity hardware clusters for the underlying architecture.*
  – *The use of the functional programming paradigm and design patterns for the design and implementation of the distributed control system.*

  The use of Linux clusters in the proposed solution has been a key feature of the project as an innovative architecture, differentiating it from most of the existing commercial solutions. The main problem was how a small team of developers were going to program such complex distributed system. What is worse, we soon realized that many requirements were not known at the very beginning of the project: set-top box or conventional desktop PCs? communication protocols? type of media? type of storage drives? Hence, the system should be as flexible as possible to adapt to these changing scenarios. We chose Erlang to program the distributed control system instead of ML or Haskell because:

  – *Nature*: Erlang has constructs for concurrent and distributed computing and it has been succesful in previous experiences with large systems [Arm96].

- *Libraries*: Erlang has a rich set of libraries and tools (*OTP, Open Telecom Platform*) that eases the development.
- *Interface*: Erlang has a nice interface with low-level languages which may be necessary for performance reasons or for interacting with devices.
- *Efficient*: Erlang is surprisingly efficient, fast enough for our purposes. If necessary, it also has a native-code compiler (*Hipe* [JPS00]).

However, Erlang has three major drawbacks for software development:

- *Type system*: Tons of simple type errors are not inmediatly caught at compile time. This is a real problem when changing a type definition or when using higher-order communications (sending/receiving a closure). We beg for just a simple type checking —optional, if you want. This has been pointed out in the past [MW97].
- *Module system*: This is twofold. Firstly, related with the type system issue, an interface/implementation module definition is advisable: it is simple not possible to check if a module satisfies a given interface. Secondly, modules have a primitive flat namespace; a hierarchical module system, like the one presented in [Car00], should be advisable.
- *Coverage*: As most of functional languages, we need more programmers, more books, more patterns, more experiences...

3.2   Initial Design

To satisfy system requirements, a distributed and hierarchical storage system running on a Linux cluster is proposed. The hierarchy in this initial proposal (figure 1), inspired by the one shown in [CT97], is composed by three specialized levels, described bottom-up as follows:

- *Tertiary Level (repository or massive storage level)*: Its main goal is to store all the available media objects in the server using tape chargers, disk arrays, or any other massive storage device. The main feature of this layer is *large capacity*. The server global performance depends on this level in terms of load time, latency, throughput, etc.. However, the secondary level will allow to reduce the global impact of these parameters acting as a cache.
- *Secondary Level (cache level)*: it is composed by a set of cluster nodes. The media object, read from the tertiary level, is stored into the node before being delivered by the primary layer. An appropriate scheduling policy should decide which are the videos that should be maintained in the cache, and for how long, in order to satisfy future user requests and reduce accesses to the massive storage level, if possible.
- *Primary Level (streaming level)*: it is composed by a set of nodes in charge of protocol adaptation and sending the final media stream with the right format to the client. This level has important requirements both in bandwidth and in response time.

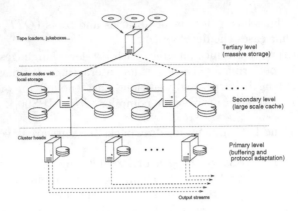

Fig. 1. Initial hierarchical structure

3.3 Design Refinement

The initial design ideas had to be modified in order to satisfy the needs of a production system. In particular, a design generalization was needed, because the static three-level hierarchical architecture (streaming, cache and massive storage) can be too complex for very small installations, and too rigid for complex network topologies like a network that interconnects some metropolitan cable networks.

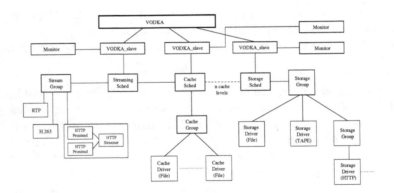

Fig. 2. VoDKA server control processes with n layers

This refinement of the hierarchical architecture gives a new one, divided into a variable number of specialized levels, all of them sharing the same standard interface (figure 2). This way, for example, the cache level can be suppressed in a given installation, or can be augmented producing a complex multilayer cache adapted to the underlying topology (figure 3) or configuring different massive storage levels physically distributed. The usual setup for a DOCSIS based cable network provides a restricted, even though sufficient under normal circumstances, bandwidth from the customer to the cable headend, but plenty of available bandwidth through high speed SDH fiber rings among cable headends and the provider central switching offices. In some cases, there are additional switching levels to the customer. So, in order to accommodate this situation, a series of distributed storage and cache servers are deployed throughout the provider network, optimizing link characteristics. Moreover, a server could be used as a storage subsystem of a different server, defining a VoD meta-server.

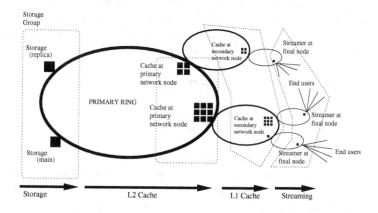

Fig. 3. Configuration of the server on a complex network topology

Besides the flexibility related to the physical distribution of the system, processes must be able to interact using heterogeneous storage and transference protocols. Hence, the communication patterns between different levels must be identified and factored out as functional abstractions (see section 4) which encapsulate protocols as functional closures. This decision is made by the control system when negotiating a new task (i.e., stream).

4   Functional Patterns in VoDKA

The use of a functional language, in particular the identification of *functional abstractions*, has been a key factor to simplify the development. As classical abstractions such as `map` or `foldr`, the identified patterns use higher-order functions to abstract particularities as functional parameters. Considering that a given pattern must be specialized with many different but related functions, two approaches can be taken:

- To define a data structure, such as a *tuple*, that collects all the functional closures needed.
- To use a *module* as a container of functions, and use the module as a function parameter.

4.1   Moving Data

One of the most recurring tasks found all along the server is the movement of data from a source to a destination. Media objects must be read from a file system, for instance, and has to feed an Erlang process delivering such media object using a socket connection. Heterogeneity plays an important role in these tasks as long as data sources and data destinations can behave rather differently: file systems, TCP connections, UDP connections, direct memory transfers, and so on. Moreover, the abstract process of moving data involves some accounting that is, in essence, independent from the nature of sources and destinations. Thus, an abstraction, *pipe*, is introduced to deal with the movement of data from a *data source*, identified by a *data source module* (behaviour of data source) and a *data source initialization data*, to a *data destination*, identified by a *data destination module* and *data destination initialization data*.

The data source module must export, among others, the following functions:

- `init(DS_initparam) -> {ok, DS_info, DS_state}`
  `                    | {error, Reason}`

  Initialization of the data source given a specific data source initial parameter. It delivers a tuple with the atom `ok`, information about the data source such as name, size, MIME type, and so on (`DS_info` structure), and the explicit state to continue reading from the data source (`DS_state`); if something goes wrong, it delivers an `error`.
- `read(DS_State) -> {ok, Data, DS_state}`
  `                 | {error, Reason}`
  `                 | {done, DS_doneparam}`

  It reads the next piece of data from the data source, delivering `ok`, the actual data read (`Data`, in principle a binary datatype), and the state for the next iteration with the data source. if we are finished with the data source, it delivers `done` and the state required for cleaning up the data source; if something goes wrong, it delivers an `error`.

- `done(DS_doneparam)  -> ok | {error, Reason}`

  It cleans up the data source after all its data has been consumed.

  The data destination module is quite similar, exporting among others:

- `init(DS_info, DD_initparam) -> {ok, DD_state}`
  `                             | {error, Reason}`

  Initialization of the data destination given a specific data destination initial parameter and the data source information. It delivers a tuple with the atom `ok` and the explicit state to continue writing the data gathered from the data source (`DD_state`); if something goes wrong, it delivers an `error`.

— `write(Data, DD_State) -> {ok, DD_state}`
`| {error, Reason}`

It writes the next piece of data (a binary datatype) to the data destination, delivering ok and the state for the next iteration with the data destination. If something goes wrong, it delivers an error.

— `done(DD_state)   -> ok | {error, Reason}`

It flushes the data destination after finishing the transference.

The following code shows a simple implementation of the pipe abstraction:

```
-module(pipe)
-export([start/2, init/2]).

start(DS, DD) ->
    spawn(pipe, init, [DS, DD]).

init({DS_module,DS_initparam}, {DD_module,DD_initparam}) ->
    {ok, DS_info, DS_state0} = DS_module:init(DS_initparam),
    {ok, DD_state0} = DD_module:init(DS_info, DD_initparam),
    {DS_statef, DD_statef} = pipe_while(DS_module, DS_state0, DD_module, DD_state0),
    ok = DS_module:done(DS_statef),
    ok = DD_module:done(DD_statef).

pipe_while(DS_module, DS_state, DD_module, DD_state) ->
    case DS_module:read(DS_state) of
        {ok, Data, DS_statenext} ->
            {ok, DD_statenext} = DD_module:write(Data, DD_state),
            pipe_while(DS_module, DS_statenext, DD_module, DD_statenext);
        {done, DS_statef} ->
            {DS_statef, DD_state}
    end.
```

To understand the concept better, the following example defines a *file copy* using pipes. Firstly, a suitable data source must be defined:

```
-module(read_file).
-export([init/1, read/1, done/1]).
-include("ds_info.hrl").

init(Filename) ->
    case file:open(Filename, [read, raw, binary]) of
        {ok, IoDevice} ->
            PreRead = file:read(IoDevice, 64*1024),
            {ok, #ds_info{name=Filename}, {IoDevice, PreRead}};
        {error, Reason} ->
            {error, Reason}
    end.

read({IoDevice, eof}) ->
    {done, IoDevice};
read({IoDevice, {error, Reason}}) ->
    {error, Reason};
read({IoDevice, {ok, Data}}) ->
    {ok, Data, {IoDevice, file:read(IoDevice, 64*1024)}}.

done(IoDevice) ->
    file:close(IoDevice).
```

The complementary data destination has the following implementation:

```
-module(write_file).
-export([init/2, write/2, done/1]).

init(_DSInfo, Filename) ->
    file:open(Filename, [write, raw, binary]).

write(Data, IoDevice) ->
    case file:write(IoDevice, Data) of
        ok ->
            {ok, IoDevice};
        Error ->
            Error
    end.

done(IoDevice) ->
    file:close(IoDevice).
```

Then, a pipe can be created as follows:

```
pipe:start_link({read_file, "oldfile.dat"}, {write_file, "newfile.dat"})
```

The actual pipe implementation is a bit more complex, including some instrumentation to gather information about the data movement, and an extra control parameter (*pipe_options*) that let us define extra features for the transference (bandwith control, for instance).

4.2   Functional Strategies

In the classical GoF collection of object-oriented design patterns [GHJV95], a *Strategy Pattern* is defined as a way of changing the behaviour of a given context object by replacing an internal strategy object which encapsulates some algorithm. Different strategies share the same interface but have different implementations.

This design pattern, for example, is applied to the replacement algorithm used in caches. Caches play the role of context objects while the different replacement algorithms are the strategies. The strategy concept can be implemented in a functional language defining the cache behaviour as a higher-order function that takes a module (collection of functions) as a parameter and the required explicit state for those functions. For instance, some of the functions required by a cache replacement strategy are `initial_state(InitData) -> ReplState`, that delivers the initial state from some initialization data; `lock(ReplState,MO) -> ReplState`, which locks a media object to avoid replacing it while it is being used; or `alloc(ReplState,MO) -> {ok, ReplState, [MO]} | {error, ReplState, Reason}` that allocates a new media object and, perhaps, chooses the media to be replaced. A simple non-efficient partial implementation of a LRU strategy is shown:

```
-module(simple_lru_replacement).
-export([initial_state/1, lock/2, unlock/2, alloc/2, ...]).

initial_state(Size) -> {Size, [], []}.
```

```
lock({Free, MOAvailable, MOLocked}, MO) ->
  {Free, lists:delete(MO, MOAvailable), [MO | MOLocked]}.

unlock({Free, MOAvailable, MOLocked}, MO) ->
  NewMOLocked = lists:delete(MO, MOLocked),    %% deletes only 1st occurrence of MO
  case lists:member(MO, NewMOLocked) of
    true ->
      {Free, MOAvailable, NewMOLocked};
    false ->
      {Free, MOAvailable ++ [MO], NewMOLocked}
  end.

alloc({Free, MOAvailable, MOLocked}, MO) ->
  case release(Free, get_size(MO), MOAvailable, []) of
    {ok, NewFree, ReleasedMOs} ->
        {ok, {NewFree, MOAvailable ++ [MO], MOLocked}, ReleasedMOs};
    {error, Reason} ->
        {error, {Free, MOAvailable, MOLocked}, Reason}
  end.

release(Free, Needed, _, ReleasedMOs) when Free >= Needed ->
  {ok, Free-Needed, ReleasedMOs};
release(Free, Needed, [MO | MoreMOs], ReleasedMOs) ->
  release(Free+get_size(MO), Needed, MoreMOs, [MO | ReleasedMOs]);
release(_, _, [], _) ->
  {error, not_enough_space};
```

The cache agent uses the replacement strategy, storing it as part of its state (`replace_strategy` field, a pair with the module and the replacement state). For example, when the cache is requested to transfer a media object, it must lock the media to avoid being replaced in future interactions while it is still in use. A simplification of such behaviour is defined as follows:

```
...
handle_call({getmo, MO, Destination, PipeOpts}, _, S) ->
  case in_cache(S,MO) of
    no ->
      {{error, not_found}, S};
    {yes, Path} ->
      {ReplModule, ReplState} = S#cache_state.replace_strategy,
      NewReplState = ReplModule:lock(ReplState),
      Source = {read_cache_multi_file, {Path, S#cache_state.file_chunk_size, ...}},
      Pid = pipe:start_link(Source, Destination, PipeOpts),
      NewS = S#cache_state{locked = [{MO,Pid} | S#cache_state.locked],
                            replace_strategy = {ReplModule, NewReplState}},
      {{ok, Pid}, NewS}
  end;
...
```

While the pipe created by the cache is transferring the media, an association between the pipe process and the media object is kept (`locked` field list). As soon as the pipe process dies, an exit signal is sent to the cache process. Then, the media can be unlocked.

```
...
handle_info({'EXIT', Pid, Reason}, S) ->
  case find(Pid, S#cache_state.locked) of
    {ok, MO} ->
      {ReplModule, ReplState} = S#cache_state.replace_strategy,
      NewReplState = ReplModule:unlock(ReplState, MO),
      NewS = S#cache_state{locked = [{M,P} || {M,P} <- S#cache_state.locked, P /= Pid],
                            replace_strategy = {ReplModule, NewReplState}},
      {noreply, NewS};
...
```

4.3   Storage Composition

Media objects are stored in several storage devices (hard disks, DVD, CD, in other servers, etc.), each one controlled by a process (*storage driver*). Clients should request the media to the appropriate storage agent. In order to simplify this search, a special storage agent, *a storage group*, is defined as a composition of several storages. Hence, a tree of storages is established while clients keep the illusion of accesing a simple storage. This homogeneous treatment of leaves and groups is the essence of the *Composite pattern* [GHJV95].

Declarative style is quite valuable when dealing with concurrent behaviour such as storage composition. For example, a synchronous (sequential) delegation on each of the children of a given group can be clearly stated by using a list comprehension. In this case, call(Pid,M) sends the message M to the process Pid and then waits for a response.

```
handle_call(Request, From, State) ->
    Combine( [ call(S, Request) || S <- State#composite_state.children ] ).
```

The process implements the Request service as a sequential delegation of the same service on all its children, and then combines the results by using Combine([Response]) -> Response. For example, a *lookup* service that finds the best location of a given media can be defined as:

```
handle_call({lookup, MO, PipeOpts}, From, State) ->
    MinCost = State#stgroup_state.min_cost,
    MinCost( [ call(S, {lookup, MO, PipeOpts} || S <- State#stgroup_state.children ] ).
```

Observe how a strategy (min_cost function) is applied in the context of a storage group to choose the best answer from all the children. This allows to change the cost selection algorithm used by the storage group.

There are many different types of interaction between the composite and its children. For example, the parallel composition sends the request to all the children in parallel, and then receives the responses. Figure 4 shows sequence diagrams explaining both interactions. This parallel delegation of a composite process can be defined as follows:

```
handle_call(Request, From, State) ->
    Combine( [ async_recv(Token)
              || Token <- [ async_call(S, Request)
                           || S <- State#composite_state.children] ] ).
```

In the example, async_call(Pid,M) -> Token sends the message M to process Pid and returns inmediately a token which can be used later to get the response using async_recv(Token) -> Response. All the requests are sent asynchronously and, after that, the responses are received. Finally, all the responses are combined using the Combine function to produce the composite response.

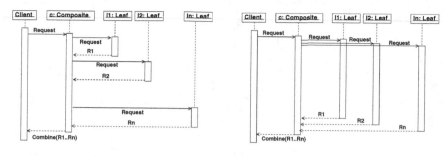

Fig. 4. Sequential and parallel interaction between composite and children

5   Performance Considerations

At the beginning of the project, we clearly decided that the distributed control system will be developed in Erlang, but I/O operations should be carried out by low-level C modules for performance reasons. In order to speed up development, some Erlang modules carrying out the basic I/O operations were implemented and it was planned to change them only when efficiency were needed (I/O 2-3 times heavier than C). However, it is noticeable that bulk performance it is not as important as we thought: quick and right implementation, and fast adaptation to new requirements are far more appreciated. Moreover, it is always possible to add new nodes to the cluster to compensate this lack of efficiency. Low-level I/O is still in our *TODO* list but there are many further features with higher priority.

In order to evaluate an Erlang based system with heavy I/O, a minimalistic configuration with a streamer and a *file driver* was defined. Both components were running in different Erlang virtual machines in a single node (Pentium II/350 384MB 2*4.5GB SCSI), interacting using TCP/IP. An AMD K7/500 256MB was connected to the server 1Gbps switch to define dummy clients performing media requests. With 100 concurrent 512 kbps video streams, the system behaves smoothly with a CPU usage of about 50% and reasonable response times. Asking for 200 concurrent streams of the same bandwidth, the server has a 99% of CPU usage, and only a few requests are delayed. With 150 concurrent requests, the performance is quite similar, the CPU occupation is about 95% and only some requests have response time problems (sometimes due to the TCP internal mechanisms). Trying with different rates, the server is able to attend 100 concurrent requests of 1Mbps, and about 50 concurrent 2Mbps.

6   Conclusions

Some experiences of using the concurrent functional language Erlang to implement a distributed video-on-demand server has been presented. Both the programming paradigm and the language have been a key success factor. The use of abstractions (functional patterns) and compositionality (both functional

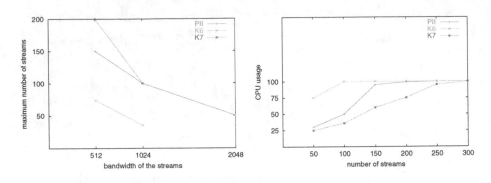

Fig. 5. Maximum number of streams and CPU usage for each of the servers

and concurrent composition) helped reduce the programming effort to adapt the system to new requirements. The available libraries and the built-in concurrent programming constructs of Erlang has simplified the development of a robust distributed control system. Even Erlang input/output issues, despite our initial concerns, were not a major problem: it was compensated with faster and cleaner development and it is always possible to replace a module with a low-level equivalent or to incorporate more cheap nodes to the cluster, if necessary. Among the criticism to the language, we should point out the lack of a static type system and a structured module system that complicates the development at large.

Even though it is still far from practical purposes, another advantage of using Erlang/OTP as the underlying platform for the system development, is that techniques coming from the formal methods area can be used in order to improve the system design and performance [AB02], and to ensure (at least partially) the system correctness [AP02]. These techniques can be used more naturally when taking as input a high level declarative language as Erlang.

The project represents a real-world application of a declarative language and we expect the system to be in production stage by early 2003.

References

[AB02]   Thomas Arts and Clara Benac Earle. Verifying Erlang code: a resource locker case-study. In *Int. Symposium on Formal Methods Europe*, volume 2391 of *LNCS*, pages 183–202. Springer-Verlag, July 2002.

[AP02]   Thomas Arts and Juan José Sánchez Penas. Global scheduler properties derived from local restrictions. In *Proceedings of ACM Sigplan Erlang Workshop*. ACM, October 2002.

[App01]   Apple Computer Inc. *About Darwin Streaming Server*, 2001.
           http://www.publicsource.apple.com/projects/streaming.

[Arm96]   J. Armstrong. Erlang — a Survey of the Language and its Industrial Applications. In *INAP'96 — The 9th Exhibitions and Symposium on Industrial Applications of Prolog*, pages 16–18, Hino, Tokyo, Japan, October 1996.

[AVWW96]   Joe Armstrong, Robert Virding, Claes Wikström, and Mike Williams. *Concurrent Programming in Erlang, Second Edition*. Prentice-Hall, 1996.

[BG99]   Miguel Barreiro and Victor M. Gulias. Cluster setup and its administration. In Rajkumar Buyya, editor, *High Performance Cluster Computing*, volume I. Prentice Hall, 1999.

[Car00]   Richard Carlsson. Extending Erlang with structured module packages. Technical Report 2000-001, Department of Information Technology, Uppsala University, January 2000.

[Cis00]   Cisco Systems, Inc. *A Distributed Video Server Architecture for Flexible Enterprise-Wide Video Delivery*, white paper edition, 2000.

[CT97]   S-H. Chan and F. Tobagi. Hierarchical storage systems for interactive video-on-demand. Technical Report CSL Technical Report CSL-TR-97-723, Computer Systems Laboratory, Stanford University, Stanford, 1997.

[GHJV95]   Gamma, Helm, Johnson, and Vlissides. *Design Patterns Elements of Reusable Object-Oriented Software*. Addison-Wesley, Massachusetts, 1995.

[Gro96]   IETF Network Working Group. Rtp: A transport protocol for real-time applications. RFC 1889 http://www.ietf.org/rfc/rfc1889.txt, January 1996.

[Gro98]   IETF Network Working Group. Real time streaming protocol (rtsp). RFC 2326 http://www.ietf.org/rfc/rfc2326.txt, April 1998.

[Hoa85]   C.A.R. Hoare. *Communicating Sequential Processes*. Prentice-Hall, Englewood Cliffs, NJ, 1985.

[JPS00]   Erik Johansson, Mikael Pettersson, and Konstantinos F. Sagonas. A high performance erlang system. In *Proceedings of the 2nd International ACM SIGPLAN Conference on Principles and Practice of Declarative Programming (PPDP-00)*, pages 32–43, N.Y., September 20–23 2000. ACM Press.

[MPW92]   R. Milner, J. Parrow, and D. Walker. A calculus of mobile processes. *Information and Computation*, 100(1):1–77, September 1992.

[MW97]   Simon Marlow and Philip Wadler. A practical subtyping system for Erlang. In *Proceedings of the 1997 ACM SIGPLAN International Conference on Functional Programming*, pages 136–149, Amsterdam, The Netherlands, 9–11 June 1997.

[Ora98]   *Oracle Video Server System Technical Overview*, oracle white paper edition, 1998.

[Phi00]   Philips, http://www.mpeg-4player.com/products/server/index.asp. *WebCine Server*, 2000.

[SGVM00]   J.J. Sanchez, V.M. Gulias, A. Valderruten, and J. Mosquera. State of the art and design of vod systems. In *International Conference on Information Systems Analysis, ISAS'00*, Orlando, FL, USA, 2000.

[Sun99]   Sun Microsystems Inc., http://www.sun.com/storage/media-central. *Sun StorEdge Media Central Streaming Server*, 1999.

[Wad98]   Philip Wadler. Functional programming: An angry half dozen. *SIGPLAN Notices*, 33(2):25–30, February 1998. Functional programming column [NB. Table of contents on the cover of this issue is wrong.].

[WDRW99]   P. Wilkinson, M. DeSisto, M. Rother, and Y. Wong. *IBM VideoCharger*. International Technical Support Organization, ibm redbook edition, 1999.

Author Index

Lecture Notes in Computer Science

For information about Vols. 1–2479

please contact your bookseller or Springer-Verlag

Vol. 2519: R. Meersman, Z. Tari, et al. (Eds.), On the Move to Meaningful Internet Systems 2002: CoopIS, DOA, and ODBASE. Proceedings, 2002. XXIII, 1367 pages. 2002.

Vol. 2521: A. Karmouch, T. Magedanz, J. Delgado (Eds.), Mobile Agents for Telecommunication Applications. Proceedings, 2002. XII, 317 pages. 2002.

Vol. 2522: T. Andreasen, A. Motro, H. Christiansen, H. Legind Larsen (Eds.), Flexible Query Answering. Proceedings, 2002. XI, 386 pages. 2002. (Subseries LNAI).

Vol. 2525: H.H. Bülthoff, S.-Whan Lee, T.A. Poggio, C. Wallraven (Eds.), Biologically Motivated Computer Vision. Proceedings, 2002. XIV, 662 pages. 2002.

Vol. 2526: A. Colosimo, A. Giuliani, P. Sirabella (Eds.), Medical Data Analysis. Proceedings, 2002. IX, 222 pages. 2002.

Vol. 2527: F.J. Garijo, J.C. Riquelme, M. Toro (Eds.), Advances in Artificial Intelligence – IBERAMIA 2002. Proceedings, 2002. XVIII, 955 pages. 2002. (Subseries LNAI).

Vol. 2528: M.T. Goodrich, S.G. Kobourov (Eds.), Graph Drawing. Proceedings, 2002. XIII, 384 pages. 2002.

Vol. 2529: D.A. Peled, M.Y. Vardi (Eds.), Formal Techniques for Networked and Distributed Sytems – FORTE 2002. Proceedings, 2002. XI, 371 pages. 2002.

Vol. 2531: J. Padget, O. Shehory, D. Parkes, N. Sadeh, W.E. Walsh (Eds.), Agent-Mediated Electronic Commerce IV. Proceedings, 2002. XVII, 341 pages. 2002. (Subseries LNAI).

Vol. 2532: Y.-C. Chen, L.-W. Chang, C.-T. Hsu (Eds.), Advances in Multimedia Information Processing – PCM 2002. Proceedings, 2002. XXI, 1255 pages. 2002.

Vol. 2533: N. Cesa-Bianchi, M. Numao, R. Reischuk (Eds.), Algorithmic Learning Theory. Proceedings, 2002. XI, 415 pages. 2002. (Subseries LNAI).

Vol. 2534: S. Lange, K. Satoh, C.H. Smith (Ed.), Discovery Science. Proceedings, 2002. XIII, 464 pages. 2002.

Vol. 2535: N. Suri (Ed.), Mobile Agents. Proceedings, 2002. X, 203 pages. 2002.

Vol. 2536: M. Parashar (Ed.), Grid Computing – GRID 2002. Proceedings, 2002. XI, 318 pages. 2002.

Vol. 2537: D.G. Feitelson, L. Rudolph, U. Schwiegelshohn (Eds.), Job Scheduling Strategies for Parallel Processing. Proceedings, 2002. VII, 237 pages. 2002.

Vol. 2538: B. König-Ries, K. Makki, S.A.M. Makki, N. Pissinou, P. Scheuermann (Eds.), Developing an Infrastructure for Mobile and Wireless Systems. Proceedings 2001. X, 183 pages. 2002.

Vol. 2539: K. Börner, C. Chen (Eds.), Visual Interfaces to Digital Libraries. X, 233 pages. 2002.

Vol. 2540: W.I. Grosky, F. Plášil (Eds.), SOFSEM 2002: Theory and Practice of Informatics. Proceedings, 2002. X, 289 pages. 2002.

Vol. 2541: T. Barkowsky, Mental Representation and Processing of Geographic Knowledge. X, 174 pages. 2002. (Subseries LNAI).

Vol. 2544: S. Bhalla (Ed.), Databases in Networked Information Systems. Proceedings 2002. X, 285 pages. 2002.

Vol. 2545: P. Forbrig, Q, Limbourg, B. Urban, J. Vanderdonckt (Eds.), Interactive Systems. Proceedings 2002. X, 269 pages. 2002.

Vol. 2546: J. Sterbenz, O. Takada, C. Tschudin, B. Plattner (Eds.), Active Networks. Proceedings, 2002. XIV, 267 pages. 2002.

Vol. 2547: R. Fleischer, B. Moret, E. Meineche Schmidt (Eds.), Experimental Algorithmics. XVII, 279 pages. 2002.

Vol. 2548: J. Hernández, Ana Moreira (Eds.), Object-Oriented Technology. Proceedings. 2002. VIII, 223 pages. 2002.

Vol. 2549: J. Cortadella, A. Yakovlev, G. Rozenberg (Eds.), Concurrency and Hardware Design. XI, 345 pages. 2002.

Vol. 2550: A. Jean-Marie (Ed.), Advances in Computing Science – ASIAN 2002. Proceedings, 2002. X, 233 pages. 2002.

Vol. 2551: A. Menezes, P. Sarkar (Eds.), Progress in Cryptology – INDOCRYPT 2002. Proceedings, 2002. XI, 437 pages. 2002.

Vol. 2552: S. Sahni, V.K. Prasanna, U. Shukla (Eds.), High Performance Computing – HiPC 2002. Proceedings, 2002. XXI, 735 pages. 2002.

Vol. 2553: B. Andersson, M. Bergholtz, P. Johannesson (Eds.), Natural Language Processing and Information Systems. Proceedings, 2002. X, 241 pages. 2002.

Vol. 2554: M. Beetz, Plan-Based Control of Robotic Agents. XI, 191 pages. 2002. (Subseries LNAI).

Vol. 2555: E.-P. Lim, S. Foo, C. Khoo, H. Chen, E. Fox, S. Urs, T. Costantino (Eds.), Digital Libraries: People, Knowledge, and Technology. Proceedings, 2002. XVII, 535 pages. 2002.

Vol. 2556: M. Agrawal, A. Seth (Eds.), FST TCS 2002: Foundations of Software Technology and Theoretical Computer Science. Proceedings, 2002. XI, 361 pages. 2002.

Vol. 2557: B. McKay, J. Slaney (Eds.), AI 2002: Advances in Artificial Intelligence. Proceedings, 2002. XV, 730 pages. 2002. (Subseries LNAI).

Vol. 2558: P. Perner, Data Mining on Multimedia Data. X, 131 pages. 2002.

Vol. 2559: M. Oivo, S. Komi-Sirviö (Eds.), Product Focused Software Process Improvement. Proceedings, 2002. XV, 646 pages. 2002.

Vol. 2560: S. Goronzy, Robust Adaptation to Non-Native Accents in Automatic Speech Recognition. Proceedings, 2002. XI, 144 pages. 2002. (Subseries LNAI).

Vol. 2561: H.C.M. de Swart (Ed.), Relational Methods in Computer Science. Proceedings, 2001. X, 315 pages. 2002.

Vol. 2562: V. Dahl, P. Wadler (Eds.), Practical Aspects of Declarative Languages. Proceedings, 2003. X, 315 pages. 2002.

Vol. 2566: T.Æ. Mogensen, D.A. Schmidt, I.H. Sudborough (Eds.), The Essence of Computation. XIV, 473 pages. 2002.

Vol. 2567: Y.G. Desmedt (Ed.), Public Key Cryptography – PKC 2003. Proceedings, 2003. XI, 365 pages. 2002.

Vol. 2569: D. Gollmann, G. Karjoth, M. Waidner (Eds.), Computer Security – ESORICS 2002. Proceedings, 2002. XIII, 648 pages. 2002. (Subseries LNAI).

Vol. 2571: S.K. Das, S. Bhattacharya (Eds.), Distributed Computing. Proceedings, 2002. XIV, 354 pages. 2002.

Vol. 2572: D. Calvanese, M. Lenzerini, R. Motwani (Eds.), Database Theory – ICDT 2003. Proceedings, 2003. XI, 455 pages. 2002.

Vol. 2575: L.D. Zuck, P.C. Attie, A. Cortesi, S. Mukhopadhyay (Eds.), Verification, Model Checking, and Abstract Interpretation. Proceedings, 2003. XI, 325 pages. 2003.